Mergers, Acquisitions, and Buyouts

Sample Acquisition Agreements with Tax and Legal Analysis

November 1999 Edition

Martin D. Ginsburg
Georgetown University Law Center

Jack S. Levin
Kirkland & Ellis

Volume 3

Volume Co-author
Douglas C. Barnard

This volume is current through November 30, 1999

A PANEL PUBLICATION
Aspen Publishers, Inc.

Copyright © 1999 by Jack S. Levin and The Chicago Classical Recording Foundation

Permissions
Panel Publishers
A Division of Aspen Publishers, Inc.
1185 Avenue of the Americas
New York, NY 10036

Printed in the United States of America

Library of Congress Catolog No. 94-74474

ISBN 0-7355-1109-8 Volume 3
ISBN 0-7355-1104-7 Set

About Panel

Panel Publishers—comprising the former Prentice Hall Law & Business, Little, Brown and Company's Professional Division, and Wiley Law Publications—is a leading publisher of authoritative treatises, practice manuals, information services, and journals written by specialists to assist attorneys, financial and tax advisors, corporate and bank directors, and other business professionals. Our mission is to provide practical solution-based how-to information keyed to the latest legislative, judicial, and regulatory developments.

We offer publications in the areas of compensation and benefits, pensions, payroll, employment, civil rights, taxation, estate planning, and elder law.

Other Panel products treating tax issues include:

Structuring Venture Capital, Private Equity, and Entrepreneurial Transactions

Multistate Corporate Tax Guide

Corporate Tax Planning: Takeovers, Leveraged Buyouts, and Restructuring

Venture Capital and Public Offering Negotiation

Corporate Finance and Securities Laws

Failing and Failed Businesses

Financial Products: Taxation, Regulation, and Design

PANEL PUBLISHERS
A Division of Aspen Publishers, Inc.
Practical Solutions for Legal and Business Professionals
www.panelpublishers.com

SUBSCRIPTION NOTICE

This Panel product is revised twice a year to reflect important changes in the subject matter. If you purchased this product directly from Panel, we have already recorded your subscription for the update service.

If, however, you purchased this product from a bookstore and wish to receive future updates and revised or related volumes billed separately with a 30-day examination review, please contact our Customer Service Department at 1-800-234-1660, or send your name, company name (if applicable), address, and the title of the product to:

PANEL PUBLISHERS
A Division of Aspen Publishers, Inc.
7201 McKinney Circle
Frederick, MD 21704

About the Authors

Martin D. Ginsburg is Professor of Law at Georgetown University Law Center in Washington, D.C. His professional corporation is of counsel to the firm of Fried, Frank, Harris, Shriver & Jacobson.

Professor Ginsburg attended Cornell University, stood very low in his class, and played on the golf team. He graduated magna cum laude from Harvard Law School which, in those years, did not field a golf team.

Professor Ginsburg entered private practice in New York City in 1958. Although beloved by partners, clients, and opposing counsel, including Mr. Levin, he withdrew from full-time practice when appointed the Beekman Professor of Law at Columbia Law School. He moved to Georgetown University in 1980 when his wife obtained a good job in Washington.

In the interim, Professor Ginsburg served as Chairman of the Tax Section of the New York State Bar Association, Chairman of the Committee on Taxation of the Association of the Bar of the City of New York, Chairman of the Committee on Simplification of the Section of Taxation of the American Bar Association, Member of the Advisory Group to the Commissioner of Internal Revenue, and Member of the Advisory Group to the Tax Division of the Department of Justice. Since 1974 Professor Ginsburg has acted as Consultant to the American Law Institute's Federal Income Tax Project on the revision of the corporate and partnership tax laws; from 1984 to 1987 he was a member of the ABA Tax Section Council where he performed no useful service at all.

In addition to Columbia and Georgetown, he has taught at New York University School of Law (Adjunct Professor 1967-79 and Visiting Professor 1993), Stanford Law School (Visiting Professor 1978), the University of Leiden in Holland (1982), the Salzburg Seminar in Austria (1984), Harvard Law School (Visiting Professor 1986), and the University of Chicago Law School (Visiting Professor 1990).

In 1986, someone who probably prefers never to be identified endowed a Chair in Taxation in his name at Georgetown; no one appears willing to occupy the Ginsburg Chair, and it remains vacant. In 1993 the National Women's Political Caucus gave Professor Ginsburg its "Good Guy" award; history reveals no prior instance of a tax lawyer held to be a "Good Guy," or even a "Decent Sort."

Professor Ginsburg is a Fellow of the American College of Tax Counsel, a frequent speaker at tax seminars, mainly in warm climates, and the author of a ghastly number of articles on corporate and partnership taxation, business acquisitions, and other stimulating things. Professor Ginsburg's spouse was a lawyer before she found better work. Their older child was a lawyer before she became a schoolteacher. The younger child, when he feels grumpy, threatens to become a lawyer.

Jack S. Levin, through his professional corporation, is a senior partner in the law firm of Kirkland & Ellis, where it is widely known that the professional corporation does more of the work than does Mr. Levin. In person he is also a lecturer at the University of Chicago Law School and the Harvard Law School, teaching a course on *Structuring Venture Capital, Private Equity, and Entrepreneurial Transactions.*

Mr. Levin graduated summa cum laude from the Northwestern University School of Business in 1958, where unlike Professor Ginsburg he was not on the golf team. In May 1958 Mr. Levin won the Illinois Gold Medal on the CPA examination, an accomplishment secretly admired by Professor Ginsburg.

In 1961 Mr. Levin graduated summa cum laude from the Harvard Law School, ranking first in a class of 500, and served as Recent Case Editor of the Harvard Law Review, a job that required no athletic prowess at all.

After graduation Mr. Levin served as law clerk to Chief Judge J. Edward Lumbard of the United States Court of Appeals for the Second Circuit and later as Assistant to the Solicitor General of the United States for tax matters under Archibald Cox and Thurgood Marshall, where he slowly began to develop a tennis game.

Mr. Levin is a member of the American College of Tax Counsel and the Tax Advisory Group to the American Law Institute's Federal Income Tax Project on the Revision of the Corporate Tax Laws.

Mr. Levin is author of a book *Structuring Venture Capital, Private Equity, and Entrepreneurial Transactions,* which he has updated and republished each year since 1994 (Panel/Aspen Publishers). He is a frequent speaker at major tax institutes, Practising Law Institute programs, ALI-ABA seminars, and venture capital and leveraged buyout conferences, and has also authored numerous articles and chapters of books on a variety of exciting tax subjects, although, to the best of his knowledge, no one has read any of them.

In past times Mr. Levin has also served as a member of the Harvard Board of Overseers Committee for visiting the Harvard Law School, Chairman of the ABA Subcommittee on Corporate Distributions, Chairman of the Chicago Federal Tax Forum, Chairman of the Harvard Law School Fund Raising Drives in 1986, 1991, and 1996, a member of the Little, Brown & Company and the CCH Tax Advisory Boards, an Executive Committee member of the Chicago Bar Association's Taxation Committee, Chairman of the Lawyers Division of the Chicago Jewish United Fund, and, more important, for 13 years as Parliamentarian of the Winnetka Town Meeting. (Winnetka, Illinois, for the very few who do not know, is the nation's model for honest and efficient government.)

Through many patient years of practice and the selection of an extraordinary partner, Mr. Levin won the Kirkland & Ellis doubles tennis tournament four successive times during the summers of 1987 through 1991, and it has been downhill ever since.

Overcoming a lifetime of fear, Mr. Levin at age 45 (through his professional corporation, in case of debilitating injury) took up downhill skiing, a sport he enthusiastically pursues shoulder-to-shoulder with a number of his venture capital clients, who (unlike Mr. Levin) are professional risk takers.

About the Authors

While neither Mr. Levin nor Professor Ginsburg has ever achieved election to any public office, Mr. Levin's wife (the family's socially useful member) has at various times been elected President of the Winnetka Public School Board and a Trustee of the Winnetka Village Council. As Winnetka elected officials serve without monetary compensation, Mr. Levin devotes most of his time to the remunerative practice of law, less to teaching, none to the professional tennis or skiing circuits. Mr. Levin's two older daughters are lawyers, while his two younger daughters have graduated from Harvard Business School.

Douglas C. Barnard is Vice President, General Counsel, and Secretary of Life-*Style* Furnishings International, which recently acquired the largest U.S. manufacturer of home furnishings in a leveraged buyout. He was formerly a partner in the Chicago office of Kirkland & Ellis (1982–92), where his law practice concentrated on mergers and acquisitions (especially leveraged buyouts and venture capital transactions). Mr. Barnard is a graduate of the Massachusetts Institute of Technology (S.B. Physics 1979), the University of Minnesota Law Center (J.D. 1982), and the University of Chicago Graduate School of Business (M.B.A. High Honors 1998).

Acknowledgments

The authors wish to thank Donald E. Rocap, William R. Welke, Patrick C. Gallagher, and Alexandra Mihalas of Kirkland & Ellis for their assistance in the preparation of this volume.

The authors are grateful to Elaine C. Crowley and Gary R. Wendorf, Legal Assistants at Kirkland & Ellis, without whose Herculean organizational endeavors this book would still be so much waste paper.

Summary of Contents

Contents

Introduction and Explanation   1

Contents

Taxable Purchase of Stock 65

Contents

Taxable Purchase of Assets   255

Taxable Purchase of Divisional Business   441

Taxable Reverse Subsidiary Merger   607

Tax-Free Merger   637

Introduction and Explanation

¶2001 INTRODUCTION TO SAMPLE ACQUISITION AGREEMENTS

This volume contains sample acquisition agreements for mergers, acquisitions, and leveraged buyouts ("LBOs") involving a purchasing corporation ("P") and a target corporation ("T"). In the case of a sale of T's stock, the sellers are T's shareholders. In the case of a sale of T's assets or a merger, the seller is T. For most sample acquisition agreements, there are pro-buyer, pro-seller, and neutral versions.

Naturally, the acquisition documents covering an actual transaction must be carefully tailored to the economic terms and the risk-sharing arrangements agreed upon by the parties. It is therefore unlikely that any sample acquisition agreement will ever be appropriate in its entirety for a particular negotiated transaction. Indeed, in preparing the acquisition documents for a particular negotiated transaction, it will frequently be necessary to mix and match between sample acquisition agreements, i.e., to use parts of several. The introductory comments in front of each sample acquisition agreement make useful suggestions along this line. When one portion of a sample acquisition agreement is changed, however, care is necessary to make sure that all appropriate changes are made in other parts of the sample acquisition agreement, because many clauses of a sample acquisition agreement are often interrelated.

Accordingly, the sample acquisition agreements in this volume are designed to suggest (often in footnotes) the principal issues encountered in each type of acquisitive transaction (e.g., a purchase of stock, a purchase of assets, a purchase of divisional assets, a reverse subsidiary taxable merger, and a tax-free reorganization) and to offer at least one resolution of each principal issue. With respect to many issues, the sample acquisition agreements contain alternative provisions (e.g., full, limited, or minimal indemnification for breaches of representations and warranties) or footnote or bracketed references discussing additional alternative resolutions.

In addition, the sample acquisition agreements contain cross-references to relevant discussions of tax and legal issues in the Transactional Analysis volume of this series.

¶2001.1   Key Issues in Preparing Acquisition Documents

Mergers, acquisitions, and LBOs begin with a business idea and are driven by economic factors. While the impact of the tax law is surely one such factor, the central concern in acquisition transactions is the commercial bargain struck by the parties, i.e., the determination of the economic benefits and burdens to be generated by the transaction and their allocation among the parties to the transaction.

All too often the parties to an acquisition erroneously believe the negotiation completed when they have settled upon the price to be paid and the medium of payment. Inevitably, they find that there are several alternative structures and contractual clauses with radically different tax and legal results so that the economics of the transaction will vary materially depending upon the structure and contractual clauses selected.

Generally, one structure or set of contractual clauses will advantage the seller and another the buyer. Hence, the parties invite serious conflict and do a disservice to themselves and their professional advisers if they settle the price and the medium of payment without giving concurrent attention to the tax and legal structuring of the transaction and such contractual issues as the scope of the seller's representations, warranties, and indemnifications.

For example, assume that P has decided to expand into widget manufacturing by acquiring T, an existing widget producer. P's and T's principals negotiate vigorously over the price to be paid and agree that P will pay $1 million in cash for T. At this point the principals, believing their job completed, leave the details to their lawyers and accountants.

Unfortunately, there are a number of unresolved economic issues. Principal nontax issues include:

(1) Will the transaction be structured so that P inherits all of T's liabilities, disclosed and undisclosed, *or* structured to maximize the likelihood that P assumes only specified T liabilities and that the remainder are left with T or inherited by its shareholders?

(2) Will T's contractual representations, warranties, and indemnifications allow P to recover back from T or its shareholders a portion of the purchase price if, after the transaction is completed, P discovers that T has undisclosed liabilities (environmental cleanup, unpaid taxes, employment discrimination, antitrust violations, product liability, patent or trademark infringement, etc.), that T lacks good title to a portion of its assets, that part of T's receivables are not collectible or part of its inventory is not saleable, that T's past financial statements are inaccurate, etc.?

(3) Will T's executives receive employment contracts, golden parachute agreements, or severance agreements, or, instead, will they receive no employment protection? Will P obtain from T's executives covenants not to compete?

Principal tax issues include:

(1) Will the transaction be structured so that P obtains a new cost basis (either a stepped-up or stepped-down basis) in T's assets (generally the purchase price paid by P plus the T liabilities inherited by P (or to which T remains subject if T becomes a P subsidiary) plus P's expenses of acquiring T), or will P take a carryover basis ("COB") in T's assets (generally T's much lower historical asset basis)?

(2) Will the transaction cause T to pay corporate-level tax on all the appreciation inherent in its assets, including goodwill and other intangibles? If so, will the economic burden of this tax fall on P or on T's shareholders?

(3) Will T's shareholders pay tax on the appreciation inherent in their stock? Can that gain be deferred by the installment method, a tax-free reorganization, or the use of Code §351?

(4) If T has a net operating loss ("NOL") or other tax attribute carryforward, will P inherit T's NOL or other tax attribute and, if so, what if any restrictions will be imposed on P's enjoyment of T's NOL or other attribute?

In the widget manufacturing transaction presented above, P's lawyer advises P (1) to purchase T's assets in a taxable transaction to obtain a stepped-up basis ("SUB") in T's assets without additional tax cost to P, and (2) to assume in the contract only specified T liabilities, i.e., to avoid assuming T's undisclosed liabilities. T's lawyer, on the other hand, advises T's shareholders to sell their stock to P (rather than have T sell its assets to P) to avoid bearing the cost of a corporate-level tax on the taxable sale of T's assets and to make no representations concerning T's undisclosed liabilities to shift the economic burden of all T's liabilities (disclosed and undisclosed) to P.

P and T thus find that their previous negotiations failed to settle significant economic issues and hence that the economic price to be paid by P (as opposed to the nominal cash price) has not yet been determined.

Because the manner in which the acquisition is structured and the terms of the contract have major economic consequences, it is important that the parties confer with counsel and resolve these issues as early in the negotiating process as possible.

Successful planning for an acquisition requires awareness of the interdependence of the issues that arise. A change in the structure of contractual terms to deal with one issue may affect the resolution of another issue or raise a new issue. In most cases, no single structure or set of contractual terms provides a perfect fit, and a balance must be struck between competing interests.

¶2001.1.1 Structuring the Transaction

¶2001.1.1.1 *The Legal Structure*

The parties will need to select a basic legal structure for the transaction. For example, the transaction might be structured as a purchase of stock, a purchase of assets, or a merger.

T's shareholder profile will frequently influence P's approach to and structuring of the acquisition. If T is closely held, P may be able to negotiate directly with all of T's shareholders to acquire 100% of T's stock. If T is publicly held (or privately held by a large diverse group of shareholders), this would be virtually impossible, necessitating an approach other than a direct purchase of T's stock (e.g., a merger with T *or* a purchase of T's assets *or* a two-step acquisition, in which T acquires a controlling block of T stock through direct purchases or a tender offer and then acquires the remainder of the T stock through a "squeeze-out" merger).

T's asset profile will also frequently influence P's approach to and structuring of the acquisition. If T has difficult-to-transfer assets (such as hundreds of parcels of real estate *or* hundreds of vehicles *or* important contracts, leases, licenses, and the like which prohibit assignment), P's purchase of T's stock or a reverse merger of a P subsidiary ("S") into T will normally obviate the need for such asset transfers. Some agreements or licenses, however, are specifically drafted to require the other party's approval for even a change in control of T (i.e., a sale of a controlling interest in T's stock) or a merger involving T.

The selection of a legal structure for the transaction may have important federal income tax and other consequences for P, the seller(s), and T. Some of the principal considerations are discussed at ¶2001.2.

If the structure selected will cause T to recognize gain on its inherent asset appreciation (generally a sale of T assets or a sale of T stock with a Code §338 election), the contract should allocate the federal, state, local, and foreign tax liabilities so created.

¶2001.1.1.2   *The Purchase Price and the Medium of Payment*

The parties need to agree upon the purchase price P will pay the seller(s).

The seller(s) may find a particular purchase price more attractive if P will purchase T "as is" than if P will require the seller(s) to make extensive representations and warranties and indemnify P against a broad range of losses and liabilities. Conversely, the seller(s) may be willing to make extensive representations and warranties and indemnify P against a broad range of losses and liabilities if P is willing to pay a premium price for T.

The parties will also need to agree upon the medium of payment (e.g., cash, P notes, P stock, or some combination thereof).

An acquisition of T in which part or all of the consideration is stock or debt instruments (i.e., "securities" within the meaning of the Securities Act of 1933 (the "1933 Act")) of P (or S) will necessitate compliance with the 1933 Act. The 1933 Act prohibits the sale of securities unless (i) such securities are registered with SEC and certain other requirements are satisfied *or* (ii) there is an applicable exemption from registration, e.g., the private placement or intrastate exemption.

If T's shareholder group is of any significant size, P (or S) will generally not be able to qualify for an exemption and will be required to register under the 1933 Act the P (or S) stock or notes being issued for T. This process is likely to require at least several weeks and more likely several months. The 1933 Act registration requirements are discussed in greater detail at ¶1502.2.8.1.

Section 4(2) of the 1933 Act exempts P (or S) from the requirement to register its stock or debt securities if the issuance does not involve a public offering (i.e., the offering constitutes a private placement). SEC Regulation D (Rules 501 through 508 under the 1933 Act) and SEC Rule 701 each provide a safe harbor for certain private placements. Regulation D and Rule 701 are discussed in greater detail at ¶¶1502.2.8.2 and 1502.2.8.3.

Section 3(a)(11) of the 1933 Act exempts intrastate offerings. SEC Rule 147 provides a safe harbor for certain intrastate offerings. Rule 147 is discussed in greater detail at ¶1502.2.8.4.

If P (or S) has issued stock or debt securities to T or T's shareholders in exchange for T's stock or assets, there are frequently SEC restrictions on resale of the P (or S) stock or debt securities (unless the parties file a 1933 Act registration statement covering such resale). These resale restrictions are discussed in greater detail at ¶1502.2.8.5.

¶2001.1.1.3   *The Terms of Any Securities the Seller(s) Will Receive*
              as Part of the Purchase Price

If part of the purchase price is payable, for example, in P notes, the acquisition documents must address maturity, interest rate, subordination, security, guaranties, prepayment rights and premiums, default provisions, and recoupment (e.g., whether P will be able to recoup its losses for breaches of the seller(s)'s representations and warranties against the notes).

Similarly, where part of the purchase price is payable in P stock, the acquisition document must address preferences (e.g., dividend preferences and priorities on liquidation), conversion rights, antidilution protection, dividend rates, participation rights, registration rights, and put and call rights.

¶2001.1.1.4   *Whether There Will Be Any Purchase Price Adjustments*

There might be a formula adjustment based, for example, on T's closing date book value *or* T's working capital in excess of (or less than) its liabilities at closing *or* a formula earnout based on T's post-closing earnings for a specified period.

¶2001.1.1.5   *The Assets and/or Stock P Will Receive from the Seller(s)*

If P is purchasing T's assets, the contract will normally specify any excluded assets (which T will retain), such as cash, cash equivalents, marketable securities, and rights to tax refunds and deposit refunds. Similarly, if P is purchasing the assets of a T division, the contract will normally specify the disposition of shared assets (assets used both in the division being sold to P and in the division(s) being retained by T). Finally, if P is purchasing T's stock, the contract will normally prohibit P from withdrawing T's assets (except possibly cash, cash equivalents, marketable securities, etc.) as a dividend or redemption prior to the closing.

¶2001.1.1.6   *The Extent to Which P Will Inherit T's Liabilities and*
              Obligations and, Conversely, the Extent to Which T's
              Old Shareholders Will Bear the Burden of T's Liabilities
              and Obligations

On the one hand, the transaction could be structured and the documents drafted so that P will inherit all of T's liabilities and obligations, including those for environmental cleanup, employment discrimination, antitrust violations, product liability, product warranty, prior years' tax deficiencies, current year's taxes, and other claims and lawsuits, even if unknown at the time the contract is signed and the acquisition closed.

On the other hand, the transaction could be structured and the documents drafted so that P will inherit only specified T liabilities and obligations, such as those shown on the latest T balance sheet available before signing the purchase agreement and those arising in the ordinary course of business thereafter (but not including lawsuits, disputed claims, and the like). If this latter approach is adopted, the contract will contain extensive representations, warranties, and indemnifications running from the seller(s) to P. *See* ¶2001.1.2.

¶2001.1.1.7   *Determining Whether to Structure a Taxable Acquisition*
              for Stepped-Up Basis

In a tax-free acquisition (*see* ¶2006—Tax-Free Merger of T into P for P Stock), T's assets inevitably take a COB. *See* Chapter 6 through Chapter 8 and ¶¶2001.2.1.1(2) and 2001.2.2.1(2). However, in a taxable acquisition, T's assets may take a COB or a stepped-up or stepped-down cost basis, depending on how the taxable transaction is structured.

The parties to a taxable acquisition should therefore determine whether to structure the acquisition so that P takes (1) a stepped-up (or stepped-down) cost basis in T's assets or (2) a COB in T's assets. If the purchase price paid (including transferred liabilities) exceeds T's asset tax basis, then this determination depends on a comparison of the front-end tax cost for an SUB to the discounted present value of later tax savings generated by an SUB. If it is determined that an SUB is desirable, it will then be necessary to allocate the purchase price paid by P for T (and other capitalizable costs) among T's assets.

There are two methods of structuring for SUB:

(1)   P purchases T's assets (or acquires T's assets in a taxable forward merger of T into P or a P subsidiary), and

(2) P purchases T's stock (or acquires T's stock in a taxable reverse subsidiary merger of P's newly formed subsidiary into T) with a Code §338 or 338(h)(10) election.

On the other hand, if P purchases T's stock (or acquires T's stock in a reverse subsidiary merger of P's newly formed subsidiary into T) with no Code §338 or 338(h)(10) election, T's assets will have COB.

After *GU* repeal in 1986, it is generally uneconomic from a tax standpoint to structure for full asset SUB except in the following situations:

(1) T has a sufficiently large NOL which may be used to offset the gain on either an asset sale or a Code §338 election. T's NOL can offset such gain, but P's NOL cannot.

(2) T is a subsidiary of a consolidated group or of an affiliated group not filing a consolidated return (the Bigco group), and Bigco's outside basis in T's stock is not significantly higher than T's inside basis in its assets, in which case Bigco may either sell T's stock with a Code §338(h)(10) election or cause T to sell its assets and liquidate under Code §332.

(3) T is a subsidiary of a consolidated group (the Bigco group) and, although Bigco's outside basis in T's stock is significantly higher than T's inside net basis in its assets, the Bigco group has a sufficiently large NOL with which to offset T's gain, in which case Bigco may either sell T's stock with a Code §338(h)(10) election or cause T to sell its assets and liquidate under Code §332.

(4) T is a Subchapter S corporation which is not subject to the penalty tax of Code §1374 (or can find a way to avoid such penalty tax). *See* ¶1103.7.

However, there are additional circumstances where it will be economically desirable to structure the transaction for partial asset SUB, i.e., to bifurcate the transaction so that P purchases a portion of T's assets (with asset SUB) and then acquires T's stock with no Code §338 or 338(h)(10) election (so that T's remaining assets take COB). See ¶¶204.3 and 1109.1.2 for a detailed discussion of these techniques.

The principal circumstances where such a bifurcated acquisition structure will be desirable are:

(1) T has an NOL sufficient to shelter a portion of the gain inherent in its assets, in which case T can sell a portion of its assets to P, selected so as to (a) trigger T gain approximately equal to T's NOL and (b) step up P's basis in purchased assets with a relatively short depreciable life in P's hands.

(2) T is an SCo with §1374 BIG in some but not all of its assets, in which case P can select assets to purchase with little or no §1374-tainted BIG.

(3) T is a Bigco 80-80 subsidiary, and Bigco has a higher outside basis in T's stock than T's inside basis in its assets, in which case the bifurcated technique is feasible only if (a) P is a partnership (not 80%-or-more owned by

a single corporation or a single corporate affiliated group) or (b) T's selected assets are sold to P and T's stock is sold to a P affiliate structured so that it is technically not a §1504 affiliate of P.

1. Desirability of structuring acquisition to obtain full stepped-up basis. In determining whether to structure the transaction for full asset SUB (or through a bifurcated transaction for partial asset SUB) rather than COB, the following factors must be taken into account:

- The discounted present value of the tax savings from the additional deductions for cost of goods sold, depreciation, and amortization resulting from the step-up.
- The extra front-end tax because the transaction was structured for asset SUB rather than asset COB.

The discounted present value of the tax savings depends on:

- the amount of step-up allocable to inventory, depreciable tangible assets, and amortizable intangibles rather than land and other non-amortizable assets,
- the useful life of the depreciable/amortizable assets,
- the degree of risk that IRS will successfully challenge (on audit) the allocation among the assets and/or the claimed useful lives,
- whether P elects FIFO or LIFO inventory,
- the applicable corporate tax rate in the future years when the additional deductions are allowable,
- the proper discount rate for computing the present value of the future tax savings, and
- whether P can obtain sufficient financing to pay the extra front-end tax (either to the seller to induce it to sell assets rather than stock or to IRS in the case of a stock purchase with a regular Code §338 election).

In structuring for full asset SUB, the amount of the extra front-end tax turns first on whether T is:

(a)   a free-standing C corporation (i.e., not an 80-80 Bigco subsidiary),
(b)   a C corporation that is a Bigco 80-80 subsidiary,
(c)   an S corporation not subject to the Code §1374 penalty tax, or
(d)   an S corporation subject to the Code §1374 penalty tax,

and second, in (b) (and, to a lesser degree, in (c) and (d)) above, on whether T's inside net asset basis (i.e., asset basis less liabilities) exceeds the outside basis of T's shareholders in their T stock.

If T is a free-standing C corporation (i.e., not an 80-80 Bigco subsidiary) so that no Code §338(h)(10) election is available (*see* ¶206), the transaction can be structured for full asset SUB in two ways, either:

(1) P purchases T's assets (or T merges into P or a P subsidiary in a taxable forward merger), or

(2) P purchases T's stock and makes a Code §338 election.

In either event, T will be subjected to corporate-level tax on its asset sale gain, except to the extent T has an NOL sufficient to shelter its asset sale gain. In addition, T's shareholders will also be subjected to shareholder-level tax on their stock sale gain except where T sells its assets to P, retains its asset sale proceeds, and does not liquidate.

2. T is a free-standing C corporation. Generally, when T is a free-standing C corporation, it will not be advantageous to structure for full asset SUB unless T has sufficient NOL to shelter all or a substantial portion of T's asset sale gain (or deemed asset sale gain in the case of a Code §338 election).

EXAMPLE 1

T owns only land with an FV of $100 and a zero basis. On 1/1/89 P purchases T's stock for $66 but makes no Code §338 election. T continues to have a zero basis in the land.

On 1/1/91 T sells the land for $100 and recognizes $100 of gain. T pays $34 of tax.

EXAMPLE 2

Same as Example 1 except that P makes a Code §338 election.

Under *GU* repeal T thus incurs a $34 corporate-level tax and its basis in the land is stepped up to $100 (i.e., $66 purchase price for the stock and $34 tax liability on the Code §338 election). P borrows $34 to pay the Code §338 tax liability.

On 1/1/91 T sells the land for $100 and recognizes no gain. T repays the $34 debt and has $66 less the interest on the borrowed fund. Under these circumstances (and assuming that tax rates do not change), a Code §338 election is not advantageous to P because it merely accelerates $34 of tax on T's land which could otherwise be deferred until sale of the land.

EXAMPLE 3

Same as Example 1 except that T has a $100 NOL. On 1/1/89 P purchases T's stock for $100 but does not make a Code §338 election.

On 1/1/91 T sells the land and recognizes a $100 gain. Whether T can use its $100 NOL to offset this gain turns on the Code §382 rules, because the sale of 100% of T's stock on 1/1/88 is a change of ownership for purposes of Code §382(g). *See* Chapter 12. T can use its NOL to offset its $100 gain if such gain is a recognized BIG under Code §382(h), i.e., if the net unrealized BIG is greater than the lesser of 15% of the FV of T's assets immediately before the ownership change, or $10,000,000. In this example T's $100 gain is a recognized BIG and T can use its entire $100 NOL to offset such gain. If T's gain was not a BIG, T's ability to use its $100 NOL to offset such gain would be severely limited by the Code §382 formula.

EXAMPLE 4

Same as Example 3 except that P makes a Code §338 election.

T may use its NOL to offset its gain on the Code §338 election without regard to any Code §382 limitation triggered by the sale of T stock to P. As a result, T has no taxable gain ($100 gain offset by $100 NOL) and its basis in the land is stepped up to $100.

3. T is a Bigco 80-80 subsidiary. If T is a C corporation which is a Bigco 80-80 subsidiary so that a Code §338(h)(10) election can be made, the transaction can be structured for full asset SUB in two ways, either:

(1) P purchases T's assets and T liquidates into Bigco in a tax-free Code §332 liquidation (or T merges into P or a P subsidiary in a taxable forward merger), or

(2) P purchases T's stock and makes a joint Code §338(h)(10) election with Bigco (in which case T is treated as if T sold its assets to a newly formed subsidiary of P ("new T") and then T liquidated into Bigco in a tax-free Code §332 liquidation).

In either case, a single tax is imposed on the gain in T's assets, and no tax is imposed on Bigco's gain in its T stock. In contrast, if P purchases the stock of T (whether or not it is owned by Bigco) and makes a regular Code §338 election, two layers of tax are imposed.[1]

¶2001   [1] *See* ¶206 for discussion of Code §338(h)(10) and ¶205 for a discussion of Code §338.

EXAMPLE 5

Bigco owns all of T's stock, which has an FV of $100 and an outside tax basis in Bigco's hands of $40. T owns depreciable equipment with a $100 FV and a $40 inside tax basis in T's hands. T has no liabilities. The Bigco group files a consolidated return. P purchases T's stock for $100 on 2/1/94. P makes neither a Code §338 election nor a joint Code §338(h)(10) election with Bigco.

Bigco recognizes $60 of gain on the sale of T's stock and pays $21 in taxes ($60 × 35%).

T sells the equipment to X for $100 on 1/1/95. T recognizes $60 of gain and pays $21 in tax ($60 × 35%).

Thus, the total tax paid is $42 (Bigco's $21 tax on the sale of T's stock plus T's $21 tax on the sale of the equipment).

EXAMPLE 6

Same as Example 5 except P makes a Code §338 election (but P and Bigco do not make a joint Code §338(h)(10) election).

Bigco recognizes $60 of gain on the sale of T's stock ($100 selling price minus Bigco's $40 outside basis in T's stock). Bigco pays $21 in federal income tax ($60 gain × 35%).

Under the ADSP formula, old T recognizes $92.31 of gain on the deemed sale of its equipment ($100 stock purchase price plus $32.31 T-level income tax liability inherited by new T minus $40 asset basis). This income cannot be included on the Bigco group's consolidated return and must be reported by old T in a separate return. *See* ¶205.4. Old T pays $32.31 in federal income tax ($92.31 gain × 35%).

New T takes an aggregate basis of $132.31 in its assets ($100 purchase price + $32.31 in T-level tax liability inherited by new T). This asset basis is allocated $100 to T's equipment and, under the residual method, the remaining $32.31 is allocated to Code §197 intangibles (since under the allocation rules, assets other than Code §197 intangibles may not be allocated basis in excess of their FV). *See* ¶¶403.3 and 403.6.

Bigco and T pay a total of $53.31 in federal income taxes and T receives a $92.31 step-up in its asset basis ($132.31 new T asset basis compared to $40 old T asset basis), $32.31 of which is allocated to Code §197 intangibles amortizable over 15 years.

T recognizes no further gain when it sells the equipment for $100 on 1/1/95. However, upon the sale of the equipment, T will have no remaining assets or business, and so T will be allowed a loss of $32.31 with respect to its Code §197 intangibles.[2] This loss will yield $11.31 (35% of $32.31) in tax savings to P.

The same total tax is imposed on Bigco and T ($42 = Bigco's $21 tax on the sale of T's stock plus T's $32.31 tax paid on the sale of the equipment minus $11.31 tax savings resulting from the loss (or amortization) of the Code §197 intangibles) in Example 6 as was imposed in Example 5. However, Example 6 is less tax efficient overall because $32.31 of tax payments have been accelerated and $11.31 of tax savings have been deferred.[3]

EXAMPLE 7

Same as Example 5 except that Bigco and P make a joint Code §338(h)(10) election.

The Bigco group (on its consolidated income tax return) recognizes $60 gain on old T's deemed sale of its equipment to new T for $100 and Bigco pays $21 in federal income tax ($60 gain × 35%). *See* ¶206.1. Bigco recognizes no gain on the deemed Code §332 liquidation of old T into Bigco.

New T takes an aggregate $100 basis in its assets ($100 purchase price + $0 inherited tax liability). All of this basis is allocated to T's equipment. T recognizes no further gain when it sells the equipment on 1/1/95.

The results are considerably more tax efficient than the results in Examples 5 and 6. Bigco and T pay a total of $21 in federal income taxes (compared to $42 in Examples 5 and 6).

EXAMPLE 8

Same as Example 5 except that P purchases T's assets for $100 and T liquidates into Bigco. The results are the same as in Example 7.

The Bigco group (on its consolidated income tax return) recognizes $60 gain on T's sale of its equipment to P for $100 and Bigco pays $21 in federal income tax ($60 gain × 35%). Bigco recognizes no gain on the Code §332 liquidation of T into Bigco.

P takes an aggregate $100 basis in T's assets ($100 purchase price + $0 inherited tax liability). All of this basis is allocated to the equipment. P recognizes no gain on the sale of the equipment on 1/1/95.

---

[2] *See* Code §197(f)(1). For the sake of simplicity, this example treats the entire $32.31 basis in Code §197 intangibles as deductible 1/1/95 and ignores the fact that some portion will be deductible earlier through amortization.

[3] The deferral would be even greater if the Code §197 intangibles were amortized over 15 years instead of, as in this Example, allowed as a loss upon a disposition of the business.

EXAMPLE 9

Same as Example 5 except that Bigco has a large NOL which it will not be able to use fully.

If P and Bigco make a joint Code §338(h)(10) election with respect to P's purchase of T's stock, T will obtain an asset basis step-up at no tax cost to either P or Bigco, because Bigco's NOL will shelter T's $60 gain on the deemed sale of its assets.

P will generally not want to make the Code §338(h)(10) election if it results in an overall step-down in basis.

P will generally want to make a Code §338(h)(10) election if it produces a step-up in the tax basis of T's assets which is allocable (1) to depreciable and amortizable assets or (2) to assets likely to be sold soon (e.g., inventory). In some cases when there is an overall asset basis step-up, however, the operation of the allocation rules may make a Code §338(h)(10) election undesirable for P (e.g., by producing a step-down in basis for T's inventory and receivables). *See* ¶403.1.2.

Whether Bigco will desire to or be willing to make a Code §338(h)(10) election depends largely on the relative magnitude of Bigco's outside basis in its T stock compared to T's inside net basis in its assets (i.e., T's asset basis less its liabilities).[4] If T's inside net asset basis is higher, a Code §338(h)(10) election will reduce Bigco's gain. If T's outside basis is higher, a stock sale without a Code §338(h)(10) will produce less gain. If outside basis and inside net asset basis are equal, the amount of Bigco's gain will be the same with or without a Code §338(h)(10) election, although the composition of the gain (i.e., capital or ordinary) will likely be different, as explained more fully below.

The consolidated return investment adjustment rules generally adjust Bigco's outside basis in T's stock in lockstep with T's changes in net inside asset basis.[5] Thus, differences between inside and outside basis are generally produced, if at all, only in the transaction in which Bigco acquired T.

Bigco's outside basis in T's stock will be higher than T's inside net asset basis at the time of the Bigco-P stock sale if Bigco previously purchased T's stock for a price greater than T's inside net asset basis at the time of such stock purchase and such stock purchase was structured so that it left T's historic asset basis unchanged. Conversely, Bigco's outside basis in T's stock will be lower than T's inside net asset basis at the time of the Bigco-P stock sale if Bigco previously purchased T's stock for a price less than T's inside net asset basis at the time of such stock purchase and such stock purchase was structured so that T's historic asset basis remained unchanged. If Bigco previously formed T by dropping cash or assets into a newly formed T or if Bigco previously purchased T's stock in a transaction structured so that T's assets took on a new cost basis (i.e., a taxable purchase of assets or a

---

[4] *See* ¶206.2 for other reasons which may cause Bigco to desire to make a Code §338(h)(10) election.
[5] *See* Reg. §1.1502-32, discussed at ¶212.3.1.

taxable purchase of stock with a Code §338 or a Code §338(h)(10) election) or if Bigco previously purchased T's stock for a price equal to T's inside net asset basis at the time of such stock purchase, then Bigco's outside basis in T's stock will be equal to T's inside net asset basis at the time of the later Bigco-P stock sale.

If Bigco previously acquired T in a tax-free reorganization, the relationship between T's inside and outside basis at the time of the Bigco-P stock sale will turn on the relationship of Bigco's outside basis and T's inside basis immediately after the tax-free reorganization. If Bigco previously acquired T in a "B" reorganization, Bigco's initial outside basis in its T stock was equal to the basis that T's shareholders had in their T stock. In contrast, if Bigco previously acquired T in a reverse subsidiary merger under Code §368(a)(2)(E), a triangular "C" reorganization, or a forward subsidiary merger under Code §368(a)(2)(D), Bigco's initial outside basis in its T stock was generally equal to T's inside net asset basis at the time of the reorganization.[6]

Even when a Code §338(h)(10) election would not affect the amount of Bigco's gain on the sale of T's stock, the character of that gain may differ depending on whether the election is made. A stock sale will generally produce all capital gain while a Code §338(h)(10) deemed asset sale will generally produce part CG (to the extent the appreciated assets are capital assets or Code §1231 assets) and part OI (e.g., recapture and gain on appreciated inventory).

EXAMPLE 10

Bigco purchases T's stock for $200 and makes no Code §338 or §338(h)(10) election. T owns inventory worth $200 with a $50 tax basis and has no liabilities. The inventory rises in FV to $225, and Bigco decides to sell T's stock to P for $225.

If Bigco sells T's stock and makes a Code §338(h)(10) election (jointly with P), Bigco's gain will be $175 ($225 selling price − T's $50 inside asset basis) and the character of the gain will be OI (because T's only asset is inventory). On the other hand, if the parties make no Code §338(h)(10) election, Bigco's gain will be $25 ($225 selling price − Bigco's $200 outside basis in T's stock), and the character will be CG, long-term or short-term, depending on the length of Bigco's holding period for T's stock. Thus, although a Code §338(h)(10) election would give P a $175 step-up in the basis of T's inventory, it would increase Bigco's gain on the sale by $150 and change its character from capital to ordinary.

---

[6] Code §362(b) ("B" reorganizations); Prop. Reg. §1.358-6 (triangular reorganizations). *See also* ¶¶602.2, 803.6, 702.1.2, and 802.5.

4. T is an S corporation. When T is an S corporation, the transaction can be structured for full asset SUB in two ways, either:

(1) P purchases T-SCo's assets and T-SCo liquidates in a taxable Code §331 liquidation (or T-SCo merges into P or a P subsidiary in a taxable forward merger), but T's shareholders' basis in their T stock has been increased by T's asset sale gain taxed to them pursuant to the S rule—*see* ¶1108, or

(2) P purchases T's stock (or a newly formed P subsidiary merges into T-SCo in a taxable reverse subsidiary merger) and P makes a joint Code §338(h)(10) election with T-SCo's shareholders, in which case T-SCo is treated as if it sold its assets to a newly formed subsidiary of P ("new T") and then T-SCo liquidated under Code §331.

In either case a single tax is imposed on the gain in T's assets and, although T-SCo's liquidation is taxable to T-SCo's selling shareholders (although not, we believe, to a T-SCo shareholder who retained his T-SCo stock), T-SCo's shareholders' basis in their T-SCo stock is stepped up for the T-SCo asset sale gain.

Several other factors are relevant in deciding whether to structure an acquisition of T-SCo for SUB, including: (1) a sale of stock structured for COB generally produces all CG, while a sale of assets or a stock sale structured for SUB produces part OI and part CG (*see* ¶1109.3.2); (2) T-SCo's shareholders' outside basis in their T-SCo stock may differ from T-SCo's inside net asset basis (because of a prior death or stock sale); (3) Code §1374 corporate-level penalty tax may apply (*see* ¶1103.7.4); and (4) the parties may structure a bifurcated purchase of T-SCo, with P purchasing part of T-SCo's assets and then purchasing T-SCo's stock (*see* ¶¶204.3 and 1109.1.2).

5. Allocation rules may make an SUB undesirable. In some cases where an SUB transaction results in an overall asset basis step-up, the operation of the allocation rules may make the SUB transaction (i.e., a purchase of T's assets or a purchase of T's stock with a Code §338 or Code §338(h)(10) election) undesirable for P (e.g., by producing a step-down in basis for T's inventory and receivables).

EXAMPLE 11

T owns inventory (FV $100 and tax basis $100) and land (FV $150 and tax basis $10). T has a contingent liability that the parties value at $50 and no other liabilities. P buys T's stock from Bigco for $200 ($100 + $150–$50).

If P and Bigco make a Code §338(h)(10) election, new T's aggregate basis in its assets will initially be $200 (since the contingent liability may not be counted unless and until it becomes fixed). *See* ¶¶206.7, 1205.7.1 and 403.5. New T's $200 of asset basis is allocated between the inventory and land based on relative FV so that the basis in the inventory is stepped down to $80 (from $100) and the basis in the land is stepped up to $120 (from $10).

When T sells its inventory for $100 shortly after the acquisition, T recognizes $20 of gain attributable to the step-down. T recognizes no benefit from the step-up on the non-depreciable land unless and until T sells the land.

The result would be the same if the purchase price were allocated under Code §1060 (which generally applies if the purchased assets constitute a trade or business) if a new P subsidiary, S, purchased T's assets for $200 and assumed the contingent liability.[7]

Such an allocation (i.e., an allocation that produces a step-down in T's inventory and receivables) may result where P acquires T's assets or T's stock (with a Code §338 election or a Code §338(h)(10) election) and (i) the purchase price plus assumed liabilities is less than the FV of T's assets, (ii) a significant portion of the purchase price paid by P is contingent, or (iii) T has significant contingent liabilities that remain with new T or are assumed by P in the acquisition. In such case, the bargain element or the shortfall in basis caused by the timing rules for including contingent liabilities is generally allocated across all of T's Class 3 assets. *See* ¶403.3.

P may wish to consider allowing Bigco to keep T's inventory or T's receivables (or other assets where the shortfall in basis is a problem) in such case, with an appropriate adjustment to the purchase price, to avoid the adverse allocation. In the case of inventory, T may wish to consider making a LIFO election to attempt to lock in any shortfall in basis in a LIFO layer that it expects not to be invaded.[8]

¶2001.1.1.8   *Subchapter S, Consolidated Return, Purchase Accounting, Fraudulent Conveyance, and Antitrust Reporting*

A number of special considerations may arise in a merger, acquisition, or LBO when one or more of the participating corporations is or becomes an S corporation. These issues are discussed in Chapter 11.

Special considerations also may arise if T was a member of a consolidated group at any time prior to the sale to P or if T will enter into P's consolidated return. These issues are discussed at ¶¶210, 211, and 212.

---

[7] The allocation rules of Code §1060 are similar to those applicable to Code §338 and Code §338(h)(10) elections under Temp. Reg. §1.338(b)-2T. Both Code §1060 and Temp. Reg §1.338(b)-2T allocate basis to assets by class and use the residual method to value goodwill and going concern value. The two methods are not identical however. The allocation produced in a purchase of T's stock with a Code §338 or Code §338(h)(10) election may be different from the allocation resulting from a purchase of T's assets under Code §1060 if T has more than one business or if T has subsidiaries. *See* ¶403.3.

[8] The making of LIFO election in this situation raises certain additional questions such as (1) the proper LIFO pool for the purchased inventory and (2) the opening inventory for new T (in the case of a Code §338 or Code §338(h)(10) election) or P (in an asset purchase). The IRS has generally taken the position that a LIFO election does not lock the shortfall of basis in new T's or P's earliest LIFO layer.

Under generally accepted accounting principles, whether P's acquisition of T is accounted for as a purchase, a part purchase, or a pooling of interests can have a material effect on P's postacquisition accounting net income, balance sheet, and other accounting results. These issues are discussed in detail at ¶1503.

Some LBO structures prejudice T's creditors, and hence might permit payments, transfers, and obligations arising out of the LBO to be attacked under fraudulent conveyance law. These issues are discussed in detail at ¶1506.

The Hart-Scott-Rodino Antitrust Improvements Act of 1976 and the rules and regulations promulgated by the Federal Trade Commission thereunder prohibit P from acquiring more than a certain percentage or dollar amount of voting securities or assets of T unless P and T have complied with the reporting and waiting periods of the Act, unless the size of P and T falls below the size-of-person criteria *or* the size of the transaction falls below the size-of-transaction criteria *or* a specific exemption applies. The statute and rules apply to acquisitions of stock, acquisitions of assets, and mergers alike (with minor timing variations for tender offers). These issues are discussed in detail at ¶1507.

¶2001.1.2   Representations and Warranties

Several of the key nontax aspects in drafting an acquisition agreement (and frequently the most disputed) are (i) the extent of the representations and warranties P will obtain from the seller(s), (ii) the extent of the seller(s)'s liability for any breach of these representations and warranties (e.g., the time period within which P must make a claim, the deductible amount, the threshold amount, the ceiling amount, and/or the significance of whether P knew of the breach at the time of closing), and (iii) P's method for recovering from the seller(s)—generally T in a sale of assets or T's shareholder(s) in a sale of stock or merger (e.g., escrow, note recoupment, lawsuit, or arbitration).

¶2001.1.2.1   *The Extent to Which the Seller(s) Will Give P Contractual Representations and Warranties*

For example, the seller(s) might give P representations and warranties concerning (i) authorization with respect to the transaction, (ii) title to the stock or assets being sold (and title to T's underlying assets in a stock sale), (iii) required governmental and third party consents (and noncontravention generally), (iv) organization and capitalization, (v) historical financial statements, (vi) intervening material adverse changes in the business, (vii) litigation and undisclosed liabilities, (viii) tax matters, (ix) adequacy and condition of T's tangible assets, (x) real estate matters, (xi) intellectual property matters, (xii) leases, licenses, and contracts, (xiii) inventory and accounts receivable, (xiv) pension and welfare benefit plans, (xv) compliance with federal, state, local, and foreign laws, (xvi) environmental matters, (xvii) product liability and warranties, (xviii) insurance, (xix) brokerage fees, and (xx) material misstatements and omissions.

¶2001.1.2.2   *The Extent to Which the Representations and Warranties*
              Will Be Qualified with References to Knowledge and
              Materiality

In drafting the seller(s)'s representations and warranties, the contract may make
the allocation of risk between P and the seller(s) turn on whether the particular
fact represented (e.g., the existence of a T liability or a defect in a T asset) is
"known" or is "material." If so, the contract should specify the person(s) whose
knowledge is relevant (e.g., any T shareholder, director, officer, or employee vs.
only certain specified high-level T executives). In addition, it may be desirable
for the contract to define "knowledge" (e.g., whether it implies a duty to investigate
and whether it includes "should have known") and "materiality" (e.g., whether
a matter involves more than $50,000).

¶2001.1.2.3   *The Extent to Which the Representations and Warranties*
              Will Survive the Closing

P will want the seller(s)'s representations and warranties to survive the closing
of the acquisition for a long time, if not indefinitely, so that P can recover for
breaches which do not become known until substantially after the closing (unless,
as discussed at ¶2001.1.2.6, P is acquiring a publicly held T).

On the other hand, the seller(s) will generally want the representations and
warranties to terminate at the closing (i.e., not to survive the closing so that they
merely function as closing conditions) or, if they do survive the closing, to survive
only for a specified short period of time within which P must make any claim
for indemnification.

Often the parties will agree on some arbitrary period of survival, perhaps
with a longer period for third party claims (such as environmental cleanup or
IRS claims).

P will seek a provision allowing it to recover for breach of representation or
warranty even if P knew about the breach at the time of closing. The seller(s),
however, will seek a provision precluding any P claim for breach of representation
or warranty if P knew (or even should have known) about the breach at the time
of closing. There may be a strong presumption that P knew (or at least should
have known) about a particular breach if P conducted extensive business, legal,
and accounting due diligence prior to closing.

¶2001.1.2.4   *The Extent to Which P's Indemnification Rights Will Be*
              Subject to a Deductible, Threshold, and/or Ceiling

Another issue is whether there will be a *deductible* (e.g., seller(s) liable only for
damages in excess of a $100,000 deductible) or a *threshold* (e.g., seller(s) liable for
the entire amount once damages exceed $100,000), and whether there will be a
ceiling (e.g., seller(s)'s liability for damages will not exceed $1 million).

¶2001.1.2.5   *The Manner in Which P Will Be Able to Recover Damages*
            from the Seller(s) for a Breach of Representation and
            Warranty

There is generally vigorous negotiation as to the method for protecting P against breaches of the seller(s)'s representations and warranties. For example, P may have the right to recover back a portion of the purchase price by lawsuit against the seller(s), the right to make a claim against an escrow of a portion of the purchase price, and/or the right to recoup its losses against any P notes issued to the seller(s). P also may have a security interest in specific seller(s)'s assets. *See* ¶2001.1.7 for a general discussion of dispute resolution alternatives (e.g., specific performance, arbitration, consent to service of process, and consent to exclusive jurisdiction).

¶2001.1.2.6   *The Extent to Which P Will Have Indemnification Rights*
            and Remedies When T Is Public

When P is acquiring a publicly held T, T's representations and warranties generally will *not* survive the closing of the acquisition (i.e., P is generally not entitled to recover any of the purchase price from the seller(s)) for two reasons: *First*, P will have the comfort of the substantial public information about T available in T's SEC filings, and hence P needs less in the way of representations and warranties. *Second*, the purchase price will generally be disbursed to T's public shareholders as soon as the acquisition is closed. Although an escrow for a portion of the purchase price is feasible, it is not frequently used.

¶2001.1.3   Restrictive and Affirmative Covenants

The parties might agree to certain pre-closing covenants requiring the seller(s) to operate the business in the ordinary course in accordance with past custom and practice (e.g., restricting acquisitions, dispositions, large capital expenditures, dividends, issuance or redemption of T securities, new material contracts, bonus payments, salary increases, etc.), requiring the seller(s) to notify P of any material adverse development, preventing the seller(s) from soliciting further offers (or responding to unsolicited proposals), imposing confidentiality requirements on P, and allocating responsibility for the satisfaction of closing conditions.

Similarly, the parties might agree to certain post-closing covenants requiring the seller(s) to refrain from competition, imposing confidentiality requirements on the seller(s), providing for mutual transition assistance, or requiring a seller to render consulting services.

If T has been a subsidiary or a division of Bigco, T may require significant transition assistance. This might be the case when Bigco performs substantial services for its subsidiaries and divisions and/or when Bigco owns various tangible and intangible assets used by its subsidiaries and divisions. For example,

T may require accounting, purchasing, payroll, risk management, and data processing services, real estate leases, or intellectual property licenses from Bigco. P and the seller(s) may also have to address the disposition of employee benefit plan assets and liabilities when T's employees have participated in Bigco-level plans.

¶2001.1.4 The Extent to Which the Respective Parties Will Have Closing Conditions, the Failure of Which Will Allow P and/or the Seller(s) to Refuse to Consummate the Transaction

For example, P might have closing conditions concerning (i) compliance with the seller(s)'s representations, warranties, and covenants, (ii) absence of a material adverse change, (iii) absence of litigation affecting the transaction, (iv) availability of financing, (v) delivery of title insurance, surveys, and third party consents, (vi) delivery of any side agreements, and (vii) delivery of an opinion of the seller(s)'s legal counsel.

Similarly, the seller(s) might have closing conditions concerning (i) compliance with P's representations, warranties, and covenants, (ii) absence of litigation affecting the transaction, (iii) delivery of any side agreements, and (iv) delivery of an opinion of P's legal counsel.

¶2001.1.5 The Circumstances Under Which the Respective Parties Will Be Able to Terminate the Contract Without Penalty

For example, any party might be able to terminate the contract (i) after a "drop-dead date" (e.g., 120 days after signing) if a condition to its obligation to close remains unsatisfied or (ii) in the interim if another party breaches any representation, warranty, or covenant in any material respect. P might also have the right to terminate the contract for a limited period (e.g., 15 days) after signing if P is not satisfied with the results of its continuing business, legal, and accounting due diligence.

¶2001.1.6 The Extent to Which P and/or the Seller(s) Will Be Entitled to Damages in the Event the Transaction Does Not Close

For example, the contract may require P to pay a specified amount of liquidated damages if it defaults. Alternatively, the seller(s) may require P to put up an earnest money deposit at the time of signing. In that event, the contract would specify the circumstances under which P would receive back this deposit if the transaction did not close.

Similarly, the contract may require the seller(s) to pay P a specified break-up fee and/or reimbursement for its out-of-pocket expenses if a seller defaults.

¶2001.1.7   The Manner in Which P and the Seller(s) Will Settle Any Disputes over the Contract

For example, the contract may (i) specify that specific performance is an appropriate remedy for a party's failure to close, (ii) call for arbitration rather than litigation to resolve a dispute regarding a party's failure to close, a party's alleged breach of representation, warranty, or covenant, or a dispute over a purchase price adjustment, or (iii) contain a consent to service of process in a particular jurisdiction's courts (and/or a limitation of suit to the courts of a particular jurisdiction).

¶2001.2   Principal Issues Associated with Certain Legal Structures

¶2001.2.1   P's Purchase of T's Stock

This volume contains several sample acquisition agreements for P's purchase of T's stock:

(i)   pro-buyer terms (*see* ¶2002.1),
(ii)   pro-seller terms (*see* ¶2002.2),
(iii) neutral terms (*see* ¶2002.3),
(iv)   additional provisions in which T is a subsidiary of Bigco filing a consolidated federal income tax return before the acquisition (*see* ¶2002.4), and
(v)   additional provisions in which there is to be a purchase price adjustment based on T's closing date balance sheet (*see* ¶2002.5).

¶2001.2.1.1   *Brief Summary of Federal Income Tax Issues in a Stock Acquisition*

1. Taxable stock acquisitions.

Taxable purchase of T's stock. P purchases all of T's stock for cash and/or P notes.

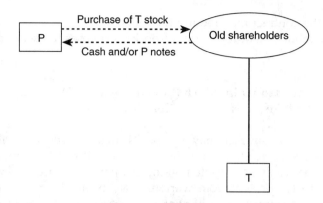

See Chapter 2 for a discussion of a taxable stock purchase and a reverse subsidiary taxable merger treated for tax purposes as a taxable stock purchase, Chapter 4 for a discussion of certain additional aspects of a taxable stock purchase or taxable reverse subsidiary merger, and Chapter 11 for a discussion of Subchapter S aspects of such a transaction where P or T (or both) is an S corporation.

In a taxable stock purchase, T's shareholders recognize the gain or loss (usually capital) realized on the sale of their T stock.[1]

T shareholders who receive P notes generally may report their gain from the stock sale on the installment method, as long as (1) the P notes received are not payable on demand or readily tradable and (2) the T stock sold was not traded on an established securities market. The tax deferral arising from a large installment sale (generally where the P note received by a T-selling shareholder exceeds $5 million) is subject to an interest charge payable annually to IRS.

P's basis in the T stock purchased is equal to the purchase price paid by P plus expenses (such as legal fees) of effectuating the acquisition.

If P delivers nontraded notes bearing inadequate stated interest to pay all or part of the purchase price of nontraded T shares, the notes are appropriately discounted under the Code, and both the sale price to T's shareholders and P's basis in the T shares will reflect the discounted (rather than the larger face) amount. If the T shares or the P notes are publicly traded, both the sale price to T's shareholders and P's basis in the T shares will derive from the market price of the T shares or the P notes, whichever is publicly traded.

¶2001.2   [1] Two significant qualifications:

First, if T's stock is owned by Bigco and T is a member of the Bigco consolidated group prior to P's purchase of T's stock, the consolidated return regulations severely restrict the allowance of any Bigco loss deduction on the sale of its T stock.

Second, if a part of the consideration is P stock (but the transaction does not qualify for reorganization or Code §351 treatment—*see* Chapter 7 through Chapter 9), the P stock is treated like cash in an amount equal to such stock's FV in computing T's shareholders' gain on the transaction and P's basis in the T stock purchased. Installment reporting is not available to T's shareholders with respect to the P stock because the P stock constitutes immediate (rather than deferred) payment.

T recognizes no gain or loss on the sale of its stock, and T's basis in its assets after the acquisition remains the same as before the acquisition (absent an election under Code §338). T's other tax attributes are generally not affected by the acquisition (absent a Code §338 election). However, T's ability thereafter to use its net operating loss, net capital loss, and excess tax credits may be limited by Code §§269, 382, and 383 and by the consolidated return regulation SRLY rules. See Chapter 12. In addition, if T has a net operating loss and will be included in P's consolidated group, P and T should consider making (on their consolidated federal income tax return for the year of the P-T acquisition) an irrevocable election to waive all or part of T's NOL to avoid a reduction in the outside basis of T's stock if and when T's NOL expires. See ¶1203.3.

If P makes a timely regular Code §338 election (on or before the 15th day of the ninth month following the month in which the acquisition date occurred) to treat T as if it had sold and also purchased its own assets:

(1) T becomes (for most tax purposes) "new T" immediately following the acquisition date;

(2) old T is taxed, effective at the close of the acquisition date, as if it had sold its assets (in a "deemed asset sale") to new T;

(3) old T therefore recognizes the full gain or loss in its assets (both tangible and intangible);

(4) old T's tax attributes, including old T's net operating loss and other carryforwards, will generally be usable to offset gain on old T's deemed asset sale to new T but will not be usable by new T or P after the deemed sale;

(5) new T's basis in its assets is stepped up (or down) to equal, in the aggregate, the purchase price paid by P plus old T's liabilities transferred to new T (including old T's tax liability generated by the deemed sale of its assets to new T for which new T is primarily liable) plus P's acquisition expenses; and

(6) old T's corporate attributes—e.g., net operating loss and other carryovers (to the extent not used to offset old T's deemed asset sale gain), E&P, and tax accounting methods—are expunged.[2]

After the 1993 enactment of Code §197 permitting 15-year amortization of goodwill and other purchased intangibles, all of T's SUB (except basis allocable to land) normally generates deductions (depreciation, amortization, cost of goods sold, and the like).

Even when P makes a regular Code §338 election, T's shareholders are still taxed on their sale of T stock, i.e., with a regular Code §338 election, only P and T (and not T's shareholders) are taxed as if there had been an asset sale. Thus, where P makes a regular Code §338 election, there is generally double tax on the transaction, i.e., T's shareholders pay tax on their stock sale gain (generally at CG rates) and T pays tax on its deemed asset sale gain (part capital and part ordinary, depending on the mix of T's assets giving rise to the gain).

There are, however, several circumstances where double tax can be avoided on a stock sale with a Code §338 election:

---

[2] If T qualifies for a Code §338(h)(10) election (generally only when T is an S corporation or when T is an 80-80 Bigco subsidiary) and such election is jointly made by T's shareholder(s) and by P, the tax rules applicable to the transaction are significantly modified as described below in text.

- There is no double taxation when (1) T is an S corporation, (2) T is not subject to Code §1374 tax (attributable to a prior C corporation history), and (3) the parties (i.e., P and T's shareholders) make a Code §338(h)(10) election (as contrasted with a regular Code §338 election discussed above) so that T's shareholders (as well as T) are taxed as if T had sold assets and distributed the proceeds to its shareholders in liquidation. This result follows because an S corporation is not subject to corporate-level tax on its asset sale gain (unless Code §1374 applies). If T-SCo is subject to Code §1374 tax, there may be double tax on only a portion of T-SCo's deemed asset sale gain.
- There is no double taxation when (1) T is a Bigco 80-80 subsidiary (whether or not Bigco and T file a consolidated return) and (2) the parties (i.e., P and Bigco) make a Code §338(h)(10) election so that Bigco (as well as T) is taxed as if T had sold assets and distributed the proceeds to Bigco in a tax-free Code §332 liquidation.
- There is no double taxation when (1) T is a C corporation, (2) T is not a Bigco 80-80 subsidiary, and (3) T has an NOL sufficient to shelter all of T's corporate-level deemed sale gain from the regular Code §338 election. When T's NOL is not sufficient to shelter all of T's corporate-level deemed sale gain, there is no double taxation to the extent T's NOL shelters T's deemed sale gain.

These volumes assume (except where otherwise stated) that T is a C corporation, is not an 80-80 Bigco subsidiary, and does not have an NOL.

2. Tax-free stock acquisitions.

P's Acquisition of T's Stock in a Tax-Free Exchange. P acquires all of T's stock in exchange for P stock (or P stock plus "boot," i.e., generally any property other than P stock) in a transaction qualifying as tax-free reorganization under Code §368, generally a "B" reorganization or a reverse subsidiary "A" reorganization.

"B" reorganization

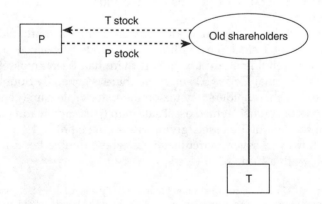

Reverse subsidiary "A" reorganization

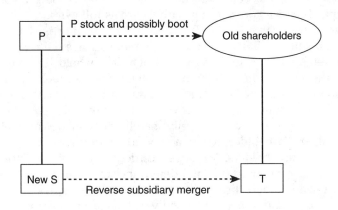

In some reorganization formats—generally those not involving a merger or subsidiary merger—only P voting stock may be received tax free and the presence of any boot or any P nonvoting stock will prevent the transaction from qualifying as a reorganization.

See Chapter 6 through Chapter 8 for a discussion of tax-free reorganizations.

T's shareholders do not recognize any gain or loss realized on the exchange of stock except that (if the reorganization employs a form that permits the delivery of boot) a T shareholder recognizes gain to the extent of any boot received, but not in excess of the gain realized on the transaction. Each T shareholder takes a substituted basis in the P stock received equal to the basis in the T stock surrendered, increased by any gain recognized and reduced by the amount of any boot received.

T's basis in its assets is unchanged and P may not elect to step up the basis of T's assets under Code §338. T recognizes no gain on the exchange and generally retains its tax attributes. However, T's ability to use its net operating loss, net capital loss, and excess tax credits may be limited by Code §§269, 382, and 383 and by the consolidated return regulation SRLY rules. See Chapter 12. In addition, if T has a net operating loss and will be included in P's consolidated group, P and T should consider making (on their consolidated federal income tax return for the year of the P-T acquisition) an irrevocable election to waive all or part of T's NOL to avoid a reduction in the outside basis of T's stock if and when T's NOL expires. See ¶1204.4 and ¶1203.3.

Depending upon the format of the reorganization, P may take a basis in the T stock acquired (1) equal to the aggregate basis T's shareholders had in the T stock exchanged or (2) equal to T's basis in its assets less its liabilities.

¶2001.2.1.2   Key Nontax Issues in a Stock Acquisition

Some of the key nontax considerations where P is purchasing T's stock (rather than acquiring T's assets or merging with T) are as follows:

(1) *Acquiring less than 100% of T.* When the acquisition is structured as P's voluntary acquisition of T's stock, each T shareholder has the right to retain his T stock or to sell his T stock to P. In the case of a closely held T, it may be possible to negotiate the acquisition of 100% of T's stock. This is much less likely in the case of a widely or publicly held T. In the latter case, P may end up owning less than 100% of T's outstanding stock, in which case P would have all the concerns associated with the presence of T minority shareholders, such as possible P liability (as T's controlling shareholder) for breach of fiduciary duties in its dealings with T or its minority shareholders. Moreover, difficult fairness and "going private" issues will generally be raised if P later determines to acquire (i.e., "squeeze out") the T minority shareholders through merger or otherwise, as discussed at ¶1502.7.

(2) *Liability for T's indebtedness.* Generally, if P acquires T's stock, T's creditors can reach only T's assets and not P's assets.

(3) *Mechanical problems in transferring T's assets.* When P acquires T's stock so that T's assets are not transferred, the difficulties involved in actually conveying title to numerous parcels of real estate, motor vehicles, or the like are generally not encountered. Certain types of agreements (e.g., loan agreements and leases) and certain types of licenses may, however, explicitly require the consent of the third party in the event of a change in T's control, i.e., a sale of a controlling interest in T's stock.

(4) *Transfer, sales, and use taxes.* There is generally no transfer, sales, or use tax on P's purchase of T's stock. Some states, however, impose a stock transfer tax. The transaction may also be subject to New York State Real Property Transfer Gains Tax (due to the transfer of a controlling interest in T's stock) if T holds real property located in New York. There may be transfer taxes on a subsequent merger between P and its subsidiary T or a subsequent liquidation of T, depending upon the laws of the particular state involved.

(5) *Non-pro-rata consideration.* In an acquisition of T stock (not constituting a public tender offer) in which P deals separately with each T shareholder, P may give different amounts or types of consideration to different T shareholders (subject to state corporate law and full disclosure under SEC Rule 10b-5). For example, P can pay $10 per share to some T shareholders and $9 per share to others. Or P can pay some T shareholders in cash, others by note, and still others with P stock.

In the case of a public tender offer, however, all of T's tendering shareholders must either receive the same consideration or have the option to receive the same consideration in a cash-option offer. *See* ¶805.

(6) *Dissenters' rights.* Because of the voluntary nature of a stock acquisition (i.e., a T shareholder is not compelled to sell his T stock to P), statutory dissenters' or appraisal rights entitling a T shareholder to sue to recover the FV of his T stock do not apply.

(7) *Shareholder vote.* Because of the voluntary nature of a stock acquisition from the perspective of T's shareholders, no vote of T's shareholders is required when P is acquiring T's stock. Approval by P's shareholders will be required only if

(a) P's charter explicitly requires the approval of P's shareholders;

(b) P is issuing stock to T's shareholders in excess of P's authorized shares (so that a vote of P's shareholders is necessary to authorize the stock);

(c) P's stock is listed on the New York Stock Exchange ("NYSE"), the American Stock Exchange ("AMEX"), the Nasdaq National Market ("Nasdaq NM") or certain regional exchanges which would de-list P's stock if it effectuated the transaction without a shareholder vote. Each of the NYSE, AMEX, Nasdaq NM, or certain regional exchange rules has slightly different substantive provisions and somewhat different wording.

The NYSE rules require a shareholder vote when:

(i) P is issuing 20% (in voting power or in number of shares) or more of its common stock (or equivalent such as warrants or convertibles), or

(ii) the acquisition is from a director, officer, or substantial shareholder of P (or of a P subsidiary, affiliate, and other closely related person), or from any company or party in which one of such persons has a substantial direct or indirect interest, and P is issuing 1% (in voting power or in number of shares) or more of its common stock (or equivalent such as warrants or convertible), or

(iii) the issuance will result in a change of control of P.

The AMEX rules require a shareholder vote when:

(i) P is issuing or potentially issuing common stock or securities convertible into its common stock which could result in an increase in its outstanding common stock of 20% or more, or

(ii) any director, officer or substantial shareholder of P has a 5% or greater interest (or such persons collectively have a 10% or greater interest), directly or indirectly, in the company or assets to be acquired or otherwise has such an interest in the consideration to be paid in the transaction and the present or potential issuance of P's common stock, or securities convertible into P's common stock, could result in an increase in outstanding P common stock of 5% or more, or

(iii) P is issuing or selling its common stock (or securities convertible into its common stock) at a price below the greater of book or market value and such issuance or sale (together with any sales by P's directors, officers or substantial shareholders) equals 20% or more of P's presently outstanding common stock, or

(iv) P is selling or issuing its common stock (or securities convertible into its common stock) equal to 20% or more of its presently outstanding stock at a price below the greater of book or market value of the stock.

The Nasdaq NM rules require a shareholder vote when:

(i)   P is issuing 20% (in voting power or in number of shares) or more of its common stock (or equivalent, such as warrants or convertibles),

(ii)   P is issuing or selling its common stock (or equivalent, such as warrants or convertibles) at a price below the greater of book or market value, and such issuance or sale (together with any sales by P's directors, officers, and substantial shareholders) represents 20% or more in voting power or in number of common shares,

(iii) any director, officer, or substantial shareholder of P has a 5%-or-greater interest (or such persons collectively have a 10%-or-greater interest), directly or indirectly, in the company or assets to be acquired or otherwise has an interest in the consideration to be paid, and P is issuing 5% (in voting power or in number of shares) or more of its common stock (or equivalent, such as warrants or convertibles), or

(iv)   the issuance will result in a change of control of P.[3]

If P is publicly held and a vote of its shareholders is necessary, P must comply with SEC's proxy rules, as described at ¶1502.2.7.6.

(8) *Application of the 1933 Act.* Acquisitions of stock are generally effected for cash, other securities (including debt and/or equity securities), or some combination thereof. Whenever part or all of the consideration is stock or debt instruments (i.e., "securities" within the meaning of the 1933 Act) of P (or S), P (or S) must comply with the 1933 Act. The 1933 Act prohibits the sale of securities unless (i) such securities are registered with the SEC and certain other requirements are satisfied *or* (ii) there is an applicable exemption from registration, e.g., the private placement, SEC Rule 701, or intrastate exemption.

If T's shareholder group is of any significant size, P (or S) will generally not be able to qualify for an exemption and will be required to register under the 1933 Act the P (or S) stock or notes being issued for T's stock. This process is likely to require at least several weeks and more likely several months. The 1933 Act registration requirements are discussed in greater detail at ¶1502.2.8.1.

Section 4(2) of the 1933 Act exempts P (or S) from the requirement to register its stock or debt securities if the issuance does not involve a public offering (i.e., the offering constitutes a private placement). SEC Regulation D (Rules 501 through 508 under the 1933 Act) and SEC Rule 701 each provide a safe harbor for certain private placements. Regulation D and Rule 701 are discussed in greater detail at ¶¶1502.2.8.2 and 1502.2.8.3.

---

[3] Under the NYSE and NASD rules, these percentage tests are calculated using (1) *as the numerator* the voting power, or the number of shares, of common stock that will be issued or sold in the transaction (assuming exercise of any warrants, and conversion of any convertibles, that will be issued or sold in the transaction), and (2) *as the denominator* the voting power of all voting securities (i.e., not merely common stock), or the number of shares of common stock, actually outstanding immediately *before* the proposed issuance or sale (this time *without* assuming exercise of any warrants, or conversion of any convertibles, whether those outstanding or those being issued or sold in the transaction).

Section 3(a)(11) of the 1933 Act exempts intrastate offerings. SEC Rule 147 provides a safe harbor for certain intrastate offerings. Rule 147 is discussed in greater detail at ¶1502.2.8.4.

If P (or S) has issued stock or debt securities to T's shareholders in exchange for T's stock, there are frequently SEC restrictions on resale of the P (or S) stock or debt securities (unless the parties file a 1933 Act registration statement covering such resale). Although recent amendments to Rule 144 have shortened the holding period for public resales of "restricted securities" to one year, other Rule 144 requirements must still be satisfied. These resale restrictions are discussed in greater detail at ¶1502.2.8.5.

(9) *Other considerations.* Care should be taken, particularly in the case of a closely held T, to insure that P's purchase of T's stock is carried out in compliance with any restrictions in T's charter or bylaws or any agreement among T's shareholders restricting the free sale of T stock to P.

Although not commonly used, some state corporation statutes authorize the shareholders of two corporations, by requisite vote of their shareholders, to adopt a "plan of exchange" which forces all T shareholders to exchange their T securities for P securities or other consideration. This sort of acquisition would require compliance with (i) the 1934 Act's proxy requirements if publicly held T's or P's shareholders are voting on the transaction (*see* ¶1502.2.7.6) and (ii) the 1933 Act's registration requirements if P securities are being issued to a group of T shareholders of any significant size (*see* ¶1502.2.8).

If T's stock is widely held, any effort by P to acquire T stock from a significant number of T shareholders on any systematic basis (other than through open market purchases and privately negotiated purchases, generally including street sweeps) would necessitate compliance with SEC tender offer disclosure requirements of the 1934 Act.

¶2001.2.2   P's Purchase of Part or All of T's Assets

This volume contains several sample acquisition agreements for P's purchase of part or all of T's assets:

(i)   pro-buyer, pro-seller, and neutral versions in which P is purchasing all of T's assets (*see* ¶2003),

(ii)   pro-buyer, pro-seller, and neutral versions in which P is purchasing a T divisional business (*see* ¶2004), and

(iii)   additional provisions in which there is to be a purchase price adjustment based on T's closing date balance sheet (*see* ¶2002.5).

¶2001.2.2.1   Brief Summary of Federal Income Tax Issues in an Asset Acquisition

1. Taxable asset acquisitions.

P's Taxable Purchase of T's Assets. P purchases T's assets (and generally assumes T's liabilities) for cash and/or P notes.

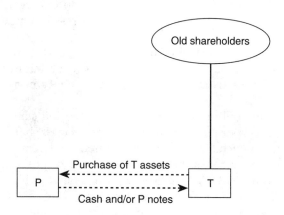

See Chapter 3 for a discussion of a taxable asset purchase and a forward taxable merger treated for tax purposes as an asset purchase, Chapter 4 for certain additional aspects of a taxable asset purchase or taxable reverse subsidiary merger, and Chapter 11 for a discussion of subchapter S aspects of such a transaction in which P or T (or both) is an S corporation.

In a taxable asset purchase, P takes a basis in T's assets equal to the purchase price paid plus any T liabilities transferred to P plus P's acquisition expenses (such as legal fees).

After the 1993 enactment of Code §197 permitting 15-year amortization of goodwill and other purchased intangibles, all of T's SUB (except basis allocable to land) normally generates deductions (depreciation, amortization, cost of goods sold, and the like).

T recognizes full gain or loss on the sale of its assets.[4] T's tax attributes—e.g., NOL and other carryovers, E&P, and tax accounting methods—are not acquired by P. T's NOLs and other carryovers are, however, generally usable by T to offset gain on the asset sale.

If T receives P notes that are not payable on demand or readily tradable, T generally may use the installment method to report the gain recognized on sale

---

[4] If a part of the consideration is P stock (but the transaction does not qualify for reorganization or Code §351 treatment—*see* Chapter 7 through Chapter 9), the P stock is treated like cash in an amount equal to such stock's FV, in computing T's gain on the transaction (and T's shareholders' gain if T is liquidated) as well as P's basis in the purchased assets. Installment reporting is not available to T or its shareholders with respect to the P stock because the P stock constitutes immediate (rather than deferred) payment.

of its assets (other than recapture, gain on marketable securities or inventory, and gain on certain other assets not qualifying for installment reporting), so long as T does not liquidate.[5] The tax deferral arising from a large installment sale (generally when the P note received by T exceeds $5 million) is subject to an interest charge payable annually to IRS.

T's shareholders do not realize taxable gain or loss on T's asset sale, unless T liquidates (except that when T is an S corporation, T's shareholders rather than T report and pay tax on T's asset sale gain). If T liquidates, its shareholders recognize gain or loss (usually capital) on the disposition of their T stock in the liquidation. However, if (1) T distributes P notes to its shareholders in a prompt complete liquidation, (2) the P notes qualify for installment reporting, and (3) T's stock is not traded on an established securities market, then T's shareholders generally may use the installment method to report their gain on the liquidation. The tax deferral arising from a large installment sale (generally where the P note received by a T shareholder exceeds $5 million) is subject to an interest charge payable annually to IRS.

There is generally double tax when P sells its assets and distributes the proceeds to its shareholders in liquidation, i.e., T pays tax on its asset sale gain (part capital and part ordinary, depending on the mix of T's assets giving rise to the gain) and T's shareholders pay tax on their stock sale gain (generally at CG rates).

There are, however, several circumstances where double tax can be avoided on T's sale of assets followed by T's liquidation:

- There is no double taxation if T (1) is an S corporation and (2) is not subject to Code §1374 tax (attributable to a prior C corporation history). If T is subject to Code §1374 tax, there may be double tax on only a portion of T-SCo's asset sale gain.
- There is no double taxation if T is a Bigco 80-80 subsidiary (whether or not Bigco and T file a consolidated return), so that T's distribution of its asset sale proceeds to Bigco is a Code §332 tax-free liquidation.
- There is no double taxation if (1) T is a C corporation, (2) T is not a Bigco 80-80 subsidiary, and (3) T has an NOL sufficient to shelter all of T's corporate-level asset sale gain. If T's NOL is not sufficient to shelter all of T's corporate-level asset sale gain, there is no double taxation to the extent T's NOL shelters T's asset sale gain.

2. Tax-free asset acquisitions.

P's Acquisition of T's Assets in a Tax-Free Exchange. P acquires all of T's assets in exchange for P stock (or P stock plus boot) in a transaction qualifying as a tax-free reorganization under Code §368, generally an "A" or "C" reorganization or a forward subsidiary "A" reorganization.

---

[5] When T is an S corporation, its liquidation may not accelerate gain on distribution to its shareholders of the P notes in a complete liquidation of T.

"C" reorganization

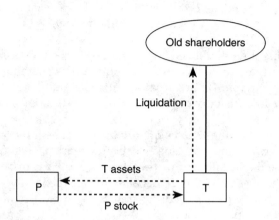

"A" reorganization

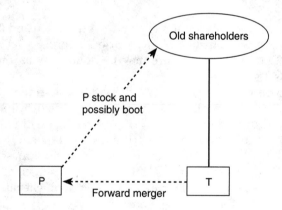

Forward subsidiary "A" reorganization

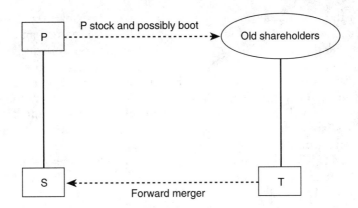

In some reorganization formats—generally those not involving a merger or subsidiary merger—only P voting stock may be received tax free and the presence of any boot or any P nonvoting stock will prevent the transaction from qualifying as a reorganization.

See Chapter 6 through Chapter 8 for a discussion of tax-free reorganizations.

T shareholders exchange their T stock for P stock (or, in some cases in which the transaction is a statutory merger, P stock and possibly boot) either because T has liquidated or because the asset acquisition was accomplished by statutory merger. T's shareholders do not recognize any gain or loss realized on the exchange except that (if the reorganization employs a form that permits the delivery of boot) gain realized by a T shareholder will be recognized to the extent of any boot received. Each T shareholder takes a substituted basis in the P stock received equal to the basis in the T stock surrendered, increased by any gain recognized and reduced by the amount of any boot received.

P takes a carryover basis in T's assets and generally acquires T's tax attributes. However, P's ability to use T's net operating loss, net capital loss, and excess tax credits may be limited by Code §§269, 382, and 383 and by the consolidated return regulation SRLY rules. See Chapter 12. In addition, if P's subsidiary S acquires T's assets in a subsidiary "A" or subsidiary "C" reorganization in exchange for P stock, (i) S's ability thereafter to use T's net operating loss, net capital loss and excess tax credits may be limited by the consolidated return regulations' SRLY rules, and (ii) P and S should consider making (on their consolidated federal income tax return for the year of the P-T acquisition) an irrevocable election to waive all or part of T's NOL (acquired by S in the reorganization) to avoid a reduction in the outside basis of S's stock if and when the NOL expires. See ¶1204.4 and ¶1203.3.

T generally recognizes no gain or loss on the transaction.

¶2001.2.2.2   *Key Nontax Issues in an Asset Acquisition*

Some of the key nontax considerations in which P is purchasing some or all of T's assets (and assuming some or all of T's liabilities), leaving T and the balance of its assets and liabilities (if any) as a separate noncontrolled company, are as follows:

(1) *Acquiring less than 100% of T.* If P acquires all or substantially all of T's assets, P will not be left to deal with any T minority shareholders following the transaction (as P will be if it buys less than all of T's stock). If the requisite vote of T's shareholders is obtained for a sale of assets, the sale takes place notwithstanding dissenting shareholders.

(2) *Liability for T's indebtedness.* If P acquires T's assets, the bulk sales provisions of the Uniform Commercial Code (UCC Article 6) generally permit T's creditors to sue P (at least up to the FV of T's assets acquired by P) for six months after the acquisition, unless notice was given to all of T's creditors (in some states by registered mail and in other states by publication) and other specified procedures were followed. The UCC bulk sales provisions generally apply regardless of any contract provision between P and T to the contrary, if T transfers the major part of the inventory of an enterprise whose principal business is the sale of merchandise from inventory.

In addition, even if the parties have complied with the notice and other requirements of the bulk sales law (so that UCC Article 6 does *not* make P liable for T's debts), courts have increasingly held P responsible for some or all of T's debts and contingent liabilities (especially tort liabilities for defective products) under the common law doctrines of "de facto merger" and "successor liability" when T's business has been transferred to P as a going concern and T goes out of existence (especially, but not exclusively, when T's shareholders receive an equity interest in P).

If S (rather than P) acquires T's assets, bulk sales law and common law doctrines may apply to make S liable for T's debts and contingent liabilities (but generally not P, unless P has done something to permit a plaintiff to pierce the corporate veil).

(3) *Mechanical problems in transferring T's assets.* When P purchases T's assets for cash, notes, or stock, substantial paperwork can be required (including recording of, e.g., real estate, vehicle, patent, trademark, and airplane transfers), and difficult problems can arise in transferring thousands of assets. In addition, significant loan agreements, leases, licenses, and other contracts may prohibit their assignment, in which case consent must be obtained from the other party to the agreement, who may seek to exact some consideration for granting consent.

(4) *Transfer, sales, and use taxes.* Most states impose transfer taxes (i) on the sale of real property (real estate transfer taxes) and (ii) on the sale of tangible personal property not for resale (sales and use taxes). Some state sales and use taxes exempt the transfer of tangible personal property in an isolated sale or a sale not in the ordinary course of business. In these states T's sale of its assets and business to P would not be subject to sales and use tax.

Some states (e.g., California), however, do *not* provide such an exemption and hence impose a sales tax on T's sale of its assets and business to P. Nevertheless, even in states which tax an isolated sale, T's sale of inventory to P would almost always be exempt because T's sale of inventory to P would be for subsequent resale by P (so that sales tax will be payable when P resells such inventory). In such states T's sale of its machinery and equipment, furniture, tools and dies, etc., to P would be subjected to sales tax. State law varies on whether less tangible property (e.g., computer software) is considered tangible personal property subject to sales tax.

(5) *Non-pro-rata consideration.* Most states do not allow the consideration received by T in a sale of assets to be distributed in liquidation so that some T common shareholders receive different amounts or different types of consideration than other holders of identical stock (without the consent of 100% of T's shareholders). The same practical result can be achieved, however, if P acquires some T stock for one amount or type of consideration and immediately thereafter follows with a purchase of T's assets with the remaining T shareholders receiving another amount or type of consideration in T's liquidation.

(6) *Dissenters' rights.* The laws of many jurisdictions permit a T shareholder who dissents from the sale, lease, exchange, or other disposition of all or substantially all of T's assets to receive in cash the appraised FV of his T stock as determined by a court. Delaware, however, is an exception, as it allows no dissenters' or appraisal rights to a T shareholder when T sells all or substantially all its assets unless T's charter otherwise provides.[6]

(7) *Shareholder vote and proxy rules.* If P acquires all or substantially all of T's assets, state law generally requires the approval of T's shareholders, with the necessary percentage for approval varying according to the law of T's jurisdiction of incorporation and the specific provisions of T's charter (which generally may require a higher percentage than applicable state law).

In Delaware, for example, the sale of all or substantially all of T's assets requires approval of a majority of T's outstanding voting stock, subject to higher requirements in T's charter.[7] Many other states require a higher percentage (frequently two-thirds) for approval.

States differ on their interpretation of "substantially all" of a corporation's assets, with some cases indicating that more than 50% may be "substantially all."

No vote of *P's* shareholders is necessary in an acquisition of T's assets, unless

(a) P's charter explicitly requires the approval of P's shareholders;

(b) P is issuing stock to T's shareholders in excess of P's authorized shares (so that a vote of P's shareholders is necessary to authorize the stock);

(c) P's stock is listed on the NYSE, the AMEX, the Nasdaq NM, or certain regional exchanges, which would de-list P's stock if it effectuated the transaction without a shareholder vote. As discussed at §2001.2.1.2 above, each of the NYSE, AMEX, Nasdaq NM, or certain regional exchange rules has slightly different substantive provisions and somewhat different wording.

[6] Del. GCL §262.
[7] Del. GCL §271(a).

If a vote of P's or T's shareholders is necessary, as in the case of an acquisition of all or substantially all of T's assets, state law generally requires that written notice of a shareholders' meeting be sent to all shareholders (in some states, whether or not entitled to vote) a specified number of days in advance of the meeting, absent attendance at the meeting or a waiver of notice (generally by 100% of the shareholders).

In Delaware, for example, 10 days' advance notice is required for most shareholders' meetings, but 20 days' advance notice is required for a shareholder vote on a sale of assets.[8] A corporation's charter may provide for a longer notice period. A shareholder generally may waive notice in writing.[9]

Most states permit a corporation, if authorized by the corporation's charter or bylaws (or, in some states, if not expressly prohibited in the charter or bylaws), to obtain shareholder approval by written consent, obviating the need for a formal shareholders' meeting. Under Delaware law (unless prohibited by charter), action may be taken by shareholder consent if written consent is obtained from the number of shareholders whose vote would have been sufficient to take such action at a shareholders' meeting (generally a majority for a sale of assets), followed by "prompt" notice to the nonconsenting shareholders.[10] Some other states require *unanimous* shareholder consent in lieu of a meeting, without regard to the percentage that would have been sufficient to take action at a meeting.

In the event that *T* is publicly held and proxies are solicited from T's shareholders regarding approval for a sale of all or substantially all of T's assets, or in the event P is publicly held and proxies are solicited from P's shareholders in connection with an acquisition of assets, an amendment to P's charter to authorize additional stock in a stock-for-assets transaction, or to obtain required shareholder approval to issue additional shares of stock in a stock-for-assets transaction, such proxies must be solicited pursuant to a proxy statement prepared, filed, and distributed to shareholders in accordance with §14(a) of the 1934 Act and SEC Regulation 14A thereunder. The proxy rules are discussed in greater detail at ¶1502.2.7.6.

(8) *Application of the 1933 Act.* Acquisitions of assets are generally effected for cash, securities (including debt and/or equity securities), or some combination thereof.

Whenever part or all of the consideration is stock or debt instruments (i.e., "securities" within the meaning of the 1933 Act) of P (or S), P (or S) must comply with the 1933 Act. The 1933 Act prohibits the sale of securities unless (i) such securities are registered with the SEC and certain other requirements are satisfied *or* (ii) there is an applicable exemption from registration, e.g., the private placement, SEC Rule 701, or intrastate exemption.

If T intends to hold such P (or S) securities without further distribution to T's shareholders or resale to the public, and T does not plan to dissolve, P (or S) may be able to rely on a private placement exemption under the 1933 Act. Otherwise,

---

[8] Del. GCL §§222(b) and 271(a).
[9] Del. GCL §229.
[10] Del. GCL §228(a).

registration of such securities may be required, depending upon the number and nature of T's shareholders.

If T's shareholder group is of any significant size, P (or S) will generally not be able to qualify for an exemption and will be required to register under the 1933 Act the P (or S) stock or notes being issued for T's assets. This process is likely to require at least several weeks and more likely several months. The 1933 Act registration requirements are discussed in greater detail at ¶1502.2.8.1.

Section 4(2) of the 1933 Act exempts P (or S) from the requirement to register its stock or debt securities if the issuance does not involve a public offering (i.e., the offering constitutes a private placement) SEC Regulation D (Rules 501 through 508 under the 1933 Act) and SEC Rule 701 each provide a safe harbor for certain private placements. Regulation D and Rule 701 are discussed in greater detail at ¶1502.2.8.2 and ¶1502.2.8.3.

Section 3(a)(11) of the 1933 Act exempts intrastate offerings. SEC Rule 147 provides a safe harbor for certain intrastate offerings, Rule 147 is discussed in greater detail at ¶1502.2.8.4.

If P (or S) has issued stock or debt securities to T's shareholders in exchange for T's assets, there are frequently SEC restrictions on resale of the P (or S) stock or debt securities (unless the parties file a 1933 Act registration statement covering such resale). Although recent amendments to Rule 144 have shortened the holding period for public resales of "restricted securities" to one year, other Rule 144 requirements must still be satisfied. These resale restrictions are discussed in greater detail at ¶1502.2.8.5.

¶2001.2.3   P's Purchase of T by a Merger

This volume contains sample acquisition agreements for P's acquisition of T through a merger:

(i)   taxable reverse subsidiary merger of P's transitory subsidiary into T for cash and notes (*see* ¶2005),

(ii)   tax-free merger of T into P for P stock (*see* ¶2006),

(iii) examples of types of representations, warranties, and other terms that would be appropriate for either (i) or (ii) if T were not publicly held and if the parties agreed upon pro-buyer terms (*see* ¶2002.1 or ¶2003.1), pro-seller terms (*see* ¶2002.2 or ¶2003.2), or neutral terms (*see* ¶2002.3 or ¶2003.3), and

(iv)   additional provisions in which there is to be a purchase price adjustment based on T's closing date balance sheet (*see* ¶2002.5).

¶2001.2.3.1   *Brief Summary of Federal Income Tax Issues in a Merger*

(1) *Taxable reverse subsidiary merger.* A taxable reverse subsidiary merger (i.e., a merger of S into T) generally will be treated for tax purposes like a taxable stock purchase. *See* ¶¶202 and 2001.2.1.1(1).

(2) *Taxable forward merger.* A taxable forward merger (i.e., a merger of T into P) generally will be treated for tax purposes like a taxable asset purchase. *See* ¶¶301 and 2001.2.2.1(1).

(3) *Tax-free merger.* A tax-free reorganization may take the form of a state-law merger. *See* ¶¶2001.2.1.1(2) and 2001.2.2.1(2) and Chapter 6 through Chapter 8.

¶2001.2.3.2   *Key Nontax Issues in a Merger*

A merger is negotiated by the constituent corporations and effectuated pursuant to state corporation statutes by one or more filings with state officials. Absent an applicable "short-form" merger procedure or other exception, a merger must be approved by shareholders of both corporations. If approved by the requisite shareholder vote, the conversion of T's securities pursuant to the terms of the merger agreement is mandatory with respect to all T shareholders except dissenters, who (depending on state law) may be entitled to receive cash equal to the FV of their T stock.

The mechanics of a merger, of course, are governed by the corporation laws of the states in which the constituent corporations are incorporated and by the charters, bylaws, and other governing documents of such corporations.

(1) *Acquiring less than 100% of T.* If P and T merge or S and T merge, P will not be left to deal with any T minority shareholders following the transaction (as P will be if it buys less than all of T's stock). If the requisite vote of T's shareholders is obtained for the merger, the transaction takes place notwithstanding dissenting shareholders.

(2) *Liability for T's indebtedness.* If T and P merge or T and S merge, most corporation laws allow T's creditors to reach both T's and P's assets (if T and P merge) or T's and S's assets (if T and S merge in a reverse or forward subsidiary merger).

(3) *Mechanical problems of transferring T's assets.* A forward merger in which T merges into P (or S) may avoid the asset transfer problems encountered in a sale of assets because a merger transfers T's assets by operation of law. Some leases, loan agreements, licenses, and other contracts, however, specifically require consent of the other party even for transfers by operation of law. Moreover, some courts have interpreted contracts, licenses, and the like to require consent to the transfer of assets pursuant to a forward merger even in the absence of specific contractual language. *See, e.g.,* PPG Ind., Inc. v. Guardian Ind. Corp. 597 F.2d 1090 (6th Cir.), *cert. denied,* 444 U.S. 930 (1979), discussed at §1502.2.3.3.

A reverse subsidiary merger of S into T will normally avoid the asset transfer problems described above because T's assets are not being transferred. A particular agreement or license, however, may explicitly require consent for a change in T's control or for a merger (even when T is the survivor) under certain circumstances (e.g., when T's net worth after the merger is lower than before, as is frequently the case in an LBO when S borrows, and hence T becomes liable for, part of the money being paid to T's shareholders).

(4) *Transfer, sales, and use taxes.* Most states do not impose sales and use taxes generally with respect to a merger, although a particular state's law may differ on this point. The formal transfers of certain assets in the merger (particularly titled assets, e.g., motor vehicles, aircraft), however, may give rise to a specific transfer tax. The transaction may also be subject to the New York State Real Property Transfer Gains Tax (due to the transfer of a controlling interest in T's stock) if T holds real property located in New York. In addition, some states impose a stock transfer and/or issuance tax, which may apply if P issues its stock in a merger.

(5) *Non-pro-rata consideration.* In a merger, most (but not all) states allow cash, property, securities, or a combination thereof to be used as consideration. There is, however, some question whether a merger agreement can (without the consent of 100% of T's shareholders) provide for some T common shareholders to receive different amounts or different types of consideration than other holders of identical stock. If not, the same practical result can be achieved if P acquires some T stock for one amount or type of consideration and immediately thereafter follows with a merger, with the remaining T shareholders receiving another amount or type of consideration in the merger.

This technique is frequently used in an LBO in which T's Mgmt is swapping its T stock for P stock in a tax-free Code §351 transaction and T's other shareholders are receiving cash (or cash and P notes) in a reverse subsidiary merger of S into T immediately after the Code §351 transaction. *See* ¶1310.

(6) *Dissenters' rights. If T and P merge,* the laws of most jurisdictions allow a T shareholder or a P shareholder who dissents to receive in cash the appraised FV of his shares as determined by a court.

Delaware, however, denies appraisal rights to a T shareholder involved in a merger if (i) the class of shares he held before the transaction is listed on a national securities exchange or held by at least 2,000 shareholders *and* (ii) he receives (a) shares of the surviving corporation, (b) shares of another corporation (e.g., the surviving corporation's parent) that are listed on a national securities exchange or held by at least 2,000 shareholders, (c) cash in lieu of fractional shares, or (d) any combination of the foregoing.[11]

Delaware also denies appraisal rights to a *P* shareholder if the class of shares held before the merger is listed on a national securities exchange or held by at least 2,000 shareholders.[12] Moreover, if P's shareholders are not required to vote on the merger, either because of the "small merger" provision (in which the

---

[11] Del. GCL §262(b).
[12] Del. GCL §262(b)(1).

amount of P stock to be issued in the merger is relatively small compared to P's outstanding stock) or because of the "short-form merger" provision (in which T is a 90%-or-greater subsidiary), P's shareholders are denied appraisal rights.[13]

When T and S merge (in a forward or reverse subsidiary merger), *P's* shareholders are not entitled to appraisal rights (because P is not a party to the merger).[14] This is true even if P's shareholders vote in connection with the T acquisition for one or more of the reasons set forth below in ¶2001.2.3.2(7).

A Delaware corporation, however, may provide additional appraisal rights in its certificate of incorporation not otherwise required by law.[15]

(7) *Shareholder vote and proxy rules. A merger of T into P or a merger of P into T* will generally require the approval of both T's shareholders and P's shareholders. The necessary percentage for approval varies from state to state and generally may be increased by a corporation's charter.

In Delaware, for example, a merger requires approval of a majority of T's and P's outstanding voting stock, subject to higher requirements in their respective charters.[16] Many other states require a higher percentage (frequently two-thirds) for approval.

When T and S merge (in a forward or reverse subsidiary merger), approval is generally necessary only from T's and S's shareholders. Since P is normally S's only shareholder, P can consent on behalf of S. Usually no approval of P's shareholders is necessary, unless:

(a) P's charter explicitly requires the approval of P's shareholders;

(b) P is issuing stock to T's shareholders in excess of P's authorized shares (so that a vote of P's shareholders is necessary to authorize the stock);

(c) P's stock is listed on the NYSE, the AMEX, the Nasdaq NM, or certain regional exchanges, which would de-list P's stock if it effectuated the transaction without a shareholder vote. As discussed at ¶2001.2.1.2 above, each of the NYSE, AMEX, Nasdaq NM, or certain regional exchange rules has slightly different substantive provisions and somewhat different wording.

Most states provide for a so-called "short-form merger"—without any shareholder vote—between a parent corporation ("P") and one of its subsidiaries ("T"), with T's minority shareholders receiving P stock, cash, or other consideration as specified in the short-form merger agreement. The precise percentage of ownership that P must have in T in order to carry out a short-form merger varies from state to state, with 90% being required in Delaware.[17] Thus, once P has acquired the requisite stock ownership in T by purchasing T stock (e.g., 90% in Delaware) in a tender offer or negotiated stock purchase, P could (if such a short-form merger statute is applicable) merge with T without a T or P

---

[13] Del. GCL §262(b).
[14] Del. GCL §262.
[15] Del. GCL §262(c).
[16] Del. GCL §251(c).
[17] Del. GCL §253(a).

shareholder vote.[18] Care should be taken to assure that the relevant state statute permits the merger in the direction desired (T into P versus P into T). Delaware, for example, allows a short-form merger to be either upstream or downstream.[19]

Delaware also provides an exception (the "small merger" exception) from the usual P-shareholder voting requirement in which T merges into P (even though P may own no T stock); the amount of P stock issued is relatively small compared to P's outstanding stock; *and* P is a Delaware corporation. Under this provision, no vote of P's shareholders is required if the merger does not involve (1) a change in P's charter, (2) a change in the stock held by P's shareholders, or (3) the issuance of P common stock (or securities convertible into P common stock), exceeding in the aggregate 20% of P's outstanding common stock immediately prior to the merger.[20] The laws of T's state of incorporation, however, may require the vote of *both* T's and P's shareholders, thus nullifying the Delaware exception. Furthermore, P's charter or a stock exchange rule (such as the NYSE 20% rule) may require a vote of P's shareholders.

When a vote of P's or T's shareholders is necessary, state law generally requires written notice of a shareholders' meeting to be sent to all shareholders (in some states, whether or not entitled to vote) a specified number of days in advance of the meeting, absent attendance at the meeting or a waiver of notice (generally by 100% of the shareholders).

In Delaware, for example, 10 days' advance notice is required for most shareholders' meetings, but 20 days' advance notice is required for a shareholder vote on a merger.[21] A corporation's charter or bylaws may provide for a longer notice period. A shareholder generally may waive notice in writing.[22]

Most states permit a corporation, if authorized by the corporation's charter (or, in some states, if not expressly prohibited in the charter) to obtain shareholder approval by written consent, obviating the need for a formal shareholders' meeting. Under Delaware law (unless prohibited by charter), action may be taken by shareholder consent if written consent is obtained from the number of shareholders whose vote would have been sufficient to take such action at a shareholders' meeting (generally a majority for a merger), followed by "prompt" notice to the nonconsenting shareholders.[23] Some other states require *unanimous* shareholder consent in lieu of a meeting without regard to the percentage that would have been sufficient to take action at a meeting.

In the event that *T* is publicly held and proxies are solicited from T's shareholders regarding approval for a merger *or* in the event P is publicly held and proxies are solicited from P's shareholders in connection with a merger or an amendment to P's charter to authorize additional stock for issuance in the

---

[18] Of course, a vote of P's shareholders would be necessary if explicitly required by P's charter or if P stock is being issued and either (1) P does not have sufficient authorized stock or (2) a listing or trading rule (such as the NYSE or NASD 20% rule) requires a P shareholder vote.

[19] Del. GCL §253(a).

[20] Del. GCL §251(f).

[21] Del. GCL §§222(b), 251(c) and 271(a).

[22] Del. GCL §229.

[23] Del. GCL §228(a).

merger or to obtain required shareholder approval to issue additional shares of stock in the merger, such proxies must be solicited pursuant to a proxy statement prepared, filed, and distributed to shareholders in accordance with §14(a) of the 1934 Act and SEC Regulation 14A thereunder. The proxy rules are discussed in greater detail at ¶1502.2.7.6.

(8) *Application of the 1933 Act.* Mergers between P (or S) and T are generally effected so that T's shareholders will receive cash, securities (including debt and/or equity securities), or some combination thereof. Whenever part or all of the merger consideration is stock or debt instruments (i.e., "securities" within the meaning of the 1933 Act) of P (or S), P (or S) must comply with the 1933 Act. The 1933 Act prohibits the sale of securities unless (i) such securities are registered with SEC and certain other requirements are satisfied, *or* (ii) there is an applicable exemption from registration, e.g., the private placement, SEC Rule 701, or intrastate exemption.

If T's shareholder group is of any significant size, P (or S) will generally not be able to qualify for an exemption and will be required to register under the 1933 Act the P (or S) stock or notes being issued in the merger. This process is likely to require at least several weeks and more likely several months. The 1933 Act registration requirements are discussed in greater detail at ¶1502.2.8.1.

Section 4(2) of the 1933 Act exempts P (or S) from the requirement to register its stock or debt securities if the issuance does not involve a public offering (i.e., the offering constitutes a private placement). SEC Regulation D (Rules 501 through 508 under the 1933 Act) and SEC Rule 701 each provide a safe harbor for certain private placements. Regulation D and Rule 701 are discussed in greater detail at ¶¶1502.2.8.2 and 1502.2.8.3.

Section 3(a)(11) of the 1933 Act exempts intrastate offerings. SEC Rule 147 provides a safe harbor for certain intrastate offerings. Rule 147 is discussed in greater detail at ¶1502.2.8.4.

When P (or S) has issued stock or debt securities in the merger, there are frequently SEC restrictions on resale of the P (or S) stock or debt securities (unless the parties file a 1933 Act registration statement covering such resale). Although recent amendments to Rule 144 have shortened the holding period for public resales of "restricted securities" to one year, other Rule 144 requirements must still be satisfied. These resale restrictions are discussed in greater detail at ¶1502.2.8.5.

¶2001.3 *Summary Overview of the Sample Acquisition Agreements*

The sample acquisition agreements are broken down by type of transaction as follows:

¶2002   **P's Purchase of T's Stock for Cash and Notes**
  ¶2002.1   **Pro-Buyer Stock Purchase**
  ¶2002.2   **Pro-Seller Stock Purchase**
  ¶2002.3   **Neutral Stock Purchase**

¶2001.3.1   P's Purchase of T's Stock for Cash and Notes

Sample acquisition agreement 2002.1 is a *pro-buyer* version of a taxable stock purchase. Sample acquisition agreement 2002.2 is a *pro-seller* version of a taxable stock purchase. Sample acquisition agreement 2002.3 is a *neutral* version of a taxable stock purchase.

Sample acquisition agreements 2002.1, 2002.2, and 2002.3 contemplate a transaction in which a corporation ("P") will purchase all of the outstanding stock of another corporation ("T") from several corporate and individual sellers for cash and P notes. If P is to pay the entire purchase price in cash (i.e., no P notes are being issued to the sellers), all of the provisions relating to the P notes can be deleted.

After P purchases the T shares, T will become a subsidiary of P (assuming P is a corporation). T will generally retain all of its assets and rights and remain responsible for all of its liabilities and obligations.[1]

It is generally not necessary to prepare asset transfer documents or liability assumption documents in a stock purchase, as it is in a purchase of assets.

See ¶2001.2.1 for a further description of the principal tax and other issues associated with a purchase of stock.

If T has so many shareholders that it would be unwieldy for all of them to become parties to a stock purchase agreement (or if T has only a few shareholders, but some minority shareholders decline to participate), the parties may wish to use sample acquisition agreement 2005 (reverse subsidiary merger),[2] adjusted to incorporate the pro-buyer, pro-seller or neutral features of sample acquisition

---

¶2001.3   [1] If T was a Subchapter S corporation before the stock purchase, however, it will generally not have paid federal income tax at the corporate level. Thus the sellers (i.e., the T shareholders) will generally remain liable for federal income taxes through the Closing. *See* Chapter 11.

[2] A reverse subsidiary merger will generally be treated as a sale of stock for federal income tax purposes. *See* ¶202.

agreement 2002.1 (*pro-buyer* stock purchase), sample acquisition agreement 2002.2 (*pro-seller* stock purchase), or sample acquisition agreement 2002.3 (*neutral* stock purchase) as appropriate. See ¶2001.2.3 for a description of the principal tax and other issues associated with a merger.

Sample acquisition agreement 2002.4 contains additional provisions which should be used (or at least considered) in tandem with either 2002.1, 2002.2, or 2002.3 when T is, before the acquisition, a subsidiary of Bigco filing a consolidated federal income tax return.

Sample acquisition agreement 2002.5 contains additional provisions for use where there is to be a post-closing purchase price adjustment based on T's net book value as of the closing. This sample acquisition agreement can be adapted for other post-closing purchase price adjustments (such as a comparison of working capital with liabilities as of the closing or a contingent earnout based on earnings for a specified period after the closing).

The parties must address a number of general issues in preparing any acquisition document. See ¶2001.1 for a discussion of these key issues.

¶2001.3.1.1   Pro-Buyer

Sample acquisition agreement 2002.1 (*pro-buyer* stock purchase) contains provisions favoring P in areas such as (i) the extent to which T will retain its cash at the time of the closing, (ii) the extent to which the sellers (i.e., T's old shareholders) will bear the burden of T's liabilities and obligations after the closing, (iii) the extent to which P will have conditions to its obligation to close, (iv) the extent to which the sellers will be required to give representations and warranties, and (v) the extent to which the sellers will be required to indemnify P against breaches of those representations and warranties.

Sample acquisition agreement 2002.1 prohibits the sellers (i.e., T's shareholders) from causing T to distribute any of its cash to them (e.g., as a dividend or in a repurchase or redemption) at or prior to the closing. This means that T will retain its cash at the time of the closing.

Sample acquisition agreement 2002.1 contains extensive representations and warranties from the sellers (i.e., T's shareholders) concerning (i) T's historical financial statements, (ii) intervening adverse changes in T's business, (iii) litigation and undisclosed liabilities, (iv) tax matters, (v) pension and welfare benefit plans, (vi) compliance with federal, state, local, and foreign laws, (vii) environmental matters, and (viii) product liability and warranties.

The sellers (i.e., T's shareholders) accordingly will be in breach of their representations and warranties and required to indemnify P if T has any undisclosed liabilities, i.e., liabilities *other than* (i) those shown on the last T balance sheet reviewed by P before signing the contract, (ii) those incurred in the ordinary course of business thereafter (but not including claims and lawsuits), and (iii) those listed on a disclosure schedule. This would generally protect P against such undisclosed T liabilities as environmental cleanup, employment discrimination, antitrust violations, product liability, product warranty, tax deficiencies, and other claims and lawsuits.

Sample acquisition agreement 2002.1 also contains extensive representations and warranties from the sellers (i.e., T's shareholders) concerning (i) authorization with respect to the transaction, (ii) title to the stock being sold (and title to T's underlying assets), (iii) required governmental and third party consents (and noncontravention generally), (iv) organization and capitalization, (v) adequacy and condition of T's tangible assets, (vi) real estate matters, (vii) intellectual property matters, (viii) leases, licenses, and contracts, (ix) inventory and accounts receivable, (x) insurance, (xi) brokerage fees, and (xii) material misstatements and omissions.

The sellers' representations and warranties are not qualified with references to materiality, but do contain occasional references to the actual knowledge of the sellers (i.e., T's shareholders) and the directors, officers, and employees of T *after reasonable investigation.*

Sample acquisition agreement 2002.1 contains alternative provisions for (i) full indemnification to P for breaches of the seller's representations and warranties (i.e., the representations and warranties concerning T survive forever and there is no deductible, threshold, or ceiling with respect to indemnification for breaches thereof) *or* (ii) limited indemnification to P for breaches of the sellers' representations and warranties (i.e., the representations and warranties with respect to tax matters survive forever, the other representations and warranties concerning T survive only for three years, and there is a threshold, but not a deductible or a ceiling, with respect to indemnification for breaches thereof). The sellers' indemnification obligation is joint and several.

P also has the right to recoup its losses against the P notes in lieu of seeking indemnification from the sellers (i.e., T's shareholders).

P's obligation to close is subject to several conditions, such as (i) compliance with the sellers' representations, warranties, and covenants, (ii) absence of a material adverse change, (iii) absence of litigation affecting the transaction, (iv) availability of financing, (v) receipt of governmental approvals, (vi) delivery of title insurance, surveys, and third party consents, (vii) delivery of any side agreements, and (viii) delivery of an opinion of the sellers' legal counsel.

P also has the right to terminate the purchase agreement for a limited period after signing if P is not satisfied with the results of its continuing business, legal, and accounting due diligence review.

There are a number of other important differences among sample acquisition agreement 2002.1 (*pro-buyer* stock purchase), sample acquisition agreement 2002.2 (*pro-seller* stock purchase), and sample acquisition agreement 2002.3 (*neutral* stock purchase). Each of these sample acquisition agreements contains extensive footnotes with cross-references pointing out the differences.

¶2001.3.1.2   Pro-Seller

Sample acquisition agreement 2002.2 (*pro-seller* stock purchase) contains provisions favoring the sellers (i.e., T's old shareholders) in areas such as (i) the extent to which the sellers will receive T's cash (net of unpaid taxes) at the time of the closing, (ii) the extent to which P will bear the burden of T's liabilities and obligations after the closing, (iii) the extent to which P will lack conditions to its obligation to close, (iv) the extent to which the sellers will be required to give representations and warranties, and (v) the extent to which the sellers will be required to indemnify P against breaches of those representations and warranties.

Sample acquisition agreement 2002.2 permits the sellers (i.e., T's shareholders) to cause T to distribute its cash (net of unpaid taxes) to them (e.g., as a dividend or in a repurchase or redemption) at the time of the closing. This means that the sellers will receive T's cash (net of unpaid taxes) at the time of the closing.

Sample acquisition agreement 2002.2 contains limited representations and warranties from the sellers (i.e., T's shareholders) concerning (i) T's historical financial statements, (ii) intervening events, (iii) litigation, (iv) tax matters, (v) pension and welfare benefit plans, and (vi) compliance with federal, state, local, and foreign laws.

Sample acquisition agreement 2002.2 *does not* contain a specific representation and warranty concerning undisclosed liabilities.

Sample acquisition agreement 2002.2 also contains limited representations and warranties from the sellers (i.e., T's shareholders) concerning (i) authorization with respect to the transaction, (ii) title to the stock being sold (and title to T's underlying assets), (iii) required governmental and third party consents (and noncontravention generally), (iv) organization and capitalization, (v) real estate matters, (vi) intellectual property matters, (vii) leases and contracts, and (viii) brokerage fees.

The sellers' representations and warranties are qualified frequently with references to materiality and to the actual knowledge of the sellers (i.e., T's shareholders), but not, for example, T's directors, officers, and employees, *without any duty of independent investigation.*

Sample acquisition agreement 2002.2 contains alternative provisions for (i) minimal indemnification to P for breaches of the seller's representations and warranties (i.e., none of the representations and warranties concerning T survive the closing and there is no indemnification for breaches thereof)[3] *or* (ii) limited indemnification to P for breaches of the sellers' representations and warranties (i.e., the representations and warranties concerning T survive only for one year and there is a deductible and a ceiling with respect to indemnification for breaches thereof). The sellers' indemnification obligation is several (rather than joint) and in proportion to their respective holdings of T shares.

P *does not* have any right to recoup its losses against the P notes in lieu of seeking indemnification from the sellers (i.e., T's shareholders).

P's obligation to close is subject to minimal conditions, such as (i) compliance with the sellers' representations, warranties, and covenants, (ii) absence of a material adverse change, (iii) absence of an injunction affecting the transaction,

---

[3] This is referred to as *minimal* indemnification (rather than *no* indemnification) because the sellers' representations and warranties about the transaction itself (e.g., organization of certain sellers, authorization of the transaction, noncontravention, absence of brokers' fees, ownership of the T shares, etc.) do survive the Closing and may give rise to indemnification.

(iv) receipt of governmental approvals, (v) delivery of any side agreements, and (vi) delivery of an opinion of the sellers' legal counsel.

P *does not* have any closing condition concerning its ability to secure financing for the transaction *or* any right to terminate the purchase agreement after signing if it is not satisfied with the results of its continuing business, legal, and accounting due diligence review.

There are a number of other important differences among sample acquisition agreement 2002.1 (*pro-buyer* stock purchase), sample acquisition agreement 2002.2 (*pro-seller* stock purchase), and sample acquisition agreement 2002.3 (*neutral* stock purchase). Each of these sample acquisition agreements contains extensive footnotes with cross-references pointing out the differences.

¶2001.3.1.3   *Neutral*

Sample acquisition agreement 2002.3 (*neutral* stock purchase) is intended to strike a reasonable balance between the conflicting interests of P and T in areas such as (i) the extent to which T will retain its cash at the time of the closing, (ii) the extent to which the sellers (i.e., T's old shareholders) will bear the burden of T's liabilities and obligations after the closing, (iii) the extent to which P will have conditions to its obligation to close, (iv) the extent to which the sellers will be required to give representations and warranties, and (v) the extent to which the sellers will be required to indemnify P against breaches of those representations and warranties.

Sample acquisition agreement 2002.3 prohibits the sellers (i.e., T's shareholders) from causing T to distribute any of its cash to them (e.g., as a dividend or in a repurchase or redemption) at or prior to the closing. This means that T will retain its cash at the time of the closing.

Sample acquisition agreement 2002.3 contains fairly extensive representations and warranties from the sellers (i.e., T's shareholders) concerning (i) T's historical financial statements, (ii) intervening material adverse changes in T's business, (iii) litigation and material undisclosed liabilities, (iv) tax matters, (v) pension and welfare benefit plans, (vi) compliance with federal, state, local, and foreign laws, (vii) environmental matters, and (viii) product liability and warranties.

The sellers (i.e., T's shareholders) accordingly will be in breach of their representations and warranties and required to indemnify P if T has any material undisclosed liabilities, i.e., liabilities *other than* (i) those shown on the last T balance sheet reviewed by P before signing the contract, (ii) those incurred in the ordinary course of business thereafter (but not including claims and lawsuits), and (iii) those listed on a disclosure schedule. This would generally protect P against such material undisclosed T liabilities as environmental cleanup, employment discrimination, antitrust violations, product liability, product warranty, tax deficiencies, and other claims and lawsuits.

Sample acquisition agreement 2002.3 also contains fairly extensive representations and warranties from the sellers (i.e., T's shareholders) concerning (i) authorization with respect to the transaction, (ii) title to the stock being sold (and title to T's underlying assets), (iii) required governmental and third party consents (and noncontravention generally), (iv) organization and capitalization, (v) adequacy and condition of T's tangible assets, (vi) real estate matters, (vii) intellectual property matters, (viii) leases, licenses, and contracts, (ix) inventory and accounts receivable, (x) insurance, (xi) brokerage fees, and (xii) material misstatements and omissions.

The sellers' representations and warranties are, however, qualified with relatively frequent references to knowledge (defined as the actual knowledge of T's shareholders, directors, and officers after reasonable investigation) and materiality.

Sample acquisition agreement 2002.3 provides that the representations and warranties with respect to the transaction itself and with respect to taxes will survive indefinitely, that the environmental representations and warranties will survive for five years, that the other representations and warranties will survive for two years, and that there will be a deductible and a ceiling with respect to indemnification against breaches of any representations and warranties that do not concern the transaction itself. The sellers' indemnification obligation is joint and several.

P *does not* have any right to recoup its losses against the P notes in lieu of seeking indemnification from the sellers (i.e., T's shareholders).

P's obligation to close is subject to several conditions, such as (i) compliance with the sellers' representations, warranties, and covenants, (ii) absence of a material adverse change, (iii) absence of litigation affecting the transaction, (iv) receipt of governmental approvals, (v) delivery of title insurance, surveys, and material third party consents, (vi) delivery of any side agreements, and (vii) delivery of an opinion of the sellers' legal counsel.

P *does not* have any closing condition concerning its ability to secure financing for the transaction *or* any right to terminate the purchase agreement after signing if it is not satisfied with the results of its continuing business, legal, and accounting due diligence review.

It is important to note that some of the provisions in sample acquisition agreement 2002.3 are neutral only in the context of the overall agreement. In part, this is due to the interplay between the sellers' representations and warranties (which are fairly extensive but qualified with references to knowledge and materiality) on the one hand and their indemnification obligations (which are subject to various deductibles, ceilings, and survival periods) on the other. Accordingly, it is not always possible to remove a provision from sample acquisition agreement 2002.3 for use in another agreement and have the provision remain neutral.

Finally, the choice of neutral provisions for sample acquisition agreement 2002.3 was necessarily subjective. Thus, in any particular transaction, it may be necessary to modify the agreement so that it strikes a different balance between the interests of P and T.

There are a number of other important differences among sample acquisition agreement 2002.1 (*pro-buyer* stock purchase), sample acquisition agreement 2002.2 (*pro-seller* stock purchase), and sample acquisition agreement 2002.3 (*neutral* stock purchase). Each of these sample acquisition agreements contains extensive footnotes with cross-references pointing out the differences.

¶2001.3.1.4   *Sale of Subsidiary Out of Consolidated Group*

Sample acquisition agreements 2002.1 (the *pro-buyer* stock purchase agreement), 2002.2 (the *pro-seller* stock purchase agreement), and 2002.3 (the *neutral* stock purchase agreement) assume that (prior to P's purchase of T's stock) T was not filing a consolidated federal income tax return with Bigco (i.e., that prior to P's purchase of T's stock, T either was not a Bigco subsidiary or, if T was a Bigco subsidiary, Bigco and T were not filing consolidated federal income tax returns). Sample acquisition agreement 2002.4 (sale of a consolidated subsidiary) contains additional provisions which should be used (or at least considered) in tandem with either sample acquisition agreement 2002.1, sample acquisition agreement 2002.2, or sample acquisition agreement 2002.3 in which T was filing a consolidated return with Bigco before P purchased T's stock. See ¶¶210 and 212 for a discussion of certain tax issues that may arise when T and Bigco were filing consolidated returns.

¶2001.3.1.5   *Purchase Price Adjustment Based on Closing Date Balance Sheet*

Sample acquisition agreements 2002.1 (*pro-buyer* stock purchase), 2002.2 (*pro-seller* stock purchase), and 2002.3 (*neutral* stock purchase) assume a fixed purchase price. Sample acquisition agreement 2002.5 (purchase price adjustment) contains additional provisions for use when there is to be a post-closing purchase price adjustment based on T's net book value as of the closing. This sample acquisition agreement can be adapted for other post-closing purchase price adjustments (such as a comparison of working capital with liabilities as of the closing *or* a contingent earnout based on earnings for a specified period after the closing).

¶2001.3.2   **P's Purchase of All T's Assets for Cash and Notes**

Sample acquisition agreement 2003.1 is a *pro-buyer* version of a taxable asset purchase. Sample acquisition agreement 2003.2 is a *pro-seller* version of a taxable asset purchase. Sample acquisition agreement 2003.3 is a *neutral* version of a taxable asset purchase.

Sample acquisition agreements 2003.1, 2003.2, and 2003.3 contemplate a transaction in which a corporation ("P") will purchase all of the assets of another corporation ("T") for cash and P notes. If P is to pay the entire purchase price in cash (i.e., no P notes are being issued to T), all of the provisions relating to the P notes can be deleted.

If P purchases T's assets, T will generally retain those assets and rights that it does not transfer and assign to P, and T will generally remain responsible for those liabilities and obligations not assumed by P.[4]

It is generally necessary to prepare asset transfer documents and liability assumption documents in an asset purchase (whether a purchase of all T's assets or a purchase of a T division), which would not be required if P purchased T's *stock*.

See ¶2001.2.2 for a further description of the principal tax and other issues associated with a purchase of assets.

If P intends to purchase only the assets of a T division rather than all of T's assets, the parties should generally use sample acquisition agreement 2004.1 (*pro-buyer* divisional asset purchase), 2004.2 (*pro-seller* divisional asset purchase), or 2004.3 (*neutral* divisional asset purchase), as appropriate.

Sample acquisition agreement 2002.5 (purchase price adjustment) contains additional provisions for use when there is to be a post-closing purchase price adjustment based on T's net book value as of the closing. This sample acquisition agreement can be adapted for other post-closing purchase price adjustments (such as a comparison of working capital with liabilities as of the closing *or* a contingent earnout based on earnings for a specified period after the closing). Sample acquisition agreement 2002.5 is, however, intended for use with sample acquisition agreements 2002.1, 2002.2, and 2002.3 (the *stock* purchase agreements) and must be modified prior to use with sample acquisition agreements 2003.1, 2003.2, and 2003.3 (the *asset* purchase agreements.)

The parties must address a number of general issues in preparing any acquisition document. See ¶2001.1 for a discussion of these key issues.

¶2001.3.2.1   Pro-Buyer

Sample acquisition agreement 2003.1 (*pro-buyer* asset purchase) contains provisions favoring P in areas such as (i) the extent to which P will receive T's cash (net of unpaid taxes) at the time of the closing, (ii) the extent to which T will bear the burden of its liabilities and obligations after the closing, (iii) the extent to which P will have conditions to its obligation to close, (iv) the extent to which T will be required to give representations and warranties, and (v) the extent to which T will be required to indemnify P against breaches of those representations and warranties.

Sample acquisition agreement 2003.1 provides that P will (i) acquire T's cash at the closing and (ii) assume T's liability for unpaid taxes with respect to periods up to the closing (but not to exceed an amount computed in accordance with T's

---

[4] P's contractual assumption of certain T liabilities and obligations generally will not preclude a third party to whom T owed the liabilities and obligations from suing T (if P has failed to pay or perform) unless the third party consents to P's assumption and agrees to look only to P for satisfaction (i.e., enters into a novation agreement). This means that if P fails to satisfy the assumed liabilities and obligations, nonconsenting third parties to whom T owed the liabilities and obligations may have a cause of action against T or, if T has liquidated and dissolved, against T's stockholders and/or directors.

past custom and practice in filing its tax returns). This means that P will receive T's cash (net of unpaid taxes) at the time of the closing.

Sample acquisition agreement 2003.1 provides that the only T liabilities P will assume are those liabilities (i) shown on the last T balance sheet reviewed by P before signing the contract, (ii) incurred in the ordinary course of business thereafter (but not including claims and lawsuits), (iii) involving certain taxes (as noted above), employee benefit plans, and executory contracts, and (iv) listed on a disclosure schedule. Thus, P would generally *not* assume such undisclosed T liabilities as environmental cleanup, employment discrimination, antitrust violations, product liability, product warranty, tax deficiencies, and other claims and lawsuits.

Sample acquisition agreement 2003.1 contains extensive representations and warranties from T concerning (i) its historical financial statements, (ii) intervening adverse changes in its business, (iii) litigation and undisclosed liabilities, (iv) tax matters, (v) pension and welfare benefit plans, (vi) compliance with federal, state, local, and foreign laws, (vii) environmental matters, and (viii) product liability and warranties.

Sample acquisition agreement 2003.1 also contains extensive representations and warranties from T concerning (i) authorization with respect to the transaction, (ii) title to the assets being sold, (iii) required governmental and third party consents (and noncontravention generally), (iv) organization, (v) adequacy and condition of its tangible assets, (vi) real estate matters, (vii) intellectual property matters, (viii) leases, licenses, and contracts, (ix) inventory and accounts receivable, (x) insurance, (xi) brokerage fees, and (xii) material misstatements and omissions.

T's representations and warranties are not qualified with references to materiality, but do contain occasional references to the actual knowledge of its shareholders, directors, officers, and employees *after reasonable investigation.*

Sample acquisition agreement 2003.1 contains alternative provisions for (i) full indemnification to P for breaches of T's representations and warranties (i.e., the representations and warranties concerning T survive forever, and there is no deductible, threshold, or ceiling with respect to indemnification for breaches thereof) *or* (ii) limited indemnification to P for breaches of T's representations and warranties (i.e., the representations and warranties with respect to tax matters survive forever; the other representations and warranties concerning T survive only for three years; and there is a threshold, but not a deductible or a ceiling, with respect to indemnification for breaches thereof).[5]

P also has the right to recoup its losses against the P notes in lieu of seeking indemnification from T and its shareholders.

---

[5] Sample acquisition agreement 2003.1 (the pro-buyer *asset* purchase agreement) assumes that T will liquidate and dissolve immediately after the Closing, so that T will not be able to perform any post-Closing covenants (including any post-Closing indemnification provisions) analogous to those contained in sample acquisition agreement 2002.1 (the pro-buyer *stock* purchase agreement). The Agreement with Target Stockholders (Exhibit A to sample acquisition agreement 2003.1) is designed to address this situation by making *T's shareholders* responsible for the post-Closing covenants (including the post-Closing indemnification provisions).

P's obligation to close is subject to several conditions, such as (i) compliance with T's representations, warranties, and covenants, (ii) absence of a material adverse change, (iii) absence of litigation affecting the transaction, (iv) availability of financing, (v) receipt of governmental approvals, (vi) delivery of title insurance, surveys, and third party consents, (vii) delivery of any side agreements, and (viii) delivery of an opinion of T's legal counsel.

P also has the right to terminate the purchase agreement for a limited period after signing if P is not satisfied with the results of its continuing business, legal, and accounting due diligence review.

There are a number of other important differences among sample acquisition agreement 2003.1 (*pro-buyer* asset purchase), sample acquisition agreement 2003.2 (*pro-seller* asset purchase), and sample acquisition agreement 2003.3 (*neutral* asset purchase). Each of these sample acquisition agreements contains extensive footnotes with cross-references pointing out the differences.

¶2001.3.2.2   Pro-Seller

Sample acquisition agreement 2003.2 (*pro-seller* asset purchase) contains provisions favoring T in areas such as (i) the extent to which T will retain its cash (net of unpaid taxes) at the time of the closing, (ii) the extent to which P will bear the burden of T's liabilities and obligations after the closing, (iii) the extent to which P will lack conditions to its obligation to close, (iv) the extent to which T will be required to give representations and warranties, and (v) the extent to which T will be required to indemnify P against breaches of those representations and warranties.

Sample acquisition agreement 2003.2 provides that T will retain all of its cash at the closing (less an amount equal to its good faith estimate of its unpaid taxes with respect to periods up to the closing computed in accordance with its past custom and practice in filing its tax returns). This means that T will retain its cash (net of unpaid taxes) at the time of the closing.

Sample acquisition agreement 2003.2 provides that P will assume substantially all of T's obligations and liabilities (whether known or unknown and whether absolute or contingent). Thus, P would generally assume such undisclosed T liabilities as environmental cleanup, employment discrimination, antitrust violations, product liability, product warranty, tax deficiencies, and other claims and lawsuits.

Sample acquisition agreement 2003.2 contains limited representations and warranties from T concerning (i) its historical financial statements, (ii) intervening events, (iii) litigation, (iv) tax matters, (v) pension and welfare benefit plans, and (vi) compliance with federal, state, local, and foreign laws.

Sample acquisition agreement 2003.2 *does not* contain a specific representation and warranty concerning undisclosed liabilities.

Sample acquisition agreement 2003.2 also contains limited representations and warranties from T concerning (i) authorization with respect to the transaction, (ii) title to the assets being sold, (iii) required governmental and third party consents (and noncontravention generally), (iv) organization, (v) real estate matters, (vi) intellectual property matters, (vii) leases and contracts, and (viii) brokerage fees.

T's representations and warranties are qualified frequently with references to materiality and to the actual knowledge of T's shareholders, but not, for example, T's directors, officers, and employees, *without any duty of independent investigation.*

Sample acquisition agreement 2003.2 contains alternative provisions for (i) minimal indemnification to P for breaches of T's representations and warranties (i.e., none of the representations and warranties concerning T survive the closing and there is no indemnification for breaches thereof)[6] or (ii) limited indemnification to P for breaches of T's representations and warranties (i.e., the representations and warranties concerning T survive only for one year, and there is a deductible and a ceiling with respect to indemnification for breaches thereof).[7]

P *does not* have any right to recoup its losses against the P notes in lieu of seeking indemnification from T and its shareholders.

P's obligation to close is subject to minimal conditions, such as (i) compliance with T's representations, warranties, and covenants, (ii) absence of a material adverse change, (iii) absence of an injunction affecting the transaction, (iv) receipt of governmental approvals, (v) delivery of any side agreements, and (vi) delivery of an opinion of T's legal counsel.

P *does not* have any closing condition concerning its ability to secure financing for the transaction *or* any right to terminate the purchase agreement after signing if it is not satisfied with the results of its continuing business, legal, and accounting due diligence review.

There are a number of other important differences among sample acquisition agreement 2003.1 (*pro-buyer* asset purchase), sample acquisition agreement 2003.2 (*pro-seller* asset purchase), and sample acquisition agreement 2003.3 (*neutral* asset purchase). Each of these sample acquisition agreements contains extensive footnotes with cross-references pointing out the differences.

¶2001.3.2.3 *Neutral*

Sample acquisition agreement 2003.3 (*neutral* asset purchase) is intended to strike a reasonable balance between the conflicting interests of P and T in areas such as (i) the extent to which P will receive T's cash (net of unpaid taxes) at the

---

[6]This is referred to as *minimal* indemnification (rather than *no* indemnification) because T's representations and warranties about the transaction itself (e.g., organization of T, authorization of the transaction, noncontravention, absence of brokers' fees, ownership of T's assets, etc.) do survive the Closing and may give rise to indemnification.

[7]Sample acquisition agreement 2003.2 (the pro-seller *asset* purchase agreement) assumes that T will liquidate and dissolve immediately after the Closing so that T will not be able to perform any post-Closing covenants (including any post-Closing indemnification provisions) analogous to those contained in sample acquisition agreement 2002.2 (the pro-seller *stock* purchase agreement). The Agreement with Target Stockholders (Exhibit A to sample acquisition agreement 2003.2) is designed to address this situation by making *T's shareholders* responsible for the post-Closing covenants (including the post-Closing indemnification provisions).

time of the closing, (ii) the extent to which T will bear the burden of its liabilities and obligations after the closing, (iii) the extent to which P will have conditions to its obligation to close, (iv) the extent to which T will be required to give representations and warranties, and (v) the extent to which T will be required to indemnify P against breaches of those representations and warranties.

Sample acquisition agreement 2003.3 provides that P will (i) acquire T's cash at the closing and (ii) assume T's liability for unpaid taxes with respect to periods up to the closing (but not to exceed an amount computed in accordance with T's past custom and practice in filing its tax returns). This means that P will receive T's cash (net of unpaid taxes) at the time of the closing.

Sample acquisition agreement 2003.3 provides that the only T liabilities P will assume are those liabilities (i) shown on the last T balance sheet reviewed by P before signing the contract, (ii) incurred in the ordinary course of business thereafter (but not including claims and lawsuits), (iii) involving certain taxes (as noted above), employee benefit plans, and executory contracts, or (iv) listed on a disclosure schedule. Thus, P would generally *not* assume such undisclosed T liabilities as environmental cleanup, employment discrimination, antitrust violations, product liability, product warranty, tax deficiencies, and other claims and lawsuits.

Sample acquisition agreement 2003.3 contains fairly extensive representations and warranties from T concerning (i) its historical financial statements, (ii) intervening material adverse changes in its business, (iii) litigation and material undisclosed liabilities, (iv) tax matters, (v) pension and welfare benefit plans, (vi) compliance with federal, state, local, and foreign laws, (vii) environmental matters, and (viii) product liability and warranties.

Sample acquisition agreement 2003.3 also contains fairly extensive representations and warranties from T concerning (i) authorization with respect to the transaction, (ii) title to the assets being sold, (iii) required governmental and third party consents (and noncontravention generally), (iv) organization, (v) adequacy and condition of its tangible assets, (vi) real estate matters, (vii) intellectual property matters, (viii) leases, licenses, and contracts, (ix) inventory and accounts receivable, (x) insurance, (xi) brokerage fees, and (xii) material misstatements and omissions.

T's representations and warranties, however, are qualified with relatively frequent references to knowledge (defined as the actual knowledge of its shareholders, directors, and officers after reasonable investigation) and materiality.

Sample acquisition agreement 2003.3 provides that the representations and warranties with respect to the transaction itself and with respect to taxes will survive indefinitely, that the environmental representations and warranties will survive for five years, that the other representations and warranties will survive for two years, and that there will be a deductible and a ceiling with respect to indemnification against breaches of any representations and warranties that do not concern the transaction itself.[8]

---

[8] Sample acquisition agreement 2003.3 (the neutral *asset* purchase agreement) assumes that T will liquidate and dissolve immediately after the Closing so that T will not be able to perform any

P *does not* have any right to recoup its losses against the P notes in lieu of seeking indemnification from T and its shareholders.

P's obligation to close is subject to several conditions, such as (i) compliance with T's representations, warranties, and covenants, (ii) absence of a material adverse change, (iii) absence of litigation affecting the transaction, (iv) receipt of governmental approvals, (v) delivery of title insurance, surveys, and material third party consents, (vi) delivery of any side agreements, and (vii) delivery of an opinion of T's legal counsel.

P *does not* have any closing condition concerning its ability to secure financing for the transaction *or* any right to terminate the purchase agreement after signing if it is not satisfied with the results of its continuing business, legal, and accounting due diligence review.

It is important to note that some of the provisions in sample acquisition agreement 2003.3 are neutral only in the context of the overall agreement. In part, this is due to the interplay between T's representations and warranties (which are fairly extensive but qualified with references to knowledge and materiality) on the one hand and the indemnification obligations of T's stockholders (which are subject to various deductibles, ceilings, and survival periods) on the other. Accordingly, it is not always possible to remove a provision from sample acquisition agreement 2003.3 for use in another agreement and have the provision remain neutral.

Finally, the choice of neutral provisions for sample acquisition agreement 2003.3 was necessarily subjective. Thus, in any particular transaction, it may be necessary to modify the agreement so that it strikes a different balance between the interests of P and T.

There are a number of other important differences among sample acquisition agreement 2003.1 (*pro-buyer* asset purchase), sample acquisition agreement 2003.2 (*pro-seller* asset purchase), and sample acquisition agreement 2003.3 (*neutral* asset purchase). Each of these sample acquisition agreements contains extensive footnotes with cross-references pointing out the differences.

¶2001.3.3   P's Purchase of T's Divisional Business for Cash and Notes

Sample acquisition agreement 2004.1 is a *pro-buyer* version of a taxable divisional asset purchase. Sample acquisition agreement 2004.2 is a *pro-seller* version of a taxable divisional asset purchase. Sample acquisition agreement 2004.3 is a *neutral* version of a taxable divisional asset purchase.

Sample acquisition agreements 2004.1, 2004.2, and 2004.3 contemplate a transaction in which a corporation ("P") will purchase all of the assets of *a division*

---

post-Closing covenants (including any post-Closing indemnification provisions) analogous to those contained in sample acquisition agreement 2002.3 (the neutral *stock* purchase agreement). The Agreement with Target Stockholders (Exhibit A to sample acquisition agreement 2003.3) is designed to address this situation by making *T's shareholders* responsible for the post-Closing covenants (including the post-Closing indemnification provisions).

of another corporation ("T") for cash and P notes.[9] If P is to pay the entire purchase price in cash (i.e., no P notes are being issued to T), all of the provisions relating to the P notes can be deleted.

If P purchases a T division, T will generally retain those assets and rights that it does not transfer and assign to P, and T will generally remain responsible for those liabilities and obligations not assumed by P.[10]

It is generally necessary to prepare asset transfer documents and liability assumption documents in an asset purchase (whether a purchase of all T's assets or a purchase of a T division), which would not be required if P purchased T's *stock*.

See ¶2001.2.2 for a further description of the principal tax and other issues associated with a purchase of assets.

If P intends to purchase all of T's assets, rather than only the assets of a T division, the parties should generally use sample acquisition agreement 2003.1 (*pro-buyer* asset purchase), 2003.2 (*pro-seller* asset purchase), or 2003.3 (*neutral* asset purchase), as appropriate.

Sample acquisition agreement 2002.5 (purchase price adjustment) contains additional provisions for use when there is to be a post-closing purchase price adjustment based on T's net book value as of the closing. This sample acquisition agreement can be adapted for other post-closing purchase price adjustments (such as a comparison of working capital with liabilities as of the closing *or* a contingent earnout based on earnings for a specified period after the closing). Sample acquisition agreement 2002.5 is, however, intended for use with sample acquisition agreements 2002.1, 2002.2, and 2002.3 (the *stock* purchase agreements) and must be modified prior to use with sample acquisition agreements 2004.1, 2004.2, and 2004.3 (the divisional *asset* purchase agreements).

The parties must address a number of general issues in preparing any acquisition document. See ¶2001.1 for a discussion of these key issues.

¶2001.3.3.1   Pro-Buyer

Sample acquisition agreement 2004.1 (*pro-buyer* divisional asset purchase) contains provisions favoring P in areas such as (i) the extent to which P will receive divisional cash (net of unpaid taxes) at the time of the closing, (ii) the extent to which T will bear the burden of the divisional liabilities and obligations after the closing, (iii) the extent to which P will have conditions to its obligation

---

[9] It may be difficult to identify and describe those rights, assets, obligations, and liabilities of T which constitute the division. This is especially likely when T does not segregate cash in a separate account for the division or when the division shares rights, assets, obligations, and liabilities with other T divisions. The parties must address the disposition of any such shared items in the purchase agreement.

[10] P's contractual assumption of certain T liabilities and obligations generally will not preclude a third party to whom T owed the liabilities and obligations from suing T (if P has failed to pay or perform) unless the third party consents to P's assumption and agrees to look only to P for satisfaction (i.e., enters into a novation agreement). This means that if P fails to satisfy the assumed liabilities and obligations, nonconsenting third parties to whom T owed the liabilities and obligations may have a cause of action against T or if T has liquidated and dissolved, against T's stockholders and/or directors.

to close, (iv) the extent to which T will be required to give representations and warranties, and (v) the extent to which T will be required to indemnify P against breaches of those representations and warranties.

Sample acquisition agreement 2004.1 provides that T will retain only so much of the divisional cash at the closing as will cover the unpaid divisional taxes with respect to periods up to the closing for which T will remain liable. This means that P will receive the divisional cash (net of unpaid taxes) at the time of the closing.

Sample acquisition agreement 2004.1 provides that the only T liabilities that P will assume are those divisional liabilities (i) shown on the last divisional balance sheet reviewed by P before signing the contract, (ii) incurred in the ordinary course of business thereafter (but not including claims and lawsuits), (iii) involving employee benefit plans and executory contracts, and (iv) listed on a disclosure schedule. Thus, P would generally *not* assume such undisclosed divisional liabilities as environmental cleanup, employment discrimination, antitrust violations, product liability, product warranty, tax deficiencies, and other claims and lawsuits.

Sample acquisition agreement 2004.1 contains extensive representations and warranties from T concerning (i) the historical divisional financial statements, (ii) intervening adverse changes in the divisional business, (iii) litigation and undisclosed liabilities, (iv) tax matters, (v) pension and welfare benefit plans, (vi) compliance with federal, state, local, and foreign laws, (vii) environmental matters, and (viii) product liability and warranties.

Sample acquisition agreement 2004.1 also contains extensive representations and warranties from T concerning (i) authorization with respect to the transaction, (ii) title to the assets being sold, (iii) required governmental and third party consents (and noncontravention generally), (iv) organization, (v) adequacy and condition of the divisional tangible assets, (vi) real estate matters, (vii) intellectual property matters, (viii) leases, licenses, and contracts, (ix) inventory and accounts receivable, (x) insurance, (xi) brokerage fees, and (xii) material misstatements and omissions.

T's representations and warranties are not qualified with references to materiality but do contain occasional references to the actual knowledge of its shareholders, directors, officers, and employees *after reasonable investigation.*

Sample acquisition agreement 2004.1 contains alternative provisions for (i) full indemnification to P for breaches of T's representation and warranties (i.e., the representations and warranties concerning the division survive forever, and there is no deductible, threshold, or ceiling with respect to indemnification for breaches thereof) *or* (ii) limited indemnification to P for breaches of T's representations and warranties (i.e., the representations and warranties with respect to tax matters survive forever; the other representations and warranties concerning the division survive only for three years; and there is a threshold, but not a deductible or a ceiling, with respect to indemnification for breaches thereof).

P also has the right to recoup its losses against the P notes in lieu of seeking indemnification from T.

P's obligation to close is subject to several conditions, such as (i) compliance with T's representations, warranties, and covenants, (ii) absence of a material adverse change, (iii) absence of litigation affecting the transaction, (iv) availability of financing, (v) receipt of governmental approvals, (vi) delivery of title insurance, surveys, and third party consents, (vii) delivery of any side agreements, and (viii) delivery of an opinion of T's legal counsel.

P also has the right to terminate the purchase agreement for a limited period after signing if P is not satisfied with the results of its continuing business, legal, and accounting due diligence review.

There are a number of other important differences among sample acquisition agreement 2004.1 (*pro-buyer* divisional asset purchase), sample acquisition agreement 2004.2 (*pro-seller* divisional asset purchase), and sample acquisition agreement 2004.3 (*neutral* divisional asset purchase). Each of these sample acquisition agreements contains extensive footnotes with cross-references pointing out the differences.

¶2001.3.3.2   Pro-Seller

Sample acquisition agreement 2004.2 (*pro-seller* divisional asset purchase) contains provisions favoring T in areas such as (i) the extent to which T will retain the divisional cash (net of unpaid taxes) at the time of the closing, (ii) the extent to which P will bear the burden of the divisional liabilities and obligations at the time of the closing, (iii) the extent to which P will lack conditions to its obligation to close, (iv) the extent to which T will be required to give representations and warranties, and (v) the extent to which T will be required to indemnify P against breaches of those representations and warranties.

Sample acquisition agreement 2004.2 provides that T will (i) retain all of the divisional cash at the closing and (ii) remain liable for the unpaid divisional taxes for periods up to the closing. This means that T will retain the divisional cash (net of unpaid taxes) at the time of the closing.

Sample acquisition agreement 2004.2 provides that P will assume substantially all of the divisional obligations and liabilities (whether known or unknown and whether absolute or contingent). Thus, P would generally assume such undisclosed divisional liabilities as environmental cleanup, employment discrimination, antitrust violations, product liability, product warranty, tax deficiencies, and other claims and lawsuits.

Sample acquisition agreement 2004.2 contains limited representations and warranties from T concerning (i) the historical divisional financial statements, (ii) intervening events, (iii) litigation, (iv) tax matters, (v) pension and welfare benefit plans, and (vi) compliance with federal, state, local, and foreign laws.

Sample acquisition agreement 2004.2 *does not* contain a specific representation and warranty concerning undisclosed divisional liabilities.

Sample acquisition agreement 2004.2 also contains limited representations and warranties from T concerning (i) authorization with respect to the transaction, (ii) title to the assets being sold, (iii) required governmental and third party consents (and noncontravention generally), (iv) organization, (v) real estate matters, (vi) intellectual property matters, (vii) leases and contracts, and (viii) brokerage fees.

T's representations and warranties are qualified frequently with references to materiality and to the actual knowledge of T's shareholders, but not, for example, T's directors, officers, and employees, *without any duty of independent investigation.*

Sample acquisition agreement 2004.2 contains alternative provisions for (i) minimal indemnification to P for breaches of T's representations and warranties (i.e., none of the representations and warranties concerning the division survive the closing and there is no indemnification for breaches thereof)[11] *or* (ii) limited indemnification to P for breaches of T's representations and warranties (i.e., the representations and warranties concerning the division survive only for one year, and there is a deductible and a ceiling with respect to indemnification for breaches thereof).

P *does not* have any right to recoup its losses against the P notes in lieu of seeking indemnification from T.

P's obligation to close is subject to minimal conditions, such as (i) compliance with T's representations, warranties, and covenants, (ii) absence of a material adverse change, (iii) absence of an injunction affecting the transaction, (iv) receipt of governmental approvals, (v) delivery of any side agreements, and (vi) delivery of an opinion of T's legal counsel.

P *does not* have any closing condition concerning its ability to secure financing for the transaction *or* any right to terminate the purchase agreement after signing if it is not satisfied with the results of its continuing business, legal, and accounting due diligence review.

There are a number of other important differences among sample acquisition agreement 2004.1 (*pro-buyer* divisional asset purchase), sample acquisition agreement 2004.2 (*pro-seller* divisional asset purchase), and sample acquisition agreement 2004.3 (*neutral* divisional asset purchase). Each of these sample acquisition agreements contains extensive footnotes with cross-references pointing out the differences.

¶2001.3.3.3 *Neutral*

Sample acquisition agreement 2004.3 (*neutral* divisional asset purchase) is intended to strike a reasonable balance between the conflicting interests of P and T in areas such as (i) the extent to which P will receive divisional cash (net of unpaid taxes) at the time of the closing, (ii) the extent to which T will bear the burden of the divisional liabilities and obligations after the closing, (iii) the extent to which P will have conditions to its obligation to close, (iv) the extent to which T will be required to give representations and warranties, and (v) the extent to

---

[11] This is referred to as *minimal* indemnification (rather than *no* indemnification) because T's representations and warranties about the transaction itself (e.g, organization of T, authorization of the transaction, noncontravention, absence of brokers' fees, ownership of the divisional assets, etc.) do survive the Closing and may give rise to indemnification.

which T will be required to indemnify P against breaches of those representations and warranties.

Sample acquisition agreement 2004.3 provides that T will retain only so much of the divisional cash at the closing as will cover the unpaid divisional taxes with respect to periods up to the closing for which T will remain liable. This means that P will receive the divisional cash (net of unpaid taxes) at the time of the closing.

Sample acquisition agreement 2004.3 provides that the only T liabilities P will assume are those divisional liabilities (i) shown on the last divisional balance sheet reviewed by P before signing the contract, (ii) incurred in the ordinary course of business thereafter (but not including claims and lawsuits), (iii) involving employee benefit plans and executory contracts, or (iv) listed on a disclosure schedule. Thus, P would generally *not* assume such undisclosed divisional liabilities as environmental cleanup, employment discrimination, antitrust violations, product liability, product warranty, tax deficiencies, and other claims and lawsuits.

Sample acquisition agreement 2004.3 contains fairly extensive representations and warranties from T concerning (i) the historical divisional financial statements, (ii) intervening material adverse changes in the divisional business, (iii) litigation and material undisclosed liabilities, (iv) tax matters, (v) pension and welfare benefit plans, (vi) compliance with federal, state, local, and foreign laws, (vii) environmental matters, and (viii) product liability and warranties.

Sample acquisition agreement 2004.3 also contains fairly extensive representations and warranties from T concerning (i) authorization with respect to the transaction, (ii) title to the assets being sold, (iii) required governmental and third party consents (and noncontravention generally), (iv) organization, (v) adequacy and condition of the divisional tangible assets, (vi) real estate matters, (vii) intellectual property matters, (viii) leases, licenses, and contracts, (ix) inventory and accounts receivable, (x) insurance, (xi) brokerage fees, and (xii) material misstatements and omissions.

T's representations and warranties, however, are qualified with relatively frequent references to knowledge (defined as the actual knowledge of its shareholders, directors, and officers after reasonable investigation) and materiality.

Sample acquisition agreement 2004.3 provides that the representations and warranties with respect to the transaction itself and with respect to taxes will survive indefinitely, that the environmental representations and warranties will survive for five years, that the other representations and warranties will survive for two years, and that there will be a deductible and a ceiling with respect to indemnification against breaches of any representations and warranties that do not concern the transaction itself.

P *does not* have any right to recoup its losses against the P notes in lieu of seeking indemnification from T.

P's obligation to close is subject to several conditions, such as (i) compliance with T's representations, warranties, and covenants, (ii) absence of a material adverse change, (iii) absence of litigation affecting the transaction, (iv) receipt of governmental approvals, (v) delivery of title insurance, surveys, and material third party consents, (vi) delivery of any side agreements, and (vii) delivery of an opinion of T's legal counsel.

P *does not* have any closing condition concerning its ability to secure financing for the transaction *or* any right to terminate the purchase agreement after signing if it is not satisfied with the results of its continuing business, legal, and accounting due diligence review.

It is important to note that some of the provisions in sample acquisition agreement 2004.3 are neutral only in the context of the overall agreement. In part, this is due to the interplay between T's representations and warranties (which are fairly extensive but qualified with references to knowledge and materiality) on the one hand and the indemnification obligations of T's stockholders (which are subject to various deductibles, ceilings, and survival periods) on the other. Accordingly, it is not always possible to remove a provision from sample acquisition agreement 2004.3 for use in another agreement and have the provision remain neutral.

Finally, the choice of neutral provisions for sample acquisition agreement 2004.3 was necessarily subjective. Thus, in any particular transaction, it may be necessary to modify the agreement so that it strikes a different balance between the interests of P and T.

There are a number of other important differences among sample acquisition agreement 2004.1 (*pro-buyer* divisional asset purchase), sample acquisition agreement 2004.2 (*pro-seller* divisional asset purchase), and sample acquisition agreement 2004.3 (*neutral* divisional asset purchase). Each of these sample acquisition agreements contains extensive footnotes with cross-references pointing out the differences.

¶2001.3.4   Reverse Subsidiary Merger of P's Transitory Subsidiary into T for Cash and Notes

Sample acquisition agreement 2005 is a taxable reverse subsidiary merger agreement (in which T's shareholders receive cash and notes) for use when T is a public reporting company. Because this sample acquisition agreement assumes that T is a publicly held company, it contains very limited representations and warranties about T (based primarily on T's SEC filings) and no post-closing indemnification from T's shareholders.

This arrangement is typical in public company acquisitions for two reasons. *First*, P will have the comfort of the substantial public information about T available in T's SEC filings, and hence P needs less in the way of representations and warranties. *Second*, the merger consideration will generally be disbursed to T's shareholders as soon as the merger is effective. Although an escrow for a portion of the merger consideration is feasible, it is not frequently used.

If T is *not* a publicly held company, P may seek extensive representations and warranties about T and post-closing indemnification from T's shareholders against any breaches thereof. Sample acquisition agreements 2002.1, 2002.2, and 2002.3

(the *stock purchase* agreements) contain provisions more favorable to P in this respect than the provisions in sample acquisition agreement 2005.

Naturally, the acquisition documents covering an actual transaction must be carefully tailored to the economic terms and the risk-sharing arrangements agreed upon by the parties. It is therefore unlikely that any sample acquisition agreement will ever be appropriate in its entirety for a particular negotiated transaction. Indeed, in preparing the acquisition documents for a particular negotiated transaction, it will frequently be necessary to mix and match between sample acquisition agreements, i.e., to use parts of several. When one portion of a sample acquisition agreement is changed, however, care is necessary to make sure that all appropriate changes are made in other parts of the sample acquisition agreement because many clauses of a sample acquisition agreement are often interrelated.

Sample acquisition agreement 2005 contemplates that P will acquire all of T's outstanding shares for cash and notes through the mechanism of a reverse subsidiary merger (i.e., a merger of P's transitory subsidiary S with and into T).[12] The reverse subsidiary merger technique is used when T has so many shareholders that it would be unwieldy for all of them to become parties to a stock purchase agreement (or when T has only a few shareholders, but some minority shareholders decline to participate).[13] If P is to pay the entire purchase price in cash (i.e., no P notes are being issued to T's shareholders in the merger), all of the provisions relating to the P notes can be deleted.

After S merges into T, T will become a subsidiary of P. T will generally retain all of its assets and rights and remain responsible for all of its liabilities and obligations.

It is generally not necessary to prepare asset transfer documents or liability assumption documents in a merger as it is in a purchase of assets.

See ¶2001.2.3 for a further description of the principal tax and other issues associated with a merger.

Sample acquisition agreement 2002.5 (purchase price adjustment) contains additional provisions for use when there is to be a post-closing purchase price adjustment based on T's net book value as of the closing. This sample acquisition agreement can be adapted for other post-closing purchase price adjustments (such as a comparison of working capital with liabilities as of the closing *or* a contingent earnout based on earnings for a specified period after the closing). Sample acquisition agreement 2002.5 is, however, intended for use with sample acquisition agreements 2002.1, 2002.2, and 2002.3 (the *stock purchase* agreements) and must be modified prior to use with sample acquisition agreement 2005 (the reverse subsidiary *merger* agreement).

The parties must address a number of general issues in preparing any acquisition document. See ¶2001.1 for a discussion of these key issues.

---

[12] A reverse subsidiary merger will generally be treated as a sale of stock for federal income tax purposes. *See* ¶202.

[13] Sample acquisition agreement 2005 contemplates a single-step reverse subsidiary merger. The parties would have to modify the agreement accordingly if the transaction involved a first-step tender offer followed by a second-step merger. *See* ¶1502.7.

¶2001.3.5   Tax-Free Merger of T into P for P Stock

Sample acquisition agreement 2006 is a tax-free merger agreement for use when T is a public reporting company. Because this sample acquisition agreement assumes that T is a publicly held company, it contains very limited representations and warranties about T (based primarily on T's SEC filings) and no post-closing indemnification from T's shareholders.

This arrangement is typical in public company acquisitions for two reasons. *First*, P will have the comfort of the substantial public information about T available in T's SEC filings, and hence P needs less in the way of representations and warranties. *Second*, the merger consideration will generally be disbursed to T's shareholders as soon as the merger is effective. Although an escrow for a portion of the merger consideration is feasible, it is not frequently used.

If T is *not* a publicly held company, P may seek extensive representations and warranties about T and post-closing indemnification from T's shareholders against any breaches thereof. Sample acquisition agreements 2003.1, 2003.2, and 2003.3 (the *asset purchase* agreements) contain provisions which are more favorable to P in this respect than the provisions in this sample acquisition agreement 2006.

Naturally, the acquisition documents covering an actual transaction must be carefully tailored to the economic terms and the risk-sharing arrangements agreed upon by the parties. It is therefore unlikely that any sample acquisition agreement will ever be appropriate in its entirety for a particular negotiated transaction. Indeed, in preparing the acquisition documents for a particular negotiated transaction, it will frequently be necessary to mix and match between sample acquisition agreements, i.e., to use parts of several. When one portion of a sample acquisition agreement is changed, however, care is necessary to make sure that all appropriate changes are made in other parts of the sample acquisition agreement because many clauses of a sample acquisition agreement are often interrelated.

Sample acquisition agreement 2006 contemplates a tax-free merger of T into P (e.g., a two-party "A" reorganization pursuant to Code §368(a)(1)(A)), with T's shareholders receiving capital stock of P in exchange for their capital stock in T. See ¶801 for a discussion of the requirements for and consequences of an "A" reorganization (including the circumstances under which P may distribute cash or other "boot" to T's shareholders in addition to P stock).[14]

There are alternative tax-free acquisition structures that P and T may wish to consider. See Chapters 6, 7, and 8 for a discussion of stock-for-stock exchanges, stock-for-assets exchanges, forward subsidiary mergers, and reverse subsidiary mergers. See also Chapter 9 for a discussion of evolving acquisition techniques using Code §351.

---

[14] A transaction which is a tax-free reorganization for tax purposes (so that the basis of T in its assets carries over to P) also may constitute a *pooling of interests* for GAAP purposes (so that the book value of T for its assets carries over to P) if it meets the very rigorous pooling requirements described at ¶1503. If the parties wish to structure the transaction as a pooling of interests for GAAP purposes, it will be necessary to add representations, warranties, covenants, and other provisions addressing the pooling requirements.

All tax-free reorganizations (including the two-party "A" reorganization) must satisfy three requirements: (i) business purpose, (ii) continuity of shareholder interest, and (iii) continuity of business enterprise. *See* ¶¶609, 610, and 611. Unless the merger of T into P satisfies all three of these requirements, the transaction will not qualify as a tax-free reorganization and instead will constitute a taxable sale of assets from T to P followed by a complete liquidation of T. *See* Rev. Rul. 69-6, 1969-1 C.B. 104, discussed at ¶301. For example, if too much of the consideration paid to T's shareholders is cash or other boot (i.e., too little of the consideration is P stock) so that the continuity of shareholder interest requirement is not satisfied, the transaction will be treated as such a taxable sale of assets.

After T merges into P, P will generally acquire all of T's assets and rights and assume all of T's liabilities and obligations by operation of law.

It is generally not necessary to prepare asset transfer documents or liability assumption documents in a merger as it is in a purchase of assets.

See ¶2001.2.3 for a further description of the principal tax and other issues associated with a merger.

Sample acquisition agreement 2002.5 (purchase price adjustment) contains additional provisions for use when there is to be a post-closing purchase price adjustment based on T's net book value as of the closing. This sample acquisition agreement can be adapted for other post-closing purchase price adjustments (such as a comparison of working capital with liabilities as of the closing *or* a contingent earnout based on earnings for a specified period after the closing). Sample acquisition agreement 2002.5, however, is intended for use with sample acquisition agreements 2002.1, 2002.2, and 2002.3 (the taxable *stock purchase* agreements) and must be modified prior to use with sample acquisition agreement 2006 (the tax-free *merger* agreement).

The parties must address a number of general issues in preparing any acquisition document. See ¶2001.1 for a discussion of these key issues.

Taxable Purchase of Stock

¶2002   P's PURCHASE OF T's STOCK FOR CASH AND NOTES

Sample acquisition agreement 2002.1 is a *pro-buyer* version of a taxable stock purchase. Sample acquisition agreement 2002.2 is a *pro-seller* version of a taxable stock purchase. Sample acquisition agreement 2002.3 is a *neutral* version of a taxable stock purchase.

Sample acquisition agreements 2002.1, 2002.2, and 2002.3 contemplate a transaction in which a corporation ("P") will purchase all of the outstanding stock of another corporation ("T") from several corporate and individual sellers for cash and P notes. If P is to pay the entire purchase price in cash (i.e., no P notes are being issued to the sellers), all of the provisions relating to the P notes can be deleted.

After P purchases the T shares, T will become a subsidiary of P (assuming P is a corporation). T will generally retain all of its assets and rights and remain responsible for all of its liabilities and obligations.[1]

It is generally not necessary to prepare asset transfer documents or liability assumption documents in a stock purchase, as it is in a purchase of assets.

See ¶2001.2.1 for a further description of the principal tax and other issues associated with a purchase of stock.

If T has so many shareholders that it would be unwieldy for all of them to become parties to a stock purchase agreement (or if T has only a few shareholders, but some minority shareholders decline to participate), the parties may wish to use sample acquisition agreement 2005 (reverse subsidiary merger),[2] adjusted to incorporate the pro-buyer, pro-seller, or neutral features of sample acquisition agreement 2002.1 (*pro-buyer* stock purchase), sample acquisition agreement 2002.2 (*pro-seller* stock purchase), or sample acquisition agreement 2002.3 (*neutral* stock purchase) as appropriate. See ¶2001.2.3 for a description of the principal tax and other issues associated with a merger.

¶2002   [1] If T was a Subchapter S corporation before the stock purchase, however, it will generally not have paid federal income tax at the corporate level. Thus the sellers (i.e., the T shareholders) will generally remain liable for federal income taxes through the Closing. *See* Chapter 11.

[2] A reverse subsidiary merger will generally be treated as a sale of stock for federal income tax purposes. *See* ¶202.

Sample acquisition agreement 2002.4 contains additional provisions which should be used (or at least considered) in tandem with either 2002.1, 2002.2, or 2002.3 where T is, before the acquisition, a subsidiary of Bigco filing a consolidated federal income tax return.

Sample acquisition agreement 2002.5 contains additional provisions for use where there is to be a post-closing purchase price adjustment based on T's net book value as of the closing. This sample acquisition agreement can be adapted for other post-closing purchase price adjustments (such as a comparison of working capital with liabilities as of the closing *or* a contingent earnout based on earnings for a specified period after the closing).

Sample acquisition agreement 2002.6 contains additional provisions which should be considered where T is an S corporation, particularly (although not exclusively) where P wishes to make a Code §338(h)(10) election with respect to its acquisition of T-SCo's stock.

The parties must address a number of general issues in preparing any acquisition document. See ¶2001.1 for a discussion of these key issues.

¶2002.1   Pro-Buyer Stock Purchase

Sample acquisition agreement 2002.1 (*pro-buyer* stock purchase) contains provisions favoring P in such areas as (i) the extent to which T will retain its cash at the time of the closing, (ii) the extent to which the sellers (i.e., T's old shareholders) will bear the burden of T's liabilities and obligations after the closing, (iii) the extent to which P will have conditions to its obligation to close, (iv) the extent to which the sellers will be required to give representations and warranties, and (v) the extent to which the sellers will be required to indemnify P against breaches of those representations and warranties.

Sample acquisition agreement 2002.1 prohibits the sellers (i.e., T's shareholders) from causing T to distribute any of its cash to them (e.g., as a dividend or in a repurchase or redemption) at or prior to the closing. This means that T will retain its cash at the time of the closing.

Sample acquisition agreement 2002.1 contains extensive representations and warranties from the sellers (i.e., T's shareholders) concerning (i) T's historical financial statements, (ii) intervening adverse changes in T's business, (iii) litigation and undisclosed liabilities, (iv) tax matters, (v) pension and welfare benefit plans, (vi) compliance with federal, state, local, and foreign laws, (vii) environmental matters, and (viii) product liability and warranties.

The sellers (i.e., T's shareholders) accordingly will be in breach of their representations and warranties and required to indemnify P if T has any undisclosed liabilities, i.e., liabilities *other than* (i) those shown on the last T balance sheet reviewed by P before signing the contract, (ii) those incurred in the ordinary course of business thereafter (but not including claims and lawsuits), and (iii) those listed on a disclosure schedule. This would generally protect P against such undisclosed T liabilities as environmental cleanup, employment discrimination, antitrust violations, product liability, product warranty, tax deficiencies, and other claims and lawsuits.

Sample acquisition agreement 2002.1 also contains extensive representations and warranties from the sellers (i.e., T's shareholders) concerning (i) authorization with respect to the transaction, (ii) title to the stock being sold (and title to T's underlying assets), (iii) required governmental and third party consents (and noncontravention generally), (iv) organization and capitalization, (v) adequacy and condition of T's tangible assets, (vi) real estate matters, (vii) intellectual property matters, (viii) leases, licenses, and contracts, (ix) inventory and accounts receivable, (x) insurance, (xi) brokerage fees, and (xii) material misstatements and omissions.

The sellers' representations and warranties are not qualified with references to materiality, but do contain occasional references to the actual knowledge of the sellers (i.e., T's shareholders) and the directors, officers, and employees of T *after reasonable investigation.*

Sample acquisition agreement 2002.1 contains alternative provisions for (i) full indemnification to P for breaches of the seller's representations and warranties (i.e., the representations and warranties concerning T survive indefinitely and there is no deductible, threshold, or ceiling with respect to indemnification for breaches thereof) *or* (ii) limited indemnification to P for breaches of the seller's representations and warranties (i.e., the representations and warranties with respect to tax matters survive indefinitely, the other representations and warranties concerning T survive only for three years, and there is a threshold, but not a deductible or a ceiling, with respect to indemnification for breaches thereof). The sellers' indemnification obligation is joint and several.

P also has the right to recoup its losses against the P notes in lieu of seeking indemnification from the sellers (i.e., T's shareholders).

P's obligation to close is subject to several conditions such as (i) compliance with the sellers' representations, warranties, and covenants, (ii) absence of a material adverse change, (iii) absence of litigation affecting the transaction, (iv) availability of financing, (v) delivery of title insurance, surveys, and third party consents, (vi) delivery of any side agreements, and (vii) delivery of an opinion of the sellers' legal counsel.

P also has the right to terminate the purchase agreement for a period of [30 days] after signing if P is not satisfied with the results of its continuing business, legal, and accounting due diligence review.

There are a number of other important differences among sample acquisition agreement 2002.1 (*pro-buyer* stock purchase), sample acquisition agreement 2002.2 (*pro-seller* stock purchase), and sample acquisition agreement 2002.3 (*neutral* stock purchase). Each of these sample acquisition agreements contains extensive footnotes with cross-references pointing out the differences.

STOCK PURCHASE AGREEMENT[1]

AMONG

_____

AND

_____, _____,

AND_____

_____, 19_____

¶2002.1   [1]The Buyer may choose to make a regular Code §338 election on a timely basis after an acquisition structured as a taxable purchase of Target Shares. *See* ¶¶107.1, 204, 205, 403, and 405.

If the Buyer makes a timely regular Code §338 election, the Target in effect becomes "New Target" immediately following the acquisition date: the Target's basis in its assets is stepped up (or down) so that the Target's aggregate asset basis equals the purchase price (plus the Target's liabilities, including tax liabilities generated in the transaction and inherited by New Target, and the Buyer's expenses of the acquisition), and "Old Target's" corporate attributes—e.g., E&P and tax accounting methods—are expunged. Concomitantly, effective upon the close of the acquisition date, "Old Target" is taxed as if it had sold its assets, i.e., the Target is taxed on its full gain or loss inherent in its tangible and intangible assets (including goodwill), with the Target's gain or loss on each asset being ordinary or capital in character, depending on the nature of each asset treated as sold.

However, even with a regular Code §338 election, the Target's selling shareholders are nevertheless taxed on the stock sale, resulting in double tax, i.e., Target is taxed on the deemed asset sale and the selling shareholders are taxed on the stock sale. *See* ¶205.

If the Buyer intends to make a Code §338 election, it may well be desirable to add language to this Agreement (and to have the board of directors of the Target adopt resolutions) stating that the New Target "expressly assumes" certain enumerated liabilities (and all other unenumerated liabilities) of the Target which have not yet matured into tax deductions. *See* ¶304 and the related footnote to ¶2001.2.1.1(1).

When (1) Target is a member of a consolidated group or (2) the acquisition of Target is consummated on or after 1/20/94 (or earlier if a retroactive election is made) and Target is a member of an affiliated (but not consolidated) group or (3) the acquisition of Target is consummated on or after 1/20/94 (or earlier if a retroactive election is made) and Target is an S corporation, the parties may have the ability to make a Code §338(h)(10) election, in which case all parties (including the selling shareholders) are treated for tax purposes as if Buyer purchased Target's assets. Hence, with a Code §338(h)(10) election (as distinguished from a regular Code §338 election), there is no double tax on the transaction, i.e., Target is treated as selling assets but Target's shareholders are not treated as selling Target's stock, and the deemed liquidation of Target will generally not produce a second tax, because of Code §332 in the consolidated or affiliated subsidiary situation or because of Subchapter S pass-through rules in the SCo situation. *See* ¶¶206.1.1, 206.2, 206.3.3, and 1109.3.

A Code §338(h)(10) election must be made jointly by Buyer and Seller(s). Hence, if either party desires such an election, it should add language to this Agreement stating that both parties agree to make such election. *See* ¶2002.4 for a number of contractual provisions which the parties may desire to add to the acquisition agreement where Target is a subsidiary of a consolidated group.

See §9 of this Agreement for sample language obligating each of the Sellers, if so directed by the Buyer, to join in making a Code §338(h)(10) election.

A purchase of stock in which the consideration is primarily cash and notes is generally treated for accounting purposes as a purchase rather than as a pooling of interests. *See* ¶1503.

TABLE OF CONTENTS

Some LBO structures prejudice the Target's creditors and hence might permit payments, transfers, liens, and obligations arising out of the LBO to be attacked under fraudulent conveyance law. *See* ¶1506.

[EXHIBITS, ANNEXES, AND SCHEDULES HAVE BEEN OMITTED FROM THIS SAMPLE ACQUISITION AGREEMENT 2002.1]

Agreement entered into on [as of] _____, 19____, by and among _____, a _____ corporation (the *"Buyer"*), and _____, and _____ (collectively the *"Sellers"*). The Buyer and the Sellers are referred to collectively herein as the *"Parties."*[2]

The Sellers in the aggregate own all of the outstanding capital stock of _____, a _____ corporation (the *"Target"*).

---

[2] If the Target has so many shareholders that it would be unwieldy for all of them to become parties to this Agreement (or if the Target has only a few shareholders, but some minority shareholders decline to participate), the Parties may wish to use sample acquisition agreement 2005 (reverse subsidiary merger of the Buyer's transitory subsidiary into the Target for cash and notes) rather than this sample acquisition agreement 2002. A reverse subsidiary merger will generally be treated as a sale of stock for federal income tax purposes. *See* ¶202.

This Agreement contemplates a transaction in which the Buyer will purchase from the Sellers, and the Sellers will sell to the Buyer, all of the outstanding capital stock of the Target in return for cash and the Buyer Notes.[3]

Now, therefore, in consideration of the premises and the mutual promises herein made, and in consideration of the representations, warranties, and covenants herein contained, the Parties agree as follows.

1. *Definitions.*

"Accredited Investor" has the meaning set forth in Regulation D promulgated under the Securities Act.

"Adverse Consequences" means all actions, suits, proceedings, hearings, investigations, charges, complaints, claims, demands, injunctions, judgments, orders, decrees, rulings, damages, dues, penalties, fines, costs, amounts paid in settlement, Liabilities, obligations, Taxes, liens, losses, expenses, and fees, including court costs and [reasonable] attorneys' fees and expenses.

"Affiliate" has the meaning set forth in Rule 12b-2 of the regulations promulgated under the Securities Exchange Act.

"Affiliated Group" means any affiliated group within the meaning of Code §1504(a) [or any similar group defined under a similar provision of state, local or foreign law].

"Applicable Rate" means the corporate base rate of interest publicly announced from time to time by [FINANCIAL INSTITUTION] [plus/minus % per annum].

"Basis" means any past or present fact, situation, circumstance, status, condition, activity, practice, plan, occurrence, event, incident, action, failure to act, or transaction that forms or could form the basis for any specified consequence.

"Buyer" has the meaning set forth in the preface above.

"Buyer Note" has the meaning set forth in §2(b) below.

"Closing" has the meaning set forth in §2(c) below.

"Closing Date" has the meaning set forth in §2(c) below.

---

[3] After the Buyer purchases the Target Shares, the Target will become a subsidiary of the Buyer (assuming the Buyer is a corporation). The Target will generally retain all of its assets and rights and remain responsible for all of its liabilities and obligations. Thus it is generally not necessary to prepare asset transfer documents or liability assumption documents in a stock purchase, as it is in a purchase of assets.

"COBRA" means the requirements of Part 6 of Subtitle B of Title I of ERISA and Code §4980B and of any similar state law.

"Code" means the Internal Revenue Code of 1986, as amended.

"Confidential Information" means any information concerning the businesses and affairs of the Target and its Subsidiaries that is not already generally available to the public.

"Controlled Group" has the meaning set forth in Code §1563.

"Deferred Intercompany Transaction" has the meaning set forth in Reg. §1.1502-13.

"Disclosure Schedule" has the meaning set forth in §4 below.

"Employee Benefit Plan" means any "employee benefit plan" (as such term is defined in ERISA §3(3)) and any other [material] employee benefit plan, program or arrangement of any kind.

"Employee Pension Benefit Plan" has the meaning set forth in ERISA §3(2).

"Employee Welfare Benefit Plan" has the meaning set forth in ERISA §3(1).

"Environmental, Health, and Safety Requirements" shall mean all federal, state, local and foreign statutes, regulations, ordinances and other provisions having the force or effect of law, all judicial and administrative orders and determinations, all contractual obligations and all common law concerning public health and safety, worker health and safety, and pollution or protection of the environment, including without limitation all those relating to the presence, use, production, generation, handling, transportation, treatment, storage, disposal, distribution, labeling, testing, processing, discharge, release, threatened release, control, or cleanup of any hazardous materials, substances or wastes, chemical substances or mixtures, pesticides, pollutants, contaminants, toxic chemicals, petroleum products or byproducts, asbestos, polychlorinated biphenyls, noise or radiation, each as amended and as now or hereafter in effect.[4]

"ERISA" means the Employee Retirement Income Security Act of 1974, as amended.

---

[4]Sample acquisition agreement 2002.2 (the *pro-seller* stock purchase agreement) excludes contractual obligations and common law from this definition and explicitly limits this definition to laws as enacted and in effect on or prior to the Closing Date.

Sample acquisition agreement 2002.3 (the *neutral* stock purchase agreement) excludes contractual obligations from this definition and is silent as to the time frame for enactment of covered "Environmental, Health, and Safety Requirements."

"ERISA Affiliate" means each entity which is treated as a single employer with the Target for purposes of Code §414.

"Excess Loss Account" has the meaning set forth in Reg. §1.1502-19.

"Fiduciary" has the meaning set forth in ERISA §3(21).

"Financial Statement" has the meaning set forth in §4(g) below.

"GAAP" means United States generally accepted accounting principles as in effect from time to time.

"Hart-Scott-Rodino Act" means the Hart-Scott-Rodino Antitrust Improvements Act of 1976, as amended.

"Indemnified Party" has the meaning set forth in §8(d) below.

"Indemnifying Party" has the meaning set forth in §8(d) below.

"Intellectual Property" means (a) all inventions (whether patentable or unpatentable and whether or not reduced to practice), all improvements thereto, and all patents, patent applications, and patent disclosures, together with all reissuances, continuations, continuations-in-part, revisions, extensions, and reexaminations thereof, (b) all trademarks, service marks, trade dress, logos, trade names, and corporate names, together with all translations, adaptations, derivations, and combinations thereof and including all goodwill associated therewith, and all applications, registrations, and renewals in connection therewith, (c) all copyrightable works, all copyrights, and all applications, registrations, and renewals in connection therewith, (d) all mask works and all applications, registrations, and renewals in connection therewith, (e) all trade secrets and confidential business information (including ideas, research and development, know-how, formulas, compositions, manufacturing and production processes and techniques, technical data, designs, drawings, specifications, customer and supplier lists, pricing and cost information, and business and marketing plans and proposals), (f) all computer software (including data and related documentation), (g) all other proprietary rights, and (h) all copies and tangible embodiments thereof (in whatever form or medium).

"Knowledge" means actual knowledge after reasonable investigation.[5]

"Liability" means any liability (whether known or unknown, whether asserted or unasserted, whether absolute or contingent, whether accrued or unaccrued,

---

[5] Sample acquisition agreement 2002.2 (the *pro-seller* stock purchase agreement) defines "Knowledge" as actual knowledge without independent investigation.

whether liquidated or unliquidated, and whether due or to become due), including any liability for Taxes.

"Most Recent Balance Sheet" means the balance sheet contained within the Most Recent Financial Statements.

"Most Recent Financial Statements" has the meaning set forth in §4(g) below.

"Most Recent Fiscal Month End" has the meaning set forth in §4(g) below.

"Most Recent Fiscal Year End" has the meaning set forth in §4(g) below.

"Multiemployer Plan" has the meaning set forth in ERISA §3(37).

"Ordinary Course of Business" means the ordinary course of business consistent with past custom and practice (including with respect to quantity and frequency).

"Party" has the meaning set forth in the preface above.

"PBGC" means the Pension Benefit Guaranty Corporation.

"Person" means an individual, a partnership, a corporation, an association, a joint stock company, a trust, a joint venture, an unincorporated organization, or a governmental entity (or any department, agency, or political subdivision thereof).

"Process Agent" has the meaning set forth in §10(p) below.

"Prohibited Transaction" has the meaning set forth in ERISA §406 and Code §4975.

"Purchase Price" has the meaning set forth in §2(b) below.

"Reportable Event" has the meaning set forth in ERISA §4043.

"Requisite Sellers" means Sellers holding [a majority] in interest of the Target Shares as set forth in §4(b) of the Disclosure Schedule.[6]

"Securities Act" means the Securities Act of 1933, as amended.

"Securities Exchange Act" means the Securities Exchange Act of 1934, as amended.

"Security Interest" means any mortgage, pledge, lien, encumbrance, charge, or other security interest, other than (a) mechanic's, materialmen's, and similar liens,

---

[6] It may be necessary to revise this definition if the Target has additional classes of capital stock.

(b) liens for Taxes not yet due and payable [or for Taxes that the taxpayer is contesting in good faith through appropriate proceedings], (c) purchase money liens and liens securing rental payments under capital lease arrangements, and (d) other liens arising in the Ordinary Course of Business and not incurred in connection with the borrowing of money.

"Seller" has the meaning set forth in the preface above.

"Subsidiary" means any corporation with respect to which a specified Person (or a Subsidiary thereof) owns a majority of the common stock or has the power to vote or direct the voting of sufficient securities to elect a majority of the directors.[7]

"Survey" has the meaning set forth in §5(i) below.

"Target" has the meaning set forth in the preface above.

"Target Share" means any share of the Common Stock, par value $_____ per share, of the Target.[8]

"Tax" means any federal, state, local, or foreign income, gross receipts, license, payroll, employment, excise, severance, stamp, occupation, premium, windfall profits, environmental (including taxes under Code §59A), customs duties, capital stock, franchise, profits, withholding, social security (or similar), unemployment, disability, real property, personal property, sales, use, transfer, registration, value added, alternative or add-on minimum, estimated, or other tax of any kind whatsoever, including any interest, penalty, or addition thereto, whether disputed or not.[9]

"Tax Return" means any return, declaration, report, claim for refund, or information return or statement relating to Taxes, including any schedule or attachment thereto, and including any amendment thereof.

"Third Party Claim" has the meaning set forth in §8(d) below.

2. *Purchase and Sale of Target Shares.*[10]

---

[7] It may be necessary to revise this definition if, for example, the Target has subsidiary *partnerships*.

[8] It may be necessary to revise this definition if the Target has additional classes of capital stock.

[9] This sample acquisition agreement 2002.1 (the *pro-buyer* stock purchase agreement) defines "Tax" broadly to include taxes of all descriptions.

Sample acquisition agreement 2002.2 (the *pro-seller* stock purchase agreement), on the other hand, defines "Tax" narrowly to include only federal, state, local, and foreign income taxes.

[10] Sample acquisition agreement 2002.2 (the *pro-seller* stock purchase agreement) contains a provision allowing the Sellers to cause the Target and its Subsidiaries to distribute their consolidated cash (net of unpaid taxes) to the Sellers at the Closing. *See* §2(c), §4(h), and §5(c) of sample acquisition agreement 2002.2. This *pro-buyer* stock purchase agreement lacks a comparable provision and indeed *prohibits* the Sellers from causing any such distribution. *See* §4(h)(xiii) and §5(c) below.

(a) *Basic Transaction.* On and subject to the terms and conditions of this Agreement, the Buyer agrees to purchase from each of the Sellers, and each of the Sellers agrees to sell to the Buyer, all of his or its Target Shares for the consideration specified below in this §2.

(b) *Purchase Price.*[11] The Buyer agrees to pay to the Sellers at the Closing $_____ (the *"Purchase Price"*) by delivery of (i) its promissory notes (the *"Buyer Notes"*) in the form of Exhibit A attached hereto in the aggregate principal amount of $_____ and (ii) cash for the balance of the Purchase Price payable by wire transfer or delivery of other immediately available funds. The Purchase Price shall be allocated among the Sellers in proportion to their respective holdings of Target Shares as set forth in §4(b) of the Disclosure Schedule.[12]

(c) *The Closing.* The closing of the transactions contemplated by this Agreement (the *"Closing"*) shall take place at the offices of in _____, _____, commencing at 9:00 a.m. local time on the [second] business day following the satisfaction or waiver of all conditions to the obligations of the Parties to consummate the transactions contemplated hereby (other than conditions with respect to actions the respective Parties will take at the Closing itself) or such other date as the Buyer and the Requisite Sellers may mutually determine (the *"Closing Date"*); *provided, however,* that the Closing Date shall be no earlier than _____, 19____.[13]

(d) *Deliveries at the Closing.* At the Closing, (i) the Sellers will deliver to the Buyer the various certificates, instruments, and documents referred to in §7(a) below, (ii) the Buyer will deliver to the Sellers the various certificates, instruments, and documents referred to in §7(b) below, (iii) each of the Sellers will deliver to the Buyer stock certificates representing all of his or its Target Shares, endorsed in blank or accompanied by duly executed assignment documents, and (iv) the Buyer will deliver to each of the Sellers the consideration specified in §2(b) above.

3. *Representations and Warranties Concerning the Transaction.*

---

[11] The Sellers may seek to have the Buyer make an earnest money deposit upon execution of this Agreement. If the transaction were thereafter completed, the deposit would be applied to the Purchase Price. If the transaction were thereafter aborted, the deposit would be refunded to the Buyer or paid to the Sellers as liquidated damages depending on the terms of this Agreement and the reasons for the termination.

[12] Sample acquisition agreement 2002.5 contains additional provisions for use when there is to be a post-Closing Purchase Price adjustment based on the consolidated net book value for the Target and its Subsidiaries as of the Closing. That sample acquisition agreement can be adapted for other post-Closing Purchase Price adjustments (such as a comparison of consolidated working capital with consolidated liabilities as of the Closing *or* a contingent earnout based on consolidated earnings for a specified period after the Closing).

[13] The Parties should determine whether the Sellers or the Buyer will owe any stock transfer or similar Tax on the transfer of the Target Shares by reason of the chosen Closing location.

(a) *Representations and Warranties of the Sellers.* Each of the Sellers represents and warrants to the Buyer that the statements contained in this §3(a) are correct and complete as of the date of this Agreement and will be correct and complete as of the Closing Date (as though made then and as though the Closing Date were substituted for the date of this Agreement throughout this §3(a)) with respect to himself or itself, except as set forth in Annex I attached hereto.

(i) *Organization of Certain Sellers.* If the Seller is a corporation, the Seller is duly organized, validly existing, and in good standing under the laws of the jurisdiction of its incorporation.[14]

(ii) *Authorization of Transaction.* The Seller has full power and authority (including, if the Seller is a corporation, full corporate power and authority) to execute and deliver this Agreement and to perform his or its obligations hereunder. This Agreement constitutes the valid and legally binding obligation of the Seller, enforceable in accordance with its terms and conditions. The Seller need not give any notice to, make any filing with, or obtain any authorization, consent, or approval of any government or governmental agency in order to consummate the transactions contemplated by this Agreement.

(iii) *Noncontravention.* Neither the execution and the delivery of this Agreement, nor the consummation of the transactions contemplated hereby, will [(A)] violate any constitution, statute, regulation, rule, injunction, judgment, order, decree, ruling, charge, or other restriction of any government, governmental agency, or court to which the Seller is subject or, if the Seller is a corporation, any provision of its charter or bylaws [or (B) conflict with, result in a breach of, constitute a default under, result in the acceleration of, create in any party the right to accelerate, terminate, modify, or cancel, or require any notice under any agreement, contract, lease, license, instrument, or other arrangement to which the Seller is a party or by which he or it is bound or to which any of his or its assets is subject].

(iv) *Brokers' Fees.* The Seller has no Liability or obligation to pay any fees or commissions to any broker, finder, or agent with respect to the transactions contemplated by this Agreement for which the Buyer could become liable or obligated.

(v) *Investment.* The Seller (A) understands that the Buyer Notes have not been, and will not be, registered under the Securities Act, or under any state securities laws, and are being offered and sold in reliance upon federal and state exemptions for transactions not involving any public offering, (B) is acquiring the Buyer Notes solely for his or its own account for investment purposes, and not with a view to the distribution thereof, (C) is a sophisticated investor

---

[14] Several representations and warranties in this §3(a) concern Sellers which are corporations. If any Sellers are partnerships, trusts, business associations, estates, or guardians, the Buyer may seek to add analogous provisions covering them.

with knowledge and experience in business and financial matters, (D) has received certain information concerning the Buyer and has had the opportunity to obtain additional information as desired in order to evaluate the merits and the risks inherent in holding the Buyer Notes, (E) is able to bear the economic risk and lack of liquidity inherent in holding the Buyer Notes, and (F) is an Accredited Investor for the reasons set forth on Annex I.[15]

(vi) *Target Shares.* The Seller holds of record and owns beneficially the number of Target Shares set forth next to his or its name in §4(b) of the Disclosure Schedule, free and clear of any restrictions on transfer (other than any restrictions under the Securities Act and state securities laws), Taxes, Security Interests, options, warrants, purchase rights, contracts, commitments, equities, claims, and demands. The Seller is not a party to any option, warrant, purchase right, or other contract or commitment that could require the Seller to sell, transfer, or otherwise dispose of any capital stock of the Target (other than this Agreement). The Seller is not a party to any voting trust, proxy, or other agreement or understanding with respect to the voting of any capital stock of the Target.

(b) *Representations and Warranties of the Buyer.*[16] The Buyer represents and warrants to the Sellers that the statements contained in this §3(b) are correct and complete as of the date of this Agreement and will be correct and complete as of the Closing Date (as though made then and as though the Closing Date were substituted for the date of this Agreement throughout this §3(b)), except as set forth in Annex II attached hereto.

(i) *Organization of the Buyer.* The Buyer is a corporation duly organized, validly existing, and in good standing under the laws of the jurisdiction of its incorporation.

(ii) *Authorization of Transaction.* The Buyer has full power and authority (including full corporate power and authority) to execute and deliver this Agreement and to perform its obligations hereunder. This Agreement constitutes the valid and legally binding obligation of the Buyer, enforceable in accordance with its terms and conditions. The Buyer need not give any notice to, make any filing with, or obtain any authorization, consent, or approval of any

---

[15] This provision contemplates that the Buyer will issue the Buyer Notes pursuant to the exemption from registration under the Securities Act contained in Regulation D. The Parties should determine whether this exemption is available in a particular transaction. If it is not, the Agreement must be modified as necessary to reflect the issuance of the Buyer Notes under a different exemption from securities registration or in an offering registered under the Securities Act.

[16] The Sellers may seek to obtain additional representations and warranties concerning the Buyer and its Subsidiaries (e.g., the typical representations and warranties contained in a loan agreement or an underwriting agreement) because the Buyer is issuing the Buyer Notes to the Sellers as part of the Purchase Price. Any such representations and warranties would normally survive the Closing and remain applicable for so long as the Buyer Notes remained outstanding.

government or governmental agency in order to consummate the transactions contemplated by this Agreement.

(iii) *Noncontravention.* Neither the execution and the delivery of this Agreement, nor the consummation of the transactions contemplated hereby, will [(A)] violate any constitution, statute, regulation, rule, injunction, judgment, order, decree, ruling, charge, or other restriction of any government, governmental agency, or court to which the Buyer is subject or any provision of its charter or bylaws [or (B) conflict with, result in a breach of, constitute a default under, result in the acceleration of, create in any party the right to accelerate, terminate, modify, or cancel, or require any notice under any agreement, contract, lease, license, instrument, or other arrangement to which the Buyer is a party or by which it is bound or to which any of its assets is subject].

(iv) *Brokers' Fees.* The Buyer has no Liability or obligation to pay any fees or commissions to any broker, finder, or agent with respect to the transactions contemplated by this Agreement for which any Seller could become liable or obligated.

(v) *Investment.* The Buyer is not acquiring the Target Shares with a view to or for sale in connection with any distribution thereof within the meaning of the Securities Act.

4. *Representations and Warranties Concerning the Target and Its Subsidiaries.*[17] The Sellers represent and warrant to the Buyer that the statements contained in this §4 are correct and complete as of the date of this Agreement and will be correct and complete as of the Closing Date (as though made then and as though the Closing Date were substituted for the date of this Agreement throughout this §4), except as set forth in the disclosure schedule delivered by the Sellers to the Buyer on the date hereof and initialed by the Parties (the *"Disclosure Schedule"*).[18] Nothing in the Disclosure Schedule shall be deemed adequate to disclose an exception to a

---

[17] The Sellers will seek to give fewer representations and warranties and to qualify the representations and warranties they do give with concepts of "knowledge" and "materiality." This *pro-buyer* §4 does not contain any unbracketed qualifications as to materiality. It does, however, contain occasional references to the actual knowledge of the Sellers and the directors, officers, and employees of the Target and its Subsidiaries after reasonable investigation. The Sellers will seek to limit the group of individuals whose knowledge is applicable and make it clear that no such individual need conduct any special investigation. Sample acquisition agreement 2002.2 (the *pro-seller* stock purchase agreement) contains comparable representations and warranties which are more favorable to the Sellers.

[18] The Buyer will have a closing condition (see §7(a)(i) below) and post-Closing indemnification rights (see §8(b) below) with respect to certain misrepresentations and breaches of warranty. The Buyer will not, however, have a closing condition or post-Closing indemnification rights with respect to any adverse matter which the Sellers disclose in the Disclosure Schedule. This is because the disclosure will cure any misrepresentation or breach of warranty that might otherwise have existed. Thus, if the Sellers disclose an adverse matter in the Disclosure Schedule, the Buyer may seek (a) to add a specific closing condition requiring an acceptable resolution of the matter and/or (b) to obtain specific post-Closing indemnification against the matter.

representation or warranty made herein, however, unless the Disclosure Schedule identifies the exception with [reasonable] particularity and describes the relevant facts in [reasonable] detail. Without limiting the generality of the foregoing, the mere listing (or inclusion of a copy) of a document or other item shall not be deemed adequate to disclose an exception to a representation or warranty made herein (unless the representation or warranty has to do with the existence of the document or other item itself). The Disclosure Schedule will be arranged in paragraphs corresponding to the lettered and numbered paragraphs contained in this §4.[19]

(a) *Organization, Qualification, and Corporate Power.* Each of the Target and its Subsidiaries is a corporation duly organized, validly existing, and in good standing under the laws of the jurisdiction of its incorporation. Each of the Target and its Subsidiaries is duly authorized to conduct business and is in good standing under the laws of each jurisdiction where such qualification is required. Each of the Target and its Subsidiaries has full corporate power and authority and all licenses, permits, and authorizations necessary to carry on the businesses in which it is engaged [and in which it presently proposes to engage] and to own and use the properties owned and used by it. §4(a) of the Disclosure Schedule lists the directors and officers of each of the Target and its Subsidiaries. The Sellers have delivered to the Buyer correct and complete copies of the charter and bylaws of each of the Target and its Subsidiaries (as amended to date). The minute books (containing the records of meetings of the stockholders, the board of directors, and any committees of the board of directors), the stock certificate books, and the stock record books of each of the Target and its Subsidiaries are correct and complete. None of the Target and its Subsidiaries is in default under or in violation of any provision of its charter or bylaws.

(b) *Capitalization.* The entire authorized capital stock of the Target consists of _____ Target Shares, of which _____ Target Shares are issued and outstanding and _____ Target Shares are held in treasury.[20] All of the issued and outstanding Target Shares have been duly authorized, are validly issued, fully paid, and nonassessable, and are held of record by the respective Sellers as set forth in §4(b) of the Disclosure Schedule. There are no outstanding or authorized options, warrants, purchase rights, subscription rights, conversion rights, exchange rights, or other contracts or commitments that could require the Target to issue, sell, or otherwise cause to become outstanding any of its capital stock. There are no outstanding or authorized stock appreciation, phantom stock, profit participation, or similar rights with respect to the Target. There are no voting trusts, proxies, or other agreements or understandings with respect to the voting of the capital stock of the Target.

---

[19] Sample acquisition agreement 2002.2 (the *pro-seller* stock purchase agreement) omits the last three sentences of this lead-in paragraph.

[20] It may be necessary to revise this sentence if the Target has more than one class of capital stock. See the definition of "Target Shares" in §1 above.

(c) *Noncontravention.* Neither the execution and the delivery of this Agreement, nor the consummation of the transactions contemplated hereby, will (i) violate any constitution, statute, regulation, rule, injunction, judgment, order, decree, ruling, charge, or other restriction of any government, governmental agency, or court to which any of the Target and its Subsidiaries is subject or any provision of the charter or bylaws of any of the Target and its Subsidiaries or (ii) conflict with, result in a breach of, constitute a default under, result in the acceleration of, create in any party the right to accelerate, terminate, modify, or cancel, or require any notice under any agreement, contract, lease, license, instrument, or other arrangement to which any of the Target and its Subsidiaries is a party or by which it is bound or to which any of its assets is subject (or result in the imposition of any Security Interest upon any of its assets). None of the Target and its Subsidiaries needs to give any notice to, make any filing with, or obtain any authorization, consent, or approval of any government or governmental agency in order for the Parties to consummate the transactions contemplated by this Agreement.

(d) *Brokers' Fees.* None of the Target and its Subsidiaries has any Liability or obligation to pay any fees or commissions to any broker, finder, or agent with respect to the transactions contemplated by this Agreement.

(e) *Title to Assets.* The Target and its Subsidiaries have good and marketable title to, or a valid leasehold interest in, the properties and assets used by them, located on their premises, or shown on the Most Recent Balance Sheet or acquired after the date thereof, free and clear of all Security Interests, except for properties and assets disposed of in the Ordinary Course of Business since the date of the Most Recent Balance Sheet.

(f) *Subsidiaries.* §4(f) of the Disclosure Schedule sets forth for each Subsidiary of the Target (i) its name and jurisdiction of incorporation, (ii) the number of shares of authorized capital stock of each class of its capital stock, (iii) the number of issued and outstanding shares of each class of its capital stock, the names of the holders thereof, and the number of shares held by each such holder, and (iv) the number of shares of its capital stock held in treasury. All of the issued and outstanding shares of capital stock of each Subsidiary of the Target have been duly authorized and are validly issued, fully paid, and nonassessable. One of the Target and its Subsidiaries holds of record and owns beneficially all of the outstanding shares of each Subsidiary of the Target, free and clear of any restrictions on transfer (other than restrictions under the Securities Act and state securities laws), Taxes, Security Interests, options, warrants, purchase rights, contracts, commitments, equities, claims, and demands. There are no outstanding or authorized options, warrants, purchase rights, subscription rights, conversion rights, exchange rights, or other contracts or commitments that could require any of the Target and its Subsidiaries to sell, transfer, or otherwise dispose of any capital stock of any of its Subsidiaries or that could require any Subsidiary of the Target to issue, sell, or otherwise cause to become outstanding any of its own capital stock. There are no outstanding stock appreciation, phantom stock, profit participation, or similar rights with respect to any Subsidiary of the Target. There are no voting trusts, proxies, or other agreements or understandings with respect to the voting of any capital stock of any Subsidiary of the Target. None of the Target and its Subsidiaries controls directly or indirectly or has any direct or indirect equity participation in any corporation, partnership, trust, or other business association which is not a Subsidiary of the Target.

(g) *Financial Statements.* Attached hereto as Exhibit B are the following financial statements (collectively the *"Financial Statements"*): (i) audited consolidated and unaudited consolidating balance sheets and statements of income, changes in stockholders' equity, and cash flow as of and for the fiscal years ended _____, 19____, _____, 19____, _____, 19____, _____, 19____, and _____, 19____ (the *"Most Recent Fiscal Year End"*) for the Target and its Subsidiaries; and (ii) unaudited consolidated and consolidating balance sheets and statements of income, changes in stockholders' equity, and cash flow (the *"Most Recent Financial Statements"*) as of and for the months ended _____, 19____ (the *"Most Recent Fiscal Month End"*) for the Target and its Subsidiaries. The Financial Statements (including the notes thereto) have been prepared in accordance with GAAP applied on a consistent basis throughout the periods covered thereby, present fairly the financial condition of the Target and its Subsidiaries as of such dates and the results of operations of the Target and its Subsidiaries for such periods, are correct and complete, and are consistent with the books and records of the Target and its Subsidiaries (which books and records are correct and complete)[21] [; provided, however, that the Most Recent Financial Statements are subject to normal year-end adjustments (which will not be material individually or in the aggregate) and lack footnotes and other presentation items].

(h) *Events Subsequent to Most Recent Fiscal Year End.* Since the Most Recent Fiscal Year End, there has not been any [material] adverse change in the business, financial condition, operations, results of operations, or future prospects of any of the Target and its Subsidiaries. Without limiting the generality of the foregoing, since that date:

(i) none of the Target and its Subsidiaries has sold, leased, transferred, or assigned any of its assets, tangible or intangible, other than for a fair consideration in the Ordinary Course of Business;

(ii) none of the Target and its Subsidiaries has entered into any agreement, contract, lease, or license (or series of related agreements, contracts, leases, and licenses) either involving more than $_____ or outside the Ordinary Course of Business;

---

[21] Sample acquisition agreement 2002.2 (the *pro-seller* stock purchase agreement) contains a narrower representation to the effect that financial statements present fairly the financial condition and results of operations of the Target and its Subsidiaries.

(iii) no party (including any of the Target and its Subsidiaries) has accelerated, terminated, modified, or cancelled any agreement, contract, lease, or license (or series of related agreements, contracts, leases, and licenses) involving more than $_____ to which any of the Target and its Subsidiaries is a party or by which any of them is bound;

(iv) none of the Target and its Subsidiaries has imposed any Security Interest upon any of its assets, tangible or intangible;

(v) none of the Target and its Subsidiaries has made any capital expenditure (or series of related capital expenditures) either involving more than $_____ or outside the Ordinary Course of Business;

(vi) none of the Target and its Subsidiaries has made any capital investment in, any loan to, or any acquisition of the securities or assets of, any other Person (or series of related capital investments, loans, and acquisitions) either involving more than $_____ or outside the Ordinary Course of Business;

(vii) none of the Target and its Subsidiaries has issued any note, bond, or other debt security or created, incurred, assumed, or guaranteed any indebtedness for borrowed money or capitalized lease obligation either involving more than $_____ singly or $_____ in the aggregate;

(viii) none of the Target and its Subsidiaries has delayed or postponed the payment of accounts payable and other Liabilities outside the Ordinary Course of Business;

(ix) none of the Target and its Subsidiaries has cancelled, compromised, waived, or released any right or claim (or series of related rights and claims) either involving more than $_____ or outside the Ordinary Course of Business;

(x) none of the Target and its Subsidiaries has granted any license or sublicense of any rights under or with respect to any Intellectual Property;

(xi) there has been no change made or authorized in the charter or bylaws of any of the Target and its Subsidiaries;

(xii) none of the Target and its Subsidiaries has issued, sold, or otherwise disposed of any of its capital stock, or granted any options, warrants, or other rights to purchase or obtain (including upon conversion, exchange, or exercise) any of its capital stock;

(xiii) none of the Target and its Subsidiaries has declared, set aside, or paid any dividend or made any distribution with respect to its capital stock (whether in cash or in kind) or redeemed, purchased, or otherwise acquired any of its capital stock;

(xiv) none of the Target and its Subsidiaries has experienced any damage, destruction, or loss (whether or not covered by insurance) to its property;

(xv) none of the Target and its Subsidiaries has made any loan to, or entered into any other transaction with, any of its directors, officers, and employees outside the Ordinary Course of Business;

(xvi) none of the Target and its Subsidiaries has entered into any employment contract or collective bargaining agreement, written or oral, or modified the terms of any existing such contract or agreement;

(xvii) none of the Target and its Subsidiaries has granted any increase in the base compensation of any of its directors, officers, and employees outside the Ordinary Course of Business;

(xviii) none of the Target and its Subsidiaries has adopted, amended, modified, or terminated any bonus, profit-sharing, incentive, severance, or other plan, contract, or commitment for the benefit of any of its directors, officers, and employees (or taken any such action with respect to any other Employee Benefit Plan);

(xix) none of the Target and its Subsidiaries has made any other change in employment terms for any of its directors, officers, and employees outside the Ordinary Course of Business;

(xx) none of the Target and its Subsidiaries has made or pledged to make any charitable or other capital contribution outside the Ordinary Course of Business;

(xxi) there has not been any other [material] occurrence, event, incident, action, failure to act, or transaction outside the Ordinary Course of Business involving any of the Target and its Subsidiaries; and

(xxii) none of the Target and its Subsidiaries has committed to any of the foregoing.

(i) *Undisclosed Liabilities.* None of the Target and its Subsidiaries has any Liability (and there is no Basis for any present or future action, suit, proceeding, hearing, investigation, charge, complaint, claim, or demand against any of them giving rise to any Liability), except for (i) Liabilities set forth on the face of the Most Recent Balance Sheet (rather than in any notes thereto) and (ii) Liabilities which have arisen after the Most Recent Fiscal Month End in the Ordinary Course of Business (none of which results from, arises out of, relates to, is in the nature of, or was caused by any breach of contract, breach of warranty, tort, infringement, or violation of law).[22]

(j) *Legal Compliance.* Each of the Target, its Subsidiaries, and their respective predecessors and Affiliates has complied with all applicable laws (including rules, regulations, codes, plans, injunctions, judgments, orders, decrees, rulings, and charges thereunder) of federal, state, local, and foreign governments (and all agencies thereof), and no action, suit, proceeding, hearing, investigation, charge, complaint, claim, demand, or notice has been filed or commenced against any of them alleging any failure so to comply.

(k) *Tax Matters.*[23]

(i) Each of the Target and its Subsidiaries has filed all Tax Returns that it was required to file. All such Tax Returns were correct and complete in all respects. All Taxes owed by any of the Target and its Subsidiaries (whether or not shown on any Tax Return) have been paid.[24] None of the Target and its Subsidiaries currently is the beneficiary of any extension of time within which to file any Tax Return. No claim has ever been made by an authority in a jurisdiction where any of the Target and its Subsidiaries does not file Tax Returns that it is or may be subject to taxation by that jurisdiction. There are no Security Interests on any of the assets of any of the Target and its Subsidiaries that arose in connection with any failure (or alleged failure) to pay any Tax.

---

[22] The lead-in language to §4 provides that the Sellers may disclose exceptions to their representations and warranties in the Disclosure Schedule. This means the Buyer will have no claim against the Sellers for breach of §4(i) with respect to any matter the Sellers have disclosed in the Disclosure Schedule. The lead-in language also provides, however, that no attempt at disclosure will be sufficient unless the Disclosure Schedule identifies the exception with (reasonable) particularity and describes the relevant facts in (reasonable) detail.

[23] Unless the Target was a Subchapter S corporation or was filing a consolidated return with a parent corporation ("Bigco") before the stock purchase, it will generally remain liable for its federal income taxes through the Closing.

If the Target was a Subchapter S corporation before the stock purchase, it will generally not have paid federal income tax at the corporate level. Thus the Sellers (i.e., the Target shareholders) will generally remain liable for federal income taxes through the Closing. When the Buyer (a corporation) purchases the Target Shares, however, the Target will cease to be an S Corporation. *See* Chapter 11.

If the Target was filing a consolidated return with Bigco before the stock purchase, the Target's liability for federal income taxes through the Closing will turn on the tax allocation agreement in effect between the Target and Bigco or on any specific provision in this Agreement. See sample acquisition agreement 2002.4 (sale of subsidiary out of consolidated group) for specific provisions in this regard.

If T has a NOL and will be included in P's consolidated group, P and T should consider making (on their consolidated federal income tax return for the year of the P-T acquisition) an irrevocable election to waive all or part of T's NOL to avoid a reduction in the outside basis of T's stock if and when T's NOL expires. See ¶1203.3.

[24] Sample acquisition agreement 2002.2 (the *pro-seller* stock purchase agreement) contains a narrower representation to the effect that each of the Target and its Subsidiaries has filed all tax returns that it was required to file and has paid all taxes *shown thereon as owing.*

(ii) Each of the Target and its Subsidiaries has withheld and paid all Taxes required to have been withheld and paid in connection with amounts paid or owing to any employee, independent contractor, creditor, stockholder, or other third party.

(iii) No Seller or director or officer (or employee responsible for Tax matters) of any of the Target and its Subsidiaries expects any authority to assess any additional Taxes for any period for which Tax Returns have been filed. There is no dispute or claim concerning any Tax Liability of any of the Target and its Subsidiaries either (A) claimed or raised by any authority in writing or (B) as to which any of the Sellers and the directors and officers (and employees responsible for Tax matters) of the Target and its Subsidiaries has Knowledge based upon personal contact with any agent of such authority. §4(k) of the Disclosure Schedule lists all federal, state, local, and foreign income Tax Returns filed with respect to any of the Target and its Subsidiaries for taxable periods ended on or after _____, 19____, indicates those Tax Returns that have been audited, and indicates those Tax Returns that currently are the subject of audit. The Sellers have delivered to the Buyer correct and complete copies of all federal income Tax Returns, examination reports, and statements of deficiencies assessed against or agreed to by any of the Target and its Subsidiaries since _____, 19____.

(iv) None of the Target and its Subsidiaries has waived any statute of limitations in respect of Taxes or agreed to any extension of time with respect to a Tax assessment or deficiency.

(v) None of the Target and its Subsidiaries has filed a consent under Code §341(f) concerning collapsible corporations. None of the Target and its Subsidiaries has made any payments, is obligated to make any payments, or is a party to any agreement that under certain circumstances could obligate it to make any payments that will not be deductible under Code §280G. None of the Target and its Subsidiaries has been a United States real property holding corporation within the meaning of Code §897(c)(2) during the applicable period specified in Code §897(c)(1)(A)(ii). [Each of the Target and its Subsidiaries has disclosed on its federal income Tax Returns all positions taken therein that could give rise to a substantial understatement of federal income Tax within the meaning of Code §6662.] None of the Target and its Subsidiaries is a party to any Tax allocation or sharing agreement. None of the Target and its Subsidiaries (A) has been a member of an Affiliated Group filing a consolidated federal income Tax Return (other than a group the common parent of which was the Target) or (B) has any Liability for the Taxes of any Person (other than any of the Target and its Subsidiaries) under Reg. §1.1502-6 (or any similar provision of state, local, or foreign law), as a transferee or successor, by contract, or otherwise.[25]

---

[25] If the Target or a Subsidiary has been a member of an Affiliated Group filing a consolidated federal income tax return, such corporation (or its successor) will be jointly and severally liable under

(vi) §4(k) of the Disclosure Schedule sets forth the following information with respect to each of the Target and its Subsidiaries (or, in the case of clause (B) below, with respect to each of the Subsidiaries) as of the most recent practicable date [(as well as on an estimated pro forma basis as of the Closing giving effect to the consummation of the transactions contemplated hereby)]: (A) the basis of the Target or Subsidiary in its assets; (B) the basis of the stockholder(s) of the Subsidiary in its stock (or the amount of any Excess Loss Account); (C) the amount of any net operating loss, net capital loss, unused investment or other credit, unused foreign tax, or excess charitable contribution allocable to the Target or Subsidiary; and (D) the amount of any deferred gain or loss allocable to the Target or Subsidiary arising out of any Deferred Intercompany Transaction.

(vii) The unpaid Taxes of the Target and its Subsidiaries (A) did not, as of the Most Recent Fiscal Month End, exceed the reserve for Tax Liability (rather than any reserve for deferred Taxes established to reflect timing differences between book and Tax income) set forth on the face of the Most Recent Balance Sheet (rather than in any notes thereto) and (B) do not exceed that reserve as adjusted for the passage of time through the Closing Date in accordance with the past custom and practice of the Target and its Subsidiaries in filing their Tax Returns.

(l) *Real Property.*[26]

(i) §4(l)(i) of the Disclosure Schedule lists and describes briefly all real property that any of the Target and its Subsidiaries owns. With respect to each such parcel of owned real property:

(A) the identified owner has good and marketable title to the parcel of real property, free and clear of any Security Interest, easement, covenant, or other restriction, except for installments of special assessments not yet delinquent and recorded easements, covenants, and other restrictions which do not impair the current use, occupancy, or value, or the marketability of title, of the property subject thereto;

Reg. §1.1502-6 for certain tax liabilities incurred by such Affiliated Group for a tax year when such corporation was a member of such Affiliated Group for all or part of such tax year. *See* ¶210.

The Target or a Subsidiary may also be liable for the unpaid taxes of third parties under similar provisions of state, local, or foreign law, as a transferee or successor, by contract (e.g., a tax sharing agreement), or otherwise.

After the Buyer acquires the stock of the Target, the Target and its Subsidiaries will remain liable for any such unpaid Tax liabilities.

This Agreement contains indemnification provisions designed to protect the Buyer against any liability for the unpaid taxes of any person other than the Target and its Subsidiaries. *See* §8(b) below.

[26] These representations and warranties concerning real property are relatively long and detailed. A condensed version of these provisions may be more appropriate when, for example, the real property of the Target and its Subsidiaries is relatively insignificant.

(B) there are no pending or[, to the Knowledge of any of the Sellers and the directors and officers (and employees with responsibility for real estate matters) of the Target and its Subsidiaries,] threatened condemnation proceedings, lawsuits, or administrative actions relating to the property or other matters affecting [materially and] adversely the current use, occupancy, or value thereof;

(C) the legal description for the parcel contained in the deed thereof describes such parcel fully and adequately, the buildings and improvements are located within the boundary lines of the described parcels of land, are not in violation of applicable setback requirements, zoning laws, and ordinances (and none of the properties or buildings or improvements thereon are subject to "permitted non-conforming use" or "permitted non-conforming structure" classifications), and do not encroach on any easement which may burden the land, and the land does not serve any adjoining property for any purpose inconsistent with the use of the land, and the property is not located within any flood plain or subject to any similar type restriction for which any permits or licenses necessary to the use thereof have not been obtained;

(D) all facilities have received all approvals of governmental authorities (including licenses and permits) required in connection with the ownership or operation thereof and have been operated and maintained in accordance with applicable laws, rules, and regulations;

(E) there are no leases, subleases, licenses, concessions, or other agreements, written or oral, granting to any party or parties the right of use or occupancy of any portion of the parcel of real property;

(F) there are no outstanding options or rights of first refusal to purchase the parcel of real property, or any portion thereof or interest therein;

(G) there are no parties (other than the Target and its Subsidiaries) in possession of the parcel of real property, other than tenants under any leases disclosed in §4(l)(i) of the Disclosure Schedule who are in possession of space to which they are entitled;

(H) all facilities located on the parcel of real property are supplied with utilities and other services necessary for the operation of such facilities, including gas, electricity, water, telephone, sanitary sewer, and storm sewer, all of which services are adequate in accordance with all applicable laws, ordinances, rules, and regulations and are provided via public roads or via permanent, irrevocable, appurtenant easements benefitting the parcel of real property; and

(I) each parcel of real property abuts on and has direct vehicular access to a public road, or has access to a public road via a permanent, irrevocable, appurtenant easement benefitting the parcel of real property, and access to the property is provided by paved public right-of-way with adequate curb cuts available.

(ii) §4(l)(ii) of the Disclosure Schedule lists and describes briefly all real property leased or subleased to any of the Target and its Subsidiaries. §4(l)(ii) of the Disclosure Schedule also identifies the leased or subleased properties for which title insurance policies are to be procured in accordance with §5(h)(ii) below. The Sellers have delivered to the Buyer correct and complete copies of the leases and subleases listed in §4(l)(ii) of the Disclosure Schedule (as amended to date). With respect to each lease and sublease listed in §4(l)(ii) of the Disclosure Schedule:

(A) the lease or sublease is legal, valid, binding, enforceable, and in full force and effect;

(B) the lease or sublease will continue to be legal, valid, binding, enforceable, and in full force and effect on identical terms following the consummation of the transactions contemplated hereby;

(C) no party to the lease or sublease is in breach or default, and no event has occurred which, with notice or lapse of time, would constitute a breach or default or permit termination, modification, or acceleration thereunder;

(D) no party to the lease or sublease has repudiated any provision thereof;

(E) there are no disputes, oral agreements, or forbearance programs in effect as to the lease or sublease;

(F) with respect to each sublease, the representations and warranties set forth in subsections (A) through (E) above are true and correct with respect to the underlying lease;

(G) none of the Target and its Subsidiaries has assigned, transferred, conveyed, mortgaged, deeded in trust, or encumbered any interest in the leasehold or subleasehold;

(H) all facilities leased or subleased thereunder have received all approvals of governmental authorities (including licenses and permits) required in connection with the operation thereof and have been operated and maintained in accordance with applicable laws, rules, and regulations;

(I) all facilities leased or subleased thereunder are supplied with utilities and other services necessary for the operation of said facilities; and

(J) the owner of the facility leased or subleased has good and marketable title to the parcel of real property, free and clear of any Security Interest, easement, covenant, or other restriction, except for installments of special easements not yet delinquent and recorded easements, covenants, and other restrictions which do not impair the current use, occupancy, or value, or the marketability of title, of the property subject thereto.

(m) *Intellectual Property.*[27]

(i) The Target and its Subsidiaries own or have the right to use pursuant to license, sublicense, agreement, or permission all Intellectual Property necessary [or desirable] for the operation of the businesses of the Target and its Subsidiaries as presently conducted [and as presently proposed to be conducted]. Each item of Intellectual Property owned or used by any of the Target and its Subsidiaries immediately prior to the Closing hereunder will be owned or available for use by the Target or the Subsidiary on identical terms and conditions immediately subsequent to the Closing hereunder. Each of the Target and its Subsidiaries has taken all necessary [and desirable] action to maintain and protect each item of Intellectual Property that it owns or uses.

(ii) None of the Target and its Subsidiaries has interfered with, infringed upon, misappropriated, or otherwise come into conflict with any Intellectual Property rights of third parties, and none of the Sellers and the directors and officers (and employees with responsibility for Intellectual Property matters) of the Target and its Subsidiaries has ever received any charge, complaint, claim, demand, or notice alleging any such interference, infringement, misappropriation, or violation (including any claim that any of the Target and its Subsidiaries must license or refrain from using any Intellectual Property rights of any third party). To the Knowledge of any of the Sellers and the directors and officers (and employees with responsibility for Intellectual Property matters) of the Target and its Subsidiaries, no third party has interfered with, infringed upon, misappropriated, or otherwise come into conflict with any Intellectual Property rights of any of the Target and its Subsidiaries.

(iii) §4(m)(iii) of the Disclosure Schedule identifies each patent or registration which has been issued to any of the Target and its Subsidiaries with respect to any of its Intellectual Property, identifies each pending patent application or application for registration which any of the Target and its Subsidiaries has made with respect to any of its Intellectual Property, and identifies each license, agreement, or other permission which any of the Target and its Subsidiaries has granted to any third party with respect to any of its Intellectual Property (together with any exceptions). The Sellers have delivered to the Buyer correct and complete copies of all such patents, registrations, applications, licenses,

---

[27] These representations and warranties concerning intellectual property are relatively long and detailed. A condensed version of these provisions may be more appropriate when, for example, the intellectual property of the Target and its Subsidiaries is relatively insignificant.

agreements, and permissions (as amended to date) [and have made available to the Buyer correct and complete copies of all other written documentation evidencing ownership and prosecution (if applicable) of each such item]. §4(m)(iii) of the Disclosure Schedule also identifies each trade name or unregistered trademark used by any of the Target and its Subsidiaries in connection with any of its businesses. With respect to each item of Intellectual Property required to be identified in §4(m)(iii) of the Disclosure Schedule:

(A) the Target and its Subsidiaries possess all right, title, and interest in and to the item, free and clear of any Security Interest, license, or other restriction;

(B) the item is not subject to any outstanding injunction, judgment, order, decree, ruling, or charge;

(C) no action, suit, proceeding, hearing, investigation, charge, complaint, claim, or demand is pending or[, to the Knowledge of any of the Sellers and the directors and officers (and employees with responsibility for Intellectual Property matters) of the Target and its Subsidiaries,] is threatened which challenges the legality, validity, enforceability, use, or ownership of the item; and

(D) none of the Target and its Subsidiaries has ever agreed to indemnify any Person for or against any interference, infringement, misappropriation, or other conflict with respect to the item.

(iv) §4(m)(iv) of the Disclosure Schedule identifies each item of Intellectual Property that any third party owns and that any of the Target and its Subsidiaries uses pursuant to license, sublicense, agreement, or permission. The Sellers have delivered to the Buyer correct and complete copies of all such licenses, sublicenses, agreements, and permissions (as amended to date). With respect to each item of Intellectual Property required to be identified in §4(m)(iv) of the Disclosure Schedule:

(A) the license, sublicense, agreement, or permission covering the item is legal, valid, binding, enforceable, and in full force and effect;

(B) the license, sublicense, agreement, or permission will continue to be legal, valid, binding, enforceable, and in full force and effect on identical terms following the consummation of the transactions contemplated hereby (including the assignments and assumptions referred to in §2 above);

(C) no party to the license, sublicense, agreement, or permission is in breach or default, and no event has occurred which with notice or lapse of time would constitute a breach or default or permit termination, modification, or acceleration thereunder;

(D) no party to the license, sublicense, agreement, or permission has repudiated any provision thereof;

(E) with respect to each sublicense, the representations and warranties set forth in subsections (A) through (D) above are true and correct with respect to the underlying license;

(F) the underlying item of Intellectual Property is not subject to any outstanding injunction, judgment, order, decree, ruling, or charge;

(G) no action, suit, proceeding, hearing, investigation, charge, complaint, claim, or demand is pending or[, to the Knowledge of any of the Sellers and the directors and officers (and employees with responsibility for Intellectual Property matters) of the Target and its Subsidiaries,] is threatened which challenges the legality, validity, or enforceability of the underlying item of Intellectual Property; and

(H) none of the Target and its Subsidiaries has granted any sublicense or similar right with respect to the license, sublicense, agreement, or permission.

(v) To the Knowledge of any of the Sellers and the directors and officers (and employees with responsibility for Intellectual Property matters) of the Target and its Subsidiaries, none of the Target and its Subsidiaries will interfere with, infringe upon, misappropriate, or otherwise come into conflict with, any Intellectual Property rights of third parties as a result of the continued operation of its businesses as presently conducted [and as presently proposed to be conducted].

(vi) [None of the Sellers and the directors and officers (and employees with responsibility for Intellectual Property matters) of the Target and its Subsidiaries has any Knowledge of any new products, inventions, procedures, or methods of manufacturing or processing that any competitors or other third parties have developed which reasonably could be expected to supersede or make obsolete any product or process of any of the Target and its Subsidiaries.]

(n) *Tangible Assets.* The Target and its Subsidiaries own or lease all buildings, machinery, equipment, and other tangible assets necessary for the conduct of their businesses as presently conducted [and as presently proposed to be conducted]. Each such tangible asset is free from defects (patent and latent), has been maintained in accordance with normal industry practice, is in good operating condition and repair (subject to normal wear and tear), and is suitable for the purposes for which it presently is used [and presently is proposed to be used].

(o) *Inventory.* The inventory of the Target and its Subsidiaries consists of raw materials and supplies, manufactured and purchased parts, goods in process, and finished goods, all of which is merchantable and fit for the purpose for which it was procured or manufactured, and none of which is slow-moving, obsolete, damaged, or defective, subject only to the reserve for inventory writedown set forth on the face of the Most Recent Balance Sheet (rather than in any notes thereto) as adjusted for the passage of time through the Closing Date in accordance with the past custom and practice of the Target and its Subsidiaries.

(p) *Contracts.* §4(p) of the Disclosure Schedule lists the following contracts and other agreements to which any of the Target and its Subsidiaries is a party:

(i) any agreement (or group of related agreements) for the lease of personal property to or from any Person providing for lease payments in excess of $_____ per annum;

(ii) any agreement (or group of related agreements) for the purchase or sale of raw materials, commodities, supplies, products, or other personal property, or for the furnishing or receipt of services, the performance of which will extend over a period of more than one year, result in a [material] loss to any of the Target and its Subsidiaries, or involve consideration in excess of $_____;

(iii) any agreement concerning a partnership or joint venture;

(iv) any agreement (or group of related agreements) under which it has created, incurred, assumed, or guaranteed any indebtedness for borrowed money, or any capitalized lease obligation, in excess of $_____ or under which it has imposed a Security Interest on any of its assets, tangible or intangible;

(v) any agreement concerning confidentiality or noncompetition;

(vi) any agreement with any of the Sellers and their Affiliates (other than the Target and its Subsidiaries);

(vii) any profit sharing, stock option, stock purchase, stock appreciation, deferred compensation, severance, or other [material] plan or arrangement for the benefit of its current or former directors, officers, and employees;

(viii) any collective bargaining agreement;

(ix) any agreement for the employment of any individual on a full-time, part-time, consulting, or other basis providing annual compensation in excess of $_____ or providing severance benefits;

(x) any agreement under which it has advanced or loaned any amount to any of its directors, officers, and employees outside the Ordinary Course of Business;

(xi) any agreement under which the consequences of a default or termination could have a [material] adverse effect on the business, financial condition, operations, results of operations, or future prospects of any of the Target and its Subsidiaries; or

(xii) any other agreement (or group of related agreements) the performance of which involves consideration in excess of $_____.

The Sellers have delivered to the Buyer a correct and complete copy of each written agreement listed in §4(p) of the Disclosure Schedule (as amended to date) and a written summary setting forth the terms and conditions of each oral agreement referred to in §4(p) of the Disclosure Schedule. With respect to each such agreement: (A) the agreement is legal, valid, binding, enforceable, and in full force and effect; (B) the agreement will continue to be legal, valid, binding, enforceable, and in full force and effect on identical terms following the consummation of the transactions contemplated hereby; (C) no party is in breach or default, and no event has occurred which with notice or lapse of time would constitute a breach or default, or permit termination, modification, or acceleration, under the agreement; and (D) no party has repudiated any provision of the agreement.

(q) *Notes and Accounts Receivable.* All notes and accounts receivable of the Target and its Subsidiaries are reflected properly on their books and records, are valid receivables subject to no setoffs or counterclaims, are current and collectible, and will be collected in accordance with their terms at their recorded amounts, subject only to the reserve for bad debts set forth on the face of the Most Recent Balance Sheet (rather than in any notes thereto) as adjusted for the passage of time through the Closing Date in accordance with the past custom and practice of the Target and its Subsidiaries.

(r) *Powers of Attorney.* There are no outstanding powers of attorney executed on behalf of any of the Target and its Subsidiaries.

(s) *Insurance.* §4(s) of the Disclosure Schedule sets forth the following information with respect to each insurance policy (including policies providing property, casualty, liability, and workers' compensation coverage and bond and surety arrangements) to which any of the Target and its Subsidiaries has been a party, a named insured, or otherwise the beneficiary of coverage at any time within the past [10] years:

(i) the name, address, and telephone number of the agent;

(ii) the name of the insurer, the name of the policyholder, and the name of each covered insured;

(iii) the policy number and the period of coverage;

(iv) the scope (including an indication of whether the coverage was on a claims made, occurrence, or other basis) and amount (including a description of how deductibles and ceilings are calculated and operate) of coverage; and

(v) a description of any retroactive premium adjustments or other loss-sharing arrangements.

With respect to each such insurance policy: (A) the policy is legal, valid, binding, enforceable, and in full force and effect; (B) the policy will continue to be legal, valid, binding, enforceable, and in full force and effect on identical terms following the consummation of the transactions contemplated hereby; (C) neither any of the Target and its Subsidiaries nor any other party to the policy is in breach or default (including with respect to the payment of premiums or the giving of notices), and no event has occurred which, with notice or the lapse of time, would constitute such a breach or default, or permit termination, modification, or acceleration, under the policy; and (D) no party to the policy has repudiated any provision thereof. Each of the Target and its Subsidiaries has been covered during the past [10] years by insurance in scope and amount customary and reasonable for the businesses in which it has engaged during the aforementioned period. §4(s) of the Disclosure Schedule describes any self-insurance arrangements affecting any of the Target and its Subsidiaries.

(t) *Litigation.* §4(t) of the Disclosure Schedule sets forth each instance in which any of the Target and its Subsidiaries (i) is subject to any outstanding injunction, judgment, order, decree, ruling, or charge or (ii) is a party or [, to the Knowledge of any of the Sellers and the directors and officers (and employees with responsibility for litigation matters) of the Target and its Subsidiaries,] is threatened to be made a party to any action, suit, proceeding, hearing, or investigation of, in, or before any court or quasi-judicial or administrative agency of any federal, state, local, or foreign jurisdiction or before any arbitrator. None of the actions, suits, proceedings, hearings, and investigations set forth in §4(t) of the Disclosure Schedule could result in any [material] adverse change in the business, financial condition, operations, results of operations, or future prospects of any of the Target and its Subsidiaries. None of the Sellers and the directors and officers (and employees with responsibility for litigation matters) of the Target and its Subsidiaries has any reason to believe that any such action, suit, proceeding, hearing, or investigation may be brought or threatened against any of the Target and its Subsidiaries.

(u) *Product Warranty.* Each product manufactured, sold, leased, or delivered by any of the Target and its Subsidiaries has been in conformity with all applicable contractual commitments and all express and implied warranties, and none of the Target and its Subsidiaries has any Liability (and there is no Basis for any present or future action, suit, proceeding, hearing, investigation, charge, complaint, claim, or demand against any of them giving rise to any Liability) for replacement or repair thereof or other damages in connection therewith, subject only to the reserve for product warranty claims set forth on the face of the Most Recent Balance Sheet (rather than in any notes thereto) as adjusted for the passage of time through the Closing Date in accordance with the past custom and practice of the Target and its Subsidiaries. No product manufactured, sold, leased, or delivered by any of the Target and its Subsidiaries is subject to any guaranty, warranty, or other indemnity beyond the applicable standard terms and conditions of sale or lease. §4(u) of the Disclosure Schedule includes copies of the standard terms and conditions of sale or lease for each of the Target and its Subsidiaries (containing applicable guaranty, warranty, and indemnity provisions).

(v) *Product Liability.* None of the Target and its Subsidiaries has any Liability (and there is no Basis for any present or future action, suit, proceeding, hearing, investigation, charge, complaint, claim, or demand against any of them giving rise to any Liability) arising out of any injury to individuals or property as a result of the ownership, possession, or use of any product manufactured, sold, leased, or delivered by any of the Target and its Subsidiaries.

(w) *Employees.* To the Knowledge of any of the Sellers and the directors and officers (and employees with responsibility for employment matters) of the Target and its Subsidiaries, no executive, key employee, or group of employees has any plans to terminate employment with any of the Target and its Subsidiaries. None of the Target and its Subsidiaries is a party to or bound by any collective bargaining agreement, nor has any of them experienced any strikes, grievances, claims of unfair labor practices, or other collective bargaining disputes. None of the Target and its Subsidiaries has committed any unfair labor practice. None of the Sellers and the directors and officers (and employees with responsibility for employment matters) of the Target and its Subsidiaries has any Knowledge of any organizational effort presently being made or threatened by or on behalf of any labor union with respect to employees of any of the Target and its Subsidiaries.

(x) *Employee Benefits.*[28]

(i) §4(x) of the Disclosure Schedule lists each Employee Benefit Plan that any of the Target and its Subsidiaries maintains, to which any of the Target and its Subsidiaries contributes or has any obligation to contribute, or with respect to which any of the Target and its Subsidiaries has any [material] Liability or potential Liability.

(A) Each such Employee Benefit Plan (and each related trust, insurance contract, or fund) has been maintained, funded and administered in accordance with the terms of such Employee Benefit Plan and complies in form and in operation in all [material] respects with the applicable requirements of ERISA, the Code, and other applicable laws.

---

[28] These representations and warranties concerning employee benefits are relatively long and detailed. A condensed version of these provisions may be more appropriate when, for example, the Target and its Subsidiaries have relatively insignificant employee benefit plans.

(B) All required reports and descriptions (including annual reports (IRS Form 5500), summary annual reports, and summary plan descriptions) have been timely filed and/or distributed in accordance with the applicable requirements of ERISA and the Code with respect to each such Employee Benefit Plan. The requirements of COBRA have been met with respect to each such Employee Benefit Plan which is an Employee Welfare Benefit Plan subject to COBRA.

(C) All contributions (including all employer contributions and employee salary reduction contributions) which are due have been made within the time period prescribed by ERISA to each such Employee Benefit Plan which is an Employee Pension Benefit Plan and all contributions for any period ending on or before the Closing Date which are not yet due have been made to each such Employee Pension Benefit Plan or accrued in accordance with the past custom and practice of the Target and its Subsidiaries. All premiums or other payments for all periods ending on or before the Closing Date have been paid with respect to each such Employee Benefit Plan which is an Employee Welfare Benefit Plan.

(D) Each such Employee Benefit Plan which is intended to meet the requirements of a "qualified plan" under Code §401(a) has received a determination from the Internal Revenue Service that such Employee Benefit Plan is so qualified, and nothing has occurred since the date of such determination that could adversely affect the qualified status of any such Employee Benefit Plan.

(E) The market value of assets under each such Employee Benefit Plan which is an Employee Pension Benefit Plan (other than any Multiemployer Plan) equals or exceeds the present value of all vested and nonvested Liabilities thereunder determined in accordance with PBGC methods, factors, and assumptions applicable to an Employee Pension Benefit Plan terminating on the date for determination.

(F) The Sellers have delivered to the Buyer correct and complete copies of the plan documents and summary plan descriptions, the most recent determination letter received from the Internal Revenue Service, the most recent annual report (IRS Form 5500, with all applicable attachments), and all related trust agreements, insurance contracts, and other funding arrangements which implement each such Employee Benefit Plan.

(ii) With respect to each Employee Benefit Plan that any of the Target, its Subsidiaries, and any ERISA Affiliate maintains, to which any of them contributes or has any obligation to contribute, or with respect to which any of them has any [material] Liability or potential Liability:

(A) No such Employee Benefit Plan which is an Employee Pension Benefit Plan (other than any Multiemployer Plan) has been completely or partially terminated or been the subject of a Reportable Event. No proceeding by the PBGC to terminate any such Employee Pension Benefit Plan (other than any Multiemployer Plan) has been instituted or [, to the Knowledge of any of the Sellers and the directors and officers (and employees with responsibility for employee benefits matters) of the Target and its Subsidiaries,] threatened.

(B) There have been no Prohibited Transactions with respect to any such Employee Benefit Plan. No Fiduciary has any Liability for breach of fiduciary duty or any other failure to act or comply in connection with the administration or investment of the assets of any such Employee Benefit Plan. No action, suit, proceeding, hearing, or investigation with respect to the administration or the investment of the assets of any such Employee Benefit Plan (other than routine claims for benefits) is pending or [, to the Knowledge of any of the Sellers and the directors and officers (and employees with responsibility for employee benefits matters) of the Target and its Subsidiaries,] threatened. None of the Sellers and the directors and officers (and employees with responsibility for employee benefits matters) of the Target and its Subsidiaries has any Knowledge of any Basis for any such action, suit, proceeding, hearing, or investigation.

(C) None of the Target and its Subsidiaries has incurred, and none of the Sellers and the directors and officers (and employees with responsibility for employee benefits matters) of the Target and its Subsidiaries has any reason to expect that any of the Target and its Subsidiaries will incur, any Liability to the PBGC (other than with respect to PBGC premium payments not yet due) or otherwise under Title IV of ERISA (including any withdrawal liability as defined in ERISA §4201) or under the Code with respect to any such Employee Benefit Plan which is an Employee Pension Benefit Plan, or under COBRA with respect to any such Employee Benefit Plan which is an Employee Welfare Benefit Plan.

(iii) ALTERNATIVE A (NO MULTIEMPLOYER PLANS): None of the Target, its Subsidiaries, and any ERISA Affiliate contributes to, has any obligation to contribute to, or has any Liability (including withdrawal liability as defined in ERISA §4201) under or with respect to any Multiemployer Plan.

ALTERNATIVE B (MULTIEMPLOYER PLANS): None of the Target, its Subsidiaries, and any ERISA Affiliate has incurred any Liability on account of a "partial withdrawal" or a "complete withdrawal" (within the meaning of ERISA §§4205 and 4203, respectively) from any Multiemployer Plan, no such Liability has been asserted, and there are no events or circumstances which could result in any such partial or complete withdrawal; and none of the Target, its Subsidiaries, and any ERISA Affiliate is bound by any contract or agreement or has any obligation or Liability described in ERISA §4204. [Each Multiemployer Plan complies in form and has been administered in accordance with the requirements of ERISA and, where applicable, the Code, and each Multiemployer Plan is qualified under Code §401(a).]

(iv) None of the Target and its Subsidiaries maintains, contributes to or has an obligation to contribute to, or has any [material] Liability or potential Liability with respect to, any Employee Welfare Benefit Plan providing medical, health, or life insurance or other welfare-type benefits for current or future retired or terminated employees, their spouses, or their dependents (other than in accordance with COBRA).

(y) *Guaranties.* None of the Target and its Subsidiaries is a guarantor or otherwise is liable for any Liability or obligation (including indebtedness) of any other Person.

(z) *Environmental, Health, and Safety Matters.*[29]

(i) Each of the Target, its Subsidiaries, and their respective predecessors and Affiliates has complied and is in compliance with all Environmental, Health, and Safety Requirements.

(ii) Without limiting the generality of the foregoing, each of the Target, its Subsidiaries and their respective Affiliates has obtained and complied with, and is in compliance with, all permits, licenses and other authorizations that are required pursuant to Environmental, Health, and Safety Requirements for the occupation of its facilities and the operation of its business; a list of all such permits, licenses and other authorizations is set forth on the attached *"Environmental and Safety Permits Schedule."*

(iii) Neither the Target, its Subsidiaries, nor their respective predecessors or Affiliates has received any written or oral notice, report or other information regarding any actual or alleged violation of Environmental, Health, and Safety Requirements, or any liabilities or potential liabilities (whether accrued, absolute, contingent, unliquidated or otherwise), including any investigatory, reme-

---

[29] These representations and warranties concerning environmental, health, and safety matters are relatively long and detailed, contain no materiality or knowledge limitations, and impose a substantial disclosure burden on the Seller. A condensed version may be more appropriate when, for example, the operations of the Target and its Subsidiaries appear to have had a relatively insignificant effect upon the environment or upon public or employee health and safety.

Sample acquisition agreement 2002.2 (the *pro-seller* stock purchase agreement) contains an environmental representation which (1) is subject to certain knowledge and materiality limitations, (2) focuses on current compliance with environmental, health, and safety laws, and (3) does not extend to strict liability for site cleanup under CERCLA or common law liability.

Sample acquisition agreement 2002.3 (the *neutral* stock purchase agreement) contains an environmental representation which (1) is subject to certain materiality limitations, (2) is generally more limited and narrowly focused than this representation, and (3) in particular, does *not* include the provisions set forth in (vii) and (viii) of this section.

dial or corrective obligations, relating to any of them or its facilities arising under Environmental, Health, and Safety Requirements.

(iv) None of the following exists at any property or facility owned or operated by the Target or its Subsidiaries: (1) underground storage tanks, (2) asbestos-containing material in any form or condition, (3) materials or equipment containing polychlorinated biphenyls, or (4) landfills, surface impoundments, or disposal areas.

(v) None of the Target, its Subsidiaries, or their respective predecessors or Affiliates has treated, stored, disposed of, arranged for or permitted the disposal of, transported, handled, or released any substance, including without limitation any hazardous substance, or owned or operated any property or facility (and no such property or facility is contaminated by any such substance) in a manner that has given or would give rise to liabilities, including any liability for response costs, corrective action costs, personal injury, property damage, natural resources damages or attorney fees, pursuant to the Comprehensive Environmental Response, Compensation and Liability Act of 1980, as amended ("CERCLA"), the Solid Waste Disposal Act, as amended ("SWDA") or any other Environmental, Health, and Safety Requirements.

(vi) Neither this Agreement nor the consummation of the transaction that is the subject of this Agreement will result in any obligations for site investigation or cleanup, or notification to or consent of government agencies or third parties, pursuant to any of the so-called "transaction-triggered" or "responsible property transfer" Environmental, Health, and Safety Requirements.

(vii) Neither the Target, its Subsidiaries, nor any of their respective predecessors or Affiliates has, either expressly or by operation of law, assumed or undertaken any liability, including without limitation any obligation for corrective or remedial action, of any other Person relating to Environmental, Health, and Safety Requirements.

(viii) No facts, events or conditions relating to the past or present facilities, properties or operations of the Target, its Subsidiaries, or any of their respective predecessors or Affiliates will prevent, hinder or limit continued compliance with Environmental, Health, and Safety Requirements, give rise to any investigatory, remedial or corrective obligations pursuant to Environmental, Health, and Safety Requirements, or give rise to any other liabilities (whether accrued, absolute, contingent, unliquidated or otherwise) pursuant to Environmental, Health, and Safety Requirements, including without limitation any relating to onsite or offsite releases or threatened releases of hazardous materials, substances or wastes, personal injury, property damage or natural resources damage.

(aa) *Euro.* All of the computer software, computer firmware and computer hardware used by the Target or its Subsidiaries (i) are capable of performing all appropriate functions necessary to process more than one currency and any common currency adopted by one or more members of the European Union (the "Euro"), (ii) comply with all legal requirements applicable to the Euro in any jurisdiction, including the rules on conversion and rounding set out in applicable European Community regulations, and (iii) are capable of displaying and printing, and incorporate in all relevant screen layouts, all symbols and codes adopted by any government or any other European Union body in relation to the Euro.[30]

(bb) *Year 2000.* None of the computer software, computer firmware, computer hardware (whether general or special purpose) or other similar or related items of automated, computerized or software systems that are used or relied on by the Target or its Subsidiaries in the conduct of their respective businesses, and none of the products and services sold, licensed, rendered, or otherwise provided by the Target and its Subsidiaries in the conduct of their respective businesses, will malfunction, cease to function, generate incorrect data or produce incorrect results when processing, providing or receiving (i) date-related data from, into and between the twentieth and twenty-first centuries or (ii) date-related data in connection with any valid date in the twentieth and twenty-first centuries.

Neither the Target nor its Subsidiaries has made any representations or warranties regarding the ability of any product or service sold, licensed, rendered, or otherwise provided by the Target or its Subsidiaries in the conduct of their respective businesses to operate without malfunction, to operate without ceasing to function, to generate correct data or to produce correct results when processing, providing or receiving (i) date-related data from, into and between the twentieth and twenty-first centuries and (ii) date-related data in connection with any valid date in the twentieth and twenty-first centuries.[31]

(cc) *Certain Business Relationships with the Target and Its Subsidiaries.* None of the Sellers and their Affiliates has been involved in any business arrangement or relationship with any of the Target and its Subsidiaries within the past 12 months, and none of the Sellers and their Affiliates owns any asset, tangible or intangible, which is used in the business of any of the Target and its Subsidiaries.

(dd) *Disclosure.* The representations and warranties contained in this §4 do not contain any untrue statement of a [material] fact or omit to state any [material]

---

[30] Sample acquisition agreements 2002.2 (the *pro-seller* stock purchase agreement) and 2002.3 (the *neutral* stock purchase agreement) do not contain this representation.

[31] This representation can be omitted for agreements entered into a sufficient period after approximately 3/1/00 so that Buyer has been able to verify that Target and its Subsidiaries have no Y2K problem.

Sample acquisition agreement 2002.2 (the *pro-seller* stock purchase agreement) does not contain this representation and 2002.3 (the *neutral* stock purchase agreement) contains a more limited representation.

fact necessary in order to make the statements and information contained in this §4 not misleading.

5. *Pre-Closing Covenants.* The Parties agree as follows with respect to the period between the execution of this Agreement and the Closing.[32]

(a) *General.* Each of the Parties will use his or its [reasonable] best efforts to take all action and to do all things necessary[, proper, or advisable] in order to consummate and make effective the transactions contemplated by this Agreement (including satisfaction, but not waiver, of the closing conditions set forth in §7 below).

(b) *Notices and Consents.* The Sellers will cause each of the Target and its Subsidiaries to give any notices to third parties, and will cause each of the Target and its Subsidiaries to use its [reasonable] best efforts to obtain any third party consents, that the Buyer [reasonably] may request in connection with the matters referred to in §4(c) above. Each of the Parties will (and the Sellers will cause each of the Target and its Subsidiaries to) give any notices to, make any filings with, and use its [reasonable] best efforts to obtain any authorizations, consents, and approvals of governments and governmental agencies in connection with the matters referred to in §3(a)(ii), §3(b)(ii), and §4(c) above. Without limiting the generality of the foregoing, each of the Parties will file (and the Sellers will cause each of the Target and its Subsidiaries to file) any Notification and Report Forms and related material that he or it may be required to file with the Federal Trade Commission and the Antitrust Division of the United States Department of Justice under the Hart-Scott-Rodino Act, will use his or its [reasonable] best efforts to obtain (and the Sellers will cause each of the Target and its Subsidiaries to use its [reasonable] best efforts to obtain) an early termination of the applicable waiting period, and will make (and the Sellers will cause each of the Target and its Subsidiaries to make) any further filings pursuant thereto that may be necessary[, proper, or advisable] in connection therewith.

(c) *Operation of Business.* The Sellers will not cause or permit any of the Target and its Subsidiaries to engage in any practice, take any action, or enter into any transaction outside the Ordinary Course of Business. Without limiting the generality of the foregoing, the Sellers will not cause or permit any of the Target

---

[32] The Buyer may seek to make the Target and its Subsidiaries parties to this Agreement for the purpose of obtaining directly their covenants applicable to the period prior to the Closing.

Whether or not the Target and its Subsidiaries become parties to this Agreement, they are likely to incur significant costs and expenses in connection with the transaction (e.g., when they and their agents prepare the Disclosure Schedule and perhaps certain of the Financial Statements, give notices to third parties and obtain their consent, make filings under the Hart-Scott-Rodino Act and respond to requests for additional information, and obtain title insurance and surveys for the Closing).

These costs and expenses of the Target and its Subsidiaries are separate and distinguishable from the costs and expenses of the Buyer on the one hand and of the Sellers on the other hand.

Section 11(l) below allocates responsibility among the respective parties for these costs and expenses through Closing.

and its Subsidiaries to (i) declare, set aside, or pay any dividend or make any distribution with respect to its capital stock or redeem, purchase, or otherwise acquire any of its capital stock, (ii) _____, or (iii) otherwise engage in any practice, take any action, or enter into any transaction of the sort described in §4(h) above.[33]

(d) *Preservation of Business.* The Sellers will cause each of the Target and its Subsidiaries to keep its business and properties substantially intact, including its present operations, physical facilities, working conditions, and relationships with lessors, licensors, suppliers, customers, and employees.[34]

(e) *Full Access.* Each of the Sellers will permit, and the Sellers will cause each of the Target and its Subsidiaries to permit, representatives of the Buyer to have full access [at all reasonable times, and in a manner so as not to interfere with the normal business operations of the Target and its Subsidiaries,] to all premises, properties, personnel, books, records (including Tax records), contracts, and documents of or pertaining to each of the Target and its Subsidiaries.[35]

(f) *Notice of Developments.* The Sellers will give prompt written notice to the Buyer of any material adverse development causing a breach of any of the representations and warranties in §4 above. Each Party will give prompt written notice to the others of any material adverse development causing a breach of any of his or its own representations and warranties in §3 above. No disclosure by any Party pursuant to this §5(f), however, shall be deemed to amend or supplement Annex I, Annex II, or the Disclosure Schedule or to prevent or cure any misrepresentation, breach of warranty, or breach of covenant.[36]

(g) *Exclusivity.* None of the Sellers will (and the Sellers will not cause or permit any of the Target and its Subsidiaries to) (i) solicit, initiate, or encourage the submission of any proposal or offer from any Person relating to the acquisition of any capital stock or other voting securities, or any substantial portion of the assets, of any of the Target and its Subsidiaries (including any acquisition structured as a merger, consolidation, or share exchange) or (ii) participate in any discussions or negotiations regarding, furnish any information with respect to, assist or participate in, or facilitate in any other manner any effort or attempt by

---

[33] The Parties may prefer to revise this covenant so that it recites specific prohibitions (rather than incorporating the matters in §4(h) above by reference).

[34] Sample acquisition agreement 2002.2 (the *pro-seller* stock purchase agreement) does not contain a comparable provision.

[35] The Sellers may seek a confidentiality and nonuse provision protecting the Confidential Information until the Buyer actually purchases the Target Shares. See sample acquisition agreement 2002.2 (the *pro-seller* stock purchase agreement) for an example of such a provision.

[36] Sample acquisition agreement 2002.2 (the *pro-seller* stock purchase agreement) provides that certain disclosures (presumably, but not necessarily, by the Sellers) between signing and Closing will supplement the previous disclosures and cure misrepresentations and breaches of warranty.

any Person to do or seek any of the foregoing.[37] None of the Sellers will vote their Target Shares in favor of any such acquisition structured as a merger, consolidation, or share exchange. The Sellers will notify the Buyer immediately if any Person makes any proposal, offer, inquiry, or contact with respect to any of the foregoing.

(h) *Title Insurance.*[38] The Sellers will cause the Target and its Subsidiaries to obtain the following title insurance commitments, policies, and riders in preparation for the Closing:

(i) with respect to each parcel of real estate that any of the Target and its Subsidiaries owns, an ALTA Owner's Policy of Title Insurance Form B-1987 (or equivalent policy [reasonably] acceptable to the Buyer if the real property is located in a state in which an ALTA Owner's Policy of Title Insurance Form B-1987 is not available) issued by a title insurer [reasonably] satisfactory to the Buyer (and, if requested by the Buyer, reinsured in whole or in part by one or more insurance companies and pursuant to a direct access agreement [reasonably] acceptable to the Buyer), in such amount as the Buyer [reasonably] may determine to be the fair market value of such real property (including all improvements located thereon), insuring title to such real property to be in the Target or its Subsidiary as of the Closing (subject only to the title exceptions described above in §4(l)(i) and in §4(l)(i) of the Disclosure Schedule); and

(ii) with respect to each parcel of real estate that any of the Target and its Subsidiaries leases or subleases and which is listed on §4(l)(ii) of the Disclosure Schedule as a property for which a title insurance policy is to be procured, an ALTA Leasehold Owner's Policy of Title Insurance-1987 (or equivalent policy [reasonably] acceptable to the Buyer if the real property is located in a state in which an ALTA Leasehold Owner's Policy of Title Insurance-1987 is not available) issued by a title insurer [reasonably] satisfactory to the Buyer (and, if requested by the Buyer, reinsured in whole or in part by one or more insurance companies and pursuant to a direct access agreement [reasonably] acceptable to the Buyer) in such amount as the Buyer [reasonably] may determine (taking into account the time cost of money using the Applicable Rate as the discount rate and such other factors as whether the fair market rental value of the premises exceeds the stipulated consideration in the lease or sublease, whether the tenant or subtenant has any option to renew or extend, whether the tenant or subtenant owns any improvements located on the premises, whether the

---

[37] Sample acquisition agreement 2002.2 (the *pro-seller* stock purchase agreement) gives the Sellers, the Target, its Subsidiaries, and their directors and officers greater latitude to respond to unsolicited proposals.

[38] These provisions concerning title insurance are relatively long and detailed. A condensed version may be more appropriate when, for example, the real property of the Target and its Subsidiaries is relatively insignificant.

Sample acquisition agreement 2002.2 (the *pro-seller* stock purchase agreement) does not have *any* title insurance closing condition for the benefit of the Buyer and contemplates that the Buyer will obtain any title insurance it requires independently and at its own expense.

tenant or subtenant is permitted to sublease, and whether the tenant or subtenant would owe any amount under the lease or sublease if evicted), insuring title to the leasehold or subleasehold estate to be in the Target or its Subsidiary as of the Closing (subject only to the title exceptions described above in §4(l)(ii) and in 4(l)(ii) of the Disclosure Schedule).

Each title insurance policy delivered under §5(h)(i) and §5(h)(ii) above shall (A) insure title to the real property and all recorded easements benefitting such real property, (B) contain an "extended coverage endorsement" insuring over the general exceptions contained customarily in such policies, (C) contain an ALTA Zoning Endorsement 3.1 (or equivalent), (D) contain an endorsement insuring that the real property described in the title insurance policy is the same real estate as shown on the Survey delivered with respect to such property, (E) contain an endorsement insuring that each street adjacent to the real property is a public street and that there is direct and unencumbered pedestrian and vehicular access to such street from the real property, (F) contain an inflation endorsement providing for annual adjustments in the amount of coverage corresponding to the annual percentage increase, if any, in the United States Department of Commerce Composite Construction Cost Index (Base Year = _____), (G) if the real property consists of more than one record parcel, contain a "contiguity" endorsement insuring that all of the record parcels are contiguous to one another, and (H) contain a "non-imputation" endorsement to the effect that title defects known to the officers, directors, and stockholders of the owner prior to the Closing shall not be deemed "facts known to the insured" for purposes of the policy.

(i) *Surveys.*[39] With respect to each parcel of real property that any of the Target and its Subsidiaries owns, leases, or subleases, and as to which a title insurance policy is to be procured pursuant to §5(h) above, the Sellers will cause the Target and its Subsidiaries to procure in preparation for the Closing a current survey of the real property certified to the Buyer, prepared by a licensed surveyor and conforming to current ALTA Minimum Detail Requirements for Land Title Surveys, disclosing the location of all improvements, easements, party walls, sidewalks, roadways, utility lines, and other matters shown customarily on such surveys, and showing access affirmatively to public streets and roads (the "*Survey*"). The Survey shall not disclose any survey defect or encroachment from or onto the real property which has not been cured or insured over prior to the Closing.

6. *Post-Closing Covenants.*[40] The Parties agree as follows with respect to the period following the Closing.

---

[39] Sample acquisition agreement 2002.2 (the *pro-seller* stock purchase agreement) does not have any survey closing condition for the benefit of the Buyer and contemplates that the Buyer will obtain any surveys it requires independently and at its own expense.

[40] The Sellers may seek to obtain additional covenants from the Buyer and its Subsidiaries (e.g., the typical covenants contained in a loan agreement or an indenture) because the Buyer is issuing the Buyer Notes to the Sellers as part of the Purchase Price. Any such covenants would remain applicable so long as the Buyer Notes remained outstanding.

(a) *General.* In case at any time after the Closing any further action is necessary [or desirable] to carry out the purposes of this Agreement, each of the Parties will take such further action (including the execution and delivery of such further instruments and documents) as any other Party [reasonably] may request, all at the sole cost and expense of the requesting Party (unless the requesting Party is entitled to indemnification therefor under §8 below).[41] The Sellers acknowledge and agree that from and after the Closing the Buyer will be entitled to possession of all documents, books, records (including Tax records), agreements, and financial data of any sort relating to the Target and its Subsidiaries.

(b) *Litigation Support.* In the event and for so long as any Party actively is contesting or defending against any action, suit, proceeding, hearing, investigation, charge, complaint, claim, or demand in connection with (i) any transaction contemplated under this Agreement or (ii) any fact, situation, circumstance, status, condition, activity, practice, plan, occurrence, event, incident, action, failure to act, or transaction on or prior to the Closing Date involving any of the Target and its Subsidiaries, each of the other Parties will cooperate with him or it and his or its counsel in the contest or defense, make available their personnel, and provide such testimony and access to their books and records as shall be necessary in connection with the contest or defense, all at the sole cost and expense of the contesting or defending Party (unless the contesting or defending Party is entitled to indemnification therefor under §8 below).[42]

(c) *Transition.* None of the Sellers will take any action that is designed or intended to have the effect of discouraging any lessor, licensor, customer, supplier, or other business associate of any of the Target and its Subsidiaries from maintaining the same business relationships with the Target and its Subsidiaries after the Closing as it maintained with the Target and its Subsidiaries prior to the Closing. Each of the Sellers will refer all customer inquiries relating to the businesses of the Target and its Subsidiaries to the Buyer from and after the Closing.

(d) *Confidentiality.*[43] Each of the Sellers will treat and hold as such all of the Confidential Information, refrain from using any of the Confidential Information except in connection with this Agreement, and deliver promptly to the Buyer or

---

[41] The Parties may prefer to allocate responsibility for these post-Closing costs and expenses in some other manner (*e.g.*, the Party incurring the costs and expenses might be responsible for their payment, the Parties might share the costs and expenses in a predetermined ratio, or one Party might be responsible for the costs and expenses up to a specified aggregate ceiling and the other Party responsible for any excess).

Compare §11(l) below which allocates responsibility among the Parties for their costs and expenses *through* the Closing.

[42] The Parties may prefer to allocate responsibility for these post-Closing costs and expenses in some other manner as discussed in the preceding footnote.

[43] Sample acquisition agreement 2002.2 (the *pro-seller* stock purchase agreement) lacks a comparable confidentiality provision affecting the Sellers after the Closing.

destroy, at the request and option of the Buyer, all tangible embodiments (and all copies) of the Confidential Information which are in his or its possession. In the event that any of the Sellers is requested or required (by oral question or request for information or documents in any legal proceeding, interrogatory, subpoena, civil investigative demand, or similar process) to disclose any Confidential Information, that Seller will notify the Buyer promptly of the request or requirement so that the Buyer may seek an appropriate protective order or waive compliance with the provisions of this §6(d). If, in the absence of a protective order or the receipt of a waiver hereunder, any of the Sellers is, on the advice of counsel, compelled to disclose any Confidential Information to any tribunal or else stand liable for contempt, that Seller may disclose the Confidential Information to the tribunal; *provided, however*, that the disclosing Seller shall use his or its [reasonable] best efforts to obtain, at the [reasonable] request of the Buyer, an order or other assurance that confidential treatment will be accorded to such portion of the Confidential Information required to be disclosed as the Buyer shall designate. The foregoing provisions shall not apply to any Confidential Information which is generally available to the public immediately prior to the time of disclosure.

(e) *Covenant Not to Compete.*[44] For a period of [five years] from and after the Closing Date, none of the Sellers will engage directly or indirectly in any business that any of the Target and its Subsidiaries conducts as of the Closing Date [in any geographic area in which any of the Target and its Subsidiaries conducts that business as of the Closing Date]; *provided, however*, that no owner of less than 1% of the outstanding stock of any publicly-traded corporation shall be deemed to engage solely by reason thereof in any of its businesses. If the final judgment of a court of competent jurisdiction declares that any term or provision of this §6(e) is invalid or unenforceable, the Parties agree that the court making the determination of invalidity or unenforceability shall have the power to reduce the scope, duration, or area of the term or provision, to delete specific words or phrases, or to replace any invalid or unenforceable term or provision with a term or provision that is valid and enforceable and that comes closest to expressing the intention of the invalid or unenforceable term or provision, and this Agreement shall be enforceable as so modified after the expiration of the time within which the judgment may be appealed.

(f) *Buyer Notes.* Each Buyer Note will be imprinted with a legend substantially in the following form:

The payment of principal and interest on this Note is subject to certain recoupment provisions set forth in a Stock Purchase Agreement dated as of _____, 19____ (the "Purchase Agreement") among the issuer of this Note, the person to whom this Note originally was issued, and certain other persons. This Note was originally issued

---

[44] Note that unless this Agreement allocates a specified amount of consideration to the covenant not to compete, applicable tax cases will preclude the Buyer from seeking to allocate a portion of the purchase price to the covenant and amortizing such amount over the covenant's life.

on _____, 19____, and has not been registered under the Securities Act of 1933, as amended. The transfer of this Note is subject to certain restrictions set forth in the Purchase Agreement. The issuer of this Note will furnish a copy of these provisions to the holder hereof without charge upon written request.

Each holder desiring to transfer a Buyer Note first must furnish the Buyer with (i) a written opinion [reasonably] satisfactory to the Buyer in form and substance from counsel [reasonably] satisfactory to the Buyer by reason of experience to the effect that the holder may transfer the Buyer Note as desired without registration under the Securities Act and (ii) a written undertaking executed by the desired transferee [reasonably] satisfactory to the Buyer in form and substance agreeing to be bound by the recoupment provisions and the restrictions on transfer contained herein.[45]

7. *Conditions to Obligation to Close.*

(a) *Conditions to Obligation of the Buyer.* The obligation of the Buyer to consummate the transactions to be performed by it in connection with the Closing is subject to satisfaction of the following conditions:[46]

(i) the representations and warranties set forth in §3(a) and §4 above shall be true and correct in all material respects at and as of the Closing Date;[47]

(ii) the Sellers shall have performed and complied with all of their covenants hereunder in all material respects through the Closing;

(iii) the Target and its Subsidiaries shall have procured all of the third party consents specified in §5(b) above, all of the title insurance commitments, policies, and riders specified in §5(h) above, and all of the surveys specified in §5(i) above;[48]

(iv) no action, suit, or proceeding shall be pending [or threatened] before any court or quasi-judicial or administrative agency of any federal, state, local,

---

[45] Certain provisions in §6(f) contemplate that the Buyer will issue the Buyer Notes pursuant to an exemption from securities registration under the Securities Act. These provisions must be eliminated if the Buyer will issue the Buyer Notes in an offering registered under the Securities Act.

[46] Note the provision in §10(a)(ii) giving the Buyer the right to terminate this Agreement within a specified period after signing if the Buyer is not [reasonably] satisfied with the results of its continuing business, legal, and accounting due diligence concerning the Target and its Subsidiaries. If this termination right were to continue through the Closing, it could be recast as an additional closing condition in §7(a).

[47] Note that this provision will not give the Buyer any closing condition with respect to any adverse matter which the Sellers may disclose in the Disclosure Schedule. This is because the disclosure will cure any misrepresentation or breach of warranty that might otherwise have existed. Thus, if the Sellers disclose an adverse matter in the Disclosure Schedule, the Buyer may seek to add a specific closing condition requiring an acceptable resolution of the matter.

[48] Sample acquisition agreement 2002.2 (the *pro-seller* stock purchase agreement) lacks a comparable closing condition with respect to third party consents, title insurance, and surveys.

or foreign jurisdiction [or before any arbitrator] wherein an unfavorable injunction, judgment, order, decree, ruling, or charge would (A) prevent consummation of any of the transactions contemplated by this Agreement, (B) cause any of the transactions contemplated by this Agreement to be rescinded following consummation, (C) affect adversely the right of the Buyer to own the Target Shares and to control the Target and its Subsidiaries, or (D) affect adversely the right of any of the Target and its Subsidiaries to own its assets and to operate its businesses (and no such injunction, judgment, order, decree, ruling, or charge shall be in effect);[49]

(v) the Sellers shall have delivered to the Buyer a certificate to the effect that each of the conditions specified above in §7(a)(i)-(iv) is satisfied in all respects;

(vi) [all applicable waiting periods (and any extensions thereof) under the Hart-Scott-Rodino Act shall have expired or otherwise been terminated and the Parties, the Target, and its Subsidiaries shall have received all other authorizations, consents, and approvals of governments and governmental agencies referred to in §3(a)(ii), §3(b)(ii), and §4(c) above];

(vii) the relevant parties shall have entered into side agreements in form and substance as set forth in Exhibits C-1 through C-_____ attached hereto and the same shall be in full force and effect;

(viii) the Buyer shall have received from counsel to the Sellers an opinion in form and substance as set forth in Exhibit D attached hereto, addressed to the Buyer, and dated as of the Closing Date;

(ix) the Buyer shall have received the resignations, effective as of the Closing, of each director and officer of the Target and its Subsidiaries other than those whom the Buyer shall have specified in writing at least [five] business days prior to the Closing;[50]

(x) the Buyer shall have obtained on terms and conditions [reasonably] satisfactory to it all of the financing it needs in order to consummate the transactions contemplated hereby [and fund the working capital requirements of the Target and its Subsidiaries after the Closing];[51] and

(xi) all actions to be taken by the Sellers in connection with consummation of the transactions contemplated hereby and all certificates, opinions, instruments,

---

[49] Sample acquisition agreement 2002.2 (the *pro-seller* stock purchase agreement) contains a narrower closing condition requiring only that there not be in effect any injunction, judgment, order, decree, ruling, or charge preventing consummation of the transactions contemplated by this Agreement.

[50] Sample acquisition agreement 2002.2 (the *pro-seller* stock purchase agreement) lacks a comparable closing condition concerning the receipt of director and officer resignations.

[51] Sample acquisition agreement 2002.2 (the *pro-seller* stock purchase agreement) lacks a comparable closing condition concerning the availability of financing for the transaction.

and other documents required to effect the transactions contemplated hereby will be [reasonably] satisfactory in form and substance to the Buyer.

The Buyer may waive any condition specified in this §7(a) if it executes a writing so stating at or prior to the Closing.

(b) *Conditions to Obligation of the Sellers.* The obligation of the Sellers to consummate the transactions to be performed by them in connection with the Closing is subject to satisfaction of the following conditions:

(i) the representations and warranties set forth in §3(b) above shall be true and correct in all material respects at and as of the Closing Date;

(ii) the Buyer shall have performed and complied with all of its covenants hereunder in all material respects through the Closing;

(iii) no action, suit, or proceeding shall be pending [or threatened] before any court or quasi-judicial or administrative agency of any federal, state, local, or foreign jurisdiction [or before any arbitrator] wherein an unfavorable injunction, judgment, order, decree, ruling, or charge would (A) prevent consummation of any of the transactions contemplated by this Agreement or (B) cause any of the transactions contemplated by this Agreement to be rescinded following consummation (and no such injunction, judgment, order, decree, ruling, or charge shall be in effect);[52]

(iv) the Buyer shall have delivered to the Sellers a certificate to the effect that each of the conditions specified above in §7(b)(i)-(iii) is satisfied in all respects;

(v) [all applicable waiting periods (and any extensions thereof) under the Hart-Scott-Rodino Act shall have expired or otherwise been terminated and the Parties, the Target, and its Subsidiaries shall have received all other authorizations, consents, and approvals of governments and governmental agencies referred to in §3(a)(ii), §3(b)(ii), and §4(c) above];

(vi) the relevant parties shall have entered into side agreements in form and substance as set forth in Exhibits C-_____, C-_____, ... and C-_____ and the same shall be in full force and effect;

(vii) the Sellers shall have received from counsel to the Buyer an opinion in form and substance as set forth in Exhibit E attached hereto, addressed to the Sellers, and dated as of the Closing Date; and

---

[52] Because this Sellers' closing condition conforms in part to the comparable Buyer's closing condition in §7(a)(iv) above, it leaves the Sellers with a relatively broad "out." Thus, the Buyer may prefer to narrow the respective closing conditions. *Compare* the narrower closing conditions in sample acquisition agreement 2002.2 (the *pro-seller* stock purchase agreement).

(viii) all actions to be taken by the Buyer in connection with consummation of the transactions contemplated hereby and all certificates, opinions, instruments, and other documents required to effect the transactions contemplated hereby will be [reasonably] satisfactory in form and substance to the Requisite Sellers.

The Requisite Sellers may waive any condition specified in this §7(b) if they execute a writing so stating at or prior to the Closing.

8. *Remedies for Breaches of This Agreement.*[53]

(a) *Survival of Representations and Warranties.*[54]

ALTERNATIVE A (FULL INDEMNIFICATION): All of the representations and warranties of the Parties contained in this Agreement shall survive the Closing hereunder (even if the damaged Party knew or had reason to know of any misrepresentation or breach of warranty or covenant at the time of Closing) and continue in full force and effect forever thereafter (subject to any applicable statutes of limitations).

ALTERNATIVE B (LIMITED INDEMNIFICATION): All of the representations and warranties of the Sellers contained in §4(a)-(j) and §4(l)-(bb) above shall survive the Closing hereunder (even if the Buyer knew or had reason to know of any

---

[53] The Buyer may seek some form of additional security covering the obligation of the Sellers to indemnify the Buyer after the Closing. The recoupment provisions contained in §8(f) provide security up to the aggregate principal amount outstanding from time to time under the Buyer Notes. The Buyer may seek additional provisions calling for (a) the Sellers to deposit a portion of the Purchase Price with a third party escrow agent, (b) the Buyer to hold back a portion of the Purchase Price (to be paid later with interest), or (c) the Buyer to obtain a security interest in certain assets of the Sellers.

[54] This Agreement contains alternative provisions for (A) *full indemnification* (the representations and warranties survive indefinitely, and there is no deductible, threshold, or ceiling with respect to indemnification against breaches thereof) and (B) *limited indemnification* (the representations and warranties with respect to the transaction itself and with respect to taxes survive indefinitely; the other representations and warranties survive only for [three years]; and there is a threshold, but not a deductible or ceiling, with respect to indemnification against breaches of the latter).

Sample acquisition agreement 2002.2 (the *pro-seller* stock purchase agreement), on the other hand, contains alternative provisions for (A) *minimal indemnification* (only the representations and warranties concerning the transaction itself survive the Closing) and (B) *limited indemnification* (the representations and warranties with respect to the transaction itself survive indefinitely; the other representations and warranties survive only for [one year]; and there is a deductible and a ceiling with respect to indemnification against breaches of the latter).

This *pro-buyer* Agreement provides that the representations and warranties will survive the Closing (*even if* the damaged Party knew or had reason to know of the misrepresentation or breach of warranty at the time of Closing).

Sample acquisition agreement 2002.2 (the *pro-seller* stock purchase agreement), on the other hand, provides that the representations and warranties of the Parties will survive the Closing (*unless* the damaged Party knew or had reason to know of the misrepresentation or breach of warranty at the time of Closing).

The Buyer will have assumed all Liabilities (whether known or unknown, and whether absolute or contingent) of the Target and its Subsidiaries if the Sellers representations and warranties in §4 above do not survive the Closing.

misrepresentation or breach of warranty at the time of Closing) and continue in full force and effect for a period of [three years] thereafter. All of the other representations and warranties of the Parties contained in this Agreement (including the representations and warranties of the Sellers contained in §4(k) above) shall survive the Closing (even if the damaged Party knew or had reason to know of any misrepresentation or breach of warranty at the time of Closing) and continue in full force and effect forever thereafter (subject to any applicable statutes of limitations).

(b) *Indemnification Provisions for Benefit of the Buyer.*[55]

(i) In the event any of the Sellers breaches (or in the event any third party alleges facts that, if true, would mean any of the Sellers has breached) any of their representations, warranties, and covenants contained herein (other than the covenants in §2(a) above and the representations and warranties in §3(a) above), and, if there is an applicable survival period pursuant to §8(a) above, provided that the Buyer makes a written claim for indemnification against any of the Sellers pursuant to §11(h) below within such survival period, then each of the Sellers agrees to indemnify the Buyer from and against the entirety of any Adverse Consequences the Buyer may suffer through and after the date of the claim for indemnification (including any Adverse Consequences the Buyer may suffer after the end of any applicable survival period) resulting from, arising out of, relating to, in the nature of, or caused by the breach (or the alleged breach)[56] [ALTERNATIVE B (LIMITED INDEMNIFICATION):; provided, however, that the Sellers shall not have any obligation to indemnify the Buyer from and against any Adverse Consequences resulting from, arising

---

[55] Section 11(a)(i) below provides that the representations, warranties, and covenants *of the individual Sellers* (e.g., each Seller agrees to sell his or its Target Shares to the Buyer and makes certain representations and warranties concerning himself or itself and his or its Target Shares) will be "several." This is defined in such a way that the particular Seller (and no other Seller) will be entirely responsible for the Buyer's Adverse Consequences if the particular Seller fails to perform his or its obligations.

On the other hand, §11(a)(ii) provides that the representations, warranties, and covenants *of the Sellers as a group* (e.g., the Sellers as a group make representations and warranties concerning the Target and its Subsidiaries) will be "joint and several." This is defined in such a way that each Seller will be responsible for *all* of the Buyer's Adverse Consequences if the Sellers as a group fail to perform their obligation.

[56] This *pro-buyer* Agreement requires an indemnifying party (presumably, but not necessarily, one of the Sellers) to indemnify an indemnified party (presumably, but not necessarily, the Buyer) from and against any Adverse Consequences the indemnified party *may* suffer through and after the date of the claim for indemnification (including any Adverse Consequences the indemnified party may suffer after the end of any applicable survival period) *resulting from, arising out of, relating to, in the nature of, or caused by* certain breaches by the indemnifying party of his or its representations, warranties, and covenants.

Sample acquisition agreement 2002.2 (the *pro-seller* stock purchase agreement), on the other hand, provides that the indemnifying party (presumably, but not necessarily, one of the Sellers) must indemnify the indemnified party (presumably, but not necessarily, the Buyer) from and against Adverse Consequences the indemnified party *shall* suffer *caused [proximately]* by certain breaches by the indemnifying party of his or its representations, warranties, and covenants.

out of, relating to, in the nature of, or caused by the breach (or alleged breach) of any representation or warranty of the Sellers contained in §4(a)-(j) and §4(l)-(bb) above until the Buyer has suffered Adverse Consequences by reason of all such breaches (or alleged breaches) in excess of a $_____ aggregate threshold (at which point the Sellers will be obligated to indemnify the Buyer from and against all such Adverse Consequences relating back to the first dollar).][57]

(ii) In the event any of the Sellers breaches (or in the event any third party alleges facts that, if true, would mean any of the Sellers has breached) any of his or its covenants in §2(a) above or any of his or its representations and warranties in §3(a) above, and, if there is an applicable survival period pursuant to §8(a) above, provided that the Buyer makes a written claim for indemnification against the Seller pursuant to §11(h) below within such survival period, then the Seller agrees to indemnify the Buyer from and against the entirety of any Adverse Consequences the Buyer may suffer through and after the date of the claim for indemnification (including any Adverse Consequences the Buyer may suffer after the end of any applicable survival period) resulting from, arising out of, relating to, in the nature of, or caused by the breach (or the alleged breach).

(iii) Each of the Sellers agrees to indemnify the Buyer from and against the entirety of any Adverse Consequences the Buyer may suffer resulting from, arising out of, relating to, in the nature of, or caused by any Liability of any of the Target and its Subsidiaries (x) for any Taxes of the Target and its Subsidiaries with respect to any Tax year or portion thereof ending on or before the Closing Date (or for any Tax year beginning before and ending after the Closing Date to the extent allocable (determined in a manner consistent with §9(c)) to the portion of such period beginning before and ending on the Closing Date), [ALTERNATIVE A WHERE THERE IS NO PURCHASE PRICE ADJUSTMENT: to the extent such Taxes are not reflected in the reserve for Tax Liability (rather than any reserve for deferred Taxes established to reflect timing differences between book and Tax income) shown on the face of the Most Recent Balance Sheet (rather than in any notes thereto)[, as such reserve is adjusted for the passage of time through the Closing Date in accordance with the past custom and practice of the Target and its Subsidiaries in filing their Tax Returns]] [ALTERNATIVE B WHERE THERE IS A PURCHASE PRICE ADJUSTMENT: to the extent such Taxes are not reflected in the reserve for Tax Liability (rather than any reserve for deferred Taxes established to reflect timing differences between book and Tax income) shown on the face of the Closing Balance

---

[57] The Sellers may seek to substitute a deductible (with no relation back to the first dollar) for the threshold in this proviso and to impose an aggregate ceiling on indemnification. *Compare* sample acquisition agreement 2002.2 (the *pro-seller* stock purchase agreement). The Sellers may also seek to impose an additional *per claim* deductible.

Sheet],[58] and (y) for the unpaid Taxes of any Person (other than any of the Target and its Subsidiaries) under Reg. §1.1502-6 (or any similar provision of state, local, or foreign law), as a transferee or successor, by contract, or otherwise.[59]

(iv) Each of the Sellers agrees to indemnify the Buyer from and against the entirety of any Adverse Consequences the Buyer may suffer resulting from, arising out of, relating to, in the nature of, or caused by _____.[60]

(c) *Indemnification Provisions for Benefit of the Sellers.* In the event the Buyer breaches (or in the event any third party alleges facts that, if true, would mean the Buyer has breached) any of its representations, warranties, and covenants contained herein, and, if there is an applicable survival period pursuant to §8(a) above, provided that any of the Sellers makes a written claim for indemnification against the Buyer pursuant to §11(h) below within such survival period, then the Buyer agrees to indemnify each of the Sellers from and against the entirety of

---

[58] Clause (x) is intended to protect the Buyer with respect to pre-Closing Taxes of the Target and its Subsidiaries. Alternative A contemplates a fixed purchase price. Alternative B contemplates that there will be a purchase price adjustment as described in ¶2002.5.

In the absence of clause (x), generally the Buyer is protected with respect to pre-Closing Taxes only to the extent the Sellers have breached one or more of the §4(k) Tax representations. Clause (x) may have little or no impact on the scope of the Buyer's protection to the extent the agreement contains an unqualified indemnity for breach of §4(k)(vii), as this pro-buyer agreement contemplates. However, a provision such as clause (x) can be useful in circumstances where (1) the Sellers are willing to give a strong Tax indemnity but are not comfortable giving unqualified Tax representations of the type shown in §4(k)(vii) and elsewhere in §4(k), (2) in contrast to the approach described in §8(a), the §4(k) Tax representations survive for only a limited period, or (3) in contrast to the approach described in §8(b)(i), the Sellers are willing to indemnify the Buyer for breaches of Tax representations only if the resulting claim (together with any claims arising from breaches of other representations) exceeds a threshold amount.

Clause (x) is best used in addition to (rather than in lieu of) an indemnity for breach of Tax representations, because certain of the §4(k) Tax representations cover matters beyond the scope of clause (x).

[59] If the Target or a Subsidiary has been a member of an Affiliated Group filing a consolidated federal income tax return, such corporation (or its successor) will be jointly and severally liable under Reg. §1.1502-6 for certain tax liabilities incurred by such Affiliated Group for a tax year when such corporation was a member of such Affiliated Group for all or part of such tax year. *See* ¶210.

The Target or a Subsidiary may also be liable for the unpaid taxes of third parties under similar provisions of state, local, or foreign law, as a transferee or successor, by contract (e.g., a tax-sharing agreement), or otherwise.

After the Buyer acquires the stock of the Target, the Target and its Subsidiaries will remain liable for any such unpaid tax liabilities. This indemnification provision is designed to protect the Buyer against any liability for the unpaid taxes of any person other than the Target and its Subsidiaries.

[60] Note that the indemnification provisions in clause (i) above will not give the Buyer any post-Closing indemnification rights with respect to any adverse matter which the Sellers may disclose in the Disclosure Schedule. This is because the disclosure will cure any misrepresentation or breach of warranty that might otherwise have existed.

Thus, if the Sellers disclose an adverse matter in the Disclosure Schedule, the Buyer may seek to add a provision conferring specific post-Closing indemnification rights with respect to the particular matter.

The Buyer normally would seek to draft such a provision so that the indemnification would not be subject to any survival period, threshold, deductible, and/or ceiling.

any Adverse Consequences the Seller may suffer through and after the date of the claim for indemnification (including any Adverse Consequences the Seller may suffer after the end of any applicable survival period) resulting from, arising out of, relating to, in the nature of, or caused by the breach (or the alleged breach).

(d) *Matters Involving Third Parties.*[61]

(i) If any third party shall notify any Party (the *"Indemnified Party"*) with respect to any matter (a *"Third Party Claim"*) which may give rise to a claim for indemnification against any other Party (the *"Indemnifying Party"*) under this §8, then the Indemnified Party shall promptly notify each Indemnifying Party thereof in writing; *provided, however,* that no delay on the part of the Indemnified Party in notifying any Indemnifying Party shall relieve the Indemnifying Party from any obligation hereunder unless (and then solely to the extent) the Indemnifying Party thereby is prejudiced.

(ii) Any Indemnifying Party will have the right to defend the Indemnified Party against the Third Party Claim with counsel of its choice [reasonably] satisfactory to the Indemnified Party so long as (A) the Indemnifying Party notifies the Indemnified Party in writing within [15 days] after the Indemnified Party has given notice of the Third Party Claim that the Indemnifying Party will indemnify the Indemnified Party from and against the entirety of any Adverse Consequences the Indemnified Party may suffer resulting from, arising out of, relating to, in the nature of, or caused by the Third Party Claim, (B) the Indemnifying Party provides the Indemnified Party with evidence [reasonably] acceptable to the Indemnified Party that the Indemnifying Party will have the financial resources to defend against the Third Party Claim and fulfill its indemnification obligations hereunder, (C) the Third Party Claim involves only money damages and does not seek an injunction or other equitable relief, (D)

---

[61] An *indemnifying* party (presumably, but not necessarily, one of the Sellers) will normally seek to control the defense of any third party claim that may give rise to a claim for indemnification under §8. However, the *indemnified* party (presumably, but not necessarily, the Buyer) will not want the indemnifying party to control the defense of any third party claim in which the indemnified party will retain a meaningful interest. For example, the indemnified party claim if the third party seeks an injunction or other equitable relief or if it is not clear that the indemnifying party will bear the entirety of any money damages or amount paid in settlement.

This *pro-buyer* Agreement provides that the indemnified party will control the defense of any third party claim *unless* (a) an indemnifying party accepts full responsibility for the matter within [15 days], (b) the indemnifying party demonstrates it has the financial resources necessary to defend against the matter and fulfill its indemnification obligations, (c) the third party seeks only money damages (as opposed to an injunction or other equitable relief), (d) settlement of, or an adverse judgment with respect to, the third party claim is not likely to establish a precedent [materially] adverse to the indemnified party, and (e) the indemnifying party conducts the defense actively and diligently.

Sample acquisition agreement 2002.2 (the *pro-seller* stock purchase agreement), on the other hand, provides that any indemnifying party may assume the defense of a third party claim *at any time* during the course of the defense and prevents the indemnified party from consenting to the entry of any judgment or entering into any settlement with respect to the matter without the consent of the indemnifying party [(not to be unreasonably withheld)].

settlement of, or an adverse judgment with respect to, the Third Party Claim is not, in the good faith judgment of the Indemnified Party, likely to establish a precedential custom or practice [materially] adverse to the continuing business interests of the Indemnified Party, and (E) the Indemnifying Party conducts the defense of the Third Party Claim actively and diligently.

(iii) So long as the Indemnifying Party is conducting the defense of the Third Party Claim in accordance with §8(d)(ii) above, (A) the Indemnified Party may retain separate co-counsel at its sole cost and expense and participate in the defense of the Third Party Claim, (B) the Indemnified Party will not consent to the entry of any judgment or enter into any settlement with respect to the Third Party Claim without the prior written consent of the Indemnifying Party [(not to be withheld unreasonably)], and (C) the Indemnifying Party will not consent to the entry of any judgment or enter into any settlement with respect to the Third Party Claim without the prior written consent of the Indemnified Party [(not to be withheld unreasonably)].

(iv) In the event any of the conditions in §8(d)(ii) above is or becomes unsatisfied, however, (A) the Indemnified Party may defend against, and consent to the entry of any judgment or enter into any settlement with respect to, the Third Party Claim in any manner it [reasonably] may deem appropriate (and the Indemnified Party need not consult with, or obtain any consent from, any Indemnifying Party in connection therewith), (B) the Indemnifying Parties will reimburse the Indemnified Party promptly and periodically for the costs of defending against the Third Party Claim (including [reasonable] attorneys' fees and expenses), and (C) the Indemnifying Parties will remain responsible for any Adverse Consequences the Indemnified Party may suffer resulting from, arising out of, relating to, in the nature of, or caused by the Third Party Claim to the fullest extent provided in this §8.

(e) *Determination of Adverse Consequences.* [The Parties shall take into account the time cost of money (using the Applicable Rate as the discount rate) in determining Adverse Consequences for purposes of this §8.] All indemnification payments under this §8 shall be deemed adjustments to the Purchase Price.

(f) *Recoupment Under Buyer Notes.* The Buyer shall have the option of recouping all or any part of any Adverse Consequences it may suffer (in lieu of seeking any indemnification to which it is entitled under this §8) by notifying any Seller that the Buyer is reducing the principal amount outstanding under his or its Buyer Note. This shall affect the timing and amount of payments required under the Buyer Note in the same manner as if the Buyer had made a permitted prepayment (without premium or penalty) thereunder.[62]

---

[62] Sample acquisition agreement 2002.2 (the *pro-seller* stock purchase agreement) lacks a comparable provision giving the Buyer a right of recoupment against the Buyer Notes.

(g) *Other Indemnification Provisions.* The foregoing indemnification provisions are in addition to, and not in derogation of, any statutory, equitable, or common law remedy (including without limitation any such remedy arising under Environmental, Health, and Safety Requirements) any Party may have with respect to the Target, its Subsidiaries, or the transactions contemplated by this Agreement.[63] Each of the Sellers hereby agrees that he or it will not make any claim for indemnification against any of the Target and its Subsidiaries by reason of the fact that he or it was a director, officer, employee, or agent of any such entity or was serving at the request of any such entity as a partner, trustee, director, officer, employee, or agent of another entity (whether such claim is for judgments, damages, penalties, fines, costs, amounts paid in settlement, losses, expenses, or otherwise and whether such claim is pursuant to any statute, charter document, bylaw, agreement, or otherwise) with respect to any action, suit, proceeding, complaint, claim, or demand brought by the Buyer against such Seller (whether such action, suit, proceeding, complaint, claim, or demand is pursuant to this Agreement, applicable law, or otherwise).[64]

9. *Tax Matters.*[65] The following provisions shall govern the allocation of responsibility as between Buyer and Sellers for certain tax matters following the Closing Date:

[63] Sample acquisition agreement 2002.2 (the *pro-seller* stock purchase agreement) states that (1) the remedies available to the Parties under the Agreement are exclusive (i.e., that the Buyer has no other statutory, equitable, or common law remedies) and (2) the Buyer specifically waives and releases the Seller from, and indemnifies the Seller with respect to, environmental, health, and safety matters.

Sample acquisition agreement 2002.3 (the *neutral* stock purchase agreement) (1) states that the remedies available to the Parties under the Agreement are exclusive (i.e., that the Buyer has no other statutory, equitable, or common law remedies), (2) contains a waiver of extra-contractual environmental remedies, but (3) does not contain an environmental indemnification of the Seller by the Buyer.

[64] This provision responds to the surprising decision in Heffernan v. Pacific Dunlop GNB Corporation, 965 F.2d 369 (7th Cir. 1992).

In *Heffernan*, the Buyer of Target's stock sued the Sellers (who had sold Target's stock to the Buyer) after the Closing of the stock sale, alleging that the Sellers failed to disclose to the Buyer certain of the Target's environmental and other liabilities. The court focused on the Buyer's claim against Seller A under §12(2) of the 1933 Act. Section 12(2) makes a seller of securities (here Seller A) liable to the purchaser (here the Buyer) for certain material misrepresentations and omissions in connection with the sale.

Seller A, who had been a director as well as a shareholder of the Target, countered that the Target (now a wholly owned subsidiary of the Buyer) should be required to indemnify him for any losses he suffered as a result of the Buyer's lawsuit. He based his argument on Delaware corporate law (which permits a corporation to indemnify its directors against third party lawsuits under certain circumstances) and the Target's bylaws (which made such director indemnification mandatory).

The federal district court dismissed Seller A's indemnification claim, holding (quite rationally) that he was not entitled to indemnification because his alleged misconduct was committed as a selling shareholder and not as a director of the Target.

On appeal, the Seventh Circuit reversed. The court noted that Seller A's duty of care under §12(2) (i.e., his duty to ascertain the truth or falsity of the Sellers' representations to the Buyer) was higher because he was a director, and hence the Buyer's claim against Seller A may have been related to his status as a former director of Target. Accordingly, the court concluded that it was premature to dismiss Seller A's indemnification claim before trial.

[65] When Target is (1) an S corporation, (2) a subsidiary member of a consolidated group, or (3) a subsidiary member of an affiliated (but not consolidated) group, the parties have the ability to make

(a) *Tax Periods Ending on or Before the Closing Date.* Buyer shall prepare or cause to be prepared and file or cause to be filed all Tax Returns for the Target and its Subsidiaries for all periods ending on or prior to the Closing Date which are filed after the Closing Date [other than income Tax Returns with respect to periods for which a consolidated, unitary or combined income Tax Return of Seller will include the operations of the Target and its Subsidiaries]. Buyer shall permit Target and its Subsidiaries to review and comment on each such Tax Return described in the preceding sentence prior to filing. Sellers shall reimburse Buyer for Taxes of the Target and its Subsidiaries with respect to such periods within fifteen (15) days after payment by Buyer or the Target and its Subsidiaries of such Taxes to the extent such Taxes are not reflected in the reserve for Tax Liability (rather than any reserve for deferred Taxes established to reflect timing differences between book and Tax income) shown on the face of the Closing Balance Sheet.[66]

(b) *Tax Periods Beginning Before and Ending After the Closing Date.* Buyer shall prepare or cause to be prepared and file or cause to be filed any Tax Returns of the Target and its Subsidiaries for Tax periods which begin before the Closing Date and end after the Closing Date. Sellers shall pay to Buyer within fifteen (15) days after the date on which Taxes are paid with respect to such periods an amount equal to the portion of such Taxes which relates to the portion of such Taxable period ending on the Closing Date to the extent such Taxes are not reflected in the reserve for Tax Liability (rather than any reserve for deferred Taxes established to reflect timing differences between book and Tax income)

---

a Code §338(h)(10) election, in which case all parties (including the selling shareholders) are treated for tax purposes as if Buyer purchased Target's assets. With a Code §338(h)(10) election (as distinguished from a regular Code §338 election), there is no double tax on the transaction, *i.e.*, Target is treated as selling assets and Target's shareholders are treated as receiving their proceeds in a deemed liquidation of Target, which deemed liquidation generally will not produce a second tax because of the consolidated return regulations in the consolidated group situation, Code §332 in the affiliated subsidiary situation, and Subchapter S pass-through rules in the S corporation situation. *See* ¶¶206.1.1, 206.3, 206.3.3, and 1109.3.

See ¶2002.4, *Sale of Subsidiary Out of a Consolidated Group*, for contractual provisions to use in connection with a Code §338(h)(10) election for a Target that is a member of a selling consolidated group. *See* ¶2002.6, *P's Purchase of T-SCo's Stock for Cash and Notes*, for contractual provisions to use in connection with a Code §338(h)(10) election for a Target that is an S corporation.

If Target is being acquired out of an affiliated (but not consolidated) group, a Code §338(h)(10) election may be made only if Buyer purchases at least 80% (by vote and by value) of Target's stock on a single day from a single member of the affiliated group of which Target is a member. In addition, the treatment of the sale of Target stock as an asset sale rather than as a stock sale applies only to the stock purchased from the member of the affiliated group that sold the requisite 80% of Target's stock. *See* ¶206.2.

[66] This provision contemplates that there will be a purchase price adjustment as described in ¶2002.5.

The neutral stock purchase agreement in ¶2002.3 also contains this provision. However, the pro-seller stock purchase agreement in ¶2002.2 does not contain any provision for the preparation of, or payment of taxes with respect to, returns filed after the Closing Date or for the payment of tax refunds received after the Closing Date. Because the pro-seller agreement does not require Sellers to indemnify Buyer against pre-Closing taxes, such taxes will be an obligation of the Target, and hence an indirect obligation of Buyer, and tax refunds will generally be received and retained by Target.

shown on the face of the Closing Balance Sheet.[67] For purposes of this Section, in the case of any Taxes that are imposed on a periodic basis and are payable for a Taxable period that includes (but does not end on) the Closing Date, the portion of such Tax which relates to the portion of such Taxable period ending on the Closing Date shall (x) in the case of any Taxes other than Taxes based upon or related to income or receipts, be deemed to be the amount of such Tax for the entire Taxable period multiplied by a fraction the numerator of which is the number of days in the Taxable period ending on the Closing Date and the denominator of which is the number of days in the entire Taxable period, and (y) in the case of any Tax based upon or related to income or receipts be deemed equal to the amount which would be payable if the relevant Taxable period ended on the Closing Date. Any credits relating to a Taxable period that begins before and ends after the Closing Date shall be taken into account as though the relevant Taxable period ended on the Closing Date. All determinations necessary to give effect to the foregoing allocations shall be made in a manner consistent with prior practice of the Target and its Subsidiaries.

(c) *Cooperation on Tax Matters.*[68]

(i) Buyer, the Target and its Subsidiaries and Sellers shall cooperate fully, as and to the extent reasonably requested by the other party, in connection with the filing of Tax Returns pursuant to this Section and any audit, litigation or other proceeding with respect to Taxes. Such cooperation shall include the retention and (upon the other party's request) the provision of records and information which are reasonably relevant to any such audit, litigation or other proceeding and making employees available on a mutually convenient basis to provide additional information and explanation of any material provided

---

[67] This provision contemplates that there will be a purchase price adjustment as described in ¶2002.5.

The neutral stock purchase agreement in ¶2002.3 also contains this provision. However, the pro-seller stock purchase agreement in ¶2002.2 does not contain any provision for the preparation of, or payment of taxes with respect to, returns filed after the Closing Date. Because the pro-seller agreement does not require Sellers to indemnify Buyer against pre-Closing taxes, such taxes will be an obligation of the Target, and hence an indirect obligation of Buyer.

[68] This pro-buyer agreement does not contain any provision addressing the treatment of tax refunds for pre-Closing tax periods. Such refunds of taxes previously paid by Target could arise in two circumstances: first, if Target overpaid its taxes for a pre-Closing period, and second, if a Target post-Closing loss can be carried back to Target's pre-Closing period. In the absence of a specific provision in the agreement, such refunds generally will be paid to Target, and hence Buyer will receive the economic benefit of such refunds, even though Sellers bear the economic burden of taxes for the pre-Closing period.

When Target was, prior to Closing, a member of Seller's consolidated group, federal income tax refunds for pre-Closing periods would be paid to the parent of Seller's consolidated group, and hence Seller would receive the economic benefit of such refunds. See ¶2002.4.4 for a discussion of this topic when Target was a member of Seller's consolidated group before the acquisition and ¶2002.4.7(f) for a sample agreement clause requiring Seller to pay over to Buyer any tax refund (or reduction of tax liability) resulting from a carryback of a postacquisition tax attribute of the Target and its Subsidiaries.

The neutral stock purchase agreement in ¶2002.3 requires Buyer to pay over to Seller any tax refunds for pre-Closing tax periods, under which circumstances Buyer would normally cause Target to elect to waive any carryback of a postacquisition loss (i.e., only to carry such loss forward).

hereunder. The Target and its Subsidiaries and Sellers agree (A) to retain all books and records with respect to Tax matters pertinent to the Target and its Subsidiaries relating to any taxable period beginning before the Closing Date until the expiration of the statute of limitations (and, to the extent notified by Buyer or Sellers, any extensions thereof) of the respective taxable periods, and to abide by all record retention agreements entered into with any taxing authority, and (B) to give the other party reasonable written notice prior to transferring, destroying or discarding any such books and records and, if the other party so requests, the Target and its Subsidiaries or Sellers, as the case may be, shall allow the other party to take possession of such books and records.

(ii) Buyer and Sellers further agree, upon request, to use their best efforts to obtain any certificate or other document from any governmental authority or any other Person as may be necessary to mitigate, reduce or eliminate any Tax that could be imposed (including, but not limited to, with respect to the transactions contemplated hereby).

(iii) Buyer and Sellers further agree, upon request, to provide the other party with all information that either party may be required to report pursuant to Section 6043 of the Code and all Treasury Department Regulations promulgated thereunder.

(d) *Tax Sharing Agreements.* All tax sharing agreements or similar agreements with respect to or involving the Target and its Subsidiaries shall be terminated as of the Closing Date and, after the Closing Date, the Target and its Subsidiaries shall not be bound thereby or have any liability thereunder.

(e) *Certain Taxes.* All transfer, documentary, sales, use, stamp, registration and other such Taxes and fees (including any penalties and interest) incurred in connection with this Agreement (including any New York State Gains Tax, New York City Transfer Tax and any similar tax imposed in other states or subdivisions), shall be paid by Sellers when due, and Sellers will, at their own expense, file all necessary Tax Returns and other documentation with respect to all such transfer, documentary, sales, use, stamp, registration and other Taxes and fees, and, if required by applicable law, Buyer will, and will cause its affiliates to, join in the execution of any such Tax Returns and other documentation.

10. *Termination.*

(a) *Termination of Agreement.* Certain of the Parties may terminate this Agreement as provided below:

(i) the Buyer and the Requisite Sellers may terminate this Agreement by mutual written consent at any time prior to the Closing;

(ii) the Buyer may terminate this Agreement by giving written notice to the Requisite Sellers on or before the [30th] day following the date of this Agreement if the Buyer is not [reasonably] satisfied with the results of its continuing business, legal, environmental, and accounting due diligence regarding the Target and its Subsidiaries;[69]

(iii) the Buyer may terminate this Agreement by giving written notice to the Requisite Sellers at any time prior to the Closing (A) in the event any of the Sellers has breached any material representation, warranty, or covenant contained in this Agreement in any material respect, the Buyer has notified the Requisite Sellers of the breach, and the breach has continued without cure for a period of [30 days] after the notice of breach or (B) if the Closing shall not have occurred on or before _____, 19_____, by reason of the failure of any condition precedent under §7(a) hereof (unless the failure results primarily from the Buyer itself breaching any representation, warranty, or covenant contained in this Agreement); and

(iv) the Requisite Sellers may terminate this Agreement by giving written notice to the Buyer at any time prior to the Closing (A) in the event the Buyer has breached any material representation, warranty, or covenant contained in this Agreement in any material respect, any of the Sellers has notified the Buyer of the breach, and the breach has continued without cure for a period of [30 days] after the notice of breach or (B) if the Closing shall not have occurred on or before _____, 19_____, by reason of the failure of any condition precedent under §7(b) hereof (unless the failure results primarily from any of the Sellers themselves breaching any representation, warranty, or covenant contained in this Agreement).

(b) *Effect of Termination.* If any Party terminates this Agreement pursuant to §10(a) above, all rights and obligations of the Parties hereunder shall terminate without any Liability of any Party to any other Party (except for any Liability of any Party then in breach).

11. *Miscellaneous.*

(a) *Nature of Certain Obligations.*

(i) The covenants of each of the Sellers in §2(a) above concerning the sale of his or its Target Shares to the Buyer and the representations and warranties of each of the Sellers in §3(a) above concerning the transaction are several obligations. This means that the particular Seller making the representation, warranty, or covenant will be solely responsible to the extent provided in §8

---

[69] Sample acquisition agreement 2002.2 (the *pro-seller* stock purchase agreement) lacks a comparable provision giving the Buyer a right to terminate the agreement for a limited period after signing if the Buyer is not [reasonably] satisfied with the results of its continuing business, legal, environmental, and accounting due diligence concerning the Target and its Subsidiaries.

above for any Adverse Consequences the Buyer may suffer as a result of any breach thereof.

(ii) The remainder of the representations, warranties, and covenants in this Agreement are joint and several obligations. This means that each Seller will be responsible to the extent provided in §8 above for the entirety of any Adverse Consequences the Buyer may suffer as a result of any breach thereof.[70]

(b) *Press Releases and Public Announcements.* No Party shall issue any press release or make any public announcement relating to the subject matter of this Agreement [prior to the Closing] without the prior written approval of the Buyer and the Requisite Sellers; *provided, however*, that any Party may make any public disclosure it believes in good faith is required by applicable law or any listing or trading agreement concerning its publicly-traded securities (in which case the disclosing Party will use its [reasonable] best efforts to advise the other Parties prior to making the disclosure).

(c) *No Third-Party Beneficiaries.* This Agreement shall not confer any rights or remedies upon any Person other than the Parties and their respective successors and permitted assigns.

(d) *Entire Agreement.* [This Agreement (including the documents referred to herein) constitutes the entire agreement among the Parties and supersedes any prior understandings, agreements, or representations by or among the Parties, written or oral, to the extent they related in any way to the subject matter hereof.]

(e) *Succession and Assignment.* This Agreement shall be binding upon and inure to the benefit of the Parties named herein and their respective successors and permitted assigns. No Party may assign either this Agreement or any of his or its rights, interests, or obligations hereunder without the prior written approval of the Buyer and the Requisite Sellers; *provided, however*, that the Buyer may (i) assign any or all of its rights and interests hereunder to one or more of its Affiliates and (ii) designate one or more of its Affiliates to perform its obligations hereunder (in any or all of which cases the Buyer nonetheless shall remain responsible for the performance of all of its obligations hereunder).

(f) *Counterparts.* This Agreement may be executed in one or more counterparts, each of which shall be deemed an original but all of which together will constitute one and the same instrument.

---

[70] The Sellers may seek to have their obligations as a group be "joint" rather than joint and several. That would be defined in such a way that each Seller would be responsible for only his or its *allocable portion* of the Buyer's Adverse Consequences (as opposed to the entire amount) if the Sellers as a group failed to perform their obligations. This would protect those Sellers who have "deep pockets" (or who otherwise are attractive defendants) from potentially having to indemnify the Buyer against a disproportionately large portion (or even all) of its Adverse Consequences. Sample acquisition agreement 2002.2 (the *pro-seller* stock purchase agreement) contains provisions more favorable to the Sellers in this regard.

(g) *Headings.* The section headings contained in this Agreement are inserted for convenience only and shall not affect in any way the meaning or interpretation of this Agreement.

(h) *Notices.*[71] All notices, requests, demands, claims, and other communications hereunder will be in writing. Any notice, request, demand, claim, or other communication hereunder shall be deemed duly given if (and then two business days after) it is sent by registered or certified mail, return receipt requested, postage prepaid, and addressed to the intended recipient as set forth below:

If to the Sellers: *Copy to:*

If to the Buyer: *Copy to:*

If to the Process Agent: *Copy to:*

Any Party may send any notice, request, demand, claim, or other communication hereunder to the intended recipient at the address set forth above using any other means (including personal delivery, expedited courier, messenger service, telecopy, telex, ordinary mail, or electronic mail), but no such notice, request, demand, claim, or other communication shall be deemed to have been duly given unless and until it actually is received by the intended recipient. Any Party may change the address to which notices, requests, demands, claims, and other communications hereunder are to be delivered by giving the other Parties notice in the manner herein set forth.

(i) *Governing Law. This Agreement shall be governed by and construed in accordance with the domestic laws of the State of _____ without giving effect to any choice or conflict of law provision or rule (whether of the State of _____ or any other jurisdiction) that would cause the application of the laws of any jurisdiction other than the State of _____.*

(j) *Amendments and Waivers.* No amendment of any provision of this Agreement shall be valid unless the same shall be in writing and signed by the Buyer and the Requisite Sellers. No waiver by any Party of any default, misrepresentation, or breach of warranty or covenant hereunder, whether intentional or not, shall be deemed to extend to any prior or subsequent default, misrepresentation, or breach of warranty or covenant hereunder or affect in any way any rights arising by virtue of any prior or subsequent such occurrence.

(k) *Severability.* Any term or provision of this Agreement that is invalid or unenforceable in any situation in any jurisdiction shall not affect the validity or enforceability of the remaining terms and provisions hereof or the validity or

---

[71] The Parties may want to add provisions designating a nominee to act on behalf of the Sellers for purposes of receiving notice, agreeing to modifications and amendments, and taking action.

enforceability of the offending term or provision in any other situation or in any other jurisdiction.

(l) *Expenses.* Each of the Parties, the Target, and its Subsidiaries will bear his or its own costs and expenses (including legal fees and expenses) incurred in connection with this Agreement and the transactions contemplated hereby. The Sellers agree that none of the Target and its Subsidiaries has borne or will bear any of the Sellers' costs and expenses (including any of their legal fees and expenses) in connection with this Agreement or any of the transactions contemplated hereby.[72]

(m) *Construction.* [The Parties have participated jointly in the negotiation and drafting of this Agreement. In the event an ambiguity or question of intent or interpretation arises, this Agreement shall be construed as if drafted jointly by the Parties and no presumption or burden of proof shall arise favoring or disfavoring any Party by virtue of the authorship of any of the provisions of this Agreement.] Any reference to any federal, state, local, or foreign statute or law shall be deemed also to refer to all rules and regulations promulgated thereunder, unless the context requires otherwise. The word "including" shall mean including without limitation. The Parties intend that each representation, warranty, and covenant contained herein shall have independent significance. If any Party has breached any representation, warranty, or covenant contained herein in any respect, the fact that there exists another representation, warranty, or covenant relating to the same subject matter (regardless of the relative levels of specificity) which the Party has not breached shall not detract from or mitigate the fact that the Party is in breach of the first representation, warranty, or covenant.[73]

(n) *Incorporation of Exhibits, Annexes, and Schedules.* The Exhibits, Annexes, and Schedules identified in this Agreement are incorporated herein by reference and made a part hereof.

(o) *Specific Performance.* Each of the Parties acknowledges and agrees that the other Parties would be damaged irreparably in the event any of the provisions

---

[72] This Agreement makes the Target responsible for the transactional cost and expenses of the Target and its Subsidiaries. This means that the Buyer will bear these costs and expenses if it consummates the stock purchase.

For this reason the Buyer may seek to have the Sellers reimburse the Target and its Subsidiaries for some or all of these costs and expenses.

The Sellers, on the other hand, may seek to make the Target and its Subsidiaries responsible not only for their own costs and expenses but also for some or all of *the Sellers'* costs and expenses. Sample acquisition agreement 2002.2 (the *pro-seller* stock purchase agreement) contains provisions more favorable to the Sellers in this regard.

The Parties may settle on a compromise allocation of responsibility (such as sharing the costs and expenses in a predetermined ratio or making one Party responsible for the costs and expenses up to a specified aggregate ceiling and the other Party responsible for any excess).

[73] Sample acquisition agreement 2002.2 (the *pro-seller* stock purchase agreement) omits the last two sentences of this paragraph.

of this Agreement are not performed in accordance with their specific terms or otherwise are breached. Accordingly, each of the Parties agrees that the other Parties shall be entitled to an injunction or injunctions to prevent breaches of the provisions of this Agreement and to enforce specifically this Agreement and the terms and provisions hereof in any action instituted in any court of the United States or any state thereof having jurisdiction over the Parties and the matter [(subject to the provisions set forth in §10(p) below)], in addition to any other remedy to which they may be entitled, at law or in equity.[74]

(p) *Submission to Jurisdiction.*[75] Each of the Parties submits to the jurisdiction of any state or federal court sitting in _____, _____, in any action or proceeding arising out of or relating to this Agreement and agrees that all claims in respect of the action or proceeding may be heard and determined in any such court. [Each Party also agrees not to bring any action or proceeding arising out of or relating to this Agreement in any other court.] Each of the Parties waives any defense of inconvenient forum to the maintenance of any action or proceeding so brought and waives any bond, surety, or other security that might be required of any other Party with respect thereto. Each Party appoints (the *"Process Agent"*) as his or its agent to receive on his or its behalf service of copies of the summons and complaint and any other process that might be served in the action or proceeding. Any Party may make service on any other Party by sending or delivering a copy of the process (i) to the Party to be served at the address and in the manner provided for the giving of notices in §10(h) above or (ii) to the Party to be served in care of the Process Agent at the address and in the manner provided for the giving of notices in §10(h) above. Nothing in this §10(p), however, shall affect the right of any Party [to bring any action or proceeding arising out of or relating to this Agreement in any other court or] to serve legal process in any other manner permitted by law or at equity. Each Party agrees that a final judgment in any action or proceeding so brought shall be conclusive and may be enforced by suit on the judgment or in any other manner provided by law or at equity.[76]

---

[74] Sample acquisition agreement 2002.2 (the *pro-seller* stock purchase agreement) omits this specific performance provision.

[75] The Parties may want to add a provision calling for optional or mandatory arbitration with respect to all or certain issues.

[76] Sample acquisition agreement 2002.2 (the *pro-seller* stock purchase agreement) omits this submission to jurisdiction provision.

* * * * *

IN WITNESS WHEREOF, the Parties hereto have executed this Agreement on [as of] the date first above written.

[BUYER]

By: _____

Title: _____

[SELLER # 1 (an entity)]

By: _____

Title: _____

[SELLER # 2 (an entity)]

By: _____

Title: _____

_____

[SELLER #3 (an individual)]

¶2002.2 *Pro-Seller Stock Purchase*

Sample acquisition agreement 2002.2 (*pro-seller* stock purchase) contains provisions favoring the sellers (i.e., T's old shareholders) in such areas as (i) the extent to which the sellers will receive T's cash (net of unpaid taxes) at the time of the closing, (ii) the extent to which P will bear the burden of T's liabilities and obligations after the closing, (iii) the extent to which P will lack conditions to its obligation to close, (iv) the extent to which the sellers will be required to give representations and warranties, and (v) the extent to which the sellers will be required to indemnify P against breaches of those representations and warranties.

Sample acquisition agreement 2002.2 permits the sellers (i.e., T's shareholders) to cause T to distribute its cash (net of unpaid taxes) to them (e.g., as a dividend or in a repurchase or redemption) at the time of the closing. This means that the sellers will receive T's cash (net of unpaid taxes) at the time of the closing.

Sample acquisition agreement 2002.2 contains limited representations and warranties from the sellers (i.e., T's shareholders) concerning (i) T's historical financial statements, (ii) intervening events, (iii) litigation, (iv) tax matters, (v) pension and welfare benefit plans, (vi) environmental, health, and safety matters, and (vii) compliance with federal, state, local, and foreign laws.

Sample acquisition agreement 2002.2 *does not* contain a specific representation and warranty concerning undisclosed liabilities.

Sample acquisition agreement 2002.2 also contains limited representations and warranties from the sellers (i.e., T's shareholders) concerning (i) authorization with respect to the transaction, (ii) title to the stock being sold (and title to T's underlying assets), (iii) required governmental and third party consents (and noncontravention generally), (iv) organization and capitalization, (v) real estate matters, (vi) intellectual property matters, (vii) leases and contracts, and (viii) brokerage fees.

The sellers' representations and warranties are qualified frequently with references to materiality and to the actual knowledge of the sellers (i.e., T's shareholders, but not, for example, T's directors, officers, and employees), *without any duty of independent investigation.*

Sample acquisition agreement 2002.2 contains alternative provisions for (i) minimal indemnification to P for breaches of the seller's representations and warranties (i.e., none of the representations and warranties concerning T survive the closing and there is no indemnification for breaches thereof)[1] *or* (ii) limited indemnification to P for breaches of the seller's representations and warranties (i.e., the representations and warranties concerning T survive only for one year and there is a deductible and a ceiling with respect to indemnification for breaches thereof). The sellers' indemnification obligation is several (rather than joint) and in proportion to their respective holdings of T shares.

¶2002.2 [1] This is referred to as *minimal* indemnification (rather than *no* indemnification) because the sellers' representations and warranties about the transaction itself (e.g., organization of certain sellers, authorization of the transaction, noncontravention, absence of brokers' fees, ownership of the T shares, etc.) do survive the closing and may give rise to indemnification.

P *does not* have any right to recoup its losses against the P notes in lieu of seeking indemnification from the sellers (i.e., T's shareholders).

P's obligation to close is subject to minimal conditions such as (i) compliance with the sellers' representations, warranties, and covenants, (ii) absence of a material adverse change, (iii) absence of an injunction affecting the transaction, (iv) delivery of any side agreements, and (v) delivery of an opinion of the sellers' legal counsel.

P *does not* have any closing condition concerning its ability to secure financing for the transaction *or* any right to terminate the purchase agreement after signing if it is not satisfied with the results of its continuing business, legal, and accounting due diligence review.

There are a number of other important differences among sample acquisition agreement 2002.1 (*pro-buyer* stock purchase), sample acquisition agreement 2002.2 (*pro-seller* stock purchase), and sample acquisition agreement 2002.3 (*neutral* stock purchase). Each of these sample forms contains extensive footnotes with cross-references pointing out the differences.

STOCK PURCHASE AGREEMENT[2]

AMONG

_____

AND

_____, _____,

AND_____

_____, 19_____

[2] The Buyer may choose to make a regular Code §338 election on a timely basis after an acquisition structured as a taxable purchase of Target Shares. *See* ¶¶107.1, 204, 205, 403, and 405.

If the Buyer makes a timely regular Code §338 election, the Target in effect becomes "New Target" immediately following the acquisition date: the Target's basis in its assets is stepped up (or down) so that the Target's aggregate asset basis equals the purchase price (plus the Target's liabilities, including tax liabilities generated in the transaction and inherited by New Target, and the Buyer's expenses of the acquisition), and "Old Target's" corporate attributes—e.g., E&P and tax accounting methods—are expunged. Concomitantly, effective upon the close of the acquisition date, "Old Target" is taxed as if it had sold its assets, *i.e.*, the Target is taxed on its full gain or loss inherent in its tangible and intangible assets (including goodwill), with the Target's gain or loss on each asset being ordinary or capital in character, depending on the nature of each asset treated as sold.

However, even with a regular Code §338 election, the Target's selling shareholders are nevertheless taxed on the stock sale, resulting in double tax, i.e., Target is taxed on the deemed asset sale and the selling shareholders are taxed on the stock sale. *See* ¶205.

If the Buyer intends to make a Code §338 election, it may well be desirable to add language to this Agreement (and to have the board of directors of the Target adopt resolutions) stating that the New Target "expressly assumes" certain enumerated liabilities (and all other unenumerated liabilities) of the Target which have not yet matured into tax deductions. See ¶304 and the related footnote to ¶2001.2.1.1(1).

If (1) Target is a member of a consolidated group or (2) the acquisition of Target is consummated on or after 1/20/94 (or earlier if a retroactive election is made) and Target is a member of an affiliated (but not consolidated) group or (3) the acquisition of Target is consummated on or after 1/20/94 (or earlier if a retroactive election is made) and Target is an S corporation, the parties may have the ability to make a Code §338(h)(10) election, in which case all parties (including the selling shareholders) are treated for tax purposes as if Buyer purchased Target's assets. Hence, with a Code §338(h)(10) election (as distinguished from a regular Code §338 election), there is no double tax on the transaction, i.e., Target is treated as selling assets but Target's shareholders are not treated as selling Target's stock, and the deemed liquidation of Target will generally not produce a second tax because of Code §332 in the consolidated or affiliated subsidiary situation or because of Subchapter S pass-through rules in the SCo situation. *See* ¶¶206.1.1, 206.2, 206.3.3, and S1109.3.

A Code §338(h)(10) election must be made jointly by Buyer and Seller(s). Hence, if either party desires such an election, it should add language to this Agreement stating that both parties agree to make such election. See ¶2002.4 for a number of contractual provisions the parties may desire to add to the acquisition agreement when Target is a subsidiary of a consolidated group.

This pro-seller form does not contain a provision obligating either Seller or Buyer to join in making a Code §338(h)(10) election. For such a provision, see §9 of the pro-buyer sample acquisition agreement in ¶2002.1.

A purchase of stock in which the consideration is primarily cash and notes is generally treated for accounting purposes as a purchase rather than as a pooling of interests. *See* ¶1503.

TABLE OF CONTENTS

Some LBO structures prejudice the Target's creditors and hence might permit payments, transfers, liens, and obligations arising out of the LBO to be attacked under fraudulent conveyance law. *See* ¶1506.

Disclosure Schedule—Exceptions to Representations and Warranties Concerning
the Target and Its Subsidiaries

**[EXHIBITS, ANNEXES, AND SCHEDULES HAVE BEEN OMITTED FROM
THIS SAMPLE FORM 2002.2]**

Agreement entered into on [as of] _____, 19____, by and
among _____, a _____ corporation (the *"Buyer"*),
and _____, _____, and _____ (collectively the
"Sellers"). The Buyer and the Sellers are referred to collectively herein as the
"Parties."[3]

The Sellers in the aggregate own all of the outstanding capital stock
of _____, a _____ corporation (the *"Target"*).

This Agreement contemplates a transaction in which the Buyer will purchase
from the Sellers, and the Sellers will sell to the Buyer, all of the outstanding capital
stock of the Target in return for cash and the Buyer Notes.[4]

Now, therefore, in consideration of the premises and the mutual promises
herein made, and in consideration of the representations, warranties, and covenants herein contained, the Parties agree as follows.

1. *Definitions.*

"Accredited Investor" has the meaning set forth in Regulation D promulgated
under the Securities Act.

"Adverse Consequences" means all actions, suits, proceedings, hearings, investigations, charges, complaints, claims, demands, injunctions, judgments, orders,
decrees, rulings, damages, dues, penalties, fines, costs, [reasonable amounts paid
in settlement,] liabilities, obligations, taxes, liens, losses, expenses, and fees, including court costs and [reasonable] attorneys' fees and expenses.

"Affiliate" has the meaning set forth in Rule 12b-2 of the regulations promulgated under the Securities Exchange Act.

---

[3] If the Target has so many shareholders that it would be unwieldy for all of them to become
parties to this Agreement (or if the Target has only a few shareholders but some minority shareholders
decline to participate), the Parties may wish to use sample acquisition agreement 2005 (reverse
subsidiary merger of the Buyer's transitory subsidiary into the Target for cash and notes) rather than
this sample acquisition agreement 2002. A reverse subsidiary merger will generally be treated as a
sale of stock for federal income tax purposes. *See* ¶202.

[4] After the Buyer purchases the Target Shares, the Target will become a subsidiary of the Buyer
(assuming the Buyer is a corporation). The Target will generally retain all of its assets and rights and
remain responsible for all of its liabilities and obligations. Thus it is generally not necessary to prepare
asset transfer documents or liability assumption documents in a stock purchase as it is in a purchase
of assets.

"Affiliated Group" means any affiliated group within the meaning of Code §1504(a) [or any similar group defined under a similar provision of state, local or foreign law].

"Allocable Portion" means with respect to the share of any Seller in a particular amount that fraction equal to the number of Target Shares the Seller holds as set forth in §4(b) of the Disclosure Schedule over the total number of outstanding Target Shares.[5]

"Applicable Rate" means the corporate base rate of interest publicly announced from time to time by [FINANCIAL INSTITUTION] [plus/minus ____ % per annum].

"Buyer" has the meaning set forth in the preface above.

"Buyer Note" has the meaning set forth in §2(b) below.

"Cash" means cash and cash equivalents (including marketable securities and short term investments) calculated in accordance with GAAP applied on a basis consistent with the preparation of the Financial Statements.

"Closing" has the meaning set forth in §2(d) below.

"Closing Date" has the meaning set forth in §2(d) below.

"COBRA" means the requirements of Part 6 of Subtitle B of Title I of ERISA and Code §4980B and of any similar state law.

"Code" means the Internal Revenue Code of 1986, as amended.

"Confidential Information" means any information concerning the businesses and affairs of the Target and its Subsidiaries that is not already generally available to the public.

"Disclosure Schedule" has the meaning set forth in §4 below.

"Employee Benefit Plan" means any "employee benefit plan" (as such term is defined in ERISA §3(3)) and any other [material] employee benefit plan, program or arrangement of any kind.

"Employee Pension Benefit Plan" has the meaning set forth in ERISA §3(2).

"Employee Welfare Benefit Plan" has the meaning set forth in ERISA §3(1).

---

[5] It may be necessary to revise this definition if the Target has more than one class of capital stock.

"Environmental, Health, and Safety Requirements" shall mean all federal, state, local and foreign statutes, regulations, and ordinances concerning public health and safety, worker health and safety, and pollution or protection of the environment, including without limitation all those relating to the presence, use, production, generation, handling, transportation, treatment, storage, disposal, distribution, labeling, testing, processing, discharge, release, threatened release, control, or cleanup of any hazardous materials, substances or wastes, as such requirements are enacted and in effect on or prior to the Closing Date.[6]

"ERISA" means the Employee Retirement Income Security Act of 1974, as amended.

"ERISA Affiliate" means each entity which is treated as a single employer with the Target for purposes of Code §414.

"Financial Statement" has the meaning set forth in §4(g) below.

"GAAP" means United States generally accepted accounting principles as in effect from time to time.

"Hart-Scott-Rodino Act" means the Hart-Scott-Rodino Antitrust Improvements Act of 1976, as amended.

"Income Tax" means any federal, state, local, or foreign income tax, including any interest, penalty, or addition thereto, whether disputed or not.

"Income Tax Return" means any return, declaration, report, claim for refund, or information return or statement relating to Income Taxes, including any schedule or attachment thereto.

"Indemnified Party" has the meaning set forth in §8(d) below.

"Indemnifying Party" has the meaning set forth in §8(d) below.

"Knowledge" means actual knowledge without independent investigation.[7]

"Most Recent Financial Statements" has the meaning set forth in §4(g) below.

---

[6] Sample acquisition agreement 2002.1 (the *pro-buyer* stock purchase agreement) explicitly extends this definition to include legal requirements enacted and in effect prior to, on, or after the Closing Date and also includes within this definition contractual obligations and common law.

Sample acquisition agreement 2002.3 (the *neutral* stock purchase agreement) is silent as to the time frame for enactment of covered Environmental, Health, and Safety Requirements and also includes within this definition common law.

[7] Sample acquisition agreement 2002.1 (the *pro-buyer* stock purchase agreement) defines "Knowledge" as actual knowledge after reasonable investigation.

"Most Recent Fiscal Month End" has the meaning set forth in §4(g) below.

"Multiemployer Plan" has the meaning set forth in ERISA §3(37).

"Ordinary Course of Business" means the ordinary course of business consistent with part custom and practice (including with respect to quantity and frequency).

"Party" has the meaning set forth in the preface above.

"PBGC" means the Pension Benefit Guaranty Corporation.

"Person" means an individual, a partnership, a corporation, an association, a joint stock company, a trust, a joint venture, an unincorporated organization, or a governmental entity (or any department, agency, or political subdivision thereof).

"Purchase Price" has the meaning set forth in §2(b) below.

"Reportable Event" has the meaning set forth in ERISA §4043.

"Requisite Sellers" means Sellers holding [a majority) in interest of the Target Shares as set forth in §4(b) of the Disclosure Schedule.[8]

"Securities Act" means the Securities Act of 1933, as amended.

"Securities Exchange Act" means the Securities Exchange Act of 1934, as amended.

"Security Interest" means any mortgage, pledge, lien, encumbrance, charge, or other security interest, other than (a) mechanic's, materialmen's, and similar liens, (b) liens for taxes not yet due and payable [or for taxes that the taxpayer is contesting in good faith through appropriate proceedings], (c) purchase money liens and liens securing rental payments under capital lease arrangements, and (d) other liens arising in the Ordinary Course of Business and not incurred in connection with the borrowing of money.

"Seller" has the meaning set forth in the preface above.

"Subsidiary" means any corporation with respect to which a specified Person (or a Subsidiary thereof) owns a majority of the common stock or has the power to vote or direct the voting of sufficient securities to elect a majority of the directors.[9]

"Target" has the meaning set forth in the preface above.

---

[8] It may be necessary to revise this definition if the Target has more than one class of capital stock.
[9] It may be necessary to revise this definition if, for example, the Target has subsidiary *partnerships*.

"Target Share" means any share of the Common Stock, par value $_____ per share, of the Target.[10]

"Third Party Claim" has the meaning set forth in §8(d) below.

2. *Purchase and Sale of Target Shares.*

(a) *Basic Transaction.* On and subject to the terms and conditions of this Agreement, the Buyer agrees to purchase from each of the Sellers, and each of the Sellers agrees to sell to the Buyer, all of his or its Target Shares for the consideration specified below in this §2.

(b) *Purchase Price.*[11] The Buyer agrees to pay to the Sellers at the Closing $_____ (the *"Purchase Price"*) by delivery of (i) its promissory notes (the *"Buyer Notes"*) in the form of Exhibit A attached hereto in the aggregate principal amount of $_____ and (ii) cash for the balance of the Purchase Price payable by wire transfer or delivery of other immediately available funds. The Purchase Price shall be allocated among the Sellers in proportion to their respective holdings of Target Shares as set forth in §4(b) of the Disclosure Schedule.[12]

(c) *Net Cash Payment to Sellers.*[13] Immediately prior to the Closing, the Sellers will cause the Target to pay the Sellers in proportion to their respective holdings of Target Shares an aggregate amount (and may cause each Subsidiary of the Target to pay to the Target any necessary component thereof) equal to the Sellers' good faith estimate of the excess (if any) of (i) the consolidated Cash of the Target and its Subsidiaries as of the Closing *over* (ii) the aggregate liability of the Target and its Subsidiaries for unpaid Income Taxes as of the Closing (computed in accordance with the past custom and practice of the Target and its Subsidiaries in filing their Income Tax Returns). The Sellers may cause (A) the Target to make any such payment to them in the form of a dividend or a redemption and (B)

---

[10] It may be necessary to revise this definition if the Target has additional classes of capital stock.

[11] The Sellers may seek to have the Buyer make an earnest money deposit upon execution of this Agreement. If the transaction were thereafter completed, the deposit would be applied to the Purchase Price. If the transaction were thereafter aborted, the deposit would be refunded to the Buyer or paid to the Sellers as liquidated damages depending on the terms of this Agreement and the reasons for the termination.

[12] Sample acquisition agreement 2002.5 contains additional provisions for use if there is to be a post-Closing Purchase Price adjustment based on the consolidated net book value for the Target and its Subsidiaries as of the Closing. That sample acquisition agreement can be adapted for other post-Closing Purchase Price adjustments (such as a comparison of consolidated working capital with consolidated liabilities as of the Closing *or* a contingent earnout based on consolidated earnings for a specified period after the Closing).

[13] Sample acquisition agreement 2002.1 (the *pro-buyer* stock purchase agreement) lacks a comparable provision allowing the Sellers to cause the Target and its Subsidiaries to distribute their consolidated cash (net of unpaid taxes) to the Sellers at the Closing and indeed *prohibits* the Sellers from causing any such distribution.

any Subsidiary of the Target to make any such payment to the Target in the form of a dividend, a redemption, or an intercompany loan.[14]

(d) *The Closing.* The closing of the transactions contemplated by this Agreement (the *"Closing"*) shall take place at the offices of _____, in _____, _____ commencing at 9:00 a.m. local time on the [second] business day following the satisfaction or waiver of all conditions to the obligations of the Parties to consummate the transactions contemplated hereby (other than conditions with respect to actions the respective Parties will take at the Closing itself) or such other date as the Buyer and the Requisite Sellers may mutually determine (the *"Closing Date"*); *provided, however,* that the Closing Date shall be no earlier than _____, 19_____.[15]

(e) *Deliveries at the Closing.* At the Closing, (i) the Sellers will deliver to the Buyer the various certificates, instruments, and documents referred to in §7(a) below, (ii) the Buyer will deliver to the Sellers the various certificates, instruments, and documents referred to in §7(b) below, (iii) each of the Sellers will deliver to the Buyer stock certificates representing all of his or its Target Shares, endorsed in blank or accompanied by duly executed assignment documents, and (iv) the Buyer will deliver to each of the Sellers the consideration specified in §2(b) above.

3. *Representations and Warranties Concerning the Transaction.*

(a) *Representations and Warranties of the Sellers.* Each of the Sellers represents and warrants to the Buyer that the statements contained in this §3(a) are correct and complete as of the date of this Agreement and will be correct and complete as of the Closing Date (as though made then and as though the Closing Date were substituted for the date of this Agreement throughout this §3(a)) with respect to himself or itself, except as set forth in Annex I attached hereto.

(i) *Organization of Certain Sellers.* If the Seller is a corporation, the Seller is duly organized, validly existing, and in good standing under the laws of the jurisdiction of its incorporation.[16]

---

[14] The Parties may want to introduce a post-Closing adjustment to the Purchase Price based on the difference between the amount the Target paid to the Sellers pursuant to this §2(c) (i.e., the Sellers' goodfaith estimate of the net cash) and the actual amount as determined later. *See* sample acquisition agreement 2002.5 for analogous provisions concerning a different type of post-Closing Purchase Price adjustment.

The Parties should determine whether there is any external restriction or prohibition on the type of cash payment by the Target and its Subsidiaries contemplated by this §2(c) (such as a loan covenant or a statutory provision concerning dividends, stock redemptions, and intercompany loans).

The Parties should also consider any possible difference in tax treatment between a cash dividend and a partial stock redemption.

[15] The Parties should determine whether the Sellers or the Buyer will owe any stock transfer or similar tax on the transfer of the Target Shares by reason of the chosen Closing location.

[16] Several representations and warranties in this §3(a) concern Sellers which are corporations. If any Sellers are partnerships, trusts, business associations, estates, or guardians, the Buyer may seek to add analogous provisions covering them.

(ii) *Authorization of Transaction.* The Seller has full power and authority (including, if the Seller is a corporation, full corporate power and authority) to execute and deliver this Agreement and to perform his or its obligations hereunder. This Agreement constitutes the valid and legally binding obligation of the Seller, enforceable in accordance with its terms and conditions. The Seller need not give any notice to, make any filing with, or obtain any authorization, consent, or approval of any government or governmental agency in order to consummate the transactions contemplated by this Agreement.

(iii) *Noncontravention.* Neither the execution and the delivery of this Agreement, nor the consummation of the transactions contemplated hereby, will [(A)] violate any constitution, statute, regulation, rule, injunction, judgment, order, decree, ruling, charge, or other restriction of any government, governmental agency, or court to which the Seller is subject or, if the Seller is a corporation, any provision of its charter or bylaws [or (B) conflict with, result in a breach of, constitute a default under, result in the acceleration of, create in any party the right to accelerate, terminate, modify, or cancel, or require any notice under any agreement, contract, lease, license, instrument, or other arrangement to which the Seller is a party or by which he or it is bound or to which any of his or its assets is subject].

(iv) *Brokers' Fees.* The Seller has no liability or obligation to pay any fees or commissions to any broker, finder, or agent with respect to the transactions contemplated by this Agreement for which the Buyer could become liable or obligated.

(v) *Investment.* The Seller (A) understands that the Buyer Notes have not been, and will not be, registered under the Securities Act, or under any state securities laws, and are being offered and sold in reliance upon federal and state exemptions for transactions not involving any public offering, (B) is acquiring the Buyer Notes solely for his or its own account for investment purposes, and not with a view to the distribution thereof, (C) is a sophisticated investor with knowledge and experience in business and financial matters, (D) has received certain information concerning the Buyer and has had the opportunity to obtain additional information as desired in order to evaluate the merits and the risks inherent in holding the Buyer Notes, (E) is able to bear the economic risk and lack of liquidity inherent in holding the Buyer Notes, and (F) is an Accredited Investor for the reasons set forth on Annex I.[17]

(vi) *Target Shares.* The Seller holds of record and owns beneficially the number of Target Shares set forth next to his or its name in §4(b) of the Disclosure

---

[17] This provision contemplates that the Buyer will issue the Buyer Notes pursuant to the exemption from registration under the Securities Act contained in Regulation D. The Parties should determine whether this exemption is available in a particular transaction. If it is not, the Agreement must be modified as necessary to reflect the issuance of the Buyer Notes under a different exemption from securities registration or in an offering registered under the Securities Act.

Schedule, free and clear of any restrictions on transfer (other than restrictions under the Securities Act and state securities laws), taxes, Security Interests, options, warrants, purchase rights, contracts, commitments, equities, claims, and demands. The Seller is not a party to any option, warrant, purchase right, or other contract or commitment that could require the Seller to sell, transfer, or otherwise dispose of any capital stock of the Target (other than this Agreement). The Seller is not a party to any voting trust, proxy, or other agreement or understanding with respect to the voting of any capital stock of the Target.

(b) *Representations and Warranties of the Buyer.*[18] The Buyer represents and warrants to the Sellers that the statements contained in this §3(b) are correct and complete as of the date of this Agreement and will be correct and complete as of the Closing Date (as though made then and as though the Closing Date were substituted for the date of this Agreement throughout this §3(b)), except as set forth in Annex II attached hereto.

(i) *Organization of the Buyer.* The Buyer is a corporation duly organized, validly existing, and in good standing under the laws of the jurisdiction of its incorporation.

(ii) *Authorization of Transaction.* The Buyer has full power and authority (including full corporate power and authority) to execute and deliver this Agreement and to perform its obligations hereunder. This Agreement constitutes the valid and legally binding obligation of the Buyer, enforceable in accordance with its terms and conditions. The Buyer need not give any notice to, make any filing with, or obtain any authorization, consent, or approval of any government or governmental agency in order to consummate the transactions contemplated by this Agreement.

(iii) *Noncontravention.* Neither the execution and the delivery of this Agreement, nor the consummation of the transactions contemplated hereby, will [(A)] violate any constitution, statute, regulation, rule, injunction, judgment, order, decree, ruling, charge, or other restriction of any government, governmental agency, or court to which the Buyer is subject or any provision of its charter or bylaws [or (B) conflict with, result in a breach of, constitute a default under, result in the acceleration of, create in any party the right to accelerate, terminate, modify, or cancel, or require any notice under any agreement, contract, lease, license, instrument, or other arrangement to which the Buyer is a party or by which it is bound or to which any of its assets is subject].

---

[18] The Sellers may seek to obtain additional representations and warranties concerning the Buyer and its Subsidiaries (e.g., the typical representations and warranties contained in a loan agreement or an underwriting agreement) because the Buyer is issuing the Buyer Notes to the Sellers as part of the Purchase Price. Any such representations and warranties would normally survive the Closing and remain applicable for so long as the Buyer Notes remained outstanding.

(iv) *Brokers' Fees.* The Buyer has no liability or obligation to pay any fees or commissions to any broker, finder, or agent with respect to the transactions contemplated by this Agreement for which any Seller could become liable or obligated.

(v) *Investment.* The Buyer is not acquiring the Target Shares with a view to or for sale in connection with any distribution thereof within the meaning of the Securities Act.

4. *Representations and Warranties Concerning the Target and Its Subsidiaries.*[19] The Sellers represent and warrant to the Buyer that the statements contained in this §4 are correct and complete as of the date of this Agreement and will be correct and complete as of the Closing Date (as though made then and as though the Closing Date were substituted for the date of this Agreement throughout this §4), except as set forth in the disclosure schedule delivered by the Sellers to the Buyer on the date hereof and initialed by the Parties (the *"Disclosure Schedule"*).[20]

(a) *Organization, Qualification, and Corporate Power.* Each of the Target and its Subsidiaries is a corporation duly organized, validly existing, and in good standing under the laws of the jurisdiction of its incorporation. Each of the Target and its Subsidiaries is duly authorized to conduct business and is in good standing under the laws of each jurisdiction where such qualification is required, except where the lack of such qualification would not have a material adverse effect on the financial condition of the Target and its Subsidiaries taken as a whole. Each of the Target and its Subsidiaries has full corporate power and authority to carry on the businesses in which it is engaged and to own and use the properties owned

---

[19] This *pro-seller* §4 contains relatively few representations and warranties by the Sellers concerning the Target and its Subsidiaries, and is qualified frequently with references to "knowledge" (defined as the actual knowledge of any Seller without independent investigation) and "materiality" (defined generally as having a material adverse effect on the financial condition of the Target and its Subsidiaries taken as a whole or on the ability of the Parties to consummate the transactions contemplated by this Agreement).

The Buyer will seek to have the Sellers make extensive representations and warranties concerning the Target and its Subsidiaries, without any qualification as to materiality and with only occasional references to knowledge (defined in a manner more favorable to the Buyer as the actual knowledge of any Seller or any director, officer, or employee of any of the Target and its Subsidiaries after reasonable investigation). Sample acquisition agreement 2002.1 (the *pro-buyer* stock purchase agreement) contains comparable representations and warranties which are more favorable to the Buyer.

[20] The Buyer will have a closing condition (*see* §7(a)(i)) and post-Closing indemnification rights (*see* §8(b)) with respect to certain misrepresentations and breaches of warranty. The Buyer will not, however, have a closing condition or post-Closing indemnification rights with respect to any adverse matter that the Sellers disclose in the Disclosure Schedule. This is because the disclosure will cure any misrepresentation or breach of warranty that might otherwise have existed. Thus, if the Sellers disclose any adverse matter in the Disclosure Schedule, the Buyer may seek (a) to add a specific closing condition requiring an acceptable resolution of the matter and/or (b) to obtain specific post-Closing indemnification against the matter.

Sample acquisition agreement 2002.1 (the *pro-buyer* stock purchase agreement) contains additional provisions to the effect that the Sellers' disclosures will be ineffective unless they meet specified standards for particularity and detail.

and used by it. §4(a) of the Disclosure Schedule lists the directors and officers of each of the Target and its Subsidiaries.

(b) *Capitalization.* The entire authorized capital stock of the Target consists of _____ Target Shares, of which _____ Target Shares are issued and outstanding and _____ Target Shares are held in treasury.[21] All of the issued and outstanding Target Shares have been duly authorized, are validly issued, fully paid, and nonassessable, and are held of record by the respective Sellers as set forth in §4(b) of the Disclosure Schedule. There are no outstanding or authorized options, warrants, purchase rights, subscription rights, conversion rights, exchange rights, or other contracts or commitments that could require the Target to issue, sell, or otherwise cause to become outstanding any of its capital stock. There are no outstanding or authorized stock appreciation, phantom stock, profit participation, or similar rights with respect to the Target.

(c) *Noncontravention.* To the Knowledge of any of the Sellers, neither the execution and the delivery of this Agreement, nor the consummation of the transactions contemplated hereby, will [(i)] violate any constitution, statute, regulation, rule, injunction, judgment, order, decree, ruling, charge, or other restriction of any government, governmental agency, or court to which any of the Target and its Subsidiaries is subject or any provision of the charter or bylaws of any of the Target and its Subsidiaries [or (ii) conflict with, result in a breach of, constitute a default under, result in the acceleration of, create in any party the right to accelerate, terminate, modify, or cancel, or require any notice under any agreement, contract, lease, license, instrument, or other arrangement to which any of the Target and its Subsidiaries is a party or by which it is bound or to which any of its assets is subject (or result in the imposition of any Security Interest upon any of its assets)], except where the violation[, conflict, breach, default, acceleration, termination, modification, cancellation, failure to give notice, or Security Interest] would not have a material adverse effect on the financial condition of the Target and its Subsidiaries taken as a whole or on the ability of the Parties to consummate the transactions contemplated by this Agreement. To the Knowledge of any of the Sellers, none of the Target and its Subsidiaries needs to give any notice to, make any filing with, or obtain any authorization, consent, or approval of any government or governmental agency in order for the Parties to consummate the transactions contemplated by this Agreement, except where the failure to give notice, to file, or to obtain any authorization, consent, or approval would not have a material adverse effect on the financial condition of the Target and its Subsidiaries taken as a whole or on the ability of the Parties to consummate the transactions contemplated by this Agreement.

(d) *Brokers' Fees.* None of the Target and its Subsidiaries has any liability or obligation to pay any fees or commissions to any broker, finder, or agent with respect to the transactions contemplated by this Agreement.

---

[21] It may be necessary to revise this sentence if the Target has more than one class of capital stock. See the definition of "Target Shares" in §1 above.

(e) *Title to Tangible Assets.* The Target and its Subsidiaries have good [and marketable] title to, or a valid leasehold interest in, the material tangible assets they use regularly in the conduct of their businesses.

(f) *Subsidiaries.* §4(f) of the Disclosure Schedule sets forth for each Subsidiary of the Target (i) its name and jurisdiction of incorporation, (ii) the number of shares of authorized capital stock of each class of its capital stock, (iii) the number of issued and outstanding shares of each class of its capital stock, the names of the holders thereof, and the number of shares held by each such holder, and (iv) the number of shares of its capital stock held in treasury. All of the issued and outstanding shares of capital stock of each Subsidiary of the Target have been duly authorized and are validly issued, fully paid, and nonassessable. One of the Target and its Subsidiaries holds of record and owns beneficially all of the outstanding shares of each Subsidiary of the Target.

(g) *Financial Statements.*[22] Attached hereto as Exhibit B are the following financial statements (collectively the *"Financial Statements"*): (i) audited consolidated balance sheets and statements of income, changes in stockholders' equity, and cash flow as of and for the fiscal years ended _____, 19____, _____, 19____, _____, 19____, _____, 19____, and _____, 19____ for the Target and its Subsidiaries; and (ii) unaudited consolidated balance sheets and statements of income, changes in stockholders' equity, and cash flow (the *"Most Recent Financial Statements"*) as of and for the months ended _____, 19____ (the *"Most Recent Fiscal Month End"*) for the Target and its Subsidiaries. The Financial Statements (including the notes thereto) have been prepared in accordance with GAAP applied on a consistent basis throughout the periods covered thereby and present fairly the financial condition of the Target and its Subsidiaries as of such dates and the results of operations of the Target and its Subsidiaries for such periods;[23] *provided, however,* that the Most Recent Financial Statements are subject to normal year-end adjustments and lack footnotes and other presentation items.

(h) *Events Subsequent to Most Recent Fiscal Month End.* Since the Most Recent Fiscal Month End, there has not been any material adverse change in the financial condition of the Target and its Subsidiaries taken as a whole. Without limiting the generality of the foregoing, since that date none of the Target and its Subsidiaries has engaged in any practice, taken any action, or entered into any transaction outside the Ordinary Course of Business the primary purpose or effect of which has been to generate or preserve Cash.[24]

---

[22] This *pro-seller* stock purchase agreement does not contain a representation and warranty concerning undisclosed liabilities. See sample acquisition agreement 2002.1 (the *pro-buyer* stock purchase agreement) for an example of such a provision.

[23] Sample acquisition agreement 2002.1 (the *pro-buyer* stock purchase agreement) contains additional representations and warranties to the effect that the financial statements are correct and complete and consistent with the books and records of the Target and its Subsidiaries.

[24] The requirement to disclose certain matters which have had an effect on the amount of cash relates to the provision in §2(c) calling for a net cash payment to the Sellers immediately prior to the Closing.

(i) *Legal Compliance.* To the Knowledge of any of the Sellers, each of the Target and its Subsidiaries has complied with all applicable laws (including rules, regulations, codes, plans, injunctions, judgments, orders, decrees, rulings, and charges thereunder) of federal, state, local, and foreign governments (and all agencies thereof), except where the failure to comply would not have a material adverse effect upon the financial condition of the Target and its Subsidiaries taken as a whole.

(j) *Tax Matters.*[25]

(i) Each of the Target and its Subsidiaries has filed all Income Tax Returns that it was required to file, and has paid all Income Taxes shown thereon as owing, except where the failure to file Income Tax Returns or to pay Income Taxes would not have a material adverse effect on the financial condition of the Target and its Subsidiaries taken as a whole.[26]

(ii) §4(j), of the Disclosure Schedule lists all Income Tax Returns filed with respect to any of the Target and its Subsidiaries for taxable periods ended on or after _____, 19____, indicates those Income Tax Returns that have been audited, and indicates those Income Tax Returns that currently are the subject of audit. The Sellers have delivered to the Buyer correct and complete copies of all federal Income Tax Returns, examination reports, and statements of deficiencies assessed against or agreed to by any of the Target and its Subsidiaries since _____, 19____.

This disclosure requirement is designed to uncover pre-Closing activities of the Target and its Subsidiaries that were outside the Ordinary Course of Business and either (a) intended to generate cash (such as borrowings, sales of assets, and collections of accounts receivable) or (b) intended to eliminate expenditures (such as failures to make loan repayments, purchase assets, pay accounts payable, perform maintenance and repairs, conduct research and development, and engage in advertising and promotion).

[25] Unless the Target was a Subchapter S corporation or was filing a consolidated return with a parent corporation ("Bigco") before the stock purchase, it will generally remain liable for its federal income taxes through the Closing.

If the Target was a Subchapter S corporation before the stock purchase, it will generally not have paid federal income tax at the corporate level. Thus, the Sellers (i.e., the Target shareholders) will generally remain liable for federal income taxes through the Closing. When the Buyer (a corporation) purchases the Target Shares, however, the Target will cease to be an S Corporation. *See* Chapter 11.

If the Target was filing a consolidated return with Bigco before the stock purchase, the Target's liability for federal income taxes through the Closing will turn on the tax allocation agreement in effect between the Target and Bigco or on any specific provision in this Agreement. *See* sample acquisition agreement 2002.4 (sale of subsidiary out of consolidated group) for specific provisions in this regard.

If T has a NOL and will be included in P's consolidated group, P and T should consider making (on their consolidated federal income tax return for the year of the P-T acquisition) an irrevocable election to waive all or part of T's NOL to avoid a reduction in the outside basis of T's stock if and when T's NOL expires. *See* ¶1203.3.

[26] Sample acquisition agreement 2002.1 (the *pro-buyer* stock purchase agreement) contains a broader representation to the effect that each of the Target and its Subsidiaries has filed all Tax Returns that it was required to file, that all such Tax Returns were correct and complete in all respects, and that

(iii) None of the Target and its Subsidiaries has waived any statute of limitations in respect of Income Taxes or agreed to any extension of time with respect to an Income Tax assessment or deficiency.

(iv) None of the Target and its Subsidiaries is a party to any Income Tax allocation or sharing agreement.

(v) [To the Knowledge of any of the Sellers, none of the Target and its Subsidiaries has been a member of an Affiliated Group filing a consolidated federal Income Tax Return (other than a group the common parent of which was the Target).][27]

(k) *Real Property.*

(i) §4(k)(i) of the Disclosure Schedule lists all real property that any of the Target and its Subsidiaries owns. With respect to each such parcel of owned real property, and except for matters which would not have a material adverse effect on the financial condition of the Target and its Subsidiaries taken as a whole:

(A) the identified owner has good and marketable title to the parcel of real property, free and clear of any Security Interest, easement, covenant, or other restriction, except for installments of special assessments not yet delinquent, recorded easements, covenants, and other restrictions, and utility easements, building restrictions, zoning restrictions, and other easements and restrictions existing generally with respect to properties of a similar character;

(B) there are no leases, subleases, licenses, concessions, or other agreements granting to any party or parties the right of use or occupancy of any portion of the parcel of real property; and

---

all taxes owed by any of the Target and its Subsidiaries (whether or not shown on any Tax Returns) have been paid.

[27] If the Target or a Subsidiary has been a member of an Affiliated Group filing a consolidated federal income tax return, such corporation (or its successor) will be jointly and severally liable under Reg. §1.1502-6 for certain tax liabilities incurred by such Affiliated Group for a tax year when such corporation was a member of such Affiliated Group for all or part of such tax year. *See* ¶210.

The Target or a Subsidiary may also be liable for the unpaid taxes of third parties under similar provisions of state, local, or foreign law, as a transferee or successor, by contract (e.g., a tax sharing agreement), or otherwise.

After the Buyer acquires the stock of the Target, the Target and its Subsidiaries will remain liable for any such unpaid tax liabilities.

The Buyer may seek additional protection from the Sellers against any liability for the unpaid taxes of any person other than the Target and its Subsidiaries. Sample acquisition agreement 2002.1 (the *pro-buyer* stock purchase agreement), for example, contains additional representations and warrant-

(C) there are no outstanding options or rights of first refusal to purchase the parcel of real property, or any portion thereof or interest therein.

(ii) §4(k)(ii) of the Disclosure Schedule lists all real property leased or subleased to any of the Target and its Subsidiaries. The Sellers have delivered to the Buyer correct and complete copies of the leases and subleases listed in §4(k)(ii) of the Disclosure Schedule (as amended to date). To the Knowledge of any of the Sellers, each lease and sublease listed in §4(k)(ii) of the Disclosure Schedule is legal, valid, binding, enforceable, and in full force and effect, except where the illegality, invalidity, nonbinding nature, unenforceability, or ineffectiveness would not have a material adverse effect on the financial condition of the Target and its Subsidiaries taken as a whole.

(l) *Intellectual Property.* §4(l) of the Disclosure Schedule identifies each patent or registration which has been issued to any of the Target and its Subsidiaries with respect to any of its intellectual property, identifies each pending patent application or application for registration which any of the Target and its Subsidiaries has made with respect to any of its intellectual property, [and identifies each license, agreement, or other permission which any of the Target and its Subsidiaries has granted to any third party with respect to any of its intellectual property].

(m) *Contracts.* §4(m) of the Disclosure Schedule lists all written contracts and other written agreements to which any of the Target and its Subsidiaries is a party the performance of which will involve consideration in excess of $_____. The Sellers have delivered to the Buyer a correct and complete copy of each contract or other agreement listed in 4(m) of the Disclosure Schedule (as amended to date).

(n) *Powers of Attorney.* To the Knowledge of any of the Sellers, there are no outstanding powers of attorney executed on behalf of any of the Target and its Subsidiaries.

(o) *Litigation.* §4(o) of the Disclosure Schedule sets forth each instance in which any of the Target and its Subsidiaries (i) is subject to any outstanding injunction, judgment, order, decree, ruling, or charge or (ii) is a party to any action, suit, proceeding, hearing, or investigation of, in, or before any court or quasi-judicial or administrative agency of any federal, state, local, or foreign jurisdiction, except where the injunction, judgment, order, decree, ruling, action, suit, proceeding, hearing, or investigation would not have a material adverse effect on the financial condition of the Target and its Subsidiaries taken as a whole.

(p) *Employee Benefits.*

---

ies on this subject and an explicit indemnification provision. *See* §4(k)(v) and §8(b)(iii) of sample acquisition agreement 2002.1.

(i) §4(p) of the Disclosure Schedule lists each Employee Benefit Plan that any of the Target and its Subsidiaries maintains or to which any of the Target and its Subsidiaries contributes.

(A) To the Knowledge of any of the Sellers, each such Employee Benefit Plan (and each related trust, insurance contract, or fund) has been maintained, funded and administered in accordance with the terms of such Employee Benefit Plan and complies in form and in operation in all respects with the applicable requirements of ERISA and the Code, except where the failure to comply would not have a material adverse effect on the financial condition of the Target and its Subsidiaries taken as a whole.

(B) All contributions (including all employer contributions and employee salary reduction contributions) which are due have been made to each such Employee Benefit Plan which is an Employee Pension Benefit Plan. All premiums or other payments which are due have been paid with respect to each such Employee Benefit Plan which is an Employee Welfare Benefit Plan.

(C) Each such Employee Benefit Plan which is intended to meet the requirements of a "qualified plan" under Code §401(a) has received a determination letter from the Internal Revenue Service to the effect that it meets the requirements of Code §401(a).

(D) As of the last day of the most recent prior plan year, the market value of assets under each such Employee Benefit Plan which is an Employee Pension Benefit Plan (other than any Multiemployer Plan) equaled or exceeded the present value of liabilities thereunder (determined in accordance with then current funding assumptions).

(E) The Sellers have delivered to the Buyer correct and complete copies of the plan documents and summary plan descriptions, the most recent determination letter received from the Internal Revenue Service, the most recent annual report (IRS Form 5500), and all related trust agreements, insurance contracts, and other funding arrangements which implement each such Employee Benefit Plan.

(ii) [With respect to each Employee Benefit Plan that any of the Target and its Subsidiaries or any ERISA Affiliate maintains or has maintained during the prior six years or to which any of them contributes, or has been required to contribute during the prior six years:

(A) No action, suit, proceeding, hearing, or investigation with respect to the administration or the investment of the assets of any such Employee Benefit Plan (other than routine claims for benefits) is pending, except where the action, suit, proceeding, hearing, or investigation would not have a material adverse effect on the financial condition of the Target and its Subsidiaries taken as a whole.

(B) None of the Target and its Subsidiaries has incurred any liability to the PBGC (other than PBGC premium payments) or otherwise under Title IV of ERISA (including any withdrawal liability) with respect to any such Employee Benefit Plan which is an Employee Pension Benefit Plan.][28]

(q) *Environmental, Health, and Safety Matters.*[29]

(i) To the Knowledge of any of the Sellers, the Target and its Subsidiaries are in compliance with Environmental, Health, and Safety Requirements, except for such noncompliance as would not have a material adverse effect on the financial condition of the Target and its Subsidiaries taken as a whole.

(ii) To the Knowledge of any of the Sellers, the Target and its Subsidiaries have not received any written notice, report or other information regarding any actual or alleged material violation of Environmental, Health, and Safety Requirements, or any material liabilities or potential material liabilities (whether accrued, absolute, contingent, unliquidated or otherwise), including any investigatory, remedial or corrective obligations, relating to the Target or its Subsidiaries or their facilities arising under Environmental, Health, and Safety Requirements, the subject of which would have a material adverse effect on the financial condition of the Target and its Subsidiaries taken as a whole.

(iii) This Section 4(q) contains the sole and exclusive representations and warranties of the Seller with respect to any environmental, health, or safety matters, including without limitation any arising under any Environmental, Health, and Safety Requirements.

---

[28] The Sellers may seek to delete or qualify some or all of §4(p)(ii).

[29] These representations and warranties concerning environmental, health, and safety matters are relatively long and detailed. A condensed version may be more appropriate when, for example, the operations of the Target and its Subsidiaries appear to have had a relatively insignificant effect upon the environment or upon public or employee health and safety.

The environmental representations in this *pro-seller* stock purchase agreement (1) are limited to matters within the Seller's knowledge, (2) are consistently limited to matters that would have a material adverse effect, (3) do not extend to strict liability for site cleanup under CERCLA or common law liability, (4) otherwise limit the disclosure and indemnification obligations of the Seller, and (5) state that these environmental representations constitute the sole representation of the Seller with respect to environmental, health, and safety matters.

Sample acquisition agreement 2002.1 (the *pro-buyer* stock purchase agreement) contains broader environmental, health, and safety representations, which (1) contain neither knowledge nor materiality limitations, (2) impose a broader disclosure obligation upon the Seller, and (3) extend to strict liability for site cleanup under CERCLA and common law liability under current and future Environmental, Health, and Safety Requirements.

Sample acquisition agreement 2002.3 (the *neutral* stock purchase agreement) contains environmental representations which are (1) subject to certain materiality limitations and (2) are slightly more limited and focused than the corresponding *pro-buyer* representations.

(r) *Certain Business Relationships with the Target and Its Subsidiaries.* None of the Sellers and their Affiliates has been involved in any material business arrangement or relationship with any of the Target and its Subsidiaries within the past 12 months and none of the Sellers and their Affiliates owns any material asset, tangible or intangible, which is used in the business of any of the Target and its Subsidiaries.

(s) *Disclaimer of Other Representations and Warranties.* Except as expressly set forth in Section 3 and this Section 4, the Sellers make no representation or warranty, express or implied, at law or in equity, in respect of the Target, its Subsidiaries, or any of their respective assets, liabilities or operations, including, without limitation, with respect to merchantability or fitness for any particular purpose, and any such other representations or warranties are hereby expressly disclaimed. Buyer hereby acknowledges and agrees that, except to the extent specifically set forth in Section 3 and this Section 4, the Buyer is purchasing the Target shares on an "as-is, where-is" basis.[30]

5. *Pre-Closing Covenants.*[31] The Parties agree as follows with respect to the period between the execution of this Agreement and the Closing.[32]

(a) *General.* Each of the Parties will use his or its reasonable best efforts to take all action and to do all things necessary [, proper, or advisable] in order to consummate and make effective the transactions contemplated by this Agreement (including satisfaction, but not waiver, of the closing conditions set forth in §7 below).

(b) *Notices and Consents.* [The Sellers will cause each of the Target and its Subsidiaries to give any notices to third parties, and will cause each of the Target and its Subsidiaries to use its reasonable best efforts to obtain any third party consents, that the Buyer reasonably may request in connection with the matters referred to in §4(c) above.] Each of the Parties will (and the Sellers will cause

---

[30] Consideration should be given to highlighting this subsection by printing it in all capital letters, particularly in jurisdictions where statutory or common law rights (e.g., implied representations and warranties) are being waived.

[31] Sample acquisition agreement 2002.1 (the *pro-buyer* stock purchase agreement) contains additional pre-Closing covenants concerning preservation of the business and obtaining title insurance and surveys in preparation for the Closing.

[32] The Buyer may seek to make the Target and its Subsidiaries parties to this Agreement for the purpose of obtaining directly their covenants applicable to the period prior to the Closing.

Whether or not the Target and its Subsidiaries become parties to this Agreement, they are likely to incur significant costs and expenses in connection with the transaction (e.g., when they and their agents prepare the Disclosure Schedule and perhaps certain of the Financial Statements, give notices to third parties and obtain their consent, and make filings under the Hart-Scott-Rodino Act and respond to requests for additional information).

These costs and expenses of the Target and its Subsidiaries are separate and distinguishable from the costs and expenses of the Buyer on the one hand and of the Sellers on the other hand.

Section 10(1) allocates responsibility among the respective parties for these costs and expenses through the Closing.

each of the Target and its Subsidiaries to) give any notices to, make any filings with, and use its reasonable best efforts to obtain any authorizations, consents, and approvals of governments and governmental agencies in connection with the matters referred to in §3(a)(ii), §3(b)(ii) and §4(c) above. Without limiting the generality of the foregoing, each of the Parties will file (and the Sellers will cause each of the Target and its Subsidiaries to file) any Notification and Report Forms and related material that he or it may be required to file with the Federal Trade Commission and the Antitrust Division of the United States Department of Justice under the Hart-Scott-Rodino Act, will use his or its reasonable best efforts to obtain (and the Sellers will cause each of the Target and its Subsidiaries to use its reasonable best efforts to obtain) a waiver from the applicable waiting period, and will make (and the Sellers will cause each of the Target and its Subsidiaries to make) any further filings pursuant thereto that may be necessary [, proper, or advisable] in connection therewith.

(c) *Operation of Business.* [The Sellers will not cause or permit any of the Target and its Subsidiaries to engage in any practice, take any action, or enter into any transaction outside the Ordinary Course of Business.[33] Without limiting the generality of the foregoing,] the Sellers will not cause or permit any of the Target and its Subsidiaries to engage in any practice, take any action, or enter into any transaction outside the Ordinary Course of Business the primary purpose or effect of which will be to generate or preserve Cash.[34]

(d) *Full Access.* [Each of the Sellers will permit, and the Sellers will cause each of the Target and its Subsidiaries to permit, representatives of the Buyer to have full access at all reasonable times, and in a manner so as not to interfere with the normal business operations of the Target and its Subsidiaries, to all premises, properties, personnel, books, records (including tax records), contracts, and documents of or pertaining to each of the Target and its Subsidiaries. The Buyer will treat and hold as such any Confidential Information it receives from any of the Sellers, the Target, and its Subsidiaries in the course of the reviews contemplated by this §5(d), will not use any of the Confidential Information except in connection with this Agreement, and, if this Agreement is terminated for any reason whatsoever, will return to the Sellers, the Target, and its Subsidiaries all tangible embodiments (and all copies) of the Confidential Information which are in its possession.]

(e) *Notice of Developments.*

---

[33] The Buyer may seek to have this covenant restrict a number of specific practices, actions, and transactions. Sample acquisition agreement 2002.1 (the *pro-buyer* stock purchase agreement) contains provisions that are more favorable to the Buyer in this regard.

[34] This covenant relates to the provision in §2(c) above calling for a net cash payment to the Sellers immediately prior to the Closing. The covenant is designed to prevent pre-Closing activities of the Target and its Subsidiaries that would be outside the Ordinary Course of Business and either (a) intended to generate cash (such as borrowings, sales of assets, and collections of accounts receivable) or (b) intended to eliminate expenditures (such as failures to make loan repayments, purchase assets, pay accounts payable, perform maintenance and repairs, conduct research and development, and engage in advertising and promotion).

(i) Any of the Sellers may elect at any time to notify the Buyer of any development causing a breach of any of the representations and warranties in §4 above. Unless the Buyer has the right to terminate this Agreement pursuant to §9(a)(ii) below by reason of the development and exercises that right within the period of [10 business days] referred to in §9(a)(ii) below, the written notice pursuant to this §5(e)(i) will be deemed to have amended the Disclosure Schedule, to have qualified the representations and warranties contained in §4 above, and to have cured any misrepresentation or breach of warranty that otherwise might have existed hereunder by reason of the development.[35]

(ii) Each Party will give prompt written notice to the others of any material adverse development causing a breach of any of his or its own representations and warranties in §3 above. No disclosure by any Party pursuant to this §5(e)(ii), however, shall be deemed to amend or supplement Annex I, Annex II, or the Disclosure Schedule or to prevent or cure any misrepresentation or breach of warranty.[36]

(f) *Exclusivity.* None of the Sellers will (and the Sellers will not cause or permit any of the Target and its Subsidiaries to) solicit, initiate, or encourage the submission of any proposal or offer from any Person relating to the acquisition of all or substantially all of the capital stock or assets of any of the Target and its Subsidiaries (including any acquisition structured as a merger, consolidation, or share exchange); *provided, however,* that the Sellers, the Target, its Subsidiaries, and their directors and officers will remain free to participate in any discussions or negotiations regarding, furnish any information with respect to, assist or participate in, or facilitate in any other manner any effort or attempt by any Person to do or seek any of the foregoing to the extent their fiduciary duties may require.[37]

6. *Post-Closing Covenants.*[38] The Parties agree as follows with respect to the period following the Closing.

---

[35] Section 5(e)(i) permits the Sellers to notify the Buyer of any development prior to the Closing that causes a breach of their representations and warranties in §4 above concerning the Target and its Subsidiaries. If the development gives the Buyer any right to terminate this Agreement pursuant to §9(a)(ii), the Buyer must exercise its termination right within [10 business days] after the notice. Unless the Buyer has such a termination right and exercises it within that period, the notice will be deemed to have cured any such breach of the representations and warranties that otherwise would have existed.

[36] Sample acquisition agreement 2002.1 (the *pro-buyer* stock purchase agreement) provides that no disclosure (presumably, but not necessarily, by the Sellers) between signing and closing will supplement the previous disclosures or cure any misrepresentation or breach of warranty.

[37] Sample acquisition agreement 2002.1 (the *pro-buyer* stock purchase agreement) lacks a comparable proviso permitting these persons to respond to unsolicited proposals to the extent their fiduciary duties may require.

[38] Sample acquisition agreement 2002.1 (the *pro-buyer* stock purchase agreement) contains an additional covenant requiring the Sellers to keep certain information regarding the Target and its Subsidiaries confidential after the Closing.

The Sellers may seek to obtain additional covenants from the Buyer and its Subsidiaries (e.g., the typical covenants contained in a loan agreement or an indenture) because the Buyer is issuing the Buyer Notes to the Sellers as part of the Purchase Price. Any such covenants would remain applicable so long as the Buyer Notes remained outstanding.

(a) *General.* In case at any time after the Closing any further action is necessary [or desirable] to carry out the purposes of this Agreement, each of the Parties will take such further action (including the execution and delivery of such further instruments and documents) as any other Party [reasonably] may request, all at the sole cost and expense of the requesting Party (unless the requesting Party is entitled to indemnification therefor under §8 below).[39]

(b) *Litigation Support.* In the event and for so long as any Party actively is contesting or defending against any action, suit, proceeding, hearing, investigation, charge, complaint, claim, or demand in connection with (i) any transaction contemplated under this Agreement or (ii) any fact, situation, circumstance, status, condition, activity, practice, plan, occurrence, event, incident, action, failure to act, or transaction on or prior to the Closing Date involving any of the Target and its Subsidiaries, each of the other Parties shall cooperate with him or it and his or its counsel in the defense or contest, make available their personnel, and provide such testimony and access to their books and records as shall be necessary in connection with the defense or contest, all at the sole cost and expense of the contesting or defending Party (unless the contesting or defending Party is entitled to indemnification therefor under §8 below).[40]

(c) *Transition.* [None of the Sellers will take any action that is designed or intended to have the effect of discouraging any lessor, licensor, customer, supplier,

---

The pro-buyer stock purchase agreement in ¶2002.1 and the neutral stock purchase agreement in ¶2002.3 both require Sellers to reimburse Buyer for Taxes of the Target and its Subsidiaries with respect to (1) tax periods ending on or before the Closing Date and (2) the pre-Closing portion of any tax periods which include the Closing Date. This pro-seller stock purchase agreement does not require Sellers to indemnify Buyer against pre-Closing Taxes. Hence such taxes will be an obligation of the Target and an indirect obligation of Buyer.

This pro-seller agreement does not contain any provision addressing the treatment of tax refunds for pre-Closing tax periods. Such refunds of taxes previously paid by Target could arise in two circumstances: first, where Target overpaid its taxes for a pre-Closing period, and second, where a target post-Closing loss can be carried back to Target's pre-Closing period. In the absence of a specific provision in the agreement, such refunds generally will be paid to Target, and hence Buyer will receive the economic benefit of such refunds. This is a fair result to Sellers because in this pro-seller agreement Sellers are not reimbursing Buyer for pre-Closing taxes of Target and its subsidiaries.

When Target was, prior to Closing, a member of Seller's consolidated group, federal income tax refunds for pre-Closing periods would be paid to the parent of Seller's consolidated group and hence Seller would receive the economic benefit of such refunds. See ¶2002.4.4 for a discussion of this topic when Target was a member of Seller's consolidated group before the acquisition and ¶2002.4.7(f) for a sample agreement clause requiring Seller to pay over to Buyer any tax refund (or reduction of tax liability) resulting from a carryback of a postacquisition tax attribute of the Target and its Subsidiaries.

[39] The Parties may prefer to allocate responsibility for these post-Closing costs and expenses in some other manner (e.g., the Party incurring the costs and expenses might be responsible for their payment; the Parties might share the costs and expenses in a predetermined ratio; or one Party might be responsible for the costs and expenses up to a specified aggregate ceiling and the other Party responsible for any excess).

Compare §10(1) which allocates responsibility among the Parties for their costs and expenses *through* the Closing.

[40] The Parties may prefer to allocate responsibility for these post-Closing costs and expenses in some other manner as discussed in the preceding footnote.

or other business associate of any of the Target and its Subsidiaries from maintaining the same business relationships with the Target and its Subsidiaries after
the Closing as it maintained with the Target and its Subsidiaries prior to the
Closing.]

(d) *Covenant Not to Compete.*[41] [For a period of one year from and after the
Closing Date, none of the Sellers will engage directly or indirectly in any business
that any of the Target and its Subsidiaries conducts as of the Closing Date in any
geographic area in which any of the Target and its Subsidiaries conducts that
business as of the Closing Date; *provided, however,* that no owner of less than 5%
of the outstanding stock of any publicly-traded corporation shall be deemed to
engage solely by reason thereof in any of its businesses. If the final judgment of
a court of competent jurisdiction declares that any term or provision of this
§6(d) is invalid or unenforceable, the Parties agree that the court making the
determination of invalidity or unenforceability shall have the power to reduce
the scope, duration, or area of the term or provision, to delete specific words or
phrases, or to replace any invalid or unenforceable term or provision with a term
or provision that is valid and enforceable and that comes closest to expressing
the intention of the invalid or unenforceable term or provision, and this Agreement
shall be enforceable as so modified after the expiration of the time within which
the judgment may be appealed.]

(e) *Buyer Notes.* Each Buyer Note will be imprinted with a legend substantially
in the following form:

This Note was originally issued on _____, 19____, *and has not been registered
under the Securities Act of 1933, as amended.*[42]

7. *Conditions to Obligation to Close.*

(a) *Conditions to Obligation of the Buyer.*[43] The obligation of the Buyer to consummate the transactions to be performed by it in connection with the Closing is
subject to satisfaction of the following conditions:

---

[41] Note that unless this Agreement allocates a specified amount of consideration to the covenant
not to compete, applicable tax cases will preclude the Buyer from seeking to allocate a portion of the
purchase price to the covenant and amortizing such amount over the covenant's life.

[42] This provision must be eliminated if the Buyer will issue the Buyer Notes in an offering registered
under the Securities Act.

Sample acquisition agreement 2001.1 (the *pro-buyer stock purchase agreement*) contains additional
provisions requiring the Sellers to obtain an opinion of counsel as to securities law matters prior to
transferring the Buyer Notes.

[43] Sample acquisition agreement 2002.1 (the *pro-buyer* stock purchase agreement) contains additional
closing conditions for the benefit of the Buyer concerning third party consents, title insurance, surveys,
director and officer resignations, and the receipt of financing for the transaction.

(i) the representations and warranties set forth in §3(a) and §4 above shall be true and correct in all material respects at and as of the Closing Date;[44]

(ii) the Sellers shall have performed and complied with all of their covenants hereunder in all material respects through the Closing;

(iii) there shall not be any injunction, judgment, order, decree, ruling, or charge in effect preventing consummation of any of the transactions contemplated by this Agreement;[45]

(iv) the Sellers shall have delivered to the Buyer a certificate to the effect that each of the conditions specified above in §7(a)(i)-(iii) is satisfied in all respects;

(v) [all applicable waiting periods (and any extensions thereof) under the Hart-Scott-Rodino Act shall have expired or otherwise been terminated and the Parties, the Target, and its Subsidiaries shall have received all other authorizations, consents, and approvals of governments and governmental agencies referred to in §3(a)(ii), §3(b)(ii), and §4(c) above];

(vi) the relevant parties shall have entered into side agreements in form and substance as set forth in Exhibits C-1 through C-_____ attached hereto and the same shall be in full force and effect;

(vii) the Buyer shall have received from counsel to the Sellers an opinion in form and substance as set forth in Exhibit D attached hereto, addressed to the Buyer, and dated as of the Closing Date; and

(viii) all actions to be taken by the Sellers in connection with consummation of the transactions contemplated hereby and all certificates, opinions, instruments, and other documents required to effect the transactions contemplated hereby will be [reasonably] satisfactory in form and substance to the Buyer.

The Buyer may waive any condition specified in this §7(a) if it executes a writing so stating at or prior to the Closing.

---

[44] Note that this provision will not give the Buyer any closing condition with respect to any adverse matter that the Sellers may disclose in the Disclosure Schedule. This is because the disclosure will cure any misrepresentation or breach of warranty that might otherwise have existed. Thus, when the Sellers disclose an adverse matter in the Disclosure Schedule, the Buyer may seek to add a specific closing condition requiring an acceptable resolution of the matter.

Section 5(e)(i) above permits the Sellers to notify the Buyer of any development prior to the Closing that causes a breach of their representations and warranties in §4 concerning the Target and its Subsidiaries. If the development gives the Buyer any right to terminate this Agreement pursuant to §9(a)(ii), the Buyer must exercise its termination right within [10 business days] after the notice. Unless the Buyer has such a termination right and exercises it within that period, the notice will be deemed to have cured any such breach of the representations and warranties that otherwise would have existed.

[45] Sample acquisition agreement 2002.1 (the *pro-buyer* stock purchase agreement) contains a broader closing condition requiring also that there not be any pending [or threatened] litigation.

(b) *Conditions to Obligation of the Sellers.* The obligation of the Sellers to consummate the transactions to be performed by them in connection with the Closing is subject to satisfaction of the following conditions:

(i) the representations and warranties set forth in §3(b) above shall be true and correct in all material respects at and as of the Closing Date;

(ii) the Buyer shall have performed and complied with all of its covenants hereunder in all material respects through the Closing;

(iii) there shall not be any injunction, judgment, order, decree, ruling, or charge in effect preventing consummation of any of the transactions contemplated by this Agreement;[46]

(iv) the Buyer shall have delivered to the Sellers a certificate to the effect that each of the conditions specified above in §7(b)(i)-(iii) is satisfied in all respects;

(v) [all applicable waiting periods (and any extensions thereof) under the Hart-Scott-Rodino Act shall have expired or otherwise been terminated and the Parties, the Target, and its Subsidiaries shall have received all other authorizations, consents, and approvals of governments and governmental agencies referred to in §3(a)(ii), §3(b)(ii), and §4(c) above];

(vi) the relevant parties shall have entered into side agreements in form and substance as set forth in Exhibits C-_____, C-_____, ... and C-_____ and the same shall be in full force and effect;

(vii) the Sellers shall have received from counsel to the Buyer an opinion in form and substance as set forth in Exhibit E attached hereto, addressed to the Sellers, and dated as of the Closing Date; and

(viii) all actions to be taken by the Buyer in connection with consummation of the transactions contemplated hereby and all certificates, opinions, instruments, and other documents required to effect the transactions contemplated hereby will be [reasonably] satisfactory in form and substance to the Requisite Sellers.

The Requisite Sellers may waive any condition specified in this §7(b) if they execute a writing so stating at or prior to the Closing.

8. *Remedies for Breaches of This Agreement.*[47]

---

[46] Because this Sellers' closing condition conforms to the comparable Buyer's closing condition in §7(a)(iii), it leaves the Sellers with a relatively narrow "out." Thus, the Sellers may prefer to broaden the respective closing conditions. Compare the broader closing conditions in sample acquisition agreement 2002.1 (the *pro-buyer* stock purchase agreement).

[47] The Buyer may seek some form of additional security covering the obligation of the Sellers to indemnify the Buyer after the Closing. This may include provisions calling for (a) the Buyer to have a recoupment remedy with respect to the Buyer Notes, (b) the Sellers to deposit a portion of the Purchase Price with a third party escrow agent, (c) the Buyer to hold back a portion of the Purchase Price (to be paid later with interest), or (d) the Buyer to obtain a security interest in certain assets of

(a) *Survival of Representations and Warranties.*[48]

ALTERNATIVE A (MINIMAL INDEMNIFICATION): None of the representations and warranties of the Sellers contained in §4 above shall survive the Closing hereunder. All of the representations and warranties of the Parties contained in §3 above shall survive the Closing (unless the damaged Party knew or had reason to know of any misrepresentation or breach of warranty at the time of Closing) and continue in full force and effect forever thereafter (subject to any applicable statutes of limitations).

ALTERNATIVE B (LIMITED INDEMNIFICATION): All of the representations and warranties of the Sellers contained in §4 above shall survive the Closing hereunder (unless the Buyer knew or had reason to know of any misrepresentation or breach of warranty at the time of Closing) and continue in full force and effect for a period of [one year] thereafter. All of the representations and warranties of the Parties contained in §3 above shall survive the Closing (unless the damaged Party knew or had reason to know of any misrepresentation or breach of warranty at the time of Closing) and continue in full force and effect forever thereafter (subject to any applicable statutes of limitations).

(b) *Indemnification Provisions for Benefit of the Buyer.*[49]

---

the Sellers. Sample acquisition agreement 2002.1 (the *pro-buyer* stock purchase agreement), for example, contains recoupment provisions applicable to the Buyer Notes.

[48] This Agreement contains alternative provisions for (a) *minimal indemnification* (only the representations and warranties concerning the transaction itself survive the closing) and (b) *limited indemnification* (the representations and warranties with respect to the transaction itself survive indefinitely; the other representations and warranties survive only for [one year]; and there is a deductible and a ceiling with respect to indemnification against breaches of the latter).

Sample acquisition agreement 2002.1 (the *pro-buyer* stock purchase agreement), on the other hand, contains alternative provisions for (a) *full indemnification* (the representations and warranties survive indefinitely, and there is no deductible, threshold, or ceiling with respect to indemnification against breaches thereof) and (b) *limited indemnification* (the representations and warranties with respect to the transaction itself and with respect to taxes survive indefinitely; the other representations and warranties survive only for [three years]; and there is a threshold, but not a deductible or ceiling, with respect to indemnification against breaches of the latter).

This *pro-seller* Agreement provides that the representations and warranties of the Parties will survive the Closing (*unless* the damaged Party knew or had reason to know of the misrepresentation or breach of warranty at the time of Closing).

Sample acquisition agreement 2002.1 (the *pro-buyer* stock purchase agreement), on the other hand, provides that the representations and warranties will survive the Closing (even if the damaged Party knew or had reason to know of the misrepresentation or breach of warranty at the time of Closing).

The Buyer will have assumed all liabilities (whether known or unknown, and whether absolute or contingent) of the Target and its Subsidiaries if the Sellers' representations and warranties in §4 do not survive the Closing.

[49] Section 10(a)(i) provides that the representations, warranties, and covenants of the *individual Sellers* (e.g., each Seller agrees to sell his or its Target Shares to the Buyer and makes certain representations and warranties concerning himself or itself and his or its Target Shares) will be "several." This is defined in such a way that the particular Seller (and no other Seller) will be entirely responsible for the Buyer's Adverse Consequences if the particular Seller fails to perform his or its obligation.

On the other hand, §10(a)(ii) provides that the representations, warranties, and covenants *of the Sellers as a group* (e.g., the Sellers as a group make representations and warranties concerning the

(i) In the event any of the Sellers breaches any of their representations, warranties, and covenants contained herein (other than the covenants in §2(a) above and the representations and warranties in §3(a) above),[50] and, if there is an applicable survival period pursuant to §8(a) above, provided that the Buyer makes a written claim for indemnification against any of the Sellers pursuant to §10(h) below within such survival period, then each of the Sellers agrees to indemnify the Buyer from and against his or its Allocable Portion of any Adverse Consequences the Buyer shall suffer through and after the date of the claim for indemnification (but *excluding* any Adverse Consequences the Buyer shall suffer after the end of any applicable survival period) caused [proximately] by the breach;[51] *provided, however,* that the Sellers shall not have any obligation to indemnify the Buyer from and against any Adverse Consequences caused by the breach of any representation or warranty or covenant of the Sellers contained in §4 above [ALTERNATIVE B (LIMITED INDEMNIFICATION): (A) until the Buyer has suffered Adverse Consequences by reason of all such breaches in excess of a $_____ aggregate deductible (after which point the Sellers will be obligated only to indemnify the Buyer from and against further such Adverse Consequences)[52] or thereafter (B) to the extent the Adverse Consequences the Buyer has suffered by reason of all such breaches exceeds a $_____ aggregate ceiling (after which point the Sellers will have no obligation to indemnify the Buyer from and against further such Adverse Consequences)].[53]

Target and its Subsidiaries) will be "joint." This is defined in such a way that each Seller will be responsible for his or its Allocable Portion of the Buyer's Adverse Consequences if the Sellers as a group fail to perform their obligation.

[50] Section 5(e)(i) permits the Sellers to notify the Buyer of any development prior to the Closing that causes a breach of their representations and warranties in §4 above concerning the Target and its Subsidiaries. If the development gives the Buyer any right to terminate this Agreement pursuant to §9(a)(ii), the Buyer must exercise its termination right within [10 business days] after the notice. Unless the Buyer has such a termination right and exercises it within that period, the notice will be deemed to have cured any such breach of the representations and warranties that otherwise would have existed.

[51] Sample acquisition agreement 2002.2 (the *pro-seller* stock purchase agreement) provides that the indemnifying party (presumably, but not necessarily, one of the Sellers) must indemnify the indemnified party (presumably, but not necessarily, the Buyer) from and against Adverse Consequences the indemnified party *shall* suffer *caused [proximately] by* certain breaches by the indemnifying party of his or its representations, warranties, and covenants.

Sample acquisition agreement 2002.1 (the *pro-buyer* stock purchase agreement), on the other hand, provides that the indemnifying party must indemnify the indemnified party from and against Adverse Consequences the indemnified party *may* suffer *resulting from, arising out of, relating to, in the nature of, or caused by* certain breaches by the indemnifying party of his or its representations, warranties, and covenants.

[52] The Sellers may also seek to impose a *per claim* deductible.

[53] The Buyer may seek to substitute a threshold (with relation back to the first dollar once the threshold is exceeded) for the deductible in this proviso and also seek to eliminate the ceiling on indemnification. *Compare* sample acquisition agreement 2002.1 (the *pro-buyer* stock purchase agreement).

(ii) In the event any of the Sellers breaches any of his or its covenants in §2(a) above or any of his or its representations and warranties in §3(a) above, and, if there is an applicable survival period pursuant to §8(a) above, provided that the Buyer makes a written claim for indemnification against the Seller pursuant to §10(h) below within such survival period, then the Seller agrees to indemnify the Buyer from and against the entirety of any Adverse Consequences the Buyer shall suffer through and after the date of the claim for indemnification (but *excluding* any Adverse Consequences the Buyer shall suffer after the end of any applicable survival period) caused [proximately] by the breach.

(c) *Indemnification Provisions for Benefit of the Sellers.* In the event the Buyer breaches any of its representations, warranties, and covenants contained herein, and, if there is an applicable survival period pursuant to §8(a) above, provided that any of the Sellers makes a written claim for indemnification against the Buyer pursuant to §10(h) below within such survival period, then the Buyer agrees to indemnify each of the Sellers from and against the entirety of any Adverse Consequences the Seller shall suffer through and after the date of the claim for indemnification (but *excluding* any Adverse Consequences the Seller shall suffer after the end of any applicable survival period) caused [proximately] by the breach.

(d) *Matters Involving Third Parties.*[54]

(i) If any third party shall notify any Party (the *"Indemnified Party"*) with respect to any matter (a *"Third Party Claim"*) which may give rise to a claim for indemnification against any other Party (the *"Indemnifying Party"*) under this §8, then the Indemnified Party shall promptly (and in any event within [five business days] after receiving notice of the Third Party Claim) notify each Indemnifying Party thereof in writing.

(ii) Any Indemnifying Party will have the right at any time to assume and thereafter conduct the defense of the Third Party Claim with counsel of his or

---

[54] An *indemnifying* party (presumably, but not necessarily, one of the Sellers) will normally seek to control the defense of any third party claim that may give rise to a claim for indemnification under §8. However, the *indemnified* party (presumably, but not necessarily, the Buyer) will not want the indemnifying party to control the defense of any third party claim in which the indemnified party will retain a meaningful interest. For example, the indemnified party may seek to control the defense of a third party claim if the third party seeks an injunction or other equitable relief or if it is not clear that the indemnifying party will bear the entirety of any money damages or amount paid in settlement.

This *pro-seller* Agreement provides that any indemnifying party may assume the defense of a third party claim *at any time* during the course of the defense, and prevents the indemnified party from consenting to the entry of any judgment or entering into any settlement with respect to the matter without the consent of the indemnifying party [(not to be unreasonably withheld)].

Sample acquisition agreement 2002.1 (the *pro-buyer* stock purchase agreement), on the other hand, provides that the indemnified party will control the defense of any third party claim *unless* (a) an indemnifying party accepts full responsibility for the matter within [15 days]; (b) the indemnifying party demonstrates it has the financial resources necessary to defend against the matter and fulfill its indemnification obligations; (c) the third party seeks only money damages (as opposed to an

its choice [reasonably satisfactory to the Indemnified Party; *provided, however,* that the Indemnifying Party will not consent to the entry of any judgment or enter into any settlement with respect to the Third Party Claim without the prior written consent of the Indemnified Party (not to be withheld unreasonably) unless the judgment or proposed settlement involves only the payment of money damages and does not impose an injunction or other equitable relief upon the Indemnified Party].

(iii) Unless and until an Indemnifying Party assumes the defense of the Third Party Claim as provided in §8(d)(ii) above, however, the Indemnified Party may defend against the Third Party Claim in any manner he or it reasonably may deem appropriate.

(iv) In no event will the Indemnified Party consent to the entry of any judgment or enter into any settlement with respect to the Third Party Claim without the prior written consent of each of the Indemnifying Parties [(not to be withheld unreasonably)].

(e) *Determination of Adverse Consequences.* The Parties shall make appropriate adjustments for tax benefits and insurance coverage [and take into account the time cost of money (using the Applicable Rate as the discount rate)] in determining Adverse Consequences for purposes of this §8. All indemnification payments under this §8 shall be deemed adjustments to the Purchase Price.

(f) *Exclusive Remedy.* The Buyer and the Seller acknowledge and agree that the foregoing indemnification provisions in this §8 shall be the exclusive remedy of the Buyer and the Seller with respect to the Target, its Subsidiaries, and the transactions contemplated by this Agreement. [ALTERNATIVE A (MINIMAL INDEMNIFICATION): Without limiting the generality of the foregoing, the Buyer acknowledges and agrees that it shall not have any remedy after the Closing for any breach of the representations and warranties in §4 above.] [ALTERNATIVE B (LIMITED INDEMNIFICATION): OMIT ALTERNATIVE A LANGUAGE ABOVE.][55]

---

injunction or other equitable relief); (d) settlement of, or an adverse judgment with respect to, the third party claim is not likely to establish a precedent [materially] adverse to the indemnified party; and (e) the indemnifying party conducts the defense actively and diligently.

[55] Sample acquisition agreement 2002.1 (the *pro-buyer* stock purchase agreement) states that the indemnification provisions in the Agreement are in addition to and not in derogation of any other statutory, equitable, or common law remedies (including any such remedies relating to environmental matters).

Sample acquisition agreement 2002.1 also contains an additional provision to the effect that no Seller will make a claim for indemnification against the Target, by reason of the fact that the Seller was, before the stock purchase, a director or other officeholder of the Target entitled to indemnification from the Target with respect to any suit or claim the Buyer might bring against the Seller in connection with the stock purchase. This provision responds to the surprising decision in Heffernan v. Pacific Dunlop GNB Corporation, 965 F.2d 369 (7th Cir. 1992). *See* §8(g) of sample acquisition agreement 2002.1 and the footnote thereto. This *pro-seller* stock purchase agreement does not contain such an anti-*Heffernan* provision, although the buyer may seek such a provision.

(g) *Environmental Remedies.*[56] [ALTERNATIVE A (MINIMAL INDEMNIFI-CATION): Without limiting the generality of (f), above, the Buyer hereby waives any right, whether arising at law or in equity, to seek contribution, cost recovery, damages, or any other recourse or remedy from the Seller, and hereby releases the Seller, from any claim, demand or liability, with respect to any environmental, health, or safety matter relating to the past, current or future facilities, properties or operations of the Target, its Subsidiaries, and all of their respective predecessors or Affiliates, including without limitation any such matter arising under any Environmental, Health, and Safety Requirements and including, without limita-tion, any arising under the Comprehensive Environmental Response, Compensa-tion, and Liability Act ("CERCLA"), any analogous state law, or the common law. The Buyer hereby unconditionally agrees to indemnify, defend, and hold harmless the Seller from any and all liability, loss, cost or expense with respect to any such environmental, health, or safety matter (including any arising under any Environmental, Health, and Safety Requirements and including, without limita-tion, CERCLA, any analogous state law, or the common law).]

ALTERNATIVE B (LIMITED INDEMNIFICATION): Without limiting the gen-erality of (f), above, the Buyer understands and agrees that its right to indemnifica-tion under §8(b) for breach of the representations and warranties contained in §4(q) hereof shall constitute its sole and exclusive remedy against the Seller with respect to any environmental, health, or safety matter relating to the past, current or future facilities, properties or operations of the Target, its Subsidiaries, and all of their respective predecessors or Affiliates, including without limitation any such matter arising under any Environmental, Health, and Safety Requirements. Aside from such right to indemnification, the Buyer hereby waives any right, whether arising at law or in equity, to seek contribution, cost recovery, damages, or any other recourse or remedy from the Seller, and hereby releases the Seller from any claim, demand or liability, with respect to any such environmental, health, or safety matter (including without limitation any arising under any Envi-ronmental, Health, and Safety Requirements and including without limitation any arising under the Comprehensive Environmental Response, Compensation, and Liability Act ("CERCLA"), any analogous state law, or the common law. Except as set forth above, the Buyer hereby unconditionally agrees to indemnify, defend, and hold harmless the Seller from any and all liability, loss, cost or expense

---

Sample acquisition agreement 2002.3 (the *neutral* stock purchase agreement) states, as does (f) above, that the remedies available to the Parties under the Agreement are exclusive (i.e., that the Buyer has no other statutory, equitable, or common law remedies) and also sets forth a waiver of extra-contractual environmental remedies, but does not contain an environmental indemnification of the Seller by the Buyer of the sort set forth in §8(g) of this *pro-seller* stock purchase agreement.

Although not so stated in this *pro-seller* stock purchase agreement, the Seller could seek to have its own statutory, equitable, and common law remedies survive while the Buyer's analogous rights are explicitly negated, although this would be unusual.

[56] This provision (1) limits the Buyer's recourse against the Seller for environmental, health, or safety matters to the Buyer's right, if any, to indemnification for breach of the environmental, health, and safety representation, and (2) grants the Seller indemnification by the Buyer for environmental, health, and safety matters.

with respect to any such environmental, health, or safety matter (including without limitation any arising under any Environmental, Health, and Safety Requirements and including without limitation CERCLA, any analogous state law, and the common law).

9. Termination.

(a) *Termination of Agreement.*[57]   Certain of the Parties may terminate this Agreement as provided below:

(i) the Buyer and the Requisite Sellers may terminate this Agreement by mutual written consent at any time prior to the Closing;

(ii) the Buyer may terminate this Agreement by giving written notice to the Requisite Sellers at any time prior to the Closing in the event (A) any of the Sellers has within the then previous [10 business days] given the Buyer any notice pursuant to §5(e)(i) above and (B) the development that is the subject of the notice has had a material adverse effect upon the financial condition of the Target and its Subsidiaries taken as a whole;[58]

(iii) the Buyer may terminate this Agreement by giving written notice to the Requisite Sellers at any time prior to the Closing (A) in the event any of the Sellers has breached any material representation, warranty, or covenant contained in this Agreement (other than the representations and warranties in §4 above) in any material respect, the Buyer has notified the Requisite Sellers of the breach, and the breach has continued without cure for a period of [30 days] after the notice of breach or (B) if the Closing shall not have occurred on or before _____, 19____, by reason of the failure of any condition precedent under §7(a) hereof (unless the failure results primarily from the Buyer itself breaching any representation, warranty, or covenant contained in this Agreement); and

(iv) the Requisite Sellers may terminate this Agreement by giving written notice to the Buyer at any time prior to the Closing (A) in the event the Buyer has breached any material representation, warranty, or covenant contained in this Agreement in any material respect, any of the Sellers has notified the Buyer

---

[57] Sample acquisition agreement 2002.1 (the *pro-buyer* stock purchase agreement) contains a provision giving the Buyer a right to terminate the agreement for a limited period after signing if the Buyer is not [reasonably] satisfied with the results of its continuing business, legal, and accounting due diligence concerning the Target and its Subsidiaries.

[58] Section 5(e)(i) permits the Sellers to notify the Buyer of any development prior to the Closing that causes a breach of their representations and warranties in §4 concerning the Target and its Subsidiaries. If the development gives the Buyer any right to terminate this Agreement pursuant to §9(a)(ii), the Buyer must exercise its termination right within [10 business days] after the notice. Unless the Buyer has such a termination right and exercises it within that period, the notice will be deemed to have cured any such breach of the representations and warranties that otherwise would have existed.

of the breach, and the breach has continued without cure for a period of [30 days] after the notice of breach or (B) if the Closing shall not have occurred on or before _____, 19_____, by reason of the failure of any condition precedent under §7(b) hereof (unless the failure results primarily from any of the Sellers themselves breaching any representation, warranty, or covenant contained in this Agreement).

(b) *Effect of Termination.* If any Party terminates this Agreement pursuant to §9(a) above, all rights and obligations of the Parties hereunder shall terminate without any liability of any Party to any other Party (except for any liability of any Party then in breach); *provided, however,* that the confidentiality provisions contained in §5(d) above shall survive termination.

10. *Miscellaneous.*[59]

(a) *Nature of Certain Obligations.*

   (i) The covenants of each of the Sellers in §2(a) above concerning the sale of his or its Target Shares to the Buyer and the representations and warranties of each of the Sellers in §3(a) above concerning the transaction are several obligations. This means that the particular Seller making the representation, warranty, or covenant will be solely responsible to the extent provided in §8 above for any Adverse Consequences the Buyer may suffer as a result of any breach thereof.

   (ii) The remainder of the representations, warranties, and covenants in this Agreement are joint obligations. This means that each Seller will be responsible to the extent provided in §8 above for his or its Allocable Portion of any Adverse Consequences the Buyer may suffer as a result of any breach thereof.[60]

(b) *Press Releases and Public Announcements.* No Party shall issue any press release or make any public announcement relating to the subject matter of this Agreement [prior to the Closing] without the prior written approval of the Buyer and the Requisite Sellers; *provided, however,* that any Party may make any public

---

[59] The Buyer may seek to add provisions whereby the Parties agree to specific performance, agree to service of process on an agent, and submit to the [exclusive] jurisdiction of the state and federal courts in a particular city. Sample acquisition agreement 2002.1 (the *pro-buyer* stock purchase agreement) contains examples of these provisions.

   The Parties may want to add a provision calling for optional or mandatory arbitration with respect to all or certain issues.

[60] The Buyer may seek to have the obligations of the Sellers as a group be "joint and several" rather than only joint. That would be defined in such a way that each Seller would be responsible for *all* of the Buyer's Adverse Consequences (instead of only for his or its Allocable Portion) if the Sellers as a group failed to perform their obligations. This would protect the Buyer from having to proceed against all of the Sellers (some of whom may be insolvent or not subject to service of process) in order to collect all of what is owing it. Sample acquisition agreement 2002.1 (the *pro-buyer* stock purchase agreement) contains provisions more favorable to the Buyer in this regard.

disclosure it believes in good faith is required by applicable law or any listing or trading agreement concerning its publicly-traded securities (in which case the disclosing Party will use its [reasonable] best efforts to advise the other Parties prior to making the disclosure).

(c) *No Third-Party Beneficiaries.* This Agreement shall not confer any rights or remedies upon any Person other than the Parties and their respective successors and permitted assigns.

(d) *Entire Agreement.* [This Agreement (including the documents referred to herein) constitutes the entire agreement among the Parties and supersedes any prior understandings, agreements, or representations by or among the Parties, written or oral, to the extent they have related in any way to the subject matter hereof.]

(e) *Succession and Assignment.* This Agreement shall be binding upon and inure to the benefit of the Parties named herein and their respective successors and permitted assigns. No Party may assign either this Agreement or any of his or its rights, interests, or obligations hereunder without the prior written approval of the Buyer and the Requisite Sellers [; *provided, however,* that the Buyer may (i) assign any or all of its rights and interests hereunder to one or more of its Affiliates and (ii) designate one or more of its Affiliates to perform its obligations hereunder (in any or all of which cases the Buyer nonetheless shall remain responsible for the performance of all of its obligations hereunder)].

(f) *Counterparts.* This Agreement may be executed in one or more counterparts, each of which shall be deemed an original but all of which together will constitute one and the same instrument.

(g) *Headings.* The section headings contained in this Agreement are inserted for convenience only and shall not affect in any way the meaning or interpretation of this Agreement.

(h) *Notices.*[61] All notices, requests, demands, claims, and other communications hereunder will be in writing. Any notice, request, demand, claim, or other communication hereunder shall be deemed duly given if (and then two business days after) it is sent by registered or certified mail, return receipt requested, postage prepaid, and addressed to the intended recipient as set forth below:

If to the Sellers: *Copy to:*

If to the Buyer: *Copy to:*

---

[61] The parties may want to add provisions designating a nominee to act on behalf of the Sellers for purposes of receiving notice, agreeing to modifications and amendments, and taking action.

Any Party may send any notice, request, demand, claim, or other communication hereunder to the intended recipient at the address set forth above using any other means (including personal delivery, expedited courier, messenger service, telecopy, telex, ordinary mail, or electronic mail), but no such notice, request, demand, claim, or other communication shall be deemed to have been duly given unless and until it actually is received by the intended recipient. Any Party may change the address to which notices, requests, demands, claims, and other communications hereunder are to be delivered by giving the other Parties notice in the manner herein set forth.

(i) *Governing Law. This Agreement shall be governed by and construed in accordance with the domestic laws of the State of* _____ *without giving effect to any choice or conflict of law provision or rule (whether of the State of* _____ *or any other jurisdiction) that would cause the application of the laws of any jurisdiction other than the State of* _____.

(j) *Amendments and Waivers.* No amendment of any provision of this Agreement shall be valid unless the same shall be in writing and signed by the Buyer and the Requisite Sellers. No waiver by any Party of any default, misrepresentation, or breach of warranty or covenant hereunder, whether intentional or not, shall be deemed to extend to any prior or subsequent default, misrepresentation, or breach of warranty or covenant hereunder or affect in any way any rights arising by virtue of any prior or subsequent such occurrence.

(k) *Severability.* Any term or provision of this Agreement that is invalid or unenforceable in any situation in any jurisdiction shall not affect the validity or enforceability of the remaining terms and provisions hereof or the validity or enforceability of the offending term or provision in any other situation or in any other jurisdiction.

(l) *Expenses.* Each of the Buyer, the Target, and the Target's Subsidiaries will bear its own costs and expenses (including legal fees and expenses) incurred in connection with this Agreement and the transactions contemplated hereby. The Target will also bear all of the Sellers' costs and expenses (including all of their legal fees and expenses) incurred in connection with this Agreement and the transactions contemplated hereby (other than any Income Tax on any gain resulting from the sale of the Target Shares hereunder).[62]

---

[62] This Agreement makes the Target responsible for the transactional costs and expenses of the Target, its Subsidiaries, *and the Sellers.* This means that the buyer will bear these costs and expenses if it consummates the stock purchase. Note, however, that allocating transactional costs and expenses to the Target may reduce the amount of cash the Sellers will be entitled to receive at the Closing pursuant to §2(c). Furthermore, any assumption of the Sellers' costs and expenses by the Target may be deemed a dividend for federal income tax purposes.

The Sellers may seek to make the Buyer *directly* responsible for these costs and expenses. In the unlikely event the Buyer agreed to this arrangement, it would be responsible for the costs and expenses of the Target, its Subsidiaries, and the Sellers whether or not it acquired the Target Shares.

The Buyer may seek to make the Sellers responsible for their own costs and expenses. Sample acquisition agreement 2002.1 (the *pro-buyer* stock purchase agreement) contains provisions more favorable to the Buyers in this regard.

(m) *Construction.* [The Parties have participated jointly in the negotiation and drafting of this Agreement. In the event an ambiguity or question of intent or interpretation arises, this Agreement shall be construed as if drafted jointly by the Parties and no presumption or burden of proof shall arise favoring or disfavoring any Party by virtue of the authorship of any of the provisions of this Agreement.] Any reference to any federal, state, local, or foreign statute or law shall be deemed also to refer to all rules and regulations promulgated thereunder, unless the context requires otherwise. The word "including" shall mean including without limitation.[63]

(n) *Incorporation of Exhibits, Annexes, and Schedules.* The Exhibits, Annexes, and Schedules identified in this Agreement are incorporated herein by reference and made a part hereof.

* * * * *

IN WITNESS WHEREOF, the Parties hereto have executed this Agreement on [as of] the date first above written.

[BUYER]

By: _____

Title: _____

[SELLER # 1 (an entity)]

By: _____

Title: _____

[SELLER # 2 (an entity)]

By: _____

Title: _____

_____

[SELLER #3 (an individual)]

The Parties may settle on a compromise allocation of responsibility (such as sharing the costs and expenses in a predetermined ratio or making one Party responsible for the costs and expenses up to a specified aggregate ceiling and the other Party responsible for any excess).

[63] Sample acquisition agreement 2002.1 (the *pro-buyer* stock purchase agreement) contains additional language construing the representations, warranties, and covenants herein in a manner more favorable to the Buyer.

¶2002.3 *Neutral Stock Purchase*

Sample acquisition agreement 2002.3 (*neutral* stock purchase) is intended to strike a reasonable balance between the conflicting interests of P and T in such areas as (i) the extent to which T will retain its cash at the time of the closing, (ii) the extent to which the sellers (i.e., T's old shareholders) will bear the burden of T's liabilities and obligations after the closing, (iii) the extent to which P will have conditions to its obligation to close, (iv) the extent to which the sellers will be required to give representations and warranties, and (v) the extent to which the sellers will be required to indemnify P against breaches of those representations and warranties.

Sample acquisition agreement 2002.3 prohibits the sellers (i.e., T's shareholders) from causing T to distribute any of its cash to them (e.g., as a dividend or in a repurchase or redemption) at or prior to the closing. This means that T will retain its cash at the time of the closing.

Sample acquisition agreement 2002.3 contains fairly extensive representations and warranties from the sellers (i.e., T's shareholders) concerning (i) T's historical financial statements, (ii) intervening material adverse changes in T's business, (iii) litigation and material undisclosed liabilities, (iv) tax matters, (v) pension and welfare benefit plans, (vi) compliance with federal, state, local, and foreign laws, (vii) environmental matters, and (viii) product liability and warranties.

The sellers (i.e., T's shareholders) accordingly will be in breach of their representations and warranties and required to indemnify P if T has any material undisclosed liabilities, i.e., liabilities *other than* (i) those shown on the last T balance sheet reviewed by P before signing the contract, (ii) those incurred in the ordinary course of business thereafter (but not including claims and lawsuits), and (iii) those listed on a disclosure schedule. This would generally protect P against such material undisclosed T liabilities as environmental clean up, employment discrimination, antitrust violations, product liability, product warranty, tax deficiencies, and other claims and lawsuits.

Sample acquisition agreement 2002.3 also contains fairly extensive representations and warranties from the sellers (i.e., T's shareholders) concerning (i) authorization with respect to the transaction, (ii) title to the stock being sold (and title to T's underlying assets), (iii) required governmental and third party consents (and noncontravention generally), (iv) organization and capitalization, (v) adequacy and condition of T's tangible assets, (vi) real estate matters, (vii) intellectual property matters, (viii) leases, licenses, and contracts, (ix) inventory and accounts receivable, (x) insurance, (xi) brokerage fees, and (xii) material misstatements and omissions.

The sellers' representations and warranties are, however, qualified with relatively frequent references to knowledge (defined as the actual knowledge of T's shareholders, directors, and officers after reasonable investigation) and materiality.

Sample acquisition agreement 2002.3 provides that the representations and warranties with respect to the transaction itself and with respect to taxes will survive indefinitely, that the environmental representations and warranties will survive for five years, that the other representations and warranties will survive for two years, and that there will be a deductible and a ceiling with respect to indemnification against breaches of any representations and warranties that do not concern the transaction itself. The sellers' indemnification obligation is joint and several.

P *does not* have any right to recoup its losses against the P notes in lieu of seeking indemnification from the sellers (i.e., T's shareholders).

P's obligation to close is subject to several conditions such as (i) compliance with the sellers' representations, warranties, and covenants, (ii) absence of a material adverse change, (iii) absence of litigation affecting the transaction, (iv) receipt of governmental approvals, (v) delivery of title insurance, surveys, and material third party consents, (vi) delivery of any side agreements, and (vii) delivery of an opinion of the sellers' legal counsel.

P *does not* have any closing condition concerning its ability to secure financing for the transaction *or* any right to terminate the purchase agreement after signing if it is not satisfied with the results of its continuing business, legal, and accounting due diligence review.

It is important to note that some of the provisions in sample acquisition agreement 2002.3 are neutral only in the context of the overall agreement. In part, this is due to the interplay between the sellers' representations and warranties (which are fairly extensive, but qualified with references to knowledge and materiality) on the one hand and their indemnification obligations (which are subject to various deductibles, ceilings, and survival periods) on the other. Accordingly, it is not always possible to remove a provision from sample acquisition agreement 2002.3 for use in another agreement and have the provision remain neutral.

Finally, the choice of neutral provisions for sample acquisition agreement 2002.3 was necessarily subjective. Thus, in any particular transaction, it may be necessary to modify the agreement so that it strikes a different balance between the interests of P and T.

There are a number of other important differences among sample acquisition agreement 2002.1 (*pro-buyer* stock purchase), sample acquisition agreement 2002.2 (*pro-seller* stock purchase), and sample acquisition agreement 2002.3 (*neutral* stock purchase). Each of these sample acquisition agreements contains extensive footnotes with cross-references pointing out the differences.

STOCK PURCHASE AGREEMENT[1]

AMONG

_____

AND

_____, _____,

AND_____

_____, 19_____

¶2002.3 [1] The Buyer may choose to make a regular Code §338 election on a timely basis after an acquisition structured as a taxable purchase of Target Shares. *See* ¶¶107.1, 204, 205, 403, and 405.

If the Buyer makes a timely regular Code §338 election, the Target in effect becomes "New Target" immediately following the acquisition date: the Target's basis in its assets is stepped up (or down) so that the Target's aggregate asset basis equals the purchase price (plus the Target's liabilities, including tax liabilities generated in the transaction and inherited by New Target, and the Buyer's expenses of the acquisition), and "Old Target's" corporate attributes—e.g., E&P and tax accounting methods—are expunged. Concomitantly, effective upon the close of the acquisition date, "Old Target" is taxed as if it had sold its assets, i.e., the Target is taxed on its full gain or loss inherent in its tangible and intangible assets (including goodwill) with the Target's gain or loss on each asset being ordinary or capital in character, depending on the nature of each asset treated as sold.

However, even with a regular Code §338 election, the Target's selling shareholders are nevertheless taxed on the stock sale, resulting in double tax, i.e., Target is taxed on the deemed asset sale and the selling shareholders are taxed on the stock sale. *See* ¶205.

If the Buyer intends to make a Code §338 election, it may well be desirable to add language to this Agreement (and to have the board of directors of the Target adopt resolutions) stating that the New Target "expressly assumes" certain enumerated liabilities (and all other unenumerated liabilities) of the Target which have not yet matured into tax deductions. *See* ¶304 and the related footnote to ¶2001.2.1.1(1).

If (1) Target is a member of a consolidated group or (2) the acquisition of Target is consummated on or after 1/20/94 (or earlier if a retroactive election is made) and Target is a member of an affiliated (but not consolidated) group or (3) the acquisition of Target is consummated on or after 1/20/94 (or earlier if a retroactive election is made) and Target is an S corporation, the parties may have the ability to make a Code §338(h)(10) election, in which case all parties (including the selling shareholders) are treated for tax purposes as if Buyer purchased Target's assets. Hence, with a Code §338(h)(10) election (as distinguished from a regular Code §338 election), there is no double tax on the transaction, i.e., Target is treated as selling assets but Target's shareholders are not treated as selling Target's stock, and the deemed liquidation of Target will generally not produce a second tax because of Code §332 in the consolidated or affiliated subsidiary situation or because of Subchapter S pass-through rules in the SCo situation. *See* ¶¶206.1.1, 206.2, 206.3.3, and 1109.3.

A Code §338(h)(10) election must be made jointly by Buyer and Seller(s). Hence, if either party desires such an election, it should add language to this Agreement stating that both parties agree to make such election. See ¶2002.4 for a number of contractual provisions the parties may desire to add to the acquisition agreement when Target is a subsidiary of a consolidated group.

See §9 of this Agreement for sample language obligating each of the Sellers, if so directed by Buyer, to join in making a Code §338(h)(10) election.

A purchase of stock in which the consideration is primarily cash and notes is generally treated for accounting purposes as a purchase rather than as a pooling of interests. *See* ¶1503.

TABLE OF CONTENTS

Some LBO structures prejudice the Target's creditors and hence might permit payments, transfers, liens, and obligations arising out of the LBO to be attacked under fraudulent conveyance law. *See* ¶1506.

Exhibit A—Form of Buyer Note
Exhibit B—Historical Financial Statements
Exhibit C—Forms of Side Agreements
Exhibit D—Form of Opinion of Counsel to the Sellers
Exhibit E—Form of Opinion of Counsel to the Buyer
Annex I—Exceptions to the Sellers' Representations and Warranties Concerning the Transaction
Annex II—Exceptions to the Buyer's Representations and Warranties Concerning the Transaction
Disclosure Schedule—Exceptions to Representations and Warranties Concerning the Target and Its Subsidiaries

[EXHIBITS, ANNEXES, AND SCHEDULES HAVE BEEN OMITTED FROM THIS SAMPLE FORM 2002.3]

Agreement entered into on [as of] _____, 19____, by and among _____, a _____ corporation (the *"Buyer"*), and _____, and _____ (collectively the *"Sellers"*). The Buyer and the Sellers are referred to collectively herein as the *"Parties."*[2]

The Sellers in the aggregate own all of the outstanding capital stock of _____, a _____ corporation (the *"Target"*).

This Agreement contemplates a transaction in which the Buyer will purchase from the Sellers, and the Sellers will sell to the Buyer, all of the outstanding capital stock of the Target in return for cash and the Buyer Notes.[3]

Now, therefore, in consideration of the premises and the mutual promises herein made, and in consideration of the representations, warranties, and covenants herein contained, the Parties agree as follows.

---

[2] If the Target has so many shareholders that it would be unwieldy for all of them to become parties to this Agreement (or if the Target has only a few shareholders but some minority shareholders decline to participate), the Parties may wish to use sample acquisition agreement 2005 (reverse subsidiary merger of the Buyer's transitory subsidiary into the Target for cash and notes) rather than sample acquisition agreement 2002. A reverse subsidiary merger will generally be treated as a sale of stock for federal income tax purposes. *See* ¶202.

[3] After the Buyer purchases the Target Shares, the Target will become a subsidiary of the Buyer (assuming the Buyer is a corporation). The Target will generally retain all of its assets and rights and remain responsible for all of its liabilities and obligations. Thus it is generally not necessary to prepare

1. *Definitions.*

"Accredited Investor" has the meaning set forth in Regulation D promulgated under the Securities Act.

"Adverse Consequences" means all actions, suits, proceedings, hearings, investigations, charges, complaints, claims, demands, injunctions, judgments, orders, decrees, rulings, damages, dues, penalties, fines, costs, [reasonable amounts paid in settlement], liabilities, obligations, taxes, liens, losses, expenses, and fees, including court costs and [reasonable] attorneys' fees and expenses.

"Affiliate" has the meaning set forth in Rule 12b-2 of the regulations promulgated under the Securities Exchange Act.

"Affiliated Group" means any affiliated group within the meaning of Code §1504(a) [or any similar group defined under a similar provision of state, local, or foreign law].

"Applicable Rate" means the corporate base rate of interest publicly announced from time to time by [FINANCIAL INSTITUTION] [plus/minus ____ % per annum].

"Basis" means any past or present fact, situation, circumstance, status, condition, activity, practice, plan, occurrence, event, incident, action, failure to act, or transaction that forms or could form the basis for any specified consequence.

"Buyer" has the meaning set forth in the preface above.

"Buyer Note" has the meaning set forth in §2(b) below.

"Closing" has the meaning set forth in §2(c) below.

"Closing Date" has the meaning set forth in §2(c) below.

"COBRA" means the requirements of Part 6 of Subtitle B of Title I of ERISA and Code §4980B and of any similar state law.

"Code" means the Internal Revenue Code of 1986, as amended.

"Confidential Information" means any information concerning the businesses and affairs of the Target and its Subsidiaries that is not already generally available to the public.

---

asset transfer documents or liability assumption documents in a stock purchase, as it is in a purchase of assets.

"Controlled Group" has the meaning set forth in Code §1563.

"Disclosure Schedule" has the meaning set forth in §4 below.

"Employee Benefit Plan" means any "employee benefit plan" (as such term is defined in ERISA §3(3)) and any other [material] employee benefit plan, program or arrangement of any kind.

"Employee Pension Benefit Plan" has the meaning set forth in ERISA §3(2).

"Employee Welfare Benefit Plan" has the meaning set forth in ERISA §3(1).

"Environmental, Health, and Safety Requirements"[4] shall mean all federal, state, local and foreign statutes, regulations, ordinances and similar provisions having the force or effect of law, all judicial and administrative orders and determinations, and all common law concerning public health and safety, worker health and safety, and pollution or protection of the environment, including without limitation all those relating to the presence, use, production, generation, handling, transportation, treatment, storage, disposal, distribution, labeling, testing, processing, discharge, release, threatened release, control, or cleanup of any hazardous materials, substances or wastes, chemical substances or mixtures, pesticides, pollutants, contaminants, toxic chemicals, petroleum products or byproducts, asbestos, polychlorinated biphenyls, noise or radiation.

"ERISA" means the Employee Retirement Income Security Act of 1974, as amended.

"ERISA Affiliate" means each entity which is treated as a single employer with the Target for purposes of Code §414.

"Fiduciary" has the meaning set forth in ERISA §3(21).

"Financial Statement" has the meaning set forth in §4(g) below.

"GAAP" means United States generally accepted accounting principles as in effect from time to time.

"Hart-Scott-Rodino Act" means the Hart-Scott-Rodino Antitrust Improvements Act of 1976, as amended.

---

[4]Sample acquisition agreement 2002.1 (the *pro-buyer* stock purchase agreement) explicitly extends this definition to include legal requirements enacted and in effect prior to, on, or after the Closing Date and also includes within this definition contractual obligations.

Sample acquisition agreement 2002.2 (the *pro-seller* stock purchase agreement) does not include either contractual obligations or common law in this definition and explicitly limits this definition to laws as enacted and in effect on or prior to the Closing Date.

"Income Tax" means any federal, state, local, or foreign income tax, including any interest, penalty, or addition thereto, whether disputed or not.[5]

"Income Tax Return" means any return, declaration, report, claim for refund, or information return or statement relating to Income Taxes, including any schedule or attachment thereto, and including any amendment thereof.

"Indemnified Party" has the meaning set forth in §8(d) below.

"Indemnifying Party" has the meaning set forth in §8(d) below.

"Intellectual Property" means (a) all inventions (whether patentable or unpatentable and whether or not reduced to practice), all improvements thereto, and all patents, patent applications, and patent disclosures, together with all reissuances, continuations, continuations-in-part, revisions, extensions, and reexaminations thereof, (b) all trademarks, service marks, trade dress, logos, trade names, and corporate names, together with all translations, adaptations, derivations, and combinations thereof and including all goodwill associated therewith, and all applications, registrations, and renewals in connection therewith, (c) all copyrightable works, all copyrights, and all applications, registrations, and renewals in connection therewith, (d) all mask works and all applications, registrations, and renewals in connection therewith, (e) all trade secrets and confidential business information (including ideas, research and development, know-how, formulas, compositions, manufacturing and production processes and techniques, technical data, designs, drawings, specifications, customer and supplier lists, pricing and cost information, and business and marketing plans and proposals), (f) all computer software (including data and related documentation), (g) all other proprietary rights, and (h) all copies and tangible embodiments thereof (in whatever form or medium).

"Knowledge" means actual knowledge after reasonable investigation.[6]

"Most Recent Balance Sheet" means the balance sheet contained within the Most Recent Financial Statements.

"Most Recent Financial Statements" has the meaning set forth in §4(g) below.

---

[5] This Agreement, like sample acquisition agreement 2002.2 (the *pro-seller* stock purchase agreement), uses the term "Income Tax," which is defined narrowly to include only federal, state, local, and foreign income taxes. Sample acquisition agreement 2002.1 (the *pro-buyer* stock purchase agreement), on the other hand, uses the term "Tax," which is defined broadly to include taxes of all descriptions.

[6] This Agreement, like sample acquisition agreement 2002.1 (the *pro-buyer* stock purchase agreement), defines "Knowledge" as actual knowledge after reasonable investigation. Sample acquisition agreement 2002.2 (the *pro-seller* stock purchase agreement), on the other hand, defines "Knowledge" as actual knowledge without independent investigation.

"Most Recent Fiscal Month End" has the meaning set forth in §4(g) below.

"Most Recent Fiscal Year End" has the meaning set forth in §4(g) below.

"Multiemployer Plan" has the meaning set forth in ERISA §3(37).

"Ordinary Course of Business" means the ordinary course of business consistent with past custom and practice (including with respect to quantity and frequency).

"Party" has the meaning set forth in the preface above.

"PBGC" means the Pension Benefit Guaranty Corporation.

"Person" means an individual, a partnership, a corporation, an association, a joint stock company, a trust, a joint venture, an unincorporated organization, or a governmental entity (or any department, agency, or political subdivision thereof).

"Prohibited Transaction" has the meaning set forth in ERISA §406 and Code §4975.

"Purchase Price" has the meaning set forth in §2(b) below.

"Reportable Event" has the meaning set forth in ERISA §4043.

"Requisite Sellers" means Sellers holding [a majority] in interest of the Target Shares as set forth in §4(b) of the Disclosure Schedule.[7]

"Securities Act" means the Securities Act of 1933, as amended.

"Securities Exchange Act" means the Securities Exchange Act of 1934, as amended.

"Security Interest" means any mortgage, pledge, lien, encumbrance, charge, or other security interest, other than (a) mechanic's, materialmen's, and similar liens, (b) liens for taxes not yet due and payable [or for taxes that the taxpayer is contesting in good faith through appropriate proceedings], (c) purchase money liens and liens securing rental payments under capital lease arrangements, and (d) other liens arising in the Ordinary Course of Business and not incurred in connection with the borrowing of money.

"Seller" has the meaning set forth in the preface above.

---

[7] It may be necessary to revise this definition if the Target has more than one class of capital stock.

"Subsidiary" means any corporation with respect to which a specified Person (or a Subsidiary thereof) owns a majority of the common stock or has the power to vote or direct the voting of sufficient securities to elect a majority of the directors.[8]

"Survey" has the meaning set forth in §5(i) below.

"Target" has the meaning set forth in the preface above.

"Target Share" means any share of the Common Stock, par value $_____ per share, of the Target.[9]

"Third Party Claim" has the meaning set forth in 8(d) below.

2. *Purchase and Sale of Target Shares.*[10]

(a) *Basic Transaction.* On and subject to the terms and conditions of this Agreement, the Buyer agrees to purchase from each of the Sellers, and each of the Sellers agrees to sell to the Buyer, all of his or its Target Shares for the consideration specified below in this §2.

(b) *Purchase Price.*[11] The Buyer agrees to pay to the Sellers at the Closing $_____ (the *"Purchase Price"*) by delivery of (i) its promissory notes (the *"Buyer Notes"*) in the form of Exhibit A attached hereto in the aggregate principal amount of $_____ and (ii) cash for the balance of the Purchase Price payable by wire transfer or delivery of other immediately available funds. The Purchase Price shall be allocated among the Sellers in proportion to their respective holdings of Target Shares as set forth in §4(b) of the Disclosure Schedule.[12]

---

[8] It may be necessary to revise this definition if, for example, the Target has subsidiary *partnerships.*

[9] It may be necessary to revise this definition if the Target has additional classes of capital stock.

[10] Sample acquisition agreement 2002.2 (the *pro-seller* stock purchase agreement) contains a provision allowing the Sellers to cause the Target and its Subsidiaries to distribute their consolidated cash (net of unpaid taxes) to the Sellers at the closing. *See* §§2(c), 4(h), and 5(c) of sample acquisition agreement 2002.2. This Agreement, like sample acquisition agreement 2002.1 (the *pro-buyer* stock purchase agreement), lacks a comparable provision and indeed prohibits the Sellers from causing any such distribution. *See* §§4(h)(xi) and 5(c).

[11] The Sellers may seek to have the Buyer make an earnest money deposit upon execution of this Agreement. If the transaction were thereafter completed, the deposit would be applied to the Purchase Price. If the transaction were thereafter aborted, the deposit would be refunded to the Buyer or paid to the Sellers as liquidated damages depending on the terms of this Agreement and the reasons for the termination.

[12] Sample acquisition agreement 2002.5 contains additional provisions for use where there is to be a post-Closing Purchase Price adjustment based on the consolidated net book value for the Target and its Subsidiaries as of the Closing. That sample acquisition agreement can be adapted for other post-Closing Purchase Price adjustments (such as a comparison of consolidated working capital with consolidated liabilities as of the Closing *or* a contingent earnout based on consolidated earnings for a specified period after the Closing).

(c) *The Closing.* The closing of the transactions contemplated by this Agreement (the *"Closing"*) shall take place at the offices of _____ in, _____ , _____, commencing at 9:00 a.m. local time on the [second] business day following the satisfaction or waiver of all conditions to the obligations of the Parties to consummate the transactions contemplated hereby (other than conditions with respect to actions the respective Parties will take at the Closing itself) or such other date as the Buyer and the Requisite Sellers may mutually determine (the *"Closing Date"*); provided, however, that the Closing Date shall be no earlier than _____, 19_____.[13]

(d) *Deliveries at the Closing.* At the Closing, (i) the Sellers will deliver to the Buyer the various certificates, instruments, and documents referred to in §7(a) below, (ii) the Buyer will deliver to the Sellers the various certificates, instruments, and documents referred to in §7(b) below, (iii) each of the Sellers will deliver to the Buyer stock certificates representing all of his or its Target Shares, endorsed in blank or accompanied by duly executed assignment documents, and (iv) the Buyer will deliver to each of the Sellers the consideration specified in §2(b) above.

3. *Representations and Warranties Concerning the Transaction.*

(a) *Representations and Warranties of the Sellers.* Each of the Sellers represents and warrants to the Buyer that the statements contained in this §3(a) are correct and complete as of the date of this Agreement and will be correct and complete as of the Closing Date (as though made then and as though the Closing Date were substituted for the date of this Agreement throughout this §3(a)) with respect to himself or itself, except as set forth in Annex I attached hereto.

(i) *Organization of Certain Sellers.* If the Seller is a corporation, the Seller is duly organized, validly existing, and in good standing under the laws of the jurisdiction of its incorporation.[14]

(ii) *Authorization of Transaction.* The Seller has full power and authority (including, if the Seller is a corporation, full corporate power and authority) to execute and deliver this Agreement and to perform his or its obligations hereunder. This Agreement constitutes the valid and legally binding obligation of the Seller, enforceable in accordance with its terms and conditions. The Seller need not give any notice to, make any filing with, or obtain any authorization, consent, or approval of any government or governmental agency in order to consummate the transactions contemplated by this Agreement.

---

[13] The Parties should determine whether the Sellers or the Buyer will owe any stock transfer or similar tax on the transfer of the Target Shares by reason of the chosen Closing location.

[14] Several representations and warranties in §3(a) concern Sellers that are corporations. If any Sellers are partnerships, trusts, business associations, estates, or guardians, the Buyer may seek to add analogous provisions covering them.

(iii) *Noncontravention.* Neither the execution and the delivery of this Agreement, nor the consummation of the transactions contemplated hereby, will [(A)] violate any constitution, statute, regulation, rule, injunction, judgment, order, decree, ruling, charge, or other restriction of any government, governmental agency, or court to which the Seller is subject or, if the Seller is a corporation, any provision of its charter or bylaws [or (B) conflict with, result in a breach of, constitute a default under, result in the acceleration of, create in any party the right to accelerate, terminate, modify, or cancel, or require any notice under any agreement, contract, lease, license, instrument, or other arrangement to which the Seller is a party or by which he or it is bound or to which any of his or its assets is subject].

(iv) *Brokers' Fees.* The Seller has no liability or obligation to pay any fees or commissions to any broker, finder, or agent with respect to the transactions contemplated by this Agreement for which the Buyer could become liable or obligated.

(v) *Investment.* The Seller (A) understands that the Buyer Notes have not been, and will not be, registered under the Securities Act, or under any state securities laws, and are being offered and sold in reliance upon federal and state exemptions for transactions not involving any public offering, (B) is acquiring the Buyer Notes solely for his or its own account for investment purposes, and not with a view to the distribution thereof, (C) is a sophisticated investor with knowledge and experience in business and financial matters, (D) has received certain information concerning the Buyer and has had the opportunity to obtain additional information as desired in order to evaluate the merits and the risks inherent in holding the Buyer Notes, (E) is able to bear the economic risk and lack of liquidity inherent in holding the Buyer Notes, and (F) is an Accredited Investor for the reasons set forth on Annex I.[15]

(vi) *Target Shares.* The Seller holds of record and owns beneficially the number of Target Shares set forth next to his or its name in §4(b) of the Disclosure Schedule, free and clear of any restrictions on transfer (other than any restrictions under the Securities Act and state securities laws), taxes, Security Interests, options, warrants, purchase rights, contracts, commitments, equities, claims, and demands. The Seller is not a party to any option, warrant, purchase right, or other contract or commitment that could require the Seller to sell, transfer, or otherwise dispose of any capital stock of the Target (other than this Agreement). The Seller is not a party to any voting trust, proxy, or other agreement or understanding with respect to the voting of any capital stock of the Target.

---

[15] This provision contemplates that the Buyer will issue the Buyer Notes pursuant to the exemption from registration under the Securities Act contained in Regulation D. The Parties should determine whether this exemption is available in a particular transaction. If it is not, the Agreement must be modified as necessary to reflect the issuance of the Buyer Notes under a different exemption from securities registration or in an offering registered under the Securities Act.

(b) *Representations and Warranties of the Buyer.*[16] The Buyer represents and warrants to the Sellers that the statements contained in this §3(b) are correct and complete as of the date of this Agreement and will be correct and complete as of the Closing Date (as though made then and as though the Closing Date were substituted for the date of this Agreement throughout this §3(b)), except as set forth in Annex II attached hereto.

(i) *Organization of the Buyer.* The Buyer is a corporation duly organized, validly existing, and in good standing under the laws of the jurisdiction of its incorporation.

(ii) *Authorization of Transaction.* The Buyer has full power and authority (including full corporate power and authority) to execute and deliver this Agreement and to perform its obligations hereunder. This Agreement constitutes the valid and legally binding obligation of the Buyer, enforceable in accordance with its terms and conditions. The Buyer need not give any notice to, make any filing with, or obtain any authorization, consent, or approval of any government or governmental agency in order to consummate the transactions contemplated by this Agreement.

(iii) *Noncontravention.* Neither the execution and the delivery of this Agreement, nor the consummation of the transactions contemplated hereby, will [(A)] violate any constitution, statute, regulation, rule, injunction, judgment, order, decree, ruling, charge, or other restriction of any government, governmental agency, or court to which the Buyer is subject or any provision of its charter or bylaws [or (B) conflict with, result in a breach of, constitute a default under, result in the acceleration of, create in any party the right to accelerate, terminate, modify, or cancel, or require any notice under any agreement, contract, lease, license, instrument, or other arrangement to which the Buyer is a party or by which it is bound or to which any of its assets is subject].

(iv) *Brokers' Fees.* The Buyer has no liability or obligation to pay any fees or commissions to any broker, finder, or agent with respect to the transactions contemplated by this Agreement for which any Seller could become liable or obligated.

(v) *Investment.* The Buyer is not acquiring the Target Shares with a view to or for sale in connection with any distribution thereof within the meaning of the Securities Act.

---

[16] The Sellers may seek to obtain additional representations and warranties concerning the Buyer and its Subsidiaries (e.g., the typical representations and warranties contained in a loan agreement or an underwriting agreement) because the Buyer is issuing the Buyer Notes to the Sellers as part of the Purchase Price. Any such representations and warranties normally would survive the Closing and remain applicable for so long as the Buyer Notes remained outstanding.

4. *Representations and Warranties Concerning the Target and Its Subsidiaries.*[17] The Sellers represent and warrant to the Buyer that the statements contained in this §4 are correct and complete as of the date of this Agreement and will be correct and complete as of the Closing Date (as though made then and as though the Closing Date were substituted for the date of this Agreement throughout this §4), except as set forth in the disclosure schedule delivered by the Sellers to the Buyer on the date hereof and initialed by the Parties (the *"Disclosure Schedule"*).[18] The Disclosure Schedule will be arranged in paragraphs corresponding to the lettered and numbered paragraphs contained in this §4.[19]

(a) *Organization, Qualification, and Corporate Power.* Each of the Target and its Subsidiaries is a corporation duly organized, validly existing, and in good standing under the laws of the jurisdiction of its incorporation. Each of the Target and its Subsidiaries is duly authorized to conduct business and is in good standing under the laws of each jurisdiction where such qualification is required, except where the lack of such qualification would not have a material adverse effect on the business, financial condition, operations, results of operations, or future prospects of the Target and its Subsidiaries. Each of the Target and its Subsidiaries has full corporate power and authority to carry on the businesses in which it is engaged and to own and use the properties owned and used by it. §4(a) of the Disclosure Schedule lists the directors and officers of each of the Target and its Subsidiaries.

(b) *Capitalization.* The entire authorized capital stock of the Target consists of _____ Target Shares, of which _____ Target Shares are issued and outstanding and _____ Target Shares are held in treasury.[20]

---

[17] The Buyer will seek to have the Sellers make extensive representations and warranties concerning the Target and its Subsidiaries with only occasional qualifications as to knowledge and without any qualification as to materiality. See §4 of sample acquisition agreement 2002.1 (the *pro-buyer* stock purchase agreement).

The Sellers, on the other hand, will seek to give fewer representations and warranties concerning the Target and its Subsidiaries with frequent qualifications as to knowledge and materiality. See §4 of sample acquisition agreement 2002.2 (the *pro-seller* stock purchase agreement).

This Agreement, which is intended to favor neither the Buyer nor the Sellers, contains fairly extensive representations and warranties *and* relatively frequent qualifications as to knowledge and materiality.

[18] The Buyer will have a closing condition (*see* §7(a)(i)) and post-Closing indemnification rights (*see* §8(b)) with respect to certain misrepresentations and breaches of warranty. The Buyer will not, however, have a closing condition or post-Closing indemnification rights with respect to any adverse matter that the Sellers disclose in the Disclosure Schedule. This is because the disclosure will cure any misrepresentation or breach of warranty that might otherwise have existed. Thus, if the Sellers disclose an adverse matter in the Disclosure Schedule, the Buyer may seek (a) to add a specific closing condition requiring an acceptable resolution of the matter and/or (b) to obtain specific post-Closing indemnification against the matter.

[19] Sample acquisition agreement 2002.1 (the *pro-buyer* stock purchase agreement) contains additional provisions to the effect that the Sellers' disclosures will be ineffective unless they meet specified standards for particularity and detail. This Agreement, like sample acquisition agreement 2002.2 (the *pro-seller* stock purchase agreement), lacks such provisions.

[20] It may be necessary to revise this sentence if the Target has more than one class of capital stock. *See* the definition of "Target Shares" in §1.

All of the issued and outstanding Target Shares have been duly authorized, are validly issued, fully paid, and nonassessable, and are held of record by the respective Sellers as set forth in §4(b) of the Disclosure Schedule. There are no outstanding or authorized options, warrants, purchase rights, subscription rights, conversion rights, exchange rights, or other contracts or commitments that could require the Target to issue, sell, or otherwise cause to become outstanding any of its capital stock. There are no outstanding or authorized stock appreciation, phantom stock, profit participation, or similar rights with respect to the Target. There are no voting trusts, proxies, or other agreements or understandings with respect to the voting of the capital stock of the Target.

(c) *Noncontravention.* Neither the execution and the delivery of this Agreement, nor the consummation of the transactions contemplated hereby, will (i) violate any constitution, statute, regulation, rule, injunction, judgment, order, decree, ruling, charge, or other restriction of any government, governmental agency, or court to which any of the Target and its Subsidiaries is subject or any provision of the charter or bylaws of any of the Target and its Subsidiaries or (ii) conflict with, result in a breach of, constitute a default under, result in the acceleration of, create in any party the right to accelerate, terminate, modify, or cancel, or require any notice under any agreement, contract, lease, license, instrument, or other arrangement to which any of the Target and its Subsidiaries is a party or by which it is bound or to which any of its assets is subject (or result in the imposition of any Security Interest upon any of its assets), except where the violation, conflict, breach, default, acceleration, termination, modification, cancellation, failure to give notice, or Security Interest would not have a material adverse effect on the business, financial condition, operations, results of operations, or future prospects of the Target and its Subsidiaries or on the ability of the Parties to consummate the transactions contemplated by this Agreement. None of the Target and its Subsidiaries needs to give any notice to, make any filing with, or obtain any authorization, consent, or approval of any government or governmental agency in order for the Parties to consummate the transactions contemplated by this Agreement, except where the failure to give notice, to file, or to obtain any authorization, consent, or approval would not have a material adverse effect on the business, financial condition, operations, results of operations, or future prospects of the Target and its Subsidiaries or on the ability of the Parties to consummate the transactions contemplated by this Agreement.

(d) *Brokers' Fees.* None of the Target and its Subsidiaries has any liability or obligation to pay any fees or commissions to any broker, finder, or agent with respect to the transactions contemplated by this Agreement.

(e) *Title to Assets.* The Target and its Subsidiaries have good and marketable title to, or a valid leasehold interest in, the properties and assets used by them, located on their premises, or shown on the Most Recent Balance Sheet or acquired after the date thereof, free and clear of all Security Interests, except for properties and assets disposed of in the Ordinary Course of Business since the date of the Most Recent Balance Sheet.

(f) *Subsidiaries.* §4(f) of the Disclosure Schedule sets forth for each Subsidiary of the Target (i) its name and jurisdiction of incorporation, (ii) the number of shares of authorized capital stock of each class of its capital stock, (iii) the number of issued and outstanding shares of each class of its capital stock, the names of the holders thereof, and the number of shares held by each such holder, and (iv) the number of shares of its capital stock held in treasury. All of the issued and outstanding shares of capital stock of each Subsidiary of the Target have been duly authorized and are validly issued, fully paid, and nonassessable. One of the Target and its Subsidiaries holds of record and owns beneficially all of the outstanding shares of each Subsidiary of the Target, free and clear of any restrictions on transfer (other than restrictions under the Securities Act and state securities laws), taxes, Security Interests, options, warrants, purchase rights, contracts, commitments, equities, claims, and demands. There are no outstanding or authorized options, warrants, purchase rights, subscription rights, conversion rights, exchange rights, or other contracts or commitments that could require any of the Target and its Subsidiaries to sell, transfer, or otherwise dispose of any capital stock of any of its Subsidiaries or that could require any Subsidiary of the Target to issue, sell, or otherwise cause to become outstanding any of its own capital stock. There are no outstanding stock appreciation, phantom stock, profit participation, or similar rights with respect to any Subsidiary of the Target. There are no voting trusts, proxies, or other agreements or understandings with respect to the voting of any capital stock of any Subsidiary of the Target. None of the Target and its Subsidiaries controls directly or indirectly or has any direct or indirect equity participation in any corporation, partnership, trust, or other business association which is not a Subsidiary of the Target.

(g) *Financial Statements.* Attached hereto as Exhibit B are the following financial statements (collectively the *"Financial Statements"*): (i) audited consolidated balance sheets and statements of income, changes in stockholders' equity, and cash flow as of and for the fiscal years ended _____, 19____, _____, 19____, _____, 19____, _____, 19____, and _____, 19____, (the *"Most Recent Fiscal Year End"*) for the Target and its Subsidiaries; and (ii) unaudited consolidated balance sheets and statements of income, changes in stockholders' equity, and cash flow (the *"Most Recent Financial Statements"*) as of and for the months ended _____, 19____ (the *"Most Recent Fiscal Month End"*) for the Target and its Subsidiaries. The Financial Statements (including the notes thereto) have been prepared in accordance with GAAP applied on a consistent basis throughout the periods covered thereby and present fairly the financial condition of the Target and its Subsidiaries as of such dates and the results of operations of the Target and its Subsidiaries for such periods;[21] *provided, however,* that the

---

[21] This Agreement, like sample acquisition agreement 2002.2 (the *pro-seller* stock purchase agreement), contains a representation and warranty to the effect that the Financial Statements have been prepared in accordance with GAAP consistently applied and fairly present the financial condition

Most Recent Financial Statements are subject to normal year-end adjustments (which will not be material individually or in the aggregate) and lack footnotes and other presentation items.

(h) *Events Subsequent to Most Recent Fiscal Year End.* Since the Most Recent Fiscal Year End, there has not been any material adverse change in the business, financial condition, operations, results of operations, or future prospects of the Target and its Subsidiaries taken as a whole. Without limiting the generality of the foregoing, since that date:

(i) none of the Target and its Subsidiaries has sold, leased, transferred, or assigned any material assets, tangible or intangible, outside the Ordinary Course of Business;

(ii) none of the Target and its Subsidiaries has entered into any material agreement, contract, lease, or license outside the Ordinary Course of Business;

(iii) no party (including any of the Target and its Subsidiaries) has accelerated, terminated, made material modifications to, or canceled any material agreement, contract, lease, or license to which any of the Target and its Subsidiaries is a party or by which any of them is bound;

(iv) none of the Target and its Subsidiaries has imposed any Security Interest upon any of its assets, tangible or intangible;

(v) none of the Target and its Subsidiaries has made any material capital expenditures outside the Ordinary Course of Business;

(vi) none of the Target and its Subsidiaries has made any material capital investment in, or any material loan to, any other Person outside the Ordinary Course of Business;

(vii) the Target and its Subsidiaries have not created, incurred, assumed, or guaranteed more than $_____ in aggregate indebtedness for borrowed money and capitalized lease obligations;

(viii) none of the Target and its Subsidiaries has granted any license or sublicense of any material rights under or with respect to any Intellectual Property;

(ix) there has been no change made or authorized in the charter or bylaws of any of the Target and its Subsidiaries;

---

and the results of operations of the Target and its Subsidiaries. Sample acquisition agreement 2002.1 (the *pro-buyer* stock purchase agreement), on the other hand, contains additional representations and warranties to the effect that the Financial Statements are correct and complete and consistent with the books and records of the Target and its Subsidiaries.

(x) none of the Target and its Subsidiaries has issued, sold, or otherwise disposed of any of its capital stock, or granted any options, warrants, or other rights to purchase or obtain (including upon conversion, exchange, or exercise) any of its capital stock;

(xi) none of the Target and its Subsidiaries has declared, set aside, or paid any dividend or made any distribution with respect to its capital stock (whether in cash or in kind) or redeemed, purchased, or otherwise acquired any of its capital stock;

(xii) none of the Target and its Subsidiaries has experienced any material damage, destruction, or loss (whether or not covered by insurance) to its property;

(xiii) none of the Target and its Subsidiaries has made any loan to, or entered into any other transaction with, any of its directors, officers, and employees outside the Ordinary Course of Business;

(xiv) none of the Target and its Subsidiaries has entered into any employment contract or collective bargaining agreement, written or oral, or modified the terms of any existing such contract or agreement;

(xv) none of the Target and its Subsidiaries has granted any increase in the base compensation of any of its directors, officers, and employees outside the Ordinary Course of Business;

(xvi) none of the Target and its Subsidiaries has adopted, amended, modified, or terminated any bonus, profit-sharing, incentive, severance, or other plan, contract, or commitment for the benefit of any of its directors, officers, and employees (or taken any such action with respect to any other Employee Benefit Plan);

(xvii) none of the Target and its Subsidiaries has made any other material change in employment terms for any of its directors, officers, and employees outside the Ordinary Course of Business; and

(xviii) none of the Target and its Subsidiaries has committed to any of the foregoing.

(i) *Undisclosed Liabilities.* None of the Target and its Subsidiaries has any material liability (whether known or unknown, whether asserted or unasserted, whether absolute or contingent, whether accrued or unaccrued, whether liquidated or unliquidated, and whether due or to become due, including any liability for taxes), except for (i) liabilities set forth on the face of the Most Recent Balance

Sheet (rather than in any notes thereto) and (ii) liabilities which have arisen after the Most Recent Fiscal Month End in the Ordinary Course of Business.[22]

(j) *Legal Compliance.* Each of the Target and its Subsidiaries has complied with all applicable laws (including rules, regulations, codes, plans, injunctions, judgments, orders, decrees, rulings, and charges thereunder) of federal, state, local, and foreign governments (and all agencies thereof), and no action, suit, proceeding, hearing, investigation, charge, complaint, claim, demand, or notice has been filed or commenced against any of them alleging any failure so to comply, except where the failure to comply would not have a material adverse effect on the business, financial condition, operations, results of operations, or future prospects of the Target and its Subsidiaries.

(k) *Tax Matters.*[23]

(i) Each of the Target and its Subsidiaries has filed all Income Tax Returns that it was required to file. All such Income Tax Returns were correct and complete in all material respects. All Income Taxes owed by any of the Target and its Subsidiaries (whether or not shown on any Income Tax Return) have been paid.[24] None of the Target and its Subsidiaries currently is the beneficiary of any extension of time within which to file any Income Tax Return.

---

[22] This Agreement, like sample acquisition agreement 2002.1 (the *pro-buyer* stock purchase agreement), contains a representation and warranty regarding undisclosed liabilities. Sample acquisition agreement 2002.2 (the *pro-seller* stock purchase agreement), on the other hand, lacks such a provision.

[23] Unless the Target was a Subchapter S corporation or was filing a consolidated return with a parent corporation ("Bigco") before the stock purchase, it will generally remain liable for its federal income taxes through the Closing.

If the Target was a Subchapter S corporation before the stock purchase, it will generally not have paid federal income tax at the corporate level. Thus, the Sellers (i.e., the Target shareholders) will generally remain liable for federal income taxes through the Closing. When the Buyer (a corporation) purchases the Target Shares, however, the Target will cease to be an S Corporation. *See* Chapter 11.

If the Target was filing a consolidated return with Bigco before the stock purchase, the Target's liability for federal income taxes through the Closing will turn on the tax allocation agreement in effect between the Target and Bigco or on any specific provision in this Agreement. See sample acquisition agreement 2002.4 (sale of subsidiary out of consolidated group) for specific provisions in this regard.

If T has a NOL and will be included in P's consolidated group, P and T should consider making (on their consolidated federal income tax return for the year of the P-T acquisition) an irrevocable election to waive all or part of T's NOL to avoid a reduction in the outside basis of T's stock if and when T's NOL expires. See ¶1203.3.

[24] Sample acquisition agreement 2002.1 (the *pro-buyer* stock purchase agreement) contains a broad representation and warranty to the effect that each of the Target and its Subsidiaries has filed all tax returns that it was required to file, that all such tax returns were correct and complete in all respects, and that all taxes owed by any of the Target and its Subsidiaries (whether or not shown on any return) have been paid.

Sample acquisition agreement 2002.2 (the *pro-seller* stock purchase agreement), on the other hand, contains a narrow representation to the effect that each of the Target and its Subsidiaries has filed all *income* tax returns that it was required to file and has paid all *income* taxes *shown thereon as owing.*

(ii) There is no material dispute or claim concerning any Income Tax liability of any of the Target and its Subsidiaries either (A) claimed or raised by any authority in writing or (B) as to which any of the Sellers and the directors and officers of the Target and its Subsidiaries has Knowledge based upon personal contact with any agent of such authority.

(iii) §4(k) of the Disclosure Schedule lists all federal, state, local, and foreign Income Tax Returns filed with respect to any of the Target and its Subsidiaries for taxable periods ended on or after _____, 19_____, indicates those Income Tax Returns that have been audited, and indicates those Income Tax Returns that currently are the subject of audit. The Sellers have delivered to the Buyer correct and complete copies of all federal Income Tax Returns, examination reports, and statements of deficiencies assessed against,or agreed to by any of the Target and its Subsidiaries since_____, 19_____. None of the Target and its Subsidiaries has waived any statute of limitations in respect of Income Taxes or agreed to any extension of time with respect to an Income Tax assessment or deficiency.

(iv) None of the Target and its Subsidiaries has filed a consent under Code §341(f) concerning collapsible corporations. None of the Target and its Subsidiaries has made any material payments, is obligated to make any material payments, or is a party to any agreement that under certain circumstances could obligate it to make any material payments that will not be deductible under Code §280G. None of the Target and its Subsidiaries has been a United States real property holding corporation within the meaning of Code §897(c)(2) during the applicable period specified in Code §897(c)(1)(A)(ii). None of the Target and its Subsidiaries is a party to any tax allocation or sharing agreement. None of the Target and its Subsidiaries (A) has been a member of an Affiliated Group filing a consolidated federal Income Tax Return (other than a group the common parent of which was the Target) or (B) has any liability for the taxes of any Person (other than any of the Target and its Subsidiaries) under Reg. §1.1502-6 (or any similar provision of state, local, or foreign law), as a transferee or successor, by contract, or otherwise.[25]

This Agreement, intended to favor neither the Buyer nor the Sellers, contains a fairly broad representation and warranty to the effect that each of the Target and its Subsidiaries has filed all *income* tax returns that it was required to file, that all such *income* tax returns were correct and complete in all *material* respects, and that all *income* taxes owed by any of the Target and its Subsidiaries (whether or not shown on any return) have been paid.

[25] If the Target or a Subsidiary has been a member of an Affiliated Group filing a consolidated federal income tax return, such corporation (or its successor) will be jointly and severally liable under Reg. §1.1502-6 for certain tax liabilities incurred by such Affiliated Group for a tax year when such corporation was a member of such Affiliated Group for all or part of such tax year. *See* ¶210.

The Target or a Subsidiary may also be liable for the unpaid taxes of third parties under similar provisions of state, local, or foreign law, as a transferee or successor, by contract (e.g., a tax sharing agreement), or otherwise.

After the Buyer acquires the stock of the Target, the Target and its Subsidiaries will remain liable for any such unpaid Tax liabilities.

This Agreement, like sample acquisition agreement 2002.1 (the *pro-buyer* agreement), contains representations and warranties (as set forth above) and indemnification provisions (*see* §8(b)(iii))

(v) The unpaid Income Taxes of the Target and its Subsidiaries (A) did not, as of the Most Recent Fiscal Month End, exceed by any material amount the reserve for Income Tax liability (rather than any reserve for deferred taxes established to reflect timing differences between book and tax income) set forth on the face of the Most Recent Balance Sheet (rather than in any notes thereto) and (B) will not exceed by any material amount that reserve as adjusted for operations and transactions through the Closing Date in accordance with the past custom and practice of the Target and its Subsidiaries in filing their Income Tax Returns.

(l) *Real Property.*[26]

(i) §4(l)(i) of the Disclosure Schedule lists and describes briefly all real property that any of the Target and its Subsidiaries owns. With respect to each such parcel of owned real property:

(A) the identified owner has good and marketable title to the parcel of real property, free and clear of any Security Interest, easement, covenant, or other restriction, except for installments of special assessments not yet delinquent, recorded easements, covenants, and other restrictions, and utility easements, building restrictions, zoning restrictions, and other easements and restrictions existing generally with respect to properties of a similar character which do not affect materially and adversely the current use, occupancy, or value, or the marketability of title, of the property subject thereto;

(B) there are no pending or, to the Knowledge of any of the Sellers and the directors and officers of the Target and its Subsidiaries, threatened condemnation proceedings, lawsuits, or administrative actions relating to the property or other matters affecting materially and adversely the current use, occupancy, or value thereof;

(C) the legal description for the parcel contained in the deed thereof describes such parcel fully and adequately, the buildings and improvements are located within the boundary lines of the described parcels of land, are not in material violation of applicable setback requirements, zoning laws, and ordinances (and none of the properties or buildings or improvements thereon are subject to "permitted non-conforming use" or "permitted non-

---

designed to protect the Buyer against any liability for the unpaid taxes of any person other than the Target and its Subsidiaries.

Sample acquisition agreement 2002.2 (the *pro-seller* stock purchase agreement), on the other hand, contains only a representation and warranty that, to the knowledge of the Sellers, none of the Target and its Subsidiaries has been a member of any Affiliated Group filing a consolidated federal income tax return (other than an Affiliated Group, the parent of which was the Target).

[26] These representations and warranties concerning real property are relatively long and detailed. A condensed version of these provisions may be more appropriate when, for example, the real property of the Target and its Subsidiaries is relatively insignificant.

conforming structure" classifications), and do not encroach on any easement which may burden the land;

(D) all facilities have received all approvals of governmental authorities (including material licenses and permits) required in connection with the ownership or operation thereof, and have been operated and maintained in accordance with applicable laws, rules, and regulations in all material respects;

(E) there are no leases, subleases, licenses, concessions, or other agreements, written or oral, granting to any party or parties the right of use or occupancy of any portion of the parcel of real property;

(F) there are no outstanding options or rights of first refusal to purchase the parcel of real property, or any portion thereof or interest therein;

(G) there are no parties (other than the Target and its Subsidiaries) in possession of the parcel of real property, other than tenants under any leases disclosed in §4(l)(i) of the Disclosure Schedule who are in possession of space to which they are entitled.

(ii) §4(l)(ii) of the Disclosure Schedule lists and describes briefly all real property leased or subleased to any of the Target and its Subsidiaries. §4(l)(ii) of the Disclosure Schedule also identifies the leased or subleased properties for which title insurance policies are to be procured in accordance with §5(h)(ii) below. The Sellers have delivered to the Buyer correct and complete copies of the leases and subleases listed in §4(l)(ii) of the Disclosure Schedule (as amended to date). With respect to each material lease and sublease listed in §4(l)(ii) of the Disclosure Schedule:

(A) the lease or sublease is legal, valid, binding, enforceable, and in full force and effect in all material respects;

(B) no party to the lease or sublease is in material breach or default, and no event has occurred which, with notice or lapse of time, would constitute a material breach or default or permit termination, modification, or acceleration thereunder;

(C) no party to the lease or sublease has repudiated any material provision thereof;

(D) there are no material disputes, oral agreements, or forbearance programs in effect as to the lease or sublease;

(E) none of the Target and its Subsidiaries has assigned, transferred, conveyed, mortgaged, deeded in trust, or encumbered any interest in the leasehold or subleasehold; and

(F) all facilities leased or subleased thereunder have received all approvals of governmental authorities (including material licenses and permits) required in connection with the operation thereof, and have been operated and maintained in accordance with applicable laws, rules, and regulations in all material respects.

(m) *Intellectual Property.*[27]

(i) None of the Target and its Subsidiaries has interfered with, infringed upon, misappropriated, or violated any material Intellectual Property rights of third parties in any material respect, and none of the Sellers and the directors and officers of the Target and its Subsidiaries has ever received any charge, complaint, claim, demand, or notice alleging any such interference, infringement, misappropriation, or violation (including any claim that any of the Target and its Subsidiaries must license or refrain from using any Intellectual Property rights of any third party). To the Knowledge of any of the Sellers and the directors and officers of the Target and its Subsidiaries, no third party has interfered with, infringed upon, misappropriated, or violated any material Intellectual Property rights of any of the Target and its Subsidiaries in any material respect.

(ii) §4(m)(ii) of the Disclosure Schedule identifies each patent or registration which has been issued to any of the Target and its Subsidiaries with respect to any of its Intellectual Property, identifies each pending patent application or application for registration which any of the Target and its Subsidiaries has made with respect to any of its Intellectual Property, and identifies each material license, agreement, or other permission which any of the Target and its Subsidiaries has granted to any third party with respect to any of its Intellectual Property (together with any exceptions). The Sellers have delivered to the Buyer correct and complete copies of all such patents, registrations, applications, licenses, agreements, and permissions (as amended to date) §4(m)(ii) of the Disclosure Schedule also identifies each material trade name or unregistered trademark used by any of the Target and its Subsidiaries in connection with any of its businesses. With respect to each item of Intellectual Property required to be identified in §4(m)(ii) of the Disclosure Schedule:

(A) the Target and its Subsidiaries possess all right, title, and interest in and to the item, free and clear of any Security Interest, license, or other restriction;

---

[27] These representations and warranties concerning intellectual property are relatively long and detailed. A condensed version of these provisions may be more appropriate when, for example, the intellectual property of the Target and its Subsidiaries is relatively insignificant.

(B) the item is not subject to any outstanding injunction, judgment, order, decree, ruling, or charge;

(C) no action, suit, proceeding, hearing, investigation, charge, complaint, claim, or demand is pending or, to the Knowledge of any of the Sellers and the directors and officers of the Target and its Subsidiaries, is threatened which challenges the legality, validity, enforceability, use, or ownership of the item; and

(D) none of the Target and its Subsidiaries has ever agreed to indemnify any Person for or against any interference, infringement, misappropriation, or other conflict with respect to the item.

(iii) §4(m)(ii) of the Disclosure Schedule identifies each material item of Intellectual Property that any third party owns and that any of the Target and its Subsidiaries uses pursuant to license, sublicense, agreement, or permission. The Sellers have delivered to the Buyer correct and complete copies of all such licenses, sublicenses, agreements, and permissions (as amended to date). With respect to each item of Intellectual Property required to be identified in §4(m)(ii) of the Disclosure Schedule:

(A) the license, sublicense, agreement, or permission covering the item is legal, valid, binding, enforceable, and in full force and effect in all material respects;

(B) no party to the license, sublicense, agreement, or permission is in material breach or default, and no event has occurred which with notice or lapse of time would constitute a material breach or default or permit termination, modification, or acceleration thereunder;

(C) no party to the license, sublicense, agreement, or permission has repudiated any material provision thereof; and

(D) none of the Target and its Subsidiaries has granted any sublicense or similar right with respect to the license, sublicense, agreement, or permission.

(n) *Tangible Assets.* The buildings, machinery, equipment, and other tangible assets that the Target and its Subsidiaries own and lease are free from material defects (patent and latent), have been maintained in accordance with normal industry practice, and are in good operating condition and repair (subject to normal wear and tear).

(o) *Inventory.* The inventory of the Target and its Subsidiaries consists of raw materials and supplies, manufactured and processed parts, work in process, and finished goods, all of which is merchantable and fit for the purpose for which it was procured or manufactured, and none of which is slow-moving, obsolete, damaged, or defective, subject only to the reserve for inventory writedown set forth on the face of the Most Recent Balance Sheet (rather than in any notes thereto) as adjusted for operations and transactions through the Closing Date in accordance with the past custom and practice of the Target and its Subsidiaries.

(p) *Contracts.* §4(p) of the Disclosure Schedule lists the following contracts and other agreements to which any of the Target and its Subsidiaries is a party:

(i) any agreement (or group of related agreements) for the lease of personal property to or from any Person providing for lease payments in excess of $_____ per annum;

(ii) any agreement (or group of related agreements) for the purchase or sale of raw materials, commodities, supplies, products, or other personal property, or for the furnishing or receipt of services, the performance of which will extend over a period of more than one year or involve consideration in excess of $_____;

(iii) any agreement concerning a partnership or joint venture;

(iv) any agreement (or group of related agreements) under which it has created, incurred, assumed, or guaranteed any indebtedness for borrowed money, or any capitalized lease obligation, in excess of $_____ or under which it has imposed a Security Interest on any of its assets, tangible or intangible;

(v) any material agreement concerning confidentiality or noncompetition;

(vi) any material agreement with any of the Sellers and their Affiliates (other than the Target and its Subsidiaries);

(vii) any profit sharing, stock option, stock purchase, stock appreciation, deferred compensation, severance, or other material plan or arrangement for the benefit of its current or former directors, officers, and employees;

(viii) any collective bargaining agreement;

(ix) any agreement for the employment of any individual on a full-time, part-time, consulting, or other basis providing annual compensation in excess of $_____ or providing material severance benefits;

(x) any agreement under which it has advanced or loaned any amount to any of its directors, officers, and employees outside the Ordinary Course of Business;

(xi) any agreement under which the consequences of a default or termination could have a material adverse effect on the business, financial condition, operations, results of operations, or future prospects of the Target and its Subsidiaries; or

(xii) any other agreement (or group of related agreements) the performance of which involves consideration in excess of $_____.

The Sellers have delivered to the Buyer a correct and complete copy of each written agreement listed in §4(p) of the Disclosure Schedule (as amended to date) and a written summary setting forth the material terms and conditions of each oral agreement referred to in §4(p) of the Disclosure Schedule. With respect to each such agreement: (A) the agreement is legal, valid, binding, enforceable, and in full force and effect in all material respects; (B) no party is in material breach or default, and no event has occurred which with notice or lapse of time would constitute a material breach or default, or permit termination, modification, or acceleration, under the agreement; and (C) no party has repudiated any material provision of the agreement.

(q) *Notes and Accounts Receivable.* All notes and accounts receivable of the Target and its Subsidiaries are reflected properly on their books and records, are valid receivables subject to no setoffs or counterclaims, are current and collectible, and will be collected in accordance with their terms at their recorded amounts, subject only to the reserve for bad debts set forth on the face of the Most Recent Balance Sheet (rather than in any notes thereto) as adjusted for operations and transactions through the Closing Date in accordance with the past custom and practice of the Target and its Subsidiaries.

(r) *Powers of Attorney.* To the Knowledge of any of the Sellers and the directors and officers of the Target and its Subsidiaries, there are no material outstanding powers of attorney executed on behalf of any of the Target and its Subsidiaries.

(s) *Insurance.* §4(s) of the Disclosure Schedule sets forth the following information with respect to each material insurance policy (including policies providing property, casualty, liability, and workers' compensation coverage and bond and surety arrangements) with respect to which any of the Target and its Subsidiaries is a party, a named insured, or otherwise the beneficiary of coverage:

(i) the name, address, and telephone number of the agent;

(ii) the name of the insurer, the name of the policyholder, and the name of each covered insured;

(iii) the policy number and the period of coverage;

(iv) the scope (including an indication of whether the coverage is on a claims made, occurrence, or other basis) and amount (including a description of how deductibles and ceilings are calculated and operate) of coverage; and

(v) a description of any retroactive premium adjustments or other material loss-sharing arrangements.

With respect to each such insurance policy: (A) the policy is legal, valid, binding, enforceable, and in full force and effect in all material respects; (B) neither any of the Target and its Subsidiaries nor any other party to the policy is in material breach or default (including with respect to the payment of premiums or the giving of notices), and no event has occurred which, with notice or the lapse of time, would constitute such a material breach or default, or permit termination, modification, or acceleration, under the policy; and (C) no party to the policy has repudiated any material provision thereof. §4(s) of the Disclosure Schedule describes any material self-insurance arrangements affecting any of the Target and its Subsidiaries.

(t) *Litigation.* §4(t) of the Disclosure Schedule sets forth each instance in which any of the Target and its Subsidiaries (i) is subject to any outstanding injunction, judgment, order, decree, ruling, or charge or (ii) is a party or, to the Knowledge of any of the Sellers and the directors and officers of the Target and its Subsidiaries, is threatened to be made a party to any action, suit, proceeding, hearing, or investigation of, in, or before any court or quasi-judicial or administrative agency of any federal, state, local, or foreign jurisdiction or before any arbitrator.

(u) *Product Warranty.* Substantially all of the products manufactured, sold, leased, and delivered by the Target and its Subsidiaries have conformed in all material respects with all applicable contractual commitments and all express and implied warranties, and none of the Target and its Subsidiaries has any material liability (whether known or unknown, whether asserted or unasserted, whether absolute or contingent, whether accrued or unaccrued, whether liquidated or unliquidated, and whether due or to become due) for replacement or repair thereof or other damages in connection therewith, subject only to the reserve for product warranty claims set forth on the face of the Most Recent Balance Sheet (rather than in any notes thereto) as adjusted for operations and transactions through the Closing Date in accordance with the past custom and practice of the Target and its Subsidiaries. Substantially all of the products manufactured, sold, leased, and delivered by the Target and its Subsidiaries are subject to standard terms and conditions of sale or lease. §4(u) of the Disclosure Schedule includes copies of the standard terms and conditions of sale or lease for each of the Target and its Subsidiaries (containing applicable guaranty, warranty, and indemnity provisions).

(v) *Product Liability.* None of the Target and its Subsidiaries has any material liability (whether known or unknown, whether asserted or unasserted, whether absolute or contingent, whether accrued or unaccrued, whether liquidated or unliquidated, and whether due or to become due) arising out of any injury to individuals or property as a result of the ownership, possession, or use of any product manufactured, sold, leased, or delivered by any of the Target and its Subsidiaries.

(w) *Employees.* To the Knowledge of any of the Sellers and the directors and officers of the Target and its Subsidiaries, no executive, key employee, or significant group of employees plans to terminate employment with any of the Target and its Subsidiaries during the next 12 months. None of the Target and its Subsidiaries is a party to or bound by any collective bargaining agreement, nor has any of them experienced any strike or material grievance, claim of unfair labor practices, or other collective bargaining dispute within the past [three] years. None of the Target and its Subsidiaries has committed any material unfair labor practice. None of the Sellers and the directors and officers of the Target and its Subsidiaries has any Knowledge of any organizational effort presently being made or threatened by or on behalf of any labor union with respect to employees of any of the Target and its Subsidiaries.

(x) *Employee Benefits.*[28]

(i) §4(x) of the Disclosure Schedule lists each Employee Benefit Plan that any of the Target and its Subsidiaries maintains or to which any of the Target and its Subsidiaries contributes or has any obligation to contribute.

(A) Each such Employee Benefit Plan (and each related trust, insurance contract, or fund) has been maintained, funded and administered in accordance with the terms of such Employee Benefit Plan and complies in form and in operation in all material respects with the applicable requirements of ERISA, the Code, and other applicable laws.

(B) All required reports and descriptions (including annual reports (IRS Form 5500), summary annual reports, and summary plan descriptions) have been timely filed and/or distributed in accordance with the applicable requirements of ERISA and the Code with respect to each such Employee Benefit Plan. The requirements of COBRA have been met in all material respects with respect to each such Employee Benefit Plan which is an Employee Welfare Benefit Plan subject to COBRA.

(C) All contributions (including all employer contributions and employee salary reduction contributions) which are due have been made within the time period prescribed by ERISA to each such Employee Benefit Plan which is an Employee Pension Benefit Plan and all contributions for any period

---

[28] These representations and warranties concerning employee benefits are relatively long and detailed. A condensed version of these provisions may be more appropriate when, for example, the Target and its Subsidiaries have relatively insignificant employee benefit plans.

ending on or before the Closing Date which are not yet due have been made to each such Employee Pension Benefit Plan or accrued in accordance with the past custom and practice of the Target and its Subsidiaries. All premiums or other payments for all periods ending on or before the Closing Date have been paid with respect to each such Employee Benefit Plan which is an Employee Welfare Benefit Plan.

(D) Each such Employee Benefit Plan intended to meet the requirements of a "qualified plan" under Code §401(a) has received a favorable determination letter from the Internal Revenue Service that it is a "qualified plan" and the Sellers are not aware of any facts or circumstances that could adversely affect the qualified status of any such Employee Benefit Plan.

(E) The market value of assets under each such Employee Benefit Plan which is an Employee Pension Benefit Plan (other than any Multiemployer Plan) equals or exceeds the present value of all vested and nonvested liabilities thereunder (determined in accordance with then current funding assumptions).

(F) The Sellers have delivered to the Buyer correct and complete copies of the plan documents and summary plan descriptions, the most recent determination letter received from the Internal Revenue Service, the most recent annual report (IRS Form 5500, with all applicable attachments), and all related trust agreements, insurance contracts, and other funding arrangements which implement each such Employee Benefit Plan.

(ii) With respect to each Employee Benefit Plan that any of the Target, its Subsidiaries, and any ERISA Affiliate maintains, to which any of them contributes, or has any obligation to contribute, or with respect to which any of them has any [material] liability or potential liability:

(A) No such Employee Benefit Plan which is an Employee Pension Benefit Plan (other than any Multiemployer Plan) has been completely or partially terminated or been the subject of a Reportable Event as to which notices would be required to be filed with the PBGC. No proceeding by the PBGC to terminate any such Employee Pension Benefit Plan (other than any Multiemployer Plan) has been instituted or, to the Knowledge of any of the Sellers and the directors and officers of the Target and its Subsidiaries, threatened.

(B) There have been no Prohibited Transactions with respect to any such Employee Benefit Plan. No Fiduciary has any liability for material breach of fiduciary duty or any other material failure to act or comply in connection with the administration or investment of the assets of any such Employee Benefit Plan. No action, suit, proceeding, hearing, or investigation with respect to the administration or the investment of the assets of any such Employee Benefit Plan (other than routine claims for benefits) is pending or, to the Knowledge of any of the Sellers and the directors and officers of the Target and its Subsidiaries, threatened.

(C) None of the Target and its Subsidiaries has incurred any material liability (whether known or unknown, whether asserted or unasserted, whether absolute or contingent, whether accrued or unaccrued, whether liquidated or unliquidated, and whether due or to become due) to the PBGC (other than with respect to PBGC premium payments not yet due) or otherwise under Title IV of ERISA (including any withdrawal liability (as defined in ERISA §4201)) or under the Code with respect to any such Employee Benefit Plan which is an Employee Pension Benefit Plan, or under COBRA with respect to any such Employee Benefit Plan which is an Employee Welfare Benefit Plan.

(iii) None of the Target, its Subsidiaries, and any ERISA Affiliate contributes to, has any obligation to contribute to, or has any material liability (whether known or unknown, whether asserted or unasserted, whether absolute or contingent, whether accrued or unaccrued, whether liquidated or unliquidated, and whether due or to become due), including any withdrawal liability (as defined in ERISA §4201), under or with respect to any Multiemployer Plan.

(iv) None of the Target and its Subsidiaries maintains, contributes to or has an obligation to contribute to, or has any [material] liability or potential liability with respect to, any Employee Welfare Benefit Plan providing medical, health, or life insurance or other welfare-type benefits for current or future retired or terminated employees, their spouses, or their dependents (other than in accordance with COBRA).

(y) *Guaranties.* None of the Target and its Subsidiaries is a guarantor or otherwise is responsible for any liability or obligation (including indebtedness) of any other Person.

(z) *Environment, Health, and Safety Matters.*[29]

(i) Each of the Target, its Subsidiaries, and their respective predecessors and Affiliates has complied and is in compliance, in each case in all material respects, with all Environmental, Health, and Safety Requirements.

---

[29] These representations and warranties concerning environmental, health, and safety matters are relatively long and detailed. A condensed version may be more appropriate when, for example, the operations of the Target and its Subsidiaries appear to have had a relatively insignificant effect upon the environment or upon public or employee health and safety.

While quite comprehensive (including coverage for strict liability for site cleanup under CERCLA and common law liability), these environmental representations and warranties contain a consistent materiality limitation and are otherwise generally more limited and narrowly focused than those in sample acquisition agreement 2002.1 (the *pro-buyer* stock purchase agreement).

The environmental representations and warranties in sample acquisition agreement 2002.2 (the *pro-seller* stock purchase agreement) are further limited to matters within the Seller's knowledge, do

(ii) Without limiting the generality of the foregoing, each of the Target, its Subsidiaries, and their respective Affiliates, has obtained, has complied, and is in compliance with, in each case in all material respects, all material permits, licenses and other authorizations that are required pursuant to Environmental, Health, and Safety Requirements for the occupation of its facilities and the operation of its business; a list of all such material permits, licenses and other authorizations is set forth on the attached *"Environmental and Safety Permits Schedule."*

(iii) None of the Target, its Subsidiaries, or their respective Affiliates has received any written or oral notice, report or other information regarding any actual or alleged material violation of Environmental, Health, and Safety Requirements, or any material liabilities or potential material liabilities (whether accrued, absolute, contingent, unliquidated or otherwise), including any material investigatory, remedial or corrective obligations, relating to any of them or its facilities arising under Environmental, Health, and Safety Requirements.

(iv) Except as set forth on the attached *"Environmental and Safety Matters Schedule,"* none of the following exists at any property or facility owned or operated by the Target or its Subsidiaries: (1) underground storage tanks, (2) asbestos-containing material in any friable and damaged form or condition, (3) materials or equipment containing polychlorinated biphenyls, or (4) landfills, surface impoundments, or disposal areas.

(v) None of the Target, its Subsidiaries, or any of their respective predecessors or Affiliates has treated, stored, disposed of, arranged for or permitted the disposal of, transported, handled, or released any substance, including without limitation any hazardous substance, or owned or operated any property or facility (and no such property or facility is contaminated by any such substance) in a manner that has given or would give rise to material liabilities, including any material liability for response costs, corrective action costs, personal injury, property damage, natural resources damages or attorney fees, pursuant to the Comprehensive Environmental Response, Compensation and Liability Act of 1980, as amended ("CERCLA") or the Solid Waste Disposal Act, as amended ("SWDA") or any other Environmental, Health, and Safety Requirements.

(vi) Neither this Agreement nor the consummation of the transaction that is the subject of this Agreement will result in any material obligations for site investigation or cleanup, or notification to or consent of government agencies or third parties, pursuant to any of the so-called "transaction-triggered" or "responsible property transfer" Environmental, Health, and Safety Requirements.

---

not extend to strict liability for site cleanup under CERCLA or common law liability, and otherwise limit the disclosure and indemnification obligations of the Seller.

(aa) *Year 2000*. None of the computer software, computer firmware, computer hardware (whether general or special purpose) or other similar or related items of automated, computerized or software systems that are material to the businesses of the Target or its Subsidiaries, will malfunction, cease to function, generate incorrect data or produce incorrect results when processing, providing or receiving (i) date-related data from, into and between the twentieth and twenty-first centuries or (ii) date-related data in connection with any valid date in the twentieth and twenty-first centuries.[30]

(bb) *Certain Business Relationships With the Target and Its Subsidiaries*. None of the Sellers and their Affiliates has been involved in any material business arrangement or relationship with any of the Target and its Subsidiaries within the past 12 months, and none of the Sellers and their Affiliates owns any material asset, tangible or intangible, which is used in the business of any of the Target and its Subsidiaries.

(cc) *Disclosure*. The representations and warranties contained in this §4 do not contain any untrue statement of a material fact or omit to state any material fact necessary in order to make the statements and information contained in this §4 not misleading.

5. *Pre-Closing Covenants*. The Parties agree as follows with respect to the period between the execution of this Agreement and the Closing.[31]

(a) *General*. Each of the Parties will use his or its reasonable best efforts to take all action and to do all things necessary [, proper, or advisable] in order to consummate and make effective the transactions contemplated by this Agreement (including satisfaction, but not waiver, of the closing conditions set forth in §7 below).

---

[30] This representation can be omitted for agreements entered into a sufficient period after approximately 3/1/00 so that Buyer has been able to verify that Target and its Subsidiaries have no Y2K problem.

Sample acquisition agreement 2002.1 (the *pro-buyer* stock purchase agreement) contains a more extensive representation on this topic and 2002.2 (the *pro-seller* stock purchase agreement) contains no representation on this topic.

[31] The Buyer may seek to make the Target and its Subsidiaries parties to this Agreement for the purpose of obtaining directly their covenants applicable to the period prior to the Closing.

Whether or not the Target and its Subsidiaries become parties to this Agreement, they are likely to incur significant costs and expenses in connection with the transaction (e.g., when they and their agents prepare the Disclosure Schedule and perhaps certain of the Financial Statements, give notices to third parties and obtain their consent, make filings under the Hart-Scott-Rodino Act and respond to requests for additional information, and obtain title insurance and surveys for the Closing).

These costs and expenses of the Target and its Subsidiaries are separate and distinguishable from the costs and expenses of the Buyer on the one hand and of the Sellers on the other hand.

Section 10(1) allocates responsibility among the respective parties for these costs and expenses through the Closing.

(b) *Notices and Consents.* The Sellers will cause each of the Target and its Subsidiaries to give any notices to third parties, and will cause each of the Target and its Subsidiaries to use its reasonable best efforts to obtain any third party consents, that the Buyer reasonably may request in connection with the matters referred to in §4(c) above. Each of the Parties will (and the Sellers will cause each of the Target and its Subsidiaries to) give any notices to, make any filings with, and use its reasonable best efforts to obtain any authorizations, consents, and approvals of governments and governmental agencies in connection with the matters referred to in §3(a)(ii), §3(b)(ii), and §4(c) above. Without limiting the generality of the foregoing, each of the Parties will file (and the Sellers will cause each of the Target and its Subsidiaries to file) any Notification and Report Forms and related material that he or it may be required to file with the Federal Trade Commission and the Antitrust Division of the United States Department of Justice under the Hart-Scott-Rodino Act, will use his or its reasonable best efforts to obtain (and the Sellers will cause each of the Target and its Subsidiaries to use its reasonable best efforts to obtain) a waiver from the applicable waiting period, and will make (and the Sellers will cause each of the Target and its Subsidiaries to make) any further filings pursuant thereto that may be necessary [, proper, or advisable] in connection therewith.

(c) *Operation of Business.* The Sellers will not cause or permit any of the Target and its Subsidiaries to engage in any practice, take any action, or enter into any transaction outside the Ordinary Course of Business. Without limiting the generality of the foregoing, the Sellers will not cause or permit any of the Target and its Subsidiaries to (i) declare, set aside, or pay any dividend or make any distribution with respect to its capital stock or redeem, purchase, or otherwise acquire any of its capital stock, (ii) _____, or (iii) otherwise engage in any practice, take any action, or enter into any transaction of the sort described in §4(h) above.[32]

(d) *Preservation of Business.* The Sellers will cause each of the Target and its Subsidiaries to keep its business and properties substantially intact, including its present operations, physical facilities, working conditions, and relationships with lessors, licensors, suppliers, customers, and employees.[33]

(e) *Full Access.* Each of the Sellers will permit, and the Sellers will cause each of the Target and its Subsidiaries to permit, representatives of the Buyer to have full access at all reasonable times, and in a manner so as not to interfere with the

---

[32] The Parties may prefer to revise this covenant so that it recites specific prohibitions (rather than incorporating the matters in §4(h) by reference).

[33] This Agreement, like sample acquisition agreement 2002.1 (the *pro-buyer* stock purchase agreement), contains a provision regarding preservation of the business of the Target and its Subsidiaries. Sample acquisition agreement 2002.2 (the *pro-seller* stock purchase agreement), on the other hand, lacks such a provision.

normal business operations of the Target and its Subsidiaries, to all premises, properties, personnel, books, records (including tax records), contracts, and documents of or pertaining to each of the Target and its Subsidiaries. The Buyer will treat and hold as such any Confidential Information it receives from any of the Sellers, the Target, and its Subsidiaries in the course of the reviews contemplated by this §5(e), will not use any of the Confidential Information except in connection with this Agreement, and, if this Agreement is terminated for any reason whatsoever, will return to the Sellers, the Target, and its Subsidiaries all tangible embodiments (and all copies) of the Confidential Information which are in its possession.[34]

(f) *Notice of Developments.* The Sellers will give prompt written notice to the Buyer of any material adverse development causing a breach of any of the representations and warranties in §4 above.[35] Each Party will give prompt written notice to the others of any material adverse development causing a breach of any of his or its own representations and warranties in §3 above. No disclosure by any Party pursuant to this §5(f), however, shall be deemed to amend or supplement Annex I, Annex II, or the Disclosure Schedule or to prevent or cure any misrepresentation, breach of warranty, or breach of covenant.[36]

(g) *Exclusivity.* None of the Sellers will (and the Sellers will not cause or permit any of the Target and its Subsidiaries to) (i) solicit, initiate, or encourage the submission of any proposal or offer from any Person relating to the acquisition of any capital stock or other voting securities, or any substantial portion of the assets, of any of the Target and its Subsidiaries (including any acquisition structured as a merger, consolidation, or share exchange) or (ii) participate in any discussions or negotiations regarding, furnish any information with respect to, assist or participate in, or facilitate in any other manner any effort or attempt by

---

[34] This Agreement, like sample acquisition agreement 2002.2 (the *pro-seller* stock purchase agreement), contains a confidentiality and nonuse provision protecting the Confidential Information until the Buyer actually purchases the Target Shares. Sample acquisition agreement 2002.1 (the *pro-buyer* stock purchase agreement), on the other hand, lacks such a provision.

[35] This Agreement, like sample acquisition agreement 2002.1 (the *pro-buyer* stock purchase agreement), requires the Sellers to notify the Buyer of any material adverse development prior to the Closing that causes a breach of any of the representations and warranties in §4.

Sample acquisition agreement 2002.2 (the *pro-seller* stock purchase agreement), on the other hand, permits (but does not require) the Sellers to notify the Buyer of any such development. Moreover, if the development gives the Buyer any right to terminate the Agreement, the Buyer must exercise its termination right within [10 business days] after the notice. Unless the Buyer has such a termination right and exercises it within such period, the notice will be deemed to have cured any breach of the representations and warranties that otherwise would have existed by reason of the adverse development.

[36] This Agreement, like sample acquisition agreement 2002.1 (the *pro-buyer* stock purchase agreement), provides that no disclosure (presumably, but not necessarily, by the Sellers) between signing and closing shall be deemed to supplement the previous disclosures or to cure any breach of the Agreement. Sample acquisition agreement 2002.2 (the *pro-seller* stock purchase agreement), on the other hand, provides that certain such disclosures *will* supplement the previous disclosures and cure breaches of the Agreement. *See* the discussion in the immediately preceding footnote.

any Person to do or seek any of the foregoing.[37] None of the Sellers will vote their Target Shares in favor of any such acquisition structured as a merger, consolidation, or share exchange.

(h) *Title Insurance*.[38] The Sellers will cause the Target and its Subsidiaries to obtain the following title insurance commitments, policies, and riders in preparation for the Closing:

(i) with respect to each parcel of real estate that any of the Target and its Subsidiaries owns, an ALTA Owner's Policy of Title Insurance Form B-1987 (or equivalent policy reasonably acceptable to the Buyer if the real property is located in a state in which an ALTA Owner's Policy of Title Insurance Form B-1987 is not available) issued by a title insurer reasonably satisfactory to the Buyer (and, if requested by the Buyer, reinsured in whole or in part by one or more insurance companies and pursuant to a direct access agreement reasonably acceptable to the Buyer), in such amount as the Buyer reasonably may determine to be the fair market value of such real property (including all improvements located thereon), insuring title to such real property to be in the Target or its Subsidiary as of the Closing (subject only to the title exceptions described above in §4(l)(i) and in §4(l)(i) of the Disclosure Schedule); and

(ii) with respect to each parcel of real estate that any of the Target and its Subsidiaries leases or subleases and which is listed on §4(l)(ii) of the Disclosure Schedule as a property for which a title insurance policy is to be procured, an ALTA Leasehold Owner's Policy of Title Insurance-1987 (or equivalent policy reasonably acceptable to the Buyer if the real property is located in a state in which an ALTA Leasehold Owner's Policy of Title Insurance-1987 is not available) issued by a title insurer reasonably satisfactory to the Buyer (and, if requested by the Buyer, reinsured in whole or in part by one or more insurance companies and pursuant to a direct access agreement reasonably acceptable to the Buyer) in such amount as the Buyer reasonably may determine (taking into account the time cost of money using the Applicable Rate as the discount rate and such other factors as whether the fair market rental value of the premises exceeds the stipulated consideration in the lease or sublease, whether the tenant or subtenant has any option to renew or extend, whether the tenant or subtenant owns any improvements located on the premises, whether the tenant or subten-

---

[37] Sample acquisition agreement 2002.2 (the *pro-seller* stock purchase agreement) permits the Sellers, the Target, its Subsidiaries, and their directors and officers to respond to unsolicited proposals to the extent their fiduciary duties may require. This Agreement, like sample acquisition agreement 2002.1 (the *pro-buyer* stock purchase agreement), lacks such a provision.

[38] This Agreement, like sample acquisition agreement 2002.1 (the *pro-buyer* stock purchase agreement), contains relatively long and detailed provisions concerning title insurance. A condensed version may be more appropriate if, for example, the real property of the Target and its Subsidiaries is relatively insignificant.

Sample acquisition agreement 2002.2 (the *pro-seller* stock purchase agreement), on the other hand, does not have *any* such provisions and contemplates that the Buyer will obtain any title insurance it requires independently and at its own expense.

ant is permitted to sublease, and whether the tenant or subtenant would owe any amount under the lease or sublease if evicted), insuring title to the leasehold or subleasehold estate to be in the Target or its Subsidiary as of the Closing (subject only to the title exceptions described above in §4(l)(ii) and in §4(l)(ii) of the Disclosure Schedule).

Each title insurance policy delivered under §5(h)(i) and §5(h)(ii) above shall (A) insure title to the real property and all recorded easements benefitting such real property, (B) contain an "extended coverage endorsement" insuring over the general exceptions contained customarily in such policies, (C) contain an ALTA Zoning Endorsement 3.1 (or equivalent), (D) contain an endorsement insuring that the real property described in the title insurance policy is the same real estate as shown on the Survey delivered with respect to such property, (E) contain an endorsement insuring that each street adjacent to the real property is a public street and that there is direct and unencumbered pedestrian and vehicular access to such street from the real property, (F) contain an inflation endorsement providing for annual adjustments in the amount of coverage corresponding to the annual percentage increase, if any, in the United States Department of Commerce Composite Construction Cost Index (Base Year = _____), (G) if the real property consists of more than one record parcel, contain a "contiguity" endorsement insuring that all of the record parcels are contiguous to one another, and (H) contain a "non-imputation" endorsement to the effect that title defects known to the officers, directors, and stockholders of the owner prior to the Closing shall not be deemed "facts known to the insured" for purposes of the policy.

(i) *Surveys.*[39] With respect to each parcel of real property that any of the Target and its Subsidiaries owns, leases, or subleases, and as to which a title insurance policy is to be procured pursuant to §5(h) above, the Sellers will cause the Target and its Subsidiaries to procure in preparation for the Closing a current survey of the real property certified to the Buyer, prepared by a licensed surveyor and conforming to current ALTA Minimum Detail Requirements for Land Title Surveys, disclosing the location of all improvements, easements, party walls, sidewalks, roadways, utility lines, and other matters shown customarily on such surveys, and showing access affirmatively to public streets and roads (the "Survey"). The Survey shall not disclose any survey defect or encroachment from or onto the real property which has not been cured or insured over prior to the Closing.

---

[39] This Agreement, like sample acquisition agreement 2002.1 (the *pro-buyer* stock purchase agreement), contains relatively long and detailed provisions concerning real property surveys. A condensed version may be more appropriate if, for example, the real property of the Target and its Subsidiaries is relatively insignificant.

Sample acquisition agreement 2002.2 (the *pro-seller* stock purchase agreement), on the other hand, does not have *any* such provisions and contemplates that the Buyer will obtain any surveys it requires independently and at its own expense.

6. *Post-Closing Covenants.*[40] The Parties agree as follows with respect to the period following the Closing.

(a) *General.* In case at any time after the Closing any further action is necessary to carry out the purposes of this Agreement, each of the Parties will take such further action (including the execution and delivery of such further instruments and documents) as any other Party reasonably may request, all at the sole cost and expense of the requesting Party (unless the requesting Party is entitled to indemnification therefor under §8 below).[41] The Sellers acknowledge and agree that from and after the Closing the Buyer will be entitled to possession of all documents, books, records (including tax records), agreements, and financial data of any sort relating to the Target and its Subsidiaries.

(b) *Litigation Support.* In the event and for so long as any Party actively is contesting or defending against any action, suit, proceeding, hearing, investigation, charge, complaint, claim, or demand in connection with (i) any transaction contemplated under this Agreement or (ii) any fact, situation, circumstance, status, condition, activity, practice, plan, occurrence, event, incident, action, failure to act, or transaction on or prior to the Closing Date involving any of the Target and its Subsidiaries, each of the other Parties will cooperate with him or it and his or its counsel in the contest or defense, make available their personnel, and provide such testimony and access to their books and records as shall be necessary in connection with the contest or defense, all at the sole cost and expense of the contesting or defending Party (unless the contesting or defending Party is entitled to indemnification therefor under §8 below).[42]

(c) *Transition.* None of the Sellers will take any action that is designed or intended to have the effect of discouraging any lessor, licensor, customer, supplier, or other business associate of any of the Target and its Subsidiaries from maintaining the same business relationships with the Target and its Subsidiaries after the Closing as it maintained with the Target and its Subsidiaries prior to the Closing.

---

[40] The Sellers may seek to obtain additional covenants from the Buyer and its Subsidiaries (e.g., the typical covenants contained in a loan agreement or an indenture) because the Buyer is issuing the Buyer Notes to the Sellers as part of the Purchase Price. Any such covenants would remain applicable so long as the Buyer Notes remained outstanding.

[41] The Parties may prefer to allocate responsibility for these post-Closing costs and expenses in some other manner (e.g., the Party incurring the costs and expenses might be responsible for their payment; the Parties might share the costs and expenses in a predetermined ratio; or one Party might be responsible for the costs and expenses up to a specified aggregate ceiling and the other Party responsible for any excess).

Compare §10(1), which allocates responsibility among the Parties for their costs and expenses *through* the Closing.

[42] The Parties may prefer to allocate responsibility for these post-Closing costs and expenses in some other manner as discussed in the preceding footnote.

(d) *Confidentiality.*[43] Each of the Sellers will treat and hold as such all of the Confidential Information, refrain from using any of the Confidential Information except in connection with this Agreement, and deliver promptly to the Buyer or destroy, at the request and option of the Buyer, all tangible embodiments (and all copies) of the Confidential Information which are in his or its possession. In the event that any of the Sellers is requested or required (by oral question or request for information or documents in any legal proceeding, interrogatory, subpoena, civil investigative demand, or similar process) to disclose any Confidential Information, that Seller will notify the Buyer promptly of the request or requirement so that the Buyer may seek an appropriate protective order or waive compliance with the provisions of this 6(d). If, in the absence of a protective order or the receipt of a waiver hereunder, any of the Sellers is, on the advice of counsel, compelled to disclose any Confidential Information to any tribunal or else stand liable for contempt, that Seller may disclose the Confidential Information to the tribunal; provided, however, that the disclosing Seller shall use his or its reasonable best efforts to obtain, at the reasonable request of the Buyer, an order or other assurance that confidential treatment will be accorded to such portion of the Confidential Information required to be disclosed as the Buyer shall designate.

(e) *Covenant Not to Compete.*[44] For a period of [three years] from and after the Closing Date, none of the Sellers will engage directly or indirectly in any business that any of the Target and its Subsidiaries conducts as of the Closing Date in any geographic area in which any of the Target and its Subsidiaries conducts that business as of the Closing Date; *provided, however,* that no owner of less than 1% of the outstanding stock of any publicly-traded corporation shall be deemed to engage solely by reason thereof in any of its businesses. If the final judgment of a court of competent jurisdiction declares that any term or provision of this §6(e) is invalid or unenforceable, the Parties agree that the court making the determination of invalidity or unenforceability shall have the power to reduce the scope, duration, or area of the term or provision, to delete specific words or phrases, or to replace any invalid or unenforceable term or provision with a term or provision that is valid and enforceable and that comes closest to expressing the intention of the invalid or unenforceable term or provision, and this Agreement shall be enforceable as so modified after the expiration of the time within which the judgment may be appealed.

(f) *Buyer Notes.* Each Buyer Note will be imprinted with a legend substantially in the following form:

---

[43] This Agreement, like sample acquisition agreement 2002.1 (the *pro-buyer* stock purchase agreement), requires the Sellers to keep certain information regarding the Target and its Subsidiaries confidential after the Closing. Sample acquisition agreement 2002.2 (the *pro-seller* stock purchase agreement), on the other hand, lacks such a provision.

[44] Note that unless this Agreement allocates a specified amount of consideration to the covenant not to compete, applicable tax cases will preclude the Buyer from seeking to allocate a portion of the purchase price to the covenant and amortizing such amount over the covenant's life.

This Note was originally issued on _____, 19____, and has not been registered under the Securities Act of 1933, as amended. The transfer of this Note is subject to certain restrictions set forth in the Purchase Agreement. The issuer of this Note will furnish a copy of these provisions to the holder hereof without charge upon written request.

Each holder desiring to transfer a Buyer Note first must furnish the Buyer with (i) a written opinion reasonably satisfactory to the Buyer in form and substance from counsel reasonably satisfactory to the Buyer by reason of experience to the effect that the holder may transfer the Buyer Note as desired without registration under the Securities Act and (ii) a written undertaking executed by the desired transferee reasonably satisfactory to the Buyer in form and substance agreeing to be bound by the restrictions on transfer contained herein.[45]

7. Conditions to Obligation to Close.

(a) *Conditions to Obligation of the Buyer.*[46] The obligation of the Buyer to consummate the transactions to be performed by it in connection with the Closing is subject to satisfaction of the following conditions:

(i) the representations and warranties set forth in §3(a) and §4 above shall be true and correct in all material respects at and as of the Closing Date;[47]

(ii) the Sellers shall have performed and complied with all of their covenants hereunder in all material respects through the Closing;

(iii) the Target and its Subsidiaries shall have procured all of the material third party consents specified in §5(b) above, all of the title insurance commitments, policies, and riders specified in §5(h) above, and all of the surveys specified in §5(i) above;[48]

---

[45] This Agreement, like sample acquisition agreement 2002.1 (the *pro-buyer* stock purchase agreement), calls for a legend on the Buyer Notes and provides that any holder who wishes to transfer the Buyer Notes must first obtain an opinion of counsel and an undertaking of the transferee (in each case as to securities law matters). Sample acquisition agreement 2002.2 (the *pro-seller* stock purchase agreement), on the other hand, only calls for a legend on the Buyer Notes. Note that any such provision would be inappropriate if the Buyer will issue the Buyer Notes in an offering registered under the Securities Act.

[46] Sample acquisition agreement 2002.1 (the *pro-buyer* stock purchase agreement) contains an additional closing condition for the benefit of the Buyer concerning the receipt of financing for the transaction. This Agreement, like sample acquisition agreement 2002.2 (the *pro-seller* stock purchase agreement), lacks a comparable provision.

[47] Note that this provision will not give the Buyer any closing condition with respect to any adverse matter that the Sellers may disclose in the Disclosure Schedule. This is because the disclosure will cure any misrepresentation or breach of warranty that might otherwise have existed. Thus, if the Sellers disclose an adverse matter in the Disclosure Schedule, the Buyer may seek to add a specific closing condition requiring an acceptable resolution of the matter.

[48] This Agreement, like sample acquisition agreement 2002.1 (the *pro-buyer* stock purchase agreement), includes a closing condition for the benefit of the Buyer regarding third party consents, title insurance, and surveys. Unlike sample acquisition agreement 2002.1, however, the closing condition in

(iv) no action, suit, or proceeding shall be pending before any court or quasi-judicial or administrative agency of any federal, state, local, or foreign jurisdiction or before any arbitrator wherein an unfavorable injunction, judgment, order, decree, ruling, or charge would (A) prevent consummation of any of the transactions contemplated by this Agreement, (B) cause any of the transactions contemplated by this Agreement to be rescinded following consummation, (C) affect adversely the right of the Buyer to own the Target Shares and to control the Target and its Subsidiaries, or (D) affect materially and adversely the right of any of the Target and its Subsidiaries to own its assets and to operate its businesses (and no such injunction, judgment, order, decree, ruling, or charge shall be in effect);[49]

(v) the Sellers shall have delivered to the Buyer a certificate to the effect that each of the conditions specified above in §7(a)(i)-(iv) is satisfied in all respects;

(vi) all applicable waiting periods (and any extensions thereof) under the Hart-Scott-Rodino Act shall have expired or otherwise been terminated and the Parties, the Target, and its Subsidiaries shall have received all other material authorizations, consents, and approvals of governments and governmental agencies referred to in §3(a)(ii), §3(b)(ii), and §4(c) above;

(vii) the relevant parties shall have entered into side agreements in form and substance as set forth in Exhibits C-1 through C-_____ attached hereto and the same shall be in full force and effect;

(viii) the Buyer shall have received from counsel to the Sellers an opinion in form and substance as set forth in Exhibit D attached hereto, addressed to the Buyer, and dated as of the Closing Date;

(ix) the Buyer shall have received the resignations, effective as of the Closing, of each director and officer of the Target and its Subsidiaries;[50] and

---

this Agreement refers only to *material* third party consents. Sample acquisition agreement 2002.2 (the *pro-seller* stock purchase agreement), on the other hand, lacks a comparable closing condition altogether.

[49] This Agreement, like sample acquisition agreement 2002.1 (the *pro-buyer* stock purchase agreement), contains a broad closing condition regarding injunctions, judgments, orders, and pending actions, suits, and proceedings that prevent or could have an adverse effect upon the transactions contemplated by the Agreement. Unlike sample acquisition agreement 2002.1, however, the closing condition in this Agreement does not cover actions, suits, and proceedings that are only threatened. Sample acquisition agreement 2002.2 (the *pro-seller* stock purchase agreement), on the other hand, contains a narrower closing condition covering only injunctions, judgments, and orders that prevent consummation of the transactions.

[50] This Agreement, like sample acquisition agreement 2002.1 (the *pro-buyer* stock purchase agreement), contains a closing condition regarding the receipt of director and officer resignations. Sample acquisition agreement 2002.2 (the *pro-seller* stock purchase agreement), on the other hand, lacks a comparable closing condition.

(x) all actions to be taken by the Sellers in connection with consummation of the transactions contemplated hereby and all certificates, opinions, instruments, and other documents required to effect the transactions contemplated hereby will be reasonably satisfactory in form and substance to the Buyer.

The Buyer may waive any condition specified in this §7(a) if it executes a writing so stating at or prior to the Closing.

(b) *Conditions to Obligation of the Sellers.* The obligation of the Sellers to consummate the transactions to be performed by them in connection with the Closing is subject to satisfaction of the following conditions:

(i) the representations and warranties set forth in §3(b) above shall be true and correct in all material respects at and as of the Closing Date;

(ii) the Buyer shall have performed and complied with all of its covenants hereunder in all material respects through the Closing;

(iii) no action, suit, or proceeding shall be pending before any court or quasi-judicial or administrative agency of any federal, state, local, or foreign jurisdiction or before any arbitrator wherein an unfavorable injunction, judgment, order, decree, ruling, or charge would (A) prevent consummation of any of the transactions contemplated by this Agreement or (B) cause any of the transactions contemplated by this Agreement to be rescinded following consummation (and no such injunction, judgment, order, decree, ruling, or charge shall be in effect);[51]

(iv) the Buyer shall have delivered to the Sellers a certificate to the effect that each of the conditions specified above in §7(b)(i)-(iii) is satisfied in all respects;

(v) all applicable waiting periods (and any extensions thereof) under the Hart-Scott-Rodino Act shall have expired or otherwise been terminated and the Parties, the Target, and its Subsidiaries shall have received all other material authorizations, consents, and approvals of governments and governmental agencies referred to in §3(a)(ii), §3(b)(ii), and §4(c) above;

(vi) the relevant parties shall have entered into side agreements in form and substance as set forth in Exhibits C-_____, C-_____, . . . and C_____ and the same shall be in full force and effect;

(vii) the Sellers shall have received from counsel to the Buyer an opinion in form and substance as set forth in Exhibit E attached hereto, addressed to the Sellers, and dated as of the Closing Date; and

---

[51] Because this Seller's closing condition conforms in part to the comparable Buyer's closing condition in §7(a)(iv), it leaves the Sellers with a relatively broad "out." Thus, the Buyer may prefer to narrow the respective closing conditions. *Compare* the narrower closing conditions in sample acquisition

(viii) all actions to be taken by the Buyer in connection with consummation of the transactions contemplated hereby and all certificates, opinions, instruments, and other documents required to effect the transactions contemplated hereby will be reasonably satisfactory in form and substance to the Requisite Sellers.

The Requisite Sellers may waive any condition specified in this §7(b) if they execute a writing so stating at or prior to the Closing.

8. *Remedies for Breaches of This Agreement.*[52]

(a) *Survival of Representations and Warranties.*[53] All of the representations and warranties of the Sellers contained in §4 above (other than §4(k) above) shall survive the Closing hereunder (even if the Buyer knew or had reason to know of any misrepresentation or breach of warranty at the time of Closing) and continue in full force and effect for a period of [two years] thereafter; *provided, however,* that the representations and warranties contained in §4(z) above shall survive the Closing hereunder (even if the Buyer knew or had reason to know of any

---

agreement 2002.2 (the *pro-seller* stock purchase agreement) and the even broader closing conditions in sample acquisition agreement 2002.1 (the *pro-buyer* stock purchase agreement).

[52] The Buyer may seek some form of additional security covering the obligation of the Sellers to indemnify the Buyer after the Closing. This may include provisions calling for (a) the Buyer to have a recoupment remedy with respect to the Buyer Notes, (b) the Sellers to deposit a portion of the Purchase Price with a third party escrow agent, (c) the Buyer to hold back a portion of the Purchase Price (to be paid later with interest), or (d) the Buyer to obtain a security interest in certain assets of the Sellers. Sample acquisition agreement 2002.1 (the *pro-buyer* stock purchase agreement), for example, contains recoupment provisions applicable to the Buyer Notes.

[53] Sample acquisition agreement 2002.1 (the *pro-buyer* stock purchase agreement) contains alternative provisions for (a) *full indemnification* (the representations and warranties survive indefinitely, and there is no deductible, threshold, or ceiling with respect to indemnification against breaches thereof) and (b) *limited indemnification* (the representations and warranties with respect to the transaction itself and with respect to taxes survive indefinitely; the other representations and warranties survive only for (three years); and there is a threshold, but not a deductible or ceiling, with respect to indemnification against breaches of the latter). The *pro-buyer* Agreement also provides that a particular representation and warranty will survive the Closing *even* if the damaged Party knew or had reason to know of a breach thereof at the time of Closing.

Sample acquisition agreement 2002.2 (the *pro-seller* stock purchase agreement), on the other hand, contains alternative provisions for (a) *minimal indemnification* (only the representations and warranties concerning the transaction itself survive the Closing) and (b) *limited indemnification* (the representations and warranties with respect to the transaction itself survive indefinitely; the other representations and warranties survive only for [one year]; and there is a deductible and a ceiling with respect to indemnification against breaches of the latter). The *pro-seller* Agreement provides, however, that a particular representation and warranty will *not* survive the Closing if the damaged Party knew or had reason to know of a breach thereof at the time of Closing.

This Agreement, intended to favor neither the Buyer nor the Sellers, provides that the representations and warranties with respect to the transaction itself and with respect to taxes will survive indefinitely; the environmental representations and warranties will survive for [five years]; the other representations and warranties will survive for [two years]; and there will be a deductible and a ceiling with respect to indemnification against breaches of any representations and warranties that do not concern the transaction itself. This Agreement, like the *pro-buyer* Agreement, also provides that a particular representation and warranty will survive the Closing *even* if the damaged Party knew or had reason to know of a breach thereof at the time of Closing.

misrepresentation or breach of warranty at the time of Closing) and continue in full force and effect for a period of [five years] thereafter. All of the other representations and warranties of the Parties contained in this Agreement (including the representations and warranties of the Parties contained in §3 above and the representations and warranties of the Sellers contained in §4(k) above) shall survive the Closing (even if the damaged Party knew or had reason to know of any misrepresentation or breach of warranty at the time of Closing) and continue in full force and effect forever thereafter (subject to any applicable statutes of limitations).

(b) *Indemnification Provisions for Benefit of the Buyer.*[54]

(i) In the event any of the Sellers breaches any of their representations, warranties, and covenants contained herein (other than the covenants in §2(a) above and the representations and warranties in §3(a) above), and, if there is an applicable survival period pursuant to §8(a) above, provided that the Buyer makes a written claim for indemnification against any of the Sellers pursuant to §10(h) below within such survival period, then each of the Sellers agrees to indemnify the Buyer from and against the entirety of any Adverse Consequences the Buyer may suffer through and after the date of the claim for indemnification (including any Adverse Consequences the Buyer may suffer after the end of any applicable survival period) resulting from, arising out of, relating to, in the nature of, or caused by the breach;[55] provided, however, that

---

[54] This Agreement, like sample acquisition agreement 2002.1 (the *pro-buyer* stock purchase agreement) and sample acquisition agreement 2002.2 (the *pro-seller* stock purchase agreement), provides that the representations, warranties, and covenants of the *individual Sellers* (e.g., each Seller agrees to sell his or its Target Shares to the Buyer and makes certain representations and warranties concerning himself or itself and his or its Target Shares) will be "several." This is defined in such a way that the particular Seller (and no other Seller) will be entirely responsible for the Buyer's Adverse Consequences if the particular Seller fails to perform his or its obligation. *See* §10(a)(i).

This Agreement, like sample acquisition agreement 2002.1 (the *pro-buyer* stock purchase agreement), also provides that the representations, warranties, and covenants *of the Sellers as a group* (e.g., the Sellers as a group make representations and warranties concerning the Target and its Subsidiaries) will be "joint and several." This is defined in such a way that each Seller will be responsible for *all* of the Buyer's Adverse Consequences if the Sellers as a group fail to perform their obligation. *See* §10(a)(ii). Sample acquisition agreement 2002.2 (the *pro-seller* stock purchase agreement), on the other hand, provides that the representations, warranties, and covenants *of the Sellers as a group* will be "joint." This is defined in such a way that each Seller will be responsible for *his or its Allocable Portion* of the Buyer's Adverse Consequences if the Sellers as a group fail to perform their obligation.

[55] This Agreement, like sample acquisition agreement 2002.1 (the *pro-buyer* stock purchase agreement), requires an indemnifying party (presumably, but not necessarily, one of the Sellers) to indemnify an indemnified party (presumably, but not necessarily, the Buyer) from and against any Adverse Consequences the indemnified party *may* suffer through and after the date of the claim for indemnification (*including* any Adverse Consequences the indemnified party may suffer after the end of any applicable survival period) *resulting from, arising out of, relating to, in the nature of, or caused by* certain breaches by the indemnifying party of his or its representations, warranties, and covenants.

Sample acquisition agreement 2002.2 (the *pro-seller* stock purchase agreement), on the other hand, provides that the indemnifying party (presumably, but not necessarily, one of the Sellers) must indemnify the indemnified party (presumably, but not necessarily, the Buyer) from and against Adverse Consequences the indemnified party *shall* suffer *caused [proximately] by* certain breaches by the indemnifying party of his or its representations, warranties, and covenants.

(A) the Sellers shall not have any obligation to indemnify the Buyer from and against any Adverse Consequences resulting from, arising out of, relating to, in the nature of, or caused by the breach of any representation or warranty of the Sellers contained in §4 above until the Buyer has suffered Adverse Consequences by reason of all such breaches in excess of a $_____ aggregate deductible (after which point the Sellers will be obligated only to indemnify the Buyer from and against further such Adverse Consequences)[56] and (B) there will be a $_____ aggregate ceiling on the obligation of the Sellers to indemnify the Buyer from and against Adverse Consequences resulting from, arising out of, relating to, in the nature of, or caused by breaches of the representations and warranties of the Sellers contained in §4 above.[57]

(ii) In the event any of the Sellers breaches any of his or its covenants in §2(a) above or any of his or its representations and warranties in §3(a) above, and, if there is an applicable survival period pursuant to §8(a) above, provided that the Buyer makes a written claim for indemnification against the Seller pursuant to §10(h) below within such survival period, then the Seller agrees to indemnify the Buyer from and against the entirety of any Adverse Consequences the Buyer may suffer through and after the date of the claim for indemnification (including any Adverse Consequences the Buyer may suffer after the end of any applicable survival period) resulting from, arising out of, relating to, in the nature of, or caused by the breach.

(iii) Each of the Sellers agrees to indemnify the Buyer from and against the entirety of any Adverse Consequences the Buyer may suffer resulting from, arising out of, relating to, in the nature of, or caused by any Liability of any of the Target and its Subsidiaries (x) for any Income Taxes of the Target and its Subsidiaries with respect to any Tax year or portion thereof ending on or before the Closing Date (or for any Tax year beginning before and ending after the Closing Date to the extent allocable (determined in a manner consistent with §9(c)) to the portion of such period beginning before and ending on the Closing Date), [ALTERNATIVE A WHERE THERE IS NO PURCHASE PRICE ADJUSTMENT: to the extent such Income Taxes are not reflected in the reserve for Income Tax Liability (rather than any reserve for deferred Taxes established to reflect timing differences between book and Tax income) shown on the face of the Most Recent Balance Sheet (rather than in any notes thereto), as such reserve is adjusted for the passage of time through the Closing Date in accordance with the past custom and practice of the Target and its Subsidiaries in filing their Tax Returns] [ALTERNATIVE B WHERE THERE IS A PURCHASE PRICE ADJUSTMENT: to the extent such Income Taxes are not reflected in

[56] The Sellers may also seek to impose a *per claim* deductible.

[57] This Agreement, like sample acquisition agreement 2002.2 (the *pro-seller* stock purchase agreement), imposes a deductible and a ceiling on indemnification for breaches of the representations and warranties in §4 above. Sample acquisition agreement 2002.1 (the *pro-buyer* stock purchase agreement), on the other hand, substitutes a threshold (with relation back to the first dollar once the threshold is exceeded) for the deductible and also eliminates the ceiling on indemnification.

the reserve for Income Tax Liability (rather than any reserve for deferred Taxes established to reflect timing differences between book and Tax income) shown on the face of the Closing Balance Sheet],[58] and (y) for the unpaid taxes of any Person (other than any of the Target and its Subsidiaries) under Reg. §1.1502-6 (or any similar provision of state, local, or foreign law), as a transferee or successor, by contract, or otherwise.[59]

(iv) Each of the Sellers agrees to indemnify the Buyer from and against the entirety of any Adverse Consequences the Buyer may suffer resulting from, arising out of, relating to, in the nature of, or caused by _____.[60]

---

[58] Clause (x) is intended to protect the Buyer with respect to pre-Closing Income Tax liabilities of the Target and its Subsidiaries. Alternative A contemplates a fixed purchase price. Alternative B contemplates that there will be a purchase price adjustment as described in ¶2002.5.

In the absence of clause (x), generally the Buyer is protected with respect to pre-Closing Taxes only to the extent the Sellers have breached one or more of the §4(k) Tax representations. For example, clause (x) provides greater protection for the Buyer than does the indemnity for breach of §4(k)(v), because that representation contains a "materiality" qualifier. Accordingly, a provision such as clause (x) can be useful in circumstances where (1) the Sellers are willing to give a strong Income Tax indemnity but are not comfortable giving unqualified Tax representations, (2) in contrast to the approach described in §8(a), the §4(k) Tax representations survive for only a limited period, or (3) as contemplated by §8(b)(i), the indemnity for breaches of Tax and other representations is subject to a deductible (in which case the parties would need to negotiate whether the clause (x) indemnity should also be subject to the deductible).

Clause (x) is best used in addition to (rather than in lieu of) an indemnity for breach of Tax representations, because certain of the §4(k) Tax representations cover matters beyond the scope of clause (x).

[59] If the Target or a Subsidiary has been a member of an Affiliated Group filing a consolidated federal income tax return, such corporation (or its successor) will be jointly and severally liable under Reg. §1.1502-6 for certain tax liabilities incurred by such Affiliated Group for a tax year when such corporation was a member of such Affiliated Group for all or part of such tax year. *See* ¶210.

The Target or a Subsidiary may also be liable for the unpaid taxes of third parties under similar provisions of state, local, or foreign law, as a transferee or successor, by contract (e.g., a tax sharing agreement), or otherwise.

After the Buyer acquires the stock of the Target, the Target and its Subsidiaries will remain liable for any such unpaid tax liabilities.

This Agreement, like sample acquisition agreement 2002.1 (the *pro-buyer* stock purchase agreement), contains an indemnification provision designed to protect the Buyer against any liability for the unpaid taxes of any person other than the Target and its Subsidiaries. Sample acquisition agreement 2002.2 (the *pro-seller* stock purchase agreement), on the other hand, contains no such provision.

[60] Note that the indemnification provisions in clause (i) above will not give the Buyer any post-Closing indemnification rights with respect to any adverse matter that the Sellers may disclose in the Disclosure Schedule. This is because the disclosure will cure any misrepresentation or breach of warranty that might otherwise have existed.

Thus, where the Sellers disclose an adverse matter in the Disclosure Schedule, the Buyer may seek to add a provision conferring specific post-Closing indemnification rights with respect to the particular matter.

The Buyer normally would seek to draft such a provision so that the indemnification would not be subject to any survival period, threshold, deductible, and/or ceiling.

This Agreement, like sample acquisition agreement 2002.1 (the *pro-buyer* stock purchase agreement), provides for such indemnification with respect to particular matters. Sample acquisition agreement 2002.2 (the *pro-seller* stock purchase agreement), on the other hand, lacks a comparable provision.

(c) *Indemnification Provisions for Benefit of the Sellers.* In the event the Buyer breaches any of its representations, warranties, and covenants contained herein, and, if there is an applicable survival period pursuant to §8(a) above, provided that any of the Sellers makes a written claim for indemnification against the Buyer pursuant to §10(h) below within such survival period, then the Buyer agrees to indemnify each of the Sellers from and against the entirety of any Adverse Consequences the Seller may suffer through and after the date of the claim for indemnification (including any Adverse Consequences the Seller may suffer after the end of any applicable survival period) resulting from, arising out of, relating to, in the nature of, or caused by the breach.

(d) *Matters Involving Third Parties.*

(i) If any third party shall notify any Party (the *"Indemnified Party"*) with respect to any matter (a *"Third Party Claim"*) which may give rise to a claim for indemnification against any other Party (the *"Indemnifying Party"*) under this §8, then the Indemnified Party shall promptly notify each Indemnifying Party thereof in writing; *provided, however,* that no delay on the part of the Indemnified Party in notifying any Indemnifying Party shall relieve the Indemnifying Party from any obligation hereunder unless (and then solely to the extent) the Indemnifying Party thereby is prejudiced.

(ii) Any Indemnifying Party will have the right to assume the defense of the Third Party Claim with counsel of his or its choice reasonably satisfactory to the Indemnified Party at any time within 15 days after the Indemnified Party has given notice of the Third Party Claim; *provided, however,* that the Indemnifying Party must conduct the defense of the Third Party Claim actively and diligently thereafter in order to preserve its rights in this regard; and *provided further* that the Indemnified Party may retain separate co-counsel at its sole cost and expense and participate in the defense of the Third Party Claim.[61]

(iii) So long as the Indemnifying Party has assumed and is conducting the defense of the Third Party Claim in accordance with §8(d)(ii) above, (A) the

---

[61] An *indemnifying* party (presumably, but not necessarily, one of the Sellers) will normally seek to control the defense of any third party claim that may give rise to a claim for indemnification under §8. However, the *indemnified* party (presumably, but not necessarily, the Buyer) will not want the indemnifying party to control the defense of any third party claim in which the indemnified party will retain a meaningful interest. For example, the indemnified party may seek to control the defense of a third party claim if the third party seeks an injunction or other equitable relief or if it is not clear that the indemnifying party will bear the entirety of any money damages or amount paid in settlement.

Sample acquisition agreement 2002.1 (the *pro-buyer* stock purchase agreement) provides that the indemnified party will control the defense of any third party claim *unless* (a) an indemnifying party accepts full responsibility for the matter within [15 days], (b) the indemnifying party demonstrates it has the financial resources necessary to defend against the matter and fulfill its indemnification obligations, (c) the third party seeks only money damages (as opposed to an injunction or other equitable relief), (d) settlement of, or an adverse judgment with respect to, the third party claim is not likely to establish a precedent [materially] adverse to the indemnified party, and (e) the indemnifying party conducts the defense actively and diligently.

Indemnifying Party will not consent to the entry of any judgment or enter into any settlement with respect to the Third Party Claim without the prior written consent of the Indemnified Party (not to be withheld unreasonably) unless the judgment or proposed settlement involves only the payment of money damages by one or more of the Indemnifying Parties and does not impose an injunction or other equitable relief upon the Indemnified Party and (B) the Indemnified Party will not consent to the entry of any judgment or enter into any settlement with respect to the Third Party Claim without the prior written consent of the Indemnifying Party (not to be withheld unreasonably).

(iv) In the event none of the Indemnifying Parties assumes and conducts the defense of the Third Party Claim in accordance with §8(d)(ii) above, however, (A) the Indemnified Party may defend against, and consent to the entry of any judgment or enter into any settlement with respect to, the Third Party Claim in any manner he or it reasonably may deem appropriate (and the Indemnified Party need not consult with, or obtain any consent from, any Indemnifying Party in connection therewith) and (B) the Indemnifying Parties will remain responsible for any Adverse Consequences the Indemnified Party may suffer resulting from, arising out of, relating to, in the nature of, or caused by the Third Party Claim to the fullest extent provided in this §8.[62]

(e) *Determination of Adverse Consequences.* The Parties shall make appropriate adjustments for tax consequences and insurance coverage and take into account

---

Sample acquisition agreement 2002.2 (the *pro-seller* stock purchase agreement), on the other hand, provides that an indemnifying party may assume the defense of a third party claim *at any time* during the course of the defense.

This Agreement, intended to favor neither the Buyer nor the Sellers, provides that an indemnifying party may assume the defense of a third party claim at any time within 15 days after the indemnified party has given notice of the third party claim but requires the indemnifying party to conduct the defense of the third party claim actively and diligently thereafter.

[62] This Agreement, like sample acquisition agreement 2002.1 (the *pro-buyer* stock purchase agreement), provides that the *indemnified party* will not consent to the entry of any judgment or enter into any settlement with respect to the third party claim without the prior written consent of the indemnifying party (not to be withheld unreasonably) unless the indemnifying party fails to assume and conduct the defense of the third party claim. Sample acquisition agreement 2002.2 (the *pro-seller* stock purchase agreement), on the other hand, provides that the indemnified party will not consent to the entry of any judgment or enter into any settlement with respect to the third party claim without the prior written consent of the indemnifying party (not to be withheld unreasonably) under any circumstances.

This Agreement, like sample acquisition agreement 2002.2 (the *pro-seller* stock purchase agreement), also provides that the *indemnifying party* will not consent to the entry of any judgment or enter into any settlement with respect to the third party claim without the prior written consent of the indemnified party (not to be withheld unreasonably) unless the judgment or proposed settlement involves only the payment of money damages by one or more of the indemnifying parties and does not impose an injunction or other equitable relief upon the indemnified party. Sample acquisition agreement 2002.1 (the *pro-buyer* stock purchase agreement), on the other hand, provides that the indemnifying party will not consent to the entry of any judgment or enter into any settlement with respect to the third party claim without the prior written consent of the indemnified party (not to be withheld unreasonably) under any circumstances.

the time cost of money (using the Applicable Rate as the discount rate) in determining Adverse Consequences for purposes of this 8. All indemnification payments under this §8 shall be deemed adjustments to the Purchase Price.

(f) *Exclusive Remedy.*[63] The Buyer and the Seller acknowledge and agree that the foregoing indemnification provisions in this §8 shall be the exclusive remedy of the Buyer and the Seller with respect to the Target, its Subsidiaries, and the transactions contemplated by this Agreement. Without limiting the generality of the foregoing, the Buyer and the Seller hereby waive any statutory, equitable, or common law rights or remedies relating to any environmental matters, including without limitation any such matters arising under any Environmental, Health, and Safety Requirements and including without limitation any arising under the Comprehensive Environmental Response, Compensation, and Liability Act "(CERCLA)". Each of the Sellers hereby agrees that he or it will not make any claim for indemnification against any of the Target and its Subsidiaries by reason of the fact that he or it was a director, officer, employee, or agent of any such entity or was serving at the request of any such entity as a partner, trustee, director, officer, employee, or agent of another entity (whether such claim is for judgments, damages, penalties, fines, costs, amounts paid in settlement, losses, expenses, or otherwise and whether such claim is pursuant to any statute, charter document, bylaw, agreement, or otherwise) with respect to any action, suit, proceeding, complaint, claim, or demand brought by the Buyer against such Seller (whether such action, suit, proceeding, complaint, claim, or demand is pursuant to this Agreement, applicable law, or otherwise).[64]

[63] Sample acquisition agreement 2002.1 (the *pro-buyer* stock purchase agreement) states that the indemnification provisions in the Agreement are in addition to and not in derogation of any other statutory, equitable, or common law remedies (including any such remedies relating to environmental matters).

As does this *neutral* stock purchase agreement, sample acquisition agreement 2002.2 (the *pro-seller* stock purchase agreement) states that the remedies available to the Parties under the Agreement are exclusive (i.e., that the Buyer has no other statutory, equitable, or common law remedies) and also contains an additional provision by which the Buyer specifically waives and releases the Seller from, and agrees to indemnify the Seller with respect to, any environmental liabilities.

[64] This Agreement, like sample acquisition agreement 2002.1 (the *pro-buyer* stock purchase agreement), contains a provision to the effect that no Seller will make a claim for indemnification against the Target by reason of the fact that the Seller was, before the stock purchase, a director or other officeholder of the Target entitled to indemnification from the Target, with respect to any suit or claim the Buyer might bring against the Seller in connection with the stock purchase. This provision responds to the surprising decision in Heffernan v. Pacific Dunlop GNB Corporation, 965 F.2d 369 (7th Cir. 1992). Sample acquisition agreement 2002.2 (the *pro-seller* stock purchase agreement), on the other hand, lacks such a provision.

In *Heffernan,* the Buyer of Target's stock sued the Sellers (who had sold Target's stock to the Buyer) after the closing of the stock sale, alleging that the Sellers failed to disclose to the Buyer certain of the Target's environmental and other liabilities. The court focused on the Buyer's claim against Seller A under §12(2) of the 1933 Act. Section 12(2) makes a seller of securities (here Seller A) liable to the purchaser (here the Buyer) for certain material misrepresentations and omissions in connection with the sale.

Seller A, who had been a director as well as a shareholder of the Target, countered that the Target (now a wholly owned subsidiary of the Buyer) should be required to indemnify him for any losses he suffered as a result of the Buyer's lawsuit. He based his argument on Delaware corporate law

9. *Tax Matters.*[65] The following provisions shall govern the allocation of responsibility as between Buyer and Sellers for certain tax matters following the Closing Date:

(a) *Tax Periods Ending on or Before the Closing Date.* Buyer shall prepare or cause to be prepared and file or cause to be filed all Tax Returns for the Target and its Subsidiaries for all periods ending on or prior to the Closing Date which are filed after the Closing Date [other than income Tax Returns with respect to periods for which a consolidated, unitary or combined income Tax Return of Seller will include the operations of the Target and its Subsidiaries]. Buyer shall permit Sellers to review and comment on each such Tax Return described in the preceding sentence prior to filing and shall make such revisions to such Tax Returns as are reasonably requested by Sellers. Sellers shall reimburse Buyer for Taxes of the Target and its Subsidiaries with respect to such periods within fifteen (15) days after payment by Buyer or the Target and its Subsidiaries of such Taxes to the extent such Taxes are not reflected in the reserve for Tax Liability (rather than any reserve for deferred Taxes established to reflect timing differences between book and Tax income) shown on the face of the Closing Balance Sheet.[66]

(which permits a corporation to indemnify its directors against third party lawsuits under certain circumstances) and the Target's bylaws (which made such director indemnification mandatory).

The federal district court dismissed Seller A's indemnification claim, holding (quite rationally) that he was not entitled to indemnification because his alleged misconduct was committed as a selling shareholder and not as a director of the Target.

On appeal, the Seventh Circuit reversed. The court noted that Seller A's duty of care under §12(2) (i.e., his duty to ascertain the truth or falsity of the Sellers representations to the Buyer) was higher because he was a director, and hence the Buyer's claim against Seller A may have been related to his status as a former director of Target. Accordingly, the court concluded that it was premature to dismiss Seller A's indemnification claim before trial.

[65] If Target is (1) an S corporation, (2) a subsidiary member of a consolidated group, or (3) a subsidiary member of an affiliated (but not consolidated) group, the parties have the ability to make a Code §338(h)(10) election, in which case all parties (including the selling shareholders) are treated for tax purposes as if Buyer purchased Target's assets. With a Code §338(h)(10) election (as distinguished from a regular Code §338 election), there is no double tax on the transaction, i.e., Target is treated as selling assets and Target's shareholders are treated as receiving their proceeds in a deemed liquidation of Target, which deemed liquidation generally will not produce a second tax because of the consolidated return regulations in the consolidated group situation, Code §332 in the affiliated subsidiary situation, and Subchapter S pass-through rules in the S corporation situation. *See* ¶¶206.1.1, 206.3, 206.3.3, and 1109.3.

See ¶2002.4, *Sale of Subsidiary Out of a Consolidated Group*, for contractual provisions to use in connection with a Code §338(h)(10) election for a Target that is a member of a selling consolidated group. See ¶2002.6, *P's Purchase of T-SCo's Stock for Cash and Notes*, for contractual provisions to use in connection with a Code §338(h)(10) election for a Target that is an S corporation.

If Target is being acquired out of an affiliated (but not consolidated) group, a Code §338(h)(10) election may be made only if Buyer purchases at least 80% (by vote and by value) of Target's stock on a single day from a single member of the affiliated group of which Target is a member. In addition, the treatment of the sale of Target stock as an asset sale rather than as a stock sale applies only to the stock purchased from the member of the affiliated group that sold the requisite 80% of Target's stock. *See* ¶206.2.

[66] This provision contemplates that there will be a purchase price adjustment as described in ¶2002.5.

The pro-buyer stock purchase agreement in ¶2002.1 also contains this provision. However, the pro-seller stock purchase agreement in ¶2002.2 does not contain any provision for the preparation

(b) *Tax Periods Beginning Before and Ending After the Closing Date.* Buyer shall prepare or cause to be prepared and file or cause to be filed any Tax Returns of the Target and its Subsidiaries for Tax periods which begin before the Closing Date and end after the Closing Date. Seller shall pay to Buyer within fifteen (15) days after the date on which Taxes are paid with respect to such periods an amount equal to the portion of such Taxes which relates to the portion of such Taxable period ending on the Closing Date to the extent such Taxes are not reflected in the reserve for Tax Liability (rather than any reserve for deferred Taxes established to reflect timing differences between book and Tax income) shown on the face of the Closing Balance Sheet.[67] For purposes of this Section, in the case of any Taxes that are imposed on a periodic basis and are payable for a Taxable period that includes (but does not end on) the Closing Date, the portion of such Tax which relates to the portion of such Taxable period ending on the Closing Date shall (x) in the case of any Taxes other than Taxes based upon or related to income or receipts, be deemed to be the amount of such Tax for the entire Taxable period multiplied by a fraction the numerator of which is the number of days in the Taxable period ending on the Closing Date and the denominator of which is the number of days in the entire Taxable period, and (y) in the case of any Tax based upon or related to income or receipts be deemed equal to the amount which would be payable if the relevant Taxable period ended on the Closing Date. Any credits relating to a Taxable period that begins before and ends after the Closing Date shall be taken into account as though the relevant Taxable period ended on the Closing Date. All determinations necessary to give effect to the foregoing allocations shall be made in a manner consistent with prior practice of the Target and its Subsidiaries.

(c) *Refunds and Tax Benefits.* Any Tax refunds that are received by Buyer or the Target and its Subsidiaries, and any amounts credited against Tax to which Buyer or the Target and its Subsidiaries become entitled, that relate to Tax periods or portions thereof ending on or before the Closing Date shall be for the account of Seller, and Buyer shall pay over to Seller any such refund or the amount of any such credit within fifteen (15) days after receipt or entitlement thereto. In addition, to the extent that a claim for refund or a proceeding results in a payment or credit against Tax by a taxing authority to the Buyer or the Target and its Subsidiaries of any amount accrued on the Closing Balance Sheet, the Buyer shall

---

of, or payment of taxes with respect to, returns filed after the Closing Date, or for the payment of tax refunds received after the Closing Date. Because the pro-seller agreement does not require Sellers to indemnify Buyer against pre-Closing taxes, such taxes will be an obligation of the Target, and hence an indirect obligation of Buyer, and tax refunds will generally be received and retained by Target.

[67] This provision contemplates that there will be a purchase price adjustment as described in ¶2002.5.

The pro-buyer stock purchase agreement in ¶2002.1 also contains this provision. However, the pro-seller stock purchase agreement in ¶2002.2 does not contain any provision for the preparation of, or payment of taxes with respect to, returns filed after the Closing Date. Because the pro-seller agreement does not require Sellers to indemnify Buyer against pre-Closing taxes, such taxes will be an obligation of the Target, and hence an indirect obligation of Buyer.

pay such amount to Seller within fifteen (15) days after receipt or entitlement thereto.[68]

(d) *Cooperation on Tax Matters.*

(i) Buyer, the Target and its Subsidiaries and Sellers shall cooperate fully, as and to the extent reasonably requested by the other party, in connection with the filing of Tax Returns pursuant to this Section and any audit, litigation or other proceeding with respect to Taxes. Such cooperation shall include the retention and (upon the other party's request) the provision of records and information which are reasonably relevant to any such audit, litigation or other proceeding and making employees available on a mutually convenient basis to provide additional information and explanation of any material provided hereunder. The Target and its Subsidiaries and Sellers agree (A) to retain all books and records with respect to Tax matters pertinent to the Target and its Subsidiaries relating to any taxable period beginning before the Closing Date until the expiration of the statute of limitations (and, to the extent notified by Buyer or Sellers, any extensions thereof) of the respective taxable periods, and to abide by all record retention agreements entered into with any taxing authority, and (B) to give the other party reasonable written notice prior to transferring, destroying or discarding any such books and records and, if the other party so requests, the Target and its Subsidiaries or Sellers, as the case may be, shall allow the other party to take possession of such books and records.

(ii) Buyer and Seller further agree, upon request, to use their best efforts to obtain any certificate or other document from any governmental authority or any other Person as may be necessary to mitigate, reduce or eliminate any Tax that could be imposed (including, but not limited to, with respect to the transactions contemplated hereby).

(iii) Buyer and Seller further agree, upon request, to provide the other party with all information that either party may be required to report pursuant §6043 of the Code and all Treasury Department Regulations promulgated thereunder.

(e) *Tax Sharing Agreements.* All tax sharing agreements or similar agreements with respect to or involving the Target and its Subsidiaries shall be terminated

---

[68] The pro-buyer stock purchase agreement in ¶2002.1 does not contain any provision addressing the treatment of tax refunds for pre-Closing tax periods. Such refunds of taxes previously paid by Target could arise in two circumstances: first, when Target overpaid its taxes for a pre-Closing period, and second, when a Target post-Closing loss can be carried back to Target's pre-Closing period. In the absence of a specific provision in the agreement, such refunds generally will be paid to Target, and hence Buyer will receive the economic benefit of such refunds, even though Sellers bear the economic burden of taxes for the pre-Closing period.

When Target was, prior to Closing, a member of Seller's consolidated group, federal income tax refunds for pre-Closing periods would be paid to the parent of Seller's consolidated group, and hence Seller would receive the economic benefit of such refunds. See ¶2002.4.4 for a discussion of this topic when Target was a member of Seller's consolidated group before the acquisition and ¶2002.4.7(f) for

as of the Closing Date and, after the Closing Date, the Target and its Subsidiaries shall not be bound thereby or have any liability thereunder.

(f) *Certain Taxes.* All transfer, documentary, sales, use, stamp, registration and other such Taxes and fees (including any penalties and interest) incurred in connection with this Agreement (including any New York State Gains Tax, New York City Transfer Tax and any similar tax imposed in other states or subdivisions), shall be paid by Sellers when due, and Sellers will, at their own expense, file all necessary Tax Returns and other documentation with respect to all such transfer, documentary, sales, use, stamp, registration and other Taxes and fees, and, if required by applicable law, Buyer will, and will cause its affiliates to, join in the execution of any such Tax Returns and other documentation.

10. *Termination.*

(a) *Termination of Agreement.*[69] Certain of the Parties may terminate this Agreement as provided below:

(i) the Buyer and the Requisite Sellers may terminate this Agreement by mutual written consent at any time prior to the Closing;

(ii) the Buyer may terminate this Agreement by giving written notice to the Requisite Sellers at any time prior to the Closing (A) in the event any of the Sellers has breached any material representation, warranty, or covenant contained in this Agreement in any material respect, the Buyer has notified the Requisite Sellers of the breach, and the breach has continued without cure for a period of [30 days] after the notice of breach or (B) if the Closing shall not have occurred on or before _____, 19____, by reason of the failure of any condition precedent under §7(a) hereof (unless the failure results primarily from the Buyer itself breaching any representation, warranty, or covenant contained in this Agreement); and

(iii) the Requisite Sellers may terminate this Agreement by giving written notice to the Buyer at any time prior to the Closing (A) in the event the Buyer has breached any material representation, warranty, or covenant contained in this Agreement in any material respect, any of the Sellers has notified the Buyer of the breach, and the breach has continued without cure for a period of [30 days] after the notice of breach or (B) if the Closing shall not have occurred on or before _____, 19____, by reason of the failure of any condition

---

a sample agreement clause requiring Seller to pay over to Buyer any tax refund (or reduction of tax liability) resulting from a carryback of a postacquisition tax attribute of the Target and its Subsidiaries.

[69] Sample acquisition agreement 2002.1 (the *pro-buyer* stock purchase agreement) contains a provision giving the Buyer a right to terminate the agreement for a limited period after signing if the Buyer is not [reasonably] satisfied with the results of its continuing business, legal, environmental, and accounting due diligence concerning the Target and its Subsidiaries. This Agreement, like sample acquisition agreement 2002.2 (the *pro-seller* stock purchase agreement), lacks a comparable provision.

precedent under §7(b) hereof (unless the failure results primarily from any of the Sellers themselves breaching any representation, warranty, or covenant contained in this Agreement).

(b) *Effect of Termination.* If any Party terminates this Agreement pursuant to §10(a) above, all rights and obligations of the Parties hereunder shall terminate without any liability of any Party to any other Party (except for any liability of any Party then in breach); *provided, however*, that the confidentiality provisions contained in §5(e) above shall survive termination.

11. *Miscellaneous.*[70]

(a) *Nature of Certain Obligations.*

(i) The covenants of each of the Sellers in §2(a) above concerning the sale of his or its Target Shares to the Buyer and the representations and warranties of each of the Sellers in §3(a) above concerning the transaction are several obligations. This means that the particular Seller making the representation, warranty, or covenant will be solely responsible to the extent provided in §8 above for any Adverse Consequences the Buyer may suffer as a result of any breach thereof.

(ii) The remainder of the representations, warranties, and covenants in this Agreement are joint and several obligations. This means that each Seller will be responsible to the extent provided in §8 above for the entirety of any Adverse Consequences the Buyer may suffer as a result of any breach thereof.[71]

(b) *Press Releases and Public Announcements.* No Party shall issue any press release or make any public announcement relating to the subject matter of this

---

[70] Sample acquisition agreement 2002.1 (the *pro-buyer* stock purchase agreement) contains provisions whereby the Parties agree to specific performance, agree to service of process of an agent, and submit to the [exclusive] jurisdiction of the state and federal courts in a particular city. This Agreement, like sample acquisition agreement 2002.2 (the *pro-seller* stock purchase agreement), lacks comparable provisions.

The Parties may want to add a provision calling for optional or mandatory arbitration with respect to all or certain issues.

[71] This Agreement, like sample acquisition agreement 2002.1 (the *pro-buyer* stock purchase agreement), provides that the obligations of the Sellers as a group will be "joint and several." That term is defined in such a way that each Seller would be responsible for *all* of the Buyer's Adverse Consequences (instead of only for his or its Allocable Portion) if the Sellers as a group failed to perform their obligations. This would protect the Buyer from having to proceed against all the Sellers (some of whom may be insolvent or not subject to service of process) in order to collect all of what is owing it.

Sample acquisition agreement 2002.2 (the *pro-seller* stock purchase agreement) on the other hand, provides that the obligations of the Sellers as a group will be "joint." That term is defined in such a way that each Seller would be responsible for only his or its *allocable portion* of the Buyer's Adverse Consequences (as opposed to the entire amount) if the Sellers as a group failed to perform their obligations. This would protect those Sellers who have "deep pockets" (or who otherwise are attractive

Agreement [prior to the Closing] without the prior written approval of the Buyer and the Requisite Sellers; *provided, however,* that any Party may make any public disclosure it believes in good faith is required by applicable law or any listing or trading agreement concerning its publicly-traded securities (in which case the disclosing Party will use its [reasonable] best efforts to advise the other Parties prior to making the disclosure).

(c) *No Third-Party Beneficiaries.* This Agreement shall not confer any rights or remedies upon any Person other than the Parties and their respective successors and permitted assigns.

(d) *Entire Agreement.* [This Agreement (including the documents referred to herein) constitutes the entire agreement among the Parties and supersedes any prior understandings, agreements, or representations by or among the Parties, written or oral, to the extent they related in any way to the subject matter hereof.]

(e) *Succession and Assignment.* This Agreement shall be binding upon and inure to the benefit of the Parties named herein and their respective successors and permitted assigns. No Party may assign either this Agreement or any of his or its rights, interests, or obligations hereunder without the prior written approval of the Buyer and the Requisite Sellers; *provided, however,* that the Buyer may (i) assign any or all of its rights and interests hereunder to one or more of its Affiliates and (ii) designate one or more of its Affiliates to perform its obligations hereunder (in any or all of which cases the Buyer nonetheless shall remain responsible for the performance of all of its obligations hereunder).

(f) *Counterparts.* This Agreement may be executed in one or more counterparts, each of which shall be deemed an original but all of which together will constitute one and the same instrument.

(g) *Headings.* The section headings contained in this Agreement are inserted for convenience only and shall not affect in any way the meaning or interpretation of this Agreement.

(h) *Notices.*[72] All notices, requests, demands, claims, and other communications hereunder will be in writing. Any notice, request, demand, claim, or other communication hereunder shall be deemed duly given if (and then two business days after) it is sent by registered or certified mail, return receipt requested, postage prepaid, and addressed to the intended recipient as set forth below:

---

defendants) from potentially having to indemnify the Buyer against a disproportionately large portion (or even all) of its Adverse Consequences.

[72] The Parties may want to add provisions designating a nominee to act on behalf of the Sellers for purposes of receiving notice, agreeing to modifications and amendments, and taking action.

If to the Sellers: *Copy to:*

If to the Buyer: *Copy to:*

Any Party may send any notice, request, demand, claim, or other communication hereunder to the intended recipient at the address set forth above using any other means (including personal delivery, expedited courier, messenger service, telecopy, telex, ordinary mail, or electronic mail), but no such notice, request, demand, claim, or other communication shall be deemed to have been duly given unless and until it actually is received by the intended recipient. Any Party may change the address to which notices, requests, demands, claims, and other communications hereunder are to be delivered by giving the other Parties notice in the manner herein set forth.

(i) *Governing Law. This Agreement shall be governed by and construed in accordance with the domestic laws of the State of _____ without giving effect to any choice or conflict of law provision or rule (whether of the State of _____ or any other jurisdiction) that would cause the application of the laws of any jurisdiction other than the State of _____.*

(j) *Amendments and Waivers.* No amendment of any provision of this Agreement shall be valid unless the same shall be in writing and signed by the Buyer and the Requisite Sellers. No waiver by any Party of any default, misrepresentation, or breach of warranty or covenant hereunder, whether intentional or not, shall be deemed to extend to any prior or subsequent default, misrepresentation, or breach of warranty or covenant hereunder or affect in any way any rights arising by virtue of any prior or subsequent such occurrence.

(k) *Severability.* Any term or provision of this Agreement that is invalid or unenforceable in any situation in any jurisdiction shall not affect the validity or enforceability of the remaining terms and provisions hereof or the validity or enforceability of the offending term or provision in any other situation or in any other jurisdiction.

(l) *Expenses.* Each of the Parties, the Target, and its Subsidiaries will bear his or its own costs and expenses (including legal fees and expenses) incurred in connection with this Agreement and the transactions contemplated hereby. The Sellers agree that none of the Target and its Subsidiaries has borne or will bear any of the Sellers' costs and expenses (including any of their legal fees and expenses) in connection with this Agreement or any of the transactions contemplated hereby.[73]

---

[73] This Agreement, like sample acquisition agreement 2002.1 (the *pro-buyer* stock purchase agreement), makes the Target responsible for the transactional costs and expenses of the Target and its Subsidiaries. This means that the Buyer will bear these costs and expenses if it consummates the stock purchase. For this reason, the Buyer may seek to have the Sellers reimburse the Target and its Subsidiaries for some or all of these costs and expenses.

(m) *Construction.* The Parties have participated jointly in the negotiation and drafting of this Agreement. In the event an ambiguity or question of intent or interpretation arises, this Agreement shall be construed as if drafted jointly by the Parties and no presumption or burden of proof shall arise favoring or disfavoring any Party by virtue of the authorship of any of the provisions of this Agreement. Any reference to any federal, state, local, or foreign statute or law shall be deemed also to refer to all rules and regulations promulgated thereunder, unless the context requires otherwise. The word "including" shall mean including without limitation.[74]

(n) *Incorporation of Exhibits, Annexes, and Schedules.* The Exhibits, Annexes, and Schedules identified in this Agreement are incorporated herein by reference and made a part hereof.

* * * * *

IN WITNESS WHEREOF, the Parties hereto have executed this Agreement on [as of] the date first above written.

[BUYER]

By: _____

Title: _____

[SELLER # 1 (an entity)]

By: _____

Title: _____

[SELLER # 2 (an entity)]

By: _____

Title: _____

_____

[SELLER #3 (an individual)]

Sample acquisition agreement 2002.2 (the *pro-seller* stock purchase agreement), on the other hand, makes the Target and its Subsidiaries responsible not only for their own costs and expenses but also for some or all of *the Sellers'* costs and expenses.

The Parties may settle on a compromise allocation of responsibility (such as sharing the costs and expenses in a predetermined ratio or making one Party responsible for the costs and expenses up to a specified aggregate ceiling and the other Party responsible for any excess).

[74] Sample acquisition agreement 2002.1 (the *pro-buyer* stock purchase agreement) contains additional provisions construing the representations, warranties, and covenants in a manner more favorable to the Buyer. This Agreement, like sample acquisition agreement 2002.2 (the *pro-seller* stock purchase agreement), lacks comparable provisions.

¶2002.4 Sale of Subsidiary Out of Consolidated Group

Sample acquisition agreements 2002.1 (the *pro-buyer* stock purchase agreement), 2002.2 (the *pro-seller* stock purchase agreement), and 2002.3 (the *neutral* stock purchase agreement) assume that (prior to P's purchase of T's stock) T was not filing a consolidated federal income tax return with Bigco (i.e., prior to P's purchase of T's stock, T either was not a Bigco subsidiary or, if T was a Bigco subsidiary, Bigco and T were not filing consolidated federal income tax returns). This sample acquisition agreement 2002.4 (sale of a consolidated subsidiary) contains additional provisions which should be used (or at least considered) in tandem with either acquisition agreement 2002.1, acquisition agreement 2002.2, or acquisition agreement 2002.3 if T was filing a consolidated return with Bigco before P purchased T's stock. See ¶210 and ¶212 for a discussion of certain tax issues that may arise if T and Bigco were filing consolidated returns.

Except when explicitly stated in 2002.4, this acquisition agreement deals only with the *federal* income tax issues arising out of filing a consolidated *federal* income tax return and not with the many *state* income tax issues arising out of filing consolidated or separate *state* income tax returns. The state income tax consequences turn, of course, on the varying income tax laws of the 50 states.

¶2002.4.1 Code §338(h)(10) Election

Because T is a member of Bigco's consolidated group, Bigco and P can make a joint election under Code §338(h)(10) to treat (for tax purposes) P's purchase of T's stock as a purchase of T's assets. If P and Bigco make such a joint Code §338(h)(10) election, the parties are treated (for tax purposes) as if T sold its assets to new T (a newly formed P subsidiary) and, after the asset sale, T liquidated upstream into Bigco in a tax-free Code §332 liquidation. Hence, Bigco would succeed to any T tax attributes (NOLs, E&P, etc.) in the Code §332 liquidation. *See* ¶206.

New T (a P subsidiary) receives an aggregate basis for old T's assets generally equal to the amount P paid for T's stock plus T's liabilities (inherited by new T) and other relevant items (e.g., fees and expenses). *See* ¶206.6. This aggregate basis is allocated to T's assets by class under the method described in ¶403.3.4 and ¶403.6. New T's basis for goodwill, going concern value and other Code §197 intangibles is determined under the residual method.

Because T's deemed liquidation into Bigco is tax-free under Code §332, only a single layer of tax is imposed on the transaction even after *GU* repeal. Thus, a Code §338(h)(10) election will generally be more attractive than a Code §338 election (which can be made by P alone) because the latter results in two layers of tax. *See* ¶205, ¶206, and ¶403.1.

EXAMPLE 1

Bigco owns all of T's stock, which has an FV of $100 and an outside tax basis in Bigco's hands of $40. T owns depreciable equipment with a $100 FV and a $40 inside tax basis in T's hands. T has no liabilities. P purchases T's stock for $100. P makes a Code §338 election (but P and Bigco do not make a joint Code §338(h)(10) election).

Bigco recognizes $60 of gain on the sale of T's stock ($100 selling price minus Bigco's $40 basis in T's stock). Bigco pays $21 in federal income tax ($60 gain × 35%).

Under the ADSP formula of the final Code §338 regulations (see ¶205.5), old T recognizes $92.31 of gain on the deemed sale of its equipment ($100 stock selling price plus $32.31 federal income tax liability inherited by new T on the deemed asset sale gain minus old T's $40 basis in its assets). This income cannot be included on the Bigco group's consolidated return and must be reported by old T in a separate return. See ¶205.4. Old T pays $32.31 in federal income tax ($92.31 gain × 35%).

New T takes an aggregate basis of $132.31 in its assets ($100 stock purchase price + $32.31 in T-level tax liability inherited by new T). This asset basis is allocated $100 to T's equipment and, under the residual method, the remaining $32.31 is allocated to Code §197 intangibles (since under the allocation rules, assets other than Code §197 intangibles may not be allocated basis in excess of their FV). See ¶¶403.3 and 403.6. Over the 15 year life of the Code §197 intangibles, new T will receive an aggregate federal income tax benefit of $11.31 (35% of $32.31) from its amortization deductions (if tax rates remain unchanged).

Thus, the total federal income tax on the acquisition is $42 ($21 Bigco tax on the sale of T stock plus $32.31 T-level tax on the deemed asset sale minus $11.31 tax benefit from the amortization of the Code §197 intangibles).

EXAMPLE 2

Same as Example 1 except that Bigco and P make a joint Code §338(h)(10) election.

The Bigco group (on its consolidated income tax return) recognizes $60 gain on old T's deemed sale of its equipment to new T for $100 and Bigco pays $21 in federal income tax ($60 gain × 35%). See ¶206.1. Bigco recognizes no gain on the deemed Code §332 liquidation of old T into Bigco.

New T takes an aggregate $100 basis in its assets ($100 purchase price plus $0 inherited tax liability). All of this basis is allocated to T's equipment.

The result in Example 2 is considerably more tax efficient than the result in Example 1. In Example 2 Bigco and T pay a total of $21 in federal income tax and new T obtains an asset basis step-up to $100 for the equipment. In Example 1 Bigco and T pay a total of $53.31 in federal income tax and new T obtains an asset basis step-up to $100 for the equipment (same as Example 2) plus a $32.31 basis for Code §197 intangibles, which will produce aggregate federal income tax savings of $11.31 (35% of $32.31) over 15 years. Hence, Example 2 results in $32.31 less front-end federal income tax and $11.31 less back-end tax savings, making Example 2 considerably more tax efficient.

Depending on the facts involved, a Code §338(h)(10) election may favor either the buyer or the seller.

P will generally want to make a Code §338(h)(10) election if it produces a step-up in the tax basis of T's assets which is allocable (i) to short-lived depreciable and amortizable assets or (ii) to assets likely to be sold soon (e.g., inventory). In some cases where there is an overall asset basis step-up, however, the operation of the allocation rules may make a Code §338(h)(10) election undesirable for P (e.g., by producing a step-down in basis for T's inventory and receivables). P will generally not want to make the election if it results in an overall step-down in basis.

EXAMPLE 3

T owns inventory (FV $100 and tax basis $100) and land (FV $150 and tax basis $10). T has a contingent liability that the parties value at $50 and no other liabilities. P buys T's stock from Bigco for $200 ($100 + $150 − $50). If P and Bigco make a Code §338(h)(10) election, new T's aggregate basis in its assets will initially be $200 (since the contingent liability may not be counted unless and until it becomes fixed). *See* ¶¶206.7, 206.7.1, and 403.5. New T's $200 of asset basis is allocated between the inventory and land based on relative FVs, so that the basis in the inventory is stepped down to $80 (from $100) and the basis in the land is stepped up to $120 (from $10).

When T sells its inventory for $100 shortly after the acquisition, T recognizes $20 of gain attributable to the step-down. T recognizes no benefit from the step-up on the nondepreciable land unless and until T sells the land.

Whether Bigco will desire to or be willing to make a Code §338(h)(10) election depends largely on the relative magnitude of Bigco's outside basis in its T stock compared to T's inside net basis in its assets (i.e., T's asset basis less its liabilities). If T's inside net asset basis is higher, a Code §338(h)(10) election will reduce Bigco's gain. If T's outside basis is higher, a stock sale without a Code §338(b)(10) election will produce less gain. If outside basis and inside net asset basis are equal, the amount of Bigco's gain will be the same with or without a Code §338(h)(10) election although the composition of the gain (i.e., capital or ordinary) likely will be different, as explained more fully below.

The consolidated return investment adjustment rules generally adjust Bigco's outside basis in T's stock in lockstep with T's changes in inside net asset basis. Thus, differences between inside and outside basis are generally produced, if at all, only in the transaction in which Bigco acquired T.

Bigco's outside basis in T's stock will be higher than T's inside net asset basis at the time of the Bigco-P stock sale if Bigco previously purchased T's stock for a price greater than T's inside net asset basis at the time of such stock purchase and such stock purchase was structured so that it left T's historic asset basis unchanged. Conversely, Bigco's outside basis in T's stock will be lower than T's inside net asset basis at the time of the Bigco-P stock sale if Bigco previously purchased T's stock for a price less than T's inside net asset basis at the time of such stock purchase and such stock purchase was structured so that T's historic asset basis remained unchanged. If Bigco previously formed T by dropping cash or assets into a newly formed T *or* if Bigco previously purchased T's stock in a transaction structured so that T's assets took on a new cost basis (i.e., a taxable purchase of assets or a taxable purchase of stock with a Code §338 or 338(h)(10) election) *or* if Bigco purchased T's stock for a price equal to T's inside net asset basis at the time of such stock purchase, Bigco's outside basis in T's stock will be equal to T's inside net asset basis at the time of the later Bigco-P stock sale.

If previously Bigco acquired T in a tax-free reorganization, the relationship between T's inside and outside basis at the time of the Bigco-P stock sale will turn on the relationship of Bigco's outside basis and T's inside basis immediately after the tax-free reorganization. If Bigco previously acquired T in a B reorganization, Bigco's initial outside basis in its T stock was equal to the basis that T's shareholders had in their T stock. In contrast, if Bigco previously acquired T in a reverse subsidiary merger under Code §368(a)(2)(E), a triangular "C" reorganization, or a forward subsidiary merger under Code §368(a)(2)(D), Bigco's initial outside basis in its T stock was generally equal to T's inside net asset basis at the time of the reorganization.[1]

Even where a Code §338(h)(10) election would not affect the amount of Bigco's gain on the sale of T's stock, the character of that gain may differ depending on whether the election is made. A stock sale will generally produce all CG while a Code §338(h)(10) deemed asset sale will generally produce part CG (to the extent the appreciated assets are capital assets or §1231 assets) and part OI (e.g., recapture and gain on appreciated inventory).

EXAMPLE 4

Bigco purchases T's stock for $200 and makes no Code §338 or 338(h)(10) election. T owns inventory worth $200 with a $50 tax basis and has no liabilities. The inventory rises in value to $225 and Bigco decides to sell T's stock to P for $225. If Bigco sells T's stock and makes a Code §338(h)(10)

¶2002.4   [1]Code §362(b) ("B" reorganizations); Prop. Reg. §1.358-6 (triangular reorganizations). *See also* ¶¶602.2, 702.1.2, 802.5, and 803.6.

election (jointly with P), Bigco's gain will be $175 ($225 selling price minus T's $50 inside asset basis), and the character of the gain will be OI (because T's only asset is inventory). On the other hand, if the parties make no Code §338(h)(10) election, Bigco's gain will be $25 ($225 selling price minus Bigco's $200 outside basis in T's stock), and the character will be CG, long-term or short-term, depending on the length of Bigco's holding period for T's stock. Thus, although a Code §338(h)(10) election would give P a $175 step up in the basis of T's inventory, it would increase Bigco's gain on the sale by $150 and change its character from capital to ordinary.

If Bigco would recognize a loss on the sale of T's stock that would be disallowed under Reg. §1.1502-20 (*see* ¶212.4), Bigco may wish to make an election under Code §338(h)(10) since a loss on a deemed sale of T's assets under Code §338(h)(10) (or on an actual sale of T's assets) is not affected by Prop. Reg. §1.1502-20. In addition, Bigco may wish to make a Code §338(h)(10) election in order to retain T's NOLs, which may be more valuable to Bigco than they would be to T (once T is a P subsidiary) because T's NOLs (with no Code §338(h)(10) election) would be subject to the limitations of Code §382, while Bigco's NOLs inherited from T (by virtue of a Code §338(h)(10) election) would not.

EXAMPLE 5

Bigco's outside basis in T's stock is $200. T's inside basis in its assets is also $200. T has an NOL carryforward of $1,000. Bigco sells T's stock to P for $150.

If Bigco and P make a joint Code §338(h)(10) election, Bigco will recognize a $50 loss on the deemed sale of T's assets. New T will take a stepped-down $150 basis in T's assets. Bigco will retain T's $1,000 NOL and such NOL will not (as a result of the sale of T's stock to P) be subject to the limitations of Code §382.

If Bigco and P make no Code §338(h)(10) election, Bigco will realize a $50 loss on the sale of T's stock. However, Reg. §1.1502-20 may prevent Bigco from using this loss, in whole or in part. *See* ¶212.4. New T will retain old T's $200 basis in its assets and will retain its $1,000 NOL carryforward. However, new T's ability to use the NOL will be limited by Code §382 and P's ability to use T's NOL on P's consolidated return will be further limited by the SRLY rules. *See* ¶1203. If the long-term tax-exempt bond rate under Code §382 is 7%, Code §382 will permit new T to use at most $10.50 of the NOL each year ($150 stock value × 7%). In addition, the $50 BIL in T's assets may be subject to the Code §382 limitation if recognized within five years of P's acquisition of T, depending on whether T's net BIL exceeds the Code §382 threshold test. *See* ¶1208.4.

Thus, under the circumstances of Example 5 Bigco will generally prefer to make a Code §338(h)(10) election. Moreover, Bigco and P, considered as a group, will generally be better off with a Code §338(h)(10) election. Thus, although P, considered alone, would generally prefer no Code §338(h)(10) election—so that new T would inherit T's Code §382-tainted NOL and T's $200 asset basis—the parties would generally negotiate an arrangement that includes a Code §338(h)(10) election, perhaps with Bigco slightly reducing the purchase price to be paid by P for T's stock in order to compensate P for losing T's Code §382-tainted NOL and $50 of T's asset tax basis. In this fashion, Bigco will be able to retain T's $1,000 NOL without any Code §382 taint.

Given that the Code §338(h)(10) election is a joint election requiring consent from both Bigco and P, any party that wants to make the election should include language in the stock acquisition agreement requiring the other party to join in making the election.

State income tax results do not automatically follow the federal Code §338(h)(10) election in all cases. In some states a similar election is available, either as a result of piggyback rules or a separately authorized election. However, some states impose additional conditions to the availability of such an election (e.g., that the Bigco-T state consolidated or combined group be identical to the Bigco federal consolidated group). In addition, some states which generally respect a Code §338(h)(10) election may nonetheless collect the tax on the deemed asset sale from T rather than from Bigco. Other states may not recognize the Code §338(h)(10) election at all or may treat it as if it were merely a regular Code §338 election. Some states do not recognize either the regular Code §338 election or the Code §338(h)(10) election. Bigco and P should determine the relevant states for state income tax purposes and their treatment of Code §338(h)(10) elections and allocate state income tax responsibilities under the acquisition agreement so as to achieve their desired results.

Finally, either P or Bigco or both may desire to insert a contractual allocation of the purchase price (grossed up for T's liabilities) among T's assets when they are making a Code §338(h)(10) election. Such an allocation may help support new T's allocation of asset basis for depreciation and amortization purposes and Bigco's allocation of the purchase price for gain or loss recognition purposes. Any such agreement is binding on P and Bigco (unless the disavowing party can meet the *Danielson* standard) although it will not bind IRS. *See* Code §1060(a); ¶403.3.3.

¶2002.4.2   T's Liability for Bigco Group's Federal Income Taxes Under Reg. §1.1502-6

T is liable under Reg. §1.1502-6 for any unpaid federal income taxes of the Bigco group (whether attributable to T or to other group members) for each year during which T was a member of the Bigco group. *See* ¶210. This exposure continues even though P purchases T's stock and P pays Bigco full value for T's stock.

Thus, P should certainly obtain a contractual indemnity from Bigco for any Bigco group tax (including interest and penalties) that new T is ultimately required to pay to IRS. However, in practice, IRS generally will seek to collect such federal income taxes from new T only if Bigco lacks the financial ability or otherwise fails to pay them. Thus, the indemnity will generally come into play only in those situations when it is unlikely that Bigco will have the financial ability to honor its indemnity obligations.

P will generally also want a representation from Bigco that all taxes (or all material taxes) of the Bigco group have been paid for years in which T was a member of the Bigco group. P may also want to conduct a due diligence review of Bigco's prior tax returns. Bigco will generally be reluctant to provide P with information on the Bigco group's tax situation (other than tax information relating to T and its subsidiaries).

P may therefore wish to seek other forms of protection against a later IRS assertion of Reg. §1.1502-6 liability against new T for unpaid income taxes of Bigco and its other subsidiaries. Such protection could include, for example, a lien on unencumbered Bigco assets, a letter of credit from a bank or other financial institution, or an escrow of a portion of the cash purchase price. However, given the long period of time generally necessary to resolve tax controversies, Bigco may well resist such solutions.

See ¶210 for a further discussion of this issue.

¶2002.4.3 Bigco's Liability for T's Pre-Closing Income Taxes

Bigco is required to include the taxable income of T (and T's subsidiaries) in the Bigco group's consolidated federal income tax return for all periods during which T is a member of the Bigco group. Reg. §1.1502-76(b)(1). Bigco remains liable as the parent of the Bigco group for any T (or T subsidiary) federal income taxes attributable to the period T was a member of the Bigco group. Reg. §1.1502-6. In general, so long as Bigco is able to pay such taxes, IRS will collect them from Bigco. 1502-77(a).

¶2002.4.3.1 *Mid-Year Acquisitions*

If P purchases T's stock from the Bigco group during a tax year of the Bigco group, T's income for such tax year must be allocated between the preacquisition period (when T was part of the Bigco group) and the postacquisition period (when T will either be part of the P's consolidated group or a freestanding corporation). The consolidated return regulations generally require T's taxable income for the year of the acquisition to be allocated between the preacquisition and the postacquisition periods by closing T's books as of the acquisition. When Bigco, T, and P elect, however, T's items of income and expense (other than certain extraordinary items) may be prorated in proportion to the number of days during the year in the preacquisition and the postacquisition periods, respectively. Reg. §1.1502-76(b)(2).

See ¶211.2 for a discussion of whether T's income and expenses for the acquisition date are included in the preacquisition or the postacquisition period.

¶2002.4.3.2   Tax Returns

Bigco, as agent for the consolidated group, is entitled to file the consolidated return which includes T's taxable income from the beginning of the tax year to the acquisition date. Reg. §1.1502-77(a). If P wants to have any input on the positions taken on this return (or on any amended tax return for the year of the sale or for a prior year in which T was a member of the Bigco group), P must see to it that such right is reflected in the acquisition agreement. In general, P may desire the right to review such returns as they relate to T and to object to return positions that are likely to adversely affect P after the acquisition.

¶2002.4.3.3   Allocation of Responsibility for Current Year's Taxes

Bigco and P must agree on the allocation of responsibility for accrued but unpaid federal income taxes on T's taxable income for the period from the beginning of the tax year to the acquisition date. The parties should normally state in the acquisition agreement that Bigco is responsible for paying all such taxes (although T will remain liable under Reg. §1.1502-6, as discussed in ¶2002.4.2, to the extent that Bigco does not pay such taxes).

It is important that this allocation of responsibility to Bigco for T's federal income taxes for the preacquisition period be consistent with the parties' economic deal. Thus, this allocation of responsibility must be harmonized with acquisition agreement provisions regarding (i) tax representations, (ii) pre-closing cash withdrawals, if any, by Bigco, and (iii) purchase price adjustments.

If Bigco is not entitled to withdraw T's earnings for the preacquisition period, Bigco may argue that it should be reimbursed by T for that portion of the Bigco group's consolidated tax liability that is attributable to T's preacquisition earnings (i.e., by receiving a payment from T in the amount of T's book tax reserve or a payment from T under a tax sharing agreement). On the other hand, Bigco will receive an adjustment to its basis (both its outside basis in T's stock for a stock sale with no Code §338(h)(10) election and T's inside asset basis for a stock sale with a Code §338(h)(10) election) for any T taxable income during the preacquisition period. Any such positive adjustment will reduce Bigco's gain on the sale of T's stock (or the deemed sale of T's assets in case of a Code §338(h)(10) election) in the same amount as the T taxable income included on Bigco's consolidated return. This positive basis adjustment will generally reduce Bigco's federal income tax on the sale in approximately the same amount as Bigco's federal income tax on T's preacquisition period income included on Bigco's consolidated return.

Proper handling of state income taxes varies depending on state law.

¶2002.4.3.4 Deferred Intercompany Gains and Excess Loss Accounts

To the extent that T has any gains that have been deferred under Reg. §1.1502-13, they will be triggered into income immediately before T leaves the Bigco group and reported on the Bigco group consolidated return. Reg. §1.1502-13(f)(1)(iii); ¶212.1. If T has any excess loss accounts with respect to stock of other Bigco group members (including its own subsidiaries), the excess loss accounts will be triggered into income immediately before T leaves the Bigco group. Reg. §1.1502-19(a)(1) and (b)(2); ¶212.2. Similarly, if Bigco (or its subsidiaries) has any excess loss accounts with respect to stock of T or its subsidiaries, the excess loss accounts will be triggered into income immediately before T leaves the Bigco group. P may want to add contractual language to the acquisition agreement making explicit the tax treatment of deferred intercompany gains and excess losses.

¶2002.4.3.5 Allocation of Responsibility for Past Unpaid Taxes

Bigco and P must agree on an allocation of the audit risk for T's preacquisition tax years. To the extent that T was in the Bigco group for all such years, Bigco will generally be liable for such federal income taxes under the regulations described above. P generally will want provisions in the acquisition agreement reinforcing by representation and indemnity the regulatory rules stated above.

Bigco may find it difficult to limit its exposure for T's preacquisition federal income tax deficiencies as much as it may be able to when selling the stock of a nonconsolidated company. For example, if Bigco desires to limit its exposure for T's preacquisition federal income tax deficiencies as much as in the pro-seller stock purchase agreement (¶2002.2), Bigco must obtain an indemnity from P relating to past T taxes.

Bigco will automatically control (as agent for the consolidated group) any IRS audit of a preacquisition T year during which T was a member of the Bigco group. Reg. §1.1502-77(a). To the extent that P wishes to limit Bigco's exercise of this authority, P should negotiate the inclusion of appropriate language in the acquisition agreement.

¶2002.4.3.6 Tax Sharing Agreements

Bigco and T are likely to be parties to a tax sharing agreement among the members of the Bigco group. A typical tax sharing agreement would generally provide that T will make a payment to Bigco equal to the federal income tax that T would owe on its separate company taxable income, if any, and that Bigco will make a payment to T to the extent that the Bigco group uses a T NOL or other attribute to reduce the Bigco group's federal income taxes.

It is generally desirable for Bigco and P to cancel any such tax sharing agreement, both as to future years and as to past years, and for the parties to allocate explicitly in the acquisition agreement Bigco's and T's relative responsibilities for T's current and past taxes. If the old Bigco-T tax sharing agreement were left in effect, it might alter the carefully drafted allocation of responsibilities in the acquisition agreement and hence upset the parties' expectations.

¶2002.4.4   T's Postacquisition Carrybacks

As discussed in ¶1206.4, certain T postacquisition tax attributes (NOLs, net CLs, and excess tax credits) realized by T after it becomes a P subsidiary may be carried back into the Bigco group's tax returns, subject to the SRLY rules. Reg. §1.1502-21(c); Prop. Reg. §1.1502-21(c). T's ability to carry back certain postacquisition NOLs may also be limited by the CERT rules of Code §172(b)(1)(E) and (h). *See* ¶1206.1.

Any refund of federal income taxes attributable to such carrybacks of T postacquisition tax attributes will be paid to Bigco under Reg. §1.1502-77(a). Thus, P will generally desire to state in the acquisition agreement that (i) P rather than Bigco will receive the benefit of any such carrybacks and (ii) Bigco will cooperate in obtaining the benefits should P and T desire to carry postacquisition tax attributes back into Bigco's returns.

Bigco will, in many cases, prefer to avoid any postacquisition T carrybacks into its return, when possible. Bigco may be concerned about the complications that such postacquisition T carrybacks could create in its return (e.g., the carryback of T NOLs could displace Bigco foreign tax credits *or* the carryback of T NOLs could fully offset Bigco's previous taxable income and hence prevent Bigco from carrying back its own subsequent NOLs) or Bigco may be concerned about its ability to obtain a refund from P if the carryback of a postacquisition T tax attribute is later disallowed on audit. If Bigco refuses to state in the acquisition agreement that P will receive the benefit of any such carrybacks, P and T may wish to elect to forgo carrybacks to the extent possible.[2]

P and Bigco should resolve this issue in the acquisition agreement.

¶2002.4.5   T's NOL Carryforwards

If T has NOL carryforwards at the time P acquires T's stock, P may desire to obtain such NOLs for use after the acquisition. This is somewhat more complicated than in the case of a nonconsolidated target.

¶2002.4.5.1   *Use by the Bigco Group*

If P acquires T during a tax year of the Bigco group, any Bigco group NOL carryforward allocated to T will be reduced if the Bigco group has net positive

---

[2] *See* §172(b)(3)(C). Prop. Reg. §1.1502-21(g) and Prop. Reg. §1.1502-21(b)(3)(i) take the position that such an election must be made for the entire P-T group and may not be made for T alone.

taxable income for the acquisition year, including taxable income earned after T leaves the Bigco group. Reg. §1.1502-79(a)(1)(ii); Prop. Reg. §1.1502-21(b)(2)(ii). T's loss for the year of acquisition, if any, will be reduced if any Bigco group member has positive taxable income for the acquisition year (even if the Bigco group as a whole has negative taxable income), including taxable income earned after T leaves the Bigco group. Reg, §1.1502-79(a)(3); Prop. §1.1502-21(b)(2)(iv). Moreover, if the Bigco group recognizes additional taxable income in prior Bigco group years (e.g., as a result of an IRS audit), such taxable income (whether it is taxable income of T or of another Bigco group member) will generally reduce the T NOL carryforwards to the extent that the income is recognized in a year to which the T NOL can be carried under the consolidated return rules.

If P desires the economic benefit of T's NOLs, P should seek a contractual provision in the acquisition agreement that would require Bigco to make a payment to P if Bigco uses any T NOLs to offset current Bigco group taxable income or a prior year's audit adjustments when the NOLs would otherwise have been available as carryforwards to T's first postacquisition year.

¶2002.4.5.2   Retention of T NOLs by the Bigco Group

Under Reg. §1.1502-20, if Bigco is unable to claim a loss on the sale of T's stock, Bigco can elect to retain all or a portion of T's NOL carryforwards (not in excess of the loss that would otherwise be disallowed). Reg. §1.1502-20(g); ¶212.4. Bigco can apparently make such an election without P's consent by obtaining T's signature on the election prior to consummating the sale of T's stock to P (although a copy of the election must be given to P). Reg. §1.1502-20(g)(5). To avoid dispute, the acquisition agreement should either state that such an election will be made (and cover the terms of such election) or that no such election will be made.

As discussed in ¶2002.4.1, Bigco may also retain T's NOL carryforwards by joining with P in making a Code §338(h)(10) election.

¶2002.4.5.3   Prior Bigco Group Code §382 Ownership Change

If the Bigco group has undergone a Code §382 ownership change prior to P's acquisition of T's stock and such ownership change occurred while T had an NOL carryforward that has not yet been used up or expired, T's use of its prechange NOL carryforwards ("tainted NOLs") will be limited by Code §382. Once T leaves the Bigco group, T's Code §382 limitation with respect to any such tainted NOLs will be zero (thus preventing T from ever using any such tainted NOLs), *unless* Bigco elects to allocate a portion of the Bigco group's Code §382 limitation with respect to the ownership change to T.[3] Prop. Reg. §1.1502-95(b)(2)(ii).

---

[3] It is not entirely clear whether or how this rule affects T's ability to use such tainted NOLs to offset recognized BIGs after leaving the Bigco group.

If P wants T to be able to use any tainted T NOLs after the acquisition, the acquisition agreement should require Bigco to elect to allocate all or a portion of the group's Code §382 limitation to T under Prop. Reg. §1.1502-95(c) and (e).

The use of T's tainted NOLs will also be limited under Code §382 by the ownership change that occurs when P purchases T's stock from Bigco. *See* ¶2002.4.5.4. T's annual limitation under Code §382 with respect to the tainted NOLs will generally be the smaller of (i) the Code §382 limitation from the earlier Bigco change of ownership and (ii) the Code §382 limitation from the T ownership change caused by P's purchase of T's stock. *See* Prop. Reg. §1.1502-95(b)(2)(iv).

¶2002.4.5.4   *Application of Code §382 and the SRLY Rules to P's Acquisition of T's Stock from Bigco*

P's acquisition of T's stock from Bigco will generally constitute an ownership change under Code §382. Thus, T's NOL carryforwards will be usable only to the extent of the annual Code §382 limitation (plus any T recognized BIG). *See* ¶¶1203 and 1208. T's NOL carryforwards will also be subject to the SRLY limitation in the P consolidated group so that T's NOLs will generally be usable only against T's income. Reg. §1.1502-21(c); Prop. Reg. §1.1502-21 (c) (making the SRLY limitation cumulative); ¶1203.

If P is acquiring more than one target corporation from Bigco, P may wish to take steps to insure that all of the targets together will constitute a loss sub-group immediately after P's acquisition because Code §382 generally applies to the members of a loss sub-group as if they were a single corporation. Prop. Reg. §1.1502-91(a) and (c). If loss sub-group treatment is advantageous but the multiple targets are not configured so as to constitute a loss sub-group, P will generally find it desirable to require (in the acquisition agreement) that Bigco contribute to T the stock of all other direct targets prior to P's acquisition of T's stock.

The SRLY rules apply to a SRLY sub-group as if it were a single entity. Prop. Reg. §1.1502-21(c) and (d). The SRLY sub-group is not necessarily the same group as the loss sub-group under Prop. Reg. §1.1502-91(a) and (c). Moreover, IRS may disregard any steps taken by Bigco and P to change the membership of a SRLY sub-group if such steps have a principal purpose of increasing the SRLY limitation. Prop. Reg. §1.1502-21(c)(2)(iv).

¶2002.4.6   **Elections to Be Signed by T**

Certain elections by a consolidated group (here the Bigco group) require the signature of all members of the group during the tax year to which the election relates. Hence, after T has left the Bigco group, Bigco may need T's signature for an election having nothing to do with T. Bigco may wish to state explicitly in the acquisition agreement that T (as a P subsidiary) will cooperate in making certain specified elections and more generally that T will join in making any election that does not adversely effect T and P in postacquisition years.

¶2002.4.7 T's Inclusion on Bigco's Return for Acquisition

Under Reg. §1.1502-76(b), T's income and deductions for the entire day on which the P-T acquisition occurs are generally reported on Bigco's tax return. However, under an exception to this rule, a transaction that is "properly allocable" to a portion of T's day after the acquisition will be treated as occurring at the beginning of the next day, and thus will not appear on Bigco's return. Reg. §1.1502-76(b)(1)(B); ¶211.3.

Bigco may wish to include in the P-Bigco stock purchase agreement

(1) a commitment that P will indemnify Bigco for the tax cost, including gross-up, to Bigco of any transaction not in the ordinary course of business (such as an unusual asset sale) occurring on the date of P's acquisition of T stock but after the time of closing (a "special asset sale") and possibly (2) a covenant that the parties will report all post-Closing special asset sales occurring on the Closing Date on the P-T postacquisition federal income tax return to the extent permitted by law or conversely that the parties will report all such special asset sales on the Bigco-T preacquisition federal income tax return. However, the P-Bigco stock purchase agreement will generally state that Bigco remains liable for federal income taxes owed due to normal transactions occurring on the acquisition date, even for transactions occurring after the sale of Bigco's T stock to P.

Under the consolidated return investment adjustment rules, Bigco's outside basis in T's stock increases by the amount of T's taxable income. *See* ¶212.3. Hence, to the extent the gain on any post-closing special asset sale occurring on the Closing Date is reported on the Bigco-T consolidated return, Bigco's outside basis in T's stock increases and Bigco's CG on the sale of T's stock is reduced. Thus, in many cases, reporting a post-Closing special asset sale gain on Bigco's consolidated return will cost Bigco no extra federal income tax—its consolidated income will increase by the amount of the special asset sale gain and its gain on the sale of T's stock will decline by the same amount. There are, however, three circumstances when reporting a post-Closing special asset sale gain on Bigco's consolidated return may increase Bigco's income tax: *first*, when the increase in Bigco's basis in T's stock creates a stock sale loss disallowed by Reg. §1.1502-20; *second*, when Bigco has CL carry forwards it desires to use against its CG, but all or part of the special asset sale gain is OI while the offsetting increase in Bigco's outside basis in T's stock reduces its CG on the stock sale; and *third*, when Bigco and T are subject to state income tax in a state that taxes the special asset sale gain but not the T stock sale gain.

For these reasons, the decision whether to attempt to allocate the post-Closing special asset sale gain to Bigco's consolidated return will depend upon the particular facts of each case and should be a subject of negotiation between the parties.

¶2002.4.8   Contractual Provisions[4]

I. Substitute the following for Section 2(c) of the pro-seller stock purchase agreement (2002.2):[5]

(c) *Cash Dividend to Sellers.* Immediately prior to the Closing, the Sellers will cause the Target to pay the Sellers in proportion to their respective holdings of Target Shares an aggregate amount (and may cause each Subsidiary of the Target to pay to the Target any necessary component thereof) equal to the Sellers' good faith estimate of the consolidated Cash of the Target and its Subsidiaries as of the Closing. The Sellers may cause (A) the Target to make any such payment to them in the form of a dividend or a redemption and (B) any Subsidiary of the Target to make any such payment to the Target in the form of a dividend, a redemption, or an intercompany loan.

II. Substitute the following for the last sentence of Section 4(k)(v) of the pro-buyer stock purchase agreement (¶2002.1) and for Section 4(j)(v) of the pro-seller stock purchase agreement (¶2002.2):[6]

Neither Target nor any of its Subsidiaries has been a member of an Affiliated Group filing a consolidated federal income Tax Return other than a group the common parent of which is Bigco.

III. Add the following to Section 4(k) of the pro-buyer stock purchase agreement (¶2002.1):[7]

(viii) Each Affiliated Group has filed all [material][8] income Tax Returns that it was required to file for each taxable period during which any of the Target and its Subsidiaries was a member of the group. [Alternative 1: All such Tax Returns were correct and complete in all respects.] [Alternative 2: All such Tax Returns were correct and complete (A) in all respects in so far as they relate

---

[4]Section 2002.4.7 assumes that Bigco is the Seller or one of the Sellers. If this is not correct, Bigco should nevertheless be added as a party to the agreement.

[5]Section 2(c) of sample acquisition agreement 2002.2 (the *pro-seller* stock purchase agreement) allows the Sellers to cause the Target and its Subsidiaries to distribute their consolidated cash (*net of unpaid taxes*) to the Sellers as of the Closing. The substitute pro-seller language in this sample acquisition agreement (sale of a consolidated subsidiary) allows the Sellers to cause the Target and its Subsidiaries to distribute their consolidated cash to the Sellers as of the Closing (*without any holdback for unpaid taxes*). The reason for the difference in language is that Bigco will remain responsible for federal income taxes of the Target and its Subsidiaries through the Closing in this sample acquisition agreement (sale of a consolidated subsidiary), whereas the Target (and indirectly the Buyer) will remain responsible for those taxes in sample acquisition agreement 2002.2 (the *pro-seller* stock purchase agreement). See new §8A(c) below. *See also* ¶2002.4.3.4.

[6]*See* ¶2002.4.2.

[7]*See* ¶2002.4.2.

[8]If the word "material" is used in these paragraphs, there should be a separate representation or indemnity on income taxes attributable to other group members to insure that Buyer has a right to recover for any such taxes asserted against the Target under Reg. §1.1502-6, whether or not such taxes are "material."

to any of the Target and its Subsidiaries and (B) in all material respects in so far as they do not relate to the Target and its Subsidiaries.] All [material] income Taxes owed by any Affiliated Group (whether or not shown on any Tax Return) have been paid for each taxable period during which any of the Target and its Subsidiaries was a member of the group.

(ix) No Seller or director or officer (or employee responsible for Tax matters) of any of Bigco and its Subsidiaries expects any authority to assess any additional [material] income Taxes against any Affiliated Group for any taxable period during which any of the Target and its Subsidiaries was a member of the group. There is no dispute or claim concerning any [material] income Tax Liability of any Affiliated Group for any taxable period during which any of the Target and its Subsidiaries was a member of the group either (A) claimed or raised by any authority in writing or (B) as to which any of the Sellers and the directors and officers (and employees responsible for Tax matters) of any of Bigco and its Subsidiaries has Knowledge based upon personal contact with any agent of such authority. Except as disclosed on §4(k) of the Disclosure Schedule, no Affiliated Group has waived any statute of limitations in respect of any [material] income Taxes or agreed to any extension of time with respect to a [material] income Tax assessment or deficiency for any taxable period during which any of the Target and its Subsidiaries was a member of the group.

(x) None of the Target and its Subsidiaries has any liability for the Taxes of any Person other than the Target and its Subsidiaries (A) under Reg. §1.1502-6 (or any similar provision of state, local, or foreign law), (B) as a transferee or successor, (C) by contract, or (D) otherwise.

IV. Add the following to Section 4(j) of the pro-seller stock purchase agreement (¶2002.2):[9]

(vi) Each Affiliated Group has filed all Tax Returns that it was required to file for each taxable period during which any of the Target and its Subsidiaries was a member of the group, and has paid all Taxes shown thereon as owing, except where a failure to file or pay Taxes would not have a material adverse effect on the financial condition of the Target and its Subsidiaries taken as a whole.

(vii) None of the Target and its Subsidiaries has any liability for the Taxes of any Person other than the Target and its Subsidiaries under Reg. §1.1502-6 (or any similar provision of state, local, or foreign law).

V. Add the following new Section 8A (Tax Matters) to the pro-buyer (¶2002.1) and the pro-seller (¶2002.2) stock purchase agreement and delete Section 8(b)(iii) of the pro-buyer and pro-seller stock purchase agreement:

[9] *See* ¶2002.4.2.

8A. *Tax Matters.*

(a) *Tax Sharing Agreements.* Any tax sharing agreement between Bigco and any of the Target and its Subsidiaries is terminated as of the Closing Date and will have no further effect for any taxable year (whether the current year, a future year, or a past year).[10]

(b) *Taxes of Other Persons.*[11] [**Pro-buyer alternative:** Each of the Sellers agrees to indemnify the Buyer from and against the entirety of any Adverse Consequences the Buyer may suffer resulting from, arising out of, relating to, in the nature of, or caused by any Liability of any of the Target and its Subsidiaries for Taxes of any Person other than any of the Target and its Subsidiaries (i) under Reg. §1.1502-6 (or any similar provision of state, local or foreign law), (ii) as a transferee or successor, (iii) by contract, or (iv) otherwise.] [**Pro-seller alternative:** Each of the Sellers agrees to indemnify the Buyer from and against his or its Allocable Portion of any Adverse Consequences the Buyer may suffer resulting from, arising out of, relating to, in the nature of, or caused by any Liability of any of the Target and its Subsidiaries for Taxes of any Person other than any of the Target and its Subsidiaries under Reg. §1.1502-6 (or any similar provision of state, local or foreign law).]

(c) *Returns for Periods Through the Closing Date.*[12] Bigco will include the income of the Target and its Subsidiaries (including any deferred income triggered into income by Reg. §1.1502-13 and Reg. §1.1502-14 and any excess loss accounts taken into income under Reg. §1.1502-19) on the Bigco consolidated federal income Tax Returns for all periods through the Closing Date and pay any federal income Taxes attributable to such income. The Target and its Subsidiaries will furnish Tax information to Bigco for inclusion in Bigco's federal consolidated income Tax Return for the period which includes the Closing Date in accordance with the Target's past custom and practice.[13] [Bigco will allow the Buyer an opportunity to review and comment upon such Tax Returns (including any amended returns) to the extent that they relate to the Target and its Subsidiaries. Bigco will take no position on such returns that relate to the Target and its Subsidiaries that would adversely affect the Target and its Subsidiaries after the Closing Date [unless such position would be reasonable in the case of a Person that owned the Target and the Subsidiaries both before and after the Closing Date].][14] The income of the

---

[10] *See* ¶2002.4.3.7.

[11] *See* ¶2002.4.2.

[12] *See* ¶¶2002.4.3, 2002.4.3.3, 2002.4.3.4, 2002.4.3.5, and 2002.4.3.6. Consider similar provisions for state taxes.

[13] The parties may wish to provide that Buyer or Bigco bears the cost of complying with this provision.

[14] Buyer will generally want to limit Bigco's ability to take positions on the Bigco group's consolidated federal income tax returns for periods that include the income of Target and its Subsidiaries that are adverse to Target and its Subsidiaries after the acquisition. Many different contractual formulations are possible, some more favorable to Buyer and some more favorable to Bigco. If a Code §338(h)(10) election is made, this protection will generally not be needed for federal income tax

Target and its Subsidiaries will be apportioned to the period up to and including the Closing Date and the period after the Closing Date by closing the books of the Target and its Subsidiaries as of the end of the Closing Date.[15]

(d) *Audits.*[16] Bigco will allow the Target and its counsel to participate [at its own expense] in any audits of Bigco consolidated federal income Tax Returns to the extent that such returns relate to the Target and its Subsidiaries. [Alternative 1: Bigco will not settle any such audit in a manner which would adversely affect the Target and its Subsidiaries after the Closing Date [unless such settlement would be reasonable in the case of a Person that owned the Target and the Subsidiaries both before and after the Closing Date].] [Alternative 2: Bigco will not settle any such audit in a manner which would adversely affect the Target and its Subsidiaries after the Closing Date without the prior written consent of the Buyer, which consent shall not unreasonably be withheld.]

(e) *Carrybacks.* Bigco will immediately pay to the Buyer any Tax refund (or reduction in Tax liability) resulting from a carryback of a postacquisition Tax attribute of any of the Target and its Subsidiaries into the Bigco consolidated Tax Return, when such refund or reduction is realized by the Bigco group. Bigco will cooperate with the Target and its Subsidiaries in obtaining such refunds (or reduction in Tax liability), including through the filing of amended Tax Returns or refund claims. The Buyer agrees to indemnify Bigco for any Taxes resulting from the disallowance of such postacquisition Tax attribute on audit or otherwise.[17]

(f) *Retention of Carryovers.*[18] [**Alternative 1:** Bigco will not elect to retain any net operating loss carryovers or capital loss carryovers of the Target and its Subsidiaries under Reg. §1.1502-20(g).] [**Alternative 2:** Bigco may elect to retain the following net operating loss carryovers and capital loss carryovers of the Target and its Subsidiaries under Reg. §1.1502-20(g): [identify net operating losses and capital loss carryovers to be retained]. At Bigco's request, the Buyer will cause any of the Target and its Subsidiaries to join with Bigco in filing any necessary elections under Reg. §1.1502-20(g).]

---

purposes since Target and its Subsidiaries will be treated as new corporations that do not inherit a tax history from the Bigco group (other than, apparently, for purposes of Reg. §1.1502-6).

[15] *See* ¶2002.4.3.1. This provision will be modified if Target's taxable income or loss on the Closing Date is not included in the Bigco group's consolidated federal income tax return. *See also* ¶211.2.

[16] *See* ¶2002.4.3.6. If a Code §338(h)(10) election is made, this protection will generally not be needed for federal income tax purposes since Target and its Subsidiaries will be treated as new corporations that do not inherit a tax history from the Bigco group (other than, apparently, for purposes of Reg. §1.1502-6).

[17] *See* ¶2002.4.4. Bigco may wish to limit its obligation in this section to postacquisition Tax attributes as to which Target and its Subsidiaries cannot elect to waive a carryback. Bigco may also wish to provide that the Tax attributes carried back by the Target and its Subsidiaries will be considered to produce a refund (or reduce liability) only after all tax attributes of Bigco and other members of Bigco's group have been used or deemed used (in the case of any such Bigco group attribute that could have been used in the absence of the carryback).

[18] *See* ¶2002.4.5.2.

(g) *Prior Ownership Changes.* Bigco will file a timely election under Prop. Reg. §1.1502-95(e) to apportion [$] of the Bigco group's annual consolidated Section 382 limitation from [identify the previous ownership change while any of the Target and its Subsidiaries was a member of the Bigco group] to the Target and its Subsidiaries. At Bigco's request, the Buyer will cause any of the Target and its Subsidiaries to join with Bigco in making any election required under Prop. Reg. §1.1502-95(e).[19]

(h) *Post-Closing Elections.*[20] At Bigco's request, the Buyer will cause any of the Target and its Subsidiaries to make and/or join with Bigco in making [specify elections] after Closing. At Bigco's request, the Buyer will cause any of the Target and its Subsidiaries to make or join with Bigco in making any other election if the making of such election does not have [an] [a material] adverse impact on the Buyer (or any of the Target and its Subsidiaries) for any postacquisition Tax period.

(i) *Section 338(h)(10) Election.*[21] [At the Buyer's/Bigco's option,][22] Bigco will join with the Buyer in making an election under Section 338(h)(10) of the Code (and any corresponding elections under state, local, or foreign tax law) (collectively a Section 338(h)(10) Election) with respect to the purchase and sale of the stock of the Target hereunder.[23] Bigco will pay any Tax attributable to the making of the Section 338(h)(10) Election and will indemnify the Buyer, the Target, and its Subsidiaries against any Adverse Consequences arising out of any failure to pay such Tax. [Bigco will also pay any state, local, or foreign Tax (and indemnify the Buyer, the Target, and its Subsidiaries against any Adverse Consequences arising out of any failure to pay such Tax) attributable to an election under state, local, or foreign law similar to the election available under Section 338(g) of the Code (or which results from the making of an election under Section 338(g) of the Code) with respect to the purchase and sale of the stock of the Target hereunder.][24]

---

[19] *See* ¶2002.4.5.3. These two sentences are needed only if the Bigco group has undergone a prior Code §382 ownership change that limits the use of the Target's (or any of its Subsidiaries') net operating loss or other carryovers that would otherwise be available after Closing. (This section assumes that Prop. Reg. §1.1502-95(e) is finalized in its current form. *Cf.* Code §1503(a).) If it is unclear whether Bigco has undergone a previous Code §382 ownership change, it may be desirable for P to obtain a representation that no such ownership change has occurred and/or an agreement that Bigco will file a "protective" election under Prop. Reg. §1.1502-95(e) to apportion all or a part of Bigco's annual consolidated Code §382 limitation to the Target and its Subsidiaries in case such an ownership change is later found to have occurred.

[20] *See* ¶2002.4.6.

[21] *See* ¶¶2002.4.1 and 206.

[22] If it is not clear at the time of signing whether a Code §338(h)(10) election is desirable, the parties may wish to allow either the Buyer or Bigco the choice of whether the election is made after closing.

[23] The parties may wish to provide a more detailed procedure for making the Code §338(h)(10) election. For example, the parties may provide that either the Buyer or Bigco will prepare the election forms and file them (after the other party has reviewed and signed the forms) and set forth the time frame for doing so.

[24] Buyer may wish to include language similar to this sentence if the Target is taxable in a state that does not recognize a Code §338(h)(10) election or does not apply its corresponding provision to the sale and purchase of the Target's stock.

VI. Consider adding the following to new Section 8A (Tax Matters) to the *pro-seller* **(¶2002.2) stock purchase agreement:**

(j) *Indemnification for Post-Closing Transactions.*[25] Buyer agrees to indemnify Seller for any additional tax owed by Seller (including tax owed by Seller due to this indemnification payment) resulting from any transaction not in the ordinary course of business occurring on the Closing Date after Buyer's purchase of Seller's Target stock.

(k) *Post-Closing Transactions not in the Ordinary Course.*[26] Buyer and Seller agree to report all transactions not in the ordinary course of business occurring on the Closing Date after Buyer's purchase of Seller's Target stock on Buyer's [alternatively: on Seller's] federal income tax return to the extent permitted by Reg. §1.1502-76(b)(1)(B).

VII. Consider adding the following paragraph to Section 10 of the *pro-buyer* **(¶2002.1) and** *pro-seller* **(¶2002.2) stock purchase agreement if a Code §338(h)(10) election is to be made:**

Allocation of Purchase Price. The Parties agree that the Purchase Price and the liabilities of the Target and its Subsidiaries (plus other relevant items) will be allocated to the assets of the Target and its Subsidiaries for all purposes (including Tax and financial accounting purposes) [as shown on the Allocation Schedule attached hereto] [in a manner consistent with the fair market values set forth in the Allocation Schedule attached hereto]. The Buyer, the Target and its Subsidiaries and Bigco will file all Tax Returns (including amended returns and claims for refund) and information reports in a manner consistent with [such allocation] [such values].

¶2002.5   Purchase Price Adjustment Based on Closing Date Balance Sheet

Sample acquisition agreements 2002.1 (*pro-buyer* stock purchase), 2002.2 (*pro-seller* stock purchase), and 2002.3 (*neutral* stock purchase) assume a fixed purchase price. Sample acquisition agreement 2002.5 (purchase price adjustment) contains additional provisions for use if there is to be a post-closing purchase price adjustment based on T's net book value as of the closing. This form can be adapted for

---

There may be some risk of double taxation in states that recognize a regular Code §338 election but do not recognize a Code §338(h)(10) election since such states may attempt to tax both the deemed sale gain and the gain on the Target's stock (provided that they have taxing jurisdiction over both the Target and Bigco). The parties should determine whether there is a risk of such double taxation and allocate that risk under the contract. The language in the text allocates any risk of double taxation to Bigco.

[25] *See* ¶2002.4.7.

[26] *See* ¶2002.4.7.

other post-closing purchase price adjustments (such as a comparison of working capital with liabilities as of the closing *or* a contingent earnout based on earnings for a specified period after the closing).

I. Add (or substitute) the following definitions in §1 of sample acquisition agreement 2002.1 (the *pro-buyer* stock purchase agreement) and sample acquisition agreement 2002.2 (the *pro-seller* stock purchase agreement).

"Actual Value" has the meaning set forth in §2(e) below.

"Closing Date Balance Sheet" has the meaning set forth in §2(e) below.

"Consolidated Net Book Value" means the excess of assets over liabilities as shown on the Closing Date Balance Sheet.

"Draft Closing Date Balance Sheet" has the meaning set forth in §2(e) below.

"Estimated Consolidated Net Book Value" means $_____.

"High Value" has the meaning set forth in §2(e) below.

"Low Value" has the meaning set forth in §2(e) below.

"Preliminary Purchase Price" has the meaning set forth in §2(b) below.

"Purchase Price" has the meaning set forth in §2(f) below.

II. Amend §2 of sample acquisition agreement 2002.1 (the *pro-buyer* stock purchase agreement) and sample acquisition agreement 2002.2 (the *pro-seller* stock purchase agreement) to read as follows. Note that §2(c) of sample acquisition agreement 2002.2 (providing for a net cash payment to the Sellers) no longer is necessary in as much as the Sellers will receive the benefit of earnings through the Closing through the mechanism of the purchase price adjustment.

Section 2. *Purchase and Sale of Target Shares.*

(a) *Basic Transaction.* On and subject to the terms and conditions of this Agreement, the Buyer agrees to purchase from each of the Sellers, and each of the Sellers agrees to sell to the Buyer, all of his or its Target Shares for the consideration specified below in this §2.

(b) *Preliminary Purchase Price.*[1] The Buyer agrees to pay to the Sellers at the Closing $_____ (the *"Preliminary Purchase Price"*) by delivery of (i) its promis-

---

¶2002.5 [1] The Sellers may seek to have the Buyer make an earnest money deposit upon execution of this Agreement. If the transaction were thereafter completed, the deposit would be applied to the Purchase Price. If the transaction were thereafter aborted, the deposit would be refunded to the Buyer

sory notes (the *"Buyer Notes"*) in the form of Exhibit A attached hereto in the aggregate principal amount of $_____ and (ii) cash for the balance of the Preliminary Purchase Price payable by wire transfer or delivery of other immediately available funds. The Preliminary Purchase Price shall be allocated among the Sellers in proportion to their respective holdings of Target Shares as set forth in §4(b) of the Disclosure Schedule. The Preliminary Purchase Price will be subject to post-Closing adjustment as set forth below in this §2.

(c) *The Closing.* The closing of the transactions contemplated by this Agreement (the *"Closing"*) shall take place at the offices of _____ in _____, _____ commencing at 9:00 a.m. local time on the [second] business day following the satisfaction or waiver of all conditions to the obligations of the Parties to consummate the transactions contemplated hereby (other than conditions with respect to actions the respective Parties will take at the Closing itself) or such other date as the Buyer and the Requisite Sellers may mutually determine (the *"Closing Date"*); *provided, however,* that the Closing Date shall be no earlier than _____, 19____.[2]

(d) *Deliveries at the Closing.* At the Closing, (i) the Sellers will deliver to the Buyer the various certificates, instruments, and documents referred to in §7(a) below, (ii) the Buyer will deliver to the Sellers the various certificates, instruments, and documents referred to in §7(b) below, (iii) each of the Sellers will deliver to the Buyer stock certificates representing all of his or its Target Shares, endorsed in blank or accompanied by duly executed assignment documents, and (iv) the Buyer will deliver to each of the Sellers the consideration specified in §2(b) above.

(e) *Preparation of Closing Date Balance Sheet.*

(i) Within [60 days] after the Closing Date, the Buyer will prepare and deliver to the Sellers[3] a draft consolidated balance sheet (the *"Draft Closing Date Balance*

---

or paid to the Sellers as liquidated damages depending on the terms of this Agreement and the reasons for the termination.

[2] The Parties should determine whether the Sellers or the Buyer will owe any stock transfer or similar tax on the transfer of the Target Shares by reason of the chosen Closing location.

[3] The Buyer normally will be in the best position after the Closing to prepare a consolidated balance sheet for the Target and its Subsidiaries as of the Closing Date (e.g., the Buyer will take possession of the books and records and frequently will inherit the appropriate financial personnel).

Accordingly, this sample acquisition agreement 2002.5 provides that the Buyer will prepare the Draft Closing Date Balance Sheet, provides that the Sellers will have an opportunity to comment thereon, and provides for a dispute resolution mechanism.

There is, of course, a practical advantage to being the Party that prepares the Draft Closing Date Balance Sheet. For example, the financial personnel of the Buyer may be able to reduce the consolidated net book value on the Draft Closing Date Balance Sheet (and ultimately the Purchase Price) through the creative application of accounting practices and principles.

Therefore, *the Sellers* may seek to prepare the Draft Closing Date Balance Sheet (particularly if they retain the appropriate financial personnel).

The Parties may also elect to have an independent accounting firm audit the Closing Date Balance Sheet.

Sheet") for the Target and its Subsidiaries as of the close of business on the Closing Date (determined on a pro forma basis as though the Parties had not consummated the transactions contemplated by this Agreement).[4] The Buyer will prepare the Draft Closing Date Balance Sheet in accordance with GAAP applied on a basis consistent with the preparation of the Financial Statements [; *provided, however*, that assets, liabilities, gains, losses, revenues, and expenses in interim periods or as of dates other than year-end (which normally are determined through the application of so-called interim accounting conventions or procedures) will be determined, for purposes of the Draft Closing Date Balance Sheet, through full application of the procedures used in preparing the most recent audited balance sheet included within the Financial Statements].

(ii) If the Requisite Sellers have any objections to the Draft Closing Date Balance Sheet, they will deliver a detailed statement describing their objections to the Buyer within [30 days] after receiving the Draft Closing Date Balance Sheet. The Buyer and the Requisite Sellers will use reasonable efforts to resolve any such objections themselves. If the Parties do not obtain a final resolution within [30 days] after the Buyer has received the statement of objections, however, the Buyer and the Requisite Sellers will select an accounting firm mutually acceptable to them to resolve any remaining objections.[5] If the Buyer and the Requisite Sellers are unable to agree on the choice of an accounting firm, they will select a nationally-recognized accounting firm by lot (after excluding their respective regular outside accounting firms). The determination of any accounting firm so selected will be set forth in writing and will be conclusive and binding upon the Parties. The Buyer will revise the Draft Closing Date Balance Sheet as appropriate to reflect the resolution of any objections thereto pursuant to this §2(e)(ii). The *"Closing Date Balance Sheet"* shall mean the Draft Closing Date Balance Sheet together with any revisions thereto pursuant to this §2(e)(ii).

(iii) In the event the Parties submit any unresolved objections to an accounting firm for resolution as provided in §2(e)(ii) above, the Buyer and the Sellers will share responsibility for the fees and expenses of the accounting firm as follows:

(A) if the accounting firm resolves all of the remaining objections in favor of the Buyer (the Consolidated Net Book Value so determined is referred to herein as the *"Low Value"*), the Sellers will be responsible for all of the fees and expenses of the accounting firm;

(B) if the accounting firm resolves all of the remaining objections in favor of the Sellers (the Consolidated Net Book Value so determined is referred

---

[4] [ALTERNATIVE: as of the opening of business on the Closing Date.]

[5] The Parties may prefer to constrain the accounting firm so that it must choose between the position of the Buyer on the one hand and the position of the Sellers on the other hand (i.e., accounting firm would select the position that was *closer* to being correct). Such an approach would encourage the Parties to be reasonable and accurate (since any Party taking an extreme position would lose altogether).

to herein as the *"High Value"*), the Buyer will be responsible for all of the fees and expenses of the accounting firm; and

(C) if the accounting firm resolves some of the remaining objections in favor of the Buyer and the rest of the remaining objections in favor of the Sellers (the Consolidated Net Book Value so determined is referred to herein as the *"Actual Value"*), the Sellers will be responsible for that fraction of the fees and expenses of the accounting firm equal to (x) the difference between the High Value and the Actual Value over (y) the difference between the High Value and the Low Value, and the Buyer will be responsible for the remainder of the fees and expenses.[6]

(iv) The Buyer will make the work papers and back-up materials used in preparing the Draft Closing Date Balance Sheet [, and the books, records, and financial staff of the Target and its Subsidiaries,] available to the Sellers and their accountants and other representatives at reasonable times and upon reasonable notice at any time during (A) the preparation by the Buyer of the Draft Closing Date Balance Sheet, (B) the review by the Sellers of the Draft Closing Date Balance Sheet, and (C) the resolution by the Parties of any objections thereto.

(f) *Adjustment to Preliminary Purchase Price.*[7] The Preliminary Purchase Price will be adjusted as follows:

(i) If the Consolidated Net Book Value exceeds the Estimated Consolidated Net Book Value, the Buyer will pay to the Sellers an amount equal to such excess [(plus interest thereon at the Applicable Rate from the Closing Date)] by wire transfer or delivery of other immediately available funds within three business days after the date on which the Consolidated Net Book Value for the Target and its Subsidiaries finally is determined pursuant to §2(e) above. This additional amount shall be allocated among the Sellers in proportion to their respective holdings of Target Shares as set forth in §4(b) of the Disclosure Schedule.

(ii) If the Consolidated Net Book Value is less than the Estimated Consolidated Net Book Value, the Sellers will pay to the Buyer an amount equal to

---

[6] This provision allocates responsibility for the fees and expenses of the accounting firm between the Sellers on the one hand and the Buyer on the other hand based upon the degree to which the accounting firm accepts the position of the other side in the dispute.

The Parties may prefer to allocate these fees and expenses in a different manner (e.g., one side might bear *all* of the fees and expenses if the accounting firm determines the position of the other side was closer to being correct, or the two sides might agree to share the fees and expenses equally no matter what the outcome).

[7] Section 2(f) prescribes a dollar-for-dollar adjustment in the Purchase Price if the Consolidated Net Book Value (determined after the Closing) differs from the Estimated Consolidated Net Book Value (determined when the Parties execute the Agreement).

The Parties may prefer a different formulation for the Purchase Price adjustment. For example if the Preliminary Purchase Price represent 1.2 times the Estimated Consolidated Net Book Value, the

such deficiency [(plus interest thereon at the Applicable Rate from the Closing Date)] by wire transfer or delivery of other immediately available funds within three business days after the date on which the Consolidated Net Book Value for the Target and its Subsidiaries finally is determined pursuant to §2(e) above. [The Buyer shall have the option of recouping all or any part of any amount the Sellers owe it pursuant to this §2(f)(ii) by notifying the Sellers that the Buyer is reducing pro rata the principal amounts outstanding under the Buyer Notes. This shall affect the timing and amount of payments required under the Buyer Notes in the same manner as if the Buyer had made a permitted prepayment (without premium or penalty) pro rata thereunder.]

The Preliminary Purchase Price as so adjusted is referred to herein as the *"Purchase Price."*

III. Amend §8(e) of sample acquisition agreement 2002.1 (the *pro-buyer* stock purchase agreement) to read as follows:

(e) *Determination of Adverse Consequences.* The Parties shall make appropriate adjustments for liabilities accrued on the Closing Date Balance Sheet (so as to reduce the Purchase Price), [, and take into account the time cost of money (using the Applicable Rate as the discount rate),] in determining Adverse Consequences for purposes of this §8. All indemnification payments under this §8 shall be deemed adjustments to the Purchase Price.

IV. Amend §8(e) of sample acquisition agreement 2002.2 (the *pro-seller* stock purchase agreement) to read as follows:

(e) *Determination of Adverse Consequences.* The Parties shall make appropriate adjustments for liabilities accrued on the Closing Date Balance Sheet (so as to reduce the Purchase Price), tax benefits, and insurance coverage [, and take into account the time cost of money (using the Applicable Rate as the discount rate),] in determining Adverse Consequences for purposes of this §8. All indemnification payments under this §8 shall be deemed adjustments to the Purchase Price.

¶2002.6   *Purchase of S Corporation Stock*

Sample acquisition agreements 2002.1 (*pro-buyer* stock purchase), 2002.2 (*pro-seller* stock purchase), and 2002.3 (*neutral* stock purchase) generally assume, except where noted, that T is a taxable C corporation. This sample acquisition agreement 2002.6 (purchase of S corporation stock) contains certain additional provisions for use if T is an S corporation, especially (but not exclusively) if P wishes to make a Code §338(h)(10) election with respect to the purchase of T-SCo's stock. See

---

Purchase Price might increase or decrease by $1.20 for each dollar by which the Consolidated Net Book Value differs from the Estimated Consolidated Net Book Value.

Chapter 11, *Special Considerations in Taxable and Tax-Free Acquisitions Involving an S Corporation*, for a discussion of the special rules regarding S corporations and their involvement in acquisitions. In particular, see ¶¶1105 and 1109 for a discussion of the consequences of P's taxable purchase of T stock where either P or T is an S corporation or both are S corporations.

¶2002.6.1   Code §338(h)(10) Election

Where P purchases T-SCo's stock, the parties have the ability to make a Code §338(h)(10) election, in which case all parties (including the selling T-SCo shareholders) are treated for tax purposes as if P purchased T-SCo's assets. Thus, a Code §338(h)(10) election treats a stock sale by T-SCo's shareholders as an asset sale by T-SCo to P followed by T-SCo's complete liquidation while still owned by T-SCo's old shareholders. This tax treatment means that (1) the Buyer obtains asset SUB for T-SCo's old assets (just as it would in an actual asset sale) and (2) unlike a regular Code §338 election, there is no double tax on the transaction (unless the Code §1374 penalty tax applies), i.e., T-SCo is treated as selling assets and T-SCo's shareholders are treated as receiving their proceeds in a deemed liquidation of T-SCo, which deemed liquidation generally will not produce a second tax because P's purchase of T-SCo's stock does not invalidate T-SCo's Subchapter S election and hence the Subchapter S pass-through rules continue to apply. See ¶¶206.3 and 1109.3.

T-SCo's deemed asset sale gain (generally a mix of CG and OI depending on the character of the T-SCo's assets) flows through under normal SCo rules to T-SCo's shareholders. T-SCo's shareholders also recognize CG or CL on T-SCo's deemed liquidation to the extent each shareholder's stock tax basis (after adjustment for T-SCo's asset-sale gain/loss) differs from the shareholder's proceeds from sale of T-SCo's stock (which are treated for tax purposes as deemed Code §331 liquidation proceeds).

For state tax purposes, T-SCo's deemed asset sale gain flowing through to T-SCo's shareholders is generally taxable in the states where T-SCo's business contacts require it to file a tax return.

In the absence of a Code §338(h)(10) election, all of the gain recognized by T-SCo's selling shareholders would likely be LTCG for federal income tax purposes (i.e., gain from sale of T-SCo's stock) and, for state tax purposes, such gain would be taxed only in the shareholder's state of residence. Thus, while the Buyer will generally prefer a Code §338(h)(10) election in order to obtain asset SUB (whenever the purchase price is sufficiently high to produce step-up), T-SCo's selling shareholders may oppose a Code §338(h)(10) election for any of five reasons:

(1)   Sellers may pay OI (rather than LTCG) federal income tax on part of their gain, e.g., depreciation recapture and inventory gain realized on the deemed asset sale,

(2)   if the states where T-SCo does business have a higher average tax rate than the Sellers' state(s) of residence, Sellers will owe more state tax,

(3)   if the Sellers are responsible for all entity-level taxes imposed on T-SCo through and including the Closing Date, a Code §338(h)(10) election may trigger entity-level federal taxes (e.g., under Code §1374) or state taxes (if a state in which T-SCo does business imposes an entity-level tax on an SCo),

(4)   if the Sellers retain part of T-SCo's stock, they will nonetheless recognize 100% of the asset sale gain for both federal and state tax purposes, and

(5)   after the President signs the pending Tax Relief Extension Act of 1999, which in general forecloses an accrual method taxpayer from installment reporting, a Code §338(h)(10) election with respect to an accrual method T-SCo will prevent a cash method T-SCo shareholder from utilizing installment reporting where the sale is in part for future payments (see ¶¶206.1.8, 1108.3, and 1108.4).

¶2002.6.2   Code §1374 Tax on Built-In Gain

As noted above, where P purchases T-SCo's stock and P and T-SCo's shareholders make a Code §338(h)(10) election, T-SCo is deemed to have sold its assets. If T-SCo's assets have any built-in gain subject to tax under Code §1374, Code §1374 will apply to the deemed sale and impose a T-SCo corporate-level tax on the built-in gain. P, as the new owner of T-SCo's stock, will bear the burden of T-SCo's corporate-level tax, unless the parties provide otherwise by contract or by reflecting the liability in determining the purchase price.[1]

Whether T-SCo's assets have built-in gain subject to tax under Code §1374 is also an important issue where P-SCo purchases T-SCo's stock and makes no Code §338(h)(10) election. In such case, if P-SCo either liquidates T-SCo or elects to treat T-SCo as a "qualified subchapter S subsidiary,"[2] post-acquisition sales of T-SCo's assets may result in Code §1374 corporate-level tax on the built-in gain.

The cost of any potential Code §1374 tax (together with any risk resulting from uncertainty as to the amount of the built-in gain subject to the tax) (1) is an economic issue that must be considered by the parties in negotiating P's acquisition of T-SCo and determining the purchase price and (2) should generally be allocated pursuant to the stock purchase agreement. There are several potential ways for the parties to allocate any Code §1374 risk. The provisions set out below generally allocate the Code §1374 risk to T-SCo's shareholders in the pro-buyer and neutral

---

¶2002.6 [1] See ¶1103.7.4 for a general discussion of Code §1374. See ¶206.3.5 and ¶1109.3.3 for a discussion of Code §1374 where a Code §338(h)(10) election is made with respect to the purchase of T-SCo's stock. See ¶1109.1.2 for a discussion of a bifurcated purchase of T-SCo's stock and assets where some, but not all, of T-SCo's assets have built-in gain subject to tax under Code §1374. See also ¶204.3 for a more general discussion of a bifurcated purchase of T's stock and assets.

[2] See ¶1102.4.3 for a discussion of "qualified subchapter S subsidiaries."

On the other hand, if P-SCo neither liquidates T-SCo nor elects to treat it as a qualified subchapter S subsidiary, T-SCo will become a regular C corporation as a result of P-SCo's acquisition of its stock and Code §1374 will cease to be relevant. See ¶1102.2.

stock purchase agreements through representations and/or indemnities. In contrast, the pro-seller stock purchase agreement allocates any Code §1374 risk to P.

¶2002.6.3 Contractual Provisions

I. Add the following item to Section 4(k), *Tax Matters,* **of sample acquisition agreement 2002.1** *(pro-buyer* **stock purchase), Section 4(j),** *Tax Matters,* **of sample acquisition agreement 2002.2** *(pro-seller* **stock purchase), and Section 4(k),** *Tax Matters,* **of sample acquisition agreement 2002.3** *(neutral* **stock purchase):**

> (viii) Target (and any predecessor of Target) has been a validly electing S corporation[3] within the meaning of Code §§1361 and 1362 at all times [during its existence] [since _____] and Target will be an S corporation up to and including [the day before][4] the Closing Date.

> (ix) The Tax Disclosure Schedule identifies each Target Subsidiary that is a "qualified subchapter S subsidiary" within the meaning of Code §1361(b)(3)(B). Each Subsidiary so identified has been a qualified subchapter S subsidiary at all time since the date shown on such schedule up to and including [the day before][5] the Closing Date.[6]

II. If a Code §338(h)(10) election will be made with respect to the acquisition of Target's stock, add the following item to Section 4(k), *Tax Matters,* **of sample acquisition agreement 2002.1** *(pro-buyer* **stock purchase) and Section 4(k),** *Tax Matters,* **of sample acquisition agreement 2002.3** *(neutral* **stock purchase):**

> (x) Target will not be liable for any Tax under Code §1374 in connection with the deemed sale of Target's assets (including the assets of any qualified subchapter S subsidiary) caused by the Section 338(h)(10) Election. Neither Target nor any qualified subchapter S subsidiary of Target has, in the past 10 years, (A) acquired assets from another corporation in a transaction in which

---

[3] See ¶1102 for a discussion of the requirements which Target must meet in order to be an S corporation. State or local S corporation status does not follow automatically from federal S corporation status in some jurisdictions. Thus, Buyer may wish to obtain a representation that Target qualifies as an S corporation for state or local income tax purposes.

[4] Include the bracketed language if no Code §338(h)(10) election will be made. In such case, Buyer's purchase of Target stock will cause Target to cease to be an S corporation beginning on the day before the Closing Date. Code §1362(d)(2). Omit the bracketed language if a Code §338(h)(10) election will be made since, in such case, Buyer's purchase of Target stock will not cause Target to cease to be an S corporation and hence, absent any other disqualifying event, Target will continue to be an S corporation with respect to the deemed sale of Target's assets on the Closing Date. See Reg. §1.338(h)(10)-1(e)(2)(ii) and (iv).

[5] Include the bracketed language if no Code §338(h)(10) election will be made. Omit the bracketed language if a Code §338(h)(10) election will be made.

[6] The 1996 Act permits T-SCo to have 80%-or-more-owned subsidiaries and allows T-SCo to elect to treat a wholly owned subsidiary as a "qualified subchapter S subsidiary." To the extent that Target has a "qualified subchapter S subsidiary," the subsidiary is not treated as a separate corporation for

Target's Tax basis for the acquired assets was determined, in whole or in part, by reference to the Tax basis of the acquired assets (or any other property) in the hands of the transferor or (B) acquired the stock of any corporation which is a qualified subchapter S subsidiary.[7]

III. If Buyer (as well as Target) is an S corporation and no Code §338(h)(10) election will be made, add the following item to Section 4(k), *Tax Matters,* **of sample acquisition agreement 2002.1 (***pro-buyer* **stock purchase) and Section 4(k),** *Tax Matters,* **of sample acquisition agreement 2002.3 (***neutral* **stock purchase):**

(x) Target would not be liable for any Tax under Code §1374 if its assets (or the assets of any qualified subchapter S subsidiary) were sold for their fair market value as of the Closing Date. Neither Target nor any qualified subchapter S subsidiary of Target has, in the past 10 years, (A) acquired assets from another corporation in a transaction in which Target's Tax basis for the acquired assets was determined, in whole or in part, by reference to the Tax basis of the acquired assets (or any other property) in the hands of the transferor or (B) acquired the stock of any corporation which is a qualified subchapter S subsidiary.[8]

IV. Substitute the following new section for Section 9 of sample acquisition agreement 2002.1 (*pro-buyer* **stock purchase) and Section 9 of sample acquisition agreement 2002.3 (***neutral* **stock purchase). Add the following as a new Section 8A to sample acquisition agreement 2002.2 (***pro-seller* **stock purchase):**

9./8A. *Certain Tax Matters.*

(a) *Section 338(h)(10) Election.*[9] [At the Buyer's/Sellers' option,][10] Target and each of the Sellers[11] will join with Buyer in making an election under Code

---

federal income tax purposes and its assets, income, gain or loss are treated as Target's assets, income, gain or loss. Code §1361(b)(3). See ¶1102.4.3 for a.discussion of "qualified subchapter S subsidiaries."

[7] If Target acquired the stock of a C corporation and elected to treat the corporation as a "qualified subchapter S subsidiary," any built-in gain in the former C corporation's assets would be subject to a corporate-level tax under Code §1374 if any of the former C corporation's assets are disposed of in a taxable transaction during the following 10 years. See Code §1361(b)(3) and Code §1374. See also ¶1102.4.3.2.

[8] If Target acquired the stock of a C corporation and elected to treat the corporation as a "qualified subchapter S subsidiary," any built-in gain in the former C corporation's assets would be subject to a corporate-level tax under Code §1374 if any of the former C corporation's assets are disposed of in a taxable transaction during the following 10 years. See Code §1361(b)(3) and Code §1374. See also ¶1102.4.3.2.

[9] Add Sections 9/8A(a) and (b) if a Code §338(h)(10) election will be made. See ¶1109.3 for a detailed discussion of the consequences of a Code §338(h)(10) election where Target is an S corporation and ¶2002.6.1 for a more summary description.

[10] If it is not clear at the time of signing whether a Code §338(h)(10) election is desirable, the parties may wish to allow either Buyer or the Sellers the choice of whether the election is made after closing.

[11] In general, each of T-SCo's shareholders (whether or not such shareholder is a Seller), according to 8/99 proposed regulations, must sign the Code §338(h)(10) election in order for it to be valid. Thus,

§338(h)(10) of the Code (and any corresponding election under state, local, and foreign tax law) with respect to the purchase and sale of the stock of Target hereunder (a "Section 338(h)(10) Election"). Sellers will include any income, gain, loss, deduction, or other tax item resulting from the Section 338(h)(10) Election on their Tax Returns to the extent required by applicable law. [**Pro-buyer and Neutral versions:** Sellers shall also pay any Tax imposed on Target or its Subsidiaries[12] attributable to the making of the Section 338(h)(10) Election, including, but not limited to, (i) any Tax imposed under Code §1374, (ii) any tax imposed under Reg. §1.338(h)(10)-1(e)(5), or (iii) any state, local or foreign Tax imposed on Target's or its Subsidiaries' gain, and Sellers shall indemnify Buyer, Target and its Subsidiaries against any Adverse Consequences arising out of any failure to pay any such Taxes.][13]

(b) *Allocation of Purchase Price.* Buyer Target and Sellers agree that the Purchase Price and the liabilities of Target and its qualified subchapter S subsidiaries (plus other relevant items) will be allocated to the assets of Target and its qualified

---

when Buyer intends a Code §338(h)(10) election to be made, it is imperative that each T-SCo shareholder (including any shareholder who is retaining T-SCo stock rather than selling to Buyer) be contractually obligated to sign the Code §338(h)(10) election (including any similar state election, where required). See ¶1109.3 for a discussion of the signature requirements for a Code §338(h)(10) election.

The parties may wish to provide a more detailed procedure for making the Code §338(h)(10) election. For example, the parties may provide that either the Buyer or the Sellers will prepare the election forms and file them (after the other party has reviewed and signed the forms) and set forth the time frame for doing so. The Buyer may wish to include as a closing condition a requirement that each Seller (as well as each old T-SCo shareholder who is retaining his T-SCo stock, if any) execute the Code §338(h)(10) election on form 8023 at the closing. In the event the form cannot be prepared by closing, Buyer might consider requesting from each old T-SCo shareholder a power of attorney to sign the election form on such person's behalf. It is doubtful, however, that such a grant of power may be made irrevocable. Even if the operative document expressly states that the contractual right may not be revoked, IRS may view such right as a revocable power of attorney. *See* Reg. §601.505.

[12] Because a qualified subchapter S subsidiary is not treated as a separate corporation, a Code §338(h)(10) election made with respect to the sale of Target's stock will also apply to the assets of the qualified subchapter S subsidiary.

[13] The consequences of a Code §338(h)(10) election for state and local tax purposes may not be the same as the federal tax consequences. The parties need to consider whether there are any additional state and local tax costs (several states impose an entity-level tax on SCos) or risks which may result from the election and allocate such risks in the contract. The bracketed language generally allocates such risk to Sellers in the pro-buyer and neutral stock purchase agreement. Omission of the bracketed language in the pro-seller agreement generally allocates such risk to Buyer. Other variations are possible.

If the contract calls for a Code §338(h)(10) election, Sellers (in addition to demanding a higher purchase price because of SUB benefit to Buyer) may demand that Buyer indemnify Sellers for any increased net taxes resulting from the election. See ¶2002.6.1 for a description of several circumstances under which a Code §338(h)(10) election may increase state and federal taxes imposed on T-SCo's shareholders.

If Buyer agrees to indemnify selling T-SCo shareholders and the contract does not specify or limit the amount of indemnification, some Buyer contractual safeguards may include: *First*, allowing Buyer to control the purchase price allocation determination. *Second*, allowing Buyer to control the preparation of T-SCo's tax returns with respect to items attributable to the Code §338(h)(10) election. *Third*, obtaining contractual representations from Sellers as to their state of residence, so there is no question as to the state income tax they would have paid in a stock sale without a Code §338(h)(10) election.

subchapter S subsidiaries for all purposes (including Tax and financial accounting) [as shown on the Allocation Schedule attached hereto] [in a manner consistent with the fair market values set forth in the Allocation Schedule attached hereto]. Buyer, Target, Target's Subsidiaries, and Sellers will file all Tax Returns (including amended returns and claims for refund) and information reports in a manner consistent with [such allocation] [such values].

(c) *S Corporation Status.* Target and Sellers will not revoke Target's election to be taxed as an S corporation within the meaning of Code §§1361 and 1362. Target and Sellers will not take or allow any action [other than the sale of Target's stock pursuant to this agreement][14] that would result in the termination of Target's status as a validly electing S corporation within the meaning of Code §§1361 and 1362.

(d) *Tax Periods Ending on or before the Closing Date.*[15] [**Pro-buyer and Neutral alternative:** Buyer shall prepare or cause to be prepared and file or cause to be filed all Tax Returns for the Target and its Subsidiaries for all periods ending on or prior to the Closing Date which are filed after the Closing Date. [**Pro-buyer alternative:** Buyer shall permit Sellers to review and comment on each such Tax Return described in the preceding sentence prior to filing.] [**Neutral alternative:** Buyer shall permit Sellers to review and comment on each such Tax Return described in the preceding sentence prior to filing and shall make such revisions to such Tax Returns as are reasonably requested by Sellers.] To the extent permitted by applicable law, Sellers shall include any income, gain, loss, deduction or other tax items for such periods on their Tax Returns in a manner consistent with the Schedule K-1s furnished by Target to the Sellers for such periods. Sellers shall reimburse Buyer for any Taxes of the Target and its Subsidiaries with respect to such periods within fifteen (15) days after payment by Buyer or the Target and its Subsidiaries of such Taxes to the extent such Taxes are not reflected in the reserve for Tax Liability (rather than any reserve for deferred Taxes established to reflect timing differences between book and Tax income) shown on the face of the Closing Balance Sheet.[16]]

[**Pro-seller alternative:** Sellers shall prepare or cause to be prepared and file or cause to be filed all Tax Returns for the Target and its Subsidiaries for all periods ending on or prior to the Closing Date which are filed after the Closing Date. Sellers shall permit Buyer to review and comment on each such Tax Return described in the preceding sentence prior to filing. To the extent permitted by applicable law, Sellers shall include any income, gain, loss, deduction or other tax items for such periods on their Tax Returns in a manner consistent with the Schedule K-1s prepared by Sellers for such periods.]

(e) *Cooperation on Tax Matters.*

[14] Use bracketed language if no Code §338(h)(10) election will be made.
[15] To the extent that Target has any tax years which begin before the Closing Date and end after the Closing Date, additional language dealing with such years may be needed. Target will generally not have such "straddle years" for federal income tax purposes, but may for state or local tax purposes.
[16] This last sentence assumes that there will be a purchase price adjustment as described in ¶2002.5.

(i) Buyer, Target and its Subsidiaries and Sellers shall cooperate fully, as and to the extent reasonably requested by the other party, in connection with the filing of Tax Returns pursuant to this Section and any audit, litigation or other proceeding with respect to Taxes. Such cooperation shall include the retention and (upon the other party's request) the provision of records and information which are reasonably relevant to any such audit, litigation or other proceeding and making employees available on a mutually convenient basis to provide additional information and explanation of any material provided hereunder. Target and its Subsidiaries and Sellers agree (A) to retain all books and records with respect to Tax matters pertinent to Target and its Subsidiaries relating to any taxable period beginning before the Closing Date until the expiration of the statute of limitations (and, to the extent notified by Buyer or Sellers, any extensions thereof) of the respective taxable periods, and to abide by all record retention agreements entered into with any taxing authority, and (B) to give the other party reasonable written notice prior to transferring, destroying or discarding any such books and records and, if the other party so requests, Target and its Subsidiaries or Sellers, as the case may be, shall allow the other party to take possession of such books and records.

(ii) Buyer and Sellers further agree, upon request, to use their best efforts to obtain any certificate or other document from any governmental authority or any other Person as may be necessary to mitigate, reduce or eliminate any Tax that could be imposed (including, but not limited to, with respect to the transactions contemplated hereby).

(f) *Tax Sharing Agreements.* All tax sharing agreements or similar agreements with respect to or involving Target and its Subsidiaries shall be terminated as of the Closing Date and, after the Closing Date, Target and its Subsidiaries shall not be bound thereby or have any liability thereunder.

(g) *Certain Taxes.*

[**Pro-buyer alternative:** All transfer, documentary, sales, use, stamp, registration and other such Taxes and fees (including any penalties and interest) incurred in connection with this Agreement (including any corporate-level gains tax triggered by the sale of Target stock, New York City Transfer Tax and any similar tax imposed in other states or subdivisions), shall be paid by Sellers when due, and Sellers will, at their own expense, file all necessary Tax Returns and other documentation with respect to all such transfer, documentary, sales, use, stamp, registration and other Taxes and fees, and, if required by applicable law, Buyer will, and will cause its affiliates to, join in the execution of any such Tax Returns and other documentation.]

[**Neutral alternative:** All transfer, documentary, sales, use, stamp, registration and other such Taxes and fees (including any penalties and interest) incurred in connection with this Agreement (including any corporate-level gains tax triggered by the sale of Target stock, New York City Transfer Tax and any similar tax imposed in other states or subdivisions), shall be paid one-half by Buyer and one-half by Sellers when due, and the party required by applicable law will file all necessary Tax Returns and other documentation with respect to all such transfer, documentary, sales, use, stamp, registration and other Taxes and fees, and, if required by applicable law, the other parties will, and will cause their affiliates to, join in the execution of any such Tax Returns and other documentation. The expense of such filings shall be paid one-half by Buyer and one-half by Sellers.]

[**Pro-seller alternative:** All transfer, documentary, sales, use, stamp, registration and other such Taxes and fees (including any penalties and interest) incurred in connection with this Agreement (including any corporate-level gains tax triggered by the sale of Target stock, New York City Transfer Tax and any similar tax imposed in other states or subdivisions), shall be paid by Buyer when due, and Buyer or Target will, at its own expense, file all necessary Tax Returns and other documentation with respect to all such transfer, documentary, sales, use, stamp, registration and other Taxes and fees, and, if required by applicable law, Sellers will join in the execution of any such Tax Returns and other documentation.]

Taxable Purchase of Assets

¶2003 P's PURCHASE OF ALL T's ASSETS FOR CASH AND NOTES

Sample acquisition agreement 2003.1 is a *pro-buyer* version of a taxable asset purchase. Sample acquisition agreement 2003.2 is a *pro-seller* version of a taxable asset purchase. Sample acquisition agreement 2003.3 is a *neutral* version of a taxable asset purchase.

Sample acquisition agreements 2003.1, 2003.2, and 2003.3 contemplate a transaction in which a corporation ("P") will purchase all of the assets of another corporation ("T") for cash and P notes. If P is to pay the entire purchase price in cash (i.e., no P notes are being issued to T), all of the provisions relating to the P notes can be deleted.

If P purchases T's assets, T will generally retain those assets and rights which it does not transfer and assign to P, and T will generally remain responsible for those liabilities and obligations not assumed by P.[1]

It is generally necessary to prepare asset transfer documents and liability assumption documents in an asset purchase (whether a purchase of all T's assets or a purchase of a T division), which would not be required if P purchased T's *stock*.

See ¶2001.2.2 for a further description of the principal tax and other issues associated with a purchase of assets.

If P intends to purchase only the assets of a T division, rather than all of T's assets, the parties should generally use sample acquisition agreement 2004.1 (*pro-buyer* divisional asset purchase) or 2004.2 (*pro-seller* divisional asset purchase) as appropriate.

Sample acquisition agreement 2002.5 (purchase price adjustment) contains additional provisions for use when there is to be a post-closing purchase price adjustment based on T's net book value as of the closing. This form can be

---

¶2003 [1] P's contractual assumption of certain T liabilities and obligations will not preclude a third party to whom T owed the liabilities and obligations from suing T (if P has failed to pay or perform) unless the third party consents to P's assumption and agrees to look only to P for satisfaction (i.e., enters into a novation agreement). This means that if P fails to satisfy the assumed liabilities and obligations, nonconsenting third parties to whom T owed the liabilities and obligations may have a cause of action against T or, if T has liquidated and dissolved, against T's stockholders and/or directors.

adapted for other post-closing purchase price adjustments (such as a comparison of working capital with liabilities as of the closing *or* a contingent earnout based on earnings for a specified period after the closing). Sample acquisition agreement 2002.5 is, however, intended for use with sample acquisition agreements 2002.1, 2002.2, and 2002.3 (the *stock* purchase agreements) and must be modified prior to use with sample acquisition agreements 2003.1, 2003.2, and 2003.3 (the asset purchase agreements).

The parties must address a number of general issues in preparing any acquisition document. See ¶2001.1 for a discussion of these key issues.

¶2003.1   Pro-Buyer Asset Purchase

Sample acquisition agreement 2003.1 (*pro-buyer* asset purchase) contains provisions favoring P in such areas as (i) the extent to which P will receive T's cash (net of unpaid taxes) at the time of the closing, (ii) the extent to which T will bear the burden of its liabilities and obligations after the closing, (iii) the extent to which P will have conditions to its obligation to close, (iv) the extent to which T will be required to give representations and warranties, and (v) the extent to which T will be required to indemnity P against breaches of those representations and warranties.

Sample acquisition agreement 2003.1 provides that P will (i) acquire T's cash at the closing and (ii) assume T's liability for unpaid taxes with respect to periods up to the closing (but not to exceed an amount computed in accordance with T's past custom and practice in filing its tax returns). This means that P will receive T's cash (net of unpaid taxes) at the time of the closing.

Sample acquisition agreement 2003.1 provides that the only T liabilities P will assume are those liabilities (i) shown on the last T balance sheet reviewed by P before signing the contract, (ii) incurred in the ordinary course of business thereafter (but not including claims and lawsuits), (iii) involving certain taxes (as noted above), employee benefit plans, and executory contracts, and (iv) listed on a disclosure schedule. Thus, P would generally *not* assume such undisclosed T liabilities as environmental cleanup, employment discrimination, antitrust violations, product liability, product warranty, tax deficiencies, and other claims and lawsuits.

Sample acquisition agreement 2003.1 contains extensive representations and warranties from T concerning (i) its historical financial statements, (ii) intervening adverse changes in its business, (iii) litigation and undisclosed liabilities, (iv) tax matters, (v) pension and welfare benefit plans, (vi) compliance with federal, state, local, and foreign laws, (vii) environmental matters, and (viii) product liability and warranties.

Sample acquisition agreement 2003.1 also contains extensive representations and warranties from T concerning (i) authorization with respect to the transaction, (ii) title to the assets being sold, (iii) required governmental and third party consents (and noncontravention generally), (iv) organization, (v) adequacy and condition of its tangible assets, (vi) real estate matters, (vii) intellectual property matters, (viii) leases, licenses, and contracts, (ix) inventory and accounts receivable, (x) insurance, (xi) brokerage fees, and (xii) material misstatements and omissions.

T's representations and warranties are not qualified with references to materiality, but do contain occasional references to the actual knowledge of its shareholders, directors, officers, and employees *after reasonable investigation.*

Sample acquisition agreement 2003.1 contains alternative provisions for (i) full indemnification to P for breaches of T's representations and warranties (i.e., the representations and warranties concerning T survive indefinitely, and there is no deductible, threshold, or ceiling with respect to indemnification for breaches thereof) *or* (ii) limited indemnification to P for breaches of T's representations and warranties (i.e., the representations and warranties with respect to tax matters survive indefinitely; the other representations and warranties concerning T survive only for three years; and there is a threshold, but not a deductible or a ceiling, with respect to indemnification for breaches thereof).[1]

P also has the right to recoup its losses against the P notes in lieu of seeking indemnification from T and its shareholders.

P's obligation to close is subject to several conditions, such as (i) compliance with T's representations, warranties, and covenants, (ii) absence of a material adverse change, (iii) absence of litigation affecting the transaction, (iv) availability of financing, (v) delivery of title insurance, surveys, and third party consents, (vi) delivery of any side agreements, and (vii) delivery of an opinion of T's legal counsel.

P also has the right to terminate the purchase agreement for a period of [30 days] after signing if P is not satisfied with the results of its continuing business, legal, and accounting due diligence review.

There are a number of other important differences among sample acquisition agreement 2003.1 (*pro-buyer* asset purchase), sample acquisition agreement 2003.2 (*pro-seller* asset purchase), and sample acquisition agreement 2003.3 (*neutral* asset purchase). Each of these sample acquisition agreements contains extensive footnotes with cross-references pointing out the differences.

¶2003.1 [1] Sample acquisition agreement 2003.1 (the pro-buyer *asset* purchase agreement) assumes that T will liquidate and dissolve immediately after the closing so that T will not be able to perform any post-closing covenants (including any post-closing indemnification provisions) analogous to those contained in sample acquisition agreement 2002.1 (the pro-buyer *stock* purchase agreement). The Agreement with Target Stockholders (Exhibit A to sample acquisition agreement 2003.1) is designed to address this situation by making *T's shareholders* responsible for the post-closing covenants (including the post-closing indemnification provisions).

ASSET PURCHASE AGREEMENT

ASSET PURCHASE AGREEMENT[2]

BETWEEN

_____

AND

_____

_____, 19_____

TABLE OF CONTENTS

[2] The Buyer generally will obtain a cost basis (i.e., the Purchase Price _plus_ the Assumed Liabilities _plus_ the expenses of the transaction) in the Acquired Assets.

A purchase of assets in which the consideration is primarily cash and notes is generally treated for accounting purposes as a purchase rather than as a pooling of interests. _See_ ¶1503.

Some LBO structures prejudice the Target's creditors and hence might permit payments, transfers, liens, and obligations arising out of the LBO to be attacked under fraudulent conveyance law. _See_ ¶1506.

[EXHIBITS B THROUGH I AND THE DISCLOSURE SCHEDULE HAVE BEEN OMITTED FROM THIS SAMPLE ACQUISITION AGREEMENT 2003.1]

Agreement entered into on [as of] _____, 19____, by and between _____, a _____ corporation (the *"Buyer"*), and _____, a _____ corporation (the *"Target"*). The Buyer and the Target are referred to collectively herein as the *"Parties."*

This Agreement contemplates a transaction in which the Buyer will purchase all of the assets (and assume certain of the liabilities) of the Target in return for cash and the Buyer Notes.[4]

---

[3] This Asset Purchase Agreement assumes that the Target will liquidate and dissolve immediately after the Closing so that the Target will not be able to perform any post-Closing covenants (including any post-Closing indemnification provisions) analogous to those contained in sample acquisition agreement 2002.1 (the pro-buyer *stock* purchase agreement). The accompanying Agreement with Target Stockholders is designed to address this situation by making the *Target Stockholders* responsible for the post-Closing covenants (including the post-Closing indemnification provisions).

[4] If the buyer purchases the Target's assets, the Target will generally retain those assets and rights which it does not transfer and assign to the Buyer, and the Target will generally remain responsible for those liabilities and obligations not assumed by the Buyer.

Now, therefore, in consideration of the premises and the mutual promises herein made, and in consideration of the representations, warranties, and covenants herein contained, the Parties agree as follows.

1. *Definitions.*

"Accredited Investor" has the meaning set forth in Regulation D promulgated under the Securities Act.

"Acquired Assets" means all right, title, and interest in and to all of the assets of the Target,[5] *including* all of its (a) real property, leaseholds and subleaseholds therein, improvements, fixtures, and fittings thereon, and easements, rights-of-way, and other appurtenants thereto (such as appurtenant rights in and to public streets), (b) tangible personal property (such as machinery, equipment, inventories of raw materials and supplies, manufactured and purchased parts, goods in process and finished goods, furniture, automobiles, trucks, tractors, trailers, tools, jigs, and dies), (c) Intellectual Property, goodwill associated therewith, licenses and sublicenses granted and obtained with respect thereto, and rights thereunder, remedies against infringements thereof, and rights to protection of interests therein under the laws of all jurisdictions, (d) leases, subleases, and rights thereunder, (e) agreements, contracts, indentures, mortgages, instruments, Security Interests, guaranties, other similar arrangements, and rights thereunder, (f) accounts, notes, and other receivables, (g) securities (such as the capital stock in its Subsidiaries), (h) claims, deposits, prepayments, refunds, causes of action, choses in action, rights of recovery, rights of set off, and rights of recoupment (including any such item relating to the payment of Taxes), (i) franchises, approvals, permits, licenses, orders, registrations, certificates, variances, and similar rights obtained from governments and governmental agencies, (j) books, records, ledgers, files, documents, correspondence, lists, plats, architectural plans, drawings, and specifications, creative materials, advertising and promotional materials, studies, reports, and other printed or written materials, (k) Cash,[6] and (l) [rights in and with respect to the

---

It is generally necessary to prepare asset transfer documents and liability assumption documents in an asset purchase (whether a purchase of all the Target's assets or a purchase of the Target's division), which would not be required if the Buyer purchased the Target's *stock*.

The Buyer's contractual assumption of certain of the Target's liabilities and obligations generally will not preclude a third party to whom the Target owed the liabilities and obligations from suing the Target (if the Buyer has failed to pay or perform) unless the third party consents to the Buyer's assumption and agrees to look only to the Buyer for satisfaction (i.e., enters into a novation agreement). This means that if the Buyer fails to satisfy the assumed liabilities and obligations, nonconsenting third parties to whom the Target owed the liabilities and obligations may have a cause of action against the Target or, if the Target has liquidated and dissolved, against the Target's stockholders and/or directors.

[5] The Target may seek to have the definition of Acquired Assets narrowed to include only so much of the right, title, and interest in and to its assets *as it possesses and has the right to transfer.* Sample acquisition agreement 2003.2 (the *pro-seller* asset purchase agreement) contains provisions more favorable to the Target in this regard.

[6] This Agreement provides that the Buyer will acquire the consolidated cash of the Target and its Subsidiaries. The Target normally will seek to retain this consolidated cash (net of unpaid taxes up

assets associated with its Employee Benefit Plans];[7] *provided, however*, that the Acquired Assets shall not include (i) the corporate charter, qualifications to conduct business as a foreign corporation, arrangements with registered agents relating to foreign qualifications, taxpayer and other identification numbers, seals, minute books, stock transfer books, blank stock certificates, and other documents relating to the organization, maintenance, and existence of the Target as a corporation or (ii) any of the rights of the Target under this Agreement (or under any side agreement between the Target on the one hand and the Buyer on the other hand entered into on or after the date of this Agreement).

"Affiliate" has the meaning set forth in Rule 12b-2 of the regulations promulgated under the Securities Exchange Act.

"Affiliated Group" means any affiliated group within the meaning of Code §1504(a) [or any similar group defined under a similar provision of state, local, or foreign law].

"Agreement with Target Stockholders" means the Agreement with Target Stockholders entered into concurrently herewith and attached hereto as Exhibit A.[8]

"Applicable Rate" means the corporate base rate of interest publicly announced from time to time by [FINANCIAL INSTITUTION] [plus/minus ____% per annum].

"Assumed Liabilities"[9] means (a) all Liabilities of the Target set forth on the face of the Most Recent Balance Sheet (rather than in any notes thereto), (b) all Liabilities of the Target which have arisen after the Most Recent Fiscal Month End in the Ordinary Course of Business (other than any Liability resulting from, arising out of, relating to, in the nature of, or caused by any breach of contract, breach of warranty, tort, infringement, violation of law, or environmental matter, including without limitation those arising under Environmental, Health, and Safety Requirements[10]), (c) all obligations of the Target under the agreements, contracts, leases,

---

to the Closing for which the Buyer will become responsible). Sample acquisition agreement 2003.2 (the *pro-seller* asset purchase agreement) contains provisions more favorable to the Target in this regard.

[7] See the provisions in §8(r) with respect to employee benefits matters.

[8] This Asset Purchase Agreement assumes that the Target will liquidate and dissolve immediately after the Closing so that the Target will not be able to perform any post-Closing covenants (including any post-Closing indemnification provisions) analogous to those contained in sample acquisition agreement 2002.1 (the pro-buyer *stock* purchase agreement). The accompanying Agreement with Target Stockholders is designed to address this situation by making the *Target Stockholders* responsible for the post-Closing covenants (including the post-Closing indemnification provisions).

[9] See the footnote to §2(b) for an important discussion of certain tax issues that may affect the drafting of this definition as it concerns liabilities of the Target that have not yet matured into a deduction for tax purposes.

[10] This provision leaves with the Target all environmental liabilities (other than those shown on the face of the Most Recent Balance Sheet) of the Target.

Sample acquisition agreement 2003.2 (the *pro-seller* asset purchase agreement) requires the Buyer to assume all environmental liabilities relating to the Target.

licenses, and other arrangements referred to in the definition of Acquired Assets either (i) to furnish goods, services, and other non-Cash benefits to another party after the Closing or (ii) to pay for goods, services, and other non-Cash benefits that another party will furnish to it after the Closing, (d) [all Liabilities and obligations of the Target under its Employee Benefit Plans],[11] and (e) [all other Liabilities and obligations of the Target set forth in an appendix to the Disclosure Schedule under an express statement (that the Buyer has initialled) to the effect that the definition of Assumed Liabilities will include the Liabilities and obligations so disclosed]; *provided, however*, that the Assumed Liabilities shall not include (i) any Liability of the Target for Taxes,[12] (ii) any Liability of the Target for the unpaid Taxes of any Person (other than any of the Target and its Subsidiaries) under Reg. §1.1502-6 (or any similar provision of state, local, or foreign law), as a transferee or successor, by contract, or otherwise,[13] (iii) any obligation of the Target to indemnify any Person (including any of the Target Stockholders) by reason of the fact that such Person was a director, officer, employee, or agent of any of the Target and its Subsidiaries or was serving at the request of any such entity as a partner, trustee, director, officer, employee, or agent of another entity (whether such indemnification is for judgments, damages, penalties, fines, costs, amounts paid in settlement, losses, expenses, or otherwise and whether such indemnification is pursuant to any statute, charter document, bylaw, agreement, or otherwise),[14] (iv) any Liability of the Target for costs and expenses incurred in

---

Sample acquisition agreement 2003.3 (the *neutral* asset purchase agreement) states that the Buyer assumes those environmental liabilities specifically set forth on the Disclosure Schedule to that agreement.

[11] See the provisions in §8(r) with respect to employee benefits matters.

[12] This provision leaves with Target the liability for all Taxes incurred by Target through the Closing. If it is desired that Buyer assume some or all of the such Taxes, this provision should be altered.

[13] If the Target has been a member of an Affiliated Group filing a consolidated federal income tax return, the Target (or its successor) will be jointly and severally liable under Reg. §1.1502-6 for certain tax liabilities incurred by such Affiliated Group for a tax year when the Target was a member of such Affiliated Group for all or part of such tax year. *See* ¶210.

The Target may also be liable for the unpaid taxes of third parties under similar provisions of state, local, or foreign law, as a transferee or successor, by contract (e.g., a tax sharing agreement), or otherwise.

This provision is designed to protect the Buyer against assuming any liability for the unpaid taxes of any person other than the Target and its Subsidiaries.

[14] This *pro-buyer* asset purchase agreement provides that the Buyer will not assume any obligation of the Target to indemnify any Person (including any of the Target Stockholders), by reason of the fact that such Person was, before the asset purchase, a director or other officeholder of the Target entitled to indemnification from the Target, with respect to any matter whatsoever.

Note that sample acquisition agreement 2002.1 (the pro-buyer *stock* purchase agreement), when the Target retains its indemnification obligation to former directors and other officeholders even after the Buyer purchases the Target Shares, may not be as favorable to the Buyer. Sample acquisition agreement 2002.1 does, however, contain a narrower provision to the effect that none of the Target Stockholders will make any claim for indemnification against the Target, by reason of the fact that the Target Stockholder was, before the stock purchase, a director or other officeholder of the Target entitled to indemnification from the Target, with respect to any suit or claim the Buyer might bring against the Target Stockholder in connection with the stock purchase.

This provision responds to the surprising decision in Heffernan v. Pacific Dunlop GNB Corporation, 965 F.2d 369 (7th Cir. 1992). *See* §8(g) of sample acquisition agreement 2002.1 (the pro-buyer *stock*

connection with this Agreement and the transactions contemplated hereby, or (v) any Liability or obligation of the Target under this Agreement (or under any side agreement between the Target on the one hand and the Buyer on the other hand entered into on or after the date of this Agreement).[15]

"Basis" means any past or present fact, situation, circumstance, status, condition, activity, practice, plan, occurrence, event, incident, action, failure to act, or transaction that forms or could form the basis for any specified consequence.

"Buyer" has the meaning set forth in the preface above.

"Buyer Note" has the meaning set forth in §2(c) below.

"Cash" means cash and cash equivalents (including marketable securities and short term investments) calculated in accordance with GAAP applied on a basis consistent with the preparation of the Financial Statements.

"Closing" has the meaning set forth in §2(d) below.

"Closing Date" has the meaning set forth in §2(d) below.

"COBRA" means the requirements of Part 6 of Subtitle B of Title I of ERISA and Code §4980B and of any similar state law.

"Code" means the Internal Revenue Code of 1986, as amended.

"Controlled Group" has the meaning set forth in Code §1563.

"Deferred Intercompany Transaction" has the meaning set forth in Reg. §1.1502-13.

"Disclosure Schedule" has the meaning set forth in §3 below.

---

purchase agreement) and the footnote thereto. Although *Heffernan* involved a purchase of stock rather than a purchase of assets, the asset purchase covered by this Agreement presents many of the same concerns. *See also* §4(g) of the Agreement with Target Stockholders accompanying this Agreement.

Sample acquisition agreement 2003.2 (the *pro-seller* asset purchase agreement), on the other hand, provides that the Buyer *will assume* all obligations of the Target to indemnify any Person (including any of the Target Stockholders), by reason of the fact that such Person was, before the asset purchase, a director or other officeholder of the Target entitled to indemnification from the Target, with respect to any matter whatsoever.

[15] This definition of Assumed Liabilities is relatively narrow. The Buyer is assuming only those liabilities set forth on the face of the Most Recent Balance Sheet or incurred thereafter in the Ordinary Course of Business *plus* certain specified liabilities and obligations involving Taxes, employee benefit plans, and executory contracts *plus* certain liabilities and obligations identified in the Disclosure Schedule. The Buyer is *not* assuming any undisclosed liabilities (with certain exceptions as noted in the preceding sentence) or any liabilities set forth in the Disclosure Schedule (unless the Disclosure Schedule contains an express assumption initialled by the Buyer). The Target may seek to have the Buyer assume additional liabilities and obligations. Sample acquisition agreement 2003.2 (the *pro-seller* asset purchase agreement) contains a broader definition of Assumed Liabilities.

"Employee Benefit Plan" means any "employee benefit plan" (as such term is defined in ERISA §3(3)) and any other [material] employee benefit plan, program or arrangement of any kind.

"Employee Pension Benefit Plan" has the meaning set forth in ERISA §3(2).

"Employee Welfare Benefit Plan" has the meaning set forth in ERISA §3(1).

"Environmental, Health, and Safety Requirements" shall mean all federal, state, local and foreign statutes, regulations, ordinances and other provisions having the force or effect of law, all judicial and administrative orders and determinations, all contractual obligations and all common law concerning public health and safety, worker health and safety, and pollution or protection of the environment, including without limitation all those relating to the presence, use, production, generation, handling, transportation, treatment, storage, disposal, distribution, labeling, testing, processing, discharge, release, threatened release, control, or cleanup of any hazardous materials, substances or wastes, chemical substances or mixtures, pesticides, pollutants, contaminants, toxic chemicals, petroleum products or byproducts, asbestos, polychlorinated biphenyls, noise or radiation, each as amended and as now or hereafter in effect.[16]

"ERISA" means the Employee Retirement Income Security Act of 1974, as amended.

"ERISA Affiliate" means each entity which is treated as a single employer with the Target for purposes of Code §414.

"Excess Loss Account" has the meaning set forth in Reg. §1.1502-19.

"Fiduciary" has the meaning set forth in ERISA §3(21).

"Financial Statement" has the meaning set forth in §3(g) below.

"GAAP" means United States generally accepted accounting principles as in effect from time to time.

"Hart-Scott-Rodino Act" means the Hart-Scott-Rodino Antitrust Improvements Act of 1976, as amended.

---

[16] Sample acquisition agreement 2003.2 (the *pro-seller* asset purchase agreement) excludes contractual obligations and common law from this definition and explicitly limits this definition to laws as enacted and in effect on or prior to the Closing Date.

Sample acquisition agreement 2003.3 (the *neutral* asset purchase agreement) excludes contractual obligations from this definition and is silent as to the time frame for enactment of covered "Environmental, Health, and Safety Requirements."

"Intellectual Property" means (a) all inventions (whether patentable or unpatentable and whether or not reduced to practice), all improvements thereto, and all patents, patent applications, and patent disclosures, together with all reissuances, continuations, continuations-in-part, revisions, extensions, and reexaminations thereof, (b) all trademarks, service marks, trade dress, logos, trade names, and corporate names, together with all translations, adaptations, derivations, and combinations thereof and including all goodwill associated therewith, and all applications, registrations, and renewals in connection therewith, (c) all copyrightable works, all copyrights, and all applications, registrations, and renewals in connection therewith, (d) all mask works and all applications, registrations, and renewals in connection therewith, (e) all trade secrets and confidential business information (including ideas, research and development, know-how, formulas, compositions, manufacturing and production processes and techniques, technical data, designs, drawings, specifications, customer and supplier lists, pricing and cost information, and business and marketing plans and proposals), (f) all computer software (including data and related documentation), (g) all other proprietary rights, and (h) all copies and tangible embodiments thereof (in whatever form or medium).

"Knowledge" means actual knowledge after reasonable investigation.[17]

"Liability" means any liability (whether known or unknown, whether asserted or unasserted, whether absolute or contingent, whether accrued or unaccrued, whether liquidated or unliquidated, and whether due or to become due), including any liability for Taxes.

"Most Recent Balance Sheet" means the balance sheet contained within the Most Recent Financial Statements.

"Most Recent Financial Statements" has the meaning set forth in §3(g) below.

"Most Recent Fiscal Month End" has the meaning set forth in §3(g) below.

"Most Recent Fiscal Year End" has the meaning set forth in §3(g) below.

"Multiemployer Plan" has the meaning set forth in ERISA §3(37).

"Ordinary Course of Business" means the ordinary course of business consistent with past custom and practice (including with respect to quantity and frequency).

"Party" has the meaning set forth in the preface above.

"PBGC" means the Pension Benefit Guaranty Corporation.

---

[17] Sample acquisition agreement 2003.2 (the *pro-seller* asset purchase agreement) defines *"Knowledge"* as actual knowledge without independent investigation.

"Person" means an individual, a partnership, a corporation, an association, a joint stock company, a trust, a joint venture, an unincorporated organization, or a governmental entity (or any department, agency, or political subdivision thereof).

"Process Agent" has the meaning set forth in §8(p) below.

"Prohibited Transaction" has the meaning set forth in ERISA §406 and Code §4975.

"Purchase Price" has the meaning set forth in §2(c) below.

"Reportable Event" has the meaning set forth in ERISA §4043.

"Securities Act" means the Securities Act of 1933, as amended.

"Securities Exchange Act" means the Securities Exchange Act of 1934, as amended.

"Security Interest" means any mortgage, pledge, lien, encumbrance, charge, or other security interest, *other than* (a) mechanic's, materialmen's, and similar liens, (b) liens for Taxes not yet due and payable [or for Taxes that the taxpayer is contesting in good faith through appropriate proceedings], (c) purchase money liens and liens securing rental payments under capital lease arrangements, and (d) other liens arising in the Ordinary Course of Business and not incurred in connection with the borrowing of money.

"Subsidiary" means any corporation with respect to which a specified Person (or a Subsidiary thereof) owns a majority of the common stock or has the power to vote or direct the voting of sufficient securities to elect a majority of the directors.[18]

"Survey" has the meaning set forth in §5(i) below.

"Target" has the meaning set forth in the preface above.

"Target Share" means any share of the Common Stock, per value $_____ per share, of the Target.[19]

"Target Stockholder" means any person who or which holds any Target Shares.

"Tax" means any federal, state, local, or foreign income, gross receipts, license, payroll, employment, excise, severance, stamp, occupation, premium, windfall profits, environmental (including taxes under Code §59A), customs duties, capital stock, franchise, profits, withholding, social security (or similar), unemployment,

---

[18] It may be necessary to revise this definition if, for example, the Target has subsidiary *partnerships*.
[19] It may be necessary to revise this definition if the Target has additional classes of capital stock.

disability, real property, personal property, sales, use, transfer, registration, value added, alternative or add-on minimum, estimated, or other tax of any kind whatsoever, including any interest, penalty, or addition thereto, whether disputed or not.[20]

"Tax Return" means any return, declaration, report, claim for refund, or information return or statement relating to Taxes, including any schedule or attachment thereto, and including any amendment thereof.

2. *Basic Transaction.*[21]

(a) *Purchase and Sale of Assets.* On and subject to the terms and conditions of this Agreement, the Buyer agrees to purchase from the Target, and the Target agrees to sell, transfer, convey, and deliver to the Buyer, all of the Acquired Assets at the Closing for the consideration specified below in this §2.

(b) *Assumption of Liabilities.* On and subject to the terms and conditions of this Agreement, the Buyer agrees to assume and become responsible for all of the Assumed Liabilities at the Closing. The Buyer will not assume or have any responsibility, however, with respect to any other obligation or Liability of the Target not included within the definition of Assumed Liabilities.[22]

---

[20] This sample acquisition agreement 2003.1 (the *pro-buyer* asset purchase agreement) defines "Tax" broadly to include taxes of all descriptions.

Sample acquisition agreement 2003.2 (the *pro-seller* asset purchase agreement), on the other hand, defines "Tax" narrowly to include only federal, state, local, and foreign income taxes.

[21] This *pro-buyer* agreement provides that the Buyer will acquire the consolidated cash of the Target and its Subsidiaries at the Closing. *See* the definition of Acquired Assets in §1.

Sample acquisition agreement 2003.2 (the *pro-seller* asset purchase agreement), on the other hand, permits the Target to retain the consolidated cash of the Target and its Subsidiaries (net of unpaid taxes for which the Buyer will become responsible) at the Closing. *See* the definition of Acquired Assets in §1 thereof.

The *pro-seller* agreement also contains a provision allowing the Target to cause its Subsidiaries to distribute their cash to the Target at the Closing in order to facilitate the intended cash retention. *See* §2(d) thereof. This *pro-buyer* Agreement lacks a comparable provision (since there is no need for the Subsidiaries to distribute their cash to the Target at the Closing if the Target will not retain any of the consolidated cash).

[22] In a taxable purchase of the Target's assets, the Target may have liabilities that have not yet matured into a deduction for tax purposes. For example, (1) a cash method Target may have accrued (but unpaid) operating liabilities, (2) a cash method or an accrual method Target may have contingent liabilities, (3) a cash method or an accrual method Target may have unfunded pension liabilities, and (4) an accrual method Target may have liabilities as to which the "all events" test has been satisfied but as to which "economic performance" (e.g., payment) has not yet occurred. The tax treatment of these and other liabilities which have not yet matured into deductions is somewhat surprising. *See* ¶304.

Under Code §461(h), an accrual method Target can deduct liabilities which otherwise satisfy the all events test (i.e., "Code §461(h) Liabilities") only as economic performance occurs. With respect to many such liabilities, economic performance occurs under the Code §461(h) regulations only when the Target has made payment with respect to the liability. *See* ¶304.4.

Reg. §1.461-4(d)(5) and -4(g)(1)(ii)(C) seems to provide that when the Target sells the Buyer a trade or business and, as part of the sale, the Buyer *"expressly assumes"* a Code §461(h) Liability, the Target can deduct that liability (assuming that the Code §461(h) regulations make payment the proper test

(c) *Purchase Price.*[23] The Buyer agrees to pay to the Target at the Closing $_____ (the *"Purchase Price"*) by delivery of (i) its promissory notes (the *"Buyer Notes"*) in the form of Exhibit B attached hereto in the aggregate principal amount of $_____ and (ii) cash for the balance of the Purchase Price payable by wire transfer or delivery of other immediately available funds.[24]

(d) *The Closing.* The closing of the transactions contemplated by this Agreement (the *"Closing"*) shall take place at the offices of _____, in _____, _____ commencing at 9:00 a.m. local time on the [second] business day following the satisfaction or waiver of all conditions to the obligations of the Parties to consummate the transactions contemplated hereby (other than conditions with respect to actions the respective Parties will take at the Closing itself) or such other date as the Parties may mutually determine (the *"Closing Date"*); *provided, however,* that the Closing Date shall be no earlier than _____, 19____.

(e) *Deliveries at the Closing.* At the Closing, (i) the Target will deliver to the Buyer the various certificates, instruments, and documents referred to in §6(a) below; (ii) the Buyer will deliver to the Target the various certificates, instruments,

---

for economic performance) in the taxable year in which the sale occurred. This favorable tax result follows from the fact that the Target will be deemed to have made payment with respect to the liability when the amount of the liability (assumed by the Buyer) is included in the Target's amount realized on the sale of assets. The regulation is, however, unclear on the meaning of the phrase "expressly assumes." *See* ¶304.4.

Cautions taxpayers should accordingly consider taking some or all of the following steps: (i) the Parties should specifically enumerate in this Agreement as many as practicable of the Code §461(h) Liabilities that the Buyer is assuming; (ii) the Parties should specifically state in this Agreement that the Buyer is "expressly assuming" not only these enumerated liabilities but also any categories of *unenumerated* Code §461(h) Liabilities that the Buyer is assuming; and (iii) the boards of directors of the respective Parties should adopt resolutions specifically stating that the Buyer is "expressly assuming" these Code §461(h) Liabilities.

Reg. §1.461-4(d)(5) and -4(g)(1)(ii)(C) is applicable by its terms only with respect to Code §461(h) Liabilities. However, its premise that the Target will be deemed to have made payment with respect to a liability when the amount of the liability (assumed by the Buyer) is included in the Target's amount realized on the sale of assets may have a broader application. For this reason, cautious taxpayers may want to apply the advice in the preceding paragraph of this footnote to cover *all* liabilities that the Buyer is assuming as to which the Target has not yet become entitled to a deduction under the Code.

[23] The Target may seek to have the Buyer make an earnest money deposit upon execution of this Agreement. If the transaction were thereafter completed, the deposit would be applied to the Purchase Price. If the transaction were thereafter aborted, the deposit would be refunded to the Buyer or paid to the Target as liquidated damages depending on the terms of this Agreement and the reasons for the termination.

[24] Sample acquisition agreement 2002.5 contains additional provisions for use when there is to be a post-Closing Purchase Price adjustment based on the consolidated net book value for the Target and its Subsidiaries as of the Closing. That sample acquisition agreement can be adapted for other post-Closing Purchase Price adjustments (such as a comparison of consolidated working capital with consolidated liabilities as of the Closing *or* a contingent earnout based on consolidated earnings for a specified period after the Closing).

Sample acquisition agreement 2002.5 is, however, intended for use with sample acquisition agreements 2002.1, 2002.2, and 2002.3 (the *stock* purchase agreements) and must be modified prior to use with this *asset* purchase agreement.

and documents referred to in §6(b) below; (iii) the Target will execute, acknowledge (if appropriate), and deliver to the Buyer (A) assignments (including real property and Intellectual Property transfer documents) in the forms attached hereto as Exhibits C-1 through C-_____ and (B) such other instruments of sale, transfer, conveyance, and assignment as the Buyer and its counsel [reasonably] may request; (iv) the Buyer will execute, acknowledge (if appropriate), and deliver to the Target (A) an assumption in the form attached hereto as Exhibit D and (B) such other instruments of assumption as the Target and its counsel [reasonably] may request; and (v) the Buyer will deliver to the Target the consideration specified in §2(c) above.

(f) *Allocation.* [The Parties agree to allocate the Purchase Price (and all other capitalizable costs) among the Acquired Assets for all purposes (including financial accounting and tax purposes) in accordance with the allocation schedule attached hereto as Exhibit E.][25]

3. *Representations and Warranties of the Target.*[26] The Target represents and warrants to the Buyer that the statements contained in this §3 are correct and complete as of the date of this Agreement and will be correct and complete as of the Closing Date (as though made then and as though the Closing Date were substituted for the date of this Agreement throughout this §3), except as set forth in the disclosure schedule accompanying this Agreement and initialed by the Parties (the *"Disclosure Schedule"*).[27] The Disclosure Schedule will be arranged in paragraphs corresponding to the lettered and numbered paragraphs contained in this §3.

---

[25] The 1986 Act generally requires the Buyer and the Target to allocate the Buyer's aggregate basis (i.e., the Purchase Price *plus* the Assumed Liabilities *plus* the expenses of the transaction) among the Acquired Assets using the residual method. *See* ¶403. The Parties should omit this provision if they do not reach agreement on a particular allocation schedule.

[26] The Target will seek to give fewer representations and warranties and to qualify the representations and warranties it does give with concepts of "knowledge" and "materiality." Section 3 of this Agreement does not contain any unbracketed qualifications as to materiality. It does, however, contain occasional references to the actual knowledge of the Target Stockholders and the directors, officers, and employees of the Target and its Subsidiaries after reasonable investigation. The Target will seek to limit the group of individuals whose knowledge is applicable and make it clear that no such individual need conduct any special investigation. Sample acquisition agreement 2003.2 (the *pro-seller* asset purchase agreement) contains comparable representations and warranties more favorable to the Target.

[27] The Buyer will have a closing condition (*see* §6(a)(i)) and post-Closing indemnification rights (*see* §4(b)) of the accompanying Agreement with Target Stockholders) with respect to certain misrepresentations and breaches of warranty. The Buyer will not, however, have a closing condition or post-Closing indemnification rights with respect to any adverse matter that the Target discloses in the Disclosure Schedule. This is because the disclosure will cure any misrepresentation or breach of warranty that might otherwise have existed. Thus, when the Target discloses an adverse matter in the Disclosure Schedule, the Buyer may seek (a) to avoid assuming responsibility for the matter (*see* the definition of Assumed Liabilities in §1), (b) to add a specific closing condition requiring an acceptable resolution of the matter, and/or (c) to obtain specific post-Closing indemnification against the matter.

(a) *Organization of the Target.* The Target is a corporation duly organized, validly existing, and in good standing under the laws of the jurisdiction of its incorporation.

(b) *Authorization of Transaction.* The Target has full power and authority (including full corporate power and authority) to execute and deliver this Agreement and to perform its obligations hereunder. Without limiting the generality of the foregoing, the board of directors of the Target and the Target Stockholders have duly authorized the execution, delivery, and performance of this Agreement by the Target.[28] This Agreement constitutes the valid and legally binding obligation of the Target, enforceable in accordance with its terms and conditions.

(c) *Noncontravention.* Neither the execution and the delivery of this Agreement, nor the consummation of the transactions contemplated hereby (including the assignments and assumptions referred to in §2 above), will (i) violate any constitution, statute, regulation, rule, injunction, judgment, order, decree, ruling, charge, or other restriction of any government, governmental agency, or court to which any of the Target and its Subsidiaries is subject or any provision of the charter or bylaws of any of the Target and its Subsidiaries or (ii) conflict with, result in a breach of, constitute a default under, result in the acceleration of, create in any party the right to accelerate, terminate, modify, or cancel, or require any notice under any agreement, contract, lease, license, instrument, or other arrangement to which any of the Target and its Subsidiaries is a party or by which it is bound or to which any of its assets is subject (or result in the imposition of any Security Interest upon any of its assets). None of the Target and its Subsidiaries needs to give any notice to, make any filing with, or obtain any authorization, consent, or approval of any government or governmental agency in order for the Parties to consummate the transactions contemplated by this Agreement (including the assignments and assumptions referred to in §2 above).

(d) *Brokers' Fees.* The Target has no Liability or obligation to pay any fees or commissions to any broker, finder, or agent with respect to the transactions contemplated by this Agreement for which the Buyer could become liable or obligated. None of the Subsidiaries of the Target has any Liability or obligation to pay any fees or commissions to any broker, finder, or agent with respect to the transactions contemplated by this Agreement.

---

[28] The Target must obtain the approval of its board of directors *and* the approval of its stockholders in order to sell all or substantially all of its assets. *See* ¶2001.2.2.2. This Agreement assumes the Target has already obtained the requisite corporate approvals.

If the Parties wish to enter into this Agreement before the Target has obtained the approval of its *stockholders,* the Parties should revise this Agreement to include (a) a covenant calling for the Target to obtain such approval prior to the Closing and (b) a closing condition for each of the Parties to the effect that the Target *has* obtained such approval. *Compare* sample acquisition agreement 2005 (the reverse subsidiary merger agreement), which contemplates that the target corporation will obtain the approval of its stockholders between the signing of the merger agreement and the Closing.

The Parties generally will not enter into an asset purchase agreement (or for that matter a merger agreement) until the Target has obtained the approval of its *board of directors.*

(e) *Title to Assets.* The Target and its Subsidiaries have good and marketable title to, or a valid leasehold interest in, the properties and assets used by them, located on their premises, or shown on the Most Recent Balance Sheet or acquired after the date thereof, free and clear of all Security Interests, except for properties and assets disposed of in the Ordinary Course of Business since the date of the Most Recent Balance Sheet. Without limiting the generality of the foregoing, the Target has good and marketable title to all of the Acquired Assets, free and clear of any Security Interest or restriction on transfer.

(f) *Subsidiaries.* §3(f) of the Disclosure Schedule sets forth for each Subsidiary of the Target (i) its name and jurisdiction of incorporation, (ii) the number of shares of authorized capital stock of each class of its capital stock, (iii) the number of issued and outstanding shares of each class of its capital stock, the names of the holders thereof, and the number of shares held by each such holder, (iv) the number of shares of its capital stock held in treasury, and (v) its directors and officers. Each Subsidiary of the Target is a corporation duly organized, validly existing, and in good standing under the laws of the jurisdiction of its incorporation. Each Subsidiary of the Target is duly authorized to conduct business and is in good standing under the laws of each jurisdiction where such qualification is required. Each Subsidiary of the Target has full corporate power and authority and all licenses, permits, and authorizations necessary to carry on the businesses in which it is engaged [and in which it presently proposes to engage] and to own and use the properties owned and used by it. The Target has delivered to the Buyer correct and complete copies of the charter and bylaws of each Subsidiary of the Target (as amended to date). All of the issued and outstanding shares of capital stock of each Subsidiary of the Target have been duly authorized and are validly issued, fully paid, and nonassessable. One of the Target and its Subsidiaries holds of record and owns beneficially all of the outstanding shares of each Subsidiary of the Target, free and clear of any restrictions on transfer (other than restrictions under the Securities Act and state securities laws), Taxes, Security Interests, options, warrants, purchase rights, contracts, commitments, equities, claims, and demands. There are no outstanding or authorized options, warrants, purchase rights, subscription rights, conversion rights, exchange rights, or other contracts or commitments that could require any of the Target and its Subsidiaries to sell, transfer, or otherwise dispose of any capital stock of any of its Subsidiaries or that could require any Subsidiary of the Target to issue, sell, or otherwise cause to become outstanding any of its own capital stock (other than this Agreement). There are no outstanding stock appreciation, phantom stock, profit participation, or similar rights with respect to any Subsidiary of the Target. There are no voting trusts, proxies, or other agreements or understandings with respect to the voting of any capital stock of any Subsidiary of the Target. The minute books (containing the records of meetings of the stockholders, the board of directors, and any committees of the board of directors), the stock certificate books, and the stock record books of each Subsidiary of the Target are correct and complete. None of the Subsidiaries of the Target is in default under or in violation of any provision of its charter or bylaws. None of the Target and its Subsidiaries controls directly or indirectly or has any direct or indirect equity participation in any corporation, partnership, trust, or other business association which is not a Subsidiary of the Target.

(g) *Financial Statements.* Attached hereto as Exhibit F are the following financial statements (collectively the *"Financial Statements"*): (i) audited consolidated and unaudited consolidating balance sheets and statements of income, changes in stockholders' equity, and cash flow as of and for the fiscal years ended _____, 19_____, _____, 19_____, _____, 19_____, _____, 19_____, and _____, 19_____ (the *"Most Recent Fiscal Year End"*) for the Target and its Subsidiaries; and (ii) unaudited consolidated and consolidating balance sheets and statements of income, changes in stockholders' equity, and cash flow (the *"Most Recent Financial Statements"*) as of and for the _____ months ended _____, 19_____ (the *"Most Recent Fiscal Month End"*) for the Target and its Subsidiaries. The Financial Statements (including the notes thereto) have been prepared in accordance with GAAP applied on a consistent basis throughout the periods covered thereby, present fairly the financial condition of the Target and its Subsidiaries as of such dates and the results of operations of the Target and its Subsidiaries for such periods, are correct and complete, and are consistent with the books and records of the Target and its Subsidiaries (which books and records are correct and complete)[29] [; *provided, however,* that the Most Recent Financial Statements are subject to normal year-end adjustments (which will not be material individually or in the aggregate) and lack footnotes and other presentation items].

(h) *Events Subsequent to Most Recent Fiscal Year End.* Since the Most Recent Fiscal Year End, there has not been any [material] adverse change in the business, financial condition, operations, results of operations, or future prospects of any of the Target and its Subsidiaries. Without limiting the generality of the foregoing, since that date:

(i) none of the Target and its Subsidiaries has sold, leased, transferred, or assigned any of its assets, tangible or intangible, other than for a fair consideration in the Ordinary Course of Business;

(ii) none of the Target and its Subsidiaries has entered into any agreement, contract, lease, or license (or series of related agreements, contracts, leases, and licenses) either involving more than $_____ or outside the Ordinary Course of Business;

(iii) no party (including any of the Target and its Subsidiaries) has accelerated, terminated, modified, or cancelled any agreement, contract, lease, or license (or series of related agreements, contracts, leases, and licenses) involving more

---

[29] Sample acquisition agreement 2003.2 (the *pro-seller* asset purchase agreement) contains a narrower representation to the effect that the financial statements present fairly the financial condition and results of operations of the Target and its Subsidiaries.

than $_____ to which any of the Target and its Subsidiaries is a party or by which any of them is bound;

(iv) none of the Target and its Subsidiaries has imposed any Security Interest upon any of its assets, tangible or intangible;

(v) none of the Target and its Subsidiaries has made any capital expenditure (or series of related capital expenditures) either involving more than $_____ or outside the Ordinary Course of Business;

(vi) none of the Target and its Subsidiaries has made any capital investment in, any loan to, or any acquisition of the securities or assets of, any other Person (or series of related capital investments, loans, and acquisitions) either involving more than $_____ or outside the Ordinary Course of Business;

(vii) none of the Target and its Subsidiaries has issued any note, bond, or other debt security or created, incurred, assumed, or guaranteed any indebtedness for borrowed money or capitalized lease obligation either involving more than $_____ singly or $_____ in the aggregate;

(viii) none of the Target and its Subsidiaries has delayed or postponed the payment of accounts payable and other Liabilities outside the Ordinary Course of Business;

(ix) none of the Target and its Subsidiaries has cancelled, compromised, waived, or released any right or claim (or series of related rights and claims) either involving more than $_____ or outside the Ordinary Course of Business;

(x) none of the Target and its Subsidiaries has granted any license or sublicense of any rights under or with respect to any Intellectual Property;

(xi) there has been no change made or authorized in the charter or bylaws of any of the Target and its Subsidiaries;

(xii) none of the Target and its Subsidiaries has issued, sold, or otherwise disposed of any of its capital stock, or granted any options, warrants, or other rights to purchase or obtain (including upon conversion, exchange, or exercise) any of its capital stock;

(xiii) none of the Target and its Subsidiaries has declared, set aside, or paid any dividend or made any distribution with respect to its capital stock (whether in cash or in kind) or redeemed, purchased, or otherwise acquired any of its capital stock;

(xiv) none of the Target and its Subsidiaries has experienced any damage, destruction, or loss (whether or not covered by insurance) to its property;

(xv) none of the Target and its Subsidiaries has made any loan to, or entered into any other transaction with, any of its directors, officers, and employees outside the Ordinary Course of Business;

(xvi) none of the Target and its Subsidiaries has entered into any employment contract or collective bargaining agreement, written or oral, or modified the terms of any existing such contract or agreement;

(xvii) none of the Target and its Subsidiaries has granted any increase in the base compensation of any of its directors, officers, and employees outside the Ordinary Course of Business;

(xviii) none of the Target and its Subsidiaries has adopted, amended, modified, or terminated any bonus, profit-sharing, incentive, severance, or other plan, contract, or commitment for the benefit of any of its directors, officers, and employees (or taken any such action with respect to any other Employee Benefit Plan);

(xix) none of the Target and its Subsidiaries has made any other change in employment terms for any of its directors, officers, and employees outside the Ordinary Course of Business;

(xx) none of the Target and its Subsidiaries has made or pledged to make any charitable or other capital contribution outside the Ordinary Course of Business;

(xxi) none of the Target and its Subsidiaries has paid any amount to any third party with respect to any Liability or obligation (including any costs and expenses the Target has incurred or may incur in connection with this Agreement and the transactions contemplated hereby) which would not constitute an Assumed Liability if in existence as of the Closing;[30]

(xxii) there has not been any other [material] occurrence, event, incident, action, failure to act, or transaction outside the Ordinary Course of Business involving any of the Target and its Subsidiaries; and

---

[30] Notice that the Buyer will bear the cost of (i.e., will in effect assume) any liability or obligation to the extent the Target pays any amount to a third party with respect thereto prior to the Closing. This is because the payment will reduce the amount of cash the Buyer otherwise would receive when it acquires the assets of the Target and its Subsidiaries at the Closing. The Buyer therefore will seek to prevent the Target from making any payment with respect to a liability and obligation the Buyer is not assuming.

This representation and warranty is designed to uncover whether the Target has made any such payment between the Most Recent Fiscal Year End and the date of this Agreement. Section 5(c) contains a comparable covenant prohibiting the Target from making any such payment between the date of this Agreement and the Closing.

(xxiii) none of the Target and its Subsidiaries has committed to any of the foregoing.

(i) *Undisclosed Liabilities.*   None of the Target and its Subsidiaries has any Liability (and there is no Basis for any present or future action, suit, proceeding, hearing, investigation, charge, complaint, claim, or demand against any of them giving rise to any Liability), except for (i) Liabilities set forth on the face of the Most Recent Balance Sheet (rather than in any notes thereto) and (ii) Liabilities which have arisen after the Most Recent Fiscal Month End in the Ordinary Course of Business (none of which results from, arises out of, relates to, is in the nature of, or was caused by any breach of contract, breach of warranty, tort, infringement, or violation of law).[31]

(j) *Legal Compliance.*   Each of the Target, its Subsidiaries, and their respective predecessors and Affiliates has complied with all applicable laws (including rules, regulations, codes, plans, injunctions, judgments, orders, decrees, rulings, and charges thereunder) of federal, state, local, and foreign governments (and all agencies thereof), and no action, suit, proceeding, hearing, investigation, charge, complaint, claim, demand, or notice has been filed or commenced against any of them alleging any failure so to comply.

(k) *Tax Matters.*[32]

---

[31] This Agreement provides that the Buyer will assume certain specified liabilities of the *Target*. *See* the definition of Assumed Liabilities in §1 (and in particular the provision making the Buyer responsible for certain liabilities the Target reveals in the Disclosure Schedule).

In addition, the Buyer may be exposed for certain liabilities of the *Target* by operation of law if the Target does not pay them (e.g., under applicable bulk sales statutes and common law doctrines of de facto merger and successor liability). *See* ¶2001.2.2.2.

Finally, the Buyer will become indirectly responsible for all of the liabilities of the *Subsidiaries* when the Buyer acquires their capital stock as part of the Acquired Assets. For this reason, the Buyer may seek (a) to purchase assets from the Target *and from each of the Subsidiaries* (i.e., a multiple entity asset sale) or (b) to have the Target liquidate and dissolve the Subsidiaries tax free under Code §332 (to the extent they are United States Corporations) and sell their assets to the Buyer.

These representations and warranties concerning undisclosed liabilities (and the post-Closing indemnification provisions in §4(b) of the accompanying Agreement with Target Stockholders) are designed to work in conjunction with the narrow definition of Assumed Liabilities in §1 to protect the Buyer against liabilities it does not intend to assume.

[32] This Agreement provides that the Buyer will assume the tax liabilities of the *Target* with respect to periods prior to the Closing for which the return is due after the Closing up to an amount computed in accordance with the past custom and practice of the Target and its Subsidiaries in filing their tax returns. *See* the definition of Assumed Liabilities in §1.

In addition, the Buyer may be exposed for certain tax liabilities of the *Target* by operation of law if the Target does not pay them (e.g., under applicable bulk sales statutes and common law doctrines of de facto merger and successor liability). *See* ¶2001.2.2.2.

Finally, the Buyer will become indirectly responsible for all of the tax liabilities of the *Subsidiaries* when the Buyer acquires their capital stock as part of the Acquired Assets. For this reason, the Buyer may seek (a) to purchase assets from the Target *and from each of the Subsidiaries* (i.e., a multiple entity asset sale) or (b) to have the Target liquidate and dissolve the Subsidiaries tax free under Code §332 (to the extent they are United States corporations) and sell their assets to the Buyer.

These representations and warranties concerning taxes (and the post-Closing indemnification provisions in §4(b) of the accompanying Agreement with Target Stockholders) are designed to work

(i) Each of the Target and its Subsidiaries has filed all Tax Returns that it was required to file. All such Tax Returns were correct and complete in all respects. All Taxes owed by any of the Target and its Subsidiaries (whether or not shown on any Tax Return) have been paid.[33] None of the Target and its Subsidiaries currently is the beneficiary of any extension of time within which to file any Tax Return. No claim has ever been made by an authority in a jurisdiction where any of the Target and its Subsidiaries does not file Tax Returns that it is or may be subject to taxation by that jurisdiction. There are no Security Interests on any of the assets of any of the Target and its Subsidiaries that arose in connection with any failure (or alleged failure) to pay any Tax.

(ii) Each of the Target and its Subsidiaries has withheld and paid all Taxes required to have been withheld and paid in connection with amounts paid or owing to any employee, independent contractor, creditor, stockholder, or other third party.

(iii) No Target Stockholder or director or officer (or employee responsible for Tax matters) of any of the Target and its Subsidiaries expects any authority to assess any additional Taxes for any period for which Tax Returns have been filed. There is no dispute or claim concerning any Tax Liability of any of the Target and its Subsidiaries either (A) claimed or raised by any authority in writing or (B) as to which any of the Target Stockholders and the directors and officers (and employees responsible for Tax matters) of the Target and its Subsidiaries has Knowledge based upon personal contact with any agent of such authority. §3(k) of the Disclosure Schedule lists all federal, state, local, and foreign income Tax Returns filed with respect to any of the Target and its Subsidiaries for taxable periods ended on or after _____, 19____, indicates those Tax Returns that have been audited, and indicates those Tax Returns that currently are the subject of audit. The Target has delivered to the Buyer correct and complete copies of all federal income Tax Returns, examination reports, and statements of deficiencies assessed against or agreed to by any of the Target and its Subsidiaries since _____, 19____.

(iv) None of the Target and its Subsidiaries has waived any statute of limitations in respect of Taxes or agreed to any extension of time with respect to a Tax assessment or deficiency.

(v) The unpaid Taxes of the Target and its Subsidiaries (A) did not, as of the Most Recent Fiscal Month End, exceed the reserve for Tax Liability (rather than any reserve for deferred Taxes established to reflect timing differences between book and Tax income) set forth on the face of the Most Recent Balance

---

in conjunction with the narrow definition of Assumed Liabilities in §1 to protect the Buyer against tax liabilities it does not intend to assume.

[33] Sample acquisition agreement 2003.2 (the *pro-seller* asset purchase agreement) contains a narrower representation to the effect that each of the Target and its Subsidiaries has filed all tax returns that it was required to file and has paid all taxes *shown thereon as owing*.

Sheet (rather than in any notes thereto) and (B) do not exceed that reserve as adjusted for the passage of time through the Closing Date in accordance with the past custom and practice of the Target and its Subsidiaries in filing their Tax Returns.

Alternative 1—Add the following paragraph if none of the Acquired Assets is stock of a Subsidiary of Target:

(vi) None of the Assumed Liabilities is an obligation to make a payment that will not be deductible under Code §280G. [Each of the Target and its Subsidiaries has disclosed on its federal income Tax Returns all positions taken therein that could give rise to a substantial understatement of federal income Tax within the meaning of Code §6662.] None of the Target and its Subsidiaries is a party to any Tax allocation or sharing agreement. None of the Target and its Subsidiaries (A) has been a member of an Affiliated Group filing a consolidated federal income Tax Return (other than a group the common parent of which was the Target) or (B) has any Liability for the Taxes of any Person (other than any of the Target and its Subsidiaries) under Reg. §1.1502-6 (or any similar provision of state, local, or foreign law), as a transferee or successor, by contract, or otherwise.[34]

Alternative 2—Add the following paragraphs if one or more of the Acquired Assets is stock of a Subsidiary of Target:

(vi) None of the Target and its Subsidiaries has filed a consent under Code §341(f) concerning collapsible corporations. None of the Target and its Subsidiaries has made any payments, is obligated to make any payments, or is a party to any agreement that under certain circumstances could obligate it to make any payments that will not be deductible under Code §280G. None of the Target and its Subsidiaries has been a United States real property holding

---

[34] If the Target or a Subsidiary has been a member of an Affiliated Group filing a consolidated federal income tax return, such corporation (or its successor) will be jointly and severally liable under Reg. §1.1502-6 for certain tax liabilities incurred by such Affiliated Group for a tax year when such corporation was a member of such Affiliated Group for all or part of such tax year. *See* ¶210.

The Target or a Subsidiary may also be liable for the unpaid taxes of third parties under similar provisions of state, local, or foreign law, as a transferee or successor, by contract (e.g., a tax sharing agreement), or otherwise.

This Agreement provides that the Buyer will not assume any liability of the *Target* for the unpaid taxes of any person other than the Target and its Subsidiaries. See the definition of "Assumed Liabilities" in §1.

However, the Buyer will become indirectly responsible for any such liability of the *Subsidiaries* when the Buyer acquires their capital stock as part of the Acquired Assets. In order to eliminate this risk altogether, the Buyer may seek (a) to purchase assets from the Target *and from each of the Subsidiaries* (i.e., a multiple entity asset sale) or (b) to have the Target liquidate and dissolve the Subsidiaries tax free under Code §332 (to the extent they are United States corporations) and sell their assets to the Buyer.

The Agreement with Target Stockholders (Exhibit A to this Agreement) contains indemnification provisions designed to protect the Buyer against any such liability for the unpaid taxes of any person other than the Target and its Subsidiaries. *See* §4(b)(iii) of Exhibit A.

corporation within the meaning of Code §897(c)(2) during the applicable period specified in Code §897(c)(1)(A)(ii). [Each of the Target and its Subsidiaries has disclosed on its federal income Tax Returns all positions taken therein that could give rise to a substantial understatement of federal income Tax within the meaning of Code §6662.] None of the Target and its Subsidiaries is a party to any Tax allocation or sharing agreement. None of the Target and its Subsidiaries (A) has been a member of an Affiliated Group filing a consolidated federal income Tax Return (other than a group the common parent of which was the Target) or (B) has any Liability for the Taxes of any Person (other than any of the Target and its Subsidiaries) under Reg. §1.1502-6 (or any similar provision of state, local, or foreign law), as a transferee or successor, by contract, or otherwise.[35]

(vii) §3(k) of the Disclosure Schedule sets forth the following information with respect to each of the Target and its Subsidiaries (or, in the case of clause (B) below, with respect to each of the Subsidiaries) as of the most recent practicable date [(as well as on an estimated pro forma basis as of the Closing giving effect to the consummation of the transactions contemplated hereby)]: (A) the basis of the Target or Subsidiary in its assets; (B) the basis of the stockholder(s) of the Subsidiary in its stock (or the amount of any Excess Loss Account); (C) the amount of any net operating loss, net capital loss, unused investment or other credit, unused foreign tax, or excess charitable contribution allocable to the Target or Subsidiary; and (D) the amount of any deferred gain or loss allocable to the Target or Subsidiary arising out of any Deferred Intercompany Transaction.

(l) *Real Property.*[36]

---

[35] If the Target or a Subsidiary has been a member of an Affiliated Group filing a consolidated federal income tax return, such corporation (or its successor) will be jointly and severally liable under Reg. §1.1502-6 for certain tax liabilities incurred by such Affiliated Group for a tax year when such corporation was a member of such Affiliated Group for all or part of such tax year. *See* ¶210.

The Target or a Subsidiary may also be liable for the unpaid taxes of third parties under similar provisions of state, local, or foreign law, as a transferee or successor, by contract (e.g., a tax sharing agreement), or otherwise.

This Agreement provides that the Buyer will not assume any liability of the *Target* for the unpaid taxes of any person other than the Target and its Subsidiaries. See the definition of "Assumed Liabilities" in §1.

However, the Buyer will become indirectly responsible for any such liability of the *Subsidiaries* when the Buyer acquires their capital stock as part of the Acquired Assets. In order to eliminate this risk altogether, the Buyer may seek (a) to purchase assets from the Target *and from each of the Subsidiaries* (i.e., a multiple entity asset sale) or (b) to have the Target liquidate and dissolve the Subsidiaries tax free under Code §332 (to the extent they are United States corporations) and sell their assets to the Buyer.

The Agreement with Target Stockholders (Exhibit A to this Agreement) contains indemnification provisions designed to protect the Buyer against any such liability for the unpaid taxes of any person other than the Target and its Subsidiaries. *See* §4(b)(iii) of Exhibit A.

[36] These representations and warranties concerning real property are relatively long and detailed. A condensed version of these provisions may be more appropriate when, for example, the real property of the Target and its Subsidiaries is relatively insignificant.

(i) §3(l)(i) of the Disclosure Schedule lists and describes briefly all real property that any of the Target and its Subsidiaries owns. With respect to each such parcel of owned real property:

(A) the identified owner has good and marketable title to the parcel of real property, free and clear of any Security Interest, easement, covenant, or other restriction, except for installments of special assessments not yet delinquent and recorded easements, covenants, and other restrictions which do not impair the current use, occupancy, or value, or the marketability of title, of the property subject thereto;

(B) there are no pending or [, to the Knowledge of any of the Target Stockholders and the directors and officers (and employees with responsibility for real estate matters) of the Target and its Subsidiaries,] threatened condemnation proceedings, lawsuits, or administrative actions relating to the property or other matters affecting [materially and] adversely the current use, occupancy, or value thereof;

(C) the legal description for the parcel contained in the deed thereof describes such parcel fully and adequately, the buildings and improvements are located within the boundary lines of the described parcels of land, are not in violation of applicable setback requirements, zoning laws, and ordinances (and none of the properties or buildings or improvements thereon are subject to "permitted non-conforming use" or "permitted non-conforming structure" classifications), and do not encroach on any easement which may burden the land, the land does not serve any adjoining property for any purpose inconsistent with the use of the land, and the property is not located within any flood plain or subject to any similar type restriction for which any permits or licenses necessary to the use thereof have not been obtained;

(D) all facilities have received all approvals of governmental authorities (including licenses and permits) required in connection with the ownership or operation thereof and have been operated and maintained in accordance with applicable laws, rules, and regulations;

(E) there are no leases, subleases, licenses, concessions, or other agreements, written or oral, granting to any party or parties the right of use or occupancy of any portion of the parcel of real property;

(F) there are no outstanding options or rights of first refusal to purchase the parcel of real property, or any portion thereof or interest therein;

(G) there are no parties (other than the Target and its Subsidiaries) in possession of the parcel of real property, other than tenants under any leases disclosed in §3(l)(i) of the Disclosure Schedule who are in possession of space to which they are entitled;

(H) all facilities located on the parcel of real property are supplied with utilities and other services necessary for the operation of such facilities, including gas, electricity, water, telephone, sanitary sewer, and storm sewer, all of which services are adequate in accordance with all applicable laws, ordinances, rules, and regulations and are provided via public roads or via permanent, irrevocable, appurtenant easements benefitting the parcel of real property; and

(I) each parcel of real property abuts on and has direct vehicular access to a public road, or has access to a public road via a permanent, irrevocable, appurtenant easement benefitting the parcel of real property, and access to the property is provided by paved public right-of-way with adequate curb cuts available.

(ii) §3(l)(ii) of the Disclosure Schedule lists and describes briefly all real property leased or subleased to any of the Target and its Subsidiaries. §3(l)(ii) of the Disclosure Schedule also identifies the leased or subleased properties for which title insurance policies are to be procured in accordance with §5(h)(ii) below. The Target has delivered to the Buyer correct and complete copies of the leases and subleases listed in §3(l)(ii) of the Disclosure Schedule (as amended to date). With respect to each lease and sublease listed in §3(l)(ii) of the Disclosure Schedule:

(A) the lease or sublease is legal, valid, binding, enforceable, and in full force and effect;

(B) the lease or sublease will continue to be legal, valid, binding, enforceable, and in full force and effect on identical terms following the consummation of the transactions contemplated hereby (including the assignments and assumptions referred to in §2 above);

(C) no party to the lease or sublease is in breach or default, and no event has occurred which, with notice or lapse of time, would constitute a breach or default or permit termination, modification, or acceleration thereunder;

(D) no party to the lease or sublease has repudiated any provision thereof;

(E) there are no disputes, oral agreements, or forbearance programs in effect as to the lease or sublease;

(F) with respect to each sublease, the representations and warranties set forth in subsections (A) through (E) above are true and correct with respect to the underlying lease;

(G) none of the Target and its Subsidiaries has assigned, transferred, conveyed, mortgaged, deeded in trust, or encumbered any interest in the leasehold or subleasehold;

(H) all facilities leased or subleased thereunder have received all approvals of governmental authorities (including licenses and permits) required in connection with the operation thereof and have been operated and maintained in accordance with applicable laws, rules, and regulations;

(I) all facilities leased or subleased thereunder are supplied with utilities and other services necessary for the operation of said facilities; and

(J) the owner of the facility leased or subleased has good and marketable title to the parcel of real property, free and clear of any Security Interest, easement, covenant, or other restriction, except for installments of special easements not yet delinquent and recorded easements, covenants, and other restrictions which do not impair the current use, occupancy, or value, or the marketability of title, of the property subject thereto.

(m) *Intellectual Property.*[37]

(i) The Target and its Subsidiaries own or have the right to use pursuant to license, sublicense, agreement, or permission all Intellectual Property necessary [or desirable] for the operation of the businesses of the Target and its Subsidiaries as presently conducted [and as presently proposed to be conducted]. Each item of Intellectual Property owned or used by any of the Target and its Subsidiaries immediately prior to the Closing hereunder will be owned or available for use by the Buyer or the Subsidiary on identical terms and conditions immediately subsequent to the Closing hereunder. Each of the Target and its Subsidiaries has taken all necessary [and desirable] action to maintain and protect each item of Intellectual Property that it owns or uses.

(ii) None of the Target and its Subsidiaries has interfered with, infringed upon, misappropriated, or otherwise come into conflict with any Intellectual Property rights of third parties, and none of the Target Stockholders and the directors and officers (and employees with responsibility for Intellectual Property matters) of the Target and its Subsidiaries has ever received any charge, complaint, claim, demand, or notice alleging any such interference, infringement, misappropriation, or violation (including any claim that any of the Target and its Subsidiaries must license or refrain from using any Intellectual Property rights of any third party). To the Knowledge of any of the Target Stockholders and the directors and officers (and employees with responsibility for Intellectual Property matters) of the Target and its Subsidiaries, no third party has interfered

---

[37] These representations and warranties concerning intellectual property are relatively long and detailed. A condensed version of these provisions may be more appropriate when, for example, the intellectual property of the Target and its Subsidiaries is relatively insignificant.

with, infringed upon, misappropriated, or otherwise come into conflict with any Intellectual Property rights of any of the Target and its Subsidiaries.

(iii) §3(m)(iii) of the Disclosure Schedule identifies each patent or registration which has been issued to any of the Target and its Subsidiaries with respect to any of its Intellectual Property, identifies each pending patent application or application for registration which any of the Target and its Subsidiaries has made with respect to any of its Intellectual Property, and identifies each license, agreement, or other permission which any of the Target and its Subsidiaries has granted to any third party with respect to any of its Intellectual Property (together with any exceptions). The Target has delivered to the Buyer correct and complete copies of all such patents, registrations, applications, licenses, agreements, and permissions (as amended to date) [and has made available to the Buyer correct and complete copies of all other written documentation evidencing ownership and prosecution (if applicable) of each such item]. §3(m)(iii) of the Disclosure Schedule also identifies each trade name or unregistered trademark used by any of the Target and its Subsidiaries in connection with any of its businesses. With respect to each item of Intellectual Property required to be identified in §3(m)(iii) of the Disclosure Schedule:

(A) the Target and its Subsidiaries possess all right, title, and interest in and to the item, free and clear of any Security Interest, license, or other restriction;

(B) the item is not subject to any outstanding injunction, judgment, order, decree, ruling, or charge;

(C) no action, suit, proceeding, hearing, investigation, charge, complaint, claim, or demand is pending or [, to the Knowledge of any of the Target Stockholders and the directors and officers (and employees with responsibility for Intellectual Property matters) of the Target and its Subsidiaries,] is threatened which challenges the legality, validity, enforceability, use, or ownership of the item; and

(D) none of the Target and its Subsidiaries has ever agreed to indemnify any Person for or against any interference, infringement, misappropriation, or other conflict with respect to the item.

(iv) §3(m)(iv) of the Disclosure Schedule identifies each item of Intellectual Property that any third party owns and that any of the Target and its Subsidiaries uses pursuant to license, sublicense, agreement, or permission. The Target has delivered to the Buyer correct and complete copies of all such licenses, sublicenses, agreements, and permissions (as amended to date). With respect to each item of Intellectual Property required to be identified in §3(m)(iv) of the Disclosure Schedule;

(A) the license, sublicense, agreement, or permission covering the item is legal, valid, binding, enforceable, and in full force and effect;

(B) the license, sublicense, agreement, or permission will continue to be legal, valid, binding, enforceable, and in full force and effect on identical terms following the consummation of the transactions contemplated hereby (including the assignments and assumptions referred to in §2 above);

(C) no party to the license, sublicense, agreement, or permission is in breach or default, and no event has occurred which with notice or lapse of time would constitute a breach or default or permit termination, modification, or acceleration thereunder;

(D) no party to the license, sublicense, agreement, or permission has repudiated any provision thereof;

(E) with respect to each sublicense, the representations and warranties set forth in subsections (A) through (D) above are true and correct with respect to the underlying license;

(F) the underlying item of Intellectual Property is not subject to any outstanding injunction, judgment, order, decree, ruling, or charge;

(G) no action, suit, proceeding, hearing, investigation, charge, complaint, claim, or demand is pending or [, to the Knowledge of any of the Target Stockholders and the directors and officers (and employees with responsibility for Intellectual Property matters) of the Target and its Subsidiaries,] is threatened which challenges the legality, validity, or enforceability of the underlying item of Intellectual Property; and

(H) none of the Target and its Subsidiaries has granted any sublicense or similar right with respect to the license, sublicense, agreement, or permission.

(v) To the Knowledge of any of the Target Stockholders and the directors and officers (and employees with responsibility for Intellectual Property matters) of the Target and its Subsidiaries, none of the Target and its Subsidiaries will interfere with, infringe upon, misappropriate, or otherwise come into conflict with, any Intellectual Property rights of third parties as a result of the continued operation of its businesses as presently conducted [and as presently proposed to be conducted].

(vi) [None of the Target Stockholders and the directors and officers (and employees with responsibility for Intellectual Property matters) of the Target and its Subsidiaries has any Knowledge of any new products, inventions, procedures, or methods of manufacturing or processing that any competitors or other third parties have developed which reasonably could be expected to supersede or make obsolete any product or process of any of the Target and its Subsidiaries.]

(n) *Tangible Assets.* The Target and its Subsidiaries own or lease all buildings, machinery, equipment, and other tangible assets necessary for the conduct of their businesses as presently conducted [and as presently proposed to be conducted]. Each such tangible asset is free from defects (patent and latent), has been maintained in accordance with normal industry practice, is in good operating condition and repair (subject to normal wear and tear), and is suitable for the purposes for which it presently is used [and presently is proposed to be used].

(o) *Inventory.* The inventory of the Target and its Subsidiaries consists of raw materials and supplies, manufactured and purchased parts, goods in process, and finished goods, all of which is merchantable and fit for the purpose for which it was procured or manufactured, and none of which is slow-moving, obsolete, damaged, or defective, subject only to the reserve for inventory writedown set forth on the face of the Most Recent Balance Sheet (rather than in any notes thereto) as adjusted for the passage of time through the Closing Date in accordance with the past custom and practice of the Target and its Subsidiaries.

(p) *Contracts.* §3(p) of the Disclosure Schedule lists the following contracts and other agreements to which any of the Target and its Subsidiaries is a party:

(i) any agreement (or group of related agreements) for the lease of personal property to or from any Person providing for lease payments in excess of $_____ per annum;

(ii) any agreement (or group of related agreements) for the purchase or sale of raw materials, commodities, supplies, products, or other personal property, or for the furnishing or receipt of services, the performance of which will extend over a period of more than one year, result in a [material] loss to any of the Target and its Subsidiaries, or involve consideration in excess of $_____;

(iii) any agreement concerning a partnership or joint venture;

(iv) any agreement (or group of related agreements) under which it has created, incurred, assumed, or guaranteed any indebtedness for borrowed money, or any capitalized lease obligation, in excess of $_____ or under which it has imposed a Security Interest on any of its assets, tangible or intangible;

(v) any agreement concerning confidentiality or noncompetition;

(vi) any agreement involving any of the Target Stockholders and their Affiliates (other than the Target and its Subsidiaries);

(vii) any profit sharing, stock option, stock purchase, stock appreciation, deferred compensation, severance, or other [material] plan or arrangement for the benefit of its current or former directors, officers, and employees;

(viii) any collective bargaining agreement;

(ix) any agreement for the employment of any individual on a full-time, part-time, consulting, or other basis providing annual compensation in excess of $_____ or providing severance benefits;

(x) any agreement under which it has advanced or loaned any amount to any of its directors, officers, and employees outside the Ordinary Course of Business;

(xi) any agreement under which the consequences of a default or termination could have a [material] adverse effect on the business, financial condition, operations, results of operations, or future prospects of any of the Target and its Subsidiaries; or

(xii) any other agreement (or group of related agreements) the performance of which involves consideration in excess of $_____.

The Target has delivered to the Buyer a correct and complete copy of each written agreement listed in §3(p) of the Disclosure Schedule (as amended to date) and a written summary setting forth the terms and conditions of each oral agreement referred to in §3(p) of the Disclosure Schedule. With respect to each such agreement: (A) the agreement is legal, valid, binding, enforceable, and in full force and effect; (B) the agreement will continue to be legal, valid, binding, enforceable, and in full force and effect on identical terms following the consummation of the transactions contemplated hereby (including the assignments and assumptions referred to in §2 above); (C) no party is in breach or default, and no event has occurred which with notice or lapse of time would constitute a breach or default, or permit termination, modification, or acceleration, under the agreement; and (D) no party has repudiated any provision of the agreement.

(q) *Notes and Accounts Receivable.* All notes and accounts receivable of the Target and its Subsidiaries are reflected properly on their books and records, are valid receivables subject to no setoffs or counterclaims, are current and collectible, and will be collected in accordance with their terms at their recorded amounts, subject only to the reserve for bad debts set forth on the face of the Most Recent Balance Sheet (rather than in any notes thereto) as adjusted for the passage of time through the Closing Date in accordance with the past custom and practice of the Target and its Subsidiaries.

(r) *Powers of Attorney.* There are no outstanding powers of attorney executed on behalf of any of the Target and its Subsidiaries.

(s) *Insurance*. §3(s) of the Disclosure Schedule sets forth the following information with respect to each insurance policy (including policies providing property, casualty, liability, and workers' compensation coverage and bond and surety arrangements) to which any of the Target and its Subsidiaries has been a party, a named insured, or otherwise the beneficiary of coverage at any time within the past [10] years:

(i) the name, address, and telephone number of the agent;

(ii) the name of the insurer, the name of the policyholder, and the name of each covered insured;

(iii) the policy number and the period of coverage;

(iv) the scope (including an indication of whether the coverage was on a claims made, occurrence, or other basis) and amount (including a description of how deductibles and ceilings are calculated and operate) of coverage; and

(v) a description of any retroactive premium adjustments or other loss-sharing arrangements.

With respect to each such insurance policy: (A) the policy is legal, valid, binding, enforceable, and in full force and effect; (B) the policy will continue to be legal, valid, binding, enforceable, and in full force and effect on identical terms following the consummation of the transactions contemplated hereby (including the assignments and assumptions referred to in §2 above); (C) neither any of the Target and its Subsidiaries nor any other party to the policy is in breach or default (including with respect to the payment of premiums or the giving of notices), and no event has occurred which, with notice or the lapse of time, would constitute such a breach or default, or permit termination, modification, or acceleration, under the policy; and (D) no party to the policy has repudiated any provision thereof. Each of the Target and its Subsidiaries has been covered during the past [10] years by insurance in scope and amount customary and reasonable for the businesses in which it has engaged during the aforementioned period. §3(s) of the Disclosure Schedule describes any self-insurance arrangements affecting any of the Target and its Subsidiaries.

(t) *Litigation*. §3(t) of the Disclosure Schedule sets forth each instance in which any of the Target and its Subsidiaries (i) is subject to any outstanding injunction, judgment, order, decree, ruling, or charge or (ii) is a party or [, to the Knowledge of any of the Target Stockholders and the directors and officers (and employees with responsibility for litigation matters) of the Target and its Subsidiaries,] is threatened to be made a party to any action, suit, proceeding, hearing, or investigation of, in, or before any court or quasi-judicial or administrative agency of any federal, state, local, or foreign jurisdiction or before any arbitrator. None of the actions, suits, proceedings, hearings, and investigations set forth in §3(t) of the

Disclosure Schedule could result in any [material] adverse change in the business, financial condition, operations, results of operations, or future prospects of any of the Target and its Subsidiaries. None of the Target Stockholders and the directors and officers (and employees with responsibility for litigation matters) of the Target and its Subsidiaries has any reason to believe that any such action, suit, proceeding, hearing, or investigation may be brought or threatened against any of the Target and its Subsidiaries.

(u) *Product Warranty.* Each product manufactured, sold, leased, or delivered by any of the Target and its Subsidiaries has been in conformity with all applicable contractual commitments and all express and implied warranties, and none of the Target and its Subsidiaries has any Liability (and there is no Basis for any present or future action, suit, proceeding, hearing, investigation, charge, complaint, claim, or demand against any of them giving rise to any Liability) for replacement or repair thereof or other damages in connection therewith, subject only to the reserve for product warranty claims set forth on the face of the Most Recent Balance Sheet (rather than in any notes thereto) as adjusted for the passage of time through the Closing Date in accordance with the past custom and practice of the Target and its Subsidiaries. No product manufactured, sold, leased, or delivered by any of the Target and its Subsidiaries is subject to any guaranty, warranty, or other indemnity beyond the applicable standard terms and conditions of sale or lease. §3(u) of the Disclosure Schedule includes copies of the standard terms and conditions of sale or lease for each of the Target and its Subsidiaries (containing applicable guaranty, warranty, and indemnity provisions).

(v) *Product Liability.* None of the Target and its Subsidiaries has any Liability (and there is no Basis for any present or future action, suit, proceeding, hearing, investigation, charge, complaint, claim, or demand against any of them giving rise to any Liability) arising out of any injury to individuals or property as a result of the ownership, possession, or use of any product manufactured, sold, leased, or delivered by any of the Target and its Subsidiaries.

(w) *Employees.* To the Knowledge of any of the Target Stockholders and the directors and officers (and employees with responsibility for employment matters) of the Target and its Subsidiaries, no executive, key employee, or group of employees has any plans to terminate employment with any of the Target and its Subsidiaries. None of the Target and its Subsidiaries is a party to or bound by any collective bargaining agreement, nor has any of them experienced any strikes, grievances, claims of unfair labor practices, or other collective bargaining disputes. None of the Target and its Subsidiaries has committed any unfair labor practice. None of the Target Stockholders and the directors and officers (and employees with responsibility for employment matters) of the Target and its Subsidiaries has any Knowledge of any organizational effort presently being made or threatened by or on behalf of any labor union with respect to employees of any of the Target and its Subsidiaries.

(x) *Employee Benefits.*[38]

(i) §3(x) of the Disclosure Schedule lists each Employee Benefit Plan that any of the Target and its Subsidiaries maintains, to which any of the Target and its Subsidiaries contributes or has any obligation to contribute, or with respect to which any of the Target and its Subsidiaries has any [material] Liability or potential Liability.

(A) Each such Employee Benefit Plan (and each related trust, insurance contract, or fund) has been maintained, funded and administered in accordance with the terms of such Employee Benefit Plan and complies in form and in operation in all [material] respects with the applicable requirements of ERISA, the Code, and other applicable laws.

(B) All required reports and descriptions (including annual reports (IRS Form 5500), summary annual reports, and summary plan descriptions) have been timely filed and/or distributed in accordance with the applicable requirements of ERISA and the Code with respect to each such Employee Benefit Plan. The requirements of COBRA have been met with respect to each such Employee Benefit Plan which is an Employee Welfare Benefit Plan subject to COBRA.

(C) All contributions (including all employer contributions and employee salary reduction contributions) which are due have been made within the time period prescribed by ERISA to each such Employee Benefit Plan which is an Employee Pension Benefit Plan and all contributions for any period ending on or before the Closing Date which are not yet due have been made to each such Employee Pension Benefit Plan or accrued in accordance with the past custom and practice of the Target and its Subsidiaries. All premiums or other payments for all periods ending on or before the Closing Date have been paid with respect to each such Employee Benefit Plan which is an Employee Welfare Benefit Plan.

(D) Each such Employee Benefit Plan which is intended to meet the requirements of a "qualified plan" under Code §401(a) has received a determination from the Internal Revenue Service that such Employee Benefit Plan is so qualified, and nothing has occurred since the date of such determination that could adversely affect the qualified status of any such Employee Benefit Plan.

(E) The market value of assets under each such Employee Benefit Plan which is an Employee Pension Benefit Plan (other than any Multiemployer Plan) equals or exceeds the present value of all vested and nonvested Liabili-

---

[38] These representations and warranties concerning employee benefits are relatively long and detailed. A condensed version of these provisions may be more appropriate when, for example, the Target and its Subsidiaries have relatively insignificant employee benefit plans.

ties thereunder determined in accordance with PBGC methods, factors, and assumptions applicable to an Employee Pension Benefit Plan terminating on the date for determination.

(F) The Target has delivered to the Buyer correct and complete copies of the plan documents and summary plan descriptions, the most recent determination letter received from the Internal Revenue Service, the most recent annual report (IRS Form 5500, with all applicable attachments), and all related trust agreements, insurance contracts, and other funding arrangements which implement each such Employee Benefit Plan.

(ii) With respect to each Employee Benefit Plan that any of the Target, its Subsidiaries, and any ERISA Affiliate maintains, to which any of them contributes, ever has contributed or has any obligation to contribute, or with respect to which any of them has any [material] Liability or potential Liability:

(A) No such Employee Benefit Plan which is an Employee Pension Benefit Plan (other than any Multiemployer Plan) has been completely or partially terminated or been the subject of a Reportable Event. No proceeding by the PBGC to terminate any such Employee Pension Benefit Plan (other than any Multiemployer Plan) has been instituted or[, to the Knowledge of any of the Target Stockholders and the directors and officers (and employees with responsibility for employee benefits matters) of the Target and its Subsidiaries,] threatened.

(B) There have been no Prohibited Transactions with respect to any such Employee Benefit Plan. No Fiduciary has any Liability for breach of fiduciary duty or any other failure to act or comply in connection with the administration or investment of the assets of any such Employee Benefit Plan. No action, suit, proceeding, hearing, or investigation with respect to the administration or the investment of the assets of any such Employee Benefit Plan (other than routine claims for benefits) is pending or[, to the Knowledge of any of the Target Stockholders and the directors and officers (and employees with responsibility for employee benefits matters) of the Target and its Subsidiaries,] threatened. None of the Target Stockholders and the directors and officers (and employees with responsibility for employee benefits matters) of the Target and its Subsidiaries has any Knowledge of any Basis for any such action, suit, proceeding, hearing, or investigation.

(C) None of the Target and its Subsidiaries has incurred, and none of the Target Stockholders and the directors and officers (and employees with responsibility for employee benefits matters) of the Target and its Subsidiaries has any reason to expect that any of the Target and its Subsidiaries will incur any Liability to the PBGC (other than with respect to PBGC premium payments not yet due) or otherwise under Title IV of ERISA (including any withdrawal liability as defined in ERISA §4201) or under the Code with respect to any such Employee Benefit Plan which is an Employee Pension Benefit Plan, or under COBRA with respect to any such Employee Benefit Plan which is an Employee Welfare Benefit Plan.

(iii) ALTERNATIVE A (NO MULTIEMPLOYER PLANS): None of the Target, its Subsidiaries, and any ERISA Affiliate contributes to, has any obligation to contribute to, or has any Liability (including withdrawal liability as defined in ERISA §4201) under or with respect to any Multiemployer Plan.

ALTERNATIVE B (MULTIEMPLOYER PLANS): None of the Target, its Subsidiaries, and any ERISA Affiliate has incurred any Liability on account of a "partial withdrawal" or a "complete withdrawal" (within the meaning of ERISA §§4205 and 4203, respectively) from any Multiemployer Plan, no such Liability has been asserted, and there are no events or circumstances which could result in any such partial or complete withdrawal; and none of the Target, its Subsidiaries, and any ERISA Affiliate is bound by any contract or agreement or has any obligation or Liability described in ERISA §4204. [Each Multiemployer Plan complies in form and has been administered in accordance with the requirements of ERISA and, where applicable, the Code, and each Multiemployer Plan is qualified under Code §401(a).]

(iv) None of the Target and its Subsidiaries maintains, contributes to or has an obligation to contribute to, or has any [material] Liability or potential Liability with respect to, any Employee Welfare Benefit Plan providing medical, health, or life insurance or other welfare-type benefits for current or future retired or terminated employees, their spouses, or their dependents (other than in accordance with COBRA).

(y) *Guaranties.* None of the Target and its Subsidiaries is a guarantor or otherwise is liable for any Liability or obligation (including indebtedness) of any other Person.

(z) *Environmental, Health, and Safety Matters.*[39]

(i) Each of the Target, its Subsidiaries, and their respective predecessors and Affiliates has complied and is in compliance with all Environmental, Health, and Safety Requirements.

---

[39] These representations and warranties concerning environmental, health, and safety matters are relatively long and detailed, contain no materiality or knowledge limitations, and impose a substantial disclosure burden on the Target. A condensed version may be more appropriate when, for example, the operations of the Target and its Subsidiaries appear to have had a relatively insignificant effect upon the environment or upon public or employee health and safety.

Sample acquisition agreement 2003.2 (the *pro-seller* asset purchase agreement) contains an environmental representation which (1) is subject to certain knowledge and materiality limitations, (2) focuses

(ii) Without limiting the generality of the foregoing, each of the Target, its Subsidiaries and their respective Affiliates has obtained and complied with, and is in compliance with, all permits, licenses and other authorizations that are required pursuant to Environmental, Health, and Safety Requirements for the occupation of its facilities and the operation of its business; a list of all such permits, licenses and other authorizations is set forth on the attached *"Environmental and Safety Permits Schedule."*

(iii) Neither the Target, its Subsidiaries, nor their respective predecessors or Affiliates has received any written or oral notice, report or other information regarding any actual or alleged violation of Environmental, Health, and Safety Requirements, or any liabilities or potential liabilities (whether accrued, absolute, contingent, unliquidated or otherwise), including any investigatory, remedial or corrective obligations, relating to any of them or its facilities arising under Environmental, Health, and Safety Requirements.

(iv) None of the following exists at any property or facility owned or operated by the Target or its Subsidiaries: (1) underground storage tanks, (2) asbestos-containing material in any form or condition, (3) materials or equipment containing polychlorinated biphenyls, or (4) landfills, surface impoundments, or disposal areas.

(v) None of the Target, its Subsidiaries, or their respective predecessors or Affiliates has treated, stored, disposed of, arranged for or permitted the disposal of, transported, handled, or released any substance, including without limitation any hazardous substance, or owned or operated any property or facility (and no such property or facility is contaminated by any such substance) in a manner that has given or would give rise to liabilities, including any liability for response costs, corrective action costs, personal injury, property damage, natural resources damages or attorney fees, pursuant to the Comprehensive Environmental Response, Compensation and Liability Act of 1980, as amended ("CERCLA"), the Solid Waste Disposal Act, as amended ("SWDA") or any other Environmental, Health, and Safety Requirements.

(vi) Neither this Agreement nor the consummation of the transaction that is the subject of this Agreement will result in any obligations for site investigation or cleanup, or notification to or consent of government agencies or third parties, pursuant to any of the so-called "transaction-triggered" or "responsible property transfer" Environmental, Health, and Safety Requirements.

---

on current compliance with environmental, health, and safety laws, and (3) does not extend to strict liability for site cleanup under CERCLA or common law liability.

Sample acquisition agreement 2003.3 (the *neutral* asset purchase agreement) contains an environmental representation which (1) is subject to certain materiality limitations, (2) is generally more limited and narrowly focused than this representation, and (3) in particular, does *not* include the provisions set forth in (vii) and (viii) of this section.

(vii) Neither the Target, its Subsidiaries, nor any of their respective predecessors or Affiliates has, either expressly or by operation of law, assumed or undertaken any liability, including without limitation any obligation for corrective or remedial action, of any other Person relating to Environmental, Health, and Safety Requirements.

(viii) No facts, events or conditions relating to the past or present facilities, properties or operations of the Target, its Subsidiaries, or any of their respective predecessors or Affiliates will prevent, hinder or limit continued compliance with Environmental, Health, and Safety Requirements, give rise to any investigatory, remedial or corrective obligations pursuant to Environmental, Health, and Safety Requirements, or give rise to any other liabilities (whether accrued, absolute, contingent, unliquidated or otherwise) pursuant to Environmental, Health, and Safety Requirements, including without limitation any relating to onsite or offsite releases or threatened releases of hazardous materials, substances or wastes, personal injury, property damage or natural resources damage.

(aa) *Euro.* All of the computer software, computer firmware and computer hardware used by the Target or its Subsidiaries (i) are capable of performing all appropriate functions necessary to process more than one currency and any common currency adopted by one or more members of the European Union (the "Euro"), (ii) comply with all legal requirements applicable to the Euro in any jurisdiction, including the rules on conversion and rounding set out in applicable European Community regulations, and (iii) are capable of displaying and printing, and incorporate in all relevant screen layouts, all symbols and codes adopted by any government or any other European Union body in relation to the Euro.[40]

(bb) *Year 2000.* None of the computer software, computer firmware, computer hardware (whether general or special purpose) or other similar or related items of automated, computerized or software systems that are used or relied on by the Target or its Subsidiaries in the conduct of their respective businesses, and none of the products and services sold, licensed, rendered, or otherwise provided by the Target and its Subsidiaries in the conduct of their respective businesses, will malfunction, cease to function, generate incorrect data or produce incorrect results when processing, providing or receiving (i) date-related data from, into and between the twentieth and twenty-first centuries or (ii) date-related data in connection with any valid date in the twentieth and twenty-first centuries.

Neither the Target nor its Subsidiaries has made any representations or warranties regarding the ability of any product or service sold, licensed, rendered, or otherwise provided by the Target or its Subsidiaries in the conduct of their respective businesses to operate without malfunction, to operate without ceasing to function, to generate correct data or to produce correct results when processing,

---

[40] Sample acquisition agreements 2003.2 (the *pro-seller* asset purchase agreement) and 2003.3 (the *neutral* asset purchase agreement) do not contain this representation.

providing or receiving (i) date-related data from, into and between the twentieth and twenty-first centuries and (ii) date-related data in connection with any valid date in the twentieth and twenty-first centuries.[41]

(cc) *Certain Business Relationships With the Target and Its Subsidiaries.*　None of the Target Stockholders and their Affiliates has been involved in any business arrangement or relationship with any of the Target and its Subsidiaries within the past 12 months, and none of the Target Stockholders and their Affiliates owns any asset, tangible or intangible, which is used in the business of any of the Target and its Subsidiaries.

(dd) *Disclosure.*　The representations and warranties contained in this §3 do not contain any untrue statement of a [material] fact or omit to state any [material] fact necessary in order to make the statements and information contained in this §3 not misleading.

(ee) *Investment.*　The Target (i) understands that the Buyer Notes have not been, and will not be, registered under the Securities Act, or under any state securities laws, and are being offered and sold in reliance upon federal and state exemptions for transactions not involving any public offering, (ii) is acquiring the Buyer Notes solely for its own account for investment purposes, and not with a view to the distribution thereof (except to the Target Stockholders), (iii) is a sophisticated investor with knowledge and experience in business and financial matters, (iv) has received certain information concerning the Buyer and has had the opportunity to obtain additional information as desired in order to evaluate the merits and the risks inherent in holding the Buyer Notes, (v) is able to bear the economic risk and lack of liquidity inherent in holding the Buyer Notes, and (vi) is an Accredited Investor for the reasons set forth in §3(cc) of the Disclosure Schedule.[42]

4. *Representations and Warranties of the Buyer.*[43]　The Buyer represents and warrants to the Target (and to the Target Stockholders for purposes of the Agreement with Target Stockholders) that the statements contained in this §4 are correct and

---

[41] This representation can be omitted for agreements entered into a sufficient period after approximately 3/1/00 so that Buyer has been able to verify that Target and its Subsidiaries have no Y2K problem.

Sample acquisition agreement 2003.2 (the *pro-seller* asset purchase agreement) does not contain this representation and 2003.3 (the *neutral* asset purchase agreement) contains a more limited representation.

[42] This provision contemplates that the Buyer will issue the Buyer Notes pursuant to the exemption from registration under the Securities Act contained in Regulation D. The Parties should determine whether this exemption is available in a particular transaction. If it is not, the Agreement must be modified as necessary to reflect the issuance of the Buyer Notes under a different exemption from securities registration or in an offering registered under the Securities Act.

[43] The Target may seek to obtain additional representations and warranties concerning the Buyer and is Subsidiaries (e.g., the typical representations and warranties contained in a loan agreement or an underwriting agreement) because the Buyer is issuing the Buyer Notes to the Target as part of the Purchase Price. Any such representations and warranties would normally survive the Closing and remain applicable for so long as the Buyer Notes remained outstanding.

complete as of the date of this Agreement and will be correct and complete as of the Closing Date (as though made then and as though the Closing Date were substituted for the date of this Agreement throughout this §4), except as set forth in the Disclosure Schedule. The Disclosure Schedule will be arranged in paragraphs corresponding to the lettered and numbered paragraphs contained in this §4.

(a) *Organization of the Buyer.* The Buyer is a corporation duly organized, validly existing, and in good standing under the laws of the jurisdiction of its incorporation.

(b) *Authorization of Transaction.* The Buyer has full power and authority (including full corporate power and authority) to execute and deliver this Agreement and to perform its obligations hereunder. This Agreement constitutes the valid and legally binding obligation of the Buyer, enforceable in accordance with its terms and conditions.

(c) *Noncontravention.* Neither the execution and the delivery of this Agreement, nor the consummation of the transactions contemplated hereby (including the assignments and assumptions referred to in §2 above), will (i) violate any constitution, statute, regulation, rule, injunction, judgment, order, decree, ruling, charge, or other restriction of any government, governmental agency, or court to which the Buyer is subject or any provision of its charter or bylaws or (ii) conflict with, result in a breach of, constitute a default under, result in the acceleration of, create in any party the right to accelerate, terminate, modify, or cancel, or require any notice under any agreement, contract, lease, license, instrument, or other arrangement to which the Buyer is a party or by which it is bound or to which any of its assets is subject. The Buyer does not need to give any notice to, make any filing with, or obtain any authorization, consent, or approval of any government or governmental agency in order for the Parties to consummate the transactions contemplated by this Agreement (including the assignments and assumptions referred to in §2 above).

(d) *Brokers' Fees.* The Buyer has no Liability or obligation to pay any fees or commissions to any broker, finder, or agent with respect to the transactions contemplated by this Agreement for which the Target could become liable or obligated.

5. *Pre-Closing Covenants.* The Parties agree as follows with respect to the period between the execution of this Agreement and the Closing.

(a) *General.* Each of the Parties will use its [reasonable] best efforts to take all action and to do all things necessary[, proper, or advisable] in order to consummate and make effective the transactions contemplated by this Agreement (including satisfaction, but not waiver, of the closing conditions set forth in §6 below).

(b) *Notices and Consents.* The Target will give (and will cause each of its Subsidiaries to give) any notices to third parties, and the Target will use its [reasonable] best efforts (and will cause each of its Subsidiaries to use its [reasonable] best efforts) to obtain any third party consents, that the Buyer [reasonably] may request in connection with the matters referred to in §3(c) above. Each of the Parties will (and the Target will cause each of its Subsidiaries to) give any notices to, make any filings with, and use its [reasonable] best efforts to obtain any authorizations, consents, and approvals of governments and governmental agencies in connection with the matters referred to in §3(c) and §4(c) above. Without limiting the generality of the foregoing, each of the Parties will file (and the Target will cause each of its Subsidiaries to file) any Notification and Report Forms and related material that it may be required to file with the Federal Trade Commission and the Antitrust Division of the United States Department of Justice under the Hart-Scott-Rodino Act, will use its [reasonable] best efforts to obtain (and the Target will cause each of its Subsidiaries to use its [reasonable] best efforts to obtain) an early termination of the applicable waiting period, and will make (and the Target will cause each of its Subsidiaries to make) any further filings pursuant thereto that may be necessary [, proper, or advisable] in connection therewith.

(c) *Operation of Business.* The Target will not (and will not cause or permit any of its Subsidiaries to) engage in any practice, take any action, or enter into any transaction outside the Ordinary Course of Business. Without limiting the generality of the foregoing, the Target will not (and will not cause or permit any of its Subsidiaries to) (i) declare, set aside, or pay any dividend or make any distribution with respect to its capital stock or redeem, purchase, or otherwise acquire any of its capital stock, (ii) pay any amount to any third party with respect to any Liability or obligation (including any costs and expenses the Target has incurred or may incur in connection with this Agreement and the transactions contemplated hereby) which would not constitute an Assumed Liability if in existence as of the Closing, (iii) _____, or (iv) otherwise engage in any practice, take any action, or enter into any transaction of the sort described in §3(h) above.[44]

(d) *Preservation of Business.* The Target will keep (and will cause each of its Subsidiaries to keep) its business and properties substantially intact, including its present operations, physical facilities, working conditions, and relationships with lessors, licensors, suppliers, customers, and employees.[45]

(e) *Full Access.* The Target will permit (and will cause each of its Subsidiaries to permit) representatives of the Buyer to have full access [at all reasonable times, and in a manner so as not to interfere with the normal business operations of the Target and its Subsidiaries,] to all premises, properties, personnel, books, records

---

[44] The Parties may prefer to revise this covenant so that it recites specific prohibitions rather than incorporating the matter in §3(h) by reference.

[45] Sample acquisition agreement 2003.2 (the *pro-seller* asset purchase agreement) does not contain a comparable provision.

(including Tax records), contracts, and documents of or pertaining to each of the Target and its Subsidiaries.[46]

(f) *Notice of Developments.* Each Party will give prompt written notice to the other Party of any material adverse development causing a breach of any of its own representations and warranties in §3 and §4 above. No disclosure by any Party pursuant to this §5(f), however, shall be deemed to amend or supplement the Disclosure Schedule or to prevent or cure any misrepresentation, breach of warranty, or breach of covenant.[47]

(g) *Exclusivity.* The Target will not (and the Target will not cause or permit any of its Subsidiaries to) (i) solicit, initiate, or encourage the submission of any proposal or offer from any Person relating to the acquisition of any capital stock or other voting securities, or any substantial portion of the assets, of any of the Target and its Subsidiaries (including any acquisition structured as a merger, consolidation, or share exchange) or (ii) participate in any discussions or negotiations regarding, furnish any information with respect to, assist or participate in, or facilitate in any other manner any effort or attempt by any Person to do or seek any of the foregoing.[48] The Target will notify the Buyer immediately if any Person makes any proposal, offer, inquiry, or contact with respect to any of the foregoing.

(h) *Title Insurance.*[49] The Target will obtain (and will cause its Subsidiaries to obtain) the following title insurance commitments, policies, and riders in preparation for the Closing:

(i) with respect to each parcel of real estate that any of the Target and its Subsidiaries owns, an ALTA Owner's Policy of Title Insurance Form B-1987 (or equivalent policy [reasonably] acceptable to the Buyer if the real property is located in a state in which an ALTA Owner's Policy of Title Insurance Form B-1987 is not available) issued by a title insurer [reasonably] satisfactory to the Buyer (and, if requested by the Buyer, reinsured in whole or in part by one or more insurance companies and pursuant to a direct access agreement [reason-

---

[46] The Target may seek a confidentiality and nonuse provision protecting this information until the Buyer actually purchases the Acquired Assets. See sample acquisition agreement 2003.2 (the *pro-seller* asset purchase agreement) for an example of such a provision.

[47] Sample acquisition agreement 2003.2 (the *pro-seller* asset purchase agreement) provides that certain disclosures (presumably, but not necessarily, by the Target) between signing and closing *will* supplement the previous disclosures and cure misrepresentations and breaches of warranty.

[48] Sample acquisition agreement 2003.2 (the *pro-seller* asset purchase agreement) gives the Target, its Subsidiaries, and their directors and officers greater latitude to respond to unsolicited proposals.

[49] These provisions concerning title insurance are relatively long and detailed. A condensed version may be more appropriate when, for example, the real property of the Target and its Subsidiaries is relatively insignificant.

Sample acquisition agreement 2003.2 (the *pro-seller* asset purchase agreement) does not have any title insurance closing condition for the benefit of the Buyer and contemplates that the Buyer will obtain any title insurance it requires independently and at its own expense.

ably] acceptable to the Buyer), in such amount as the Buyer [reasonably] may determine to be the fair market value of such real property (including all improvements located thereon), insuring title to such real property to be in the Buyer or the Subsidiary as of the Closing (subject only to the title exceptions described above in §3(l)(i) and in §3(l)(i) of the Disclosure Schedule); and

(ii) with respect to each parcel of real estate that any of the Target and its Subsidiaries leases or subleases and which is listed on §3(l)(ii) of the Disclosure Schedule as a property for which a title insurance policy is to be procured, an ALTA Leasehold Owner's Policy of Title Insurance-1987 (or equivalent policy [reasonably] acceptable to the Buyer if the real property is located in a state in which an ALTA Leasehold Owner's Policy of Title Insurance-1987 is not available) issued by a title insurer [reasonably] satisfactory to the Buyer (and, if requested by the Buyer, reinsured in whole or in part by one or more insurance companies and pursuant to a direct access agreement [reasonably] acceptable to the Buyer) in such amount as the Buyer [reasonably] may determine (taking into account the time cost of money using the Applicable Rate as the discount rate and such other factors as whether the fair market rental value of the premises exceeds the stipulated consideration in the lease or sublease, whether the tenant or subtenant has any option to renew or extend, whether the tenant or subtenant owns any improvements located on the premises, whether the tenant or subtenant is permitted to sublease, and whether the tenant or subtenant would owe any amount under the lease or sublease if evicted), insuring title to the leasehold or subleasehold estate to be in the Buyer or the Subsidiary as of the Closing (subject only to the title exceptions described above in §3(l)(ii) and in §3(l)(ii) of the Disclosure Schedule).

Each title insurance policy delivered under §5(h)(i) and §5(h)(ii) above shall (A) insure title to the real property and all recorded easements benefitting such real property, (B) contain an "extended coverage endorsement" insuring over the general exceptions contained customarily in such policies, (C) contain an ALTA Zoning Endorsement 3.1 (or equivalent), (D) contain an endorsement insuring that the real property described in the title insurance policy is the same real estate as shown on the Survey delivered with respect to such property, (E) contain an endorsement insuring that each street adjacent to the real property is a public street and that there is direct and unencumbered pedestrian and vehicular access to such street from the real property, (F) contain an inflation endorsement providing for annual adjustments in the amount of coverage corresponding to the annual percentage increase, if any, in the United States Department of Commerce Composite Construction Cost Index (Base Year = _____), (G) if the real property consists of more than one record parcel, contain a "contiguity" endorsement insuring that all of the record parcels are contiguous to one another, and (H) contain a "non-imputation" endorsement to the effect that title defects known to the officers, directors, and stockholders of the owner prior to the Closing shall not be deemed "facts known to the insured" for purposes of the policy.

(i) *Surveys.*[50] With respect to each parcel of real property that any of the Target and its Subsidiaries owns, leases, or subleases, and as to which a title insurance policy is to be procured pursuant to §5(h) above, the Target will procure (and will cause its Subsidiaries to procure) in preparation for the Closing a current survey of the real property certified to the Buyer, prepared by a licensed surveyor and conforming to current ALTA Minimum Detail Requirements for Land Title Surveys, disclosing the location of all improvements, easements, party walls, sidewalks, roadways, utility lines, and other matters shown customarily on such surveys, and showing access affirmatively to public streets and roads (the "*Survey*"). The Survey shall not disclose any survey defect or encroachment from or onto the real property which has not been cured or insured over prior to the Closing.

6. *Conditions to Obligation to Close.*

(a) *Conditions to Obligation of the Buyer.* The obligation of the Buyer to consummate the transactions to be performed by it in connection with the Closing is subject to satisfaction of the following conditions:[51]

(i) the representations and warranties set forth in §3 above shall be true and correct in all material respects at and as of the Closing Date;[52]

(ii) the Target shall have performed and complied with all of its covenants hereunder in all material respects through the Closing;

(iii) the Target and its Subsidiaries shall have procured all of the third party consents specified in §5(b) above, all of the title insurance commitments, policies, and riders specified in §5(h) above, and all of the surveys specified in §5(i) above;[53]

(iv) no action, suit, or proceeding shall be pending [or threatened] before any court or quasi-judicial or administrative agency of any federal, state, local, or foreign jurisdiction [or before any arbitrator] wherein an unfavorable injunc-

---

[50] Sample acquisition agreement 2003.2 (the *pro-seller* asset purchase agreement) does not have any survey closing condition for the benefit of the Buyer and contemplates that the Buyer will obtain any surveys it requires independently and at its own expense.

[51] Note the provision in §7(a)(ii) giving the Buyer the right to terminate this Agreement within a specified period after signing if the Buyer is not [reasonably] satisfied with the results of its continuing business, legal, and accounting due diligence concerning the Target and its Subsidiaries. If this termination right were to continue through the Closing, it could be recast as an additional closing condition in §6(a).

[52] Note that this provision will not give the Buyer any closing condition with respect to any adverse matter that the Target may disclose in the Disclosure Schedule. This is because the disclosure will cure any misrepresentation or breach of warranty that might otherwise have existed. Thus, if the Target discloses an adverse matter in the Disclosure Schedule, the Buyer may seek to add a specific closing condition requiring an acceptable resolution of the matter.

[53] Sample acquisition agreement 2003.2 (the *pro-seller* asset purchase agreement) lacks a comparable closing condition with respect to third party consents, title insurance, and surveys.

tion, judgment, order, decree, ruling, or charge would (A) prevent consummation of any of the transactions contemplated by this Agreement, (B) cause any
of the transactions contemplated by this Agreement to be rescinded following
consummation, (C) affect adversely the right of the Buyer to own the Acquired
Assets, to operate the former businesses of the Target, and to control the Target's
Subsidiaries, or (D) affect adversely the right of any of the Target's Subsidiaries
to own its assets and to operate its businesses (and no such injunction, judgment,
order, decree, ruling, or charge shall be in effect);[54]

(v) the Target shall have delivered to the Buyer a certificate to the effect that
each of the conditions specified above in §6(a)(i)-(iv) is satisfied in all respects;

(vi) [all applicable waiting periods (and any extensions thereof) under the
Hart-Scott-Rodino Act shall have expired or otherwise been terminated and
the Target, its Subsidiaries, and the Buyer shall have received all other authorizations, consents, and approvals of governments and governmental agencies
referred to in §3(c) and §4(c) above];

(vii) the relevant parties shall have entered into side agreements in form
and substance as set forth in Exhibits G-1 through G-_____ attached
hereto and the same shall be in full force and effect;[55]

(viii) the Buyer shall have received from counsel to the Target an opinion
in form and substance as set forth in Exhibit H attached hereto, addressed to
the Buyer, and dated as of the Closing Date;

(ix) the Buyer shall have received the resignations, effective as of the Closing,
of each director and officer of the Target's Subsidiaries other than those whom
the Buyer shall have specified in writing at least [five] business days prior to
the Closing;[56]

(x) the Buyer shall have obtained on terms and conditions [reasonably]
satisfactory to it all of the financing it needs in order to consummate the
transactions contemplated hereby [and fund the working capital requirements
of the acquired businesses after the Closing];[57] and

---

[54] Sample acquisition agreement 2003.2 (the *pro-seller* asset purchase agreement) contains a narrower
closing condition requiring only that there not be in effect any injunction, judgment, order, decree,
ruling, or charge preventing consummation of the transactions contemplated by this Agreement.

[55] If the Target has been a subsidiary of Bigco, the Buyer may require significant transition assistance.
This might be the case if Bigco performs substantial services for its subsidiaries and/or where Bigco
owns various tangible and intangible assets used by its subsidiaries. For example, the Buyer may
require real estate leases, intellectual property licenses, and accounting, purchasing, payroll, risk
management, and data processing services from Bigco.

[56] Sample acquisition agreement 2003.2 (the *pro-seller* asset purchase agreement) lacks a comparable
closing condition concerning the receipt of director and officer resignations.

[57] Sample acquisition agreement 2003.2 (the *pro-seller* asset purchase agreement) lacks a comparable
closing condition concerning the availability of financing for the transaction.

(xi) all actions to be taken by the Target in connection with consummation of the transactions contemplated hereby and all certificates, opinions, instruments, and other documents required to effect the transactions contemplated hereby will be [reasonably] satisfactory in form and substance to the Buyer.

The Buyer may waive any condition specified in this §6(a) if it executes a writing so stating at or prior to the Closing.

(b) *Conditions to Obligation of the Target.* The obligation of the Target to consummate the transactions to be performed by it in connection with the Closing is subject to satisfaction of the following conditions:

(i) the representations and warranties set forth in §4 above shall be true and correct in all material respects at and as of the Closing Date;

(ii) the Buyer shall have performed and complied with all of its covenants hereunder in all material respects through the Closing;

(iii) no action, suit, or proceeding shall be pending [or threatened] before any court or quasi-judicial or administrative agency of any federal, state, local, or foreign jurisdiction [or before any arbitrator] wherein an unfavorable injunction, judgment, order, decree, ruling, or charge would (A) prevent consummation of any of the transactions contemplated by this Agreement or (B) cause any of the transactions contemplated by this Agreement to be rescinded following consummation (and no such injunction, judgment, order, decree, ruling, or charge shall be in effect);[58]

(iv) the Buyer shall have delivered to the Target a certificate to the effect that each of the conditions specified above in §6(b)(i)-(iii) is satisfied in all respects;

(v) [all applicable waiting periods (and any extensions thereof) under the Hart-Scott-Rodino Act shall have expired or otherwise been terminated and the Target, its Subsidiaries, and the Buyer shall have received all other authorizations, consents, and approvals of governments and governmental agencies referred to in §3(c) and §4(c) above];

(vi) the relevant parties shall have entered into side agreements in form and substance as set forth in Exhibits G-_____, G-_____, . . . and G-_____ and the same shall be in full force and effect;

---

[58] Because this Target's closing condition conforms in part to the comparable Buyer's closing condition in §6(a)(iv), it leaves the Target with a relatively broad "out." Thus, the Buyer may prefer to narrow the respective closing conditions. *Compare* the narrower closing conditions in sample acquisition agreement 2003.2 (the *pro-seller* asset purchase agreement).

(vii) the Target shall have received from counsel to the Buyer an opinion in form and substance as set forth in Exhibit I attached hereto, addressed to the Target, and dated as of the Closing Date; and

(viii) all actions to be taken by the Buyer in connection with consummation of the transactions contemplated hereby and all certificates, opinions, instruments, and other documents required to effect the transactions contemplated hereby will be [reasonably] satisfactory in form and substance to the Target.

The Target may waive any condition specified in this §6(b) if it executes a writing so stating at or prior to the Closing.

7. *Termination.*

(a) *Termination of Agreement.*   Certain of the Parties may terminate this Agreement as provided below:

(i) the Buyer and the Target may terminate this Agreement by mutual written consent at any time prior to the Closing;

(ii) the Buyer may terminate this Agreement by giving written notice to the Target on or before the [30th] day following the date of this Agreement if the Buyer is not [reasonably] satisfied with the results of its continuing business, legal, and accounting due diligence regarding the Target and its Subsidiaries;[59]

(iii) the Buyer may terminate this Agreement by giving written notice to the Target at any time prior to the Closing (A) in the event the Target has breached any material representation, warranty, or covenant contained in this Agreement in any material respect, the Buyer has notified the Target of the breach, and the breach has continued without cure for a period of [30 days] after the notice of breach or (B) if the Closing shall not have occurred on or before _____, 19____, by reason of the failure of any condition precedent under §6(a) hereof (unless the failure results primarily from the Buyer itself breaching any representation, warranty, or covenant contained in this Agreement); and

(iv) the Target may terminate this Agreement by giving written notice to the Buyer at any time prior to the Closing (A) in the event the Buyer has breached any material representation, warranty, or covenant contained in this Agreement in any material respect, the Target has notified the Buyer of the breach, and the breach has continued without cure for a period of [30 days] after the notice of breach or (B) if the Closing shall not have occurred on or before _____, 19____, by reason of the failure of any condition precedent

---

[59] Sample acquisition agreement 2003.2 (the *pro-seller* asset purchase agreement) lacks a comparable provision giving the Buyer a right to terminate the agreement for a limited period after signing if the Buyer is not [reasonably] satisfied with the results of its continuing business, legal, environmental, and accounting due diligence concerning the Target and its Subsidiaries.

under §6(b) hereof (unless the failure results primarily from the Target itself breaching any representation, warranty, or covenant contained in this Agreement).

(b) *Effect of Termination.* If any Party terminates this Agreement pursuant to §7(a) above, all rights and obligations of the Parties hereunder shall terminate without any Liability of any Party to any other Party (except for any Liability of any Party then in breach).

8. *Miscellaneous.*

(a) *Survival of Representations and Warranties.* All of the representations and warranties of the Parties contained in this Agreement shall survive the Closing hereunder as and to the extent provided in the Agreement with Target Stockholders.

(b) *Press Releases and Public Announcements.* No Party shall issue any press release or make any public announcement relating to the subject matter of this Agreement [prior to the Closing] without the prior written approval of the other Party; *provided, however,* that any Party may make any public disclosure it believes in good faith is required by applicable law or any listing or trading agreement concerning its publicly-traded securities (in which case the disclosing Party will use its [reasonable] best efforts to advise the other Party prior to making the disclosure).

(c) *No Third-Party Beneficiaries.* This Agreement shall not confer any rights or remedies upon any Person other than the Parties and their respective successors and permitted assigns.

(d) *Entire Agreement.* [This Agreement (including the documents referred to herein) constitutes the entire agreement between the Parties and supersedes any prior understandings, agreements, or representations by or between the Parties, written or oral, to the extent they related in any way to the subject matter hereof.]

(e) *Succession and Assignment.* This Agreement shall be binding upon and inure to the benefit of the Parties named herein and their respective successors and permitted assigns. No Party may assign either this Agreement or any of its rights, interests, or obligations hereunder without the prior written approval of the other Party; *provided, however,* that the Buyer may (i) assign any or all of its rights and interests hereunder to one or more of its Affiliates and (ii) designate one or more of its Affiliates to perform its obligations hereunder (in any or all of which cases the Buyer nonetheless shall remain responsible for the performance of all of its obligations hereunder).

(f) *Counterparts.* This Agreement may be executed in one or more counterparts, each of which shall be deemed an original but all of which together will constitute one and the same instrument.

(g) *Headings.* The section headings contained in this Agreement are inserted for convenience only and shall not affect in any way the meaning or interpretation of this Agreement.

(h) *Notices.* All notices, requests, demands, claims, and other communications hereunder will be in writing. Any notice, request, demand, claim, or other communication hereunder shall be deemed duly given if (and then two business days after) it is sent by registered or certified mail, return receipt requested, postage prepaid, and addressed to the intended recipient as set forth below:

If to the Target: *Copy to:*

If to the Buyer: *Copy to:*

If to the Process Agent: *Copy to:*

Any Party may send any notice, request, demand, claim, or other communication hereunder to the intended recipient at the address set forth above using any other means (including personal delivery, expedited courier, messenger service, telecopy, telex, ordinary mail, or electronic mail), but no such notice, request, demand, claim, or other communication shall be deemed to have been duly given unless and until it actually is received by the intended recipient. Any Party may change the address to which notices, requests, demands, claims, and other communications hereunder are to be delivered by giving the other Party notice in the manner herein set forth.

(i) *Governing Law. This Agreement shall be governed by and construed in accordance with the domestic laws of the State of _____ without giving effect to any choice or conflict of law provision or rule (whether of the State of _____ or any other jurisdiction) that would cause the application of the laws of any jurisdiction other than the State of _____.*

(j) *Amendments and Waivers.* No amendment of any provision of this Agreement shall be valid unless the same shall be in writing and signed by the Buyer and the Target. The Target may consent to any such amendment at any time prior to the Closing with the prior authorization of its board of directors; *provided, however,* that any amendment effected after the Target Stockholders have approved this Agreement will be subject to the restrictions contained in the [APPLICABLE CORPORATION STATUTE]. No waiver by any Party of any default, misrepresentation, or breach of warranty or covenant hereunder, whether intentional or not, shall be deemed to extend to any prior or subsequent default, misrepresentation, or breach of warranty or covenant hereunder or affect in any way any rights arising by virtue of any prior or subsequent such occurrence.

(k) *Severability.* Any term or provision of this Agreement that is invalid or unenforceable in any situation in any jurisdiction shall not affect the validity or enforceability of the remaining terms and provisions hereof or the validity or enforceability of the offending term or provision in any other situation or in any other jurisdiction.

(l) *Expenses.* Each of the Buyer, the Target, its Subsidiaries, and the Target Stockholders will bear his or its own costs and expenses (including legal fees and expenses) incurred in connection with this Agreement and the transactions contemplated hereby. The Target agrees that none of its Subsidiaries has borne or will bear any of the costs and expenses of the Target and the Target Stockholders (including any of their legal fees and expenses) in connection with this Agreement or any of the transactions contemplated hereby.[60] The Target also agrees that it has not paid any amount to any third party, and will not pay any amount to any third party until after the Closing, with respect to any of the costs and expenses of the Target and the Target Stockholders (including any of their legal fees and expenses) in connection with this Agreement or any of the transactions contemplated hereby.[61]

(m) *Construction.* [The Parties have participated jointly in the negotiation and drafting of this Agreement. In the event an ambiguity or question of intent or interpretation arises, this Agreement shall be construed as if drafted jointly by the Parties and no presumption or burden of proof shall arise favoring or disfavoring any Party by virtue of the authorship of any of the provisions of this Agreement.] Any reference to any federal, state, local, or foreign statute or law

[60] This Agreement makes the Target Subsidiaries responsible for their own transactional costs and expenses. This means the Buyer will bear these costs and expenses if it consummates the asset purchase.

The Subsidiaries may incur significant costs and expenses if they prepare portions of the Disclosure Schedule and the Financial Statements, give notices to third parties and obtain their consent, make filings under the Hart-Scott-Rodino Act and respond to requests for additional information, and/or obtain title insurance and surveys for the Closing.

For this reason, the Buyer may seek to have the Target reimburse its Subsidiaries for some or all of these costs and expenses *after the Closing* (i.e., out of the sale proceeds rather than out of cash the Buyer otherwise would acquire).

The Target, on the other hand, may seek to make the Buyer responsible for some or all of the costs and expenses of the Target and the Target Stockholders. Sample acquisition agreement 2003.2 (the *pro-seller* asset purchase agreement) contains provisions more favorable to the Target in this regard.

The Parties may settle on a compromise allocation of responsibility (such as sharing the costs and expenses in a predetermined ratio or making one Party responsible for the costs and expenses up to a specified aggregate ceiling and the other Party responsible for any excess).

[61] Notice that the Buyer will bear the costs and expenses of the Target and the Target Stockholders to the extent the Target pays any amount to a third party with respect thereto prior to the Closing. This is because the payment will reduce the amount of cash the Buyer otherwise would receive when it acquires the assets of the Target and its Subsidiaries at the Closing. This provision is designed to protect the Buyer from having to bear any of the costs and expenses of the Target and the Target Stockholders.

shall be deemed also to refer to all rules and regulations promulgated thereunder, unless the context requires otherwise. The word "including" shall mean including without limitation. Nothing in the Disclosure Schedule shall be deemed adequate to disclose an exception to a representation or warranty made herein unless the Disclosure Schedule identifies the exception with [reasonable] particularity and describes the relevant facts in [reasonable] detail. Without limiting the generality of the foregoing, the mere listing (or inclusion of a copy) of a document or other item shall not be deemed adequate to disclose an exception to a representation or warranty made herein (unless the representation or warranty has to do with the existence of the document or other item itself). The Parties intend that each representation, warranty, and covenant contained herein shall have independent significance. If any Party has breached any representation, warranty, or covenant contained herein in any respect, the fact that there exists another representation, warranty, or covenant relating to the same subject matter (regardless of the relative levels of specificity) which the Party has not breached shall not detract from or mitigate the fact that the Party is in breach of the first representation, warranty, or covenant.[62]

(n) *Incorporation of Exhibits and Schedules.* The Exhibits and Schedules identified in this Agreement are incorporated herein by reference and made a part hereof.

(o) *Specific Performance.* Each of the Parties acknowledges and agrees that the other Party would be damaged irreparably in the event any of the provisions of this Agreement are not performed in accordance with their specific terms or otherwise are breached. Accordingly, each of the Parties agrees that the other Party shall be entitled to an injunction or injunctions to prevent breaches of the provisions of this Agreement and to enforce specifically this Agreement and the terms and provisions hereof in any action instituted in any court of the United States or any state thereof having jurisdiction over the Parties and the matter [(subject to the provisions set forth in §8(p) below)], in addition to any other remedy to which it may be entitled, at law or in equity.[63]

(p) *Submission to Jurisdiction.*[64] Each of the Parties submits to the jurisdiction of any state or federal court sitting in _____, _____, in any action or proceeding arising out of or relating to this Agreement and agrees that all claims in respect of the action or proceeding may be heard and determined in any such court. [Each Party also agrees not to bring any action or proceeding arising out of or relating to this Agreement in any other court.] Each of the Parties waives any defense of inconvenient forum to the maintenance of any action or proceeding so brought and waives any bond, surety, or other security that might

---

[62] Sample acquisition agreement 2003.2 (the *pro-seller* asset purchase agreement) omits the last four sentences of this paragraph.

[63] Sample acquisition agreement 2003.2 (the *pro-seller* asset purchase agreement) omits this specific performance provision.

[64] The Parties may want to add a provision calling for optional or mandatory arbitration with respect to all or certain issues.

be required of any other Party with respect thereto. Each Party appoints _____ (the *"Process Agent"*) as its agent to receive on its behalf service of copies of the summons and complaint and any other process that might be served in the action or proceeding. Any Party may make service on the other Party by sending or delivering a copy of the process (i) to the Party to be served at the address and in the manner provided for the giving of notices in §8(h) above or (ii) to the Party to be served in care of the Process Agent at the address and in the manner provided for the giving of notices in §8(h) above. Nothing in this §8(p), however, shall affect the right of any Party [to bring any action or proceeding arising out of or relating to this Agreement in any other court or] to serve legal process in any other manner permitted by law or in equity. Each Party agrees that a final judgment in any action or proceeding so brought shall be conclusive and may be enforced by suit on the judgment or in any other manner provided by law or in equity.[65]

(q) *Tax Matters.* [Any agreement between the Target and any of its Subsidiaries regarding allocation or payment of Taxes or amounts in lieu of Taxes shall be deemed terminated at and as of the Closing. The Buyer and the Target will (A) cooperate in the preparation and filing of an election under Code §338(h)(10) with respect to the sale of the stock of the Subsidiaries hereunder and (B) take all such action as is required in order to give effect to the election for state, local, and foreign Tax purposes to the greatest extent permitted by law.][66]

(r) *Employee Benefits Matters.* [The Buyer will adopt and assume at and as of the Closing each of the Employee Benefit Plans that the Target maintains and each trust, insurance contract, annuity contract, or other funding arrangement that the Target has established with respect thereto. The Target will transfer (or cause the plan administrators to transfer) at and as of the Closing all of the corresponding assets associated with the Employee Benefit Plans that the Buyer

---

[65] Sample acquisition agreement 2003.2 (the *pro-seller* asset purchase agreement) omits this submission to jurisdiction provision.

[66] The Buyer may seek to have the Parties make an election under Code §338(h)(10) (i.e., to have the sale of the stock of the Subsidiaries taxed as though the Subsidiaries instead had sold their *assets* to the Buyer). *See* ¶205.

This differs from any other election the Buyer might make under Code §338 in that the *Target* will be responsible for any federal income tax on the deemed sale of assets. Note, however, that the Target will incur no federal income tax on the sale of the *stock* of the Subsidiaries (i.e., only on the deemed sale of their *assets*) if the Parties make a Code §338(h)(10) election.

This Agreement provides that the Target will remain responsible for any incremental tax arising out of the Code §338(h)(10) election. See the definition of Assumed Liabilities in §1. The Target, of course, will seek to make the Buyer responsible for the incremental tax. Sample acquisition agreement 2003.2 (the *pro-seller* asset purchase agreement) contains provisions more favorable to the Target in this regard.

is adopting and assuming. With respect to each Multiemployer Plan, the Parties shall take all actions necessary to comply with the requirements of ERISA §4204.][67]

(s) *Bulk Transfer Laws.* The Buyer acknowledges that the Target will not comply with the provisions of any bulk transfer laws of any jurisdiction in connection with the transactions contemplated by this Agreement.[68]

*   *   *   *   *

IN WITNESS WHEREOF, the Parties hereto have executed this Agreement on [as of] the date first above written.

[BUYER]

By: _____
Title: _____

[TARGET]

By: _____
Title: _____

---

[67] This Agreement provides for a transfer of all Employee Benefit Plan assets (including overfundings) and liabilities (including underfundings) to the Buyer. There are many other approaches to splitting and matching plan assets and liabilities that would cause the Buyer to share to various degrees in plan overfundings and underfundings.

If the Buyer did not want to share in any plan overfundings and underfundings, the Buyer could establish substantially identical plans for future benefit accruals and count past service with any of the Target and its Subsidiaries for purposes of eligibility and vesting thereunder. The Target would then continue its previously established plans on a "frozen" basis and retain the benefit of any overfunding (or the detriment of any underfunding) thereunder.

If the Buyer wanted to share in only certain plan overfundings and underfundings, the Buyer and the Target could proceed as set forth in the preceding paragraph, except that the Buyer would assume the liability for certain past service benefits under the Target plans as of the Closing Date and the Target would transfer certain corresponding plan assets to the Buyer.

In any event, the Purchase Price should reflect the intended disposition of Employee Benefit Plan assets and liabilities.

[68] The Buyer may seek to have the Target comply with the applicable bulk transfer laws in certain circumstances. *See* ¶2001.2.2.2.

EXHIBIT A[69]—AGREEMENT WITH TARGET STOCKHOLDERS[70]

TABLE OF CONTENTS

[69] This is Exhibit A to sample acquisition agreement 2003.1 (the *pro-buyer* asset purchase agreement).

[70] Sample acquisition agreements 2003.1.1, 2003.2.1, and 2003.3.1 (the *asset* purchase agreements) assume that the Target will liquidate and dissolve immediately after the Closing. Each of these forms therefore includes an Agreement with Target Stockholders containing indemnification provisions and other covenants analogous to those contained in sample acquisition agreements 2002.1, 2002.2, and 2003.3 (the *stock* purchase agreements) respectively.

The Parties should eliminate this document (and return the indemnification provisions and other covenants to the Asset Purchase Agreement) if the Target will *not* liquidate and dissolve after the Closing. *Compare* sample acquisition agreements 2004.1 and 2004.2 (the *divisional* asset purchase agreements).

Agreement dated [as of] _____, 19____ among _____, a _____ corporation (the *"Buyer"*), and the stockholders (the *"Target Stockholders"*) of _____, a _____ corporation (the *"Target"*). The Buyer and the Target Stockholders are referred to collectively herein as the *"Parties."*

The Buyer and the Target are entering into an Asset Purchase Agreement concurrently herewith (the *"Asset Purchase Agreement"*). Certain terms used herein without definition are used herein as defined in the Asset Purchase Agreement.

The Asset Purchase Agreement contemplates a transaction in which the Buyer will purchase the Acquired Assets (and accept responsibility for the Assumed Liabilities) of the Target in return for cash and the Buyer Notes.

The Buyer and the Target make certain representations, warranties, and covenants in the Asset Purchase Agreement which will survive the Closing for purposes of potential indemnification. The Target Stockholders, however, intend to cause the Target to liquidate and dissolve immediately after the Closing. The Buyer and the Target Stockholders therefore wish to provide for post-Closing indemnification against breaches of these representations, warranties, and covenants and to make certain other covenants among themselves.

Now, therefore, in consideration of the premises and the mutual promises herein made, the Buyer and the Target Stockholders agree as follows.

1. *Definitions.*

"Adverse Consequences" means all actions, suits, proceedings, hearings, investigations, charges, complaints, claims, demands, injunctions, judgments, orders, decrees, rulings, damages, dues, penalties, fines, costs, amounts paid in settlement, Liabilities, obligations, Taxes, liens, losses, expenses, and fees, including court costs and [reasonable] attorneys' fees and expenses.

"Annex" has the meaning set forth in §2 below.

"Asset Purchase Agreement" has the meaning set forth in the preface above.

"Confidential Information" means any information concerning the businesses and affairs of the Target and its Subsidiaries that is not already generally available to the public.

"Indemnified Party" has the meaning set forth in §4(d) below.

"Indemnifying Party" has the meaning set forth in §4(d) below.

"Party" has the meaning set forth in the preface above.

"Requisite Target Stockholders" means Target Stockholders holding [a majority] in interest of the total number of Target Shares that all of the Target Stockholders hold in the aggregate as set forth in the Annex.[71]

"Third Party Claim" has the meaning set forth in §4(d) below.

2. *Representations and Warranties of the Target Stockholders.* Each of the Target Stockholders represents and warrants to the Buyer that the statements contained in this §2 are correct and complete as of the date of this Agreement and will be correct and complete as of the Closing Date (as though made then and as though the Closing Date were substituted for the date of this Agreement throughout this §2) with respect to himself or itself, except as set forth in the Annex attached hereto (the "Annex").

(a) *Organization of Certain Target Stockholders.* If the Target Stockholder is a corporation, the Target Stockholder is duly organized, validly existing, and in good standing under the laws of the jurisdiction of its incorporation.[72]

(b) *Authorization.* The Target Stockholder has full power and authority (including, if the Target Stockholder is a corporation, full corporate power and authority) to execute and deliver this Agreement and to perform his or its obligations hereunder. This Agreement constitutes the valid and legally binding obligation of the Target Stockholder, enforceable in accordance with its terms and conditions.

(c) *Noncontravention.* Neither the execution and the delivery of this Agreement by the Target Stockholder, nor the performance by the Target Stockholder of his or its obligations hereunder, will (i) violate any constitution, statute, regulation, rule, injunction, judgment, order, decree, stipulation, ruling, charge, or other restriction of any government, governmental agency, or court to which the Target Stockholder is subject (or, if the Target Stockholder is a corporation, any provision of its charter or bylaws) or (ii) conflict with, result in a breach of, constitute a default under, result in the acceleration of, create in any party the right to acceler-

---

[71] It may be necessary to revise this definition if the Target has additional classes of capital stock.

[72] Several representations and warranties in §2 concern Target Stockholders which are corporations. If any Target Stockholders are partnerships, trusts, business associations, estates, or guardians, the Buyer may seek to add analogous provisions covering them.

ate, terminate, modify, or cancel, or require any notice under any agreement, contract, lease, license, instrument, or other arrangement to which the Target Stockholder is a party or by which he or it is bound or to which any of his or its assets is subject.

(d) *Investment.* The Target Stockholder (i) understands that the Buyer Notes have not been, and will not be, registered under the Securities Act, or under any state securities laws, and are being offered and sold in reliance upon federal and state exemptions for transactions not involving any public offering, (ii) is acquiring the Buyer Notes solely for his or its own account for investment purposes, and not with a view to the distribution thereof, (iii) is a sophisticated investor with knowledge and experience in business and financial matters, (iv) has received certain information concerning the Buyer and has had the opportunity to obtain additional information as desired in order to evaluate the merits and the risks inherent in holding the Buyer Notes, (v) is able to bear the economic risk and lack of liquidity inherent in holding the Buyer Notes, and (vi) is an Accredited Investor for the reasons set forth on the Annex.[73]

(e) *Target Shares.* The Target Stockholder holds of record the number of Target Shares set forth next to his or its name on the Annex.

3. *Post-Closing Covenants.*[74] The Parties agree as follows with respect to the period following the Closing.

(a) *General.* In case at any time after the Closing any further action is necessary [or desirable] to carry out the purposes of the Asset Purchase Agreement, each of the Parties will take such further action (including the execution and delivery of such further instruments and documents) as any other Party [reasonably] may request, all the sole cost and expense of the requesting Party (unless the requesting Party is entitled to indemnification therefor under §4 below).[75] The Target Stockholders acknowledge and agree that from and after the Closing the Buyer will

---

[73] This provision contemplates that the Buyer will issue the Buyer Notes pursuant to the exemption from registration under the Securities Act contained in Regulation D. The Parties should determine whether this exemption is available in a particular transaction. If it is not, the Agreement must be modified as necessary to reflect the issuance of the Buyer Notes under a different exemption from securities registration or in an offering registered under the Securities Act.

[74] The Target Stockholders may seek to obtain additional covenants from the Buyer and its Subsidiaries (e.g., the typical covenants contained in a loan agreement or an indenture) because the Buyer is issuing the Buyer Notes to the Target Stockholders as part of the Purchase Price. Any such covenants would remain applicable so long as the Buyer Notes remained outstanding.

[75] The Parties may prefer to allocate responsibility for these particular costs and expenses in some other manner (e.g., the Party incurring the costs and expenses might be responsible for their payment; the Parties might share the costs and expenses in a predetermined ratio; or one Party might be responsible for the costs and expenses up to a specified aggregate ceiling and the other Party responsible for any excess).

Compare §6(l) (which allocates responsibility among the Parties for their costs and expenses generally) and §8(l) of the Asset Purchase Agreement (which allocates responsibility between the Buyer and the Target for their costs and expenses through the Closing).

be entitled to possession of all documents, books, records (including Tax records), agreements, and financial data of any sort relating to the Target and its Subsidiaries.

(b) *Litigation Support.* In the event and for so long as any Party actively is contesting or defending against any action, suit, proceeding, hearing, investigation, charge, complaint, claim, or demand in connection with (i) any transaction contemplated under the Asset Purchase Agreement or (ii) any fact, situation, circumstance, status, condition, activity, practice, plan, occurrence, event, incident, action, failure to act, or transaction on or prior to the Closing Date involving any of the Target and its Subsidiaries, each of the other Parties will cooperate with the contesting or defending Party and his or its counsel in the contest or defense, make available his or its personnel, and provide such testimony and access to his or its books and records as shall be necessary in connection with the contest or defense, all at the sole cost and expense of the contesting or defending Party (unless the contesting or defending Party is entitled to indemnification therefor under §4 below).[76]

(c) *Transition.* None of the Target Stockholders will take any action that is designed or intended to have the effect of discouraging any lessor, licensor, customer, supplier, or other business associate of any of the Target and its Subsidiaries from maintaining the same business relationships with the Buyer and the Subsidiaries after the Closing as it maintained with the Target and its Subsidiaries prior to the Closing. Each of the Target Stockholders will refer all customer inquiries relating to the businesses of the Target and its Subsidiaries to the Buyer from and after the Closing.

(d) *Confidentiality.*[77] Each of the Target Stockholders will treat and hold as such all of the Confidential Information, refrain from using any of the Confidential Information except in connection with this Agreement, and deliver promptly to the Buyer or destroy, at the request and option of the Buyer, all tangible embodiments (and all copies) of the Confidential Information which are in his or its possession. In the event that any of the Target Stockholders is requested or required (by oral question or request for information or documents in any legal proceeding, interrogatory, subpoena, civil investigative demand, or similar process) to disclose any Confidential Information, that Target Stockholder will notify the Buyer promptly of the request or requirement so that the Buyer may seek an appropriate protective order or waive compliance with the provisions of this §3(d). If, in the absence of a protective order or the receipt of a waiver hereunder, any of the Target Stockholders is, on the advice of counsel, compelled to disclose any Confidential Information to any tribunal or else stand liable for contempt, that Target Stockholder may disclose the Confidential Information to the tribunal; *provided, however,*

---

[76] The Parties may prefer to allocate responsibility for these particular costs and expenses in some other manner as discussed in the preceding footnote.

[77] The *pro-seller* Agreement (Exhibit A to sample acquisition agreement 2003.2) lacks a comparable confidentiality Provision affecting the Target Stockholders after the Closing.

that the disclosing Target Stockholder shall use his or its [reasonable] best efforts to obtain, at the [reasonable] request of the Buyer, an order or other assurance that confidential treatment will be accorded to such portion of the Confidential Information required to be disclosed as the Buyer shall designate.

(e) *Covenant Not to Compete.*[78] For a period of [five years] from and after the Closing Date, none of the Target Stockholders will engage directly or indirectly in any business that any of the Target and its Subsidiaries conducts as of the Closing Date [in any geographic area in which any of the Target and its Subsidiaries conducts that business as of the Closing Date]; *provided, however*, that no owner of less than 1% of the outstanding stock of any publicly traded corporation shall be deemed to engage solely by reason thereof in any of its businesses. If the final judgment of a court of competent jurisdiction declares that any term or provision of this §3(e) is invalid or unenforceable, the Parties agree that the court making the determination of invalidity or unenforceability shall have the power to reduce the scope, duration, or area of the term or provision, to delete specific words or phrases, or to replace any invalid or unenforceable term or provision with a term or provision that is valid and enforceable and that comes closest to expressing the intention of the invalid or unenforceable term or provision, and this Agreement shall be enforceable as so modified after the expiration of the time within which the judgment may be appealed.

(f) *Buyer Notes.* Each Buyer Note will be imprinted with a legend substantially in the following form:

The payment of principal and interest on this Note is subject to certain recoupment provisions set forth in an Agreement with Target Stockholders dated as of _____, 19____ (the "Agreement") among the issuer of this Note and certain other persons. This Note was originally issued on _____, 19____, and has not been registered under the Securities Act of 1933, as amended. The transfer of this Note is subject to certain restrictions set forth in the Agreement. The issuer of this Note will furnish a copy of these provisions to the holder hereof without charge upon written request.

Each holder desiring to transfer a Buyer Note first must furnish the Buyer with (i) a written opinion [reasonably] satisfactory to the Buyer in form and substance from counsel [reasonably] satisfactory to the Buyer by reason of experience to the effect that the holder may transfer the Buyer Note as desired without registration under the Securities Act and (ii) a written undertaking executed by the desired transferee [reasonably] satisfactory to the Buyer in form and substance agreeing

---

[78] Note that unless this Agreement states that a specified amount of consideration is being paid for the covenant not to compete, applicable tax cases will preclude the Buyer from seeking to allocate a portion of the Purchase Price to the covenant and amortizing such amount over the covenant's life.

to be bound by the recoupment provisions and the restrictions on transfer contained herein.[79]

4. *Remedies for Breaches of this Agreement and the Asset Purchase Agreement.*[80]

(a) *Survival of Representations and Warranties.*[81]

ALTERNATIVE A (FULL INDEMNIFICATION): All of the representations and warranties of the Buyer, the Target, and the Target Stockholders contained in the Asset Purchase Agreement and in this Agreement shall survive the Closing (even if the damaged Party knew or had reason to know of any misrepresentation or breach of warranty at the time of Closing) and continue in full force and effect forever thereafter (subject to any applicable statutes of limitations).

ALTERNATIVE B (LIMITED INDEMNIFICATION): All of the representations and warranties of the Target contained in §3(g)-(j) and §3(l)-(cc) of the Asset Purchase Agreement shall survive the Closing (even if the Buyer knew or had reason to know of any misrepresentation or breach of warranty at the time of

---

[79] Certain provisions in §3(f) contemplate that the Buyer will issue the Buyer Notes pursuant to an exemption from securities registration under the Securities Act. These provisions must be eliminated if the Buyer will issue the Buyer Notes in an offering registered under the Securities Act.

[80] The Buyer may seek some form of additional security covering the obligation of the Target Stockholders to indemnity the Buyer after the Closing. The recoupment provisions contained in §4(f) provide security up to the aggregate principal amount outstanding from time to time under the Buyer Notes. The Buyer may seek additional provisions calling for (a) the Target Stockholders to deposit a portion of the Purchase Price with a third party escrow agent, (b) the Buyer to hold back a portion of the Purchase Price (to be paid later with interest), or (c) the Buyer to obtain a security interest in certain assets of the Target Stockholders.

[81] This *pro-buyer* Agreement contains alternative provisions for (a) *full indemnification* to the Buyer for breaches of the representations and warranties of the Target and the Target Stockholders (i.e., all representations and warranties survive indefinitely, and there is no deductible, threshold, or ceiling with respect to indemnification against breaches thereof) and (b) *limited indemnification* to the Buyer for breaches of the representations and warranties of the Target and the Target Stockholders (i.e., the representations and warranties with respect to the transaction itself and with respect to taxes survive indefinitely; the other representations and warranties survive only for [three years]; and there is a threshold, but not a deductible or ceiling, with respect to indemnification against breaches of the latter).

The *pro-seller* Agreement (Exhibit A to sample acquisition agreement 2003.2), on the other hand, contains alternative provisions for (a) *minimal indemnification* to the Buyer for breaches of the representations and warranties of the Target and the Target Stockholders (i.e., only the representations and warranties concerning the transaction itself survive the Closing) and (b) *limited indemnification* to the Buyer for breaches of the representations and warranties of the Target and the Target Stockholders (i.e., the representations and warranties with respect to the transaction itself survive indefinitely; the other representations and warranties survive only for [one year]; and there is a deductible and a ceiling with respect to indemnification against breaches of the latter).

This *pro-buyer* Agreement provides that the representations and warranties will survive the Closing (*even if* the damaged Party knew or had reason to know of the misrepresentation or breach of warranty at the time of Closing).

The *pro-seller* Agreement (Exhibit A to sample acquisition agreement 2003.2), on the other hand, provides that the representations and warranties of the Parties will survive the Closing (*unless* the damaged Party knew or had reason to know of the misrepresentation or breach of warranty at the time of Closing).

Closing) and continue in full force and effect for a period of [three years] thereafter. All of the other representations and warranties of the Buyer, the Target, and the Target Stockholders contained in the Asset Purchase Agreement (including the representations and warranties of the Target contained in §3(a)-(f) and §3(k) thereof) and in this Agreement shall survive the Closing (even if the damaged Party knew or had reason to know of any misrepresentation or breach of warranty at the time of Closing) and continue in full force and effect forever thereafter (subject to any applicable statutes of limitations).

(b) *Indemnification Provisions for Benefit of the Buyer.*[82]

(i) In the event the Target breaches (or in the event any third party alleges facts that, if true, would mean the Target has breached) any of its representations, warranties, and covenants contained in the Asset Purchase Agreement, and, if there is an applicable survival period pursuant to §4(a) above, provided that the Buyer makes a written claim for indemnification against any of the Target Stockholders pursuant to §6(h) below within such survival period, then each of the Target Stockholders agrees to indemnify the Buyer from and against the entirety of any Adverse Consequences the Buyer may suffer[83] through and after the date of the claim for indemnification (including any Adverse Consequences the Buyer may suffer after the end of any applicable survival period) resulting from, arising out of, relating to, in the nature of, or caused by the breach (or the alleged breach)[84] [ALTERNATIVE B (LIMITED

---

[82] The Buyer will become indirectly responsible for all of the liabilities of the *Subsidiaries* if the Buyer acquires their capital stock as part of the Acquired Assets. For this reason, the Buyer may seek (a) to purchase assets from the Target *and from each of the Subsidiaries* (i.e., a multiple entity asset sale) or (b) to have the Target liquidate and dissolve the Subsidiaries tax free under Code §332 (to the extent they are United States corporations) and sell their assets to the Buyer.

In addition, the Asset Purchase Agreement provides that the Buyer will assume certain specified liabilities of the *Target*. *See* the definition of Assumed Liabilities in §1 thereof (and in particular the provision making the Buyer responsible for certain liabilities the Target reveals in the Disclosure Schedule).

Finally, the Buyer may be exposed for certain liabilities of the *Target* by operation of law if the Target does not pay them (e.g., under applicable bulk sales statutes and common law doctrines of de facto merger and successor liability). *See* ¶2001.2.2.2.

These post-Closing indemnification provisions are designed to work in conjunction with the narrow definition of Assumed Liabilities in §1 of the Asset Purchase Agreement and the extensive representations and warranties in §3 of the Asset Purchase Agreement to protect the Buyer against liabilities it does not intend to assume.

[83] The Target Stockholders may seek to have each Target Stockholder be responsible for only his or its *allocable portion* of the Buyer's Adverse Consequences (as opposed to the entire amount) if the Target breaches any of its representations, warranties, and covenants. This would protect those Target Stockholders who have "deep pockets" (or who otherwise are attractive defendants) from potentially having to indemnify the Buyer against a disproportionately large portion (or even all) of its Adverse Consequences. The *pro-seller* Agreement (Exhibit A to sample acquisition agreement 2003.2) contains provisions more favorable to the Target Stockholders in this regard.

[84] This *pro-buyer* Agreement requires an indemnifying party (presumably, but not necessarily, one of the Target Stockholders) to indemnify an indemnified party (presumably, but not necessarily, the Buyer) from and against any Adverse Consequences the indemnified party *may* suffer through and

INDEMNIFICATION):; *provided, however,* that the Target Stockholders shall not have any obligation to indemnify the Buyer from and against any Adverse Consequences resulting from, arising out of, relating to, in the nature of, or caused by the breach (or alleged breach) of any representation or warranty of the Target contained in §3(g)-(j) and §3(l)-(cc) of the Asset Purchase Agreement until the Buyer has suffered Adverse Consequences by reason of all such breaches (or alleged breaches) in excess of a $_____ aggregate threshold (at which point the Target Stockholders will be obligated to indemnify the Buyer from and against all such Adverse Consequences relating back to the first dollar).][85]

(ii) In the event any of the Target Stockholders breaches (or in the event any third party alleges facts that, if true, would mean any of the Target Stockholders has breached) any of his or its representations, warranties, and covenants contained in this Agreement, and, if there is an applicable survival period pursuant to §4(a) above, provided that the Buyer makes a written claim for indemnification against the Target Stockholder pursuant to §6(h) below within such survival period, then the Target Stockholder agrees to indemnify the Buyer from and against the entirety of any Adverse Consequences the Buyer may suffer through and after the date of the claim for indemnification (including any Adverse Consequences the Buyer may suffer after the end of any applicable survival period) resulting from, arising out of, relating to, in the nature of, or caused by the breach (or the alleged breach).

(iii) Each of the Target Stockholders agrees to indemnify the Buyer from and against the entirety of any Adverse Consequences the Buyer may suffer resulting from, arising out of, relating to, in the nature of, or caused by:

(A) any Liability of the Target which is not an Assumed Liability (including any Liability of the Target that becomes a Liability of the Buyer under any bulk transfer law of any jurisdiction, under any common law doctrine

---

after the date of the claim for indemnification (*including* any Adverse Consequences the indemnified party may suffer after the end of any applicable survival period) *resulting from, arising out of, relating to, in the nature of, or caused by* certain breaches by the indemnifying party of its representations, warranties, and covenants.

The *pro-seller* Agreement (Exhibit A to sample acquisition agreement 2003.2), on the other hand, requires an indemnifying party to indemnify an indemnified party from and against any Adverse Consequences the indemnified party *shall* suffer through and after the date of the claim for indemnification (but *excluding* any Adverse Consequences the indemnified party shall suffer after the end of any applicable survival period) *caused [proximately] by* certain breaches by the indemnifying party of its representations, warranties, and covenants.

[85] The Target Stockholders may seek to substitute a deductible (with no relation back to the first dollar) for the threshold in this proviso and to impose an aggregate ceiling on indemnification. *Compare* the *pro-seller* Agreement (Exhibit A to sample acquisition agreement 2003.2). The Target Stockholders may also seek to impose an additional *per claim* deductible.

of de facto merger or successor liability, under Environmental, Health, and Safety Requirements, or otherwise by operation of law);[86]

(B) any Liability of any of the Target's Subsidiaries for unpaid Taxes with respect to any Tax year or portion thereof ending on or before the Closing Date (or for any Tax year beginning before and ending after the Closing Date to the extent allocable to the portion of such period beginning before and ending on the Closing Date), [ALTERNATIVE A WHERE THERE IS NO PURCHASE PRICE ADJUSTMENT: to the extent such Taxes are not reflected in the reserve for Tax Liability (rather than any reserve for deferred Taxes established to reflect timing differences between book and Tax income) shown on the face of the Most Recent Balance Sheet (rather than in any notes thereto)[, as such reserve is adjusted for the passage of time through the Closing Date in accordance with the past custom and practice of the Target and its Subsidiaries in filing their Tax Returns]] [ALTERNATIVE B WHERE THERE IS A PURCHASE PRICE ADJUSTMENT: to the extent such Taxes are not reflected in the reserve for Tax Liability (rather than any reserve for deferred Taxes established to reflect timing differences between book and Tax income) shown on the face of the Closing Balance Sheet],[87] or

(C) any Liability of any of the Target's Subsidiaries for the unpaid Taxes of any Person (other than any of the Target and its Subsidiaries) under

---

[86] The Buyer may be exposed for certain liabilities of the Target by operation of law if the Target does not pay them (e.g., under applicable bulk sales statutes, common law doctrines of de facto merger and successor liability, and environmental laws). See ¶2001.2.2.2. This post-Closing indemnification provision is designed to protect the Buyer against liabilities arising by operation of law that it does not intend to assume.

[87] Clause (B) is intended to protect the Buyer with respect to pre-Closing Taxes of any Subsidiaries. Alternative A contemplates a fixed purchase price. Alternative B contemplates that there will be a purchase price adjustment as described in ¶2002.5.

This indemnity is limited to unpaid Taxes of the Subsidiaries. It does not cover unpaid Taxes of the Target itself, because Taxes of the Target are expressly excluded from the definition of "Assumed Liabilities" in the Asset Purchase Agreement and therefore are indemnified under §4(b)(iii)(A) of this agreement.

In the absence of clause (B), generally the Buyer is protected with respect to pre-Closing Taxes of the Subsidiaries only to the extent the Target has breached one or more of the Tax representations contained in §3(k) of the Asset Purchase Agreement. Clause (B) may have little or no impact on the scope of the Buyer's protection to the extent the agreement contains an unqualified indemnity for breach of §3(k)(v) of the Asset Purchase Agreement, as this pro-buyer agreement contemplates. However, a provision such as clause (B) can be useful in circumstances where (1) the Target Stockholders are willing to give a strong Tax indemnity but are not comfortable giving unqualified Tax representations of the type shown in §3(k)(v) of the Asset Purchase Agreement, (2) in contrast to the approach described in §4(a) of this agreement, the Tax representations survive for only a limited period, or (3) in contrast to the approach described in §4(b)(i) of this agreement, the Target Stockholders are willing to indemnify the Buyer for breaches of Tax representations only if the resulting claim (together with any claims arising from breaches of other representations) exceeds a threshold amount.

Clause (B) is best used in addition to (rather than in lieu of) an indemnity for breach of Tax representations, because certain of the Tax representations contained in §3(k) of the Asset Purchase Agreement cover matters beyond the scope of clause (B).

Reg. §1.1502-6 (or any similar provision of state, local, or foreign law), as a transferee or successor, by contract, or otherwise.[88]

(iv) Each of the Target Stockholders agrees to indemnify the Buyer from and against the entirety of any Adverse Consequences the Buyer may suffer resulting from, arising out of, relating to, in the nature of, or caused by _____.[89]

(c) *Indemnification Provisions for Benefit of the Target Stockholders.*

(i) In the event the Buyer breaches (or in the event any third party alleges facts that, if true, would mean the Buyer has breached) any of its representations, warranties, and covenants contained in the Asset Purchase Agreement and in this Agreement, and, if there is an applicable survival period pursuant to §4(a) above, provided that any of the Target Stockholders makes a written claim for indemnification against the Buyer pursuant to §6(h) below within such survival period, then the Buyer agrees to indemnify each of the Target Stockholders from and against the entirety of any Adverse Consequences the Target Stockholder may suffer through and after the date of the claim for indemnification (including any Adverse Consequences the Target Stockholder may suffer after the end of any applicable survival period) resulting from, arising out of, relating to, in the nature of, or caused by the breach (or the alleged breach).

(ii) The Buyer agrees to indemnify each of the Target Stockholders from and against the entirety of any Adverse Consequences the Target Stockholder may suffer resulting from, arising out of, relating to, in the nature of, or caused by any Assumed Liability.

[88] If any of the Subsidiaries has been a member of an Affiliated Group filing a consolidated federal income tax return (including, if applicable, the Target's Affiliated Group), such Subsidiary (or its successor) will be jointly and severally liable under Reg. §1.1502-6 for certain tax liabilities incurred by such Affiliated Group for a tax year when such Subsidiary was a member of such Affiliated Group for all or part of such tax year. *See* ¶210. A Subsidiary may also be liable for the unpaid taxes of third parties under similar provisions of state, local, or foreign law, as a transferee or successor, by contract (e.g., a tax sharing agreement), or otherwise. After the Buyer acquires the stock of any such Subsidiary, the Subsidiary will remain liable for any such unpaid tax liabilities.

This post-Closing indemnification provision is designed to protect the Buyer against any liability for the unpaid taxes of any person other than the Target and its Subsidiaries.

In order to eliminate this risk altogether, the Buyer may seek (a) to purchase assets from the Target *and from each of the Subsidiaries* (i.e., a multiple entity asset sale) or (b) to have the Target liquidate and dissolve the Subsidiaries tax free under Code §332 (to the extent they are United States corporations) and sell their assets to the Buyer.

[89] Note that the indemnification provisions in clause (i) above will not give the Buyer any post-Closing indemnification rights with respect to any adverse matter which the Target may disclose in the Disclosure Schedule. This is because the disclosure will cure any misrepresentation or breach of warranty that might otherwise have existed.

Thus, if the Target discloses an adverse matter in the Disclosure Schedule, the Buyer may seek to add a provision conferring specific post-Closing indemnification rights with respect to the particular matter.

The Buyer normally would seek to draft such a provision so that the indemnification would not be subject to any survival period, threshold, deductible, and/or ceiling.

(d) *Matters Involving Third Parties.*[90]

(i) If any third party shall notify any Party (the *"Indemnified Party"*) with respect to any matter (a *"Third Party Claim"*) which may give rise to a claim for indemnification against any other Party (the *"Indemnifying Party"*) under this §4, then the Indemnified Party shall promptly notify each Indemnifying Party thereof in writing; *provided, however,* that no delay on the part of the Indemnified Party in notifying any Indemnifying Party shall relieve the Indemnifying Party from any obligation hereunder unless (and then solely to the extent) the Indemnifying Party thereby is prejudiced.

(ii) Any Indemnifying Party will have the right to defend the Indemnified Party against the Third Party Claim with counsel of its choice [reasonably] satisfactory to the Indemnified Party so long as (A) the Indemnifying Party notifies the Indemnified Party in writing within [15 days] after the Indemnified Party has given notice of the Third Party Claim that the Indemnifying Party will indemnify the Indemnified Party from and against the entirety of any Adverse Consequences the Indemnified Party may suffer resulting from, arising out of, relating to, in the nature of, or caused by the Third Party Claim, (B) the Indemnifying Party provides the Indemnified Party with evidence [reasonably] acceptable to the Indemnified Party that the Indemnifying Party will have the financial resources to defend against the Third Party Claim and fulfill its indemnification obligations hereunder, (C) the Third Party Claim involves only money damages and does not seek an injunction or other equitable relief, (D) settlement of, or an adverse judgment with respect to, the Third Party Claim is not, in the good faith judgment of the Indemnified Party, likely to establish a precedential custom or practice [materially] adverse to the continuing business

---

[90] An *indemnifying* party (presumably, but not necessarily, one of the Target Stockholders) will normally seek to control the defense of any third party claim that may give rise to a claim for indemnification under §4. However, the *indemnified* party (presumably, but not necessarily, the Buyer) will not want the indemnifying party to control the defense of any third party claim in which the indemnified party will retain a meaningful interest. For example, the indemnified party may seek to control the defense of a third party claim if the third party seeks an injunction or other equitable relief or if it is not clear that the indemnifying party will bear the entirety of any money damages or amount paid in settlement.

This *pro-buyer* Agreement provides that the indemnified party will control the defense of any third party claim *unless* (a) an indemnifying party accepts full responsibility for the matter within [15 days], (b) the indemnifying party demonstrates it has the financial resources necessary to defend against the matter and fulfill its indemnification obligations, (c) the third party seeks only money damages (as opposed to an injunction or other equitable relief), (d) settlement of, or an adverse judgment with respect to, the third party claim is not likely to establish a precedent [materially] adverse to the indemnified party, and (e) the indemnifying party conducts the defense actively and diligently.

The *pro-seller* agreement (Exhibit A to sample acquisition agreement 2003.2), on the other hand, provides that any indemnifying party may assume the defense of a third party claim *at any time* during the course of the defense, and prevents the indemnified party from consenting to the entry of any judgment or entering into any settlement with respect to the matter without the consent of the indemnifying party [(not to be unreasonably withheld)].

interests of the Indemnified Party, and (E) the Indemnifying Party conducts the defense of the Third Party Claim actively and diligently.

(iii) So long as the Indemnifying Party is conducting the defense of the Third Party Claim in accordance with §4(d)(ii) above, (A) the Indemnified Party may retain separate co-counsel at its sole cost and expense and participate in the defense of the Third Party Claim, (B) the Indemnified Party will not consent to the entry of any judgment or enter into any settlement with respect to the Third Party Claim without the prior written consent of the Indemnifying Party [(not to be withheld unreasonably)], and (C) the Indemnifying Party will not consent to the entry of any judgment or enter into any settlement with respect to the Third Party Claim without the prior written consent of the Indemnified Party [(not to be withheld unreasonably)].

(iv) In the event any of the conditions in §4(d)(ii) above is or becomes unsatisfied, however, (A) the Indemnified Party may defend against, and consent to the entry of any judgment or enter into any settlement with respect to, the Third Party Claim in any manner it [reasonably] may deem appropriate (and the Indemnified Party need not consult with, or obtain any consent from, any Indemnifying Party in connection therewith), (B) the Indemnifying Parties will reimburse the Indemnified Party promptly and periodically for the costs of defending against the Third Party Claim (including [reasonable] attorneys' fees and expenses), and (C) the Indemnifying Parties will remain responsible for any Adverse Consequences the Indemnified Party may suffer resulting from, arising out of, relating to, in the nature of, or caused by the Third Party Claim to the fullest extent provided in this §4.

(e) *Determination of Adverse Consequences.* [The Parties shall take into account the time cost of money (using the Applicable Rate as the discount rate) in determining Adverse Consequences for purposes of this §4.] All indemnification payments under this §4 shall be deemed adjustments to the Purchase Price.

(f) *Recoupment Under Buyer Notes.* The Buyer shall have the option of recouping all or any part of any Adverse Consequences it may suffer (in lieu of seeking any indemnification to which it is entitled under this §4) by notifying any Target Stockholder that the Buyer is reducing the principal amount outstanding under his or its Buyer Note. This shall affect the timing and amount of payments required under the Buyer Note in the same manner as if the Buyer had made a permitted prepayment (without premium or penalty) thereunder.[91]

(g) *Other Indemnification Provisions.* The foregoing indemnification provisions are in addition to, and not in derogation of, any statutory, equitable, or common law remedy (including without limitation any such remedy arising under Environ-

---

[91] The *pro-seller* Agreement (Exhibit A to sample acquisition agreement 2003.2) lacks a comparable provision giving the Buyer a right of recoupment against the Buyer Notes.

mental, Health, and Safety Requirements) any Party may have with respect to the Target, its Subsidiaries, or the transactions contemplated by this Agreement.[92] Each of the Target Stockholders hereby agrees that he or it will not make any claim for indemnification against any of the Buyer and its Subsidiaries by reason of the fact that he or it was a director, officer, employee, or agent of any of the Target and its Subsidiaries or was serving at the request of any such entity as a partner, trustee, director, officer, employee, or agent of another entity (whether such claim is for judgments, damages, penalties, fines, costs, amounts paid in settlement, losses, expenses, or otherwise and whether such claim is pursuant to any statute, charter document, bylaw, agreement, or otherwise) with respect to any action, suit, proceeding, complaint, claim, or demand brought by the Buyer against such Target Stockholder (whether such action, suit, proceeding, complaint, claim, or demand is pursuant to this Agreement, applicable law, or otherwise).[93]

5. *Termination.* This Agreement shall terminate if and only if the Asset Purchase Agreement is terminated prior to the Closing in accordance with and pursuant to the terms thereof.

6. *Miscellaneous.*

(a) *Exclusivity.* None of the Target Stockholders will (i) solicit, initiate, or encourage the submission of any proposal or offer from any Person relating to the acquisition of any capital stock or other voting securities, or any substantial portion of the assets, of any of the Target and its Subsidiaries (including any acquisition structured as a merger, consolidation, or share exchange) or (ii) participate in any discussions or negotiations regarding, furnish any information with respect to, assist or participate in, or facilitate in any other manner any effort or attempt by any Person to do or seek any of the foregoing.[94] Each Target Stockholder will notify the Buyer immediately if he or it becomes aware that any Person has made any proposal, offer, inquiry, or contact with respect to any of the foregoing.

---

[92] Sample acquisition agreement 2003.2 (the *pro-seller* asset purchase agreement) states that (1) the remedies available to the Parties under the Agreement are exclusive (i.e., that the Buyer has no other statutory, equitable, or common law remedies) and (2) the Buyer specifically waives and releases the Target Stockholders from, and indemnifies the Target Shareholders with respect to, environmental, health, and safety matters.

Sample acquisition agreement 2003.3 (the *neutral* asset purchase agreement) (1) states that the remedies available to the Parties under the Agreement are exclusive (i.e., that the Buyer has no other statutory, equitable, or common law remedies), (2) contains a waiver of extra-contractual environmental remedies, but (3) does not contain an environmental indemnification of the Target Shareholders by the Buyer.

[93] This provision responds to the surprising decision in Heffernan v. Pacific Dunlop GNB Corporation, 965 F.2d 369 (7th Cir. 1992). Although *Heffernan* involved a purchase of stock rather than a purchase of assets, the instant structure presents many of the same concerns. See §8(g) of sample acquisition agreement 2002.1 (the pro-buyer *stock* purchase agreement) and the footnote thereto. See *also* the definition of "Assumed Liabilities" in the accompanying Asset Purchase Agreement (sample acquisition agreement 2003.1.1).

[94] The *pro-seller* Agreement (Exhibit A to sample acquisition agreement 2003.2) gives the Target Stockholders greater latitude to respond to unsolicited proposals.

(b) *Press Releases and Public Announcements.* None of the Target Stockholders shall issue any press release or make any public announcement relating to the subject matter of the Asset Purchase Agreement [prior to the Closing] without the prior written approval of the Buyer; *provided, however,* that any Target Stockholder may make any public disclosure it believes in good faith is required by applicable law or any listing or trading agreement concerning its publicly-traded securities (in which case the disclosing Party will use its [reasonable] best efforts to advise the other Parties prior to making the disclosure).

(c) *No Third-Party Beneficiaries.* This Agreement shall not confer any rights or remedies upon any Person other than the Parties and their respective successors and permitted assigns.

(d) *Entire Agreement.* [This Agreement (including the documents referred to herein) constitutes the entire agreement among the Parties and supersedes any prior understandings, agreements, or representations by or among the Parties, written or oral, to the extent they related in any way to the subject matter hereof].

(e) *Succession and Assignment.* This Agreement shall be binding upon and inure to the benefit of the Parties named herein and their respective successors and permitted assigns. No Party may assign either this Agreement or any of his or its rights, interests, or obligations hereunder without the prior written approval of the Buyer and the Requisite Target Stockholders; provided, however, that the Buyer may (i) assign any or all of its rights and interests hereunder to one or more of its Affiliates and (ii) designate one or more of its Affiliates to perform its obligations hereunder (in any or all of which cases the Buyer nonetheless shall remain liable and responsible for the performance of all of its obligations hereunder).

(f) *Counterparts.* This Agreement may be executed in one or more counterparts, each of which shall be deemed an original but all of which together will constitute one and the same instrument.

(g) *Headings.* The section headings contained in this Agreement are inserted for convenience only and shall not affect in any way the meaning or interpretation of this Agreement.

(h) *Notices.*[95] All notices, requests, demands, claims, and other communications hereunder will be in writing. Any notice, request, demand, claim, or other communication hereunder shall be deemed duly given if (and then two business days after) it is sent by registered or certified mail, return receipt requested, postage prepaid, and addressed to the intended recipient as set forth below:

---

[95] The Parties may want to add provisions designating a nominee to act on behalf of the Target Stockholders for purposes of receiving notice, agreeing to modifications and amendments, and taking action.

If to the Target Stockholders: *Copy to:*

If to the Buyer: *Copy to:*

If to the Process Agent: *Copy to:*

Any Party may send any notice, request, demand, claim, or other communication hereunder to the intended recipient at the address set forth above using any other means (including personal delivery, expedited courier, messenger service, telecopy, telex, ordinary mail, or electronic mail), but no such notice, request, demand, claim, or other communication shall be deemed to have been duly given unless and until it actually is received by the intended recipient. Any Party may change the address to which notices, requests, demands, claims, and other communications hereunder are to be delivered by giving the other Parties notice in the manner herein set forth.

(i) *Governing Law. This Agreement shall be governed by and construed in accordance with the domestic laws of the State of* _____ *without giving effect to any choice or conflict of law provision or rule (whether of the State of* _____ *or any other jurisdiction) that would cause the application of the laws of any jurisdiction other than the State of* _____.

(j) *Amendments and Waivers.* No amendment of any provision of this Agreement shall be valid unless the same shall be in writing and signed by the Buyer and the Requisite Target Stockholders. No waiver by any Party of any default, misrepresentation, or breach of warranty or covenant hereunder, whether intentional or not, shall be deemed to extend to any prior or subsequent default, misrepresentation, or breach of warranty or covenant hereunder or affect in any way any rights arising by virtue of any prior or subsequent such occurrence.

(k) *Severability.* Any term or provision of this Agreement that is invalid or unenforceable in any situation in any jurisdiction shall not affect the validity or enforceability of the remaining terms and provisions hereof or the validity or enforceability of the offending term or provision in any other situation or in any other jurisdiction.

(l) *Expenses.* Each of the Parties will bear his or its own costs and expenses (including legal fees and expenses) incurred in connection with this Agreement and the transactions contemplated hereby (except as otherwise provided herein).

(m) *Construction.* [The Parties have participated jointly in the negotiation and drafting of this Agreement. In the event an ambiguity or question of intent or interpretation arises, this Agreement shall be construed as if drafted jointly by the Parties and no presumption or burden of proof shall arise favoring or disfavoring any Party by virtue of the authorship of any of the provisions of this Agreement.] Any reference to any federal, state, local, or foreign statute or law shall be deemed also to refer to all rules and regulations promulgated thereunder, unless the context requires otherwise. The word "including" shall mean including without limitation.

(n) *Incorporation of Annex.* The Annex is incorporated herein by reference and made a part hereof.

(o) *Specific Performance.* Each of the Parties acknowledges and agrees that the other Parties would be damaged irreparably in the event any of the provisions of this Agreement are not performed in accordance with their specific terms or otherwise are breached. Accordingly, each of the Parties agrees that the other Parties shall be entitled to an injunction or injunctions to prevent breaches of the provisions of this Agreement and to enforce specifically this Agreement and the terms and provisions hereof in any action instituted in any court of the United States or any state thereof having jurisdiction over the Parties and the matter [(subject to the provisions set forth in §6(p) below)] in addition to any other remedy to which they may be entitled, at law or in equity.[96]

(p) *Submission to Jurisdiction.*[97] Each of the Parties submits to the jurisdiction of any state or federal court sitting in _____, _____, in any action or proceeding arising out of or relating to this Agreement and agrees that all claims in respect of the action or proceeding may be heard and determined in any such court. [Each Party also agrees not to bring any action or proceeding arising out of or relating to this Agreement in any other court.] Each of the Parties waives any defense of inconvenient forum to the maintenance of any action or proceeding so brought and waives any bond, surety, or other security that might be required of any other Party with respect thereto. Each Party appoints the Process Agent as his or its agent to receive on his or its behalf service of copies of the summons and complaint and any other process that might be served in the action or proceeding. Any Party may make service on any other Party by sending or delivering a copy of the process (i) to the Party to be served at the address and in the manner provided for the giving of notices in §6(h) above or (ii) to the Party to be served in care of the Process Agent at the address and in the manner provided for the giving of notices in §6(h) above. Nothing in this §6(p), however, shall affect the right of any Party [to bring any action or proceeding arising out of or relating to this Agreement in any other court or] to serve legal process in any other manner permitted by law or in equity. Each Party agrees that a final judgment in any action or proceeding so brought shall be conclusive and may be enforced by suit on the judgment or in any other manner provided by law or in equity.[98]

---

[96] The *pro-seller* Agreement (Exhibit A to sample acquisition agreement 2003.2) omits this specific performance provision.

[97] The Parties may want to add a provision calling for optional or mandatory arbitration with respect to all or certain issues.

[98] The *pro-seller* Agreement (Exhibit A to sample acquisition agreement 2003.2) omits this submission to jurisdiction provision.

* * * * *

IN WITNESS WHEREOF, the Parties hereto have executed this Agreement on [as of] the date first above written.

[BUYER]

By: _____

Title: _____

[TARGET STOCKHOLDER # 1 (an entity)]

By: _____

Title: _____

[TARGET STOCKHOLDER # 2 (an entity)]

By: _____

Title: _____

_____

[TARGET STOCKHOLDER # 3 (an individual)]

¶2003.2   Pro-Seller Asset Purchase

Sample acquisition agreement 2003.2 (*pro-seller* asset purchase) contains provisions favoring T in such areas as (i) the extent to which T will retain its cash (net of unpaid taxes) at the time of the closing, (ii) the extent to which P will bear the burden of T's liabilities and obligations after the closing, (iii) the extent to which P will lack conditions to its obligation to close, (iv) the extent to which T will be required to give representations and warranties, and (v) the extent to which T will be required to indemnify P against breaches of those representations and warranties.

Sample acquisition agreement 2003.2 provides that T will retain all of its cash at the closing (less an amount equal to its good faith estimate of its unpaid taxes with respect to periods up to the closing computed in accordance with its past custom and practice in filing its tax returns). This means that T will retain its cash (net of unpaid taxes) at the time of the closing.

Sample acquisition agreement 2003.2 provides that P will assume substantially all of T's obligations and liabilities (whether known or unknown, and whether absolute or contingent). Thus, P would generally assume such undisclosed T liabilities as environmental cleanup, employment discrimination, antitrust violations, product liability, product warranty, tax deficiencies, and other claims and lawsuits.

Sample acquisition agreement 2003.2 contains limited representations and warranties from T concerning (i) its historical financial statements, (ii) intervening events, (iii) litigation, (iv) tax matters, (v) pension and welfare benefit plans, (vi) environmental, health, and safety matters, and (vii) compliance with federal, state, local, and foreign laws.

Sample acquisition agreement 2003.2 *does not* contain a specific representation and warranty concerning undisclosed liabilities.

Sample acquisition agreement 2003.2 also contains limited representations and warranties from T concerning (i) authorization with respect to the transaction, (ii) title to the assets being sold, (iii) required governmental and third party consents (and noncontravention generally), (iv) organization, (v) real estate matters, (vi) intellectual property matters, (vii) leases and contracts, and (viii) brokerage fees.

T's representations and warranties are qualified frequently with references to materiality and to the actual knowledge of T's shareholders, but not, for example, T's directors, officers, and employees, *without any duty of independent investigation.*

Sample acquisition agreement 2003.2 contains alternative provisions for (i) minimal indemnification to P for breaches of T's representations and warranties (i.e., none of the representations and warranties concerning T survive the closing and there is no indemnification for breaches thereof)[1] *or* (ii) limited indemnification to P for breaches of T's representations and warranties (i.e., the representations

---

¶2003.2   [1] This is referred to as *minimal* indemnification (rather than *no* indemnification) because the seller's representations and warranties about the transaction itself (*e.g.,* organization of T, authorization of the transaction, noncontravention, absence of brokers' fees, ownership of T's assets, etc.) do survive the closing and may give rise to indemnification.

and warranties concerning T survive only for one year and there is a deductible and a ceiling with respect to indemnification for breaches thereof).[2]

P *does not* have any right to recoup its losses against the P notes in lieu of seeking indemnification from T and its shareholders.

P's obligation to close is subject to minimal conditions such as (i) compliance with T's representations, warranties, and covenants, (ii) absence of a material adverse change, (iii) absence of an injunction affecting the transaction, (iv) delivery of any side agreements, and (v) delivery of an opinion of T's legal counsel.

P *does not* have any closing condition concerning its ability to secure financing for the transaction *or* any right to terminate the purchase agreement after signing if it is not satisfied with the results of its continuing business, legal, and accounting due diligence review.

There are a number of other important differences among sample acquisition agreement 2003.1 (*pro-buyer* asset purchase), sample acquisition agreement 2003.2 (*pro-seller* asset purchase), and sample acquisition agreement 2003.3 (*neutral* asset purchase). Each of these sample acquisition agreements contains extensive footnotes with cross-references pointing out the differences.

Asset Purchase Agreement

ASSET PURCHASE AGREEMENT[3]

BETWEEN

_____

AND

_____

_____, 19____

---

[2] Sample acquisition agreement 2003.2 (the pro-seller *asset* purchase agreement) assumes that T will liquidate and dissolve immediately after the closing, so that T will not be able to perform any post-closing covenants (including any post-closing indemnification provisions) analogous to those contained in sample acquisition agreement 2002.2 (the pro-seller *stock* purchase agreement). The Agreement with Target Stockholders (Exhibit A to sample acquisition agreement 2003.2) is designed to address this situation by making *T's shareholders* responsible for the post-closing covenants (including the post-closing indemnification provisions).

[3] The Buyer generally will obtain a cost basis (i.e., the Purchase Price *plus* the Assumed Liabilities *plus* the expenses of the transaction) in the Acquired Assets.

A purchase of assets in which the consideration is primarily cash and notes is generally treated for accounting purposes as a purchase rather than as a pooling of interests. *See* ¶1503.

Some LBO structures prejudice the Target's creditors and hence might permit payments, transfers, liens, and obligations arising out of the LBO to be attacked under fraudulent conveyance law. *See* ¶1504.

TABLE OF CONTENTS

[EXHIBITS B THROUGH I AND THE DISCLOSURE SCHEDULE HAVE BEEN OMITTED FROM THIS SAMPLE ACQUISITION AGREEMENT 2003.2]

Agreement entered into on [as of] _____, 19____, by and between _____, a _____ corporation (the *"Buyer"*)

---

[4] This Asset Purchase Agreement assumes that the Target will liquidate and dissolve immediately after the Closing, so that the Target will not be able to perform any post-Closing covenants (including any post-Closing indemnification provisions) analogous to those contained in sample acquisition agreement 2002.2 (the pro-seller *stock* purchase agreement). The accompanying Agreement with Target

and _____, a _____ corporation (the *"Target"*). The Buyer and the Target are referred to collectively herein as the *"Parties."*

This Agreement contemplates a transaction in which the Buyer will purchase substantially all of the assets (and assume substantially all of the liabilities) of the Target in return for cash and the Buyer Notes.[5]

Now, therefore, in consideration of the premises and the mutual promises herein made, and in consideration of the representations, warranties, and covenants herein contained, the Parties agree as follows.

1. *Definitions.*

"Accredited Investor" has the meaning set forth in Regulation D promulgated under the Securities Act.

"Acquired Assets" means all of the right, title, and interest that the Target possesses and has the right to transfer in and to all of its assets,[6] *including* all of its (a) real property, leaseholds and subleaseholds therein, improvements, fixtures, and fittings thereon, and easements, rights-of-way, and other appurtenants thereto (such as appurtenant rights in and to public streets), (b) tangible personal property (such as machinery, equipment, inventories of raw materials and supplies, manufactured and purchased parts, goods in process and finished goods, furniture, automobiles, trucks, tractors, trailers, tools, jigs, and dies), (c) intellectual property, goodwill associated therewith, licenses and sublicenses granted and obtained with respect thereto, and rights thereunder, remedies against infringements thereof, and rights to protection of interests therein under the laws of all jurisdictions, (d) leases, subleases, and rights thereunder, (e) agreements, contracts, indentures, mortgages, instruments, Security Interests, guaranties, other similar arrangements, and rights thereunder, (f) accounts, notes, and other receivables, (g) securities

---

Stockholders is designed to address this situation by making the *Target Stockholders* responsible for the post-Closing covenants (including the post-Closing indemnification provisions).

[5] Where the Buyer purchases Target's assets, the Target will generally retain those assets and rights which it does not transfer and assign to the Buyer, and the Target will generally remain responsible for those liabilities and obligations not assumed by the Buyer.

It is generally necessary to prepare asset transfer documents and liability assumption documents in an asset purchase (whether a purchase of all the Target's assets or a purchase of the Target's division), which would not be required if the Buyer purchased the Target's *stock.*

The Buyer's contractual assumption of certain of the Target's liabilities and obligations generally will not preclude a third party to whom the Target owed the liabilities and obligations from suing the Target (if the Buyer has failed to pay or perform) unless the third party consents to the Buyer's assumption and agrees to look only to the Buyer for satisfaction (i.e., enters into a novation agreement). This means that, if the Buyer fails to satisfy the assumed liabilities and obligations, nonconsenting third parties to whom the Target owed the liabilities and obligations may have a cause of action against the Target or, if the Target has liquidated and dissolved, against the Target's stockholders and/or directors.

[6] The Buyer may seek to have the definition of Acquired Assets broadened to include *all* right, title, and interest in and to the Target's assets (rather than only so much as the Target possesses and has the right to transfer). Sample acquisition agreement 2003.1 (the *pro-buyer* asset purchase agreement) contains provisions which are more favorable to the Buyer in this regard.

(such as the capital stock in its Subsidiaries), (h) claims, deposits, prepayments, refunds, causes of action, choses in action, rights of recovery, rights of set off, and rights of recoupment (including any such item relating to the payment of taxes), (i) franchises, approvals, permits, licenses, orders, registrations, certificates, variances, and similar rights obtained from governments and governmental agencies, (j) books, records, ledgers, files, documents, correspondence, lists, plats, architectural plans, drawings, and specifications, creative materials, advertising and promotional materials, studies, reports, and other printed or written materials, (k) Cash up to an amount equal to the Target's good faith estimate of the aggregate liability of the Target and its Subsidiaries for unpaid taxes as of the Closing (computed in accordance with the past custom and practice of the Target and its Subsidiaries in filing their tax returns), and (l) [rights in and with respect to the assets associated with its Employee Benefit Plans];[7] *provided, however,* that the Acquired Assets shall not include (i) the corporate charter, qualifications to conduct business as a foreign corporation, arrangements with registered agents relating to foreign qualifications, taxpayer and other identification numbers, seals, minute books, stock transfer books, blank stock certificates, and other documents relating to the organization, maintenance, and existence of the Target as a corporation, (ii) any Cash in excess of the amount referred to in clause (k) of this definition,[8] or (iii) any of the rights of the Target under this Agreement (or under any side agreement between the Target on the one hand and the Buyer on the other hand entered into on or after the date of this Agreement).

"*Affiliate*" has the meaning set forth in Rule 12b-2 of the regulations promulgated under the Securities Exchange Act.

"*Affiliated Group*" means any affiliated group within the meaning of Code §1504(a) [or any similar group defined under a similar provision of state, local, or foreign law].

"*Agreement with Target Stockholders*" means the Agreement with Target Stockholders entered into concurrently herewith and attached hereto as Exhibit A.[9]

---

[7] *See* the provisions in §8(p) below with respect to employee benefits matters.

[8] This Agreement provides that the Target will retain the consolidated cash of the Target and its Subsidiaries (net of unpaid Taxes for which the Buyer will become responsible) at the Closing. §2(d) below permits the Target to cause its Subsidiaries to distribute all of their cash to the Target at the Closing in order to facilitate the intended cash retention. The Buyer normally will seek to obtain *all* of the consolidated cash at the Closing. Sample acquisition agreement 2003.1 (the *pro-buyer* asset purchase agreement) contains provisions which are more favorable to the Buyer in this regard.

The Parties may want to introduce a post-Closing adjustment to the Purchase Price based on the difference between the amount of cash the Target will retain at the Closing (i.e., the Target's good faith estimate of the consolidated cash net of unpaid taxes through the Closing) and the actual amount as determined later. *See* sample acquisition agreement 2002.5 for analogous provisions concerning a different type of post-Closing Purchase Price adjustment.

[9] This Asset Purchase Agreement assumes that the Target will liquidate and dissolve immediately after the Closing, so that the Target will not be able to perform any post-Closing covenants (including any post-Closing indemnification provisions) analogous to those contained in sample acquisition agreement 2002.2 (the pro-seller stock purchase agreement). The accompanying Agreement with Target

"Applicable Rate" means the corporate base rate of interest publicly announced from time to time by [FINANCIAL INSTITUTION] [plus/minus _____% per annum].

"Assumed Liabilities"[10] means all liabilities and obligations of the Target (whether known or unknown, whether asserted or unasserted, whether absolute or contingent, whether accrued or unaccrued, whether liquidated or unliquidated, and whether due or to become due), including (a) all liabilities of the Target for unpaid taxes with respect to periods prior to the Closing, (b) all liabilities of the Target for income, transfer, sales, use, and other taxes arising in connection with the consummation of the transactions contemplated hereby (including any Income Taxes arising because the Target is transferring the Acquired Assets, because any of its Subsidiaries is deemed to be transferring its assets pursuant to an election under Code §338(h)(10), because the Target has an Excess Loss Account in the stock of any of its Subsidiaries, or because the Target has deferred gain on any Deferred Intercompany Transaction),[11] (c) all liabilities of the Target for the unpaid taxes of Persons other than the Target and its Subsidiaries under Reg. §1.1502-6 (or any similar provision of state, local, or foreign law), as a transferee or successor, by contract, or otherwise,[12] (d) all liabilities of the Target for costs and expenses (including legal fees and expenses) the Target and the Target Stockholders have incurred in connection with this Agreement and the transactions contemplated hereby, (e) [all liabilities and obligations of the Target under its Employee Benefit Plans],[13] (f) all liabilities and obligations of the Target under the agreements, contracts, leases, licenses, and other arrangements referred to in the definition of Acquired Assets, (g) all liabilities and obligations of or relating to the Target with respect to environmental matters, including without limitation those arising under

---

Stockholders is designed to address this situation by making the *Target Stockholders* responsible for the post-Closing covenants (including the post-Closing indemnification provisions).

[10] *See* the footnote to §2(b) below for an important discussion of certain tax issues which may affect the drafting of this definition as it concerns liabilities of the Target which have not yet matured into a deduction for tax purposes.

[11] This Agreement provides that the *Buyer* will be responsible for the Target-level income tax on the sale of assets. This means the Target Stockholders will receive approximately the same after-tax sales proceeds (i.e., when the Target liquidates and dissolves) as if they had sold their Target Shares directly to the Buyer. *See* ¶107.1 for a discussion of this corporate-level tax (i.e., after GU Repeal) on transactions structured as a sale of assets.

The Buyer, of course, will seek to avoid assuming this Target-level tax. Sample acquisition agreement 2003.1 (the *pro-buyer* asset purchase agreement) contains provisions that are more favorable to the Buyer in this regard.

[12] If the Target has been a member of an Affiliated Group filing a consolidated federal income tax return, the Target (or its successor) will be jointly and severally liable under Reg. §1.1502-6 for certain tax liabilities incurred by such Affiliated Group for a tax year when the Target was a member of such Affiliated Group for all or part of such tax year. *See* ¶210.

The Target may also be liable for the unpaid taxes of third parties under similar provisions of state, local, or foreign law, as a transferee or successor, by contract (e.g., a tax sharing agreement), or otherwise.

This provision is designed to ensure that the Buyer will assume all such liability for the unpaid taxes of persons other than the Target and its Subsidiaries.

[13] *See* the provisions in §8(p) below with respect to employee benefits matters.

Environmental, Health, and Safety Requirements[14], (h) all obligations of the Target to indemnify any Person (including any of the Target Stockholders) by reason of the fact that such Person was a director, officer, employee, or agent of the Target or was serving at the request of the Target as a partner, trustee, director, officer, employee, or agent of another entity (whether such indemnification is for judgments, damages, penalties, fines, costs, amounts paid in settlement, losses, expenses, or otherwise and whether such indemnification is pursuant to any statute, charter document, bylaw, agreement, or otherwise),[15] and (i) all other liabilities and obligations of the Target set forth in the Disclosure Schedule; *provided, however*, that the Assumed Liabilities shall not include any liability or obligation of the Target under this Agreement (or under any side agreement between the Target on the one hand and the Buyer on the other hand entered into on or after the date of this Agreement).[16]

"Buyer" has the meaning set forth in the preface above.

"Buyer Note" has the meaning set forth in §2(c) below.

---

[14] This provision requires the Buyer to assume all environmental liabilities relating to the Target.

Sample acquisition agreement 2003.1 (the *pro-buyer* asset purchase agreement) leaves with the Target all environmental liabilities (other than those shown on the face of the Most Recent Balance Sheet) of the Target.

Sample acquisition agreement 2003.3 (the *neutral* asset purchase agreement) states that the Buyer assumes those environmental liabilities specifically set forth on the Disclosure Schedule to that agreement.

[15] This *pro-seller* asset purchase agreement provides that the Buyer will assume all obligations of the Target to indemnify any Person (including any of the Target Stockholders), by reason of the fact that such Person was, before the asset purchase, a director or other officeholder of the Target entitled to indemnification from the Target, with respect to any matter whatsoever. Since the Target will liquidate and dissolve immediately after the Closing, this assumption of its indemnification obligations may be necessary in order to protect its former directors and other officeholders with respect to their service through the Closing. The provision is also consistent with sample acquisition agreement 2002.2 (the pro-seller *stock* purchase agreement), where the Target will retain its indemnification obligations with respect to former directors and other officeholders even after the Buyer purchases the Target Shares.

Sample acquisition agreement 2003.1 (the *pro-buyer* asset purchase agreement), on the other hand, provides that the Buyer will not assume any obligation of the Target to indemnify any Person (including any of the Target Stockholders), by reason of the fact that such Person was, before the asset purchase, a director or other officeholder of the Target entitled to indemnification from the Target, with respect to any matter whatsoever. This provision relates in part to the surprising decision in Heffernan v. Pacific Dunlop GNB Corporation, 965 F.2d 369 (7th Cir. 1992). *See* §8(g) of sample acquisition agreement 2002.1 (the pro-buyer *stock* purchase agreement) and the footnote thereto. Although *Heffernan* involved a purchase of stock, rather than a purchase of assets, the asset purchase covered by this Agreement presents many of the same concerns. *See also* §4(g) of the Agreement with Target Stockholders (sample acquisition agreement 2003.1.2) accompanying sample acquisition agreement 2003.1.

This *pro-seller* asset purchase agreement does not contain such an anti-*Heffernan* provision, although the Buyer may seek such a provision.

[16] This definition of Assumed Liabilities is relatively broad. The Buyer is assuming all liabilities and obligations of the Target (whether known or unknown, whether asserted or unasserted, whether absolute or contingent, whether accrued or unaccrued, whether liquidated or unliquidated, and whether due or to become due), including (i) unpaid taxes for periods prior to the Closing, (ii) income, transfer, sales, use, and other taxes arising in connection with the transaction, (iii) costs and expenses

"Cash" means cash and cash equivalents (including marketable securities and short term investments) calculated in accordance with GAAP applied on a basis consistent with the preparation of the Financial Statements.

"Closing" has the meaning set forth in §2(e) below.

"Closing Date" has the meaning set forth in §2(e) below.

"COBRA" means the requirements of Part 6 of Subtitle B of Title I of ERISA and Code §4980B and of any similar state law.

"Code" means the Internal Revenue Code of 1986, as amended.

"Confidential Information" means any information concerning the businesses and affairs of the Target and its Subsidiaries that is not already generally available to the public.

"Deferred Intercompany Transaction" has the meaning set forth in Reg. §1. 1502-13.

"Disclosure Schedule" has the meaning set forth in §3 below.

"Employee Benefit Plan" means any "employee benefit plan" (as such term is defined in ERISA §3(3)) and any other [material] employee benefit plan, program or arrangement of any kind.

"Employee Pension Benefit Plan" has the meaning set forth in ERISA §3(2).

"Employee Welfare Benefit Plan" has the meaning set forth in ERISA §3(1).

"Environmental, Health, and Safety Requirements" shall mean all federal, state, local and foreign statutes, regulations, and ordinances concerning public health and safety, worker health and safety, and pollution or protection of the environment, including without limitation all those relating to the presence, use, production, generation, handling, transportation, treatment, storage, disposal, distribution, labeling, testing, processing, discharge, release, threatened release, control, or cleanup of any hazardous materials, substances or wastes, as such requirements are enacted and in effect on or prior to the Closing Date.[17]

---

arising in connection with the transaction, (iv) contracts with third parties, (v) employee benefit plans, and (vi) matters set forth in the Disclosure Schedule. The Buyer may seek to assume only certain specified liabilities and obligations. Sample acquisition agreement 2003.1 (the *pro-buyer* asset purchase agreement) contains a narrower definition of Assumed Liabilities.

[17] Sample acquisition agreement 2003.1 (the *pro-buyer* asset purchase agreement) explicitly extends this definition to include legal requirements enacted and in effect prior to, on, or after the Closing Date and also includes within this definition contractual obligations and common law.

Sample acquisition agreement 2003.3 (the *neutral* asset purchase agreement) is silent as to the time frame for enactment of covered Environmental, Health, and Safety Requirements and also includes within this definition common law.

"ERISA" means the Employee Retirement Income Security Act of 1974, as amended.

"ERISA Affiliate" means each entity which is treated as a single employer with the Target for purposes of Code §414.

"Excess Loss Account" has the meaning set forth in Reg. §1.1502-19.

"Financial Statement" has the meaning set forth in §3(g) below.

"GAAP" means United States generally accepted accounting principles as in effect from time to time.

"Hart-Scott-Rodino Act" means the Hart-Scott-Rodino Antitrust Improvements Act of 1976, as amended.

"Income Tax" means any federal, state, local, or foreign income tax, including any interest, penalty, or addition thereto, whether disputed or not.

"Income Tax Return" means any return, declaration, report, claim for refund, or information return or statement relating to Income Taxes, including any schedule or attachment thereto.

"Knowledge" means actual knowledge without independent investigation.[18]

"Most Recent Financial Statements" has the meaning set forth in §3(g) below.

"Most Recent Fiscal Month End" has the meaning set forth in §3(g) below.

"Multiemployer Plan" has the meaning set forth in ERISA §3(37).

"Ordinary Course of Business" means the ordinary course of business consistent with past custom and practice (including with respect to quantity and frequency).

"Party" has the meaning set forth in the preface above.

"PBGC" means the Pension Benefit Guaranty Corporation.

"Person" means an individual, a partnership, a corporation, an association, a joint stock company, a trust, a joint venture, an unincorporated organization, or a governmental entity (or any department, agency, or political subdivision thereof).

---

[18] Sample acquisition agreement 2003.1 (the *pro-buyer* asset purchase agreement) defines "Knowledge" as actual knowledge after reasonable investigation.

"Purchase Price" has the meaning set forth in §2(c) below.

"Reportable Event" has the meaning set forth in ERISA §4043.

"Securities Act" means the Securities Act of 1933, as amended.

"Securities Exchange Act" means the Securities Exchange Act of 1934, as amended.

"Security Interest" means any mortgage, pledge, lien, encumbrance, charge, or other security interest, *other than* (a) mechanic's, materialmen's, and similar liens, (b) liens for taxes not yet due and payable [or for taxes that the taxpayer is contesting in good faith through appropriate proceedings], (c) purchase money liens and liens securing rental payments under capital lease arrangements, and (d) other liens arising in the Ordinary Course of Business and not incurred in connection with the borrowing of money.

"Subsidiary" means any corporation with respect to which a specified Person (or a Subsidiary thereof) owns a majority of the common stock or has the power to vote or direct the voting of sufficient securities to elect a majority of the directors.[19]

"Target" has the meaning set forth in the preface above.

"Target Share" means any share of the Common Stock, par value $_____ per share, of the Target.[20]

"Target Stockholder" means any person who or which holds any Target Shares.

2. *Basic Transaction.*

(a) *Purchase and Sale of Assets.* On and subject to the terms and conditions of this Agreement, the Buyer agrees to purchase from the Target, and the Target agrees to sell, transfer, convey, and deliver to the Buyer, all of the Acquired Assets at the Closing for the consideration specified below in this §2.

(b) *Assumption of Liabilities.* On and subject to the terms and conditions of this Agreement, the Buyer agrees to assume and become responsible for all of the Assumed Liabilities at the Closing. The Buyer will not assume or have any responsibility, however, with respect to any other obligation or liability of the Target not included within the definition of Assumed Liabilities.[21]

---

[19] It may be necessary to revise this definition if, for example, the Target has subsidiary *partnerships.*

[20] It may be necessary to revise this definition if the Target has additional classes of capital stock.

[21] In a taxable purchase of the Target's assets, the Target may have liabilities which have not yet matured into a deduction for tax purposes. For example, (1) a cash method Target may have accrued (but unpaid) operating liabilities, (2) a cash method or an accrual method Target may have contingent liabilities, (3) a cash method or an accrual method Target may have unfunded pension liabilities, and (4) an accrual method Target may have liabilities as to which the "all events" test has been satisfied

(c) *Purchase Price.*[22] The Buyer agrees to pay to the Target at the Closing $_____ (the *"Purchase Price"*) by delivery of (i) its promissory notes (the *"Buyer Notes"*) in the form of Exhibit B attached hereto in the aggregate principal amount of $_____ and (ii) cash for the balance of the Purchase Price payable by wire transfer or delivery of other immediately available funds.[23]

(d) *Cash Payment to Target.*[24] Immediately prior to the Closing, the Target will cause its Subsidiaries to pay the Target an aggregate amount equal to the consoli-

---

but as to which "economic performance " (*e.g.*, payment) has not yet occurred. The tax treatment of these and other liabilities which have not yet matured into deductions is somewhat surprising. See ¶304.

Under Code §461(h), an accrual method Target can deduct liabilities which otherwise satisfy the all events test (*i.e.*, "Code §461(h) Liabilities") only as economic performance occurs. With respect to many such liabilities, economic performance occurs under the Code §461(h) regulations only when the Target has made payment with respect to the liability. See ¶304.4.

Reg. §1.461-4(d)(5) and -4(g)(1)(ii)(C) seems to provide that when the Target sells the Buyer a trade or business and, as part of the sale, the Buyer *"expressly assumes"* a Code §461(h) Liability, the Target can deduct that liability (assuming that the Code §461(h) regulations make payment the proper test for economic performance) in the taxable year in which the sale occurred. This favorable tax result follows from the fact that the Target will be deemed to have made payment with respect to the liability when the amount of the liability (assumed by the Buyer) is included in the Target's amount realized on the sale of assets. The regulation is, however, unclear on the meaning of the phrase "expressly assumes." See ¶304.4.

Cautious taxpayers should accordingly consider taking some or all of the following steps: (i) the Parties should specifically enumerate in this Agreement as many as practicable of the Code §461(h) Liabilities which the Buyer is assuming; (ii) the Parties should specifically state in this Agreement that the Buyer is "expressly assuming" not only these enumerated liabilities but also any categories of *unenumerated* Code §461(h) Liabilities which the Buyer is assuming; and (iii) the boards of directors of the respective Parties should adopt resolutions specifically stating that the Buyer is "expressly assuming" these Code §461(h) Liabilities.

Reg. §1.461-4(d)(5) and -4(g)(1)(ii)(C) is applicable by its terms only with respect to Code §461(h) Liabilities. However, its premise that the Target will be deemed to have made payment with respect to a liability when the amount of the liability (assumed by the Buyer) is included in the Target's amount realized on the sale of assets may have a broader application. For this reason, cautious taxpayers may want to apply the advice in the preceding paragraph of this footnote to cover *all* liabilities which the Buyer is assuming as to which the Target has not yet become entitled to a deduction under the Code.

[22] The Target may seek to have the Buyer make an earnest money deposit upon execution of this Agreement. If the transaction were thereafter completed, the deposit would be applied to the Purchase Price. If the transaction were thereafter aborted, the deposit would be refunded to the Buyer or paid to the Target as liquidated damages depending on the terms of this Agreement and the reasons for the termination.

[23] Sample acquisition agreement 2002.5 contains additional provisions for use where there is to be a post-Closing Purchase Price adjustment based on the consolidated net book value for the Target and its Subsidiaries as of the Closing. That sample acquisition agreement can be adapted for other post-Closing Purchase Price adjustments (such as a comparison of consolidated working capital with consolidated liabilities as of the Closing *or* a contingent earnout based on consolidated earnings for a specified period after the Closing).

Sample acquisition agreement 2002.5 is, however, intended for use with sample acquisition agreements 2002.1, 2002.2, and 2002.3 (the *stock* purchase agreements) and must be modified prior to use with this *asset* purchase agreement.

[24] This *pro-seller* Agreement permits the Target to retain the consolidated cash of the Target and its Subsidiaries (net of unpaid Taxes for which the Buyer will become responsible) at the Closing. See

dated Cash of its Subsidiaries as of the Closing. The Target may cause any of its Subsidiaries to make any such payment to the Target in the form of a dividend or a redemption.[25]

(e) *The Closing.* The closing of the transactions contemplated by this Agreement (the *"Closing"*) shall take place at the offices of _____ in _____, _____ commencing at 9:00 a.m. local time on the [second] business day following the satisfaction or waiver of all conditions to the obligations of the Parties to consummate the transactions contemplated hereby (other than conditions with respect to actions the respective Parties will take at the Closing itself) or such other date as the Parties may mutually determine (the *"Closing Date"*); *provided, however* that the Closing Date shall be no earlier than _____, 19____.

(f) *Deliveries at the Closing.* At the Closing, (i) the Target will deliver to the Buyer the various certificates, instruments, and documents referred to in §6(a) below; (ii) the Buyer will deliver to the Target the various certificates, instruments, and documents referred to in §6(b) below; (iii) the Target will execute, acknowledge (if appropriate), and deliver to the Buyer (A) assignments (including real property and intellectual property transfer documents) in the forms attached hereto as Exhibits C-1 through C-_____ and (B) such other instruments of sale, transfer, conveyance, and assignment as the Buyer and its counsel [reasonably] may request; (iv) the Buyer will execute, acknowledge (if appropriate), and deliver to the Target (A) an assumption in the form attached hereto as Exhibit D and (B) such other instruments of assumption as the Target and its counsel [reasonably] may request; and (v) the Buyer will deliver to the Target the consideration specified in §2(c) above.

(g) *Allocation.* [The Parties agree to allocate the Purchase Price (and all other capitalizable costs) among the Acquired Assets for all purposes (including financial accounting and tax purposes) in accordance with the allocation schedule attached hereto as Exhibit E.][26]

---

the definition of Acquired Assets in §1 above. This §2(d) permits the Target to cause its Subsidiaries to distribute all of their cash to the Target at the Closing in order to facilitate the intended cash retention.

Sample acquisition agreement 2003.1 (the *pro-buyer* asset purchase agreement), on the other hand, provides that the Buyer will acquire the consolidated cash of the Target and its Subsidiaries. *See* the definition of Acquired Assets in §1 thereof. The *pro-buyer* agreement lacks a provision comparable to this §2(d) (since there is no need for the Subsidiaries to distribute their cash to the Target at the Closing if the Target will not retain any of the consolidated cash).

[25] The Parties should determine whether there is any external restriction or prohibition on the type of cash payment by the Subsidiaries contemplated by this §2(d) (such as a loan covenant or a statutory provision concerning dividends and stock redemptions). The Parties should also consider any possible difference in tax treatment between a cash dividend and a partial stock redemption.

[26] The 1986 Act generally requires the Buyer and the Target to allocate the Buyer's aggregate basis (i.e., the Purchase Price *plus* the Assumed Liabilities *plus* the expenses of the transaction) among the Acquired Assets using the residual method. *See* ¶403. The Parties should omit this provision if they do not reach agreement on a particular allocation schedule.

3. *Representations and Warranties of the Target.*[27] The Target represents and warrants to the Buyer that the statements contained in this §3 are correct and complete as of the date of this Agreement and will be correct and complete as of the Closing Date (as though made then and as though the Closing Date were substituted for the date of this Agreement throughout this §3), except as set forth in the disclosure schedule accompanying this Agreement and initialed by the Parties (the *"Disclosure Schedule"*).[28] The Disclosure Schedule will be arranged in paragraphs corresponding to the lettered and numbered paragraphs contained in this §3.

(a) *Organization of the Target.* The Target is a corporation duly organized, validly existing, and in good standing under the laws of the jurisdiction of its incorporation.

(b) *Authorization of Transaction.* The Target has full power and authority (including full corporate power and authority) to execute and deliver this Agreement and to perform its obligations hereunder. Without limiting the generality of the foregoing, the board of directors of the Target and the Target Stockholders have duly authorized the execution, delivery, and performance of this Agreement by the Target.[29] This Agreement constitutes the valid and legally binding obligation of the Target, enforceable in accordance with its terms and conditions.

---

[27] This *pro-seller* §3 contains relatively few representations and warranties concerning the Target and its Subsidiaries, and is qualified frequently with references to "knowledge" (defined as the actual knowledge of any Target Stockholder without independent investigation) and "materiality" (defined generally as having a material adverse effect on the financial condition of the Target and its Subsidiaries taken as a whole or on the ability of the Parties to consummate the transactions contemplated by this Agreement).

The Buyer will seek to have the Target make extensive representations and warranties concerning the Target and its Subsidiaries, without any qualification as to materiality and with only occasional references to knowledge (defined in a manner more favorable to the Buyer as the actual knowledge of any Target Stockholder or any director, officer, or employee of any of the Target and its Subsidiaries after reasonable investigation). Sample acquisition agreement 2003.1 (the *pro-buyer* asset purchase agreement) contains comparable representations and warranties which are more favorable to the Buyer.

[28] The Buyer will have a closing condition (*see* §6(a)(i) below) and post-Closing indemnification rights (*see* §4(b) of the accompanying Agreement with Target Stockholders) with respect to certain misrepresentations and breaches of warranty. The Buyer will not, however, have a closing condition or post-Closing indemnification rights with respect to any adverse matter which the Target discloses in the Disclosure Schedule. This is because the disclosure will cure any misrepresentation or breach of warranty that might otherwise have existed. Thus, where the Target discloses an adverse matter in the Disclosure Schedule, the Buyer may seek (a) to avoid assuming responsibility for the matter (see the definition of Assumed Liabilities in §1 above), (b) to add a specific closing condition requiring an acceptable resolution of the matter, and/or (c) to obtain specific post-Closing indemnification against the matter.

Sample acquisition agreement 2003.1 (the *pro-buyer* asset purchase agreement) contains additional provisions to the effect that the Target's disclosures will be ineffective unless they meet specified standards for particularity and detail. *See* §8(m) of sample acquisition agreement 2003.1.

[29] The Target must obtain the approval of its board of directors *and* the approval of its stockholders in order to sell all or substantially all of its assets. *See* ¶2001.2.2.2. This Agreement assumes the Target has already obtained the requisite corporate approvals.

If the Parties wish to enter into this Agreement before the Target has obtained the approval of its *stockholders*, the Parties should revise this Agreement to include (a) a covenant calling for the Target to obtain such approval prior to the Closing and (b) a closing condition for each of the parties to the

(c) *Noncontravention.* [To the Knowledge of any of the Target Stockholders,] neither the execution and the delivery of this Agreement, nor the consummation of the transactions contemplated hereby (including the assignments and assumptions referred to in §2 above), will [(i)] violate any constitution, statute, regulation, rule, injunction, judgment, order, decree, ruling, charge, or other restriction of any government, governmental agency, or court to which any of the Target and its Subsidiaries is subject or any provision of the charter or bylaws of any of the Target and its Subsidiaries [or (ii) conflict with, result in a breach of, constitute a default under, result in the acceleration of, create in any party the right to accelerate, terminate, modify, or cancel, or require any notice under any agreement, contract, lease, license, instrument, or other arrangement to which any of the Target and its Subsidiaries is a party or by which it is bound or to which any of its assets is subject (or result in the imposition of any Security Interest upon any of its assets), except where the violation, conflict, breach, default, acceleration, termination, modification, cancellation, failure to give notice, or Security Interest would not have a material adverse effect on the financial condition of the Target and its Subsidiaries taken as a whole or on the ability of the Parties to consummate the transactions contemplated by this Agreement]. [To the Knowledge of any of the Target Stockholders,] none of the Target and its Subsidiaries needs to give any notice to, make any filing with, or obtain any authorization, consent, or approval of any government or governmental agency in order for the Parties to consummate the transactions contemplated by this Agreement (including the assignments and assumptions referred to in §2 above) [, except where the failure to give notice, to file, or to obtain any authorization, consent, or approval would not have a material adverse effect on the financial condition of the Target and its Subsidiaries taken as a whole or on the ability of the Parties to consummate the transactions contemplated by this Agreement].[30]

(d) *Brokers' Fees.* The Target has no liability or obligation to pay any fees or commissions to any broker, finder, or agent with respect to the transactions contemplated by this Agreement for which the Buyer could become liable or obligated. None of the Subsidiaries of the Target has any liability or obligation to pay any fees or commissions to any broker, finder, or agent with respect to the transactions contemplated by this Agreement.

---

effect that the Target *has* obtained the approval. *Compare* sample acquisition agreement 2005 (the reverse subsidiary merger agreement) which contemplates the target corporation will obtain the approval of its stockholders between the signing of the merger agreement and the Closing.

The Parties generally will not enter into an asset purchase agreement (or for that matter a merger agreement) until the Target has obtained the approval of its *board of directors.*

[30] The Buyer may seek to have the Target include the bracketed language concerning required notices and consents under arrangements with third parties. The Target, on the other hand, may seek to include the bracketed language concerning knowledge and materiality (particularly if the language concerning required notices and consents is included). *Compare* the representation and warranty from the *Buyer* in §4(c) below.

(e) *Title to Tangible Assets.* The Target and its Subsidiaries have good title to, or a valid leasehold interest in, the material tangible assets they use regularly in the conduct of their businesses.

(f) *Subsidiaries.* §3(f) of the Disclosure Schedule sets forth for each Subsidiary of the Target (i) its name and jurisdiction of incorporation, (ii) the number of shares of authorized capital stock of each class of its capital stock, (iii) the number of issued and outstanding shares of each class of its capital stock, the names of the holders thereof, and the number of shares held by each such holder, (iv) the number of shares of its capital stock held in treasury, and (v) its directors and officers. Each Subsidiary of the Target is a corporation duly organized, validly existing, and in good standing under the laws of the jurisdiction of its incorporation. Each Subsidiary of the Target is duly authorized to conduct business and is in good standing under the laws of each jurisdiction where such qualification is required, except where the lack of such qualification would not have a material adverse effect on the financial condition of the Target and its Subsidiaries taken as a whole. Each Subsidiary of the Target has full corporate power and authority to carry on the businesses in which it is engaged and to own and use the properties owned and used by it. All of the issued and outstanding shares of capital stock of each Subsidiary of the Target have been duly authorized and are validly issued, fully paid, and nonassessable. One of the Target and its Subsidiaries holds of record and owns beneficially all of the outstanding shares of each Subsidiary of the Target.

(g) *Financial Statements.*[31] Attached hereto as Exhibit F are the following financial statements (collectively the *"Financial Statements"*): (i) audited consolidated balance sheets and statements of income, changes in stockholders' equity, and cash flow as of and for the fiscal years ended _____, 19_____, _____, 19_____, _____, 19_____, _____, 19_____, and _____, 19_____ for the Target and its Subsidiaries; and (ii) unaudited consolidated balance sheets and statements of income, changes in stockholders' equity, and cash flow (the *"Most Recent Financial Statements"* as of and for the _____ months ended _____, 19_____ (the *"Most Recent Fiscal Month End"*) for the Target and its Subsidiaries. The Financial Statements (including the notes thereto) have been prepared in accordance with GAAP applied on a consistent basis throughout the periods covered thereby and present fairly the financial condition of the Target and its Subsidiaries as of such dates and the results of operations of the Target and its Subsidiaries for such periods;[32] *provided, however,* that the Most Recent Financial Statements are subject to normal year-end adjustments and lack footnotes and other presentation items.

---

[31] This *pro-seller* asset purchase agreement does not contain a representation and warranty concerning undisclosed liabilities. *See* sample acquisition agreement 2003.1 (the *pro-buyer* asset purchase agreement) for an example of such a provision.

[32] Sample acquisition agreement 2003.1 (the *pro-buyer* asset purchase agreement) contains additional representations and warranties to the effect that the financial statements are correct and complete and consistent with the books and records of the Target and its Subsidiaries.

(h) *Events Subsequent to Most Recent Fiscal Month End.* Since the Most Recent Fiscal Month End, there has not been any material adverse change in the financial condition of the Target and its Subsidiaries taken as a whole. Without limiting the generality of the foregoing, since that date none of the Target and its Subsidiaries has engaged in any practice, taken any action, or entered into any transaction outside the Ordinary Course of Business the primary purpose or effect of which has been to generate or preserve Cash.[33]

(i) *Legal Compliance.* To the Knowledge of any of the Target Stockholders, each of the Target and its Subsidiaries has complied with all applicable laws (including rules, regulations, codes, plans, injunctions, judgments, orders, decrees, rulings, and charges thereunder) of federal, state, local, and foreign governments (and all agencies thereof), except where the failure to comply would not have a material adverse effect upon the financial condition of the Target and its Subsidiaries taken as a whole.

(j) *Tax Matters.*[34]

(i) Each of the Target and its Subsidiaries has filed all Income Tax Returns that it was required to file, and has paid all Income Taxes shown thereon as owing, except where the failure to file Income Tax Returns or to pay Income Taxes would not have a material adverse effect on the financial condition of the Target and its Subsidiaries taken as a whole.[35]

(ii) §3(j) of the Disclosure Schedule lists all Income Tax Returns filed with respect to any of the Target and its Subsidiaries for taxable periods ended on or after _____, 19____, indicates those Income Tax Returns that have been

---

[33] The requirement to disclose certain matters which have had an effect on the amount of cash relates to the fact that the Target will retain the consolidated cash of the Target and its Subsidiaries (net of unpaid Taxes for which the Buyer will become responsible) at the Closing. *See* §2(d) above and the definition of Acquired Assets in §1 above.

This disclosure requirement is designed to uncover pre-Closing activities of the Target and its Subsidiaries which were outside the Ordinary Course of Business and either (a) intended to generate cash (such as borrowings, sales of assets, and collections of accounts receivable) or (b) intended to eliminate expenditures (such as failures to make loan repayments, purchase assets, pay accounts payable, perform maintenance and repairs, conduct research and development, and engage in advertising and promotion).

[34] This Agreement provides that the Buyer will assume all tax liabilities of the Target with respect to periods prior to the Closing. *See* the definition of Assumed Liabilities in §1 above. In addition, the Buyer will become indirectly responsible for all of the tax liabilities of the *Subsidiaries* when the Buyer acquires their capital stock as part of the Acquired Assets. These representations and warranties concerning taxes (and the post-Closing indemnification provisions in §4(b) of the accompanying Agreement with Target Stockholders) are designed to protect the Buyer against tax liabilities it does not intend to assume.

[35] Sample acquisition agreement 2003.1 (the *pro-buyer* asset purchase agreement) contains a broader representation to the effect that each of the Target and its Subsidiaries has filed all Tax Returns that it was required to file, that all such Tax Returns were correct and complete in all respects, and that all taxes owed by any of the Target and its Subsidiaries (whether or not shown on any Tax Return) have been paid.

audited, and indicates those Income Tax Returns that currently are the subject of audit. The Target has delivered to the Buyer correct and complete copies of all federal Income Tax Returns, examination reports, and statements of deficiencies assessed against or agreed to by any of the Target and its Subsidiaries since _____, 19___.

(iii) None of the Target and its Subsidiaries has waived any statute of limitations in respect of Income Taxes or agreed to any extension of time with respect to an Income Tax assessment or deficiency.

(iv) None of the Target and its Subsidiaries is a party to any Income Tax allocation or sharing agreement.

(v) [To the Knowledge of any of the Target Stockholders, none of the Target and its Subsidiaries has been a member of an Affiliated Group filing a consolidated federal Income Tax Return (other than a group the common parent of which was the Target).][36]

(k) *Real Property.*

(i) §3(k)(i) of the Disclosure Schedule lists all real property that any of the Target and its Subsidiaries owns. With respect to each such parcel of owned real property, and except for matters which would not have a material adverse effect on the financial condition of the Target and its Subsidiaries taken as a whole:

(A) the identified owner has good and marketable title to the parcel of real property, free and clear of any Security Interest, easement, covenant, or other restriction, except for installments of special assessments not yet delinquent, recorded easements, covenants, and other restrictions, and utility easements, building restrictions, zoning restrictions, and other easements

---

[36] If the Target or a Subsidiary has been a member of an Affiliated Group filing a consolidated federal income tax return, such corporation (or its successor) will be jointly and severally liable under Reg. §1.1502-6 for certain tax liabilities incurred by such Affiliated Group for a tax year when such corporation was a member of such Affiliated Group for all or part of such tax year. *See* ¶210.

The Target or a Subsidiary may also be liable for the unpaid taxes of third parties under similar provisions of state, local, or foreign law, as a transferee or successor, by contract (e.g., a tax sharing agreement), or otherwise.

This Agreement provides that the Buyer will assume any such liability of the *Target* for the unpaid taxes of third parties. *See* the definition of "Assumed Liabilities" in §1 above. In addition, the Buyer will become responsible for any such liability of the *Subsidiaries* when the Buyer acquires their capital stock as part of the Acquired Assets.

The Buyer may seek additional protection from the Target and the Target Stockholders against any liability for the unpaid taxes of third parties. Sample acquisition agreement 2003.1 (the *pro-buyer* asset purchase agreement), for example, contains a narrower definition of "Assumed Liabilities," a broader representation and warranty, and specific post-closing indemnification provisions in this regard. *See* §1 and §3(k)(v) of sample acquisition agreement 2003.1 and §4(b)(iii) of Exhibit A thereto.

and restrictions existing generally with respect to properties of a similar character;

(B) there are no leases, subleases, licenses, concessions, or other agreements granting to any party or parties the right of use or occupancy of any portion of the parcel of real property; and

(C) there are no outstanding options or rights of first refusal to purchase the parcel of real property, or any portion thereof or interest therein.

(ii) §3(k)(ii) of the Disclosure Schedule lists all real property leased or subleased to any of the Target and its Subsidiaries. The Target has delivered to the Buyer correct and complete copies of the leases and subleases listed in §3(k)(ii) of the Disclosure Schedule (as amended to date). To the Knowledge of any of the Target Stockholders, each lease and sublease listed in §3(k)(ii) of the Disclosure Schedule is legal, valid, binding, enforceable, and in full force and effect, except where the illegality, invalidity, nonbinding nature, unenforceability, or ineffectiveness would not have a material adverse effect on the financial condition of the Target and its Subsidiaries taken as a whole.

(l) *Intellectual Property.* §3(l) of the Disclosure Schedule identifies each patent or registration which has been issued to any of the Target and its Subsidiaries with respect to any of its intellectual property, identifies each pending patent application or application for registration which any of the Target and its Subsidiaries has made with respect to any of its intellectual property, [and identifies each license, agreement, or other permission which any of the Target and its Subsidiaries has granted to any third party with respect to any of its intellectual property].

(m) *Contracts.* §3(m) of the Disclosure Schedule lists all written contracts and other written agreements to which any of the Target and its Subsidiaries is a party the performance of which will involve consideration in excess of $_____. The Target has delivered to the Buyer a correct and complete copy of each contract or other agreement listed in §3(m) of the Disclosure Schedule (as amended to date).

(n) *Powers of Attorney.* To the Knowledge of any of the Target Stockholders, there are no outstanding powers of attorney executed on behalf of any of the Target and its Subsidiaries.

(o) *Litigation.* §3(o) of the Disclosure Schedule sets forth each instance in which any of the Target and its Subsidiaries (i) is subject to any outstanding injunction, judgment, order, decree, ruling, or charge or (ii) is a party to any action, suit, proceeding, hearing, or investigation of, in, or before any court or quasi-judicial or administrative agency of any federal, state, local, or foreign jurisdiction, except where the injunction, judgment, order, decree, ruling, action, suit, proceeding, hearing, or investigation would not have a material adverse effect on the financial condition of the Target and its Subsidiaries taken as a whole.

(p) *Employee Benefits.*

(i) §3(p) of the Disclosure Schedule lists each Employee Benefit Plan that any of the Target and its Subsidiaries maintains or to which any of the Target and its Subsidiaries contributes.

(A) To the Knowledge of any of the Target Stockholders, each such Employee Benefit Plan (and each related trust, insurance contract, or fund) has been maintained, funded and administered in accordance with the terms of such Employee Benefit Plan and complies in form and in operation in all respects with the applicable requirements of ERISA and the Code, except where the failure to comply would not have a material adverse effect on the financial condition of the Target and its Subsidiaries taken as a whole.

(B) All contributions (including all employer contributions and employee salary reduction contributions) which are due have been made to each such Employee Benefit Plan which is an Employee Pension Benefit Plan. All premiums or other payments which are due have been paid with respect to each such Employee Benefit Plan which is an Employee Welfare Benefit Plan.

(C) Each such Employee Benefit Plan which is intended to meet the requirements of a "qualified plan" under Code §401(a) has received a determination letter from the Internal Revenue Service to the effect that it meets the requirements of Code §401(a).

(D) As of the last day of the most recent prior plan year, the market value of assets under each such Employee Benefit Plan which is an Employee Pension Benefit Plan (other than any Multiemployer Plan) equaled or exceeded the present value of liabilities thereunder (determined in accordance with then current funding assumptions).

(E) The Target has delivered to the Buyer correct and complete copies of the plan documents and summary plan descriptions, the most recent determination letter received from the Internal Revenue Service, the most recent annual report (IRS Form 5500), and all related trust agreements, insurance contracts, and other funding arrangements which implement each such Employee Benefit Plan.

(ii) [With respect to each Employee Benefit Plan that any of the Target and its Subsidiaries or any ERISA affiliate maintains or has maintained during the prior six years or to which any of them contributes, or has been required to contribute during the prior six years:

(A) No action, suit, proceeding, hearing, or investigation with respect to the administration or the investment of the assets of any such Employee Benefit Plan (other than routine claims for benefits) is pending, except where the action, suit, proceeding, hearing, or investigation would not have a material adverse effect on the financial condition of the Target and its Subsidiaries taken as a whole.

(B) None of the Target and its Subsidiaries has incurred any liability to the PBGC (other than PBGC premium payments) or otherwise under Title IV of ERISA (including any withdrawal liability) with respect to any such Employee Benefit Plan which is an Employee Pension Benefit Plan.][37]

(q) *Environmental, Health, and Safety Matters.*[38]

(i) To the Knowledge of any of the Target Stockholders, the Target and its Subsidiaries are in compliance with Environmental, Health, and Safety Requirements, except for such noncompliance as would not have a material adverse effect on the financial condition of the Target and its Subsidiaries taken as a whole.

(ii) To the Knowledge of any of the Target Stockholders, the Target and its Subsidiaries have not received any written notice, report or other information regarding any actual or alleged material violation of Environmental, Health, and Safety Requirements, or any material liabilities or potential material liabilities (whether accrued, absolute, contingent, unliquidated or otherwise), including any investigatory, remedial or corrective obligations, relating to the Target or its Subsidiaries or their facilities arising under Environmental, Health, and Safety Requirements, the subject of which would have a material adverse effect on the financial condition of the Target and its Subsidiaries taken as a whole.

(iii) This Section 3(q) contains the sole and exclusive representations and warranties of the Target with respect to any environmental, health, or safety

---

[37] The Target may seek to delete or qualify some or all of this §3(p)(ii).

[38] These representations and warranties concerning environmental, health, and safety matters are relatively long and detailed. A condensed version may be more appropriate when, for example, the operations of the Target and its Subsidiaries appear to have had a relatively insignificant effect upon the environment or upon public or employee health and safety.

The environmental representations in this *pro-seller* asset purchase agreement (1) are limited to matters within the Target Stockholder's knowledge, (2) are consistently limited to matters that would have a material adverse effect, (3) do not extend to strict liability for site cleanup under CERCLA or common law liability, (4) otherwise limit the disclosure and indemnification obligations of the Target, and (5) state that these environmental representations constitute the sole representation of the Target with respect to environmental, health, and safety matters.

Sample acquisition agreement 2003.1 (the *pro-buyer* asset purchase agreement) contain broader environmental, health, and safety representations, which (1) contain neither knowledge nor materiality limitations, (2) impose a broader disclosure obligation upon the Target, and (3) extend to strict liability for site cleanup under CERCLA and common law liability under current and future Environmental, Health, and Safety Requirements.

Sample acquisition agreement 2003.3 (the *neutral* asset purchase agreement) contains environmental representations which are (1) subject to certain materiality limitations and (2) are slightly more limited and focused than the corresponding *pro-buyer* representations.

matters, including without limitation any arising under any Environmental, Health, and Safety Requirements.

(r) *Certain Business Relationships with the Target and Its Subsidiaries.* None of the Target Stockholders and their Affiliates has been involved in any material business arrangement or relationship with any of the Target and its Subsidiaries within the past 12 months, and none of the Target Stockholders and their Affiliates owns any material asset, tangible or intangible, which is used in the business of any of the Target and its Subsidiaries.

(s) *Investment.* The Target (i) understands that the Buyer Notes have not been, and will not be, registered under the Securities Act, or under any state securities laws, and are being offered and sold in reliance upon federal and state exemptions for transactions not involving any public offering, (ii) is acquiring the Buyer Notes solely for its own account for investment purposes, and not with a view to the distribution thereof (except to the Target Stockholders), (iii) is a sophisticated investor with knowledge and experience in business and financial matters, (iv) has received certain information concerning the Buyer and has had the opportunity to obtain additional information as desired in order to evaluate the merits and the risks inherent in holding the Buyer Notes, (v) is able to bear the economic risk and lack of liquidity inherent in holding the Buyer Notes, and (vi) is an Accredited Investor for the reasons set forth in §3(r) of the Disclosure Schedule.[39]

(t) *Disclaimer of Other Representations and Warranties.* Except as expressly set forth in this Section 3, the Target makes no representation or warranty, express or implied, at law or in equity, in respect of any of its assets (including, without limitation, the Acquired Assets), liabilities or operations, including, without limitation, with respect to merchantability or fitness for any particular purpose, and any such other representations or warranties are hereby expressly disclaimed. Buyer hereby acknowledges and agrees that, except to the extent specifically set forth in this Section 3, the Buyer is purchasing the Acquired Assets on an "as-is, where-is" basis. Without limiting the generality of the foregoing, the Target makes no representation or warranty regarding any assets other than the Acquired Assets or any liabilities other than the Assumed Liabilities, and none shall be implied at law or in equity.[40]

---

[39] This provision contemplates that the Buyer will issue the Buyer Notes pursuant to the exemption from registration under the Securities Act contained in Regulation D. The Parties should determine whether this exemption is available in a particular transaction. If it is not, the Agreement must be modified as necessary to reflect the issuance of the Buyer Notes under a different exemption from securities registration or in an offering registered under the Securities Act.

[40] Consideration should be given to highlighting this subsection by printing it in all capital letters, particularly in jurisdictions where statutory or common law rights (e.g., implied representations and warranties) are being waived.

4. *Representations and Warranties of the Buyer.*[41] The Buyer represents and warrants to the Target (and to the Target Stockholders for purposes of the Agreement with Target Stockholders) that the statements contained in this §4 are correct and complete as of the date of this Agreement and will be correct and complete as of the Closing Date (as though made then and as though the Closing Date were substituted for the date of this Agreement throughout this §4), except as set forth in the Disclosure Schedule. The Disclosure Schedule will be arranged in paragraphs corresponding to the lettered and numbered paragraphs contained in this §4.

(a) *Organization of the Buyer.* The Buyer is a corporation duly organized, validly existing, and in good standing under the laws of the jurisdiction of its incorporation.

(b) *Authorization of Transaction.* The Buyer has full power and authority (including full corporate power and authority) to execute and deliver this Agreement and to perform its obligations hereunder. This Agreement constitutes the valid and legally binding obligation of the Buyer, enforceable in accordance with its terms and conditions.

(c) *Noncontravention.* Neither the execution and the delivery of this Agreement, nor the consummation of the transactions contemplated hereby (including the assignments and assumptions referred to in §2 above), will [(i)] violate any constitution, statute, regulation, rule, injunction, judgment, order, decree, ruling, charge, or other restriction of any government, governmental agency, or court to which the Buyer is subject or any provision of its charter or bylaws [or (ii) conflict with, result in a breach of, constitute a default under, result in the acceleration of, create in any party the right to accelerate, terminate, modify, or cancel, or require any notice under any agreement, contract, lease, license, instrument, or other arrangement to which the Buyer is a party or by which it is bound or to which any of its assets is subject]. The Buyer does not need to give any notice to, make any filing with, or obtain any authorization, consent, or approval of any government or governmental agency in order for the Parties to consummate the transactions contemplated by this Agreement (including the assignments and assumptions referred to in §2 above).

(d) *Brokers' Fees.* The Buyer has no liability or obligation to pay any fees or commissions to any broker, finder, or agent with respect to the transactions contemplated by this Agreement for which the Target could become liable or obligated.

---

[41] The Target may seek to obtain additional representations and warranties concerning the Buyer and its Subsidiaries (*e.g.,* the typical representations and warranties contained in a loan agreement or an underwriting agreement) because the Buyer is issuing the Buyer Notes to the Target as part of the Purchase Price. Any such representations and warranties would normally survive the Closing and remain applicable for so long as the Buyer Notes remained outstanding.

5. *Pre-Closing Covenants.*[42] The Parties agree as follows with respect to the period between the execution of this Agreement and the Closing.

(a) *General.* Each of the Parties will use its reasonable best efforts to take all action and to do all things necessary [, proper, or advisable] in order to consummate and make effective the transactions contemplated by this Agreement (including satisfaction, but not waiver, of the closing conditions set forth in §6 below).

(b) *Notices and Consents.* [The Target will give (and will cause each of its Subsidiaries to give) any notices to third parties, and the Target will use its reasonable best efforts (and will cause each of its Subsidiaries to use its reasonable best efforts) to obtain any third party consents, that the Buyer reasonably may request in connection with the matters referred to in §3(c) above.] Each of the Parties will (and the Target will cause each of its Subsidiaries to) give any notices to, make any filings with, and use its reasonable best efforts to obtain any authorizations, consents, and approvals of governments and governmental agencies in connection with the matters referred to in §3(c) and §4(c) above. Without limiting the generality of the foregoing, each of the Parties will file (and the Target will cause each of its Subsidiaries to file) any Notification and Report Forms and related material that it may be required to file with the Federal Trade Commission and the Antitrust Division of the United States Department of Justice under the Hart-Scott-Rodino Act, will use its reasonable best efforts to obtain (and the Target will cause each of its Subsidiaries to use its reasonable best efforts to obtain) a waiver from the applicable waiting period, and will make (and the Target will cause each of its Subsidiaries to make) any further filings pursuant thereto that may be necessary [, proper, or advisable] in connection therewith.

(c) *Operation of Business.* [The Target will not (and will not cause or permit any of its Subsidiaries to) engage in any practice, take any action, or enter into any transaction outside the Ordinary Course of Business.[43] Without limiting the generality of the foregoing,] the Target will not (and will not cause or permit any of its Subsidiaries to) engage in any practice, take any action, or enter into any transaction outside the Ordinary Course of Business the primary purpose or effect of which will be to generate or preserve Cash.[44]

---

[42] Sample acquisition agreement 2003.1 (the *pro-buyer* asset purchase agreement) contains additional pre-Closing covenants concerning preservation of the business and obtaining title insurance and surveys in preparation for the Closing.

[43] The Buyer may seek to have this covenant restrict a number of specific practices, actions, and transactions. Sample acquisition agreement 2003.1 (the *pro-buyer* asset purchase agreement) contains provisions which are more favorable to the Buyer in this regard.

[44] This covenant relates to the fact that the Target will retain the consolidated cash of the Target and its Subsidiaries (net of unpaid taxes for which the Buyer will become responsible) at the Closing. *See* §2(d) above and the definition of Acquired Assets in §1 above. The covenant is designed to prevent pre-Closing activities of the Target and its Subsidiaries which would be outside the Ordinary Course of Business and either (a) intended to generate cash (such as borrowings, sales of assets, and collections of accounts receivable) or (b) intended to eliminate expenditures (such as failures to make loan repayments, purchase assets, pay accounts payable, perform maintenance and repairs, conduct research and development, and engage in advertising and promotion).

(d) *Full Access.* [The Target will permit (and will cause each of its Subsidiaries to permit) representatives of the Buyer to have full access at all reasonable times, and in a manner so as not to interfere with the normal business operations of the Target and its Subsidiaries, to all premises, properties, personnel, books, records (including tax records), contracts, and documents of or pertaining to each of the Target and its Subsidiaries. The Buyer will treat and hold as such any Confidential Information it receives from any of the Target Stockholders, the Target, and its Subsidiaries in the course of the reviews contemplated by this §5(d), will not use any of the Confidential Information except in connection with this Agreement, and, if this Agreement is terminated for any reason whatsoever, will return to the Target and its Subsidiaries all tangible embodiments (and all copies) of the Confidential Information which are in its possession.]

(e) *Notice of Developments.*

(i) The Target may elect at any time to notify the Buyer of any development causing a breach of any of its representations and warranties in §3(g)-(p) above. Unless the Buyer has the right to terminate this Agreement pursuant to §7(a)(ii) below by reason of the development and exercises that right within the period of [10 business days] referred to in §7(a)(ii) below, the written notice pursuant to this §5(e)(i) will be deemed to have amended the Disclosure Schedule, to have qualified the representations and warranties contained in §3 above, and to have cured any misrepresentation or breach of warranty that otherwise might have existed hereunder by reason of the development.[45]

(ii) Each Party will give prompt written notice to the other Party of any material adverse development causing a breach of any of its own representations and warranties in §3(a)-(f) and §4 above. No disclosure by any Party pursuant to this §5(e)(ii), however, shall be deemed to amend or supplement the Disclosure Schedule or to prevent or cure any misrepresentation or breach of warranty.[46]

(f) *Exclusivity.* The Target will not (and will not cause or permit any of its Subsidiaries to) solicit, initiate, or encourage the submission of any proposal or offer from any Person relating to the acquisition of all or substantially all of the capital stock or assets of any of the Target and its Subsidiaries (including any acquisition structured as a merger, consolidation, or share exchange); *provided,*

---

[45] This §5(e)(i) permits the Target to notify the Buyer of any development prior to the Closing that causes a breach of the representations and warranties in §3(g)-(p) above concerning the Target and its Subsidiaries. If the development gives the Buyer any right to terminate this Agreement pursuant to §7(a)(ii) below, the Buyer must exercise its termination right within [10 business days] after the notice. Unless the Buyer has such a termination right and exercises it within that period, the notice will be deemed to have cured any such breach of the representations and warranties that otherwise would have existed.

[46] Sample acquisition agreement 2003.1 (the *pro-buyer* asset purchase agreement) provides that *no* disclosure (presumably, but not necessarily, by the Target) between signing and Closing will supplement the previous disclosures or cure any misrepresentation or breach of warranty.

however, that the Target, its Subsidiaries, and their directors and officers will remain free to participate in any discussions or negotiations regarding, furnish any information with respect to, assist or participate in, or facilitate in any other manner any effort or attempt by any Person to do or seek any of the foregoing to the extent their fiduciary duties may require.[47]

6. *Conditions to Obligation to Close.*

(a) *Conditions to Obligation of the Buyer.* [48] The obligation of the Buyer to consummate the transactions to be performed by it in connection with the Closing is subject to satisfaction of the following conditions:

(i) the representations and warranties set forth in §3 above shall be true and correct in all material respects at and as of the Closing Date;[49]

(ii) the Target shall have performed and complied with all of its covenants hereunder in all material respects through the Closing;

(iii) there shall not be any injunction, judgment, order, decree, ruling, or charge in effect preventing consummation of any of the transactions contemplated by this Agreement;[50]

(iv) the Target shall have delivered to the Buyer a certificate to the effect that each of the conditions specified above in §6(a)(i)-(iii) is satisfied in all respects;

(v) [all applicable waiting periods (and any extensions thereof) under the Hart-Scott-Rodino Act shall have expired or otherwise been terminated and the Target, its Subsidiaries, and the Buyer shall have received all other authori-

---

[47] Sample acquisition agreement 2003.1 (the *pro-buyer* asset purchase agreement) lacks a comparable proviso permitting these persons to respond to unsolicited proposals to the extent their fiduciary duties may require.

[48] Sample acquisition agreement 2003.1 (the *pro-buyer* asset purchase agreement) contains additional closing conditions for the benefit of the Buyer concerning third party consents, title insurance, surveys. director and officer resignations, and the receipt of financing for the transaction.

[49] Note that this provision will not give the Buyer any closing condition with respect to any adverse matter which the Target may disclose in the Disclosure Schedule. This is because the disclosure will cure any misrepresentation or breach of warranty that might otherwise have existed. Thus, where the Target discloses an adverse matter in the Disclosure Schedule, the Buyer may seek to add a specific closing condition requiring an acceptable resolution of the matter.

Section 5(e)(i) above permits the Target to notify the Buyer of any development prior to the Closing that causes a breach of its representations and warranties in §3(g)-(p) above concerning the Target and its Subsidiaries. If the development gives the Buyer any right to terminate this Agreement pursuant to §7(a)(ii) below, the Buyer must exercise its termination right within [10 business days] after the notice. Unless the Buyer has such a termination right and exercises it within that period, the notice will be deemed to have cured any such breach of the representations and warranties that otherwise would have existed.

[50] Sample acquisition agreement 2003.1 (the *pro-buyer* asset purchase agreement) contains a broader closing condition requiring also that there not be any pending [or threatened] litigation.

zations, consents, and approvals of governments and governmental agencies referred to in §3(c) and §4(c) above];

(vi) the relevant parties shall have entered into side agreements in form and substance as set forth in Exhibits G-1 through G-_____ attached hereto and the same shall be in full force and effect;[51]

(vii) the Buyer shall have received from counsel to the Target an opinion in form and substance as set forth in Exhibit H attached hereto, addressed to the Buyer, and dated as of the Closing Date; and

(viii) all actions to be taken by the Target in connection with consummation of the transactions contemplated hereby and all certificates, opinions, instruments, and other documents required to effect the transactions contemplated hereby will be [reasonably] satisfactory in form and substance to the Buyer.

The Buyer may waive any condition specified in this §6(a) if it executes a writing so stating at or prior to the Closing.

(b) *Conditions to Obligation of the Target.* The obligation of the Target to consummate the transactions to be performed by it in connection with the Closing is subject to satisfaction of the following conditions:

(i) the representations and warranties set forth in §4 above shall be true and correct in all material respects at and as of the Closing Date;

(ii) the Buyer shall have performed and complied with all of its covenants hereunder in all material respects through the Closing;

(iii) there shall not be any injunction, judgment, order, decree, ruling, or charge in effect preventing consummation of any of the transactions contemplated by this Agreement;[52]

(iv) the Buyer shall have delivered to the Target a certificate to the effect that each of the conditions specified above in §6(b)(i)-(iii) is satisfied in all respects;

(v) [all applicable waiting periods (and any extensions thereof) under the Hart-Scott-Rodino Act shall have expired or otherwise been terminated and

---

[51] Where the Target has been a subsidiary of Bigco, the Buyer may require significant transition assistance. This might be the case where Bigco performs substantial services for its subsidiaries and/or where Bigco owns various tangible and intangible assets used by its subsidiaries. For example, the Buyer may require real estate leases, intellectual property licenses, and accounting, purchasing, payroll, risk management, and data processing services from Bigco.

[52] Because this Target's closing condition conforms to the comparable Buyer's closing condition in §6(a)(iii) above, it leaves the Target with a relatively narrow "out." Thus, the Target may prefer to broaden the respective closing conditions. *Compare* the broader closing conditions in sample acquisition agreement 2003.1 (the *pro-buyer* asset purchase agreement).

the Target, its Subsidiaries, and the Buyer shall have received all other authorizations, consents, and approvals of governments and governmental agencies referred to in §3(c) and §4(c) above];

(vi) the relevant parties shall have entered into side agreements in form and substance as set forth in Exhibits G-_____, G-_____, . . . and G-_____ and the same shall be in full force and effect;

(vii) the Target shall have received from counsel to the Buyer an opinion in form and substance as set forth in Exhibit I attached hereto, addressed to the Target, and dated as of the Closing Date; and

(viii) all actions to be taken by the Buyer in connection with consummation of the transactions contemplated hereby and all certificates, opinions, instruments, and other documents required to effect the transactions contemplated hereby will be [reasonably] satisfactory in form and substance to the Target.

The Target may waive any condition specified in this §6(b) if it executes a writing so stating at or prior to the Closing.

7. *Termination.*

(a) *Termination of Agreement.*[53] Certain of the Parties may terminate this Agreement as provided below:

(i) the Buyer and the Target may terminate this Agreement by mutual written consent at any time prior to the Closing;

(ii) the Buyer may terminate this Agreement by giving written notice to the Target at any time prior to the Closing in the event (A) the Target has within the then previous [10 business days] given the Buyer any notice pursuant to §5(e)(i) above and (B) the development that is the subject of the notice has had a material adverse effect upon the financial condition of the Target and its Subsidiaries taken as a whole.[54]

---

[53] Sample acquisition agreement 2003.1 (the *pro-buyer* asset purchase agreement) contains a provision giving the Buyer a right to terminate the agreement for a limited period after signing if the Buyer is not [reasonably] satisfied with the results of its continuing business, legal, and accounting due diligence concerning the Target and its Subsidiaries.

[54] Section 5(e)(i) above permits the Target to notify the Buyer of any development prior to the Closing that causes a breach of the representations and warranties in §3(g)-(p) above concerning the Target and its Subsidiaries. If the development gives the Buyer any right to terminate this Agreement pursuant to this §7(a)(ii), the Buyer must exercise its termination right within [10 business days] after the notice. Unless the Buyer has such a termination right and exercises it within that period, the notice will be deemed to have cured any such breach of the representations and warranties that otherwise would have existed.

(iii) the Buyer may terminate this Agreement by giving written notice to the Target at any time prior to the Closing (A) in the event the Target has breached any material representation, warranty, or covenant contained in this Agreement (other than the representations and warranties in §3(g)-(p) above) in any material respect, the Buyer has notified the Target of the breach, and the breach has continued without cure for a period of [30 days] after the notice of breach or (B) if the Closing shall not have occurred on or before _____, 19____, by reason of the failure of any condition precedent under §6(a) hereof (unless the failure results primarily from the Buyer itself breaching any representation, warranty, or covenant contained in this Agreement); and

(iv) the Target may terminate this Agreement by giving written notice to the Buyer at any time prior to the Closing (A) in the event the Buyer has breached any material representation, warranty, or covenant contained in this Agreement in any material respect, the Target has notified the Buyer of the breach, and the breach has continued without cure for a period of [30 days] after the notice of breach or (B) if the Closing shall not have occurred on or before _____, 19____, by reason of the failure of any condition precedent under §6(b) hereof (unless the failure results primarily from the Target itself breaching any representation, warranty, or covenant contained in this Agreement).

(b) *Effect of Termination.* If any Party terminates this Agreement pursuant to §7(a) above, all rights and obligations of the Parties hereunder shall terminate without any liability of any Party to any other Party (except for any liability of any Party then in breach); *provided, however*, that the confidentiality provisions contained in §5(d) above shall survive termination.

8. *Miscellaneous.*[55]

(a) *Survival of Representations and Warranties.* All of the representations and warranties of the Parties contained in this Agreement shall survive the Closing hereunder as and to the extent provided in the Agreement with Target Stockholders.

(b) *Press Releases and Public Announcements.* No Party shall issue any press release or make any public announcement relating to the subject matter of this Agreement [prior to the Closing] without the prior written approval of the other Party; *provided, however*, that any Party may make any public disclosure it believes in good faith is required by applicable law or any listing or trading agreement

[55] The Buyer may seek to add provisions whereby the Parties agree to specific performance, agree to service of process on an agent, and submit to the [exclusive] jurisdiction of the state and federal courts in a particular city. Sample acquisition agreement 2003.1 (the *pro-buyer* asset purchase agreement) contains examples of these provisions.

The Parties may want to add a provision calling for optional or mandatory arbitration with respect to all or certain issues.

concerning its publicly-traded securities (in which case the disclosing Party will use its [reasonable] best efforts to advise the other Party prior to making the disclosure).

(c) *No Third-Party Beneficiaries.* This Agreement shall not confer any rights or remedies upon any Person other than the Parties and their respective successors and permitted assigns.

(d) *Entire Agreement.* [This Agreement (including the documents referred to herein) constitutes the entire agreement between the Parties and supersedes any prior understandings, agreements, or representations by or between the Parties, written or oral, to the extent they related in any way to the subject matter hereof.]

(e) *Succession and Assignment.* This Agreement shall be binding upon and inure to the benefit of the Parties named herein and their respective successors and permitted assigns. No Party may assign either this Agreement or any of its rights, interests, or obligations hereunder without the prior written approval of the other Party [*provided, however,* that the Buyer may (i) assign any or all of its rights and interests hereunder to one or more of its Affiliates and (ii) designate one or more of its Affiliates to perform its obligations hereunder (in any or all of which cases the Buyer nonetheless shall remain responsible for the performance of all of its obligations hereunder)].

(f) *Counterparts.* This Agreement may be executed in one or more counterparts, each of which shall be deemed an original but all of which together will constitute one and the same instrument.

(g) *Headings.* The section headings contained in this Agreement are inserted for convenience only and shall not affect in any way the meaning or interpretation of this Agreement.

(h) *Notices.* All notices, requests, demands, claims, and other communications hereunder will be in writing. Any notice, request, demand, claim, or other communication hereunder shall be deemed duly given if (and then two business days after) it is sent by registered or certified mail, return receipt requested, postage prepaid, and addressed to the intended recipient as set forth below:

If to the Target: *Copy to:*

If to the Buyer: *Copy to:*

Any Party may send any notice, request, demand, claim, or other communication hereunder to the intended recipient at the address set forth above using any other means (including personal delivery, expedited courier, messenger service, telecopy, telex, ordinary mail, or electronic mail), but no such notice, request, demand, claim, or other communication shall be deemed to have been duly given unless and until it actually is received by the intended recipient. Any Party may change the address to which notices, requests, demands, claims, and other communications hereunder are to be delivered by giving the other Party notice in the manner herein set forth.

(i) *Governing Law. This Agreement shall be governed by and construed in accordance with the domestic laws of the State of _____ without giving effect to any choice or conflict of law provision or rule (whether of the State of _____ or any other jurisdiction) that would cause the application of the laws of any jurisdiction other than the State of _____.*

(j) *Amendments and Waivers.* No amendment of any provision of this Agreement shall be valid unless the same shall be in writing and signed by the Buyer and the Target. The Target may consent to any such amendment at any time prior to the Closing with the prior authorization of its board of directors; *provided, however,* that any amendment effected after the Target Stockholders have approved this Agreement will be subject to the restrictions contained in the [APPLICABLE CORPORATION STATUTE]. No waiver by any Party of any default, misrepresentation, or breach of warranty or covenant hereunder, whether intentional or not, shall be deemed to extend to any prior or subsequent default, misrepresentation, or breach of warranty or covenant hereunder or affect in any way any rights arising by virtue of any prior or subsequent such occurrence.

(k) *Severability.* Any term or provision of this Agreement that is invalid or unenforceable in any situation in any jurisdiction shall not affect the validity or enforceability of the remaining terms and provisions hereof or the validity or enforceability of the offending term or provision in any other situation or in any other jurisdiction.

(l) *Expenses.* Each of the Buyer, the Target, and the Target's Subsidiaries will bear its own costs and expenses (including legal fees and expenses) incurred in connection with this Agreement and the transactions contemplated hereby. The Target will also bear all of the Target Stockholders' costs and expenses (including all of their legal fees and expenses) incurred in connection with this Agreement and the transactions contemplated hereby (other than any Income Tax on any income or gain the Target Stockholders may realize if the Target makes any dividend or distribution to them).[56]

---

[56] This Agreement makes the Target responsible for the transactional costs and expenses of the Target, and the Target Stockholders, but treats these costs and expenses as Assumed Liabilities. This means that the Buyer will bear these costs and expenses if it consummates the asset purchase. *See* §2(b) above and the related definition of "Assumed Liabilities" in §1 above.

Furthermore, this Agreement leaves the Target's Subsidiaries responsible for their own transactional costs and expenses. This means the Buyer will bear these costs and expenses if it acquires their capital stock as part of the Acquired Assets.

Note, however, that allocating transactional costs and expenses to the Target and its Subsidiaries may reduce the amount of cash the Target (and indirectly the Target Stockholders) will be entitled to retain at the Closing. *See* §2(a) and §2(d) above and the related definition of "Acquired Assets" in

(m) *Construction.* [The Parties have participated jointly in the negotiation and drafting of this Agreement. In the event an ambiguity or question of intent or interpretation arises, this Agreement shall be construed as if drafted jointly by the Parties and no presumption or burden of proof shall arise favoring or disfavoring any Party by virtue of the authorship of any of the provisions of this Agreement.] Any reference to any federal, state, local, or foreign statute or law shall be deemed also to refer to all rules and regulations promulgated thereunder, unless the context requires otherwise. The word "including" shall mean including without limitation.[57]

(n) *Incorporation of Exhibits and Schedules.* The Exhibits and Schedules identified in this Agreement are incorporated herein by reference and made a part hereof.

(o) *Tax Matters.* [Any agreement between the Target and any of its Subsidiaries regarding allocation or payment of taxes or amounts in lieu of taxes shall be deemed terminated at and as of the Closing. The Buyer and the Target will (A) cooperate in the preparation and filing of an election under Code §338(h)(10) with respect to the sale of the stock of the Subsidiaries hereunder and (B) take all such action as is required in order to give effect to the election for state, local, and foreign tax purposes to the greatest extent permitted by law.][58]

(p) *Employee Benefits Matters.* [The Buyer will adopt and assume at and as of the Closing each of the Employee Benefit Plans that the Target maintains and

---

§1 above. Furthermore, any assumption of the Target Stockholders' costs and expenses by the Target may be deemed a dividend for federal income tax purposes.

The Target may seek to make the Buyer *directly* responsible for these costs and expenses. In the unlikely event the Buyer agreed to this arrangement, it would be responsible for costs and expenses of the Target Stockholders, the Target, and the Target's Subsidiaries whether or not it consummated the asset purchase.

The Buyer may seek to make the Target and the Target Stockholders responsible for their own costs and expenses. Sample acquisition agreement 2003.1 (the *pro-buyer* asset purchase agreement) contains provisions more favorable to the Buyer in this regard.

The Parties may settle on a compromise allocation of responsibility (such as sharing the costs and expenses in a predetermined ratio or making one Party responsible for the costs and expenses up to a specified aggregate ceiling and the other Party responsible for any excess).

[57] Sample acquisition agreement 2003.1 (the *pro-buyer* asset purchase agreement) contains additional language construing the representations, warranties, and covenants herein in a manner more favorable to the Buyer.

[58] The Buyer may seek to have the Parties make an election under Code §338(h)(10) (*i.e.*, to have the sale of the stock of the Subsidiaries taxed as though the Subsidiaries instead had sold their *assets* to the Buyer). *See* ¶205.

This differs from any other election the Buyer might make under Code §338 in that the *Target* will be responsible for any federal income tax on the deemed sale of assets. Note, however, that the Target will incur no federal income tax on the sale of the *stock* of the Subsidiaries (*i.e.*, only on the deemed sale of their *assets*) if the Parties make a Code §338(h)(10) election.

This Agreement makes the Buyer responsible for any incremental tax arising out of the Code §338(h)(10) election. *See* the definition of Assumed Liabilities in §1 above. The Buyer, of course, will seek to have the Target remain responsible for the incremental tax. Sample acquisition agreement 2003.1 (the *pro-buyer* asset purchase agreement) contains provisions that are more favorable to the Buyer in this regard.

each trust, insurance contract, annuity contract, or other funding arrangement that the Target has established with respect thereto. The Buyer will ensure that the Employee Benefit Plans treat employment with any of the Target and its Subsidiaries prior to the Closing Date the same as employment with any of the Buyer and its Subsidiaries from and after the Closing Date for purposes of eligibility, vesting, and benefit accrual. The Target will transfer (or cause the plan administrators to transfer) at and as of the Closing all of the corresponding assets associated with the Employee Benefit Plans that the Buyer is adopting and assuming. With respect to each Multiemployer Plan, the Parties shall take all actions necessary to comply with the requirements of ERISA §4204.][59]

(q) *Bulk Transfer Laws.* The Buyer acknowledges that the Target will not comply with the provisions of any bulk transfer laws of any jurisdiction in connection with the transactions contemplated by this Agreement.[60]

* * * * *

IN WITNESS WHEREOF, the Parties hereto have executed this Agreement on [as of] the date first above written.

[BUYER]

By: _____

Title: _____

[TARGET]

By: _____

Title: _____

[59] This Agreement provides for a transfer of all employee benefit plan assets (including overfundings) and liabilities (including underfundings) to the Buyer. There are many other approaches to splitting and matching plan assets and liabilities which would cause the Buyer to share to various degrees in plan overfundings and underfundings.

If the Buyer did not want to share in any plan overfundings and underfundings, the Buyer could establish substantially identical plans for future benefit accruals and count past service with any of the Target and its Subsidiaries for purposes of eligibility and vesting thereunder. The Target would then continue its previously established plans on a "frozen" basis and retain the benefit of any overfunding (or the detriment of any underfunding) thereunder.

If the Buyer wanted to share in only certain plan overfundings and underfundings, the Buyer and the Target could proceed as set forth in the preceding paragraph, except that the Buyer would assume the liability for certain past service benefits under the Target plans as of the Closing Date and the Target would transfer certain corresponding plan assets to the Buyer.

In any event, the Purchase Price should reflect the intended disposition of employee benefit plan assets and liabilities.

[60] The Buyer may seek to have the Target comply with the applicable bulk transfer laws in certain circumstances. *See* ¶2001.2.2.2.

EXHIBIT A⁶¹—AGREEMENT WITH
TARGET STOCKHOLDERS⁶²

---

⁶¹ This is Exhibit A to sample acquisition agreement 2003.2 (the *pro-seller* asset purchase agreement).

⁶² Sample acquisition agreements 2003.1.1, 2003.2.1, and 2003.3.1 (the *asset* purchase agreements) assume that the Target will liquidate and dissolve immediately after the Closing. Each of these sample acquisition agreements therefore includes an Agreement with Target Stockholders containing indemnification provisions and other covenants analogous to those contained in sample acquisition agreements 2002.1, 2002.2, and 2002.3 (the *stock* purchase agreements) respectively.

The Parties should eliminate this document (and return the indemnification provisions and other covenants to the Asset Purchase Agreement) if the Target will *not* liquidate and dissolve after the Closing. *Compare* sample acquisition agreements 2004.1 and 2004.2 (the *divisional* asset purchase agreements).

Agreement dated [as of] _____, 19____ among _____, a _____ corporation (the *"Buyer"*), and the stockholders (the *"Target Stockholders"*) of _____, a _____ corporation (the *"Target"*). The Buyer and the Target Stockholders are referred to collectively herein as the *"Parties."*

The Buyer and the Target are entering into an Asset Purchase Agreement concurrently herewith (the *"Asset Purchase Agreement"*). Certain terms used herein without definition are used herein as defined in the Asset Purchase Agreement.

The Asset Purchase Agreement contemplates a transaction in which the Buyer will purchase the Acquired Assets (and accept responsibility for the Assumed Liabilities) of the Target in return for cash and the Buyer Notes.

The Buyer and the Target make certain representations, warranties, and covenants in the Asset Purchase Agreement which will survive the Closing for purposes of potential indemnification. The Target Stockholders, however, intend to cause the Target to liquidate and dissolve immediately after the Closing. The Buyer and the Target Stockholders therefore wish to provide for post-Closing indemnification against breaches of these representations, warranties, and covenants and to make certain other covenants among themselves.

Now, therefore, in consideration of the premises and the mutual promises herein made, the Buyer and the Target Stockholders agree as follows.

1. *Definitions.*

"Adverse Consequences" means all actions, suits, proceedings, hearings, investigations, charges, complaints, claims, demands, injunctions, judgments, orders, decrees, rulings, damages, dues, penalties, fines, costs, [reasonable amounts paid in settlement,] liabilities, obligations, taxes, liens, losses, expenses, and fees, including court costs and [reasonable] attorneys' fees and expenses.

"Allocable Portion" means, with respect to the share of any Target Stockholder in a particular amount, that fraction equal to the number of Target Shares the Target Stockholder holds over the total number of Target Shares that all of the Target Stockholders hold in the aggregate, in each case as set forth in the Annex.[63]

---

[63] If any stockholder refuses to become a party to this Agreement, then the Parties will need to determine who, as between the Target Stockholders (i.e., those stockholders who *do* become parties) and the Buyer, will suffer from the shortfall. The formulation in this definition will increase the Allocable Portion for each Target Stockholder (so that the Allocable Portions will still add to 100% and the *Target Stockholders* will suffer from the shortfall). The Target Stockholders may seek to substitute

"Annex" has the meaning set forth in §2 below.

"Asset Purchase Agreement" has the meaning set forth in the preface above.

"Indemnified Party" has the meaning set forth in §4(d) below.

"Indemnifying Party" has the meaning set forth in §4(d) below.

"Party" has the meaning set forth in the preface above.

"Requisite Target Stockholders" means Target Stockholders holding [a majority] in interest of the total number of Target Shares that all of the Target Stockholders hold in the aggregate as set forth in the "Annex."[64]

"Third Party Claim" has the meaning set forth in §4(d) below.

2. *Representations and Warranties of the Target Stockholders.* Each of the Target Stockholders represents and warrants to the Buyer that the statements contained in this §2 are correct and complete as of the date of this Agreement and will be correct and complete as of the Closing Date (as though made then and as though the Closing Date were substituted for the date of this Agreement throughout this §2) with respect to himself or itself, except as set forth in the Annex attached hereto (the "Annex").

(a) *Organization of Certain Target Stockholders.* If the Target Stockholder is a corporation, the Target Stockholder is duly organized, validly existing, and in good standing under the laws of the jurisdiction of its incorporation.[65]

(b) *Authorization.* The Target Stockholder has full power and authority (including, if the Target Stockholder is a corporation, full corporate power and authority) to execute and deliver this Agreement and to perform his or its obligations hereunder. This Agreement constitutes the valid and legally binding obligation of the Target Stockholder, enforceable in accordance with its terms and conditions.

(c) *Noncontravention.* Neither the execution and the delivery of this Agreement by the Target Stockholder, nor the performance by the Target Stockholder of his or its obligations hereunder, will [(i)] violate any constitution, statute, regulation, rule, injunction, judgment, order, decree, ruling, charge, or other restriction of

---

the *total number of outstanding Target Shares* in the denominator (so that the Allocable Portions will *not* add to 100% and the *Buyer* will suffer from any shortfall). *See* §4(b) below where this definition is used. It may be necessary to revise this definition if the Target has more than one class of capital stock.

[64] It may be necessary to revise this definition if the Target has more than one class of capital stock.

[65] Several representations and warranties in this §2 concern Target Stockholders which are corporations. If any Target Stockholders are partnerships, trusts, business associations, estates, or guardians, the Buyer may seek to add analogous provisions covering them.

any government, governmental agency, or court to which the Target Stockholder is subject (or, if the Target Stockholder is a corporation, any provision of its charter or bylaws) [or (ii) conflict with, result in a breach of, constitute a default under, result in the acceleration of, create in any party the right to accelerate, terminate, modify, or cancel, or require any notice under any agreement, contract, lease, license, instrument, or other arrangement to which the Target Stockholder is a party or by which he or it is bound or to which any of his or its assets is subject].

(d) *Investment.* The Target Stockholder (i) understands that the Buyer Notes have not been, and will not be, registered under the Securities Act, or under any state securities laws, and are being offered and sold in reliance upon federal and state exemptions for transactions not involving any public offering, (ii) is acquiring the Buyer Notes solely for his or its own account for investment purposes, and not with a view to the distribution thereof, (iii) is a sophisticated investor with knowledge and experience in business and financial matters, (iv) has received certain information concerning the Buyer and has had the opportunity to obtain additional information as desired in order to evaluate the merits and the risks inherent in holding the Buyer Notes, (v) is able to bear the economic risk and lack of liquidity inherent in holding the Buyer Notes, and (vi) is an Accredited Investor for the reasons set forth on the Annex.[66]

(e) *Target Shares.* The Target Stockholder holds of record the number of Target Shares set forth next to his or its name on the Annex.

3. *Post-Closing Covenants.*[67] The Parties agree as follows with respect to the period following the Closing.

(a) *General.* In case at any time after the Closing any further action is necessary [or desirable] to carry out the purposes of the Asset Purchase Agreement, each of the Parties will take such further action (including the execution and delivery of such further instruments and documents) as any other Party [reasonably] may request, all at the sole cost and expense of the requesting Party (unless the requesting Party is entitled to indemnification therefor under §4 below).[68]

---

[66] This provision contemplates that the Buyer will issue the Buyer Notes pursuant to the exemption from registration under the Securities Act contained in Regulation D. The Parties should determine whether this exemption is available in a particular transaction. If it is not, the Agreement must be modified as necessary to reflect the issuance of the Buyer Notes under a different exemption from securities registration or in an offering registered under the Securities Act.

[67] The *pro-buyer* Agreement (Exhibit A to sample acquisition agreement 2003.1) contains an additional covenant requiring the Target Stockholders to keep certain information regarding the Target and its Subsidiaries confidential after the Closing.

The Target Stockholders may seek to obtain additional covenants from the Buyer and its Subsidiaries (*e.g.,* the typical covenants contained in a loan agreement or an indenture) because the Buyer is issuing the Buyer Notes to the Target Stockholders as part of the Purchase Price. Any such covenants would remain applicable so long as the Buyer Notes remained outstanding.

[68] The Parties may prefer to allocate responsibility for these particular costs and expenses in some other manner (*e.g.,* the Party incurring the costs and expenses might be responsible for their payment, the Parties might share the costs and expenses in a predetermined ratio, or one Party might be

(b) *Litigation Support.* In the event and for so long as any Party actively is contesting or defending against any action, suit, proceeding, hearing, investigation, charge, complaint, claim, or demand in connection with (i) any transaction contemplated under the Asset Purchase Agreement or (ii) any fact, situation, circumstance, status, condition, activity, practice, plan, occurrence, event, incident, action, failure to act, or transaction on or prior to the Closing Date involving any of the Target and its Subsidiaries, each of the other Parties will cooperate with the contesting or defending Party and his or its counsel in the contest or defense, make available his or its personnel, and provide such testimony and access to his or its books and records as shall be necessary in connection with the contest or defense, all at the sole cost and expense of the contesting or defending Party (unless the contesting or defending Party is entitled to indemnification therefor under §4 below).[69]

(c) *Transition.* [None of the Target Stockholders will take any action that is designed or intended to have the effect of discouraging any lessor, licensor, customer, supplier, or other business associate of any of the Target and its Subsidiaries from maintaining the same business relationships with the Buyer and the Subsidiaries after the Closing as it maintained with the Target and its Subsidiaries prior to the Closing.]

(d) *Covenant Not to Compete.*[70] [For a period of one year from and after the Closing Date, none of the Target Stockholders will engage directly or indirectly in any business that any of the Target and its Subsidiaries conducts as of the Closing Date in any geographic area in which any of the Target and its Subsidiaries conducts that business as of the Closing Date; *provided, however,* that no owner of less than 5% of the outstanding stock of any publicly traded corporation shall be deemed to engage solely by reason thereof in any of its businesses. If the final judgment of a court of competent jurisdiction declares that any term or provision of this §3(d) is invalid or unenforceable, the Parties agree that the court making the determination of invalidity or unenforceability shall have the power to reduce the scope, duration, or area of the term or provision, to delete specific words or phrases, or to replace any invalid or unenforceable term or provision with a term or provision that is valid and enforceable and that comes closest to expressing the intention of the invalid or unenforceable term or provision, and this Agreement shall be enforceable as so modified after the expiration of the time within which the judgment may be appealed.]

---

responsible for the costs and expenses up to a specified aggregate ceiling and the other Party responsible for any excess).

Compare §6(l) below (which allocates responsibility among the Parties for their costs and expenses generally) and §8(l) of the Asset Purchase Agreement (which allocates responsibility between the Buyer and the Target for their costs and expenses through the Closing).

[69] The Parties may prefer to allocate responsibility for these particular costs and expenses in some other manner as discussed in the preceding footnote.

[70] Note that unless this Agreement states that a specified amount of consideration is being paid for the covenant not to compete, applicable tax cases will preclude the Buyer from seeking to allocate a portion of the Purchase Price to the covenant and amortizing such amount over the covenant's life.

(e) *Buyer Notes.* Each Buyer Note will be imprinted with a legend substantially in the following form:

This Note was originally issued on _____, 19____, and has not been registered under the Securities Act of 1933, as amended.[71]

4. *Remedies for Breaches of this Agreement and the Asset Purchase Agreement.*[72]

(a) *Survival of Representations and Warranties.*[73]

ALTERNATIVE A (MINIMAL INDEMNIFICATION): None of the representations and warranties of the Target contained in §3(g)-(r) of the Asset Purchase Agreement shall survive the Closing. All of the other representations and warranties of the Buyer, the Target, and the Target Stockholders contained in the Asset Purchase Agreement (including the representations and warranties of the Target

---

[71] This provision must be eliminated if the Buyer will issue the Buyer Notes in an offering registered under the Securities Act.

The *pro-buyer* Agreement (Exhibit A to sample acquisition agreement 2003.1) contains additional provisions requiring the Target Stockholders to obtain an opinion of counsel as to securities law matters prior to transferring the Buyer Notes.

[72] The Buyer may seek some form of additional security covering the obligation of the Target Stockholders to indemnify the Buyer after the Closing. This may include provisions calling for (a) the Buyer to have a recoupment remedy with respect to the Buyer Notes, (b) the Target Stockholders to deposit a portion of the Purchase Price with a third party escrow agent, (c) the Buyer to hold back a portion of the Purchase Price (to be paid later with interest), or (d) the Buyer to obtain a security interest in certain assets of the Target Stockholders. The *pro-buyer* Agreement (Exhibit A to sample acquisition agreement 2003.1), for example, contains recoupment provisions applicable to the Buyer Notes.

[73] This *pro-seller* Agreement contains alternative provisions for (A) *minimal indemnification* to the Buyer for breaches of the representations and warranties of the Target and the Target Stockholders (i.e., only the representations and warranties concerning the transaction itself survive the Closing) and (B) *limited indemnification* to the Buyer for breaches of the representations and warranties of the Target and the Target Stockholders (*i.e.*, the representations and warranties with respect to the transaction itself survive indefinitely, the other representations and warranties survive only for [one year], and there is a deductible and a ceiling with respect to indemnification against breaches of the latter).

The *pro-buyer* Agreement (Exhibit A to sample acquisition agreement 2003.1), on the other hand, contains alternative provisions for (A) *full indemnification* to the Buyer for breaches of the representations and warranties of the Target and the Target Stockholders (i.e., all representations and warranties survive indefinitely and there is no deductible, threshold, or ceiling with respect to indemnification against breaches thereof) and (B) *limited indemnification* to the Buyer for breaches of the representations and warranties of the Target and the Target Stockholders (i.e., the representations and warranties with respect to the transaction itself and with respect to taxes survive indefinitely, the other representations and warranties survive only for [three years], and there is a threshold, but not a deductible or ceiling, with respect to indemnification against breaches of the latter).

This *pro-seller* Agreement provides that the representations and warranties of the Parties will survive the Closing (*unless* the damaged Party knew or had reason to know of the misrepresentation or breach of warranty at the time of Closing).

The *pro-buyer* Agreement (Exhibit A to sample acquisition agreement 2003.1), on the other hand, provides that the representations and warranties will survive the Closing (*even* if the damaged Party knew or had reason to know of the misrepresentation or breach of warranty at the time of Closing).

contained in §3(a)-(f) thereof) and in this Agreement shall survive the Closing (unless the damaged Party knew or had reason to know of any misrepresentation or breach of warranty or covenant at the time of Closing) and continue in full force and effect forever thereafter (subject to any applicable statutes of limitations).

ALTERNATIVE B (LIMITED INDEMNIFICATION): All of the representations and warranties of the Target contained in §3(g)-(r) of the Asset Purchase Agreement shall survive the Closing (unless the Buyer knew or had reason to know of any misrepresentation or breach of warranty at the time of Closing) and continue in full force and effect for a period of [one year] thereafter. All of the other representations and warranties of the Buyer, the Target, and the Target Stockholders contained in the Asset Purchase Agreement (including the representations and warranties of the Target contained in §3(a)-(f) thereof) and in this Agreement shall survive the Closing (unless the damaged Party knew or had reason to know of any misrepresentation or breach of warranty at the time of Closing) and continue in full force and effect forever thereafter (subject to any applicable statutes of limitations).

(b) *Indemnification Provisions for Benefit of the Buyer.*[74]

(i) In the event the Target breaches any of its representations, warranties, and covenants contained in the Asset Purchase Agreement,[75] and, if there is an applicable survival period pursuant to §4(a) above, provided that the Buyer makes a written claim for indemnification against any of the Target Stockholder pursuant to §6(h) below within such survival period, then each of the Target Stockholder agrees to indemnify the Buyer from and against his or its Allocable

---

[74] The Buyer will become indirectly responsible for all of the liabilities of the *Subsidiaries* if the Buyer acquires their capital stock as part of the Acquired Assets. For this reason, the Buyer may seek (a) to purchase assets from the Target *and from each of the Subsidiaries* (i.e., a multiple entity asset sale) or (b) to have the Target liquidate and dissolve the Subsidiaries tax free under Code §332 (to the extent they are United States corporations) and sell their assets to the Buyer.

In addition, the Asset Purchase Agreement provides that the Buyer will assume substantially all of the liabilities of the *Target* (whether known or unknown, whether asserted or unasserted, whether absolute or contingent, whether accrued or unaccrued, whether liquidated or unliquidated, and whether due or to become due). *See* the definition of Assumed Liabilities in §1 thereof.

Finally, the Buyer may be exposed for certain liabilities of the *Target* by operation of law if the Target does not pay them (e.g., under applicable bulk sales statutes and common law doctrines of de facto merger and successor liability). *See* ¶2001.2.2.2.

These post-Closing indemnification provisions are designed to work in conjunction with the definition of Assumed Liabilities in §1 of the Asset Purchase Agreement and the representations and warranties in §3 of the Asset Purchase Agreement to protect the Buyer against liabilities it does not intend to assume.

[75] Section 5(e)(i) of the Asset Purchase Agreement permits the Target to notify the Buyer of any development prior to the Closing that causes a breach of the representations and warranties in §3(g)-(p) thereof concerning the Target and its Subsidiaries. If the development gives the Buyer any right to terminate the Asset Purchase Agreement pursuant to §7(a)(ii) thereof, the Buyer must exercise its termination right within [10 business days] after the notice. Unless the Buyer has such a termination right and exercises it within that period, the notice will be deemed to have cured any such breach of the representations and warranties that otherwise would have existed.

Portion of any Adverse Consequences the Buyer shall suffer[76] through and after the date of the claim for indemnification (but *excluding* any Adverse Consequences the Buyer shall suffer after the end of any applicable survival period) caused [proximately] by the breach;[77] *provided, however,* that the Target Stockholders shall not have any obligation to indemnify the Buyer from and against any Adverse Consequences caused by the breach of any representation or warranty of the Target contained in §3(g)-(p) of the Asset Purchase Agreement [*ALTERNATIVE B (LIMITED INDEMNIFICATION)*]: (A) until the Buyer has suffered Adverse Consequences by reason of all such breaches in excess of a $_____ aggregate deductible (after which point the Target Stockholders will be obligated only to indemnify the Buyer from and against further such Adverse Consequences)[78] or thereafter (B) to the extent the Adverse Consequences the Buyer has suffered by reason of all such breaches exceeds a $_____ aggregate ceiling (after which point the Target Stockholders will have no obligation to indemnify the Buyer from and against further such Adverse Consequences)].[79]

(ii) In the event any of the Target Stockholders breaches any of his or its representations, warranties, and covenants in this Agreement, and, if there is an applicable survival period pursuant to §4(a) above, provided that the Buyer makes a written claim for indemnification against the Target Stockholder pursuant to §6(h) below within such survival period, then the Target Stockholder agrees to indemnify the Buyer from and against the entirety of any Adverse Consequences the Buyer shall suffer through and after the date of the claim for indemnification (but *excluding* any Adverse Consequences the Buyer shall suffer after the end of any applicable survival period) caused [proximately] by the breach.

---

[76] The Buyer may seek to have each Target Stockholder be responsible for *all* of the Buyer's Adverse Consequences (instead of only for his or its Allocable Portion) if the Target breaches any of its representations, warranties, and covenants. This would protect the Buyer from having to proceed against all of the Target Stockholders (some of whom may be insolvent or not subject to service of process) in order to collect all of what is owing it. The *pro-buyer* Agreement (Exhibit A to sample acquisition agreement 2003.1) contains provisions more favorable to the Buyer in this regard.

[77] This *pro-seller* Agreement requires an indemnifying party (presumably, but not necessarily, one of the Target Stockholders) to indemnify an indemnified party (presumably, but not necessarily, the Buyer) from and against any Adverse Consequences the indemnified party *shall* suffer through and after the date of the claim for indemnification (but *excluding* any Adverse Consequences the indemnified party shall suffer after the end of any applicable survival period) *caused [proximately] by* certain breaches by the indemnifying party of his or its representations, warranties, and covenants.

The *pro-buyer* Agreement (Exhibit A to sample acquisition agreement 2003.1), on the other hand, requires an indemnifying party to indemnify an indemnified party from and against any Adverse Consequences the indemnified party *may* suffer through and after the date of the claim for indemnification *(including* any Adverse Consequences the indemnified party may suffer after the end of any applicable survival period) *resulting from, arising out of, relating to, in the nature of, or caused by* certain breaches by the indemnifying party of his or its representations, warranties, and covenants.

[78] The Target Stockholders may also seek to impose a *per claim* deductible.

[79] The Buyer may seek to substitute a threshold (with relation back to the first dollar once the threshold is exceeded) for the deductible in this proviso and also seek to eliminate the ceiling on indemnification. *Compare* the *pro-buyer* Agreement (Exhibit A to sample acquisition agreement 2003.1).

(iii) Each of the Target Stockholders agrees to indemnify the Buyer from and against his or its Allocable Portion of any Adverse Consequences the Buyer shall suffer caused [proximately] by any liability of the Target which is not an Assumed Liability (including any liability of the Target that becomes a liability of the Buyer under any bulk transfer law of any jurisdiction, under any common law doctrine of de facto merger or successor liability, or otherwise by operation of law).[80]

(c) *Indemnification Provisions for Benefit of the Target Stockholders.*

(i) In the event the Buyer breaches any of its representations, warranties, and covenants contained in the Asset Purchase Agreement and in this Agreement, and, if there is an applicable survival period pursuant to §4(a) above, provided that any of the Target Stockholders makes a written claim for indemnification against the Buyer pursuant to §6(h) below within such survival period, then the Buyer agrees to indemnify each of the Target Stockholders from and against the entirety of any Adverse Consequences the Target Stockholder shall suffer through and after the date of the claim for indemnification (but *excluding* any Adverse Consequences the Target Stockholder shall suffer after the end of any applicable survival period) caused [proximately] by the breach.

(ii) The Buyer agrees to indemnify each of the Target Stockholders from and against the entirety of any Adverse Consequences the Target Stockholder shall suffer caused [proximately] by any liability of the Target which is an Assumed Liability.

(d) *Matters Involving Third Parties.*[81]

---

[80] The Buyer may be exposed for certain liabilities of the Target by operation of law if the Target does not pay them (e.g., under applicable bulk sales statutes and common law doctrines of de facto merger and successor liability). *See* ¶2001.2.2.2. This post-Closing indemnification provision is designed to protect the Buyer against liabilities of the Target which the Buyer does not intend to assume.

[81] An *indemnifying* party (presumably, but not necessarily, one of the Target Stockholders) will normally seek to control the defense of any third party claim that may give rise to a claim for indemnification under this §4. However, the *indemnified* party (presumably, but not necessarily, the Buyer) will not want the indemnifying party to control the defense of any third party claim in which the indemnified party will retain a meaningful interest. For example, the indemnified party may seek to control the defense of a third party claim if the third party seeks an injunction or other equitable relief or if it is not clear that the indemnifying party will bear the entirety of any money damages or amount paid in settlement.

This *pro-seller* Agreement provides that any indemnifying party may assume the defense of a third party claim *at any time* during the course of the defense, and prevents the indemnified party from consenting to the entry of any judgment or entering into any settlement with respect to the matter without the consent of the indemnifying party [(not to be unreasonably withheld)].

The *pro-buyer* Agreement (Exhibit A to sample acquisition agreement 2003.1), on the other hand, provides that the indemnified party will control the defense of any third party claim *unless* (a) an indemnifying party accepts full responsibility for the matter within [15 days], (b) the indemnifying party demonstrates it has the financial resources necessary to defend against the matter and fulfill its indemnification obligations, (c) the third party seeks only money damages (as opposed to an

(i) If any third party shall notify any Party (the *"Indemnified Party"*) with respect to any matter (a *"Third Party Claim"*) which may give rise to a claim for indemnification against any other Party (the *"Indemnifying Party"*) under this §4, then the Indemnified Party shall promptly (and in any event within [five business days] after receiving notice of the Third Party Claim) notify each Indemnifying Party thereof in writing.

(ii) Any Indemnifying Party will have the right at any time to assume and thereafter conduct the defense of the Third Party Claim with counsel of his or its choice [reasonably satisfactory to the Indemnified Party; *provided, however,* that the Indemnifying Party will not consent to the entry of any judgment or enter into any settlement with respect to the Third Party Claim without the prior written consent of the Indemnified Party (not to be withheld unreasonably) unless the judgment or proposed settlement involves only the payment of money damages and does not impose an injunction or other equitable relief upon the Indemnified Party].

(iii) Unless and until an Indemnifying Party assumes the defense of the Third Party Claim as provided in §4(d)(ii) above, however, the Indemnified Party may defend against the Third Party Claim in any manner he or it reasonably may deem appropriate.

(iv) In no event will the Indemnified Party consent to the entry of any judgment or enter into any settlement with respect to the Third Party Claim without the prior written consent of each of the Indemnifying Parties [(not to be withheld unreasonably)].

(e) *Determination of Adverse Consequences.* The Parties shall make appropriate adjustments for tax benefits and insurance coverage [and take into account the time cost of money (using the Applicable Rate as the discount rate)] in determining Adverse Consequences for purposes of this §4. All indemnification payments under this §4 shall be deemed adjustments to the Purchase Price.

(f) *Exclusive Remedy.* The Buyer and the Target Stockholders acknowledge and agree that the foregoing indemnification provisions in this §4 shall be the exclusive remedy of the Buyer and the Target Stockholders with respect to the Target, its Subsidiaries, and the transactions contemplated by this Agreement. [ALTERNATIVE A (MINIMAL INDEMNIFICATION): Without limiting the generality of the foregoing, the Buyer acknowledges and agrees that it shall not have any remedy after the Closing for any breach of the representations and warranties in §3(g)-(q)

---

injunction or other equitable relief), (d) settlement of, or an adverse judgment with respect to, the third party claim is not likely to establish a precedent [materially] adverse to the indemnified party, and (e) the indemnifying party conducts the defense actively and diligently.

of the Asset Purchase Agreement.] [ALTERNATIVE B (LIMITED INDEMNIFICATION): OMIT ALTERNATIVE A LANGUAGE ABOVE.][82]

(g) *Environmental Remedies.*[83]

[*ALTERNATIVE A (MINIMAL INDEMNIFICATION):* Without limiting the generality of (f), above, the Buyer hereby waives any right, whether arising at law or in equity, to seek contribution, cost recovery, damages, or any other recourse or remedy from the Target Stockholders, and hereby releases the Target Stockholders, from any claim, demand or liability, with respect to any environmental, health, or safety matter relating to the past, current or future facilities, properties or operations of the Target, its Subsidiaries, and all of their respective predecessors or Affiliates, including without limitation any such matter arising under any Environmental, Health, and Safety Requirements and including, without limitation, any arising under the Comprehensive Environmental Response, Compensation, and Liability Act ("CERCLA"), any analogous state law, or the common law. The Buyer hereby unconditionally agrees to indemnify, defend, and hold harmless the Target Stockholders from any and all liability, loss, cost or expense with respect to any such environmental, health, or safety matter (including any arising

---

[82] Exhibit A to sample acquisition agreement 2003.1 (the *pro-buyer* asset purchase agreement) states that the indemnification provisions in the Agreement are in addition to and not in derogation of any other statutory, equitable, or common law remedies (including any such remedies relating to environmental matters).

Exhibit A to the *pro-buyer* asset purchase agreement also contains an additional provision to the effect that no Target Stockholder will make a claim for indemnification against the Buyer, by reason of the fact that the Target Stockholder was, before the asset purchase, a director or other officeholder of the Target entitled to indemnification from the Target, with respect to any suit or claim the Buyer might bring against the Target Stockholder in connection with the asset purchase. This provision responds to the surprising decision in Heffernan v. Pacific Dunlop GNB Corporation, 965 F.2d 369 (7th Cir. 1992). Although *Heffernan* involved a purchase of stock, rather than a purchase of assets, the instant structure presents many of the same concerns. *See* §8(g) of sample acquisition agreement 2002.1 (the pro-buyer *stock* purchase agreement) and the footnote thereto. *See also* the definition of "Assumed Liabilities" in the accompanying Asset Purchase Agreement (sample acquisition agreement 2003.2.1).

The Buyer may seek such an anti-*Heffernan* provision similar to §4(g) of the *pro-buyer* Agreement with Target Stockholders which accompanies the *pro-buyer* asset purchase agreement (sample acquisition agreement 2003.1.2).

Exhibit A to sample acquisition agreement 2003.3 (the *neutral* asset purchase agreement) states, as does (f) above, that the remedies available to the Parties under the Agreement are exclusive (i.e., that the Buyer has no other statutory, equitable, or common law remedies) and also sets forth a waiver of extra-contractual environmental remedies, but does not contain an environmental indemnification of the Target Stockholders by the Buyer of the sort set forth in §4(g) of this Exhibit A to the *pro-seller* asset purchase agreement.

Although not so stated in this Exhibit A to the *pro-seller* asset purchase agreement, the Target Stockholders could seek to have their own statutory, equitable, and common law remedies survive while the Buyer's analogous rights are explicitly negated, although this would be unusual.

[83] This provision (1) limits the Buyer's recourse against the Target Stockholders for environmental, health, or safety matters to the Buyer's right, if any, to indemnification for breach of the environmental, health, and safety representation, and (2) grants the Target Stockholders indemnification by the Buyer for environmental, health, and safety matters.

under any Environmental, Health, and Safety Requirements and including, without limitation, CERCLA, any analogous state law, or the common law).]

[ALTERNATIVE B (LIMITED INDEMNIFICATION): Without limiting the generality of (f), above, the Buyer understands and agrees that its right to indemnification under §4(b) for breach of the representations and warranties contained in §3(q) of the Asset Purchase Agreement shall constitute its sole and exclusive remedy against the Target Stockholders with respect to any environmental, health, or safety matter relating to the past, current or future facilities, properties or operations of the Target, its Subsidiaries, and all of their respective predecessors or Affiliates, including without limitation any such matter arising under any Environmental, Health, and Safety Requirements. Aside from such right to indemnification, the Buyer hereby waives any right, whether arising at law or in equity, to seek contribution, cost recovery, damages, or any other recourse or remedy from the Target Stockholders, and hereby releases the Target Stockholders from any claim, demand or liability, with respect to any such environmental, health, or safety matter (including without limitation any arising under any Environmental, Health, and Safety Requirements and including without limitation any arising under the Comprehensive Environmental Response, Compensation, and Liability Act ("CERCLA"), any analogous state law, or the common law. Except as set forth above, the Buyer hereby unconditionally agrees to indemnify, defend, and hold harmless the Target Stockholders from any and all liability, loss, cost or expense with respect to any such environmental, health, or safety matter (including without limitation any arising under any Environmental, Health, and Safety Requirements and including without limitation CERCLA, any analogous state law, and the common law).]

5. *Termination.* This Agreement shall terminate if and only if the Asset Purchase Agreement is terminated prior to the Closing in accordance with and pursuant to the terms thereof.

6. *Miscellaneous.*[84]

(a) *Exclusivity.* None of the Target Stockholders will solicit, initiate, or encourage the submission of any proposal or offer from any Person relating to any acquisition of all or substantially all of the capital stock or assets of any of the Target and its Subsidiaries (including any acquisition structured as a merger, consolidation, or share exchange); *provided, however,* that the target stockholders

---

[84] The Buyer may seek to add provisions whereby the Parties agree to specific performance, agree to service of process on an agent, and submit to the [exclusive] jurisdiction of the state and federal courts in a particular city. The *pro-buyer* Agreement (Exhibit A to sample acquisition agreement 2003.1) contains examples of these provisions.

The Parties may want to add a provision calling for optional or mandatory arbitration with respect to all or certain issues.

will remain free to participate in any discussions or negotiations regarding, furnish any information with respect to, assist or participate in, or facilitate in any other manner any effort or attempt by any Person to do or seek any of the foregoing to the extent their fiduciary duties may require.[85]

(b) *Press Releases and Public Announcements.* None of the Target Stockholders shall issue any press release or make any public announcement relating to the subject matter of the Asset Purchase Agreement [prior to the Closing] without the prior written approval of the Buyer; *provided, however,* that any Target Stockholder may make any public disclosure it believes in good faith is required by applicable law or any listing or trading agreement concerning its publicly-traded securities (in which case the disclosing Party will use its [reasonable] best efforts to advise the other Parties prior to making the disclosure).

(c) *No Third-Party Beneficiaries.* This Agreement shall not confer any rights or remedies upon any Person other than the Parties and their respective successors and permitted assigns.

(d) *Entire Agreement.* [This Agreement (including the documents referred to herein) constitutes the entire agreement among the Parties and supersedes any prior understandings, agreements, or representations by or among the Parties, written or oral, to the extent they related in any way to the subject matter hereof.]

(e) *Succession and Assignment.* This Agreement shall be binding upon and inure to the benefit of the Parties named herein and their respective successors and permitted assigns. No Party may assign either this Agreement or any of his or its rights, interests, or obligations hereunder without the prior written approval of the Buyer and the Requisite Target Stockholders; [; *provided, however,* that the Buyer may (i) assign any or all of its rights and interests hereunder to one or more of its Affiliates and (ii) designate one or more of its Affiliates to perform its obligations hereunder (in any or all of which cases the Buyer nonetheless shall remain responsible for the performance of all of its obligations hereunder)].

(f) *Counterparts.* This Agreement may be executed in one or more counterparts, each of which shall be deemed an original but all of which together will constitute one and the same instrument.

(g) *Headings.* The section headings contained in this Agreement are inserted for convenience only and shall not affect in any way the meaning or interpretation of this Agreement.

---

[85] The *pro-buyer* agreement (Exhibit A to sample acquisition agreement 2003.1) lacks a comparable proviso permitting the Target Stockholders to respond to unsolicited proposals to the extent their fiduciary duties may require.

(h) *Notices.*[86] All notices, requests, demands, claims, and other communications hereunder will be in writing. Any notice, request, demand, claim, or other communication hereunder shall be deemed duly given if (and then two business days after) it is sent by registered or certified mail, return receipt requested, postage prepaid, and addressed to the intended recipient as set forth below:

If to the Target Stockholders: *Copy to:*

If to the Buyer: *Copy to:*

Any Party may send any notice, request, demand, claim, or other communication hereunder to the intended recipient at the address set forth above using any other means (including personal delivery, expedited courier, messenger service, telecopy, telex, ordinary mail, or electronic mail), but no such notice, request, demand, claim, or other communication shall be deemed to have been duly given unless and until it actually is received by the intended recipient. Any Party may change the address to which notices, requests, demands, claims, and other communications hereunder are to be delivered by giving the other Parties notice in the manner herein set forth.

(i) *Governing Law. This Agreement shall be governed by and construed in accordance with the domestic laws of the State of* _____ *without giving effect to any choice or conflict of law provision or rule (whether of the State of* _____ *or any other jurisdiction) that would cause the application of the laws of any jurisdiction other than the State of* _____.

(j) *Amendments and Waivers.* No amendment of any provision of this Agreement shall be valid unless the same shall be in writing and signed by the Buyer and the Requisite Target Stockholders. No waiver by any Party of any default, misrepresentation, or breach of warranty or covenant hereunder, whether intentional or not, shall be deemed to extend to any prior or subsequent default, misrepresentation, or breach of warranty or covenant hereunder or affect in any way any rights arising by virtue of any prior or subsequent such occurrence.

(k) *Severability.* Any term or provision of this Agreement that is invalid or unenforceable in any situation in any jurisdiction shall not affect the validity or enforceability of the remaining terms and provisions hereof or the validity or enforceability of the offending term or provision in any other situation or in any other jurisdiction.

(l) *Expenses.* Each of the Parties will bear his or its own costs and expenses (including legal fees and expenses) incurred in connection with this Agreement and the transactions contemplated hereby (except as otherwise provided herein).

---

[86] The parties may want to add provisions designating a nominee to act on behalf of the Target Stockholders for purposes of receiving notice, agreeing to modifications and amendments, and taking action.

(m) *Construction.* [The Parties have participated jointly in the negotiation and drafting of this Agreement. In the event an ambiguity or question of intent or interpretation arises, this Agreement shall be construed as if drafted jointly by the Parties and no presumption or burden of proof shall arise favoring or disfavoring any Party by virtue of the authorship of any of the provisions of this Agreement.] Any reference to any federal, state, local, or foreign statute or law shall be deemed also to refer to all rules and regulations promulgated thereunder, unless the context requires otherwise. The word "including" shall mean including without limitation.

(n) *Incorporation of Annex.* The Annex is incorporated herein by reference and made a part hereof.

*   *   *   *   *

IN WITNESS WHEREOF, the Parties hereto have executed this Agreement on [as of] the date first above written.

[BUYER]

By: _____
Title: _____

[TARGET STOCKHOLDER # 1 (an entity)]

By: _____
Title: _____

[TARGET STOCKHOLDER # 2 (an entity)]

By: _____
Title: _____

_____
[TARGET STOCKHOLDER # 3 (an individual)]

¶2003.3   *Neutral Asset Purchase*

Sample acquisition agreement 2003.3 (*neutral asset purchase*) is intended to strike a reasonable balance between the conflicting interests of P and T in such areas as (i) the extent to which P will receive T's cash (net of unpaid taxes) at the time of the closing, (ii) the extent to which T will bear the burden of its liabilities and obligations after the closing, (iii) the extent to which P will have conditions to its obligation to close, (iv) the extent to which T will be required to give representations and warranties, and (v) the extent to which T will be required to indemnify P against breaches of those representations and warranties.

Sample acquisition agreement 2003.3 provides that P will (i) acquire T's cash at the closing and (ii) assume T's liability for unpaid taxes with respect to periods up to the closing (but not to exceed an amount computed in accordance with T's past custom and practice in filing its tax returns). This means that P will receive T's cash (net of unpaid taxes) at the time of the closing.

Sample acquisition agreement 2003.3 provides that the only T liabilities P will assume are those liabilities (i) shown on the last T balance sheet reviewed by P before signing the contract, (ii) incurred in the ordinary course of business thereafter (but not including claims and lawsuits), (iii) involving certain taxes (as noted above), employee benefit plans, and executory contracts, or (iv) listed on a disclosure schedule. Thus, P would generally *not* assume such undisclosed T liabilities as environmental cleanup, employment discrimination, antitrust violations, product liability, product warranty, tax deficiencies, and other claims and lawsuits.

Sample acquisition agreement 2003.3 contains fairly extensive representations and warranties from T concerning (i) its historical financial statements, (ii) intervening material adverse changes in its business, (iii) litigation and material undisclosed liabilities, (iv) tax matters, (v) pension and welfare benefit plans, (vi) compliance with federal, state, local, and foreign laws, (vii) environmental matters, and (viii) product liability and warranties.

Sample acquisition agreement 2003.3 also contains fairly extensive representations and warranties from T concerning (i) authorization with respect to the transaction, (ii) title to the assets being sold, (iii) required governmental and third party consents (and noncontravention generally), (iv) organization, (v) adequacy and condition of its tangible assets, (vi) real estate matters, (vii) intellectual property matters, (viii) leases, licenses, and contracts, (ix) inventory and accounts receivable, (x) insurance, (xi) brokerage fees, and (xii) material misstatements and omissions.

T's representations and warranties are, however, qualified with relatively frequent references to knowledge (defined as the actual knowledge of its shareholders, directors, and officers after reasonable investigation) and materiality.

Sample acquisition agreement 2003.3 provides that the representations and warranties with respect to the transaction itself and with respect to taxes will survive indefinitely, that the environmental representations and warranties will survive for five years, that the other representations and warranties will survive for two years, and that there will be a deductible and a ceiling with respect to indemnification against breaches of any representations and warranties that do not concern the transaction itself.[1]

P *does not* have any right to recoup its losses against the P notes in lieu of seeking indemnification from T and its shareholders.

P's obligation to close is subject to several conditions such as (i) compliance with T's representations, warranties, and covenants, (ii) absence of a material adverse change, (iii) absence of litigation affecting the transaction, (iv) receipt of governmental approvals, (v) delivery of title insurance, surveys, and material third party consents, (vi) delivery of any side agreements, and (vii) delivery of an opinion of T's legal counsel.

P *does not* have any closing condition concerning its ability to secure financing for the transaction *or* any right to terminate the purchase agreement after signing if it is not satisfied with the results of its continuing business, legal, and accounting due diligence review.

It is important to note that some of the provisions in sample acquisition agreement 2003.3 are neutral only in the context of the overall agreement. In part, this is due to the interplay between T's representations and warranties (which are fairly extensive, but qualified with references to knowledge and materiality) on the one hand and the indemnification obligations of T's stockholders (which are subject to various deductibles, ceilings, and survival periods) on the other. Accordingly, it is not always possible to remove a provision from sample acquisition agreement 2003.3 for use in another agreement and have the provision remain neutral.

Finally, the choice of neutral provisions for sample acquisition agreement 2003.3 was necessarily subjective. Thus, in any particular transaction, it may be necessary to modify the agreement so that it strikes a different balance between the interests of P and T.

There are a number of other important differences among sample acquisition agreement 2003.1 (*pro-buyer* asset purchase), sample acquisition agreement 2003.2 (*pro-seller* asset purchase), and sample acquisition agreement 2003.3 (*neutral* asset purchase). Each of these sample acquisition agreements contains extensive footnotes with cross-references pointing out the differences.

¶2003.3 [1]Sample acquisition agreement 2003.3 (the neutral *asset* purchase agreement) assumes that T will liquidate and dissolve immediately after the closing, so that the Target will not be able to perform any post-Closing covenants (including any post-Closing indemnification provisions) analogous to those contained in sample acquisition agreement 2002.3 (the neutral *stock* purchase agreement). The Agreement with Target Stockholders is designed to address this situation by making the Target *shareholders* responsible for the post-Closing covenants (including the post-Closing indemnification provisions).

ASSET PURCHASE AGREEMENT[2]

BETWEEN

_____

AND

_____

_____, 19____

TABLE OF CONTENTS

---

[2] The Buyer generally will obtain a cost basis (i.e., the Purchase Price *plus* the Assumed Liabilities *plus* the expenses of the transaction) in the Acquired Assets.

A purchase of assets in which the consideration is primarily cash and notes is generally treated for accounting purposes as a purchase rather than as a pooling of interests. *See* ¶1503.

Some LBO structures prejudice the Target's creditors and hence might permit payments, transfers, liens, and obligations arising out of the LBO to be attacked under fraudulent conveyance law. *See* ¶1506.

[EXHIBITS B THROUGH I AND THE DISCLOSURE SCHEDULE HAVE BEEN OMITTED FROM THIS SAMPLE ACQUISITION AGREEMENT 2003.3]

Agreement entered into on [as of] _____, 19____, by and between _____, a _____ corporation (the *"Buyer"*), and _____, a _____ corporation (the*"Target"*). The Buyer and the Target are referred to collectively herein as the *"Parties."*

This Agreement contemplates a transaction in which the Buyer will purchase all of the assets (and assume certain of the liabilities) of the Target in return for cash and the Buyer Notes.[4]

---

[3] This Asset Purchase Agreement assumes that the Target will liquidate and dissolve immediately after the Closing, so that the Target will not be able to perform any post-Closing covenants (including any post-Closing indemnification provisions) analogous to those contained in sample acquisition agreement 2002.3 (the neutral stock purchase agreement). The accompanying Agreement with Target Stockholders is designed to address this situation by making the Target Stockholders responsible for the post-Closing covenants (including the post-Closing indemnification provisions).

[4] Where the Buyer purchases the Target's assets, the Target will generally retain those assets and rights which it does not transfer and assign to the Buyer, and the Target will generally remain responsible for those liabilities and obligations not assumed by the Buyer.

It is generally necessary to prepare asset transfer documents and liability assumption documents in an asset purchase (whether a purchase of all the Target's assets or a purchase of the Target's division), which would not be required if the Buyer purchased the Target's *stock.*

The Buyer's contractual assumption of certain of the Target's liabilities and obligations generally will not preclude a third party to whom the Target owed the liabilities and obligations from suing

Now, therefore, in consideration of the premises and the mutual promises herein made, and in consideration of the representations, warranties, and covenants herein contained, the Parties agree as follows.

1. *Definitions.*

"Accredited Investor" has the meaning set forth in Regulation D promulgated under the Securities Act.

"Acquired Assets" means all right, title, and interest in and to all of the assets of the Target,[5] including all of its (a) real property, leaseholds and subleaseholds therein, improvements, fixtures, and fittings thereon, and easements, rights-of-way, and other appurtenants thereto (such as appurtenant rights in and to public streets), (b) tangible personal property (such as machinery, equipment, inventories of raw materials and supplies, manufactured and purchased parts, goods in process and finished goods, furniture, automobiles, trucks, tractors, trailers, tools, jigs, and dies), (c) Intellectual Property, goodwill associated therewith, licenses and sublicenses granted and obtained with respect thereto, and rights thereunder, remedies against infringements thereof, and rights to protection of interests therein under the laws of all jurisdictions, (d) leases, subleases, and rights thereunder, (e) agreements, contracts, indentures, mortgages, instruments, Security Interests, guaranties, other similar arrangements, and rights thereunder, (f) accounts, notes, and other receivables, (g) securities (such as the capital stock in its Subsidiaries), (h) claims, deposits, prepayments, refunds, causes of action, choses in action, rights of recovery, rights of set off, and rights of recoupment (including any such item relating to the payment of taxes), (i) franchises, approvals, permits, licenses, orders, registrations, certificates, variances, and similar rights obtained from governments and governmental agencies, (j) books, records, ledgers, files, documents, correspondence, lists, plats, architectural plans, drawings, and specifications, creative materials, advertising and promotional materials, studies, reports, and other printed or written materials, (k) Cash,[6] and (l) [rights in and with respect to the

---

the Target (if the Buyer has failed to pay or perform) unless the third party consents to the Buyer's assumption and agrees to look only to the Buyer for satisfaction (i.e., enters into a novation agreement). This means that, if the Buyer fails to satisfy the assumed liabilities and obligations, nonconsenting third parties to whom the Target owed the liabilities and obligations may have a cause of action against the Target or, if the Target has liquidated and dissolved, against the Target's stockholders and/or directors.

[5] This Agreement, like sample acquisition agreement 2003.1 (the *pro-buyer* asset purchase agreement), defines "Acquired Assets" broadly to include all right, title, and interest in and to the Target's assets.

Sample acquisition agreement 2003.2 (the *pro-seller* asset purchase agreement), on the other hand, defines "Acquired Assets" more narrowly to include only so much of the Target's right, title, and interest in and to its assets *as it possesses and has the right to transfer.*

[6] This Agreement, like sample acquisition agreement 2003.1 (the *pro-buyer* asset purchase agreement), provides that the Buyer will acquire the consolidated cash of the Target and its Subsidiaries.

Sample acquisition agreement 2003.2 (the *pro-seller* asset purchase agreement), on the other hand, provides that the Target will retain this consolidated cash (net of unpaid taxes up to the Closing for which the Buyer will become responsible).

assets associated with its Employee Benefit Plans];[7] *provided, however,* that the Acquired Assets shall not include (i) the corporate charter, qualifications to conduct business as a foreign corporation, arrangements with registered agents relating to foreign qualifications, taxpayer and other identification numbers, seals, minute books, stock transfer books, blank stock certificates, and other documents relating to the organization, maintenance, and existence of the Target as a corporation or (ii) any of the rights of the Target under this Agreement (or under any side agreement between the Target on the one hand and the Buyer on the other hand entered into on or after the date of this Agreement).

"Affiliate" has the meaning set forth in Rule 12b-2 of the regulations promulgated under the Securities Exchange Act.

"Affiliated Group" means any affiliated group within the meaning of Code §1504(a) [or any similar group defined under a similar provision of state, local, or foreign law].

"Agreement with Target Stockholders" means the Agreement with Target Stockholders entered into concurrently herewith and attached hereto as Exhibit A.[8]

"Applicable Rate" means the corporate base rate of interest publicly announced from time to time by [FINANCIAL INSTITUTION] [plus/minus ____% per annum].

"Assumed Liabilities"[9] means (a) all liabilities of the Target set forth on the face of the Most Recent Balance Sheet (rather than in any notes thereto), (b) all liabilities of the Target which have arisen after the Most Recent Fiscal Month End in the Ordinary Course of Business (other than any liability resulting from, arising out of, relating to, in the nature of, or caused by any breach of contract, breach of warranty, tort, infringement, violation of law, or environmental matter, including without limitation those arising under Environmental, Health, and Safety Requirements), (c) all obligations of the Target under the agreements, contracts, leases, licenses, and other arrangements referred to in the definition of Acquired Assets either (i) to furnish goods, services, and other non-Cash benefits to another party after the Closing or (ii) to pay for goods, services, and other non-Cash benefits that another party will furnish to it after the Closing, (d) [all liabilities

---

[7] *See* the provisions in §8(p) below with respect to employee benefits matters.

[8] This Asset Purchase Agreement assumes that the Target will liquidate and dissolve immediately after the Closing, so that the Target will not be able to perform any post-Closing covenants (including any post-Closing indemnification provisions) analogous to those contained in sample acquisition agreement 2002.3 (the neutral *stock* purchase agreement). The accompanying Agreement with Target Stockholders is designed to address this situation by making the *Target Stockholders* responsible for the post-Closing covenants (including the post-Closing indemnification provisions).

[9] *See* the footnote to §2(b) below for an important discussion of certain tax issues which may affect the drafting of this definition as it concerns liabilities of the Target which have not yet matured into a deduction for tax purposes.

and obligations of the Target under its Employee Benefit Plans],[10] and (e) [all other liabilities and obligations of or relating to the Target (including such liabilities and obligations relating to environmental matters[11]) specifically set forth in an appendix to the Disclosure Schedule under an express statement (that the Buyer has initialled) to the effect that the definition of Assumed Liabilities will include the liabilities and obligations so disclosed]; *provided, however*, that the Assumed Liabilities shall not include (i) any liability of the Target for Income Taxes,[12] (ii) any liability of the Target for transfer, sales, use, and other taxes arising in connection with the consummation of the transactions contemplated hereby, (iii) any liability of the Target for the unpaid taxes of any Person (other than any of the Target and its Subsidiaries) under Reg. §1.1502-6 (or any similar provision of state, local, or foreign law), as a transferee or successor, by contract, or otherwise,[13] (iv) any obligation of the Target to indemnify any Person (including any of the Target Stockholders) by reason of the fact that such Person was a director, officer, employee, or agent of any of the Target and its Subsidiaries or was serving at the request of any such entity as a partner, trustee, director, officer, employee, or agent of another entity (whether such indemnification is for judgments, damages, penalties, fines, costs, amounts paid in settlement, losses, expenses, or otherwise and whether such indemnification is pursuant to any statute, charter document, bylaw, agreement, or otherwise),[14] (v) any liability of the Target for costs and

[10] *See* the provisions in §8(p) below with respect to employee benefits matters.

[11] This provision states that Buyer assumes liabilities and obligations (including those relating to environmental matters) specifically set forth in the Disclosure Schedule.

Sample acquisition agreement 2003.1 (the *pro-buyer* asset purchase agreement) leaves with the Target all environmental liabilities (other than those shown on the face of the Most Recent Balance Sheet) of the Target.

Sample acquisition agreement 2003.2 (the *pro-seller* asset purchase agreement) requires the Buyer to assume all environmental liabilities relating to the Target.

[12] This provision leaves with Target the liability for all Income Taxes incurred by Target through the Closing. If it is desired that Buyer assume some or all of the such Income Taxes, this provision should be altered.

[13] If the Target has been a member of an Affiliated Group filing a consolidated federal income tax return, the target (or its successor) will be jointly and severally liable under Reg. §1.1502-6 for certain tax liabilities incurred by such Affiliated Group for a tax year when the Target was a member of such Affiliated Group for all or part of such tax year. *See* ¶210.

The Target may also be liable for the unpaid taxes of third parties under similar provisions of state, local, or foreign law, as a transferee or successor, by contract (e.g., a tax sharing agreement), or otherwise.

This provision is designed to protect the Buyer against assuming any liability for the unpaid taxes of any person other than the Target and its Subsidiaries.

[14] This Agreement, like sample acquisition agreement 2003.1 (the *pro-buyer* asset purchase agreement), provides that the Buyer will not assume any obligation of the Target to indemnify any Person (including any of the Target Stockholders), by reason of the fact that such Person was, before the asset purchase, a director or other officeholder of the Target entitled to indemnification from the Target, with respect to any matter whatsoever.

Note that sample acquisition agreement 2002.1 (the pro-buyer *stock* purchase agreement), where the Target retains its indemnification obligation to former directors and other officeholders even after the Buyer purchases the Target Shares, may not be as favorable to the Buyer. Sample acquisition agreement 2002.1 does, however, contain a narrower provision to the effect that none of the Target Stockholders will make any claim for indemnification against the Target, by reason of the fact that the Target Stockholder was, before the stock purchase, a director or other officeholder of the Target

expenses incurred in connection with this Agreement and the transactions contemplated hereby, or (vi) any liability or obligation of the Target under this Agreement (or under any side agreement between the Target on the one hand and the Buyer on the other hand entered into on or after the date of this Agreement).[15]

"Basis" means any past or present fact, situation, circumstance, status, condition, activity, practice, plan, occurrence, event, incident, action, failure to act, or transaction that forms or could form the basis for any specified consequence.

"Buyer" has the meaning set forth in the preface above.

"Buyer Note" has the meaning set forth in §2(c) below.

"Cash" means cash and cash equivalents (including marketable securities and short term investments) calculated in accordance with GAAP applied on a basis consistent with the preparation of the Financial Statements.

"Closing" has the meaning set forth in §2(d) below.

"Closing Date" has the meaning set forth §2(d) below.

"COBRA" means the requirements of Part 6 of Subtitle B of Title I of ERISA and Code §4980B and of any similar state law.

---

entitled to indemnification from the Target, with respect to any suit or claim the Buyer might bring against the Target Stockholder in connection with the stock purchase. This provision responds to the surprising decision in Heffernan v. Pacific Dunlop GNB Corporation, 965 F.2d 369 (7th Cir. 1992). *See* §8(g) of sample acquisition agreement 2002.1 (the pro-buyer *stock* purchase agreement) and the footnote thereto. Although *Heffernan* involved a purchase of stock, rather than a purchase of assets, the asset purchase covered by this Agreement presents many of the same concerns. *See also* §4(g)of the Agreement with Target Stockholders accompanying this Agreement.

Sample acquisition agreement 2003.2 (the *pro-seller* asset purchase agreement), on the other hand, provides that the Buyer *will assume* all obligations of the Target to indemnify any Person (including any of the Target Stockholders), by reason of the fact that such Person was, before the asset purchase, a director or other officeholder of the Target entitled to indemnification from the Target, with respect to any matter whatsoever.

[15] This Agreement, like sample acquisition agreement 2003.1 (the *pro-buyer* asset purchase agreement), contains a relatively narrow definition of Assumed Liabilities. The Buyer is assuming only those liabilities set forth on the face of the Most Recent Balance Sheet or incurred thereafter in the Ordinary Course of Business *plus* certain specified liabilities and obligations involving taxes, employee benefit plans, and executory contracts *plus* certain liabilities and obligations identified in the Disclosure Schedule. The Buyer is *not* assuming any undisclosed liabilities (with certain exceptions as noted in the preceding sentence) or any liabilities set forth in the Disclosure Schedule (unless the Disclosure Schedule contains an express assumption initialled by the Buyer).

Sample acquisition agreement 2003.2 (the *pro-seller* asset purchase agreement), on the other hand, contains a broad definition of Assumed Liabilities. In that form, the Buyer assumes substantially all liabilities and obligations of the Target (whether known or unknown, whether asserted or unasserted, whether absolute or contingent, whether accrued or unaccrued, whether liquidated or unliquidated, and whether due or to become due), including (i) unpaid taxes for periods prior to the Closing, (ii) income, transfer, sales, use, and other taxes arising in connection with the transaction (expressly including the *Target-level* income tax on the sale assets), (iii) costs and expenses arising in connection

"Code" means the Internal Revenue Code of 1986, as amended.

"Confidential Information" means any information concerning the businesses and affairs of the Target and its Subsidiaries that is not already generally available to the public.

"Controlled Group" has the meaning set forth in Code §1563.

"Deferred Intercompany Transaction" has the meaning set forth in Reg. §1.1502-13.

"Disclosure Schedule" has the meaning set forth in §3 below.

"Employee Benefit Plan" means any "employee benefit plan" (as such term is defined in ERISA §3(3)) and any other [material] employee benefit plan, program or arrangement of any kind.

"Employee Pension Benefit Plan" has the meaning set forth in ERISA §3(2).

"Employee Welfare Benefit Plan" has the meaning set forth in ERISA §3(1).

"Environmental, Health, and Safety Requirements"[16] shall mean all federal, state, local and foreign statutes, regulations, ordinances and similar provisions having the force or effect of law, all judicial and administrative orders and determinations, and all common law concerning public health and safety, worker health and safety, and pollution or protection of the environment, including without limitation all those relating to the presence, use, production, generation, handling, transportation, treatment, storage, disposal, distribution, labeling, testing, processing, discharge, release, threatened release, control, or cleanup of any hazardous materials, substances or wastes, chemical substances or mixtures, pesticides, pollutants, contaminants, toxic chemicals, petroleum products or byproducts, asbestos, polychlorinated biphenyls, noise or radiation.

"ERISA" means the Employee Retirement Income Security Act of 1974, as amended.

"ERISA Affiliate" means each entity which is treated as a single employer with the Target for purposes of Code §414.

---

with the transaction, (iv) contracts with third parties, (v) employee benefit plans, and (vi) matters set forth in the Disclosure Schedule.

[16] Sample acquisition agreement 2003.1 (the *pro-buyer* asset purchase agreement) explicitly extends this definition to include legal requirements enacted and in effect prior to, on, or after the Closing Date and also includes within this definition contractual obligations.

Sample acquisition agreement 2003.2 (the *pro-seller* asset purchase agreement) does not include either contractual obligations or common law in this definition and explicitly limits this definition to laws as enacted and in effect on or prior to the Closing Date.

"Excess Loss Account" has the meaning set forth in Reg. §1.1502-19.

"Fiduciary" has the meaning set forth in ERISA §3(21).

"Financial Statement" has the meaning set forth in §3(g) below.

"GAAP" means United States generally accepted accounting principles as in effect from time to time.

"Hart-Scott-Rodino Act" means the Hart-Scott-Rodino Antitrust Improvements Act of 1976, as amended.

"Income Tax" means any federal, state, local, or foreign income tax, including any interest, penalty, or addition thereto, whether disputed or not.[17]

"Income Tax Return" means any return, declaration, report, claim for refund, or information return or statement relating to Income Taxes, including any schedule or attachment thereto, and including any amendment thereof.

"Intellectual Property" means (a) all inventions (whether patentable or unpatentable and whether or not reduced to practice), all improvements thereto, and all patents, patent applications, and patent disclosures, together with all reissuances, continuations, continuations-in-part, revisions, extensions, and reexaminations thereof, (b) all trademarks, service marks, trade dress, logos, trade names, and corporate names, together with all translations, adaptations, derivations, and combinations thereof and including all goodwill associated therewith, and all applications, registrations, and renewals in connection therewith, (c) all copyrightable works, all copyrights, and all applications, registrations, and renewals in connection therewith, (d) all mask works and all applications, registrations, and renewals in connection therewith, (e) all trade secrets and confidential business information (including ideas, research and development, know-how, formulas, compositions, manufacturing and production processes and techniques, technical data, designs, drawings, specifications, customer and supplier lists, pricing and cost information, and business and marketing plans and proposals), (f) all computer software (including data and related documentation), (g) all other proprietary rights, and (h) all copies and tangible embodiments thereof (in whatever form or medium).

"Knowledge" means actual knowledge after reasonable investigation.[18]

---

[17] This Agreement, like sample acquisition agreement 2003.2 (the *pro-seller* asset purchase agreement), uses the term "Income Tax," which is defined narrowly to include only federal, state, local, and foreign income taxes. Sample acquisition agreement 2003.1 (the *pro-buyer* asset purchase agreement), on the other hand, uses the term "Tax," which is defined broadly to include taxes of all descriptions.

[18] This Agreement, like sample acquisition agreement 2003.1 (the *pro-buyer* asset purchase agreement), defines "Knowledge" as actual knowledge after reasonable investigation. Sample acquisi-

"Most Recent Balance Sheet" means the balance sheet contained within the Most Recent Financial Statements.

"Most Recent Financial Statements" has the meaning set forth in §3(g) below.

"Most Recent Fiscal Month End" has the meaning set forth in §3(g) below.

"Most Recent Fiscal Year End" has the meaning set forth in §3(g) below.

"Multiemployer Plan" has the meaning set forth in ERISA §3(37).

"Ordinary Course of Business" means the ordinary course of business consistent with past custom and practice (including with respect to quantity and frequency).

"Party" has the meaning set forth in the preface above.

"PBGC" means the Pension Benefit Guaranty Corporation.

"Person" means an individual, a partnership, a corporation, an association, a joint stock company, a trust, a joint venture, an unincorporated organization, or a governmental entity (or any department, agency, or political subdivision thereof).

"Prohibited Transaction" has the meaning set forth in ERISA §406 and Code §4975.

"Purchase Price" has the meaning set forth in §2(c) below.

"Reportable Event" has the meaning set forth in ERISA §4043.

"Securities Act" means the Securities Act of 1933, as amended.

"Securities Exchange Act" means the Securities Exchange Act of 1934, as amended.

"Security Interest" means any mortgage, pledge, lien, encumbrance, charge, or other security interest, *other than* (a) mechanic's, materialmen's, and similar liens, (b) liens for taxes not yet due and payable [or for taxes that the taxpayer is contesting in good faith through appropriate proceedings], (c) purchase money liens and liens securing rental payments under capital lease arrangements, and (d) other liens arising in the Ordinary Course of Business and not incurred in connection with the borrowing of money.

---

tion agreement 2003.2 (the *pro-seller* asset purchase agreement), on the other hand, defines "Knowledge" as actual knowledge without independent investigation.

"Subsidiary" means any corporation with respect to which a specified Person (or a Subsidiary thereof) owns a majority of the common stock or has the power to vote or direct the voting of sufficient securities to elect a majority of the directors.[19]

"Survey" has the meaning set forth in §5(i) below.

"Target" has the meaning set forth in the preface above.

"Target Share" means any share of the Common Stock, par value $_____ per share, of the Target.[20]

"Target Stockholder" means any person who or which holds any Target Shares.

2. *Basic Transaction.*[21]

(a) *Purchase and Sale of Assets.* On and subject to the terms and conditions of this Agreement, the Buyer agrees to purchase from the Target, and the Target agrees to sell, transfer, convey, and deliver to the Buyer, all of the Acquired Assets at the Closing for the consideration specified below in this §2.

(b) *Assumption of Liabilities.* On and subject to the terms and conditions of this Agreement, the Buyer agrees to assume and become responsible for all of the Assumed Liabilities at the Closing. The Buyer will not assume or have any responsibility, however, with respect to any other obligation or liability of the Target not included within the definition of Assumed Liabilities.[22]

---

[19] It may be necessary to revise this definition if, for example, the Target has subsidiary *partnerships*.

[20] It may be necessary to revise this definition if the Target has additional classes of capital stock.

[21] This Agreement, like sample acquisition agreement 2003.1 (the *pro-buyer* asset purchase agreement), provides that the Buyer will acquire the consolidated cash of the Target and its Subsidiaries at the Closing. *See* the definition of Acquired Assets in §1 above.

Sample acquisition agreement 2003.2 (the *pro-seller* asset purchase agreement), on the other hand, permits the Target to retain the consolidated cash of the Target and its Subsidiaries (net of unpaid taxes for which the Buyer will become responsible) at the Closing. *See* the definition of Acquired Assets in §1 thereof.

The *pro-seller* agreement also contains a provision allowing the Target to cause its Subsidiaries to distribute their cash to the Target at the Closing in order to facilitate the intended cash retention. *See* §2(d) thereof. This Agreement lacks a comparable provision (since there is no need for the Subsidiaries to distribute their cash to the Target at the Closing if the Target will not retain any of the consolidated cash).

[22] In a taxable purchase of the Target's assets, the Target may have liabilities which have not yet matured into a deduction for tax purposes. For example, (1) a cash method Target may have accrued (but unpaid) operating liabilities, (2) a cash method or an accrual method Target may have contingent liabilities, (3) a cash method or an accrual method Target may have unfunded pension liabilities, and (4) an accrual method Target may have liabilities as to which the "all events" test has been satisfied but as to which "economic performance" (e.g., payment) has not yet occurred. The tax treatment of these and other liabilities which have not yet matured into deductions is somewhat surprising. *See* ¶304.

Under Code §461(h), an accrual method Target can deduct liabilities which otherwise satisfy the all events test (i.e., "Code §461(h) Liabilities") only as economic performance occurs. With respect to many such liabilities, economic performance occurs under the proposed Code §461(h) regulations only when the Target has made payment with respect to the liability. *See* ¶304.4.

(c) *Purchase Price*.[23] The Buyer agrees to pay to the Target at the Closing $_____ (the *"Purchase Price"*) by delivery of (i) its promissory notes (the *"Buyer Notes"*) in the form of Exhibit B attached hereto in the aggregate principal amount of $_____ and (ii) cash for the balance of the Purchase Price payable by wire transfer or delivery of other immediately available funds.[24]

(d) *The Closing.* The closing of the transactions contemplated by this Agreement (the *"Closing"*) shall take place at the offices of _____ in _____, _____ commencing at 9:00 a.m. local time on the [second] business day following the satisfaction or waiver of all conditions to the obligations of the Parties to consummate the transactions contemplated hereby (other than conditions with respect to actions the respective Parties will take at the Closing itself) or such other date as the Parties may mutually determine (the *"Closing Date"*); *provided, however*, that the Closing Date shall be no earlier than _____, 19____.

(e) *Deliveries at the Closing.* At the Closing, (i) the Target will deliver to the Buyer the various certificates, instruments, and documents referred to in §6(a)

Reg. §§1.461-4(d)(5) and -4(g)(1)(ii)(C) seem to provide that when the Target sells the Buyer a trade or business and, as part of the sale, the Buyer *"expressly assumes"* a Code §461(h) Liability, the, Target can deduct that liability (assuming that the Code §461(h) regulations make payment the proper test for economic performance) in the taxable year in which the sale occurred. This favorable tax result follows from the fact that the Target will be deemed to have made payment with respect to the liability when the amount of the liability (assumed by the Buyer) is included in the Target's amount realized on the sale of assets. The proposed regulation is, however, unclear on the meaning of the phrase "expressly assumes." *See* ¶304.4.

Cautious taxpayers should accordingly consider taking some or all of the following steps: (i) the Parties should specifically enumerate in this Agreement as many as practicable of the Code §461(h) Liabilities which the Buyer is assuming; (ii) the Parties should specifically state in this Agreement that the Buyer is "expressly assuming" not only these enumerated liabilities, but also any categories of *unenumerated* Code §461(h) Liabilities which the Buyer is assuming; and (iii) the boards of directors of the respective Parties should adopt resolutions specifically stating that the Buyer is "expressly assuming" these Code §461(h) Liabilities.

Reg. §§1.461-4(d)(5) and -4(g)(1)(ii)(C) are applicable by their terms only with respect to Code §461(h) Liabilities. However, their premise that the Target will be deemed to have made payment with respect to a liability when the amount of the liability (assumed by the Buyer) is included in the Target's amount realized on the sale of assets may have a broader application. For this reason, cautious taxpayers may want to apply the advice in the preceding paragraph of this footnote to cover *all* liabilities which the Buyer is assuming as to which the Target has not yet become entitled to a deduction under the Code.

[23] The Target may seek to have the Buyer make an earnest money deposit upon execution of this Agreement. If the transaction were thereafter completed, the deposit would be applied to the Purchase Price. If the transaction were thereafter aborted, the deposit would be refunded to the Buyer or paid to the Target as liquidated damages depending on the terms of this Agreement and the reasons for termination.

[24] Sample acquisition agreement 2002.5 contains additional provisions for use where there is to be a post-Closing Purchase Price adjustment based on the consolidated net book value for the Target and its Subsidiaries as of the Closing. That sample acquisition agreement can be adapted for other post-Closing Purchase Price adjustments (such as a comparison of consolidated working capital with consolidated liabilities as of the Closing *or* a contingent earnout based on consolidated earnings for a specified period after the Closing).

below; (ii) the Buyer will deliver to the Target the various certificates, instruments, and documents referred to in §6(b) below; (iii) the Target will execute, acknowledge (if appropriate), and deliver to the Buyer (A) assignments (including real property and Intellectual Property transfer documents) in the forms attached hereto as Exhibits C-1 through C-_____ and (B) such other instruments of sale, transfer, conveyance, and assignment as the Buyer and its counsel [reasonably] may request; (iv) the Buyer will execute, acknowledge (if appropriate), and deliver to the Target (A) an assumption in the form attached hereto as Exhibit D and (B) such other instruments of assumption as the Target and its counsel [reasonably] may request; and (v) the Buyer will deliver to the Target the consideration specified in §2(c) above.

(f) *Allocation.* [The Parties agree to allocate the Purchase Price (and all other capitalizable costs) among the Acquired Assets for all purposes (including financial accounting and tax purposes) in accordance with the allocation schedule attached hereto as Exhibit E.][25]

3. *Representations and Warranties of the Target.*[26] The Target represents and warrants to the Buyer that the statements contained in this §3 are correct and complete as of the date of this Agreement and will be correct and complete as of the Closing Date (as though made then and as though the Closing Date were substituted for the date of this Agreement throughout this §3), except as set forth in the disclosure schedule accompanying this Agreement and initialed by the Parties (the *"Disclosure Schedule"*).[27] The Disclosure Schedule will be arranged in paragraphs corresponding to the lettered and numbered paragraphs contained in this §3.

Sample acquisition agreement 2002.5 is, however, intended for use with sample acquisition agreements 2002.1, 2002.2, and 2002.3 (the *stock* purchase agreements) and must be modified prior to use with this *asset* purchase agreement.

[25] The 1986 Act generally requires the Buyer and the Target to allocate the Buyer's aggregate basis (i.e., the Purchase Price *plus* the Assumed Liabilities *plus* the expenses of the transaction) among the Acquired Assets using the residual method. *See* ¶403. The Parties should omit this provision if they do not reach agreement on a particular allocation schedule.

[26] The Buyer will seek to have the Target make extensive representations and warranties concerning the Target and its Subsidiaries, with only occasional qualifications as to knowledge and without any qualification as to materiality. *See* §3 of sample acquisition agreement 2003.1 (the *pro-buyer* asset purchase agreement).

The Target, on the other hand, will seek to give fewer representations and warranties concerning the Target and its Subsidiaries, with frequent qualifications as to knowledge and materiality. *See* §3 of sample acquisition agreement 2003.2 (the *pro-seller* asset purchase agreement).

This Agreement, which is intended to favor neither the Buyer nor the Target, contains fairly extensive representations and warranties *and* relatively frequent qualifications as to knowledge and materiality.

[27] The Buyer will have a closing condition (*see* §6(a)(i) below) and post-Closing indemnification rights (*see* §4(b) of the accompanying Agreement with Target Stockholders) with respect to certain misrepresentations and breaches of warranty. The Buyer will not, however, have a closing condition or post-Closing indemnification rights with respect to any adverse matter which the Target discloses in the Disclosure Schedule. This is because the disclosure will cure any misrepresentation or breach of warranty that might otherwise have existed. Thus, where the Target discloses an adverse matter in the Disclosure Schedule, the Buyer may seek (a) to avoid assuming responsibility for the matter (*see* the definition of Assumed Liabilities in §1 above), (b) to add a specific closing condition requiring

(a) *Organization of the Target.* The Target is a corporation duly organized, validly existing, and in good standing under the laws of the jurisdiction of its incorporation.

(b) *Authorization of Transaction.* The Target has full power and authority (including full corporate power and authority) to execute and deliver this Agreement and to perform its obligations hereunder. Without limiting the generality of the foregoing, the board of directors of the Target and the Target Stockholders have duly authorized the execution, delivery, and performance of this Agreement by the Target.[28] This Agreement constitutes the valid and legally binding obligation of the Target, enforceable in accordance with its terms and conditions.

(c) *Noncontravention.* Neither the execution and the delivery of this Agreement, nor the consummation of the transactions contemplated hereby (including the assignments and assumptions referred to in §2 above), will (i) violate any constitution, statute, regulation, rule, injunction, judgment, order, decree, ruling, charge, or other restriction of any government, governmental agency, or court to which any of the Target and its Subsidiaries is subject or any provision of the charter or bylaws of any of the Target and its Subsidiaries or (ii) conflict with, result in a breach of, constitute a default under, result in the acceleration of, create in any party the right to accelerate, terminate, modify, or cancel, or require any notice under any agreement, contract, lease, license, instrument, or other arrangement to which any of the Target and its Subsidiaries is a party or by which it is bound or to which any of its assets is subject (or result in the imposition of any Security Interest upon any of its assets), except where the violation, conflict, breach, default, acceleration, termination, modification, cancellation, failure to give notice, or Security Interest would not have a material adverse effect on the business, financial condition, operations, results of operations, or future prospects of the Target and its Subsidiaries or on the ability of the Parties to consummate the transactions contemplated by this Agreement. None of the Target and its Subsidiaries needs to give any notice to, make any filing with, or obtain any authorization, consent, or approval of any government or governmental agency in order for the Parties to consummate the transactions contemplated by this Agreement (including the assignments and assumptions referred to in §2 above), except where the failure

---

an acceptable resolution of the matter, and/or (c) to obtain specific post-Closing indemnification against the matter.

[28] The Target must obtain the approval of its board of directors *and* the approval of its stockholders in order to sell all or substantially all of its assets. *See* ¶2001.2.2.2. This Agreement assumes the Target has already obtained the requisite corporate approvals.

If the Parties wish to enter into this Agreement before the Target has obtained the approval of its *stockholders,* the Parties should revise this Agreement to include (a) a covenant calling for the Target to obtain such approval prior to the Closing and (b) a closing condition for each of the Parties to the effect that the Target *has* obtained such approval. *Compare* sample acquisition agreement 2005 (the reverse subsidiary merger agreement) which contemplates the target corporation will obtain the approval of its stockholders between the signing of the merger agreement and the Closing.

The Parties generally will not enter into an asset purchase agreement (or for that matter a merger agreement) of until the Target has obtained the approval its *board of directors.*

to give notice, to file, or to obtain any authorization, consent, or approval would not have a material adverse effect on the business, financial condition, operations, results of operations, or future prospects of the Target and its Subsidiaries or on the ability of the Parties to consummate the transactions contemplated by this Agreement.

(d) *Brokers' Fees.* The Target has no liability or obligation to pay any fees or commissions to any broker, finder, or agent with respect to the transactions contemplated by this Agreement for which the Buyer could become liable or obligated. None of the Subsidiaries of the Target has any liability or obligation to pay any fees or commissions to any broker, finder, or agent with respect to the transactions contemplated by this Agreement.

(e) *Title to Assets.* The Target and its Subsidiaries have good and marketable title to, or a valid leasehold interest in, the properties and assets used by them, located on their premises, or shown on the Most Recent Balance Sheet or acquired after the date thereof, free and clear of all Security Interests, except for properties and assets disposed of in the Ordinary Course of Business since the date of the Most Recent Balance Sheet. Without limiting the generality of the foregoing, the Target has good and marketable title to all of the Acquired Assets, free and clear of any Security Interest or restriction on transfer.

(f) *Subsidiaries.* §3(f) of the Disclosure Schedule sets forth for each Subsidiary of the Target (i) its name and jurisdiction of incorporation, (ii) the number of shares of authorized capital stock of each class of its capital stock, (iii) the number of issued and outstanding shares of each class of its capital stock, the names of the holders thereof, and the number of shares held by each such holder, (iv) the number of shares of its capital stock held in treasury, and (v) its directors and officers. Each Subsidiary of the Target is a corporation duly organized, validly existing, and in good standing under the laws of the jurisdiction of its incorporation. Each Subsidiary of the Target is duly authorized to conduct business and is in good standing under the laws of each jurisdiction where such qualification is required, except where the lack of such qualification would not have a material adverse effect on the business, financial condition, operations, results of operations, or future prospects of the Target and its Subsidiaries. Each Subsidiary of the Target has full corporate power and authority to carry on the businesses in which it is engaged and to own and use the properties owned and used by it. All of the issued and outstanding shares of capital stock of each Subsidiary of the Target have been duly authorized and are validly issued, fully paid, and nonassessable. One of the Target and its Subsidiaries holds of record and owns beneficially all of the outstanding shares of each Subsidiary of the Target, free and clear of any restrictions on transfer (other than restrictions under the Securities Act and state securities laws), taxes, Security Interests, options, warrants, purchase rights, contracts, commitments, equities, claims, and demands. There are no outstanding or authorized options, warrants, purchase rights, subscription rights, conversion rights, exchange rights, or other contracts or commitments that could require any of the Target and its Subsidiaries to sell, transfer, or otherwise dispose of any capital stock of any of its Subsidiaries or that could require any Subsidiary of the Target to issue, sell, or otherwise cause to become outstanding any of its own capital stock (other than this Agreement). There are no outstanding stock appreciation, phantom stock, profit participation, or similar rights with respect to any Subsidiary of the Target. There are no voting trusts, proxies, or other agreements or understandings with respect to the voting of any capital stock of any Subsidiary of the Target. None of the Target and its Subsidiaries controls directly or indirectly or has any direct or indirect equity participation in any corporation, partnership, trust, or other business association which is not a Subsidiary of the Target.

(g) *Financial Statements.* Attached hereto as Exhibit F are the following financial statements (collectively the *"Financial Statements"*): (i) audited consolidated balance sheets and statements of income, changes in stockholders' equity, and cash flow as of and for the fiscal years ended _____, 19____, _____, 19____, _____, 19____, _____, 19____, and _____, 19____ (the *"Most Recent Fiscal Year End"*) for the Target and its Subsidiaries; and (ii) unaudited consolidated balance sheets and statements of income, changes in stockholders' equity, and cash flow (the *"Most Recent Financial Statements"*) as of and for the _____ months ended _____, 19____ (the *"Most Recent Fiscal Month End"*) for the Target and its Subsidiaries. The Financial Statements (including the notes thereto) have been prepared in accordance with GAAP applied on a consistent basis throughout the periods covered thereby, present fairly the financial condition of the Target and its Subsidiaries as of such dates and the results of operations of the Target and its Subsidiaries for such periods;[29] *provided, however,* that the Most Recent Financial Statements are subject to normal year-end adjustments (which will not be material individually or in the aggregate) and lack footnotes and other presentation items.

(h) *Events Subsequent to Most Recent Fiscal Year End.* Since the Most Recent Fiscal Year End, there has not been any material adverse change in the business, financial condition, operations, results of operations, or future prospects of the Target and its Subsidiaries taken as a whole. Without limiting the generality of the foregoing, since that date:

(i) none of the Target and its Subsidiaries has sold, leased, transferred, or assigned any material assets, tangible or intangible, outside the Ordinary Course of Business;

(ii) none of the Target and its Subsidiaries has entered into any material agreement, contract, lease, or license outside the Ordinary Course of Business;

---

[29] This Agreement, like sample acquisition agreement 2003.2 (the *pro-seller* asset purchase agreement), contains a representation and warranty to the effect that the Financial Statements have been prepared in accordance with GAAP consistently applied and fairly present the financial condition and the results of operations of the Target and its Subsidiaries. Sample acquisition agreement 2003.1

(iii) no party (including any of the Target and its Subsidiaries) has accelerated, terminated, made material modifications to, or cancelled any material agreement, contract, lease, or license to which any of the Target and its Subsidiaries is a party or by which any of them is bound;

(iv) none of the Target and its Subsidiaries has imposed any Security Interest upon any of its assets, tangible or intangible;

(v) none of the Target and its Subsidiaries has made any material capital expenditures outside the Ordinary Course of Business;

(vi) none of the Target and its Subsidiaries has made any material capital investment in, or any material loan to, any other Person outside the Ordinary Course of Business;

(vii) the Target and its Subsidiaries have not created, incurred, assumed, or guaranteed more than $_____ in aggregate indebtedness for borrowed money and capitalized lease obligations;

(viii) none of the Target and its Subsidiaries has granted any license or sublicense of any material rights under or with respect to any Intellectual Property;

(ix) there has been no change made or authorized in the charter or bylaws of any of the Target and its Subsidiaries;

(x) none of the Target and its Subsidiaries has issued, sold, or otherwise disposed of any of its capital stock, or granted any options, warrants, or other rights to purchase or obtain (including upon conversion, exchange, or exercise) any of its capital stock;

(xi) none of the Target and its Subsidiaries has declared, set aside, or paid any dividend or made any distribution with respect to its capital stock (whether in cash or in kind) or redeemed, purchased, or otherwise acquired any of its capital stock;

(xii) none of the Target and its Subsidiaries has experienced any material damage, destruction, or loss (whether or not covered by insurance) to its property;

(xiii) none of the Target and its Subsidiaries has made any loan to, or entered into any other transaction with, any of its directors, officers, and employees outside the Ordinary Course of Business;

(the *pro-buyer* asset purchase agreement), on the other hand, contains additional representations and warranties to the effect that the Financial Statements are correct and complete and consistent with the books and records of the Target and its Subsidiaries.

(xiv) none of the Target and its Subsidiaries has entered into any employment contract or collective bargaining agreement, written or oral, or modified the terms of any existing such contract or agreement;

(xv) none of the Target and its Subsidiaries has granted any increase in the base compensation of any of its directors, officers, and employees outside the Ordinary Course of Business;

(xvi) none of the Target and its Subsidiaries has adopted, amended, modified, or terminated any bonus, profit-sharing, incentive, severance, or other plan, contract, or commitment for the benefit of any of its directors, officers, and employees (or taken any such action with respect to any other Employee Benefit Plan);

(xvii) none of the Target and its Subsidiaries has made any other material change in employment terms for any of its directors, officers, and employees outside the Ordinary Course of Business;

(xviii) none of the Target and its Subsidiaries has paid any amount to any third party with respect to any liability or obligation (including any costs and expenses the Target has incurred or may incur in connection with this Agreement and the transactions contemplated hereby) which would not constitute an Assumed Liability if in existence as of the Closing;[30] and

(xix) none of the Target and its Subsidiaries has committed to any of the foregoing.

(i) *Undisclosed Liabilities.* None of the Target and its Subsidiaries has any material liability (whether known or unknown, whether asserted or unasserted, whether absolute or contingent, whether accrued or unaccrued, whether liquidated or unliquidated, and whether due or to become due, including any liability for taxes), except for (i) liabilities set forth on the face of the Most Recent Balance Sheet (rather than in any notes thereto) and (ii) liabilities which have arisen after the Most Recent Fiscal Month End in the Ordinary Course of Business.[31]

---

[30] Notice that the Buyer will bear the cost of (i.e., will in effect assume) any liability or obligation to the extent the Target pays any amount to a third party with respect thereto prior to the Closing. This is because the payment will reduce the amount of cash the Buyer otherwise would receive when it acquires the assets of the Target and its Subsidiaries at the Closing. The Buyer therefore will seek to prevent the Target from making any payment with respect to a liability or obligation the Buyer is not assuming.

This representation and warranty is designed to uncover whether the Target has made any such payment between the Most Recent Fiscal Year End and the date of this Agreement. §5(c) below contains a comparable covenant prohibiting the Target from making any such payment between the date of this Agreement and the Closing.

[31] This Agreement, like sample acquisition agreement 2003.1 (the *pro-buyer* asset purchase agreement), contains a representation and warranty regarding undisclosed liabilities. Sample acquisition agreement 2003.2 (the *pro-seller* asset purchase agreement), on the other hand, lacks such a provision.

(j) *Legal Compliance.* Each of the Target and its Subsidiaries has complied with all applicable laws (including rules, regulations, codes, plans, injunctions, judgments, orders, decrees, rulings, and charges thereunder) of federal, state, local, and foreign governments (and all agencies thereof), and no action, suit, proceeding, hearing, investigation, charge, complaint, claim, demand, or notice has been filed or commenced against any of them alleging any failure so to comply, except where the failure to comply would not have a material adverse effect on the business, financial condition, operations, results of operations, or future prospects of the Target and its Subsidiaries.

(k) *Tax Matters.*[32]

(i) Each of the Target and its Subsidiaries has filed all Income Tax Returns that it was required to file. All such Income Tax Returns were correct and complete in all material respects. All Income Taxes owed by any of the Target and its Subsidiaries (whether or not shown on any Income Tax Return) have been paid.[33] None of the Target and its Subsidiaries currently is the beneficiary of any extension of time within which to file any Income Tax Return.

(ii) There is no material dispute or claim concerning any Income Tax liability of any of the Target and its Subsidiaries either (A) claimed or raised by any

---

[32] This Agreement provides that the Buyer will assume the tax liabilities of the *Target* with respect to periods prior to the Closing for which the return is due after the Closing up to an amount computed in accordance with the past custom and practice of the Target and its Subsidiaries in filing their tax returns. *See* the definition of Assumed Liabilities in §1 above.

In addition, the Buyer may be exposed for certain tax liabilities of the *Target* by operation of law if the Target does not pay them (e.g., under applicable bulk sales statutes and common law doctrines of de facto merger and successor liability). *See* ¶2001.2.2.2.

Finally, the Buyer will become indirectly responsible for all of the tax liabilities of the *Subsidiaries* when the Buyer acquires their capital stock as part of the Acquired Assets. For this reason, the Buyer may seek (a) to purchase assets from the Target *and from each of the Subsidiaries* (i.e., a multiple entity asset sale) or (b) to have the Target liquidate and dissolve the Subsidiaries tax free under Code §332 (to the extent they are United States corporations) and sell their assets to the Buyer.

These representations and warranties concerning taxes (and the post-Closing indemnification provisions in §4(b) of the accompanying Agreement with Target Stockholders) are designed to work in conjunction with the narrow definition of Assumed Liabilities in §1 above to protect the Buyer against tax liabilities it does not intend to assume.

[33] Sample acquisition agreement 2003.1 (the *pro-buyer* asset purchase agreement) contains a broad representation and warranty to the effect that each of the Target and its Subsidiaries has filed all tax returns that it was required to file, that all such tax returns were correct and complete in all respects, and that all taxes owed by any of the Target and its Subsidiaries (whether or not shown on any return) have been paid.

Sample acquisition agreement 2003.2 (the *pro-seller* asset purchase agreement), on the other hand, contains a narrow representation to the effect that each of the Target and its Subsidiaries has filed all *income* tax returns that it was required to file and has paid all *income* taxes *shown thereon as owing.*

This Agreement, which is intended to favor neither the Buyer nor the Target, contains a fairly broad representation and warranty to the effect that each of the Target and its Subsidiaries has filed all *income* tax returns that it was required to file, that all such *income* tax returns were correct and complete in all *material* respects, and that all *income* taxes owed by any of the Target and its Subsidiaries (whether or not shown on any return) have been paid.

authority in writing or (B) as to which any of the Target Stockholders and the directors and officers of the Target and its Subsidiaries has Knowledge based upon personal contact with any agent of such authority.

(iii) 3(k) of the Disclosure Schedule lists all federal, state, local, and foreign Income Tax Returns filed with respect to any of the Target and its Subsidiaries for taxable periods ended on or after _____, 19____, indicates those Income Tax Returns that have been audited, and indicates those Income Tax Returns that currently are the subject of audit. The Target has delivered to the Buyer correct and complete copies of all federal Income Tax Returns, examination reports, and statements of deficiencies assessed against or agreed to by any of the Target and its Subsidiaries since _____, 19____. None of the Target and its Subsidiaries has waived any statute of limitations in respect of Income Taxes or agreed to any extension of time with respect to an Income Tax assessment or deficiency.

(iv) None of the Target and its Subsidiaries has filed a consent under Code §341(f) concerning collapsible corporations. None of the Target and its Subsidiaries has made any material payments, is obligated to make any material payments, or is a party to any agreement that under certain circumstances could obligate it to make any material payments that will not be deductible under Code §280G. None of the Target and its Subsidiaries has been a United States real property holding corporation within the meaning of Code §897(c)(2) during the applicable period specified in Code §897(c)(1)(A)(ii). None of the Target and its Subsidiaries is a party to any tax allocation or sharing agreement. None of the Target and its Subsidiaries (A) has been a member of an Affiliated Group filing a consolidated federal Income Tax Return (other than a group the common parent of which was the Target) or (B) has any liability for the taxes of any Person (other than any of the Target and its Subsidiaries) under Reg. §1.1502-6 (or any similar provision of state, local, or foreign law), as a transferee or successor, by contract, or otherwise.[34]

---

[34] If the Target or a Subsidiary has been a member of an Affiliated Group filing a consolidated federal income tax return, such corporation (or its successor) will be jointly and severally liable under Reg. §1.1502-6 for certain tax liabilities incurred by such Affiliated Group for a tax year when such corporation was a member of such Affiliated Group for all or part of such tax year. *See* ¶210.

The Target or a Subsidiary may also be liable for the unpaid taxes of third parties under similar provisions of state, local, or foreign law, as a transferee or successor, by contract (e.g., a tax sharing agreement), or otherwise.

This Agreement, like sample acquisition agreement 2003.1 (the *pro-buyer* asset purchase agreement), contains extensive provisions designed to protect the Buyer against any such liability for the unpaid taxes of any person other than the Target and its Subsidiaries.

First, this Agreement provides that the Buyer will not assume any liability of the *Target* for the unpaid taxes of any third party. *See* the definition of "Assumed Liabilities" in §1 above. However, the Buyer will become indirectly responsible for any such liability of the *Subsidiaries* when the Buyer acquires their capital stock as part of the Acquired Assets. In order to eliminate this risk altogether, the Buyer may seek (a) to purchase assets from the Target *and from each of the Subsidiaries* (i.e., a multiple entity asset sale) or (b) to have the Target liquidate and dissolve the Subsidiaries tax free under Code §332 (to the extent they are United States corporations) and sell their assets to the Buyer.

(v) The unpaid Income Taxes of the Target and its Subsidiaries (A) did not, as of the Most Recent Fiscal Month End, exceed by any material amount the reserve for Income Tax liability (rather than any reserve for deferred taxes established to reflect timing differences between book and tax income) set forth on the face of the Most Recent Balance Sheet (rather than in any notes thereto) and (B) will not exceed by any material amount that reserve as adjusted for operations and transactions through the Closing Date in accordance with the past custom and practice of the Target and its Subsidiaries in filing their Income Tax Returns.

(l) *Real Property.*[35]

(i) §3(l)(i) of the Disclosure Schedule lists and describes briefly all real property that any of the Target and its Subsidiaries owns. With respect to each such parcel of owned real property:

(A) the identified owner has good and marketable title to the parcel of real property, free and clear of any Security Interest, easement, covenant, or other restriction, except for installments of special assessments not yet delinquent, recorded easements, covenants, and other restrictions, and utility easements, building restrictions, zoning restrictions, and other easements and restrictions existing generally with respect to properties of a similar character which do not affect materially and adversely the current use, occupancy, or value, or the marketability of title, of the property subject thereto;

(B) there are no pending or, to the Knowledge of any of the Target Stockholders and the directors and officers of the Target and its Subsidiaries, threatened condemnation proceedings, lawsuits, or administrative actions relating to the property or other matters affecting materially and adversely the current use, occupancy, or value thereof;

(C) the legal description for the parcel contained in the deed thereof describes such parcel fully and adequately, the buildings and improvements

---

In addition, this Agreement contains a representation (set forth above) to the effect that none of the Target and its Subsidiaries has any liability for the unpaid taxes of any third party (as a former member of another Affiliated Group or otherwise).

Finally, the Agreement with Target Stockholders (Exhibit A to this Agreement) contains indemnification provisions designed to protect the Buyer against any such liability for the unpaid taxes of third parties. *See* §4(b)(iii) of Exhibit A.

Sample acquisition agreement 2003.2 (the *pro-seller* asset purchase agreement), on the other hand, provides that the Buyer *will* assume any liability of the Target for the unpaid taxes of third parties, contains a narrower representation (qualified by knowledge) to the effect that none of the Target and its Subsidiaries has belonged to another Affiliated Group, and lacks indemnification provisions designed to protect the Buyer against any such liability for the unpaid taxes of third parties.

[35] These representations and warranties concerning real property are relatively long and detailed. A condensed version of these provision may be more appropriate where, for example, the real property of the Target and its Subsidiaries is relatively insignificant.

are located within the boundary lines of the described parcels of land, are not in material violation of applicable setback requirements, zoning laws, and ordinances (and none of the properties or buildings or improvements thereon are subject to "permitted non-conforming use" or "permitted non-conforming structure" classifications), and do not encroach on any easement which may burden the land;

(D) all facilities have received all approvals of governmental authorities (including material licenses and permits) required in connection with the ownership or operation thereof, and have been operated and maintained in accordance with applicable laws, rules, and regulations in all material respects;

(E) there are no leases, subleases, licenses, concessions, or other agreements, written or oral, granting to any party or parties the right of use or occupancy of any portion of the parcel of real property;

(F) there are no outstanding options or rights of first refusal to purchase the parcel of real property, or any portion thereof or interest therein;

(G) there are no parties (other than the Target and its Subsidiaries) in possession of the parcel of real property, other than tenants under any leases disclosed in §3(l)(i) of the Disclosure Schedule who are in possession of space to which they are entitled.

(ii) 3(l)(ii) of the Disclosure Schedule lists and describes briefly all real property leased or subleased to any of the Target and its Subsidiaries. §3(l)(ii) of the Disclosure Schedule also identifies the leased or subleased properties for which title insurance policies are to be procured in accordance with §5(h)(ii) below. The Target has delivered to the Buyer correct and complete copies of the leases and subleases listed in §3(l)(ii) of the Disclosure Schedule (as amended to date). With respect to each material lease and sublease listed in §3(l)(ii) of the Disclosure Schedule:

(A) the lease or sublease is legal, valid, binding, enforceable, and in full force and effect in all material respects;

(B) no party to the lease or sublease is in material breach or default, and no event has occurred which, with notice or lapse of time, would constitute a material breach or default or permit termination, modification, or acceleration thereunder;

(C) no party to the lease or sublease has repudiated any material provision thereof;

(D) there are no material disputes, oral agreements, or forbearance programs in effect as to the lease or sublease;

(E) none of the Target and its Subsidiaries has assigned, transferred, conveyed, mortgaged, deeded in trust, or encumbered any interest in the leasehold or subleasehold; and

(F) all facilities leased or subleased thereunder have received all approvals of governmental authorities (including material licenses and permits) required in connection with the operation thereof, and have been operated and maintained in accordance with applicable laws, rules, and regulations in all material respects.

(m) *Intellectual Property.*[36]

(i) None of the Target and its Subsidiaries has interfered with, infringed upon, misappropriated, or violated any material Intellectual Property rights of third parties in any material respect, and none of the Target Stockholders and the directors and officers of the Target and its Subsidiaries has ever received any charge, complaint, claim, demand, or notice alleging any such interference, infringement, misappropriation, or violation (including any claim that any of the Target and its Subsidiaries must license or refrain from using any Intellectual Property rights of any third party). To the Knowledge of any of the Target Stockholders and the directors and officers of the Target and its Subsidiaries, no third party has interfered with, infringed upon, misappropriated, or violated any material Intellectual Property rights of any of the Target and its Subsidiaries in any material respect.

(ii) §3(m)(ii) of the Disclosure Schedule identifies each patent or registration which has been issued to any of the Target and its Subsidiaries with respect to any of its Intellectual Property, identifies each pending patent application or application for registration which any of the Target and its Subsidiaries has made with respect to any of its Intellectual Property, and identifies each material license, agreement, or other permission which any of the Target and its Subsidiaries has granted to any third party with respect to any of its Intellectual Property (together with any exceptions). The Target has delivered to the Buyer correct and complete copies of all such patents, registrations, applications, licenses, agreements, and permissions (as amended to date). §3(m)(ii) of the Disclosure Schedule also identifies each material trade name or unregistered trademark used by any of the Target and its Subsidiaries in connection with any of its businesses. With respect to each item of Intellectual Property required to be identified in §3(m)(ii) of the Disclosure Schedule:

---

[36] These representations and warranties concerning intellectual property are relatively long and detailed. A condensed version of these provisions may be more appropriate where, for example, the intellectual property of the Target and its Subsidiaries is relatively insignificant.

(A) the Target and its Subsidiaries possess all right, title, and interest in and to the item, free and clear of any Security Interest, license, or other restriction;

(B) the item is not subject to any outstanding injunction, judgment, order, decree, ruling, or charge;

(C) no action, suit, proceeding, hearing, investigation, charge, complaint, claim, or demand is pending or, to the Knowledge of any of the Target Stockholders and the directors and officers of the Target and its Subsidiaries, is threatened which challenges the legality, validity, enforceability, use, or ownership of the item; and

(D) none of the Target and its Subsidiaries has ever agreed to indemnify any Person for or against any interference, infringement, misappropriation, or other conflict with respect to the item.

(iii) §3(m)(iii) of the Disclosure Schedule identifies each material item of Intellectual Property that any third party owns and that any of the Target and its Subsidiaries uses pursuant to license, sublicense, agreement, or permission. The Target has delivered to the Buyer correct and complete copies of all such licenses, sublicenses, agreements, and permissions (as amended to date). With respect to each such item of used Intellectual Property required to be identified in §3(m)(iii) of the Disclosure Schedule:

(A) the license, sublicense, agreement, or permission covering the item is legal, valid, binding, enforceable, and in full force and effect in all material respects;

(B) no party to the license, sublicense, agreement, or permission is in material breach or default, and no event has occurred which with notice or lapse of time would constitute a material breach or default or permit termination, modification, or acceleration thereunder;

(C) no party to the license, sublicense, agreement, or permission has repudiated any material provision thereof; and

(D) none of the Target and its Subsidiaries has granted any sublicense or similar right with respect to the license, sublicense, agreement, or permission.

(n) *Tangible Assets.* The buildings, machinery, equipment, and other tangible assets that the Target and its Subsidiaries own and lease are free from material defects (patent and latent), have been maintained in accordance with normal industry practice, and are in good operating condition and repair (subject to normal wear and tear).

(o) *Inventory.* The inventory of the Target and its Subsidiaries consists of raw materials and supplies, manufactured and processed parts, work in process, and finished goods, all of which is merchantable and fit for the purpose for which it was procured or manufactured, and none of which is slow-moving, obsolete, damaged, or defective, subject only to the reserve for inventory writedown set forth on the face of the Most Recent Balance Sheet (rather than in any notes thereto) as adjusted for operations and transactions through the Closing Date in accordance with the past custom and practice of the Target and its Subsidiaries.

(p) *Contracts.* §3(p) of the Disclosure Schedule lists the following contracts and other agreements to which any of the Target and its Subsidiaries is a party:

(i) any agreement (or group of related agreements) for the lease of personal property to or from any Person providing for lease payments in excess of $_____ per annum;

(ii) any agreement (or group of related agreements) for the purchase or sale of raw materials, commodities, supplies, products, or other personal property, or for the furnishing or receipt of services, the performance of which will extend over a period of more than one year or involve consideration in excess of $_____;

(iii) any agreement concerning a partnership or joint venture;

(iv) any agreement (or group of related agreements) under which it has created, incurred, assumed, or guaranteed any indebtedness for borrowed money, or any capitalized lease obligation, in excess of $_____ or under which it has imposed a Security Interest on any of its assets, tangible or intangible;

(v) any material agreement concerning confidentiality or noncompetition;

(vi) any material agreement involving any of the Target Stockholders and their Affiliates (other than the Target and its Subsidiaries);

(vii) any profit sharing, stock option, stock purchase, stock appreciation, deferred compensation, severance, or other material plan or arrangement for the benefit of its current or former directors, officers, and employees;

(viii) any collective bargaining agreement;

(ix) any agreement for the employment of any individual on a full-time, part-time, consulting, or other basis providing annual compensation in excess of $_____ or providing material severance benefits;

(x) any agreement under which it has advanced or loaned any amount to any of its directors, officers, and employees outside the Ordinary Course of Business;

(xi) any agreement under which the consequences of a default or termination could have a material adverse effect on the business, financial condition, operations, results of operations, or future prospects of the Target and its Subsidiaries; or

(xii) any other agreement (or group of related agreements) the performance of which involves consideration in excess of $_____.

The Target has delivered to the Buyer a correct and complete copy of each written agreement listed in §3(p) of the Disclosure Schedule (as amended to date) and a written summary setting forth the material terms and conditions of each oral agreement referred to in §3(p) of the Disclosure Schedule. With respect to each such agreement: (A) the agreement is legal, valid, binding, enforceable, and in full force and effect in all material respects; (B) no party is in material breach or default, and no event has occurred which with notice or lapse of time would constitute a material breach or default, or permit termination, modification, or acceleration, under the agreement; and (C) no party has repudiated any material provision of the agreement.

(q) *Notes and Accounts Receivable.* All notes and accounts receivable of the Target and its Subsidiaries are reflected properly on their books and records, are valid receivables subject to no setoffs or counterclaims, are current and collectible, and will be collected in accordance with their terms at their recorded amounts, subject only to the reserve for bad debts set forth on the face of the Most Recent Balance Sheet (rather than in any notes thereto) as adjusted for operations and transactions through the Closing Date in accordance with the past custom and practice of the Target and its Subsidiaries.

(r) *Powers of Attorney.* To the Knowledge of any of the Target Stockholders and the directors and officers of the Target and its Subsidiaries, there are no material outstanding powers of attorney executed on behalf of any of the Target and its Subsidiaries.

(s) *Insurance.* §3(s) of the Disclosure Schedule sets forth the following information with respect to each material insurance policy (including policies providing property, casualty, liability, and workers' compensation coverage and bond and surety arrangements) with respect to which any of the Target and its Subsidiaries is a party, a named insured, or otherwise the beneficiary of coverage:

(i) the name, address, and telephone number of the agent;

(ii) the name of the insurer, the name of the policyholder, and the name of each covered insured;

(iii) the policy number and the period of coverage;

(iv) the scope (including an indication of whether the coverage is on a claims made, occurrence, or other basis) and amount (including a description of how deductibles and ceilings are calculated and operate) of coverage; and

(v) a description of any retroactive premium adjustments or other material loss-sharing arrangements.

With respect to each such insurance policy: (A) the policy is legal, valid, binding, enforceable, and in full force and effect in all material respects; (B) neither any of the Target and its Subsidiaries nor any other party to the policy is in material breach or default (including with respect to the payment of premiums or the giving of notices), and no event has occurred which, with notice or the lapse of time, would constitute such a material breach or default, or permit termination, modification, or acceleration, under the policy; and (C) no party to the policy has repudiated any material provision thereof. §3(s) of the Disclosure Schedule describes any material self-insurance arrangements affecting any of the Target and its Subsidiaries.

(t) *Litigation.* §3(t) of the Disclosure Schedule sets forth each instance in which any of the Target and its Subsidiaries (i) is subject to any outstanding injunction, judgment, order, decree, ruling, or charge or (ii) is a party or, to the Knowledge of any of the Target Stockholders and the directors and officers of the Target and its Subsidiaries, is threatened to be made a party to any action, suit, proceeding, hearing, or investigation of, in, or before any court or quasi-judicial or administrative agency of any federal, state, local, or foreign jurisdiction or before any arbitrator.

(u) *Product Warranty.* Substantially all of the products manufactured, sold, leased, and delivered by the Target and its Subsidiaries have conformed in all material respects with all applicable contractual commitments and all express and implied warranties, and none of the Target and its Subsidiaries has any material liability (whether known or unknown, whether asserted or unasserted, whether absolute or contingent, whether accrued or unaccrued, whether liquidated or unliquidated, and whether due or to become due) for replacement or repair thereof or other damages in connection therewith, subject only to the reserve for product warranty claims set forth on the face of the Most Recent Balance Sheet (rather than in any notes thereto) as adjusted for operations and transactions through the Closing Date in accordance with the past custom and practice of the Target and its Subsidiaries. Substantially all of the products manufactured, sold, leased, and delivered by the Target and its Subsidiaries are subject to standard terms and conditions of sale or lease.§4(u) of the Disclosure Schedule includes copies of the standard terms and conditions of sale or lease for each of the Target and its Subsidiaries (containing applicable guaranty, warranty, and indemnity provisions).

(v) *Product Liability.* None of the Target and its Subsidiaries has any material liability (whether known or unknown, whether asserted or unasserted, whether absolute or contingent, whether accrued or unaccrued, whether liquidated or unliquidated, and whether due or to become due) arising out of any injury to individuals or property as a result of the ownership, possession, or use of any product manufactured, sold, leased, or delivered by any of the Target and its Subsidiaries.

(w) *Employees.* To the Knowledge of any of the Target Stockholders and the directors and officers of the Target and its Subsidiaries, no executive, key employee, or significant group of employees plans to terminate employment with any of the Target and its Subsidiaries during the next 12 months. None of the Target and its Subsidiaries is a party to or bound by any collective bargaining agreement, nor has any of them experienced any strike or material grievance, claim of unfair labor practices, or other collective bargaining dispute within the past [three] years. None of the Target and its Subsidiaries has committed any material unfair labor practice. None of the Target Stockholders and the directors and officers of the Target and its Subsidiaries has any Knowledge of any organizational effort presently being made or threatened by or on behalf of any labor union with respect to employees of any of the Target and its Subsidiaries.

(x) *Employee Benefits.*[37]

(i) §3(x) of the Disclosure Schedule lists each Employee Benefit Plan that any of the Target and its Subsidiaries maintains or to which any of the Target and its Subsidiaries contributes or has any obligation to contribute.

(A) Each such Employee Benefit Plan (and each related trust, insurance contract, or fund) has been maintained, funded and administered in accordance with the terms of such Employee Benefit Plan and complies in form and in operation in all material respects with the applicable requirements of ERISA, the Code, and other applicable laws.

(B) All required reports and descriptions (including annual reports (IRS Form 5500), summary annual reports, and summary plan descriptions) have been timely filed and/or distributed in accordance with the applicable requirements of ERISA and the Code with respect to each such Employee Benefit Plan. The requirements of COBRA have been met in all material

---

[37] These representations and warranties concerning employee benefits are relatively long and detailed. A condensed version of these provisions may be more appropriate where, for example, the Target and its Subsidiaries have relatively insignificant employee benefit plans.

respects with respect to each such Employee Benefit Plan which is an Employee Welfare Benefit Plan subject to COBRA.

(C) All contributions (including all employer contributions and employee salary reduction contributions) which are due have been made within the time period prescribed by ERISA to each such Employee Benefit Plan which is an Employee Pension Benefit Plan and all contributions for any period ending on or before the Closing Date which are not yet due have been made to each such Employee Pension Benefit Plan or accrued in accordance with the past custom and practice of the Target and its Subsidiaries. All premiums or other payments for all periods ending on or before the Closing Date have been paid with respect to each such Employee Benefit Plan which is an Employee Welfare Benefit Plan.

(D) Each such Employee Benefit Plan which is intended to meet the requirements of a "qualified plan" under Code §401(a), has received a favorable determination letter from the Internal Revenue Service that it is a "qualified plan," and the Target stockholders are not aware of any facts or circumstances that could adversely affect the qualified status of any such Employee Benefit Plan.

(E) The market value of assets under each such Employee Benefit Plan which is an Employee Pension Benefit Plan (other than any Multiemployer Plan) equals or exceeds the present value of all vested and nonvested liabilities thereunder (determined in accordance with then current funding assumptions).

(F) The Target has delivered to the Buyer correct and complete copies of the plan documents and summary plan descriptions, the most recent determination letter received from the Internal Revenue Service, the most recent annual report (IRS Form 5500, with all applicable attachments), and all related trust agreements, insurance contracts, and other funding arrangements which implement each such Employee Benefit Plan.

(ii) With respect to each Employee Benefit Plan that any of the Target, its Subsidiaries, and any ERISA Affiliate maintains, to which any of them contributes, or has any obligation to contribute, or with respect to which any of them has any [material] liability or potential liability:

(A) No such Employee Benefit Plan which is an Employee Pension Benefit Plan (other than any Multiemployer Plan) has been completely or partially terminated or been the subject of a Reportable Event as to which notices would be required to be filed with the PBGC. No proceeding by the PBGC to terminate any such Employee Pension Benefit Plan (other than any Multiemployer Plan) has been instituted or, to the Knowledge of any of the

Target Stockholders and the directors and officers of the Target and its Subsidiaries, threatened.

(B) There have been no Prohibited Transactions with respect to any such Employee Benefit Plan. No Fiduciary has any liability for material breach of fiduciary duty or any other material failure to act or comply in connection with the administration or investment of the assets of any such Employee Benefit Plan. No action, suit, proceeding, hearing, or investigation with respect to the administration or the investment of the assets of any such Employee Benefit Plan (other than routine claims for benefits) is pending or, to the Knowledge of any of the Target Stockholders and the directors and officers of the Target and its Subsidiaries, threatened.

(C) None of the Target and its Subsidiaries has incurred any material liability (whether known or unknown, whether asserted or unasserted, whether absolute or contingent, whether accrued or unaccrued, whether liquidated or unliquidated, and whether due or to become due) to the PBGC (other than with respect to PBGC premium payments not yet due) or otherwise under Title IV of ERISA (including any withdrawal liability as defined in ERISA §4201) or under the Code with respect to any such Employee Benefit Plan which is an Employee Pension Benefit Plan, or under COBRA with respect to any such Employee Benefit Plan which is an Employee Welfare Benefit Plan.

(iii) None of the Target, its Subsidiaries, and any ERISA Affiliate contributes to, has any obligation to contribute to, or has any material liability (whether known or unknown, whether asserted or unasserted, whether absolute or contingent, whether accrued or unaccrued, whether liquidated or unliquidated, and whether due or to become due), including any withdrawal liability (as defined in ERISA §4201), under or with respect to any Multiemployer Plan.

(iv) None of the Target and its Subsidiaries maintains, contributes to or has an obligation to contribute to, or has any [material] liability or potential liability with respect to, any Employee Welfare Benefit Plan providing medical, health, or life insurance or other welfare-type benefits for current or future retired or terminated employees, their spouses, or their dependents (other than in accordance with COBRA).

(y) *Guaranties.* None of the Target and its Subsidiaries is a guarantor or otherwise is responsible for any liability or obligation (including indebtedness) of any other Person.

(z) *Environmental, Health, and Safety Matters.*[38]

---

[38] These representations and warranties concerning environmental, health, and safety matters are relatively long and detailed. A condensed version may be more appropriate when, for example, the

(i) Each of the Target, its Subsidiaries, and their respective predecessors and Affiliates has complied and is in compliance, in each case in all material respects, with all Environmental, Health, and Safety Requirements.

(ii) Without limiting the generality of the foregoing, each of the Target, its Subsidiaries, and their respective Affiliates, has obtained, has complied, and is in compliance with, in each case in all material respects, all material permits, licenses and other authorizations that are required pursuant to Environmental, Health, and Safety Requirements for the occupation of its facilities and the operation of its business; a list of all such material permits, licenses and other authorizations is set forth on the attached *"Environmental and Safety Permits Schedule."*

(iii) None of the Target, its Subsidiaries, or their respective Affiliates has received any written or oral notice, report or other information regarding any actual or alleged material violation of Environmental, Health, and Safety Requirements, or any material liabilities or potential material liabilities (whether accrued, absolute, contingent, unliquidated or otherwise), including any material investigatory, remedial or corrective obligations, relating to any of them or its facilities arising under Environmental, Health, and Safety Requirements.

(iv) Except as set forth on the attached *"Environmental and Safety Matters Schedule,"* none of the following exists at any property or facility owned or operated by the Target or its Subsidiaries: (1) underground storage tanks, (2) asbestos-containing material in any friable and damaged form or condition, (3) materials or equipment containing polychlorinated biphenyls, or (4) landfills, surface impoundments, or disposal areas.

(v) None of the Target, its Subsidiaries, or any of their respective predecessors or Affiliates has treated, stored, disposed of, arranged for or permitted the disposal of, transported, handled, or released any substance, including without limitation any hazardous substance, or owned or operated any property or facility (and no such property or facility is contaminated by any such substance) in a manner that has given or would give rise to material liabilities, including any material liability for response costs, corrective action costs, personal injury, property damage, natural resources damages or attorney fees, pursuant to the

---

operations of the Target and its Subsidiaries appear to have had a relatively insignificant effect upon the environment or upon public or employee health and safety.

While quite comprehensive (including coverage for strict liability for site cleanup under CERCLA and common law liability), these environmental representations and warranties contain a consistent materiality limitation and are otherwise generally more limited and narrowly focused than those in sample acquisition agreement 2003.1 (the *pro-buyer* asset purchase agreement).

The environmental representations and warranties in sample acquisition agreement 2003.2 (the *pro-seller* asset purchase agreement) are further limited to matters within the Target Stockholder's knowledge, do not extend to strict liability for site cleanup under CERCLA or common law liability, and otherwise limit the disclosure and indemnification obligations of the Target.

Comprehensive Environmental Response, Compensation and Liability Act of 1980, as amended ("CERCLA") or the Solid Waste Disposal Act, as amended ("SWDA") or any other Environmental, Health, and Safety Requirements.

(vi) Neither this Agreement nor the consummation of the transaction that is the subject of this Agreement will result in any material obligations for site investigation or cleanup, or notification to or consent of government agencies or third parties, pursuant to any of the so-called "transaction-triggered" or "responsible property transfer" Environmental, Health, and Safety Requirements.

(aa) *Year 2000.* None of the computer software, computer firmware, computer hardware (whether general or special purpose) or other similar or related items of automated, computerized or software systems that are material to the businesses of the Target or its Subsidiaries, will malfunction, cease to function, generate incorrect data or produce incorrect results when processing, providing or receiving (i) date-related data from, into and between the twentieth and twenty-first centuries or (ii) date-related data in connection with any valid date in the twentieth and twenty-first centuries.[39]

(bb) *Certain Business Relationships With the Target and Its Subsidiaries.* None of the Target Stockholders and their Affiliates has been involved in any material business arrangement or relationship with any of the Target and its Subsidiaries within the past 12 months, and none of the Target Stockholders and their Affiliates owns any material asset, tangible or intangible, which is used in the business of any of the Target and its Subsidiaries.

(cc) *Disclosure.* The representations and warranties contained in this §3 do not contain any untrue statement of a material fact or omit to state any material fact necessary in order to make the statements and information contained in this §3 not misleading.

(dd) *Investment.* The Target (i) understands that the Buyer Notes have not been, and will not be, registered under the Securities Act, or under any state securities laws, and are being offered and sold in reliance upon federal and state exemptions for transactions not involving any public offering, (ii) is acquiring the Buyer Notes solely for its own account for investment purposes, and not with a view to the distribution thereof (except to the Target Stockholders), (iii) is a sophisticated investor with knowledge and experience in business and financial matters, (iv) has received certain information concerning the Buyer and has had

---

[39] This representation can be omitted for agreements entered into a sufficient period after approximately 3/1/00 so that Buyer has been able to verify that Target and its Subsidiaries have no Y2K problem.

Sample acquisition agreement 2003.1 (the *pro-buyer* asset purchase agreement) contains a more extensive representation on this topic and 2003.2 (the *pro-seller* asset purchase agreement) contains no representation on this topic.

the opportunity to obtain additional information as desired in order to evaluate the merits and the risks inherent in holding the Buyer Notes, (v) is able to bear the economic risk and lack of liquidity inherent in holding the Buyer Notes, and (vi) is an Accredited Investor for the reasons set forth in §3(cc) of the Disclosure Schedule.[40]

4. *Representations and Warranties of the Buyer*.[41] The Buyer represents and warrants to the Target (and to the Target Stockholders for purposes of the Post-Closing Agreement with Target Stockholders) that the statements contained in this §4 are correct and complete as of the date of this Agreement and will be correct and complete as of the Closing Date (as though made then and as though the Closing Date were substituted for the date of this Agreement throughout this §4), except as set forth in the Disclosure Schedule. The Disclosure Schedule will be arranged in paragraphs corresponding to the lettered and numbered paragraphs contained in this §4.

(a) *Organization of the Buyer*. The Buyer is a corporation duly organized, validly existing, and in good standing under the laws of the jurisdiction of its incorporation.

(b) *Authorization of Transaction*. The Buyer has full power and authority (including full corporate power and authority) to execute and deliver this Agreement and to perform its obligations hereunder. This Agreement constitutes the valid and legally binding obligation of the Buyer, enforceable in accordance with its terms and conditions.

(c) *Noncontravention*. Neither the execution and the delivery of this Agreement, nor the consummation of the transactions contemplated hereby (including the assignments and assumptions referred to in §2 above), will (i) violate any constitution, statute, regulation, rule, injunction, judgment, order, decree, ruling, charge, or other restriction of any government, governmental agency, or court to which the Buyer is subject or any provision of its charter or bylaws or (ii) conflict with, result in a breach of, constitute a default under, result in the acceleration of, create in any party the right to accelerate, terminate, modify, or cancel, or require any notice under any agreement, contract, lease, license, instrument, or other arrangement to which the Buyer is a party or by which it is bound or to which any of its assets is subject. The Buyer does not need to give any notice to, make any

[40] This provision contemplates that the Buyer will issue the Buyer Notes pursuant to the exemption from registration under the Securities Act contained in Regulation D. The Parties should determine whether this exemption is available in a particular transaction. If it is not, the Agreement must be modified as necessary to reflect the issuance of the Buyer Notes under a different exemption from securities registration or in an offering registered under the Securities Act.

[41] The Target may seek to obtain additional representations and warranties concerning the Buyer and its Subsidiaries (e.g., the typical representations and warranties contained in a loan agreement or an underwriting agreement) because the Buyer is issuing the Buyer Notes to the Target as part of the Purchase Price. Any such representations and warranties would normally survive the Closing and remain applicable for so long as the Buyer Notes remained outstanding.

filing with, or obtain any authorization, consent, or approval of any government or governmental agency in order for the Parties to consummate the transactions contemplated by this Agreement (including the assignments and assumptions referred to in §2 above).

(d) *Brokers' Fees.* The Buyer has no liability or obligation to pay any fees or commissions to any broker, finder, or agent with respect to the transactions contemplated by this Agreement for which the Target could become liable or obligated.

5. *Pre-Closing Covenants.* The Parties agree as follows with respect to the period between the execution of this Agreement and the Closing.

(a) *General.* Each of the Parties will use its reasonable best efforts to take all action and to do all things necessary [,proper, or advisable] in order to consummate and make effective the transactions contemplated by this Agreement (including satisfaction, but not waiver, of the closing conditions set forth in §6 below).

(b) *Notices and Consents.* The Target will give (and will cause each of its Subsidiaries to give) any notices to third parties, and the Target will use its reasonable best efforts (and will cause each of its Subsidiaries to use its reasonable best efforts) to obtain any third party consents, that the Buyer reasonably may request in connection with the matters referred to in §3(c) above. Each of the Parties will (and the Target will cause each of its Subsidiaries to) give any notices to, make any filings with, and use its reasonable best efforts to obtain any authorizations, consents, and approvals of governments and governmental agencies in connection with the matters referred to in §3(c) and §4(c) above. Without limiting the generality of the foregoing, each of the Parties will file (and the Target will cause each of its Subsidiaries to file) any Notification and Report Forms and related material that it may be required to file with the Federal Trade Commission and the Antitrust Division of the United States Department of Justice under the Hart-Scott-Rodino Act, will use its reasonable best efforts to obtain (and the Target will cause each of its Subsidiaries to use its reasonable best efforts to obtain) a waiver from the applicable waiting period, and will make (and the Target will cause each of its Subsidiaries to make) any further filings pursuant thereto that may be necessary [,proper, or advisable] in connection therewith.

(c) *Operation of Business.* The Target will not (and will not cause or permit any of its Subsidiaries to) engage in any practice, take any action, or enter into any transaction outside the Ordinary Course of Business. Without limiting the generality of the foregoing, the Target will not (and will not cause or permit any of its Subsidiaries to) (i) declare, set aside, or pay any dividend or make any distribution with respect to its capital stock or redeem, purchase, or otherwise acquire any of its capital stock, (ii) pay any amount to any third party with respect to any liability or obligation (including any costs and expenses the Target has incurred or may incur in connection with this Agreement and the transactions contemplated hereby) which would not constitute an Assumed Liability if in existence as of the Closing, (iii) _____, or (iv) otherwise engage in any practice, take any action, or enter into any transaction of the sort described in §3(h) above.[42]

(d) *Preservation of Business.* The Target will keep (and will cause each of its Subsidiaries to keep) its business and properties substantially intact, including its present operations, physical facilities, working conditions, and relationships with lessors, licensors, suppliers, customers, and employees.[43]

(e) *Full Access.* The Target will permit (and will cause each of its Subsidiaries to permit) representatives of the Buyer to have full access at all reasonable times, and in a manner so as not to interfere with the normal business operations of the Target and its Subsidiaries, to all premises, properties, personnel, books, records (including tax records), contracts, and documents of or pertaining to each of the Target and its Subsidiaries. The Buyer will treat and hold as such any Confidential Information it receives from any of the Target Stockholders, the Target, and its Subsidiaries in the course of the reviews contemplated by this §5(e), will not use any of the Confidential Information except in connection with this Agreement, and, if this Agreement is terminated for any reason whatsoever, will return to the Target Stockholders, the Target, and its Subsidiaries all tangible embodiments (and all copies) of the Confidential Information which are in its possession.[44]

(f) *Notice of Developments.* Each Party will give prompt written notice to the other Party of any material adverse development causing a breach of any of its own representations and warranties in §3 and §4 above.[45] No disclosure by any Party pursuant to this §5(f), however, shall be deemed to amend or supplement

---

[42] The Parties may prefer to revise this covenant so that it recites specific prohibitions (rather than incorporating the matters in §3(h) above by reference).

[43] This Agreement, like sample acquisition agreement 2003.1 (the *pro-buyer* asset purchase agreement), contains a provision regarding preservation of the business of the Target and its Subsidiaries. Sample acquisition agreement 2003.2 (the *pro-seller* asset purchase agreement), on the other hand, lacks such a provision.

[44] This Agreement, like sample acquisition agreement 2003.2 (the *pro-seller* asset purchase agreement), contains a confidentiality and non-use provision protecting the Confidential Information until the Buyer actually purchases the Target's assets. Sample acquisition agreement 2003.1 (the *pro-buyer* asset purchase agreement), on the other hand, lacks such a provision.

[45] This Agreement, like sample acquisition agreement 2003.1 (the *pro-buyer* asset purchase agreement), requires the Target to notify the Buyer of any material adverse development prior to the Closing that causes a breach of any of the representations and warranties in §3 above.

Sample acquisition agreement 2003.2 (the *pro-seller* asset purchase agreement), on the other hand, permits (but does not require) the Target to notify the Buyer of any such development. Moreover, if the development gives the Buyer any right to terminate the *pro-seller* Agreement, the Buyer must exercise its termination right within [10 business days] after the notice. Unless the Buyer has such a termination right and exercises it within such period, the notice will be deemed to have cured any breach of the representations and warranties that otherwise would have existed by reason of the adverse development.

the Disclosure Schedule or to prevent or cure any misrepresentation, breach of warranty, or breach of covenant.[46]

(g) *Exclusivity.* The Target will not (and the Target will not cause or permit any of its Subsidiaries to) (i) solicit, initiate, or encourage the submission of any proposal or offer from any Person relating to the acquisition of any capital stock or other voting securities, or any substantial portion of the assets, of any of the Target and its Subsidiaries (including any acquisition structured as a merger, consolidation, or share exchange) or (ii) participate in any discussions or negotiations regarding, furnish any information with respect to, assist or participate in, or facilitate in any other manner any effort or attempt by any Person to do or seek any of the foregoing.[47]

(h) *Title Insurance.*[48] The Target will obtain (and will cause its Subsidiaries to obtain) the following title insurance commitments, policies, and riders in preparation for the Closing:

(i) with respect to each parcel of real estate that any of the Target and its Subsidiaries owns, an ALTA Owner's Policy of Title Insurance Form B-1987 (or equivalent policy reasonably acceptable to the Buyer if the real property is located in a state in which an ALTA Owner's Policy of Title Insurance Form B-1987 is not available) issued by a title insurer reasonably satisfactory to the Buyer (and, if requested by the Buyer, reinsured in whole or in part by one or more insurance companies and pursuant to a direct access agreement reasonably acceptable to the Buyer), in such amount as the Buyer reasonably may determine to be the fair market value of such real property (including all improvements located thereon), insuring title to such real property to be in the Buyer or the Subsidiary as of the Closing (subject only to the title exceptions described above in §3(l)(i) and in §3(l)(i) of the Disclosure Schedule); and

---

[46] This Agreement, like sample acquisition agreement 2003.1 (the *pro-buyer* asset purchase agreement), provides that no disclosure (presumably, but not necessarily, by the Target) between signing and closing shall be deemed to supplement the previous disclosures or to cure any breach of the Agreement. Sample acquisition agreement 2003.2 (the *pro-seller* asset purchase agreement), on the other hand, provides that certain such disclosures *will* supplement the previous disclosures and cure breaches of the Agreement. *See* the discussion in the immediately preceding footnote.

[47] Sample acquisition agreement 2003.2 (the *pro-seller* asset purchase agreement) permits the Target, its subsidiaries, and their directors and officers to respond to unsolicited proposals to the extent their fiduciary duties may require. This Agreement, like sample acquisition agreement 2003.1 (the *pro-buyer* asset purchase agreement), lacks such a provision.

[48] This Agreement, like sample acquisition agreement 2003.1 (the *pro-buyer* asset purchase agreement), contains relatively long and detailed provisions concerning title insurance. A condensed version may be more appropriate where, for example, the real property of the Target and its Subsidiaries is relatively insignificant.

Sample acquisition agreement 2003.2 (the *pro-seller* asset purchase agreement), on the other hand, does not have any such provisions and contemplates that the Buyer will obtain any title insurance it requires independently and at its own expense.

(ii) with respect to each parcel of real estate that any of the Target and its Subsidiaries leases or subleases and which is listed on §3(l)(ii) of the Disclosure Schedule as a property for which a title insurance policy is to be procured, an ALTA Leasehold Owner's Policy of Title Insurance-1987 (or equivalent policy reasonably acceptable to the Buyer if the real property is located in a state in which an ALTA Leasehold Owner's Policy of Title Insurance-1987 is not available) issued by a title insurer reasonably satisfactory to the Buyer (and, if requested by the Buyer, reinsured in whole or in part by one or more insurance companies and pursuant to a direct access agreement reasonably acceptable to the Buyer) in such amount as the Buyer reasonably may determine (taking into account the time cost of money using the Applicable Rate as the discount rate and such other factors as whether the fair market rental value of the premises exceeds the stipulated consideration in the lease or sublease, whether the tenant or subtenant has any option to renew or extend, whether the tenant or subtenant owns any improvements located on the premises, whether the tenant or subtenant is permitted to sublease, and whether the tenant or subtenant would owe any amount under the lease or sublease if evicted), insuring title to the leasehold or subleasehold estate to be in the Buyer or the Subsidiary as of the Closing (subject only to the title exceptions described above in §3(l)(ii) and in §3(l)(ii) of the Disclosure Schedule).

Each title insurance policy delivered under §5(h)(i) and §5(h)(ii) above shall (A) insure title to the real property and all recorded easements benefitting such real property, (B) contain an "extended coverage endorsement" insuring over the general exceptions contained customarily in such policies, (C) contain an ALTA Zoning Endorsement 3.1 (or equivalent), (D) contain an endorsement insuring that the real property described in the title insurance policy is the same real estate as shown on the Survey delivered with respect to such property, (E) contain an endorsement insuring that each street adjacent to the real property is a public street and that there is direct and unencumbered pedestrian and vehicular access to such street from the real property, (F) contain an inflation endorsement providing for annual adjustments in the amount of coverage corresponding to the annual percentage increase, if any, in the United States Department of Commerce Composite Construction Cost Index (Base Year = _____), (G) if the real property consists of more than one record parcel, contain a "contiguity" endorsement insuring that all of the record parcels are contiguous to one another, and (H) contain a "non-imputation" endorsement to the effect that title defects known to the officers, directors, and stockholders of the owner prior to the Closing shall not be deemed "facts known to the insured" for purposes of the policy.

(i) *Surveys*.[49] With respect to each parcel of real property that any of the Target and its Subsidiaries owns, leases, or subleases, and as to which a title insurance

---

[49] This Agreement, like sample acquisition agreement 2003.1 (the *pro-buyer* asset purchase agreement), contains relatively long and detailed provisions concerning real property surveys. A condensed version may be more appropriate where, for example, the real property of the Target and its Subsidiaries is relatively insignificant.

policy is to be procured pursuant to §5(h) above, the Target will procure (and will cause its Subsidiaries to procure) in preparation for the Closing a current survey of the real property certified to the Buyer, prepared by a licensed surveyor and conforming to current ALTA Minimum Detail Requirements for Land Title Surveys, disclosing the location of all improvements, easements, party walls, sidewalks, roadways, utility lines, and other matters shown customarily on such surveys, and showing access affirmatively to public streets and roads (the *"Survey"*). The Survey shall not disclose any survey defect or encroachment from or onto the real property which has not been cured or insured over prior to the Closing.

6. *Conditions to Obligation to Close.*

(a) *Conditions to Obligation of the Buyer.*[50] The obligation of the Buyer to consummate the transactions to be performed by it in connection with the Closing is subject to satisfaction of the following conditions:

(i) the representations and warranties set forth in §3 above shall be true and correct in all material respects at and as of the Closing Date;[51]

(ii) the Target shall have performed and complied with all of its covenants hereunder in all material respects through the Closing;

(iii) the Target and its Subsidiaries shall have procured all of the material third party consents specified in §5(b) above, all of the title insurance commitments, policies, and riders specified in §5(h) above, and all of the surveys specified in §5(i) above;[52]

(iv) no action, suit, or proceeding shall be pending before any court or quasi-judicial or administrative agency of any federal, state, local, or foreign jurisdiction or before any arbitrator wherein an unfavorable injunction, judg-

---

Sample acquisition agreement 2003.2 (the *pro-seller* asset purchase agreement), on the other hand, does not have any such provisions and contemplates that the Buyer will obtain any surveys it requires independently and at its own expense.

[50] Sample acquisition agreement 2003.1 (the *pro-buyer* asset purchase agreement) contains an additional closing condition for the benefit of the Buyer concerning the receipt of financing for the transaction. This Agreement, like sample acquisition agreement 2003.2 (the *pro-seller* asset purchase agreement), lacks a comparable provision.

[51] Note that this provision will not give the Buyer any closing condition with respect to any adverse matter which the Target may disclose in the Disclosure Schedule. This is because the disclosure will cure any misrepresentation or breach of warranty that might otherwise have existed. Thus, where the Target discloses an adverse matter in the Disclosure Schedule, the Buyer may seek to add a specific closing condition requiring an acceptable resolution of the matter.

[52] This Agreement, like sample acquisition agreement 2003.1 (the *pro-buyer* asset purchase agreement), includes a closing condition for the benefit of the Buyer regarding third party consents, title insurance, and surveys. Unlike sample acquisition agreement 2003.1, however, the closing condition in this Agreement refers only to *material* third party consents. Sample acquisition agreement 2003.2 (the *pro-seller* asset purchase agreement), on the other hand, lacks a comparable closing condition altogether.

ment, order, decree, ruling, or charge would (A) prevent consummation of any of the transactions contemplated by this Agreement, (B) cause any of the transactions contemplated by this Agreement to be rescinded following consummation, (C) affect adversely the right of the Buyer to own the Acquired Assets, to operate the former businesses of the Target, and to control the Target's Subsidiaries, or (D) affect materially and adversely the right of any of the Target's Subsidiaries to own its assets and to operate its businesses (and no such injunction, judgment, order, decree, ruling, or charge shall be in effect);[53]

(v) the Target shall have delivered to the Buyer a certificate to the effect that each of the conditions specified above in §6(a)(i)-(iv) is satisfied in all respects;

(vi) all applicable waiting periods (and any extensions thereof) under the Hart-Scott-Rodino Act shall have expired or otherwise been terminated and the Target, its Subsidiaries, and the Buyer shall have received all other material authorizations, consents, and approvals of governments and governmental agencies referred to in §3(c) and §4(c) above;

(vii) the relevant parties shall have entered into side agreements in form and substance as set forth in Exhibits G-1 through G-_____ attached hereto and the same shall be in full force and effect;[54]

(viii) the Buyer shall have received from counsel to the Target an opinion in form and substance as set forth in Exhibit H attached hereto, addressed to the Buyer, and dated as of the Closing Date;

(ix) the Buyer shall have received the resignations, effective as of the Closing, of each director and officer of the Target's Subsidiaries;[55] and

(x) all actions to be taken by the Target in connection with consummation of the transactions contemplated hereby and all certificates, opinions, instruments,

---

[53] This Agreement, like sample acquisition agreement 2003.1 (the *pro-buyer* asset purchase agreement), contains a broad closing condition regarding injunctions, judgments, orders, and pending actions, suits, and proceedings that prevent or could have an adverse effect upon the transactions contemplated by the Agreement. Unlike sample acquisition agreement 2003.1, however, the closing condition in this Agreement does not cover actions, suits, and proceedings that are only threatened. Sample acquisition agreement 2003.2 (the *pro-seller* asset purchase agreement), on the other hand, contains a narrower closing condition covering only injunctions, judgments, and orders that prevent consummation of the transactions.

[54] Where the Target has been a subsidiary of Bigco, the Buyer may require significant transition assistance. This might be the case where Bigco performs substantial services for its subsidiaries and/or where Bigco owns various tangible and intangible assets used by its subsidiaries. For example, the Buyer may require real estate leases, intellectual property licenses, and accounting, purchasing, payroll, risk management, and data processing services from Bigco.

[55] This Agreement like sample acquisition agreement 2003.1 (the *pro-buyer* asset purchase agreement), contains a closing condition regarding the receipt of director and officer resignations. Sample acquisition agreement 2003.2 (the *pro-seller* asset purchase agreement), on the other hand, lacks a comparable closing condition.

and other documents required to effect the transactions contemplated hereby will be reasonably satisfactory in form and substance to the Buyer.

The Buyer may waive any condition specified in this §6(a) if it executes a writing so stating at or prior to the Closing.

(b) *Conditions to Obligation of the Target.* The obligation of the Target to consummate the transactions to be performed by it in connection with the Closing is subject to satisfaction of the following conditions:

(i) the representations and warranties set forth in §4 above shall be true and correct in all material respects at and as of the Closing Date;

(ii) the Buyer shall have performed and complied with all of its covenants hereunder in all material respects through the Closing;

(iii) no action, suit, or proceeding shall be pending before any court or quasi-judicial or administrative agency of any federal, state, local, or foreign jurisdiction or before any arbitrator wherein an unfavorable injunction, judgment, order, decree, ruling, or charge would (A) prevent consummation of any of the transactions contemplated by this Agreement or (B) cause any of the transactions contemplated by this Agreement to be rescinded following consummation (and no such injunction, judgment, order, decree, ruling, or charge shall be in effect);[56]

(iv) the Buyer shall have delivered to the Target a certificate to the effect that each of the conditions specified above in §6(b)(i)-(iii) is satisfied in all respects;

(v) all applicable waiting periods (and any extensions thereof) under the Hart-Scott-Rodino Act shall have expired or otherwise been terminated and the Target, its Subsidiaries, and the Buyer shall have received all other material authorizations, consents, and approvals of governments and governmental agencies referred to in §3(c) and §4(c) above;

(vi) the relevant parties shall have entered into side agreements in form and substance as set forth in Exhibits G_____, and G_____, . . . and G_____ and the same shall be in full force and effect;

---

[56] Because this closing condition for the Target conforms in part to the comparable Buyer's closing condition in §6(a)(iv) above, it leaves the Target with a relatively broad "out." Thus, the Buyer may prefer to narrow the respective closing conditions. Compare the broad closing conditions in this *neutral* agreement with the narrower closing conditions in sample acquisition agreement 2003.2 (the *pro-seller* asset purchase agreement) and the even broader closing conditions in sample acquisition agreement 2003.1 (the *pro-buyer* asset purchase agreement).

(vii) the Target shall have received from counsel to the Buyer an opinion in form and substance as set forth in Exhibit I attached hereto, addressed to the Target, and dated as of the Closing Date; and

(viii) all actions to be taken by the Buyer in connection with consummation of the transactions contemplated hereby and all certificates, opinions, instruments, and other documents required to effect the transactions contemplated hereby will be reasonably satisfactory in form and substance to the Target.

The Target may waive any condition specified in this §6(b) if it executes a writing so stating at or prior to the Closing.

7. *Termination.*

(a) *Termination of Agreement.*[57] Certain of the Parties may terminate this Agreement as provided below:

(i) the Buyer and the Target may terminate this Agreement by mutual written consent at any time prior to the Closing;

(ii) the Buyer may terminate this Agreement by giving written notice to the Target at any time prior to the Closing (A) in the event the Target has breached any material representation, warranty, or covenant contained in this Agreement in any material respect, the Buyer has notified the Target of the breach, and the breach has continued without cure for a period of [30 days] after the notice of breach or (B) if the Closing shall not have occurred on or before _____, 19____, by reason of the failure of any condition precedent under §6(a) hereof (unless the failure results primarily from the Buyer itself breaching any representation, warranty, or covenant contained in this Agreement); and

(iii) the Target may terminate this Agreement by giving written notice to the Buyer at any time prior to the Closing (A) in the event the Buyer has breached any material representation, warranty, or covenant contained in this Agreement in any material respect, the Target has notified the Buyer of the breach, and the breach has continued without cure for a period of [30 days] after the notice of breach or (B) if the Closing shall not have occurred on or before _____, 19____, by reason of the failure of any condition precedent under §6(b) hereof (unless the failure results primarily from the Target itself breaching any representation, warranty, or covenant contained in this Agreement).

(b) *Effect of Termination.* If any Party terminates this Agreement pursuant to §7(a) above, all rights and obligations of the Parties hereunder shall terminate

---

[57] Sample acquisition agreement 2003.1 (the *pro-buyer* asset purchase agreement) contains a provision giving the Buyer a right to terminate the agreement for a limited period after signing if the Buyer is not [reasonably] satisfied with the results of its continuing business, legal, and accounting due diligence

without any liability of any Party to any other Party (except for any liability of any Party then in breach); *provided, however*, that the confidentiality provisions contained in §5(e) above shall survive termination.

8. *Miscellaneous.*[58]

(a) *Survival of Representations and Warranties.* All of the representations and warranties of the Parties contained in this Agreement shall survive the Closing hereunder as and to the extent provided in the Agreement with Target Stockholders.

(b) *Press Releases and Public Announcements.* No Party shall issue any press release or make any public announcement relating to the subject matter of this Agreement [prior to the Closing] without the prior written approval of the other Party; *provided, however*, that any Party may make any public disclosure it believes in good faith is required by applicable law or any listing or trading agreement concerning its publicly-traded securities (in which case the disclosing Party will use its [reasonable] best efforts to advise the other Party prior to making the disclosure).

(c) *No Third-Party Beneficiaries.* This Agreement shall not confer any rights or remedies upon any Person other than the Parties and their respective successors and permitted assigns.

(d) *Entire Agreement.* [This Agreement (including the documents referred to herein) constitutes the entire agreement between the Parties and supersedes any prior understandings, agreements, or representations by or between the Parties, written or oral, to the extent they related in any way to the subject matter hereof].

(e) *Succession and Assignment.* This Agreement shall be binding upon and inure to the benefit of the Parties named herein and their respective successors and permitted assigns. No Party may assign either this Agreement or any of its rights, interests, or obligations hereunder without the prior written approval of the other Party; *provided, however*, that the Buyer may (i) assign any or all of its rights and interests hereunder to one or more of its Affiliates and (ii) designate one or more of its Affiliates to perform its obligations hereunder (in any or all of which cases the Buyer nonetheless shall remain responsible for the performance of all of its obligations hereunder).

---

concerning the Target and its Subsidiaries. This Agreement, like sample acquisition agreement 2003.2 (the *pro-seller* asset purchase agreement), lacks a comparable provision.

[58] Sample acquisition agreement 2003.1 (the *pro-buyer* asset purchase agreement) contains provisions whereby the Parties agree to specific performance, agree to service of process on an agent, and submit to the [exclusive] jurisdiction of the state and federal courts in a particular city. This Agreement, like sample acquisition agreement 2003.2 (the *pro-seller* asset purchase agreement), lacks comparable provisions.

The Parties may want to add a provision calling for optional or mandatory arbitration with respect to all or certain issues.

(f) *Counterparts.* This Agreement may be executed in one or more counterparts, each of which shall be deemed an original but all of which together will constitute one and the same instrument.

(g) *Headings.* The section headings contained in this Agreement are inserted for convenience only and shall not affect in any way the meaning or interpretation of this Agreement.

(h) *Notices.* All notices, requests, demands, claims, and other communications hereunder will be in writing. Any notice, request, demand, claim, or other communication hereunder shall be deemed duly given if (and then two business days after) it is sent by registered or certified mail, return receipt requested, postage prepaid, and addressed to the intended recipient as set forth below:

If to the Target: *Copy to:*

If to the Buyer: *Copy to:*

If to the Process Agent: *Copy to:*

Any Party may send any notice, request, demand, claim, or other communication hereunder to the intended recipient at the address set forth above using any other means (including personal delivery, expedited courier, messenger service, telecopy, telex, ordinary mail, or electronic mail), but no such notice, request, demand, claim, or other communication shall be deemed to have been duly given unless and until it actually is received by the intended recipient. Any Party may change the address to which notices, requests, demands, claims, and other communications hereunder are to be delivered by giving the other Party notice in the manner herein set forth.

(i) *Governing Law. This Agreement shall be governed by and construed in accordance with the domestic laws of the State of _____ without giving effect to any choice or conflict of law provision or rule (whether of the State of _____ or any other jurisdiction) that would cause the application of the laws of any jurisdiction other than the State of _____.*

(j) *Amendments and Waivers.* No amendment of any provision of this Agreement shall be valid unless the same shall be in writing and signed by the Buyer and the Target. The Target may consent to any such amendment at any time prior to the Closing with the prior authorization of its board of directors; provided, however, that any amendment effected after the Target Stockholders have approved this Agreement will be subject to the restrictions contained in the [APPLICABLE CORPORATION STATUTE]. No waiver by any Party of any default, misrepresentation, or breach of warranty or covenant hereunder, whether intentional or not, shall be deemed to extend to any prior or subsequent default, misrepresentation, or breach of warranty or covenant hereunder or affect in any way any rights arising by virtue of any prior or subsequent such occurrence.

(k) *Severability.* Any term or provision of this Agreement that is invalid or unenforceable in any situation in any jurisdiction shall not affect the validity or enforceability of the remaining terms and provisions hereof or the validity or enforceability of the offending term or provision in any other situation or in any other jurisdiction.

(l) *Expenses.* Each of the Buyer, the Target, its Subsidiaries, and the Target Stockholders will bear his or its own costs and expenses (including legal fees and expenses) incurred in connection with this Agreement and the transactions contemplated hereby. The Target agrees that none of its Subsidiaries has borne or will bear any of the costs and expenses of the Target and the Target Stockholders (including any of their legal fees and expenses) in connection with this Agreement or any of the transactions contemplated hereby.[59] The Target also agrees that it has not paid any amount to any third party, and will not pay any amount to any third party until after the Closing, with respect to any of the costs and expenses of the Target and the Target Stockholders (including any of their legal fees and expenses) in connection with this Agreement or any of the transactions contemplated hereby.[60]

(m) *Construction.* The Parties have participated jointly in the negotiation and drafting of this Agreement. In the event an ambiguity or question of intent or interpretation arises, this Agreement shall be construed as if drafted jointly by the Parties and no presumption or burden of proof shall arise favoring or disfavoring any Party by virtue of the authorship of any of the provisions of this

---

[59] This Agreement, like sample acquisition agreement 2003.1 (the *pro-buyer* asset purchase agreement), provides that the Buyer will not assume or otherwise bear the transactional costs and expenses of the Target and the Target Stockholders. *See* the definition of "Assumed Liabilities" in §1 above, and the related provisions in §3(h)(xviii) and §5(c)(ii).

Sample acquisition agreement 2003.2 (the *pro-seller* asset purchase agreement), on the other hand, provides that the Buyer *will* assume the transactional costs and expenses of the Target and the Target Stockholders. This means that the Buyer will bear these costs and expenses if it consummates the asset purchase. *See* the definition of "Assumed Liabilities" in §1 of the *pro-seller* agreement.

Note that the Target Subsidiaries will remain responsible for their own transactional costs and expenses under either approach. As a result, the Buyer will bear these (possibly significant) costs and expenses if it consummates the asset purchase. For this reason, the Buyer may seek to have the Target reimburse its Subsidiaries for some or all of these costs and expenses *after the Closing* (i.e., out of the sale proceeds rather than out of cash the Buyer otherwise would acquire).

The Parties may settle on a compromise allocation of responsibility (such as sharing the costs and expenses in a predetermined ratio or making one Party responsible for the costs and expenses up to a specified aggregate ceiling and the other Party responsible for any excess).

[60] Notice that the Buyer will bear the costs and expenses of the Target and the Target Stockholders to the extent the Target pays any amount to a third party with respect thereto prior to the Closing. This is because the payment will reduce the amount of cash the Buyer otherwise would receive when it acquires the assets of the Target and its Subsidiaries at the Closing. This provision is designed to protect the Buyer from having to bear any of the costs and expenses of the Target and the Target Stockholders.

Agreement. Any reference to any federal, state, local, or foreign statute or law shall be deemed also to refer to all rules and regulations promulgated thereunder, unless the context requires otherwise. The word "including" shall mean including without limitation.[61]

(n) *Incorporation of Exhibits and Schedules.* The Exhibits and Schedules identified in this Agreement are incorporated herein by reference and made a part hereof.

(o) *Tax Matters.* [Any agreement between the Target and any of its Subsidiaries regarding allocation or payment of taxes or amounts in lieu of taxes shall be deemed terminated at and as of the Closing. The Buyer and the Target will (A) cooperate in the preparation and filing of an election under Code §338(h)(10) with respect to the sale of the stock of the Subsidiaries hereunder and (B) take all such action as is required in order to give effect to the election for state, local, and foreign tax purposes to the greatest extent permitted by law.][62]

(p) *Employee Benefits Matters.* [The Buyer will adopt and assume at and as of the Closing each of the Employee Benefit Plans that the Target maintains and each trust, insurance contract, annuity contract, or other funding arrangement that the Target has established with respect thereto. The Buyer will ensure that the Employee Benefit Plans treat employment with any of the Target and its Subsidiaries prior to the Closing Date the same as employment with any of the Buyer and its Subsidiaries from and after the Closing Date for purposes of eligibility, vesting, and benefit accrual. The Target will transfer (or cause the plan administrators to transfer) at and as of the Closing all of the corresponding assets associated with the Employee Benefit Plans that the Buyer is adopting and assuming. With respect to each Multiemployer Plan, the Parties shall take all actions necessary to comply with the requirements of ERISA §4204.)][63]

---

[61] Sample acquisition agreement 2003.1 (the *pro-buyer* asset purchase agreement) contains additional provisions construing the representations, warranties, and covenants in a manner more favorable to the Buyer. This Agreement, like sample acquisition agreement 2003.2 (the *pro-seller* asset purchase agreement), lacks comparable provisions.

[62] The Buyer may seek to have the Parties make an election under Code §338(h)(10) (i.e., to have the sale of the stock of the Subsidiaries taxed as though the Subsidiaries instead had sold their assets to the Buyer). *See* ¶205.

This differs from any other election the Buyer might make under Code §338 in that the *Target* will be responsible for any federal income tax on the deemed sale of assets. Note, however, that the Target will incur no federal income tax on the sale of the *stock* of the Subsidiaries (i.e., only on the deemed sale of their *assets*) if the Parties make a Code §338(h)(10) election.

This Agreement, like sample acquisition agreement 2003.1 (the *pro-buyer* asset purchase agreement), provides that the Target will remain responsible for any incremental tax arising out of the Code §338(h)(10) election. *See* the definition of "Assumed Liabilities" in §1 above.

Sample acquisition agreement 2003.2 (the *pro-seller* asset purchase agreement), on the other hand, provides that the Buyer will be responsible for any incremental tax. *See* the definition of "Assumed Liabilities" in §1 of the pro-seller agreement.

[63] This Agreement provides for a transfer of all Employee Benefit Plan assets (including overfundings) and liabilities (including underfundings) to the Buyer. There are many other approaches to splitting and matching plan assets and liabilities which would cause the Buyer to share to various degrees in plan overfundings and underfundings.

(q) *Bulk Transfer Laws.* The Buyer acknowledges that the Target will not comply with the provisions of any bulk transfer laws of any jurisdiction in connection with the transactions contemplated by this Agreement.[64]

* * * * *

IN WITNESS WHEREOF, the Parties hereto have executed this Agreement on [as of] the date first above written.

[BUYER]

By: _____
Title: _____

[TARGET]

By: _____
Title: _____

If the Buyer did not want to share in any plan overfundings and underfundings, the Buyer could establish substantially identical plans for future benefit accruals and count past service with any of the Target and its Subsidiaries for purposes of eligibility and vesting thereunder. The Target would then continue its previously established plans on a "frozen" basis and retain the benefit of any overfunding (or the detriment of any underfunding) thereunder.

If the Buyer wanted to share in only certain plan overfundings and underfundings, the Buyer and the Target could proceed as set forth in the preceding paragraph, except that the Buyer would assume the liability for certain past service benefits under the Target plans as of the Closing Date and the Target would transfer certain corresponding plan assets to the Buyer.

In any event, the Purchase Price should reflect the intended disposition of Employee Benefit Plan assets and liabilities.

[64] The Buyer may seek to have the Target comply with the applicable bulk transfer laws in certain circumstances. *See* ¶2001.2.2.2.

EXHIBIT A[65] — AGREEMENT WITH TARGET STOCKHOLDERS[66]

---

[65] This is Exhibit A to sample acquisition agreement 2003.3 (the *neutral* asset purchase agreement).

[66] Sample acquisition agreements 2003.1.1, 2003.2.1, and 2003.3.1 (the *asset* purchase agreements) assume that the Target will liquidate and dissolve immediately after the Closing. Each of these sample acquisition agreements therefore includes an Agreement with Target Stockholders containing indemnification provisions and other covenants analogous to those contained in sample acquisition agreements 2002.1, 2002.2, and 2002.3 (the *stock* purchase agreements) respectively.

The Parties should eliminate this document (and return the indemnification provisions and other covenants to the Asset Purchase Agreement) if the Target will *not* liquidate and dissolve after the Closing. *Compare* sample acquisition agreements 2004.1 and 2004.2 (the *divisional* asset purchase agreements).

Agreement dated [as of] _____, 19____ among _____, a _____ corporation the *"Buyer"*), and the stockholders (the *"Target Stockholders"*) of _____, a _____ corporation (the *"Target"*). The Buyer and the Target Stockholders are referred to collectively herein as the *"Parties."*

The Buyer and the Target are entering into an Asset Purchase Agreement concurrently herewith (the *"Asset Purchase Agreement"*). Certain terms used herein without definition are used herein as defined in the Asset Purchase Agreement.

The Asset Purchase Agreement contemplates a transaction in which the Buyer will purchase the Acquired Assets (and accept responsibility for the Assumed Liabilities) of the Target in return for cash and the Buyer Notes.

The Buyer and the Target make certain representations, warranties, and covenants in the Asset Purchase Agreement which will survive the Closing for purposes of potential indemnification. The Target Stockholders, however, intend to cause the Target to liquidate and dissolve immediately after the Closing. The Buyer and the Target Stockholders therefore wish to provide for post-Closing indemnification against breaches of these representations, warranties, and covenants and to make certain other covenants among themselves.

Now, therefore, in consideration of the premises and the mutual promises herein made, the Buyer and the Target Stockholders agree as follows.

1. *Definitions.*

"Adverse Consequences" means all actions, suits, proceedings, hearings, investigations, charges, complaints, claims, demands, injunctions, judgments, orders, decrees, rulings, damages, dues, penalties, fines, costs, [reasonable amounts paid in settlement], liabilities, obligations, taxes, liens, losses, expenses, and fees, including court costs and [reasonable] attorneyes' fees and expenses.

"Annex" has the meaning set forth in §2 below.

"Asset Purchase Agreement" has the meaning set forth in the preface above.

"Confidential Information" means any information concerning the businesses and affairs of the Target and its Subsidiaries that is not already generally available to the public.

"Indemnified Party" has the meaning set forth in §4(d) below.

"Indemnifying Party" has the meaning set forth in §4(d) below.

"Party" has the meaning set forth in the preface above.

"Requisite Target Stockholders" means Target Stockholders holding [a majority] in interest of the total number of Target Shares that all of the Target Stockholders hold in the aggregate as set forth in the Annex.[67]

"Third Party Claim" has the meaning set forth in §4(d) below.

2. *Representations and Warranties of the Target Stockholders.* Each of the Target Stockholders represents and warrants to the Buyer that the statements contained in this §2 are correct and complete as of the date of this Agreement and will be correct and complete as of the Closing Date (as though made then and as though the Closing Date were substituted for the date of this Agreement throughout this §2) with respect to himself or itself, except as set forth in the Annex attached hereto (the "Annex").

(a) *Organization of Certain Target Stockholders.* If the Target Stockholder is a corporation, the Target Stockholder is duly organized, validly existing, and in good standing under the laws of the jurisdiction of its incorporation.[68]

(b) *Authorization.* The Target Stockholder has full power and authority (including, if the Target Stockholder is a corporation, full corporate power and authority) to execute and deliver this Agreement and to perform his or its obligations hereunder. This Agreement constitutes the valid and legally binding obligation of the Target Stockholder, enforceable in accordance with its terms and conditions.

(c) *Noncontravention.* Neither the execution and the delivery of this Agreement by the Target Stockholder, nor the performance by the Target Stockholder of his or its obligations hereunder, will (i) violate any constitution, statute, regulation, rule, injunction, judgment, order, decree, ruling, charge, or other restriction of any government, governmental agency, or court to which the Target Stockholder is subject (or, if the Target Stockholder is a corporation, any provision of its charter or bylaws) or (ii) conflict with, result in a breach of, constitute a default under, result in the acceleration of, create in any party the right to accelerate, terminate, modify, or cancel, or require any notice under any agreement, contract, lease, license, instrument, or other arrangement to which the Target Stockholder is a party or by which he or it is bound or to which any of his or its assets is subject.

---

[67] It may be necessary to revise this definition if the Target has additional classes of capital stock.

[68] Several representations and warranties in this §2 concern Target Stockholders which are corporations. If any Target Stockholders are partnerships, trusts, business associations, estates, or guardians, the Buyer may seek to add analogous provisions covering them.

(d) *Investment.* The Target Stockholder (i) understands that the Buyer Notes have not been, and will not be, registered under the Securities Act, or under any state securities laws, and are being offered and sold in reliance upon federal and state exemptions for transactions not involving any public offering, (ii) is acquiring the Buyer Notes solely for his or its own account for investment purposes, and not with a view to the distribution thereof, (iii) is a sophisticated investor with knowledge and experience in business and financial matters, (iv) has received certain information concerning the Buyer and has had the opportunity to obtain additional information as desired in order to evaluate the merits and the risks inherent in holding the Buyer Notes, (v) is able to bear the economic risk and lack of liquidity inherent in holding the Buyer Notes, and (vi) is an Accredited Investor for the reasons set forth on the Annex.[69]

(e) *Target Shares.* The Target Stockholder holds of record the number of Target Shares set forth next to his or its name on the Annex.

3. *Post-Closing Covenants.*[70] The Parties agree as follows with respect to the period following the Closing.

(a) *General.* In case at any time after the Closing any further action is necessary to carry out the purposes of the Asset Purchase Agreement, each of the Parties will take such further action (including the execution and delivery of such further instruments and documents) as any other Party reasonably may request, all at the sole cost and expense of the requesting Party (unless the requesting Party is entitled to indemnification therefor under §4 below).[71] The Target Stockholders acknowledge and agree that from and after the Closing the Buyer will be entitled to possession of all documents, books, records (including tax records), agreements, and financial data of any sort relating to the Target and its Subsidiaries.

(b) *Litigation Support.* In the event and for so long as any Party actively is contesting or defending against any action, suit, proceeding, hearing, investiga-

---

[69] This provision contemplates that the Buyer will issue the Buyer Notes pursuant to the exemption from registration under the Securities Act contained in Regulation D. The Parties should determine whether this exemption is available in a particular transaction. If it is not, the Agreement must be modified as necessary to reflect the issuance of the Buyer Notes under a different exemption from securities registration or in an offering registered under the Securities Act.

[70] The Target Stockholders may seek to obtain additional covenants from the Buyer and its Subsidiaries (e.g., the typical covenants contained in a loan agreement or an indenture) because the Buyer is issuing the Buyer Notes to the Target Stockholders as part of the Purchase Price. Any such covenants would remain applicable so long as the Buyer Notes remained outstanding.

[71] The Parties may prefer to allocate responsibility for these particular costs and expenses in some other manner (e.g., the Party incurring the costs and expenses might be responsible for their payment, the Parties might share the costs and expenses in a predetermined ratio, or one Party might be responsible for the costs and expenses up to a specified aggregate ceiling and the other Party responsible for any excess).

Compare §6(l) below (which allocates responsibility among the Parties for their costs and expenses generally) and §8(l) of the Asset Purchase Agreement (which allocates responsibility between the Buyer and the Target for their costs and expenses through the Closing).

tion, charge, complaint, claim, or demand in connection with (i) any transaction contemplated under the Asset Purchase Agreement or (ii) any fact, situation, circumstance, status, condition, activity, practice, plan, occurrence, event, incident, action, failure to act, or transaction on or prior to the Closing Date involving any of the Target and its Subsidiaries, each of the other Parties will cooperate with the contesting or defending Party and his or its counsel in the contest or defense, make available his or its personnel, and provide such testimony and access to his or its books and records as shall be necessary in connection with the contest or defense, all at the sole cost and expense of the contesting or defending Party (unless the contesting or defending Party is entitled to indemnification therefor under §4 below).[72]

(c) *Transition.* None of the Target Stockholders will take any action that is designed or intended to have the effect of discouraging any lessor, licensor, customer, supplier, or other business associate of any of the Target and its Subsidiaries from maintaining the same business relationships with the Buyer and the Subsidiaries after the Closing as it maintained with the Target and its Subsidiaries prior to the Closing.

(d) *Confidentiality.*[73] Each of the Target Stockholders will treat and hold as such all of the Confidential Information, refrain from using any of the Confidential Information except in connection with this Agreement, and deliver promptly to the Buyer or destroy, at the request and option of the Buyer, all tangible embodiments (and all copies) of the Confidential Information which are in his or its possession. In the event that any of the Target Stockholders is requested or required (by oral question or request for information or documents in any legal proceeding, interrogatory, subpoena, civil investigative demand, or similar process) to disclose any Confidential Information, that Target Stockholder will notify the Buyer promptly of the request or requirement so that the Buyer may seek an appropriate protective order or waive compliance with the provisions of this §3(d). If, in the absence of a protective order or the receipt of a waiver hereunder, any of the Target Stockholders is, on the advice of counsel, compelled to disclose any Confidential Information to any tribunal or else stand liable for contempt, that Target Stockholder may disclose the Confidential Information to the tribunal; *provided, however,* that the disclosing Target Stockholder shall use his or its reasonable best efforts to obtain, at the reasonable request of the Buyer, an order or other assurance that confidential treatment will be accorded to such portion of the Confidential Information required to be disclosed as the Buyer shall designate.

---

[72] The Parties may prefer to allocate responsibility for these particular costs and expenses in some other manner as discussed in the preceding footnote.

[73] This Agreement, like sample acquisition agreement 2003.1 (the *pro-buyer* asset purchase agreement), requires the Target Stockholders to keep certain information regarding the Target and its Subsidiaries confidential after the Closing. Sample acquisition agreement 2003.2 (the *pro-seller* asset purchase agreement), on the other hand, lacks such a provision.

(e) *Covenant Not to Compete*.[74] For a period of [three years] from and after the Closing Date, none of the Target Stockholders will engage directly or indirectly in any business that any of the Target and its Subsidiaries conducts as of the Closing Date in any geographic area in which any of the Target and its Subsidiaries conducts that business as of the Closing Date; *provided, however,* that no owner of less than 1% of the outstanding stock of any publicly traded corporation shall be deemed to engage solely by reason thereof in any of its businesses. If the final judgment of a court of competent jurisdiction declares that any term or provision of this §3(e) is invalid or unenforceable, the Parties agree that the court making the determination of invalidity or unenforceability shall have the power to reduce the scope, duration, or area of the term or provision, to delete specific words or phrases, or to replace any invalid or unenforceable term or provision with a term or provision that is valid and enforceable and that comes closest to expressing the intention of the invalid or unenforceable term or provision, and this Agreement shall be enforceable as so modified after the expiration of the time within which the judgment may be appealed.

(f) *Buyer Notes.* Each Buyer Note will be imprinted with a legend substantially in the following form:

> *This Note was originally issued on _____, 19_____, and has not been registered under the Securities Act of 1933, as amended. The transfer of this Note is subject to certain restrictions set forth in the Agreement. The issuer of this Note will furnish a copy of these provisions to the holder hereof without charge upon written request.*

Each holder desiring to transfer a Buyer Note first must furnish the Buyer with (i) a written opinion reasonably satisfactory to the Buyer in form and substance from counsel reasonably satisfactory to the Buyer by reason of experience to the effect that the holder may transfer the Buyer Note as desired without registration under the Securities Act and (ii) a written undertaking executed by the desired transferee reasonably satisfactory to the Buyer in form and substance agreeing to be bound by the restrictions on transfer contained herein.[75]

4. *Remedies for Breaches of This Agreement and the Asset Purchase Agreement.*[76]

---

[74] Note that unless this Agreement states that a specified amount of consideration is being paid for the covenant not to compete, applicable tax cases will preclude the Buyer from seeking to allocate a portion of the Purchase Price to the covenant and amortizing such amount over the covenant's life.

[75] This Agreement, like sample acquisition agreement 2003.1 (the *pro-buyer* asset purchase agreement), calls for a legend on the Buyer Notes and provides that any holder who wishes to transfer the Buyer Notes must first obtain an opinion of counsel and an undertaking of the transferee (in each case as to securities law matters). Sample acquisition agreement 2003.2 (the *pro-seller* asset purchase agreement), on the other hand, only calls for a legend on the Buyer Notes. Note that any such provision would be inappropriate if the Buyer will issue the Buyer Notes in an offering registered under the Securities Act.

[76] The Buyer may seek some form of additional security covering the obligation of the Target Stockholders to indemnify the Buyer after the Closing. This may include provisions calling for (a) the Buyer to have a recoupment remedy with respect to the Buyer Notes, (b) the Target Stockholders to deposit a portion of the Purchase Price with a third party escrow agent, (c) the Buyer to hold back

(a) *Survival of Representations and Warranties.*[77] All of the representations and warranties of the Target contained in §3(g)-(j) and §3(l)-(cc) of the Asset Purchase Agreement shall survive the Closing (even if the Buyer knew or had reason to know of any misrepresentation or breach of warranty at the time of Closing) and continue in full force and effect for a period of [two years] thereafter; *provided, however,* that the representations and warranties contained in §3(z) of the Asset Purchase Agreement shall survive the Closing (even if the Buyer knew or had reason to know of any misrepresentation or breach of warranty at the time of Closing) and continue in full force and effect for a period of [five years] thereafter. All of the other representations and warranties of the Buyer, the Target, and the Target Stockholders contained in the Asset Purchase Agreement (including the representations and warranties of the Target contained in §3(a)-(f) and §3(k) thereof) and in this Agreement shall survive the Closing (even if the damaged Party knew or had reason to know of any misrepresentation or breach of warranty at the time of Closing) and continue in full force and effect forever thereafter (subject to any applicable statutes of limitations).

(b) *Indemnification Provisions for Benefit of the Buyer.*[78]

---

a portion of the Purchase Price (to be paid later with interest), or (d) the Buyer to obtain a security interest in certain assets of the Target Stockholders. Sample acquisition agreement 2003.1 (the *pro-buyer* asset purchase agreement), for example, contains recoupment provisions applicable to the Buyer Notes.

[77] Sample acquisition agreement 2003.1 (the *pro-buyer* asset purchase agreement) contains alternative provisions for (A) *full indemnification* (the representations and warranties survive indefinitely and there is no deductible, threshold, or ceiling with respect to indemnification against breaches thereof) and (B) *limited indemnification* (the representations and warranties with respect to the transaction itself and with respect to taxes survive indefinitely, the other representations and warranties survive only for [three years], and there is a threshold, but not a deductible or ceiling, with respect to indemnification against breaches of the latter). The *pro-buyer* Agreement also provides that a particular representation and warranty will survive the Closing *even if* the damaged Party knew or had reason to know of a breach thereof at the time of Closing.

Sample acquisition agreement 2003.2 (the *pro-seller* asset purchase agreement), on the other hand, contains alternative provisions for (A) *minimal indemnification* (only the representations and warranties concerning the transaction itself survive the Closing) and (B) *limited indemnification* (the representations and warranties with respect to the transaction itself survive indefinitely, the other representations and warranties survive only for [one year], and there is a deductible and a ceiling with respect to indemnification against breaches of the latter). The *pro-seller* Agreement provides, however, that a particular representation and warranty will *not* survive the Closing if the damaged Party knew or had reason to know of a breach thereof at the time of Closing.

This Agreement, which is intended to favor neither the Buyer nor the Target Stockholders, provides that the representations and warranties with respect to the transaction itself and with respect to taxes will survive indefinitely, the environmental representations and warranties will survive for [five years], the other representations and warranties will survive for [two years], and there will be a deductible and a ceiling with respect to indemnification against breaches of any representations and warranties that do not concern the transaction itself. This Agreement, like the *pro-buyer* Agreement, also provides that a particular representation and warranty will survive the Closing *even if* the damaged Party knew or had reason to know of a breach thereof at the time of Closing.

[78] The Buyer will become indirectly responsible for all of the liabilities of the *Subsidiaries* if the Buyer acquires their capital stock as part of the Acquired Assets. For this reason, the Buyer may seek (a) to purchase assets from the Target *and from each of the Subsidiaries* (i.e., a multiple entity asset sale) or (b) to have the Target liquidate and dissolve the Subsidiaries tax free under Code §332 (to the extent they are United States corporations) and sell their assets to the Buyer.

(i) In the event the Target breaches any of its representations, warranties, and covenants contained in the Asset Purchase Agreement, and, if there is an applicable survival period pursuant to §4(a) above, provided that the Buyer makes a written claim for indemnification against any of the Target Stockholders pursuant to §6(h) below within such survival period, then each of the Target Stockholders agrees to indemnify the Buyer from and against the entirety of any Adverse Consequences the Buyer may suffer[79] through and after the date of the claim for indemnification (including any Adverse Consequences the Buyer may suffer after the end of any applicable survival period) resulting from, arising out of, relating to, in the nature of, or caused by the breach;[80] *provided, however,* that (A) the Target Stockholders shall not have any obligation to indemnify the Buyer from and against any Adverse Consequences resulting from, arising out of, relating to, in the nature of, or caused by the breach of any representation or warranty of the Target contained in §3(g)-(cc) of the Asset Purchase Agreement until the Buyer has suffered Adverse Consequences

---

In addition, the Asset Purchase Agreement provides that the Buyer will assume certain specified liabilities of the *Target. See* the definition of Assumed Liabilities in §1 thereof (and in particular the provision making the Buyer responsible for certain liabilities the Target reveals in the Disclosure Schedule).

Finally, the Buyer may be exposed for certain liabilities of the *Target* by operation of law if the Target does not pay them (e.g., under applicable bulk sales statutes and common law doctrines of de facto merger and successor liability). *See* ¶2001.2.2.2.

These post-Closing indemnification provisions are designed to work in conjunction with the narrow definition of Assumed Liabilities in §1 of the Asset Purchase Agreement and the extensive representations and warranties in §3 of the Asset Purchase Agreement to protect the Buyer against liabilities it does not intend to assume.

[79] This Agreement, like the *pro-buyer* Agreement (Exhibit A to sample acquisition agreement 2003.1), provides that each Target Stockholder will be responsible for *all* (as opposed to only his or its allocable portion) of the Buyer's Adverse Consequences if the Target breaches any of its representations, warranties, and covenants. This protects the Buyer from having to proceed against all of the Target Stockholders (some of whom may be insolvent or not subject to service of process) in order to collect all of what is owing it.

The *pro-seller* Agreement (Exhibit A to sample acquisition agreement 2003.2), on the other hand, provides that each Target Stockholder will be responsible for only his or its *allocable portion* (as opposed to all) of the Buyer's Adverse Consequences if the Target breaches any of its representations, warranties, and covenants. This would protect those Target Stockholders who have "deep pockets" (or who otherwise are attractive defendants) from potentially having to indemnify the Buyer against a disproportionately large portion (or even all) of its Adverse Consequences.

[80] This Agreement, like the *pro-buyer* Agreement (Exhibit A to sample acquisition agreement 2003.1), requires an indemnifying party (presumably, but not necessarily, one of the Target Stockholders) to indemnify an indemnified party (presumably, but not necessarily, the Buyer) from and against any Adverse Consequences the indemnified party *may* suffer through and after the date of the claim for indemnification (*including* any Adverse Consequences the indemnified party may suffer after the end of any applicable survival period) *resulting from, arising out of, relating to, in the nature of, or caused by* certain breaches by the indemnifying party of its representations, warranties, and covenants.

The *pro-seller* Agreement (Exhibit A to sample acquisition agreement 2003.2), on the other hand, requires an indemnifying party to indemnify an indemnified party from and against any Adverse Consequences the indemnified party *shall* suffer through and after the date of the claim for indemnification (but *excluding* any Adverse Consequences the indemnified party shall suffer after the end of any applicable survival period) *caused [proximately] by* certain breaches by the indemnifying party of its representations, warranties, and covenants.

by reason of all such breaches in excess of a $_____ aggregate deductible (after which point the Target Stockholders will be obligated only to indemnify the Buyer from and against further such Adverse Consequences)[81] and (B) there will be a $_____ aggregate ceiling on the obligation of the Target Stockholders to indemnify the Buyer from and against Adverse Consequences resulting from, arising out of, relating to, in the nature of, or caused by breaches of the representations and warranties of the Target contained in §3(g)-(cc) of the Asset Purchase Agreement.[82]

(ii) In the event any of the Target Stockholders breaches any of his or its representations, warranties, and covenants contained in this Agreement, and, if there is an applicable survival period pursuant to §4(a) above, provided that the Buyer makes a written claim for indemnification against the Target Stockholder pursuant to §6(h) below within such survival period, then the Target Stockholder agrees to indemnify the Buyer from and against the entirety of any Adverse Consequences the Buyer may suffer through and after the date of the claim for indemnification (including any Adverse Consequences the Buyer may suffer after the end of any applicable survival period) resulting from, arising out of, relating to, in the nature of, or caused by the breach.

(iii) Each of the Target Stockholders agrees to indemnify the Buyer from and against the entirety of any Adverse Consequences the Buyer may suffer resulting from, arising out of, relating to, in the nature of, or caused by:

(A) any liability of the Target which is not an Assumed Liability (including any liability of the Target that becomes a liability of the Buyer under any bulk transfer law of any jurisdiction, under any common law doctrine of de facto merger or successor liability, or otherwise by operation of law);[83]

(B) any Liability of any of the Target's Subsidiaries for unpaid Income Taxes with respect to any Tax year or portion thereof ending on or before the Closing Date (or for any Tax year beginning before and ending after the Closing Date to the extent allocable to the portion of such period beginning before and ending on the Closing Date), [ALTERNATIVE A WHERE THERE IS NO PURCHASE PRICE ADJUSTMENT: to the extent such Income Taxes are not reflected in the reserve for Income Tax Liability (rather than any

---

[81] The Target Stockholders may also seek to impose an additional *per claim* deductible.

[82] This Agreement, like sample acquisition agreement 2003.2 (the *pro-seller* asset purchase agreement), imposes a deductible and a ceiling on indemnification for breaches of the representations and warranties in §3(g)-(cc) of the Asset Purchase Agreement. Sample acquisition agreement 2003.1 (the *pro-buyer* asset purchase agreement), on the other hand, substitutes a threshold (with relation back to the first dollar once the threshold is exceeded) for the deductible and also eliminates the ceiling on indemnification.

[83] The Buyer may be exposed for certain liabilities of the Target by operation of law if the Target does not pay them (e.g., under applicable bulk sales statutes and common law doctrines of de facto merger and successor liability). *See* ¶2001.2.2.2. This indemnification provision is designed to protect the Buyer against liabilities arising by operation of law which it does not intend to assume.

reserve for deferred Taxes established to reflect timing differences between book and Tax income) shown on the face of the Most Recent Balance Sheet (rather than in any notes thereto), as such reserve is adjusted for the passage of time through the Closing Date in accordance with the past custom and practice of the Target and its Subsidiaries in filing their Tax Returns] [ALTERNATIVE B WHERE THERE IS A PURCHASE PRICE ADJUSTMENT: to the extent such Income Taxes are not reflected in the reserve for Income Tax Liability (rather than any reserve for deferred Taxes established to reflect timing differences between book and Tax income) shown on the face of the Closing Balance Sheet],[84] or

(C) any liability of any of the Target's Subsidiaries for the unpaid taxes of any Person (other than any of the Target and its Subsidiaries) under Reg. §1.1502-6 (or any similar provision of state, local, or foreign law), as a transferee or successor, by contract, or otherwise.[85]

---

[84] Clause (B) is intended to protect the Buyer with respect to pre-Closing Income Taxes of any Subsidiaries. Alternative A contemplates a fixed purchase price. Alternative B contemplates that there will be a purchase price adjustment as described in ¶2002.5.

This indemnity is limited to unpaid Income Taxes of the Subsidiaries. It does not cover unpaid Taxes of the Target itself, because Income Taxes of the Target are expressly excluded from the definition of "Assumed Liabilities" in the Asset Purchase Agreement and therefore are indemnified under §4(b)(iii)(A) of this agreement.

In the absence of clause (B), generally the Buyer is protected with respect to pre-Closing Taxes of the Subsidiaries only to the extent the Target has breached one or more of the Tax representations contained in §3(k) of the Asset Purchase Agreement. For example, clause (B) provides greater protection for the Buyer than does the indemnity for breach of §3(k)(v) of the Asset Purchase Agreement, because that representation contains a "materiality" qualifier. Accordingly, a provision such as clause (B) can be useful in circumstances where (1) the Sellers are willing to give a strong Income Tax indemnity but are not comfortable giving unqualified Tax representations, (2) in contrast to the approach described in §4(a) of this agreement, the Tax representations survive for only a limited period, or (3) as contemplated by §4(b)(i) of this Agreement, the indemnity for breaches of Tax and other representations is subject to a deductible (in which case the parties would need to negotiate whether the clause (B) indemnity should also be subject to the deductible).

Clause (B) is best used in addition to (rather than in lieu of) an indemnity for breach of Tax representations, because certain of the Tax representations contained in §4(k) of the Asset Purchase Agreement cover matters beyond the scope of clause (B).

[85] If any of the Subsidiaries has been a member of an Affiliated Group filing a consolidated federal income tax return (including, if applicable, the Target's Affiliated Group), such Subsidiary (or its successor) will be jointly and severally liable under Reg. §1.1502-6 for certain tax liabilities incurred by such Affiliated Group for a tax year when such Subsidiary was a member of such Affiliated Group for all or part of such tax year. *See* ¶210. A Subsidiary may also be liable for the unpaid taxes of third parties under similar provisions of state, local, or foreign law, as a transferee or successor, by contract (e.g., a tax sharing agreement), or otherwise. After the Buyer acquires the stock of any such Subsidiary, the Subsidiary will remain liable for any such unpaid tax liabilities.

This Agreement, like the *pro-buyer* Agreement (Exhibit A to sample acquisition agreement 2003.1), contains a post-Closing indemnification provision designed to protect the Buyer against any liability for the unpaid taxes of any person other than the Target and its Subsidiaries. The *pro-seller* Agreement (Exhibit A to sample acquisition agreement 2003.2), on the other hand, contains no such provision.

In order to eliminate this risk altogether, the Buyer may seek (a) to purchase assets from the Target *and from each of the Subsidiaries* (i.e., a multiple entity asset sale) or (b) to have the Target liquidate and dissolve the Subsidiaries tax free under Code §332 (to the extent they are United States corporations) and sell their assets to the Buyer.

(iv) Each of the Target Stockholders agrees to indemnify the Buyer from and against the entirety of any Adverse Consequences the Buyer may suffer resulting from, arising out of, relating to, in the nature of, or caused by _____.[86]

(c) *Indemnification Provisions for Benefit of the Target Stockholders.*

(i) In the event the Buyer breaches any of its representations, warranties, and covenants contained in the Asset Purchase Agreement and in this Agreement, and, if there is an applicable survival period pursuant to §4(a) above, provided that any of the Target Stockholders makes a written claim for indemnification against the Buyer pursuant to §6(h) below within such survival period, then the Buyer agrees to indemnify each of the Target Stockholders from and against the entirety of any Adverse Consequences the Target Stockholder may suffer through and after the date of the claim for indemnification (including any Adverse Consequences the Target Stockholder may suffer after the end of any applicable survival period) resulting from, arising out of, relating to, in the nature of, or caused by the breach.

(ii) The Buyer agrees to indemnify each of the Target Stockholders from and against the entirety of any Adverse Consequences the Target Stockholder may suffer resulting from, arising out of, relating to, in the nature of, or caused by any Assumed Liability.

(d) *Matters Involving Third Parties.*

(i) If any third party shall notify any Party (the *"Indemnified Party"*) with respect to any matter (a *"Third Party Claim"*) which may give rise to a claim for indemnification against any other Party (the *"Indemnifying Party"*) under this §4, then the Indemnified Party shall promptly notify each Indemnifying Party thereof in writing; *provided, however*, that no delay on the part of the Indemnified Party in notifying any Indemnifying Party shall relieve the Indemnifying Party from any obligation hereunder unless (and then solely to the extent) the Indemnifying Party thereby is prejudiced.

---

[86] Note that the indemnification provisions in clause (i) above will not give the Buyer any post-Closing indemnification rights with respect to any adverse matter which the Target may disclose in the Disclosure Schedule. This is because the disclosure will cure any misrepresentation or breach of warranty that might otherwise have existed.

Thus, where the Target discloses an adverse matter in the Disclosure Schedule, the Buyer may seek to add a provision conferring specific post-Closing indemnification rights with respect to the particular matter.

The Buyer normally would seek to draft such a provision so that the indemnification would not be subject to any survival period, threshold, deductible, and/or ceiling.

This Agreement, like the *pro-buyer* Agreement (Exhibit A to sample acquisition agreement 2003.1), provides for such indemnification with respect to particular matters. The *pro-seller* Agreement (Exhibit A to sample acquisition agreement 2003.2), on the other hand, lacks a comparable provision.

(ii) Any Indemnifying Party will have the right to assume the defense of the Third Party Claim with counsel of his or its choice reasonably satisfactory to the Indemnified Party at any time within 15 days after the Indemnified Party has given notice of the Third Party Claim; *provided, however,* that the Indemnifying Party must conduct the defense of the Third Party Claim actively and diligently thereafter in order to preserve its rights in this regard; and *provided further* that the Indemnified Party may retain separate co-counsel at its sole cost and expense and participate in the defense of the Third Party Claim.[87]

(iii) So long as the Indemnifying Party has assumed and is conducting the defense of the Third Party Claim in accordance with §4(d)(ii) above, (A) the Indemnifying Party will not consent to the entry of any judgment or enter into any settlement with respect to the Third Party Claim without the prior written consent of the Indemnified Party (not to be withheld unreasonably) unless the judgment or proposed settlement involves only the payment of money damages by one or more of the Indemnifying Parties and does not impose an injunction or other equitable relief upon the Indemnified Party and (B) the Indemnified Party will not consent to the entry of any judgment or enter into any settlement with respect to the Third Party Claim without the prior written consent of the Indemnifying Party (not to be withheld unreasonably).

(iv) In the event none of the Indemnifying Parties assumes and conducts the defense of the Third Party Claim in accordance with §4(d)(ii) above, however, (A) the Indemnified Party may defend against, and consent to the entry of any judgment or enter into any settlement with respect to, the Third Party Claim in any manner he or it reasonably may deem appropriate (and the

---

[87] An *indemnifying* party (presumably, but not necessarily, one of the Target Stockholders) will normally seek to control the defense of any third party claim that may give rise to a claim for indemnification under this §4. However, the *indemnified* party (presumably, but not necessarily, the Buyer) will not want the indemnifying party to control the defense of any third party claim in which the indemnified party will retain a meaningful interest. For example, the indemnified party may seek to control the defense of a third party claim if the third party seeks an injunction or other equitable relief or if it is not clear that the indemnifying party will bear the entirety of any money damages or amount paid in settlement.

The *pro-buyer* Agreement (Exhibit A to sample acquisition agreement 2003.1) provides that the indemnified party will control the defense of any third party claim *unless* (a) an indemnifying party accepts full responsibility for the matter within [15 days], (b) the indemnifying party demonstrates it has the financial resources necessary to defend against the matter and fulfill its indemnification obligations, (c) the third party seeks only money damages (as opposed to an injunction or other equitable relief), (d) settlement of, or an adverse judgment with respect to, the third party claim is not likely to establish a precedent [materially] adverse to the indemnified party, and (e) the indemnifying party conducts the defense actively and diligently.

The *pro-seller* Agreement (Exhibit A to sample acquisition agreement 2003.2), on the other hand, provides that an indemnifying party may assume the defense of a third party claim *at any time* during the course of the defense.

This Agreement, which is intended to favor neither the Buyer nor the Target Stockholders, provides that an indemnifying party may assume the defense of a third party claim at any time within 15 days after the indemnified party has given notice of the third party claim, but requires the indemnifying party to conduct the defense of the third party claim actively and diligently thereafter.

Indemnified Party need not consult with, or obtain any consent from, any Indemnifying Party in connection therewith) and (B) the Indemnifying Parties will remain responsible for any Adverse Consequences the Indemnified Party may suffer resulting from, arising out of, relating to, in the nature of, or caused by the Third Party Claim to the fullest extent provided in this §4.[88]

(e) *Determination of Adverse Consequences.* The Parties shall make appropriate adjustments for tax consequences and insurance coverage and take into account the time cost of money (using the Applicable Rate as the discount rate) in determining Adverse Consequences for purposes of this §4. All indemnification payments under this §4 shall be deemed adjustments to the Purchase Price.

(f) *Exclusive Remedy.*[89] The Buyer and the Target Stockholders acknowledge and agree that the foregoing indemnification provisions in this §4 shall be the exclusive remedy of the Buyer and the Target Stockholders with respect to the Target, its Subsidiaries, and the transactions contemplated by this Agreement. Without limiting the generality of the foregoing, the Buyer and the Target Stockholders hereby waive any statutory, equitable, or common law rights or remedies relating to any environmental matters, including without limitation any such matters arising under any Environmental, Health, and Safety Requirements and including without limitation any arising under the Comprehensive Environmental Response, Compensation, and Liability Act ("CERCLA"). Each of the Target Stock-

---

[88] This Agreement, like the *pro-buyer* Agreement (Exhibit A to sample acquisition agreement 2003.1), provides that the *indemnified party* will not consent to the entry of any judgment or enter into any settlement with respect to the third party claim without the prior written consent of the indemnifying party (not to be withheld unreasonably) unless the indemnifying party fails to assume and conduct the defense of the third party claim. The *pro-seller* Agreement (Exhibit A to sample acquisition agreement 2003.2), on the other hand, provides that the indemnified party will not consent to the entry of any judgment or enter into any settlement with respect to the third party claim without the prior written consent of the indemnifying party (not to be withheld unreasonably) under any circumstances.

This Agreement, like the *pro-buyer* Agreement (Exhibit A to sample acquisition agreement 2003.1), also provides that the *indemnifying party* will not consent to the entry of any judgment or enter into any settlement with respect to the third party claim without the prior written consent of the indemnified party (not to be withheld unreasonably) unless the judgment or proposed settlement involves only the payment of money damages by one or more of the indemnifying parties and does not impose an injunction or other equitable relief upon the indemnified party. The *pro-seller* Agreement (Exhibit A to sample acquisition agreement 2003.2), on the other hand, provides that the indemnifying party will not consent to the entry of any judgment or enter into any settlement with respect to the third party claim without the prior written consent of the indemnified party (not to be withheld unreasonably) under any circumstances.

[89] Exhibit A to sample acquisition agreement 2003.1 (the *pro-buyer* asset purchase agreement) states that the indemnification provisions in the Agreement are in addition to and not in derogation of any other statutory, equitable, or common law remedies (including any such remedies relating to environmental matters).

As does this Exhibit A to the *neutral* asset purchase agreement, Exhibit A to sample acquisition agreement 2003.2 (the *pro-seller* asset purchase agreement) states that the remedies available to the Parties under the Agreement are exclusive (i.e., that the Buyer has no other statutory, equitable, or common law remedies) and also contains an additional provision by which the Buyer specifically waives and releases the Target Stockholders from, and agrees to indemnify the Target Stockholders with respect to, any environmental liabilities.

holders hereby agrees that he or it will not make any claim for indemnification against any of the Buyer and its Subsidiaries by reason of the fact that he or it was a director, officer, employee, or agent of any of the Target and its Subsidiaries or was serving at the request of any such entity as a partner, trustee, director, officer, employee, or agent of another entity (whether such claim is for judgments, damages, penalties, fines, costs, amounts paid in settlement, losses, expenses, or otherwise and whether such claim is pursuant to any statute, charter document, bylaw, agreement, or otherwise) with respect to any action, suit, proceeding, complaint, claim, or demand brought by the Buyer against such Target Stockholder (whether such action, suit, proceeding, complaint, claim, or demand is pursuant to this Agreement, applicable law, or otherwise).[90]

5. *Termination.* This Agreement shall terminate if and only if the Asset Purchase Agreement is terminated prior to the Closing in accordance with and pursuant to the terms thereof.

6. *Miscellaneous.*

(a) *Exclusivity.* None of the Target Stockholders will (i) solicit, initiate, or encourage the submission of any proposal or offer from any Person relating to the acquisition of any capital stock or other voting securities, or any substantial portion of the assets, of any of the Target and its Subsidiaries (including any acquisition structured as a merger, consolidation, or share exchange) or (ii) partici- pate in any discussions or negotiations regarding, furnish any information with respect to, assist or participate in, or facilitate in any other manner any effort or attempt by any Person to do or seek any of the foregoing.[91] None of the Target Stockholders will vote their Target Shares in favor of any such acquisition struc- tured as a merger, consolidation, or share exchange.

(b) *Press Releases and Public Announcements.* None of the Target Stockholders shall issue any press release or make any public announcement relating to the subject matter of the Asset Purchase Agreement [prior to the Closing] without

---

[90] This Agreement, like the *pro-buyer* Agreement (Exhibit A to sample acquisition agreement 2003.1), contains a provision to the effect that no Target Stockholder will make a claim for indemnification against the Target, by reason of the fact that the Target Stockholder was, before the stock purchase, a director or other officeholder of the Target entitled to indemnification from the Target, with respect to any suit or claim the Buyer might bring against the Target Stockholder in connection with the stock purchase. This provision responds to the surprising decision in Heffernan v. Pacific Dunlop GNB Corporation, 965 F.2d 369 (7th Cir. 1992). The *pro-seller* Agreement (Exhibit A to sample acquisition agreement 2003.2), on the other hand, lacks such a provision.

Although *Heffernan* involved a purchase of stock, rather than a purchase of assets, the instant structure presents many of the same concerns. *See* §8(g) of sample acquisition agreement 2002.1 (the pro-buyer *stock* purchase agreement) and the footnote thereto. *See also* the definition of "Assumed Liabilities" in the accompanying Asset Purchase Agreement (sample acquisition agreement 2003.1.1).

[91] The *pro-seller* Agreement (Exhibit A to sample acquisition agreement 2003.2) permits the Target Stockholders to respond to unsolicited proposals to the extent their fiduciary duties may require. This Agreement, like the *pro-buyer* Agreement (Exhibit A to sample acquisition agreement 2003.1), lacks such a provision.

the prior written approval of the Buyer; *provided, however*, that any Target Stock-holder may make any public disclosure it believes in good faith is required by applicable law or any listing or trading agreement concerning its publicly-traded securities (in which case the disclosing Party will use its [reasonable] best efforts to advise the other Parties prior to making the disclosure).

(c) *No Third-Party Beneficiaries.* This Agreement shall not confer any rights or remedies upon any Person other than the Parties and their respective successors and permitted assigns.

(d) *Entire Agreement.* [This Agreement (including the documents referred to herein) constitutes the entire agreement among the Parties and supersedes any prior understandings, agreements, or representations by or among the Parties, written or oral, to the extent they related in any way to the subject matter hereof].

(e) *Succession and Assignment.* This Agreement shall be binding upon and inure to the benefit of the Parties named herein and their respective successors and permitted assigns. No Party may assign either this Agreement or any of his or its rights, interests, or obligations hereunder without the prior written approval of the Buyer and the Requisite Target Stockholders; *provided, however*, that the Buyer may (i) assign any or all of its rights and interests hereunder to one or more of its Affiliates and (ii) designate one or more of its Affiliates to perform its obligations hereunder (in any or all of which cases the Buyer nonetheless shall remain liable and responsible for the performance of all of its obligations hereunder).

(f) *Counterparts.* This Agreement may be executed in one or more counterparts, each of which shall be deemed an original but all of which together will constitute one and the same instrument.

(g) *Headings.* The section headings contained in this Agreement are inserted for convenience only and shall not affect in any way the meaning or interpretation of this Agreement.

(h) *Notices.*[92] All notices, requests, demands, claims, and other communications hereunder will be in writing. Any notice, request, demand, claim, or other communication hereunder shall be deemed duly given if (and then two business days after) it is sent by registered or certified mail, return receipt requested, postage prepaid, and addressed to the intended recipient as set forth below:

If to the Target Stockholders: *Copy to:*

If to the Buyer: *Copy to:*

---

[92] The Parties may want to add provisions designating a nominee to act on behalf of the Target Stockholders for purposes of receiving notice, agreeing to modifications and amendments, and taking action.

Any Party may send any notice, request, demand, claim, or other communication hereunder to the intended recipient at the address set forth above using any other means (including personal delivery, expedited courier, messenger service, telecopy, telex, ordinary mail, or electronic mail), but no such notice, request, demand, claim, or other communication shall be deemed to have been duly given unless and until it actually is received by the intended recipient. Any Party may change the address to which notices, requests, demands, claims, and other communications hereunder are to be delivered by giving the other Parties notice in the manner herein set forth.

(i) *Governing Law. This Agreement shall be governed by and construed in accordance with the domestic laws of the State of _____ without giving effect to any choice or conflict of law provision or rule (whether of the State of _____ or any other jurisdiction) that would cause the application of the laws of any jurisdiction other than the State of _____.*

(j) *Amendments and Waivers.* No amendment of any provision of this Agreement shall be valid unless the same shall be in writing and signed by the Buyer and the Requisite Target Stockholders. No waiver by any Party of any default, misrepresentation, or breach of warranty or covenant hereunder, whether intentional or not, shall be deemed to extend to any prior or subsequent default, misrepresentation, or breach of warranty or covenant hereunder or affect in any way any rights arising by virtue of any prior or subsequent such occurrence.

(k) *Severability.* Any term or provision of this Agreement that is invalid or unenforceable in any situation in any jurisdiction shall not affect the validity or enforceability of the remaining terms and provisions hereof or the validity or enforceability of the offending term or provision in any other situation or in any other jurisdiction.

(l) *Expenses.* Each of the Parties will bear his or its own costs and expenses (including legal fees and expenses) incurred in connection with this Agreement and the transactions contemplated hereby (except as otherwise provided herein).

(m) *Construction.* The Parties have participated jointly in the negotiation and drafting of this Agreement. In the event an ambiguity or question of intent or interpretation arises, this Agreement shall be construed as if drafted jointly by the Parties and no presumption or burden of proof shall arise favoring or disfavoring any Party by virtue of the authorship of any of the provisions of this Agreement. Any reference to any federal, state, local, or foreign statute or law shall be deemed also to refer to all rules and regulations promulgated thereunder, unless the context requires otherwise. The word "including" shall mean including without limitation.

(n) *Incorporation of Annex.* The Annex is incorporated herein by reference and made a part hereof.

* * * * *

IN WITNESS WHEREOF, the Parties hereto have executed this Agreement on [as of] the date first above written.

[BUYER]

By: _____

Title: _____

[TARGET STOCKHOLDER # 1 (an entity)]

By: _____

Title: _____

[TARGET STOCKHOLDER # 2 (an entity)]

By: _____

Title: _____

_____

[TARGET STOCKHOLDER # 3 (an individual)]

Taxable Purchase of Divisional Business

¶2004 P's PURCHASE OF T's DIVISIONAL BUSINESS FOR CASH AND NOTES

Sample acquisition agreement 2004.1 is a *pro-buyer* version of a taxable divisional asset purchase. Sample acquisition agreement 2004.2 is a *pro-seller* version of a taxable divisional asset purchase.

Sample acquisition agreements 2004.1 and 2004.2 contemplate a transaction in which a corporation ("P") will purchase all of the assets of *a division* of another corporation ("T") for cash and P notes.[1] If P is to pay the entire purchase price in cash (i.e., no P notes are being issued to T), all of the provisions relating to the P notes can be deleted.

If P purchases a T division, T will generally retain those assets and rights which it does not transfer and assign to P, and T will generally remain responsible for those liabilities and obligations not assumed by P.[2]

It is generally necessary to prepare asset transfer documents and liability assumption documents in an asset purchase (whether a purchase of all T's assets or a purchase of a T division), which would not be required if P purchased T's *stock*.

See ¶2001.2.2 for a further description of the principal tax and other issues associated with a purchase of assets.

¶2004 [1] It may be difficult to identify and describe those rights, assets, obligations, and liabilities of T that constitute the division. This is especially likely when T does not segregate cash in a separate account for the division or when the division shares rights, assets, obligations, and liabilities with other T divisions. The parties must address the disposition of any such shared items in the purchase agreement.

[2] P's contractual assumption of certain T liabilities and obligations generally will not preclude a third party to whom T owed the liabilities and obligations from suing T (if P has failed to pay or perform) unless the third party consents to P's assumption and agrees to look only to P for satisfaction (i.e., enters into a novation agreement). This means that, if P fails to satisfy the assumed liabilities and obligations, nonconsenting third parties to whom T owed the liabilities and obligations may have a cause of action against T or, if T has liquidated and dissolved, against T's stock-holders and/or directors.

If P intends to purchase all of T's assets, rather than only the assets of a T division, the parties should generally use sample acquisition agreement 2003.1 (*pro-buyer* asset purchase), 2003.2 (*pro-seller* asset purchase), or 2003.3 (*neutral* asset purchase), as appropriate.

Sample acquisition agreement 2002.5 (purchase price adjustment) contains additional provisions for use when there is to be a post-closing purchase price adjustment based on T's net book value as of the closing. This form can be adapted for other post-closing purchase price adjustments (such as a comparison of working capital with liabilities as of the closing *or* a contingent earnout based on earnings for a specified period after the closing). Sample acquisition agreement 2002.5 is, however, intended for use with sample acquisition agreements 2002.1, 2002.2, and 2002.3 (the *stock* purchase agreements) and must be modified prior to use with sample acquisition agreements 2004.1 and 2004.2 (the divisional *asset* purchase agreements).

The parties must address a number of general issues in preparing any acquisition document. See ¶2001.1 for a discussion of these key issues.

¶2004.1   Pro-Buyer Divisional Purchase

Sample acquisition agreement 2004.1 (*pro-buyer* divisional asset purchase) contains provisions favoring P in such areas as (i) the extent to which P will receive the divisional cash (net of unpaid taxes) at the time of the closing, (ii) the extent to which T will bear the burden of the divisional liabilities and obligations after the closing, (iii) the extent to which P will have conditions to its obligation to close, (iv) the extent to which T will be required to give representations and warranties, and (v) the extent to which T will be required to indemnify P against breaches of those representations and warranties.

Sample acquisition agreement 2004.1 provides that T will retain only so much of the divisional cash at the closing as will cover the unpaid divisional taxes with respect to periods up to the closing for which T will remain liable. This means that P will receive the divisional cash (net of unpaid taxes) at the time of the closing.

Sample acquisition agreement 2004.1 provides that the only T liabilities P will assume are those divisional liabilities (i) shown on the last divisional balance sheet reviewed by P before signing the contract, (ii) incurred in the ordinary course of business thereafter (but not including claims and lawsuits), (iii) involving employee benefit plans and executory contracts, and (iv) listed on a disclosure schedule. Thus, P would generally *not* assume such undisclosed divisional liabilities as environmental cleanup, employment discrimination, antitrust violations, product liability, product warranty, tax deficiencies, and other claims and lawsuits.

Sample acquisition agreement 2004.1 contains extensive representations and warranties from T concerning (i) the historical divisional financial statements, (ii) intervening adverse changes in the divisional business, (iii) litigation and undisclosed liabilities, (iv) tax matters, (v) pension and welfare benefit plans, (vi) compliance with federal, state, local, and foreign laws, (vii) environmental matters, and (viii) product liability and warranties.

Sample acquisition agreement 2004.1 also contains extensive representations and warranties from T concerning (i) authorization with respect to the transaction, (ii) title to the assets being sold, (iii) required governmental and third party consents (and noncontravention generally), (iv) organization, (v) adequacy and condition of the divisional tangible assets, (vi) real estate matters, (vii) intellectual property matters, (viii) leases, licenses, and contracts, (ix) inventory and accounts receivable, (x) insurance, (xi) brokerage fees, and (xii) material misstatements and omissions.

T's representations and warranties are not qualified with references to materiality, but do contain occasional references to the actual knowledge of its shareholders, directors, officers, and employees *after reasonable investigation.*

Sample acquisition agreement 2004.1 contains alternative provisions for (i) full indemnification to P for breaches of T's representations and warranties (i.e., the representations and warranties concerning the division survive indefinitely, and there is no deductible, threshold, or ceiling with respect to indemnification for breaches thereof) *or* (ii) limited indemnification to P for breaches of T's representations and warranties (i.e., the representations and warranties with respect to tax matters survive indefinitely; the other representations and warranties concerning the division survive only for three years; and there is a threshold, but not a deductible or a ceiling, with respect to indemnification for breaches thereof).

P also has the right to recoup its losses against the P notes in lieu of seeking indemnification from T.

P's obligation to close is subject to several conditions, such as (i) compliance with T's representations, warranties, and covenants, (ii) absence of a material adverse change, (iii) absence of litigation affecting the transaction, (iv) availability of financing, (v) delivery of title insurance, surveys, and third party consents, (vi) delivery of any side agreements, and (vii) delivery of an opinion of T's legal counsel.

P also has the right to terminate the purchase agreement for a period of [30 days] after signing if P is not satisfied with the results of its continuing business, legal, and accounting due diligence review.

There are a number of other important differences between sample acquisition agreement 2004.1 (*pro-buyer* divisional asset purchase) and sample acquisition agreement 2004.2 (*pro-seller* divisional asset purchase). Each of these sample acquisition agreements contains extensive footnotes with cross-references pointing out the differences.

ASSET PURCHASE AGREEMENT[1]

BETWEEN

_____

AND

_____

_____, 19____

TABLE OF CONTENTS

¶2004.1　[1]The Buyer generally will obtain a cost basis (i.e., the Purchase Price *plus* the Assumed Liabilities *plus* the expenses of the transaction) in the Acquired Assets.

A purchase of assets in which the consideration is primarily cash and notes is generally treated for accounting purposes as a purchase rather than as a pooling of interests. *See* ¶1503.

Some LBO structures prejudice the Target's creditors and hence might permit payments, transfers, liens, and obligations arising out of the LBO to be attacked under fraudulent conveyance law. *See* ¶1506.

Exhibit A—Form of Buyer Note
Exhibit B—Forms of Assignments
Exhibit C—Form of Assumption
Exhibit D—Allocation Schedule
Exhibit E—Historical Financial Statements
Exhibit F—Forms of Side Agreements
Exhibit G—Form of Opinion of Counsel to the Target
Exhibit H—Form of Opinion of Counsel to the Buyer
Disclosure Schedule—Exceptions to Representations and Warranties

[EXHIBITS AND SCHEDULES HAVE BEEN OMITTED FROM THIS SAMPLE ACQUISITION AGREEMENT 2004.1]

Agreement entered into on [as of] _____, 19____, by and between _____, a _____ corporation (the *"Buyer"*), and _____, a _____ corporation (the *"Target"*). The Buyer and the Target are referred to collectively herein as the *"Parties."*

This Agreement contemplates a transaction in which the Buyer will purchase all of the assets (and assume certain of the liabilities) of the Division of the Target in return for cash and the Buyer Notes.[2]

Now, therefore, in consideration of the premises and the mutual promises herein made, and in consideration of the representations, warranties, and covenants herein contained, the Parties agree as follows.

1. *Definitions.*

"Accredited Investor" has the meaning set forth in Regulation D promulgated under the Securities Act.

"Acquired Assets" means all right, title, and interest in and to all of the assets constituting the Division,[3] *including* all of its (a) real property, leaseholds and subleaseholds therein, improvements, fixtures, and fittings thereon, and easements, rights-of-way, and other appurtenants thereto (such as appurtenant rights in and to public streets), (b) tangible personal property (such as machinery, equipment, inventories of raw materials and supplies, manufactured and purchased parts, goods in process and finished goods, furniture, automobiles, trucks, tractors, trailers, tools, jigs, and dies), (c) Intellectual Property, goodwill associated therewith, licenses and sublicenses granted and obtained with respect thereto, and rights thereunder, remedies against infringements thereof, and rights to protection of interests therein under the laws of all jurisdictions, (d) leases, subleases, and rights thereunder, (e) agreements, contracts, indentures, mortgages, instruments, Security Interests, guaranties, other similar arrangements, and rights thereunder, (f) accounts, notes, and other receivables, (g) securities (such as the capital stock in the Division Subsidiaries), (h) claims, deposits, prepayments, refunds, causes of action, choses in action, rights of recovery, rights of set off, and rights of recoupment (including any such item relating to the payment of Taxes), (i) franchises, approvals, permits, licenses, orders, registrations, certificates, variances,

---

[2] If the Buyer purchases a division of the Target, the Target will generally retain those assets and rights which it does not transfer and assign to the Buyer, and the Target will generally remain responsible for those liabilities and obligations not assumed by the Buyer.

It is generally necessary to prepare asset transfer documents and liability assumption documents in an asset purchase (whether a purchase of all the Target's assets or a purchase of the Target's division), which would not be required if the Buyer purchased the Target's *stock.*

The Buyer's contractual assumption of certain divisional liabilities and obligations generally will not preclude a third party to whom the Target owed the liabilities and obligations from suing the Target (if the Buyer has failed to pay or perform) unless the third party consents to the Buyer's assumption and agrees to look only to the Buyer for satisfaction (i.e., enters into a novation agreement). This means that, if the Buyer fails to satisfy the assumed liabilities and obligations, nonconsenting third parties to whom the Target owed the liabilities and obligations may have a cause of action against the Target or, if the Target has liquidated and dissolved, against the Target's stockholders and/or directors.

[3] The Target may seek to have the definition of Acquired Assets narrowed to include only so much of the right, title, and interest in and to the divisional assets *as it possesses and has the right to transfer.* Sample acquisition agreement 2004.2 (the *pro-seller* divisional asset purchase agreement) contains provisions more favorable to the Target in this regard.

and similar rights obtained from governments and governmental agencies, (j) books, records, ledgers, files, documents, correspondence, lists, plats, architectural plans, drawings, and specifications, creative materials, advertising and promotional materials, studies, reports, and other printed or written materials, (k) any Cash in excess of an amount equal to the Target's good faith estimate of the unpaid Taxes of the Division and the Division Subsidiaries (net of any amount the Division and the Division Subsidiaries shall have paid to the Target with respect thereto under any Tax sharing arrangement) with respect to periods prior to the Closing for which the return is due after the Closing[4] (computed on a pro forma stand-alone basis in accordance with the past custom and practice of the Division and the Division Subsidiaries in filing their Tax Returns),[5] and (l) [rights in and with respect to the assets associated with its Employee Benefit Plans];[6] *provided, however*, that the Acquired Assets shall not include (i) the corporate charter, qualifications to conduct business as a foreign corporation, arrangements with registered agents relating to foreign qualifications, taxpayer and other identification numbers, seals, minute books, stock transfer books, blank stock certificates, and other documents relating to the organization, maintenance, and existence of the Target as a corporation or (ii) any of the rights of the Target under this Agreement (or under any side agreement between the Target on the one hand and the Buyer on the other hand entered into on or after the date of this Agreement).[7]

"Adverse Consequences" means all actions, suits, proceedings, hearings, investigations, charges, complaints, claims, demands, injunctions, judgments, orders, decrees, rulings, damages, dues, penalties, fines, costs, amounts paid in settlement,

---

[4] This Agreement provides that the Buyer will acquire the consolidated cash of the Division and the Division Subsidiaries (net of unpaid taxes up to the Closing for which the Target will remain liable). Section 2(d) permits the Target to cause the Division Subsidiaries to distribute some or all of their cash to the Target as of the Closing in order to facilitate the intended cash retention for unpaid taxes. This would be necessary if, for example, the Division itself lacked sufficient cash to cover the aggregate unpaid taxes for the Division and the Division subsidiaries.

The Target normally will seek to retain *all* of the consolidated cash of the Division and the Division Subsidiaries. Sample acquisition agreement 2004.2 (the *pro-seller* divisional asset purchase agreement) contains provisions more favorable to the Target in this regard.

The Parties may want to introduce a post-Closing adjustment to the Purchase Price based on the difference between the Target's good faith estimate of the consolidated cash (net of unpaid taxes through the Closing) and the actual amount as determined later. See sample acquisition agreement 2002.5 for analogous provisions concerning a different type of post-Closing Purchase Price adjustment.

[5] This definition provides that the unpaid taxes of the Division and the Division Subsidiaries will be computed on a pro forma *stand-alone* basis in accordance with their past custom and practice in filing their tax returns. This means that the unpaid taxes of the Division and the Division Subsidiaries will not be reduced by any net operating loss attributable to other divisions and subsidiaries of the Target.

[6] See the provisions in §10(q) below with respect to employee benefits matters.

[7] It may be difficult to identify and describe those rights, assets, obligations, and liabilities of the Target which constitute the Division. This is especially likely when the Target does not segregate cash in a separate account for the Division or when the Division shares rights, assets, obligations, and liabilities with the Target and its Affiliates. The Parties may wish to expand upon the definitions of Acquired Assets and Assumed Liabilities to include schedules showing the disposition of specific items.

Liabilities, obligations, Taxes, liens, losses, expenses, and fees, including court costs and [reasonable] attorneys' fees and expenses.

"Affiliate" has the meaning set forth in Rule 12b-2 of the regulations promulgated under the Securities Exchange Act.

"Affiliated Group" means any affiliated group within the meaning of Code §1504(a) [or any similar group defined under a similar provision of state, local, or foreign law].

"Applicable Rate" means the corporate base rate of interest publicly announced from time to time by [FINANCIAL INSTITUTION] [plus/minus _____% per annum].

"Assumed Liabilities"[8] means (a) all Liabilities of the Division set forth on the face of the Most Recent Balance Sheet (rather than in any notes thereto), (b) all Liabilities of the Division which have arisen after the Most Recent Fiscal Month End in the Ordinary Course of Business (other than any Liability resulting from, arising out of, relating to, in the nature of, or caused by any breach of contract, breach of warranty, tort, infringement, violation of law, or environmental matter, including without limitation those arising under Environmental, Health, and Safety Requirements[9]), (c) all obligations of the Division under the agreements, contracts, leases, licenses, and other arrangements referred to in the definition of Acquired Assets either (i) to furnish goods, services, and other non-Cash benefits to another party after the Closing or (ii) to pay for goods, services, and other non-Cash benefits that another party will furnish to it after the Closing, (d) [all Liabilities and obligations of the Division under its Employee Benefit Plans],[10] and (e) [all other Liabilities and obligations of the Division set forth in an appendix to the Disclosure Schedule under an express statement (that the Buyer has initialled) to the effect that the definition of Assumed Liabilities will include the Liabilities and obligations so disclosed]; *provided, however,* that the Assumed Liabilities shall not include (i) any Liability of the Target for unpaid Taxes (with respect to the Division or otherwise) for periods prior to the Closing, (ii) any Liability of the Target for income, transfer, sales, use, and other Taxes arising in connection with the consummation of the transactions contemplated hereby (including any income Taxes arising because the Target is transferring the Ac-

---

[8] See the footnote to §2(b) below for an important discussion of certain tax issues that may affect the drafting of this definition as it concerns liabilities of the Division that have not yet matured into a deduction for tax purposes.

[9] This provision leaves with the Target all environmental liabilities (other than those shown on the face of the Most Recent Balance Sheet) of the Division.

Sample acquisition agreement 2004.2 (the *pro-seller* divisional purchase agreement) requires the Buyer to assume all environmental liabilities relating to the Division.

Sample acquisition agreement 2004.3 (the *neutral* divisional purchase agreement) states that the Buyer assumes those environmental liabilities specifically set forth on the Disclosure Schedule to that agreement.

[10] See the provisions in §10(q) below with respect to employee benefits matters.

quired Assets, because any of its Subsidiaries is deemed to be transferring its assets pursuant to an election under Code §338(h)(10), because the Target has an Excess Loss Account in the stock of any of its Subsidiaries, or because the Target has deferred gain on any Deferred Intercompany Transaction), (iii) any Liability of the Target for the unpaid Taxes of any Person other than the Target under Reg. §1.1502-6 (or any similar provision of state, local, or foreign law), as a transferee or successor, by contract or otherwise,[11] (iv) any obligation of the Target to indemnify any Person by reason of the fact that such Person was a director, officer, employee, or agent of the Target or was serving at the request of the Target as a partner, trustee, director, officer, employee, or agent of another entity (whether such indemnification is for judgments, damages, penalties, fines, costs, amounts paid in settlement, losses, expenses, or otherwise and whether such indemnification is pursuant to any statute, charter document, bylaw, agreement, or otherwise),[12] (v) any Liability of the Target for costs and expenses incurred in connection with this Agreement and the transactions contemplated hereby, or (vi) any Liability or obligation of the Target under this Agreement (or under any side agreement between the Target on the one hand and the Buyer on the other hand entered into on or after the date of this Agreement).[13]

"Basis" means any past or present fact, situation, circumstance, status, condition, activity, practice, plan, occurrence, event, incident, action, failure to act, or transaction that forms or could form the basis for any specified consequence.

"Buyer" has the meaning set forth in the preface above.

---

[11] If the Target has been a member of an Affiliated Group filing a consolidated federal income tax return, the Target (or its successor) will be jointly and severally liable under Reg. §1.1502-6 for certain tax liabilities incurred by such Affiliated Group for a tax year when the Target was a member of such Affiliated Group for all or part of such tax year. *See* ¶210.

The Target may also be liable for the unpaid taxes of third parties under similar provisions of state, local, or foreign law, as a transferee or successor, by contract (e.g., a tax sharing agreement), or otherwise.

This provision is designed to protect the Buyer against assuming any liability for the unpaid taxes of any person other than the Target.

[12] This *pro-buyer* divisional asset purchase agreement provides that the Buyer will not assume any obligation of the Target to indemnify its directors and other officeholders. This provision relates marginally to the surprising decision in Heffernan v. Pacific Dunlop GNB Corporation, 965 F.2d 369 (7th Cir. 1992). *See* §8(g) of sample acquisition agreement 2002.1 (the pro-buyer *stock* purchase agreement) and the footnote thereto. Although *Heffernan* involved a purchase of stock, rather than a purchase of divisional assets, the instant structure presents some of the same concerns.

[13] This definition of Assumed Liabilities is relatively narrow. The Buyer is assuming only those liabilities set forth on the face of the Most Recent Balance Sheet or incurred thereafter in the Ordinary Course of Business *plus* certain specified liabilities and obligations involving employee benefit plans and executory contracts *plus* certain liabilities and obligations identified in the Disclosure Schedule. The Buyer is *not* assuming any undisclosed liabilities (with certain exceptions as noted in the preceding sentence), any liabilities set forth in the Disclosure Schedule (unless the Disclosure Schedule contains an express assumption initialled by the Buyer), or any liability for unpaid taxes with respect to periods prior to the Closing. The Target may seek to have the Buyer assume additional liabilities and obligations. Sample acquisition agreement 2004.2 (the *pro-seller* divisional asset purchase agreement) contains a broader definition of Assumed Liabilities.

"Buyer Note" has the meaning set forth in §2(c) below.

"Cash" means cash and cash equivalents (including marketable securities and short term investments) calculated in accordance with GAAP applied on a basis consistent with the preparation of the Financial Statements.

"Closing" has the meaning set forth in §2(e) below.

"Closing Date" has the meaning set forth in §2(e) below.

"COBRA" means the requirements of Part 6 of Subtitle B of Title I of ERISA and Code §4980B and of any similar state law.

"Code" means the Internal Revenue Code of 1986, as amended.

"Confidential Information" means any information concerning the businesses and affairs of the Division and the Division Subsidiaries that is not already generally available to the public.

"Controlled Group" has the meaning set forth in Code §1563.

"Deferred Intercompany Transaction" has the meaning set forth in Reg. §1.1502-13.

"Disclosure Schedule" has the meaning set forth in §3 below.

"Division" means the Target with respect to its _____ Division.

"Division Subsidiary" means any Subsidiary of the Target included within the Division.

"Employee Benefit Plan" means any "employee benefit plan" (as such term is defined in ERISA §3(3)) and any other [material] employee benefit plan, program or arrangement of any kind.

"Employee Pension Benefit Plan" has the meaning set forth in ERISA §3(2).

"Employee Welfare Benefit Plan" has the meaning set forth in ERISA §3(1).

"Environmental, Health, and Safety Requirements" shall mean all federal, state, local and foreign statutes, regulations, ordinances and other provisions having the force or effect of law, all judicial and administrative orders and determinations, all contractual obligations and all common law concerning public health and safety, worker health and safety, and pollution or protection of the environment, including without limitation all those relating to the presence, use, production, generation, handling, transportation, treatment, storage, disposal, distribution, labeling, testing, processing, discharge, release, threatened release, control, or

cleanup of any hazardous materials, substances or wastes, chemical substances or mixtures, pesticides, pollutants, contaminants, toxic chemicals, petroleum products or byproducts, asbestos, polychlorinated biphenyls, noise or radiation, each as amended and as now or hereafter in effect.[14]

"ERISA" means the Employee Retirement Income Security Act of 1974, as amended.

"ERISA Affiliate" means each entity which is treated as a single employer with the Target for purposes of Code §414.

"Excess Loss Account" has the meaning set forth in Reg. §1.1502-19.

"Fiduciary" has the meaning set forth in ERISA §3(21).

"Financial Statement" has the meaning set forth in §3(g) below.

"GAAP" means United States generally accepted accounting principles as in effect from time to time.

"Hart-Scott-Rodino Act" means the Hart-Scott-Rodino Antitrust Improvements Act of 1976, as amended.

"Indemnified Party" has the meaning set forth in §8(d) below.

"Indemnifying Party" has the meaning set forth in §8(d) below.

"Intellectual Property" means (a) all inventions (whether patentable or unpatentable and whether or not reduced to practice), all improvements thereto, and all patents, patent applications, and patent disclosures, together with all reissuances, continuations, continuations-in-part, revisions, extensions, and reexaminations thereof, (b) all trademarks, service marks, trade dress, logos, trade names, and corporate names, together with all translations, adaptations, derivations, and combinations thereof and including all goodwill associated therewith, and all applications, registrations, and renewals in connection therewith, (c) all copyrightable works, all copyrights, and all applications, registrations, and renewals in connection therewith, (d) all mask works and all applications, registrations, and renewals in connection therewith, (e) all trade secrets and confidential business information (including ideas, research and development, know-how, formulas, compositions, manufacturing and production processes and techniques, technical

---

[14]Sample acquisition agreement 2004.2 (the *pro-seller* divisional purchase agreement) excludes contractual obligations and common law from this definition and explicitly limits this definition to laws as enacted and in effect on or prior to the Closing Date.

Sample acquisition agreement 2004.3 (the *neutral* divisional purchase agreement) excludes contractual obligations from this definition and is silent as to the time frame for enactment of covered "Environmental, Health, and Safety Requirements."

data, designs, drawings, specifications, customer and supplier lists, pricing and cost information, and business and marketing plans and proposals), (f) all computer software (including data and related documentation), (g) all other proprietary rights, and (h) all copies and tangible embodiments thereof (in whatever form or medium).

"Knowledge" means actual knowledge after reasonable investigation.[15]

"Liability" means any liability (whether known or unknown, whether asserted or unasserted, whether absolute or contingent, whether accrued or unaccrued, whether liquidated or unliquidated, and whether due or to become due), including any liability for Taxes.

"Most Recent Balance Sheet" means the balance sheet contained within the Most Recent Financial Statements.

"Most Recent Financial Statements" has the meaning set forth in §3(g) below.

"Most Recent Fiscal Month End" has the meaning set forth in §3(g) below.

"Most Recent Fiscal Year End" has the meaning set forth in §3(g) below.

"Multiemployer Plan" has the meaning set forth in ERISA §3(37).

"Ordinary Course of Business" means the ordinary course of business consistent with past custom and practice (including with respect to quantity and frequency).

"Party" has the meaning set forth in the preface above.

"PBGC" means the Pension Benefit Guaranty Corporation.

"Person" means an individual, a partnership, a corporation, an association, a joint stock company, a trust, a joint venture, an unincorporated organization, or a governmental entity (or any department, agency, or political subdivision thereof).

"Process Agent" has the meaning set forth in §10(o) below.

"Prohibited Transaction" has the meaning set forth in ERISA §406 and Code §4975.

"Purchase Price" has the meaning set forth in §2(c) below.

"Reportable Event" has the meaning set forth in ERISA §4043.

---

[15] Sample acquisition agreement 2004.2 (the *pro-seller* divisional asset purchase agreement) defines "Knowledge" as actual knowledge without independent investigation.

"*Securities Act*" means the Securities Act of 1933, as amended.

"*Securities Exchange Act*" means the Securities Exchange Act of 1934, as amended.

"*Security Interest*" means any mortgage, pledge, lien, encumbrance, charge, or other security interest, *other than* (a) mechanic's, materialmen's, and similar liens, (b) liens for Taxes not yet due and payable [or for Taxes that the taxpayer is contesting in good faith through appropriate proceedings], (c) purchase money liens and liens securing rental payments under capital lease arrangements, and (d) other liens arising in the Ordinary Course of Business and not incurred in connection with the borrowing of money.

"*Subsidiary*" means any corporation with respect to which a specified Person (or a Subsidiary thereof) owns a majority of the common stock or has the power to vote or direct the voting of sufficient securities to elect a majority of the directors.[16]

"*Survey*" has the meaning set forth in §5(i) below.

"*Target*" has the meaning set forth in the preface above.

"*Target Share*" means any share of the Common Stock, par value $_____ per share, of the Target.[17]

"*Target Stockholder*" means any person who or which holds any Target Shares.

"*Tax*" means any federal, state, local, or foreign income, gross receipts, license, payroll, employment, excise, severance, stamp, occupation, premium, windfall profits, environmental (including taxes under Code §59A), customs duties, capital stock, franchise, profits, withholding, social security (or similar), unemployment, disability, real property, personal property, sales, use, transfer, registration, value added, alternative or add-on minimum, estimated, or other tax of any kind whatsoever, including any interest, penalty, or addition thereto, whether disputed or not.[18]

"*Tax Return*" means any return, declaration, report, claim for refund, or information return or statement relating to Taxes, including any schedule or attachment thereto, and including any amendment thereof.

"*Third Party Claim*" has the meaning set forth in §8(d) below.

---

[16] It may be necessary to revise this definition if, for example, the Target has subsidiary *partnerships*.

[17] It may be necessary to revise this definition if the Target has additional classes of capital stock.

[18] This sample acquisition agreement 2004.1 (the *pro-buyer* divisional asset purchase agreement) defines "Tax" broadly to include taxes of all descriptions.

Sample acquisition agreement 2004.2 (the *pro-seller* divisional asset purchase agreement), on the other hand, defines "Tax" narrowly to include only federal, state, local, and foreign income taxes.

2. *Basic Transaction.*

(a) *Purchase and Sale of Assets.* On and subject to the terms and conditions of this Agreement, the Buyer agrees to purchase from the Target, and the Target agrees to sell, transfer, convey, and deliver to the Buyer, all of the Acquired Assets at the Closing for the consideration specified below in this §2.

(b) *Assumption of Liabilities.* On and subject to the terms and conditions of this Agreement, the Buyer agrees to assume and become responsible for all of the Assumed Liabilities at the Closing. The Buyer will not assume or have any responsibility, however, with respect to any other obligation or Liability of the Target not included within the definition of Assumed Liabilities.[19]

(c) *Purchase Price.*[20] The Buyer agrees to pay to the Target at the Closing $_____ (the *"Purchase Price"*) by delivery of (i) its promissory note (the *"Buyer*

---

[19] In a taxable purchase of the Target's divisional assets, the Division may have liabilities that have not yet matured into a deduction for tax purposes. For example, (1) a cash method Target may have accrued (but unpaid) operating liabilities, (2) a cash method or an accrual method Target may have contingent liabilities, (3) a cash method or an accrual method Target may have unfunded pension liabilities, and (4) an accrual method Target may have liabilities as to which the "all events" test has been satisfied but as to which "economic performance" (e.g., payment) has not yet occurred. The tax treatment of these and other liabilities which have not yet matured into deductions is somewhat surprising. *See* ¶304.

Under Code §461(h), an accrual method Target can deduct liabilities that otherwise satisfy the all events test (i.e., "Code §461(h) Liabilities") only as economic performance occurs. With respect to many liabilities, economic performance occurs under the Code §461(h) regulations only when the Target has made payment with respect to the liability. *See* ¶304.4.

Reg. §§1.461-4(d)(5) and -4(g)(1)(ii)(C) seem to provide that when the Target sells the Buyer a trade or business and, as part of the sale, the Buyer *"expressly assumes"* a Code §461(h) Liability, the Target can deduct that liability (assuming that the Code §461(h) regulations make payment the proper test for economic performance) in the taxable year in which the sale occurred. This favorable tax result follows from the fact that the Target will be deemed to have made payment with respect to the liability when the amount of the liability (assumed by the Buyer) is included in the Target's amount realized on the sale of divisional assets. The regulation is, however, unclear on the meaning of the phrase "expressly assumes." *See* ¶304.4.

Cautious taxpayers should accordingly consider taking some or all of the following steps: (i) the Parties should specifically enumerate in this Agreement as many as practicable of the Code §461(h) Liabilities that the Buyer is assuming; (ii) the Parties should specifically state in this Agreement that the Buyer is "expressly assuming" not only these enumerated liabilities but also any categories of *unenumerated* Code §461(h) Liabilities that the Buyer is assuming; and (iii) the boards of directors of the respective Parties should adopt resolutions specifically stating that the Buyer is "expressly assuming" these Code §461(h) Liabilities.

Reg. §§1.461-4(d)(5) and -4(g)(1)(ii)(C) are applicable by their terms only with respect to Code §461(h) Liabilities. However, their premise that the Target will be deemed to have made payment with respect to a liability when the amount of the liability (assumed by the Buyer) is included in the Target's amount realized on the sale of divisional assets may have a broader application. For this reason, cautious taxpayers may want to apply the advice in the preceding paragraph of this footnote to cover *all* liabilities that the Buyer is assuming as to which the Target has not yet become entitled to a deduction under the Code.

[20] The Target may seek to have the Buyer make an earnest money deposit upon execution of this Agreement. If the transaction were thereafter completed, the deposit would be applied to the Purchase Price. If the transaction were thereafter aborted, the deposit would be refunded to the Buyer or paid

Note") in the form of Exhibit A attached hereto in the principal amount of
$_____ and (ii) cash for the balance of the Purchase Price payable by wire
transfer or delivery of other immediately available funds.[21]

(d) *Cash Distribution to Target.*[22] Immediately prior to the Closing, the Target
may cause one or more of the Division Subsidiaries to pay the Target an aggregate
amount equal to the Target's good faith estimate of the amount by which the
unpaid Taxes of the Division and the Division Subsidiaries (net of any amount
the Division and the Division Subsidiaries shall have paid to the Target with
respect thereto under any Tax sharing arrangement) with respect to periods prior
to the Closing for which the return is due after the Closing (computed on a pro
forma stand-alone basis in accordance with the past custom and practice of the
Division and the Division Subsidiaries in filing their Tax Returns)[23] exceeds the
Cash of the Division.[24] The Target may cause any of the Division Subsidiaries to
make any such payment to the Target in the form of a dividend or a redemption.[25]

---

to the Target as liquidated damages depending on the terms of this Agreement and the reasons for
the termination.

[21] Sample acquisition agreement 2002.5 contains additional provisions for use when there is to be
a post-Closing Purchase Price adjustment based on the consolidated net book value for the Target
and its Subsidiaries as of the Closing. That sample acquisition agreement can be adapted for other
post-Closing Purchase Price adjustments (such as a comparison of consolidated working capital with
consolidated liabilities as of the Closing *or* a contingent earnout based on consolidated earnings for
a specified period after the Closing).

Sample acquisition agreement 2002.5 is, however, intended for use with sample acquisition
agreements 2002.1, 2002.2, and 2002.3 (the *stock* purchase agreements) and must be modified prior to
use with this *asset* purchase agreement.

[22] This *pro-buyer* Agreement provides that the Target will retain only so much of the consolidated
cash of the Division and the Division Subsidiaries as will cover their aggregate unpaid taxes up to
the Closing for which the Target will remain liable. *See* the definition of Acquired Assets in §1 above.
Section 2(d) permits the Target to cause the Division Subsidiaries to distribute some or all of their
cash to the Target at the Closing if the cash of the Division alone will not be enough to cover the
aggregate unpaid taxes of the Division and the Division Subsidiaries.

Sample acquisition agreement 2004.2 (the *pro-seller* divisional asset purchase agreement), on the
other hand, provides that the Target will retain *all* of the consolidated cash of the Division and the
Division Subsidiaries. See the definition of Acquired Assets in §1 thereof and the provision for a cash
distribution from the Division Subsidiaries to the Target in §2(d) thereof.

[23] This definition provides that the unpaid taxes of the Division and the Division Subsidiaries will
be computed on a pro forma *stand-alone* basis in accordance with their past custom and practice in
filing their tax returns. This means that the unpaid taxes of the Division and the Division Subsidiaries
will not be reduced by any net operating loss attributable to other divisions and subsidiaries of
the Target.

[24] The Parties may want to introduce a post-Closing adjustment to the Purchase Price based on
the difference between the amount of cash the Target will retain at the Closing (i.e., the Target's good
faith estimate of the consolidated cash net of unpaid taxes through the Closing) and the actual amount
as determined later. *See* sample acquisition agreement 2002.5 for analogous provisions concerning a
different type of post-Closing Purchase Price adjustment.

[25] The Parties should determine whether there is any external restriction or prohibition on the type
of cash payment by the Division Subsidiaries contemplated by §2(d) (such as a loan covenant or a
statutory provision concerning dividends and stock redemptions). The Parties should also consider
any possible difference in tax treatment between a cash dividend and a partial stock redemption.

(e) *The Closing.* The closing of the transactions contemplated by this Agreement (the *"Closing"*) shall take place at the offices of _____ in _____, _____ commencing at 9:00 a.m. local time on the [second] business day following the satisfaction or waiver of all conditions to the obligations of the Parties to consummate the transactions contemplated hereby (other than conditions with respect to actions the respective Parties will take at the Closing itself) or such other date as the Parties may mutually determine (the *"Closing Date"*); *provided, however,* that the Closing Date shall be no earlier than _____, 19____.

(f) *Deliveries at the Closing.* At the Closing, (i) the Target will deliver to the Buyer the various certificates, instruments, and documents referred to in §7(a) below; (ii) the Buyer will deliver to the Target the various certificates, instruments, and documents referred to in §7(b) below; (iii) the Target will execute, acknowledge (if appropriate), and deliver to the Buyer (A) assignments (including real property and Intellectual Property transfer documents) in the forms attached hereto as Exhibits B-1 through B-____ and (B) such other instruments of sale, transfer, conveyance, and assignment as the Buyer and its counsel [reasonably] may request; (iv) the Buyer will execute, acknowledge (if appropriate), and deliver to the Target (A) an assumption in the form attached hereto as Exhibit C and (B) such other instruments of assumption as the Target and its counsel [reasonably] may request; and (v) the Buyer will deliver to the Target the consideration specified in §2(c) above.

(g) *Allocation.* [The Parties agree to allocate the Purchase Price (and all other capitalizable costs) among the Acquired Assets for all purposes (including financial accounting and tax purposes) in accordance with the allocation schedule attached hereto as Exhibit D.][26]

3. *Representations and Warranties of the Target.*[27] The Target represents and warrants to the Buyer that the statements contained in this §3 are correct and complete as of the date of this Agreement and will be correct and complete as of the Closing Date (as though made then and as though the Closing Date were substituted for the date of this Agreement throughout this §3), except as set forth in the disclosure schedule accompanying this Agreement and initialed by the

---

[26] The 1986 Act generally requires the Buyer and the Target to allocate the Buyer's aggregate basis (i.e., the Purchase Price *plus* the Assumed Liabilities *plus* the expenses of the transaction) among the Acquired Assets using the residual method. *See* ¶403. The Parties should omit this provision if they do not reach agreement on a particular allocation schedule.

[27] The Target will seek to give fewer representations and warranties and to qualify the representations and warranties it does give with concepts of "knowledge" and "materiality." *Pro-buyer* §3 does not contain any unbracketed qualifications as to materiality. It does, however, contain occasional references to the actual knowledge of the Target Stockholders and the directors, officers, and employees of the Target and its Subsidiaries after reasonable investigation. The Target will seek to limit the group of individuals whose knowledge is applicable and make it clear that no such individual need conduct any special investigation. Sample acquisition agreement 2004.2 (the *pro-seller* divisional asset purchase agreement) contains comparable representations and warranties more favorable to the Target.

Parties (the *Disclosure Schedule*).[28] The Disclosure Schedule will be arranged in paragraphs corresponding to the lettered and numbered paragraphs contained in this §3.

(a) *Organization of the Target.* The Target is a corporation duly organized, validly existing, and in good standing under the laws of the jurisdiction of its incorporation.

(b) *Authorization of Transaction.* The Target has full power and authority (including full corporate power and authority) to execute and deliver this Agreement and to perform its obligations hereunder. [Without limiting the generality of the foregoing, the board of directors of the Target and the Target Stockholders have duly authorized the execution, delivery, and performance of this Agreement by the Target.[29]] This Agreement constitutes the valid and legally binding obligation of the Target, enforceable in accordance with its terms and conditions.

(c) *Noncontravention.* Neither the execution and the delivery of this Agreement, nor the consummation of the transactions contemplated hereby (including the assignments and assumptions referred to in §2 above), will (i) violate any constitution, statute, regulation, rule, injunction, judgment, order, decree, ruling, charge, or other restriction of any government, governmental agency, or court to which any of the Target and the Division Subsidiaries is subject or any provision of the charter or bylaws of any of the Target and the Division Subsidiaries or (ii) conflict with, result in a breach of, constitute a default under, result in the acceleration of, create in any party the right to accelerate, terminate, modify, or cancel, or require any notice under any agreement, contract, lease, license, instrument, or

---

[28] The Buyer will have a closing condition (*see* §7(a)(i)) and post-Closing indemnification rights (*see* §8(b)) with respect to certain misrepresentations and breaches of warranty. The Buyer will not, however, have a closing condition or post-Closing indemnification rights with respect to any adverse matter that the Target discloses in the Disclosure Schedule. This is because the disclosure will cure any misrepresentation or breach of warranty that might otherwise have existed. Thus, when the Target discloses an adverse matter in the Disclosure Schedule, the Buyer may seek (a) to avoid assuming responsibility for the matter (*see* the definition of Assumed Liabilities in §1), (b) to add a specific closing condition requiring an acceptable resolution of the matter, and/or (c) to obtain specific post-Closing indemnification against the matter.

[29] The Target must obtain the approval of its board of directors *and* the approval of its stockholders in order to sell all or substantially all of its assets. *See* ¶2001.2.2.2. A sale of the *divisional* assets may trigger this requirement, depending on the size of the divisional assets relative to the Target's other assets.

This Agreement assumes the Target has already obtained any requisite corporate approvals.

If approval of the Target's stockholders is necessary, but the Parties wish to enter into this Agreement before the Target has obtained such approval, the Parties should revise this Agreement to include (a) a covenant calling for the Target to obtain such approval prior to the Closing and (b) a closing condition for each of the Parties to the effect that the Target *has* obtained such approval. Compare sample acquisition agreement 2005 (the reverse subsidiary merger agreement), which contemplates the target corporation will obtain the approval of its stockholders between the signing of the merger agreement and the Closing.

The Parties generally will not enter into an asset purchase agreement (or for that matter a merger agreement) until the Target has obtained any requisite approval of its *board of directors*.

other arrangement to which any of the Target and the Division Subsidiaries is a party or by which it is bound or to which any of its assets is subject (or result in the imposition of any Security Interest upon any of its assets). None of the Target and the Division Subsidiaries needs to give any notice to, make any filing with, or obtain any authorization, consent, or approval of any government or governmental agency in order for the Parties to consummate the transactions contemplated by this Agreement (including the assignments and assumptions referred to in §2 above).

(d) *Brokers' Fees.* The Target has no Liability or obligation to pay any fees or commissions to any broker, finder, or agent with respect to the transactions contemplated by this Agreement for which the Buyer could become liable or obligated. None of the Division Subsidiaries has any Liability or obligation to pay any fees or commissions to any broker, finder, or agent with respect to the transactions contemplated by this Agreement.

(e) *Title to Assets.* The Division and the Division Subsidiaries have good and marketable title to, or a valid leasehold interest in, the properties and assets used by them, located on their premises, or shown on the Most Recent Balance Sheet or acquired after the date thereof, free and clear of all Security Interests, except for properties and assets disposed of in the Ordinary Course of Business since the date of the Most Recent Balance Sheet. Without limiting the generality of the foregoing, the Division has good and marketable title to all of the Acquired Assets, free and clear of any Security Interest or restriction on transfer.

(f) *Subsidiaries.* §3(f) of the Disclosure Schedule sets forth for each Division Subsidiary (i) its name and jurisdiction of incorporation, (ii) the number of shares of authorized capital stock of each class of its capital stock, (iii) the number of issued and outstanding shares of each class of its capital stock, the names of the holders thereof, and the number of shares held by each such holder, (iv) the number of shares of its capital stock held in treasury, and (v) its directors and officers. Each Division Subsidiary is a corporation duly organized, validly existing, and in good standing under the laws of the jurisdiction of its incorporation. Each Division Subsidiary is duly authorized to conduct business and is in good standing under the laws of each jurisdiction where such qualification is required. Each Division Subsidiary has full corporate power and authority and all licenses, permits, and authorizations necessary to carry on the businesses in which it is engaged [and in which it presently proposes to engage] and to own and use the properties owned and used by it. The Target has delivered to the Buyer correct and complete copies of the charter and bylaws of each Division Subsidiary (as amended to date). All of the issued and outstanding shares of capital stock of each Division Subsidiary have been duly authorized and are validly issued, fully paid, and nonassessable. One of the Target and the Division Subsidiaries holds of record and owns beneficially all of the outstanding shares of each Division Subsidiary, free and clear of any restrictions on transfer (other than restrictions under the Securities Act and state securities laws), Taxes, Security Interests, options, warrants, purchase rights, contracts, commitments, equities, claims, and demands. There are no outstanding or authorized options, warrants, purchase rights, subscription rights, conversion rights, exchange rights, or other contracts or commitments that could require any of the Target and its Subsidiaries to sell, transfer, or otherwise dispose of any capital stock of any of the Division Subsidiaries or that could require any Division Subsidiary to issue, sell, or otherwise cause to become outstanding any of its own capital stock (other than this Agreement). There are no outstanding stock appreciation, phantom stock, profit participation, or similar rights with respect to any Division Subsidiary. There are no voting trusts, proxies, or other agreements or understandings with respect to the voting of any capital stock of any Division Subsidiary. The minute books (containing the records of meetings of the stockholders, the board of directors, and any committees of the board of directors), the stock certificate books, and the stock record books of each Division Subsidiary are correct and complete. None of the Division Subsidiaries is in default under or in violation of any provision of its charter or bylaws. None of the Target and the Division Subsidiaries controls directly or indirectly or has any direct or indirect equity participation in any corporation, partnership, trust, or other business association with respect to the Division which is not a Division Subsidiary.

(g) *Financial Statements.* Attached hereto as Exhibit E are the following financial statements (collectively the *"Financial Statements"*): (i) audited consolidated and unaudited consolidating balance sheets and statements of income, changes in control account, and cash flow as of and for the fiscal years ended _____, 19____, _____, 19____, _____, 19____, _____, 19____, and _____, 19____ (the *"Most Recent Fiscal Year End"*) for the Division and the Division Subsidiaries; and (ii) unaudited consolidated and consolidating balance sheets and statements of income, changes in control account, and cash flow (the *"Most Recent Financial Statements"*) as of and for the _____ months ended _____ , 19____ (the *"Most Recent Fiscal Month End"*) for the Division and the Division Subsidiaries.[30] The Financial Statements (including the notes thereto) have been prepared in accordance with GAAP applied on a consistent basis throughout the periods covered thereby, present fairly the financial condition of the Division and the Division Subsidiaries as of such dates and the results of operations of the Division and the Division Subsidiaries for such periods, are correct and complete, and are consistent with the books and records of the Division and the Division

---

[30] In the event the Target is unable to satisfy its retained liabilities and obligations after the Closing (i.e., the liabilities and obligations the Buyer did not assume), the Buyer may be exposed for certain of those liabilities and obligations by operation of law (e.g., under statutes and common law doctrines imposing successor liability). *See* ¶2001.2.2.2.

For this reason, the Buyer may seek additional representations and warranties about the *Target's* financial statements and undisclosed liabilities. *Compare* sample acquisition agreement 2003.1 (the *pro-buyer* asset purchase agreement), which contains representations and warranties for use when the Buyer is acquiring *all* of the assets of a target corporation.

Subsidiaries (which books and records are correct and complete)[31] [; *provided, however,* that the Most Recent Financial Statements are subject to normal year-end adjustments (which will not be material individually or in the aggregate) and lack footnotes and other presentation items]. The Target maintains a separate Cash account for the Division (into which the Target deposits all of the receipts of the Division and out of which the Target makes all of the disbursements of the Division).

(h) *Events Subsequent to Most Recent Fiscal Year End.* Since the Most Recent Fiscal Year End, there has not been any [material] adverse change in the business, financial condition, operations, results of operations, or future prospects of any of the Division and the Division Subsidiaries. Without limiting the generality of the foregoing, since that date:

(i) none of the Division and the Division Subsidiaries has sold, leased, transferred, or assigned any of its assets, tangible or intangible, other than for a fair consideration in the Ordinary Course of Business;

(ii) none of the Division and the Division Subsidiaries has entered into any agreement, contract, lease, or license (or series of related agreements, contracts, leases, and licenses) either involving more than $_____ or outside the Ordinary Course of Business;

(iii) no party (including any of the Division and the Division Subsidiaries) has accelerated, terminated, modified, or cancelled any agreement, contract, lease, or license (or series of related agreements, contracts, leases, and licenses) involving more than $_____ to which any of the Division and the Division Subsidiaries is a party or by which any of them is bound;

(iv) none of the Division and the Division Subsidiaries has imposed any Security Interest upon any of its assets, tangible or intangible;

(v) none of the Division and the Division Subsidiaries has made any capital expenditure (or series of related capital expenditures) either involving more than $_____ or outside the Ordinary Course of Business;

(vi) none of the Division and the Division Subsidiaries has made any capital investment in, any loan to, or any acquisition of the securities or assets of, any other Person (or series of related capital investments, loans, and acquisitions) either involving more than $_____ or outside the Ordinary Course of Business;

---

[31] Sample acquisition agreement 2004.2 (the *pro-seller* divisional asset purchase agreement) contains a narrower representation to the effect that the financial statements present fairly the financial condition and results of operations of the Division and the Division Subsidiaries.

(vii) none of the Division and the Division Subsidiaries has issued any note, bond, or other debt security or created, incurred, assumed, or guaranteed any indebtedness for borrowed money or capitalized lease obligation either involving more than $_____ singly or $_____ in the aggregate;

(viii) none of the Division and the Division Subsidiaries has delayed or postponed the payment of accounts payable and other Liabilities outside the Ordinary Course of Business;

(ix) none of the Division and the Division Subsidiaries has cancelled, compromised, waived, or released any right or claim (or series of related rights and claims) either involving more than $_____ or outside the Ordinary Course of Business;

(x) none of the Division and the Division Subsidiaries has granted any license or sublicense of any rights under or with respect to any Intellectual Property;

(xi) there has been no change made or authorized in the charter or bylaws of any of the Division Subsidiaries;

(xii) none of the Division Subsidiaries has issued, sold, or otherwise disposed of any of its capital stock, or granted any options, warrants, or other rights to purchase or obtain (including upon conversion, exchange, or exercise) any of its capital stock;

(xiii) none of the Division Subsidiaries has declared, set aside, or paid any dividend or made any distribution with respect to its capital stock (whether in cash or in kind) or redeemed, purchased, or otherwise acquired any of its capital stock;

(xiv) none of the Division and the Division Subsidiaries has experienced any damage, destruction, or loss (whether or not covered by insurance) to its property;

(xv) none of the Division and the Division Subsidiaries has made any loan to, or entered into any other transaction with, any of the directors, officers, and employees of the Target and its Subsidiaries (including the Division Subsidiaries) outside the Ordinary Course of Business;

(xvi) none of the Division and the Division Subsidiaries has entered into any employment contract or collective bargaining agreement, written or oral, or modified the terms of any existing such contract or agreement;

(xvii) none of the Division and the Division Subsidiaries has granted any increase in the base compensation of any of the directors, officers, and employees of the Target and its Subsidiaries (including the Division Subsidiaries) outside the Ordinary Course of Business;

(xviii) none of the Division and the Division Subsidiaries has adopted, amended, modified, or terminated any bonus, profit-sharing, incentive, severance, or other plan, contract, or commitment for the benefit of any of the directors, officers, and employees of the Target and its Subsidiaries (including the Division Subsidiaries), or taken any such action with respect to any other Employee Benefit Plan;

(xix) none of the Division and the Division Subsidiaries has made any other change in employment terms for any of the directors, officers, and employees of the Target and its Subsidiaries (including the Division Subsidiaries) outside the Ordinary Course of Business;

(xx) none of the Division and the Division Subsidiaries has made or pledged to make any charitable or other capital contribution outside the Ordinary Course of Business;

(xxi) the Division has not paid any amount to any third party with respect to any Liability or obligation (including any costs and expenses the Target has incurred or may incur in connection with this Agreement and the transactions contemplated hereby) which would not constitute an Assumed Liability if in existence as of the Closing;[32]

(xxii) there has not been any other [material] occurrence, event, incident, action, failure to act, or transaction outside the Ordinary Course of Business involving any of the Division and the Division Subsidiaries; and

(xxiii) none of the Division and the Division Subsidiaries has committed to any of the foregoing.

(i) *Undisclosed Liabilities.* None of the Division and the Division Subsidiaries has any Liability (and there is no Basis for any present or future action, suit, proceeding, hearing, investigation, charge, complaint, claim, or demand against any of them giving rise to any Liability), except for (i) Liabilities set forth on the face of the Most Recent Balance Sheet (rather than in any notes thereto) and (ii) Liabilities which have arisen after the Most Recent Fiscal Month End in the

---

[32] Notice that the Buyer will bear the cost of (i.e., will in effect assume) any liability or obligation to the extent the Division pays any amount to a third party with respect thereto prior to the Closing. This is because the payment will reduce the amount of cash the Buyer otherwise would receive when it acquires the assets of the Division at the Closing. The Buyer therefore will seek to prevent the Division from making any payment with respect to a liability or obligation the Buyer is not assuming.

This representation and warranty is designed to uncover whether the Division has made any such payment between the Most Recent Fiscal Year End and the date of this Agreement. Section 5(c) contains a comparable covenant prohibiting the Division from making any such payment between the date of this Agreement and the Closing.

Ordinary Course of Business (none of which results from, arises out of, relates to, is in the nature of, or was caused by any breach of contract, breach of warranty, tort, infringement, or violation of law).[33]

(j) *Legal Compliance.* Each of the Division, the Division Subsidiaries, and their respective predecessors and Affiliates has complied with all applicable laws (including rules, regulations, codes, plans, injunctions, judgments, orders, decrees, rulings, and charges thereunder) of federal, state, local, and foreign governments (and all agencies thereof), and no action, suit, proceeding, hearing, investigation, charge, complaint, claim, demand, or notice has been filed or commenced against any of them alleging any failure so to comply.

(k) *Tax Matters.*[34]

(i) Each of the Division and the Division Subsidiaries[35] has filed all Tax Returns that it was required to file. All such Tax Returns were correct and complete in all respects. All Taxes owed by any of the Division and the Division

---

[33] This Agreement provides that the Buyer will assume certain specified liabilities of the *Division*. *See* the definition of Assumed Liabilities in §1 (and in particular the provision making the Buyer responsible for certain liabilities the Target reveals in the Disclosure Schedule).

In addition, the Buyer may be exposed for certain liabilities of the *Division* by operation of law if the Target does not pay them (e.g., under applicable bulk sales statutes and common law doctrines of de facto merger and successor liability). *See* ¶2001.2.2.2.

Finally, the Buyer will become indirectly responsible for all of the liabilities of the *Division Subsidiaries* not paid by the Target when the Buyer acquires their capital stock as part of the Acquired Assets. For this reason, the Buyer may seek (a) to purchase assets from the Target *and from each of the Division Subsidiaries* (i.e., a multiple entity asset sale) or (b) to have the Target liquidate and dissolve the Division Subsidiaries tax free under Code §332 (to the extent they are United States corporations) and sell their assets to the Buyer.

These representations and warranties concerning undisclosed liabilities (and the post-Closing indemnification provisions in §8(b)) are designed to work in conjunction with the narrow definition of Assumed Liabilities in §1 to protect the Buyer against liabilities it does not intend to assume.

[34] This Agreement provides that the Buyer will not assume any liability of the *Target (including the Division)* for unpaid taxes through the Closing. See the definition of Assumed Liabilities in §1. This Agreement also provides that the Target will be responsible for the unpaid taxes of the *Division Subsidiaries* through the Closing. See the tax allocation provisions in §10(p).

The Buyer may, however, have (i) exposure for the tax liabilities of the Target (including the Division) by operation of law if the Target does not pay them (e.g., under applicable bulk sales statutes and common law doctrines of de facto merger and successor liability) and (ii) indirect exposure for the tax liabilities of the Division Subsidiaries not paid by the Target when the Buyer acquires their capital stock as part of the Acquired Assets. In order to eliminate the latter risk, the Buyer may seek (a) to purchase assets from the Target and *from each of the Division Subsidiaries* (i.e., a multiple entity asset sale) or (b) to have the Target liquidate and dissolve the Division Subsidiaries tax free under Code §332 (to the extent they are United States corporations) and sell their assets to the Buyer.

[35] This Agreement contains a considerably abbreviated version of the tax provisions found in sample acquisition agreement 2002.4 (sale of subsidiary out of consolidated group). The Parties may wish to incorporate some or all of the unabridged provisions from sample acquisition agreement 2002.4 into this Agreement.

Subsidiaries (whether or not shown on any Tax Return) have been paid.[36] None of the Division and the Division Subsidiaries currently is the beneficiary of any extension of time within which to file any Tax Return. No claim has ever been made by an authority in a jurisdiction where any of the Division and the Division Subsidiaries does not file Tax Returns that it is or may be subject to taxation by that jurisdiction. There are no Security Interests on any of the assets of any of the Division and the Division Subsidiaries that arose in connection with any failure (or alleged failure) to pay any Tax.

(ii) Each of the Division and the Division Subsidiaries has withheld and paid all Taxes required to have been withheld and paid in connection with amounts paid or owing to any employee, independent contractor, creditor, stockholder, or other third party.

(iii) No Target Stockholder or director or officer (or employee responsible for Tax matters) of any of the Target and its Subsidiaries expects any authority to assess any additional Taxes with respect to the Division and the Division Subsidiaries for any period for which Tax Returns have been filed. There is no dispute or claim concerning any Tax Liability of any of the Division and the Division Subsidiaries either (A) claimed or raised by any authority in writing or (B) as to which any of the Target Stockholders and the directors and officers (and employees responsible for Tax matters) of the Target and its Subsidiaries has Knowledge based upon personal contact with any agent of such authority. §3(k) of the Disclosure Schedule lists, all federal, state, local, and foreign income Tax Returns filed with respect to any of the Division and the Division Subsidiaries for taxable periods ended on or after _____, 19____, indicates those Tax Returns that have been audited, and indicates those Tax Returns that currently are the subject of audit. The Target has delivered to the Buyer correct and complete copies of all federal income Tax Returns, examination reports, and statements of deficiencies assessed against or agreed to by any of the Division and the Division Subsidiaries since _____, 19____.

(iv) None of the Division and the Division Subsidiaries has waived any statute of limitations in respect of Taxes or agreed to any extension of time with respect to a Tax assessment or deficiency.

(v) None of the Division and the Division Subsidiaries has filed a consent under Code §341(f) concerning collapsible corporations. None of the Division and the Division Subsidiaries has made any payments, is obligated to make any payments, or is a party to any agreement that under certain circumstances could obligate it to make any payments that will not be deductible under Code §280G. None of the Division and the Division Subsidiaries has been a United States real property holding corporation within the meaning of Code §897(c)(2)

---

[36] Sample acquisition agreement 2004.2 (the *pro-seller* divisional asset purchase agreement) contains a narrower representation to the effect that each of the Division and the Division Subsidiaries has filed all tax returns that it was required to file and has paid all taxes *shown thereon as owing.*

during the applicable period specified in Code §897(c)(1)(A)(ii). [Each of the Division and the Division Subsidiaries has disclosed on its federal income Tax Returns all positions taken therein that could give rise to a substantial understatement of federal income Tax within the meaning of Code §6662]. None of the Division and the Division Subsidiaries is a party to any Tax allocation or sharing agreement. None of the Target and its Subsidiaries (A) has been a member of an Affiliated Group filing a consolidated federal income Tax Return (other than a group the common parent of which was the Target) or (B) has any Liability for the Taxes of any Person (other than any of the Target and its Subsidiaries) under Reg. §1.1502-6 (or any similar provision of state, local, or foreign law), as a transferee or successor, by contract, or otherwise.[37]

(vi) §3(k) of the Disclosure Schedule sets forth the following information with respect to each of the Division and the Division Subsidiaries (or, in the case of clause (B) below, with respect to each of the Division Subsidiaries) as of the most recent practicable date [(as well as on an estimated pro forma basis as of the Closing giving effect to the consummation of the transactions contemplated hereby)]: (A) the basis of the Division or Division Subsidiary in its assets; (B) the basis of the stockholder(s) of the Division Subsidiary in its stock (or the amount of any Excess Loss Account); (C) the amount of any net operating loss, net capital loss, unused investment or other credit, unused foreign tax, or excess charitable contribution allocable to the Division or Division Subsidiary; and (D) the amount of any deferred gain or loss allocable to the Division or Division Subsidiary arising out of any Deferred Intercompany Transaction.

(vii) The unpaid Taxes of the Division and the Division Subsidiaries (A) did not, as of the Most Recent Fiscal Month End, exceed the reserve for Tax Liability (rather than any reserve for deferred Taxes established to reflect timing differences between book and Tax income) set forth on the face of the Most Recent

---

[37] If the Target or a Subsidiary has been a member of an Affiliated Group filing a consolidated federal income tax return, such corporation (or its successor) will be jointly and severally liable under Reg. §1.1502-6 for certain tax liabilities incurred by such Affiliated Group for a tax year when such corporation was a member of such Affiliated Group for all or part of such tax year. See ¶210.

The Target or a Subsidiary may also be liable for the unpaid taxes of third parties under similar provisions of state, local, or foreign law, as a transferee or successor, by contract (e.g., a tax sharing agreement), or otherwise.

This Agreement provides that the Buyer will not assume any liability of the Target for the unpaid taxes of the Target or any other person. See the definition of "Assumed Liabilities" in §1.

However, the Buyer will become indirectly responsible for any such liability of the *Division Subsidiaries* when the Buyer acquires their capital stock as part of the Acquired Assets. In order to eliminate this risk altogether, the Buyer may seek (a) to purchase assets from the Target *and from each of the Division Subsidiaries* (i.e., a multiple entity asset sale) or (b) to have the Target liquidate and dissolve the Division Subsidiaries tax free under Code §332 (to the extent they are United States corporations) and sell their assets to the Buyer.

This Agreement contains indemnification provisions designed to protect the Buyer against any such liability for the unpaid taxes of the Target or any other person. See §8(b)(ii).

Balance Sheet (rather than in any notes thereto) and (B) do not exceed that reserve as adjusted for the passage of time through the Closing Date in accordance with the past custom and practice of the Division and the Division Subsidiaries in filing their Tax Returns.

(l) *Real Property.*[38]

(i) §3(l)(i) of the Disclosure Schedule lists and describes briefly all real property that any of the Division and the Division Subsidiaries owns. With respect to each such parcel of owned real property:

(A) the identified owner has good and marketable title to the parcel of real property, free and clear of any Security Interest, easement, covenant, or other restriction, except for installments of special assessments not yet delinquent and recorded easements, covenants, and other restrictions which do not impair the current use, occupancy, or value, or the marketability of title, of the property subject thereto;

(B) there are no pending or [, to the Knowledge of any of the Target Stockholders and the directors and officers (and employees with responsibility for real estate matters) of the Target and its Subsidiaries,] threatened condemnation proceedings, lawsuits, or administrative actions relating to the property, or other matters affecting [materially and] adversely the current use, occupancy, or value thereof;

(C) the legal description for the parcel contained in the deed thereof describes such parcel fully and adequately, the buildings and improvements are located within the boundary lines of the described parcels of land, are not in violation of applicable setback requirements, zoning laws, and ordinances (and none of the properties or buildings or improvements thereon are subject to "permitted non-conforming use" or "permitted non-conforming structure" classifications), and do not encroach on any easement which may burden the land, the land does not serve any adjoining property for any purpose inconsistent with the use of the land, and the property is not located within any flood plain or subject to any similar type restriction for which any permits or licenses necessary to the use thereof have not been obtained;

(D) all facilities have received all approvals of governmental authorities (including licenses and permits) required in connection with the ownership or operation thereof and have been operated and maintained in accordance with applicable laws, rules, and regulations;

---

[38] These representations and warranties concerning real property are relatively long and detailed. A condensed version of these provisions may be more appropriate when, for example, the real property of the Division and the Division Subsidiaries is relatively insignificant.

(E) there are no leases, subleases, licenses, concessions, or other agreements, written or oral, granting to any party or parties the right of use or occupancy of any portion of the parcel of real property;

(F) there are no outstanding options or rights of first refusal to purchase the parcel of real property, or any portion thereof or interest therein;

(G) there are no parties (other than the Division and the Division Subsidiaries) in possession of the parcel of real property, other than tenants under any leases disclosed in §3(l)(i) of the Disclosure Schedule who are in possession of space to which they are entitled;

(H) all facilities located on the parcel of real property are supplied with utilities and other services necessary for the operation of such facilities, including gas, electricity, water, telephone, sanitary sewer, and storm sewer, all of which services are adequate in accordance with all applicable laws, ordinances, rules, and regulations and are provided via public roads or via permanent, irrevocable, appurtenant easements benefitting the parcel of real property; and

(I) each parcel of real property abuts on and has direct vehicular access to a public road, or has access to a public road via a permanent, irrevocable, appurtenant easement benefitting the parcel of real property, and access to the property is provided by paved public right-of-way with adequate curb cuts available.

(ii) §3(l)(ii) of the Disclosure Schedule lists and describes briefly all real property leased or subleased to any of the Division and the Division Subsidiaries. §3(l)(ii) of the Disclosure Schedule also identifies the leased or subleased properties for which title insurance policies are to be procured in accordance with §5(h)(ii) below. The Target has delivered to the Buyer correct and complete copies of the leases and subleases listed in §3(l)(ii) of the Disclosure Schedule (as amended to date). With respect to each lease and sublease listed in §3(l)(ii) of the Disclosure Schedule:

(A) the lease or sublease is legal, valid, binding, enforceable, and in full force and effect;

(B) the lease or sublease will continue to be legal, valid, binding, enforceable, and in full force and effect on identical terms following the consummation of the transactions contemplated hereby (including the assignments and assumptions referred to in §2 above);

(C) no party to the lease or sublease is in breach or default, and no event has occurred which, with notice or lapse of time, would constitute a breach or default or permit termination, modification, or acceleration thereunder;

(D) no party to the lease or sublease has repudiated any provision thereof;

(E) there are no disputes, oral agreements, or forbearance programs in effect as to the lease or sublease;

(F) with respect to each sublease, the representations and warranties set forth in subsections (A) — (E) above are true and correct with respect to the underlying lease;

(G) none of the Division and the Division Subsidiaries has assigned, transferred, conveyed, mortgaged, deeded in trust, or encumbered any interest in the leasehold or subleasehold;

(H) all facilities leased or subleased thereunder have received all approvals of governmental authorities (including licenses and permits) required in connection with the operation thereof and have been operated and maintained in accordance with applicable laws, rules, and regulations;

(I) all facilities leased or subleased thereunder are supplied with utilities and other services necessary for the operation of said facilities; and

(J) the owner of the facility leased or subleased has good and marketable title to the parcel of real property, free and clear of any Security Interest, easement, covenant, or other restriction, except for installments of special easements not yet delinquent and recorded easements, covenants, and other restrictions which do not impair the current use, occupancy, or value, or the marketability of title, of the property subject thereto.

(m) *Intellectual Property.*[39]

(i) The Division and the Division Subsidiaries own or have the right to use pursuant to license, sublicense, agreement, or permission all Intellectual Property necessary [or desirable] for the operation of its businesses as presently conducted [and as presently proposed to be conducted]. Each item of Intellectual Property owned or used by any of the Division and the Division Subsidiaries immediately prior to the Closing hereunder will be owned or available for use by the Buyer or the Subsidiary on identical terms and conditions immediately subsequent to the Closing hereunder. Each of the Division and the Division Subsidiaries has taken all necessary [and desirable] action to maintain and protect each item of Intellectual Property that it owns or uses.

(ii) None of the Division and the Division Subsidiaries has interfered with, infringed upon, misappropriated, or otherwise come into conflict with any

---

[39] These representations and warranties concerning intellectual property are relatively long and detailed. A condensed version of these provisions may be more appropriate when, for example, the intellectual property of the Division and the Division Subsidiaries is relatively insignificant.

Intellectual Property rights of third parties, and none of the Target Stockholders and the directors and officers (and employees with responsibility for Intellectual Property matters) of the Target and its Subsidiaries has ever received any charge, complaint, claim, demand, or notice alleging any such interference, infringement, misappropriation, or violation (including any claim that any of the Division and the Division Subsidiaries must license or refrain from using any Intellectual Property rights of any third party). To the Knowledge of any of the Target Stockholders and the directors and officers (and employees with responsibility for Intellectual Property matters) of the Target and its Subsidiaries, no third party has interfered with, infringed upon, misappropriated, or otherwise come into conflict with any Intellectual Property rights of any of the Division and the Division Subsidiaries.

(iii) §3(m)(iii) of the Disclosure Schedule identifies each patent or registration which has been issued to any of the Division and the Division Subsidiaries with respect to any of its Intellectual Property, identifies each pending patent application or application for registration which any of the Division and the Division Subsidiaries has made with respect to any of its Intellectual Property, and identifies each license, agreement, or other permission which any of the Division and the Division Subsidiaries has granted to any third party with respect to any of its Intellectual Property (together with any exceptions). The Target has delivered to the Buyer correct and complete copies of all such patents, registrations, applications, licenses, agreements, and permissions (as amended to date) [and has made available to the Buyer correct and complete copies of all other written documentation evidencing ownership and prosecution (if applicable) of each such item]. §3(m)(iii) of the Disclosure Schedule also identifies each trade name or unregistered trademark used by any of the Division and the Division Subsidiaries in connection with any of its businesses. With respect to each item of Intellectual Property required to be identified in §3(m)(iii) of the Disclosure Schedule:

(A) the Division and the Division Subsidiaries possess all right, title, and interest in and to the item, free and clear of any Security Interest, license, or other restriction;

(B) the item is not subject to any outstanding injunction, judgment, order, decree, ruling, or charge;

(C) no action, suit, proceeding, hearing, investigation, charge, complaint, claim, or demand is pending or [, to the Knowledge of any of the Target Stockholders and the directors and officers (and employees with responsibility for Intellectual Property matters) of the Target and its Subsidiaries,] is threatened which challenges the legality, validity, enforceability, use, or ownership of the item; and

(D) none of the Division and the Division Subsidiaries has ever agreed to indemnify any Person for or against any interference, infringement, misappropriation, or other conflict with respect to the item.

(iv) §3(m)(iv) of the Disclosure Schedule identifies each item of Intellectual Property that any third party owns and that any of the Division and the Division Subsidiaries uses pursuant to license, sublicense, agreement, or permission. The Target has delivered to the Buyer correct and complete copies of all such licenses, sublicenses, agreements, and permissions (as amended to date). With respect to each item of Intellectual Property required to be identified in §3(m)(iv) of the Disclosure Schedule:

(A) the license, sublicense, agreement, or permission covering the item is legal, valid, binding, enforceable, and in full force and effect;

(B) the license, sublicense, agreement, or permission will continue to be legal, valid, binding, enforceable, and in full force and effect on identical terms following the consummation of the transactions contemplated hereby (including the assignments and assumptions referred to in §2 above);

(C) no party to the license, sublicense, agreement, or permission is in breach or default, and no event has occurred which with notice or lapse of time would constitute a breach or default or permit termination, modification, or acceleration thereunder;

(D) no party to the license, sublicense, agreement, or permission has repudiated any provision thereof;

(E) with respect to each sublicense, the representations and warranties set forth in subsections (A) through (D) above are true and correct with respect to the underlying license;

(F) the underlying item of Intellectual Property is not subject to any outstanding injunction, judgment, order, decree, ruling, or charge;

(G) no action, suit, proceeding, hearing, investigation, charge, complaint, claim, or demand is pending or [, to the Knowledge of any of the Target Stockholders and the directors and officers (and employees with responsibility for Intellectual Property matters) of the Target and its Subsidiaries,] is threatened which challenges the legality, validity, or enforceability of the underlying item of Intellectual Property; and

(H) none of the Division and the Division Subsidiaries has granted any sublicense or similar right with respect to the license, sublicense, agreement, or permission.

(v) To the Knowledge of any of the Target Stockholders and the directors and officers (and employees with responsibility for Intellectual Property matters) of the Target and its Subsidiaries, none of the Division and the Division Subsidiaries will interfere with, infringe upon, misappropriate, or otherwise come into conflict with, any Intellectual Property rights of third parties as a result of the continued operation of its businesses as presently conducted [and as presently proposed to be conducted].

(vi) [None of the Target Stockholders and the directors and officers (and employees with responsibility for Intellectual Property matters) of the Target and its Subsidiaries has any Knowledge of any new products, inventions, procedures, or methods of manufacturing or processing that any competitors or other third parties have developed which reasonably could be expected to supersede or make obsolete any product or process of any of the Division and the Division Subsidiaries.]

(n) *Tangible Assets.* The Division and the Division Subsidiaries own or lease all buildings, machinery, equipment, and other tangible assets necessary for the conduct of their businesses as presently conducted [and as presently proposed to be conducted]. Each such tangible asset is free from defects (patent and latent), has been maintained in accordance with normal industry practice, is in good operating condition and repair (subject to normal wear and tear), and is suitable for the purposes for which it presently is used [and presently is proposed to be used].

(o) *Inventory.* The inventory of the Division and the Division Subsidiaries consists of raw materials and supplies, manufactured and purchased parts, goods in process, and finished goods, all of which is merchantable and fit for the purpose for which it was procured or manufactured, and none of which is slow-moving, obsolete, damaged, or defective, subject only to the reserve for inventory writedown set forth on the face of the Most Recent Balance Sheet (rather than in any notes thereto) as adjusted for the passage of time through the Closing Date in accordance with the past custom and practice of the Division and the Division Subsidiaries.

(p) *Contracts.* §3(p) of the Disclosure Schedule lists the following contracts and other agreements to which any of the Division and the Division Subsidiaries is a party:

(i) any agreement (or group of related agreements) for the lease of personal property to or from any Person providing for lease payments in excess of $_____ per annum;

(ii) any agreement (or group of related agreements) for the purchase or sale of raw materials, commodities, supplies, products, or other personal property, or for the furnishing or receipt of services, the performance of which will extend over a period of more than one year, result in a [material] loss to any of the Division and the Division Subsidiaries, or involve consideration in excess of $_____;

(iii) any agreement concerning a partnership or joint venture;

(iv) any agreement (or group of related agreements) under which it has created, incurred, assumed, or guaranteed any indebtedness for borrowed money, or any capitalized lease obligation, in excess of $_____ or under which it has imposed a Security Interest on any of its assets, tangible or intangible;

(v) any agreement concerning confidentiality or noncompetition;

(vi) any agreement involving any of the Target Stockholders and their Affiliates (including the Target and its Subsidiaries other than the Division Subsidiaries);

(vii) any profit sharing, stock option, stock purchase, stock appreciation, deferred compensation, severance, or other [material] plan or arrangement for the benefit of the current or former directors, officers, and employees of the Target and its Subsidiaries (including the Division Subsidiaries);

(viii) any collective bargaining agreement;

(ix) any agreement for the employment of any individual on a full-time, part-time, consulting, or other basis providing annual compensation in excess of $_____ or providing severance benefits;

(x) any agreement under which it has advanced or loaned any amount to any of the directors, officers, and employees of the Target and its Subsidiaries (including the Division Subsidiaries) outside the Ordinary Course of Business;

(xi) any agreement under which the consequences of a default or termination could have a [material] adverse effect on the business, financial condition, operations, results of operations, or future prospects of any of the Division and the Division Subsidiaries; or

(xii) any other agreement (or group of related agreements) the performance of which involves consideration in excess of $_____.

The Target has delivered to the Buyer a correct and complete copy of each written agreement listed in §3(p) of the Disclosure Schedule (as amended to date) and a written summary setting forth the terms and conditions of each oral agreement referred to in §3(p) of the Disclosure Schedule. With respect to each such agreement: (A) the agreement is legal, valid, binding, enforceable, and in full force and effect; (B) the agreement will continue to be legal, valid, binding, enforceable, and in full force and effect on identical terms following the consummation of the transactions contemplated hereby (including the assignments and assumptions referred to in §2 above); (C) no party is in breach or default, and no event has occurred which with notice or lapse of time would constitute a breach or default, or permit termination, modification, or acceleration, under the agreement; and (D) no party has repudiated any provision of the agreement.

(q) *Notes and Accounts Receivable.* All notes and accounts receivable of the Division and the Division Subsidiaries are reflected properly on their books and records, are valid receivables subject to no setoffs or counterclaims, are current and collectible, and will be collected in accordance with their terms at their recorded amounts, subject only to the reserve for bad debts set forth on the face of the Most Recent Balance Sheet (rather than in any notes thereto) as adjusted for the passage of time through the Closing Date in accordance with the past custom and practice of the Division and the Division Subsidiaries.

(r) *Powers of Attorney.* There are no outstanding powers of attorney executed on behalf of any of the Division and the Division Subsidiaries.

(s) *Insurance.* §3(s) of the Disclosure Schedule sets forth the following information with respect to each insurance policy (including policies providing property, casualty, liability, and workers' compensation coverage and bond and surety arrangements) to which any of the Division and the Division Subsidiaries has been a party, a named insured, or otherwise the beneficiary of coverage at any time within the past [10] years:

(i) the name, address, and telephone number of the agent;

(ii) the name of the insurer, the name of the policyholder, and the name of each covered insured;

(iii) the policy number and the period of coverage;

(iv) the scope (including an indication of whether the coverage was on a claims made, occurrence, or other basis) and amount (including a description of how deductibles and ceilings are calculated and operate) of coverage; and

(v) a description of any retroactive premium adjustments or other loss-sharing arrangements.

With respect to each such insurance policy: (A) the policy is legal, valid, binding, enforceable, and in full force and effect; (B) the policy will continue to be legal, valid, binding, enforceable, and in full force and effect on identical terms following the consummation of the transactions contemplated hereby (including the assignments and assumptions referred to in §2 above); (C) neither any of the Division and the Division Subsidiaries nor any other party to the policy is in breach or default (including with respect to the payment of premiums or the giving of notices), and no event has occurred which, with notice or the lapse of time, would constitute such a breach or default, or permit termination, modification, or acceleration, under the policy; and (D) no party to the policy has repudiated any provision thereof. Each of the Division and the Division Subsidiaries has been covered during the past [10] years by insurance in scope and amount customary and reasonable for the businesses in which it has engaged during the aforementioned period. §3(s) of the Disclosure Schedule describes any self-insurance arrangements affecting any of the Division and the Division Subsidiaries.

(t) *Litigation.* §3(t) of the Disclosure Schedule sets forth each instance in which any of the Division and the Division Subsidiaries (i) is subject to any outstanding injunction, judgment, order, decree, ruling, or charge or (ii) is a party or [, to the Knowledge of any of the Target Stockholders and the directors and officers (and employees with responsibility for litigation matters) of the Target and its Subsidiaries,] is threatened to be made a party to any action, suit, proceeding, hearing, or investigation of, in, or before any court or quasi-judicial or administrative agency of any federal, state, local, or foreign jurisdiction or before any arbitrator. None of the actions, suits, proceedings, hearings, and investigations set forth in §3(t) of the Disclosure Schedule could result in any [material] adverse change in the business, financial condition, operations, results of operations, or future prospects of any of the Division and the Division Subsidiaries. None of the Target Stockholders and the directors and officers (and employees with responsibility for litigation matters) of the Target and its Subsidiaries has any reason to believe that any such action, suit, proceeding, hearing, or investigation may be brought or threatened against any of the Division and the Division Subsidiaries.

(u) *Product Warranty.* Each product manufactured, sold, leased, or delivered by any of the Division and the Division Subsidiaries has been in conformity with all applicable contractual commitments and all express and implied warranties, and none of the Division and the Division Subsidiaries has any Liability (and there is no Basis for any present or future action, suit, proceeding, hearing, investigation, charge, complaint, claim, or demand against any of them giving rise to any Liability) for replacement or repair thereof or other damages in connection therewith, subject only to the reserve for product warranty claims set forth on the face of the Most Recent Balance Sheet (rather than in any notes thereto) as adjusted for the passage of time through the Closing Date in accordance with the past custom and practice of the Division and the Division Subsidiaries. No product manufactured, sold, leased, or delivered by any of the Division and the Division Subsidiaries is subject to any guaranty, warranty, or other indemnity beyond the applicable standard terms and conditions of sale or lease. §3(u) of the Disclosure Schedule includes copies of the standard terms and conditions of sale or lease for each of the Division and the Division Subsidiaries (containing applicable guaranty, warranty, and indemnity provisions).

(v) *Product Liability.* None of the Division and the Division Subsidiaries has any Liability (and there is no Basis for any present or future action, suit, proceeding, hearing, investigation, charge, complaint, claim, or demand against any of them giving rise to any Liability) arising out of any injury to individuals or property as a result of the ownership, possession, or use of any product manufactured, sold, leased, or delivered by any of the Division and the Division Subsidiaries.

(w) *Employees.* To the Knowledge of any of the Target Stockholders and the directors and officers (and employees with responsibility for employment matters) of the Division and the Division Subsidiaries, no executive, key employee, or group of employees has any plans to terminate employment with any of the Division and the Division Subsidiaries. None of the Division and the Division Subsidiaries is a party to or bound by any collective bargaining agreement, nor has any of them experienced any strikes, grievances, claims of unfair labor practices, or other collective bargaining disputes. None of the Division and the Division Subsidiaries has committed any unfair labor practice. None of the Target Stockholders and the directors and officers (and employees with responsibility for employment matters) of the Target and its Subsidiaries has any Knowledge of any organizational effort presently being made or threatened by or on behalf of any labor union with respect to employees of any of the Division and the Division Subsidiaries.

(x) *Employee Benefits.*[40]

(i) §3(x) of the Disclosure Schedule lists each Employee Benefit Plan that any of the Division and the Division Subsidiaries maintains, to which any of the Division and the Division Subsidiaries contributes or has any obligation to contribute, or with respect to which any of the Division and the Division Subsidiaries has any [material] Liability or potential Liability.

(A) Each such Employee Benefit Plan (and each related trust, insurance contract, or fund) has been maintained, funded and administered in accordance with the terms of such Employee Benefit Plan and complies in form and in operation in all [material] respects with the applicable requirements of ERISA, the Code, and other applicable laws.

(B) All required reports and descriptions (including annual reports (IRS Form 5500), summary annual reports, and summary plan descriptions) have been timely filed and/or distributed in accordance with the applicable requirements of ERISA and the Code with respect to each such Employee Benefit Plan. The requirements of COBRA have been met with respect to

---

[40] These representations and warranties concerning employee benefits are relatively long and detailed. A condensed version of these provisions may be more appropriate when, for example, the Division and the Division Subsidiaries have relatively insignificant employee benefit plans.

each such Employee Benefit Plan which is an Employee Welfare Benefit Plan subject to COBRA.

(C) All contributions (including all employer contributions and employee salary reduction contributions) which are due have been made within the time period prescribed by ERISA to each such Employee Benefit Plan which is an Employee Pension Benefit Plan and all contributions for any period ending on or before the Closing Date which are not yet due have been made to each such Employee Pension Benefit Plan or accrued in accordance with the past custom and practice of the Division and the Division Subsidiaries. All premiums or other payments for all periods ending on or before the Closing Date have been paid with respect to each such Employee Benefit Plan which is an Employee Welfare Benefit Plan.

(D) Each such Employee Benefit Plan which is intended to meet the requirements of a "qualified plan" under Code §401(a) has received a determination from the Internal Revenue Service that such Employee Benefit Plan is so qualified, and nothing has occurred since the date of such determination that could adversely affect the qualified status of any such Employee Benefit Plan.

(E) The market value of assets under each such Employee Benefit Plan which is an Employee Pension Benefit Plan (other than any Multiemployer Plan) equals or exceeds the present value of all vested and nonvested Liabilities thereunder determined in accordance with PBGC methods, factors, and assumptions applicable to an Employee Pension Benefit Plan terminating on the date for determination.

(F) The Target has delivered to the Buyer correct and complete copies of the plan documents and summary plan descriptions, the most recent determination letter received from the Internal Revenue Service, the most recent annual report (IRS Form 5500, with all applicable attachments), and all related trust agreements, insurance contracts, and other funding arrangements which implement each such Employee Benefit Plan.

(ii) With respect to each Employee Benefit Plan that any of the Division, the Division Subsidiaries, and any ERISA Affiliate maintains, or to which any of them contributes, or has any obligation to contribute, or with respect to which any of them has any [material] Liability or potential Liability:

(A) No such Employee Benefit Plan which is an Employee Pension Benefit Plan (other than any Multiemployer Plan) has been completely or partially terminated or been the subject of a Reportable Event. No proceeding by the PBGC to terminate any such Employee Pension Benefit Plan (other than any Multiemployer Plan) has been instituted or [, to the Knowledge of any of the Target Stockholders and the directors and officers (and employees with responsibility for employee benefits matters) of the Target and its Subsidiaries,] threatened.

(B) There have been no Prohibited Transactions with respect to any such Employee Benefit Plan. No Fiduciary has any Liability for breach of fiduciary duty or any other failure to act or comply in connection with the administration or investment of the assets of any such Employee Benefit Plan. No action, suit, proceeding, hearing, or investigation with respect to the administration or the investment of the assets of any such Employee Benefit Plan (other than routine claims for benefits) is pending or [, to the Knowledge of any of the Target Stockholders and the directors and officers (and employees with responsibility for employee benefits matters) of the Target and its Subsidiaries,] threatened. None of the Target Stockholders and the directors and officers (and employees with responsibility for employee benefits matters) of the Target and its Subsidiaries has any Knowledge of any Basis for any such action, suit, proceeding, hearing, or investigation.

(C) None of the Target and its Subsidiaries has incurred, and none of the Target Stockholders and the directors and officers (and employees with responsibility for employee benefits matters) of the Target and its Subsidiaries has any reason to expect that any of the Target and its Subsidiaries will incur, any Liability with respect to the PBGC (other than PBGC premium payments not yet due) or otherwise under Title IV of ERISA (including any withdrawal liability as defined in ERISA §4201) or under the Code with respect to any such Employee Benefit Plan which is an Employee Pension Benefit Plan, or under COBRA with respect to any such Employee Benefit Plan which is an Employee Welfare Benefit Plan.

(iii) ALTERNATIVE A (NO MULTIEMPLOYER PLANS): None of the Target, its Subsidiaries, and any ERISA Affiliate contributes to, has any obligation to contribute to, or has any Liability (including withdrawal liability as defined in ERISA §4201) under or with respect to any Multiemployer Plan.

ALTERNATIVE B (MULTIEMPLOYER PLANS): None of the Target, its Subsidiaries, and any ERISA Affiliate has incurred any Liability on account of a "partial withdrawal" or a "complete withdrawal" (within the meaning of ERISA §§4205 and 4203, respectively) from any Multiemployer Plan, no such Liability has been asserted, and there are no events or circumstances which could result in any such partial or complete withdrawal; and none of the Target, its Subsidiaries, and any ERISA Affiliate is bound by any contract or agreement or has any obligation or Liability described in ERISA §4204. [Each Multiemployer Plan complies in form and has been administered in accordance with the requirements of ERISA and, where applicable, the Code, and each Multiemployer Plan is qualified under Code §401(a).]

(iv) None of the Division and the Division Subsidiaries maintains, contributes to or has an obligation to contribute to, or has any [material] Liability or potential Liability with respect to, any Employee Welfare Benefit Plan providing medical, health, or life insurance or other welfare-type benefits for current or future retired or terminated employees, their spouses, or their dependents (other than in accordance with COBRA).

(y) *Guaranties.* None of the Division and the Division Subsidiaries is a guarantor or otherwise is liable for any Liability or obligation (including indebtedness) of any other Person.

(z) *Environment, Health, and Safety Matters.*[41]

(i) Each of the Division, the Division Subsidiaries, and their respective predecessors and Affiliates has complied and is in compliance with all Environmental, Health, and Safety Requirements.

(ii) Without limiting the generality of the foregoing, each of the Division, the Division Subsidiaries and their respective Affiliates has obtained and complied with, and is in compliance with, all permits, licenses and other authorizations that are required pursuant to Environmental, Health, and Safety Requirements for the occupation of its facilities and the operation of its business; a list of all such permits, licenses and other authorizations is set forth on the attached *"Environmental and Safety Permits Schedule."*

(iii) Neither the Division, the Division Subsidiaries, nor their respective predecessors or Affiliates has received any written or oral notice, report or other information regarding any actual or alleged violation of Environmental, Health, and Safety Requirements, or any liabilities or potential liabilities (whether accrued, absolute, contingent, unliquidated or otherwise), including any investigatory, remedial or corrective obligations, relating to any of them or its facilities arising under Environmental, Health, and Safety Requirements.

---

[41] These representations and warranties concerning environmental, health, and safety matters are relatively long and detailed, contain no materiality or knowledge limitations, and impose a substantial disclosure burden on the Target. A condensed version may be more appropriate when, for example, the operations of the Division and the Division Subsidiaries appear to have had a relatively insignificant effect upon the environment or upon public or employee health and safety.

Sample acquisition agreement 2004.2 (the *pro-seller* divisional purchase agreement) contains an environmental representation which (1) is subject to certain knowledge and materiality limitations, (2) focuses on current compliance with environmental, health, and safety laws, and (3) does not extend to strict liability for site cleanup under CERCLA or common law liability.

Sample acquisition agreement 2004.3 (the *neutral* divisional purchase agreement) contains an environmental representation which (1) is subject to certain materiality limitations, (2) is generally more limited and narrowly focused than this representation, and (3) in particular, does *not* include the provisions set forth in (vii) and (viii) of this section.

(iv) None of the following exists at any property or facility owned or operated by the Division or the Division Subsidiaries: (1) underground storage tanks, (2) asbestos-containing material in any form or condition, (3) materials or equipment containing polychlorinated biphenyls, or (4) landfills, surface impoundments, or disposal areas.

(v) None of the Division, the Division Subsidiaries, or their respective predecessors or Affiliates has treated, stored, disposed of, arranged for or permitted the disposal of, transported, handled, or released any substance, including without limitation any hazardous substance, or owned or operated any property or facility (and no such property or facility is contaminated by any such substance) in a manner that has given or would give rise to liabilities, including any liability for response costs, corrective action costs, personal injury, property damage, natural resources damages or attorney fees, pursuant to the Comprehensive Environmental Response, Compensation and Liability Act of 1980, as amended ("CERCLA"), the Solid Waste Disposal Act, as amended ("SWDA") or any other Environmental, Health, and Safety Requirements.

(vi) Neither this Agreement nor the consummation of the transaction that is the subject of this Agreement will result in any obligations for site investigation or cleanup, or notification to or consent of government agencies or third parties, pursuant to any of the so-called "transaction-triggered" or "responsible property transfer" Environmental, Health, and Safety Requirements.

(vii) Neither the Division, the Division Subsidiaries, nor any of their respective predecessors or Affiliates has, either expressly or by operation of law, assumed or undertaken any liability, including without limitation any obligation for corrective or remedial action, of any other Person relating to Environmental, Health, and Safety Requirements.

(viii) No facts, events or conditions relating to the past or present facilities, properties or operations of the Division, the Division Subsidiaries, or any of their respective predecessors or Affiliates will prevent, hinder or limit continued compliance with Environmental, Health, and Safety Requirements, give rise to any investigatory, remedial or corrective obligations pursuant to Environmental, Health, and Safety Requirements, or give rise to any other liabilities (whether accrued, absolute, contingent, unliquidated or otherwise) pursuant to Environmental, Health, and Safety Requirements, including without limitation any relating to onsite or offsite releases or threatened releases of hazardous materials, substances or wastes, personal injury, property damage or natural resources damage.

(aa) *Euro.* All of the computer software, computer firmware and computer hardware used by the Division or a Division Subsidiary (i) are capable of performing all appropriate functions necessary to process more than one currency and any common currency adopted by one or more members of the European

Union (the "Euro"), (ii) comply with all legal requirements applicable to the Euro in any jurisdiction, including the rules on conversion and rounding set out in applicable European Community regulations, and (iii) are capable of displaying and printing, and incorporate in all relevant screen layouts, all symbols and codes adopted by any government or any other European Union body in relation to the Euro.[42]

(bb) *Year 2000.* None of the computer software, computer firmware, computer hardware (whether general or special purpose) or other similar or related items of automated, computerized or software systems that are used or relied on by the Division or a Division Subsidiary in the conduct of their respective businesses, and none of the products and services sold, licensed, rendered, or otherwise provided by the Division or a Division Subsidiary in the conduct of their respective businesses, will malfunction, cease to function, generate incorrect data or produce incorrect results when processing, providing or receiving (i) date-related data from, into and between the twentieth and twenty-first centuries or (ii) date-related data in connection with any valid date in the twentieth and twenty-first centuries.

Neither the Division or a Division Subsidiary has made any representations or warranties regarding the ability of any product or service sold, licensed, rendered, or otherwise provided by the Division or a Division Subsidiary in the conduct of their respective businesses to operate without malfunction, to operate without ceasing to function, to generate correct data or to produce correct results when processing, providing or receiving (i) date-related data from, into and between the twentieth and twenty-first centuries and (ii) date-related data in connection with any valid date in the twentieth and twenty-first centuries.[43]

(cc) *Certain Business Relationships with the Division and the Division Subsidiaries.* None of the Target Stockholders and their Affiliates has been involved in any business arrangement or relationship with any of the Division and the Division Subsidiaries within the past 12 months, and none of the Target Stockholders and their Affiliates owns any asset, tangible or intangible, which is used in the business of any of the Division and the Division Subsidiaries.

(dd) *Disclosure.* The representations and warranties contained in this §3 do not contain any untrue statement of a [material] fact or omit to state any [material] fact necessary in order to make the statements and information contained in this §3 not misleading.

---

[42] Sample acquisition agreements 2004.2 (the *pro-seller* divisional purchase agreement) and 2004.3 (the *neutral* divisional purchase agreement) do not contain this representation.

[43] This representation can be omitted for agreements entered into a sufficient period after approximately 3/1/00 so that Buyer has been able to verify that the Division and the Division Subsidiaries have no Y2K problem.

Sample acquisition agreement 2004.2 (the *pro-seller* divisional purchase agreement) does not contain this representation and 2004.3 (the *neutral* divisional purchase agreement) contains a more limited representation.

(ee) *Investment.* The Target (i) understands that the Buyer Note has not been, and will not be, registered under the Securities Act, or under any state securities laws, and is being offered and sold in reliance upon federal and state exemptions for transactions not involving any public offering, (ii) is acquiring the Buyer Note solely for its own account for investment purposes, and not with a view to the distribution thereof, (iii) is a sophisticated investor with knowledge and experience in business and financial matters, (iv) has received certain information concerning the Buyer and has had the opportunity to obtain additional information as desired in order to evaluate the merits and the risks inherent in holding the Buyer Note, (v) is able to bear the economic risk and lack of liquidity inherent in holding the Buyer Note, and (vi) is an Accredited Investor for the reasons set forth in §3(cc) of the Disclosure Schedule.[44]

4. *Representations and Warranties of the Buyer.*[45] The Buyer represents and warrants to the Target that the statements contained in this §4 are correct and complete as of the date of this Agreement and will be correct and complete as of the Closing Date (as though made then and as though the Closing Date were substituted for the date of this Agreement throughout this §4), except as set forth in the Disclosure Schedule. The Disclosure Schedule will be arranged in paragraphs corresponding to the lettered and numbered paragraphs contained in this §4.

(a) *Organization of the Buyer.* The Buyer is a corporation duly organized, validly existing, and in good standing under the laws of the jurisdiction of its incorporation.

(b) *Authorization of Transaction.* The Buyer has full power and authority (including full corporate power and authority) to execute and deliver this Agreement and to perform its obligations hereunder. This Agreement constitutes the valid and legally binding obligation of the Buyer, enforceable in accordance with its terms and conditions.

(c) *Noncontravention.* Neither the execution and the delivery of this Agreement, nor the consummation of the transactions contemplated hereby (including the assignments and assumptions referred to in §2 above), will (i) violate any constitution, statute, regulation, rule, injunction, judgment, order, decree, ruling, charge, or other restriction of any government, governmental agency, or court to which the Buyer is subject or any provision of its charter or bylaws or (ii) conflict with,

---

[44] This provision contemplates that the Buyer will issue the Buyer Note pursuant to the exemption from registration under the Securities Act contained in Regulation D. The Parties should determine whether this exemption is available in a particular transaction. If it is not, the Agreement must be modified as necessary to reflect the issuance of the Buyer Note under a different exemption from securities registration or in an offering registered under the Securities Act.

[45] The Target may seek to obtain additional representations and warranties concerning the Buyer and its Subsidiaries (e.g., the typical representations and warranties contained in a loan agreement or an underwriting agreement) because the Buyer is issuing the Buyer Note to the Target as part of the Purchase Price. Any such representations and warranties would normally survive the Closing and remain applicable for so long as the Buyer Note remained outstanding.

result in a breach of, constitute a default under, result in the acceleration of, create in any party the right to accelerate, terminate, modify, or cancel, or require any notice under any agreement, contract, lease, license, instrument, or other arrangement to which the Buyer is a party or by which it is bound or to which any of its assets is subject. The Buyer does not need to give any notice to, make any filing with, or obtain any authorization, consent, or approval of any government or governmental agency in order for the Parties to consummate the transactions contemplated by this Agreement (including the assignments and assumptions referred to in §2 above).

(d) *Brokers' Fees.* The Buyer has no Liability or obligation to pay any fees or commissions to any broker, finder, or agent with respect to the transactions contemplated by this Agreement for which the Target could become liable or obligated.

5. *Pre-Closing Covenants.* The Parties agree as follows with respect to the period between the execution of this Agreement and the Closing.

(a) *General.* Each of the Parties will use its [reasonable] best efforts to take all action and to do all things necessary [, proper, or advisable] in order to consummate and make effective the transactions contemplated by this Agreement (including satisfaction, but not waiver, of the Closing conditions set forth in §7 below).

(b) *Notices and Consents.* The Target will give (and will cause each of the Division Subsidiaries to give) any notices to third parties, and the Target will use its [reasonable] best efforts (and will cause each of the Division Subsidiaries to use its [reasonable] best efforts) to obtain any third party consents, that the Buyer [reasonably] may request in connection with the matters referred to in §3(c) above. Each of the Parties will (and the Target will cause each of the Division Subsidiaries to) give any notices to, make any filings with, and use its [reasonable] best efforts to obtain any authorizations, consents, and approvals of governments and governmental agencies in connection with the matters referred to in §3(c) and §4(c) above. Without limiting the generality of the foregoing, each of the Parties will file (and the Target will cause each of the Division Subsidiaries to file) any Notification and Report Forms and related material that it may be required to file with the Federal Trade Commission and the Antitrust Division of the United States Department of Justice under the Hart-Scott-Rodino Act, will use its [reasonable] best efforts to obtain (and the Target will cause each of the Division Subsidiaries to use its [reasonable] best efforts to obtain) an early termination of the applicable waiting period, and will make (and the Target will cause each of the Division Subsidiaries to make) any further filings pursuant thereto that may be necessary [, proper, or advisable] in connection therewith.

(c) *Operation of Business.* The Target will not cause or permit any of the Division and the Division Subsidiaries to engage in any practice, take any action, or enter into any transaction outside the Ordinary Course of Business. Without limiting the generality of the foregoing, the Target will not cause or permit any of the Division and the Division Subsidiaries to (i) pay any amount to any third party with respect to any Liability or obligation (including any costs and expenses the Target and its Subsidiaries have incurred or may incur in connection with this Agreement and the transactions contemplated hereby) which would not constitute an Assumed Liability if in existence as of the Closing, (ii) _____, or (iii) otherwise engage in any practice, take any action, or enter into any transaction of the sort described in §3(h) above.[46]

(d) *Preservation of Business.* The Target will cause each of the Division and the Division Subsidiaries to keep its business and properties substantially intact, including its present operations, physical facilities, working conditions, and relationships with lessors, licensors, suppliers, customers, and employees.[47]

(e) *Full Access.* The Target will permit (and will cause each of the Division and the Division Subsidiaries to permit) representatives of the Buyer to have full access [at all reasonable times, and in a manner so as not to interfere with the normal business operations of the Division and the Division Subsidiaries,] to all premises, properties, personnel, books, records (including Tax records), contracts, and documents of or pertaining to each of the Division and the Division Subsidiaries.[48]

(f) *Notice of Developments.* Each Party will give prompt written notice to the other Party of any material adverse development causing a breach of any of its own representations and warranties in §3 and §4 above. No disclosure by any Party pursuant to this §5(f), however, shall be deemed to amend or supplement the Disclosure Schedule or to prevent or cure any misrepresentation, breach of warranty, or breach of covenant.[49]

(g) *Exclusivity.* The Target will not (and the Target will not cause or permit any of the Division and the Division Subsidiaries to) (i) solicit, initiate, or encourage the submission of any proposal or offer from any Person relating to the acquisition of any capital stock or other voting securities, or any substantial portion of the assets, of any of the Division and the Division Subsidiaries (including any acquisition structured as a merger, consolidation, or share exchange) or (ii) participate in any discussions or negotiations regarding, furnish any information with respect to, assist or participate in, or facilitate in any other manner any effort or attempt

---

[46] The Parties may prefer to revise this covenant so that it recites specific prohibitions (rather than incorporating the matters in §3(h) by reference).

[47] Sample acquisition agreement 2004.2 (the *pro-seller* divisional asset purchase agreement) does not contain a comparable provision.

[48] The Target may seek a confidentiality and nonuse provision protecting this information until the Buyer actually purchases the Acquired Assets. *See* sample acquisition agreement 2004.2 (the *pro-seller* divisional asset purchase agreement) for an example of such a provision.

[49] Sample acquisition agreement 2004.2 (the *pro-seller* divisional asset purchase agreement) provides that certain disclosures (presumably, but not necessarily, by the Target) between signing and closing *will* supplement the previous disclosures and cure misrepresentations and breaches of warranty.

by any Person to do or seek any of the foregoing.[50] The Target will notify the Buyer immediately if any Person makes any proposal, offer, inquiry, or contact with respect to any of the foregoing.

(h) *Title Insurance.*[51] The Target will cause each of the Division and the Division Subsidiaries to obtain the following title insurance commitments, policies, and riders in preparation for the Closing:

(i) with respect to each parcel of real estate that any of the Division and the Division Subsidiaries owns, an ALTA Owner's Policy of Title Insurance Form B-1987 (or equivalent policy [reasonably] acceptable to the Buyer if the real property is located in a state in which an ALTA Owner's Policy of Title Insurance Form B-1987 is not available) issued by a title insurer [reasonably] satisfactory to the Buyer (and, if requested by the Buyer, reinsured in whole or in part by one or more insurance companies and pursuant to a direct access agreement [reasonably] acceptable to the Buyer), in such amount as the Buyer [reasonably] may determine to be the fair market value of such real property (including all improvements located thereon), insuring title to such real property to be in the Buyer or the Subsidiary as of the Closing (subject only to the title exceptions described above in §3(l)(i) and in §3(l)(i) of the Disclosure Schedule); and

(ii) with respect to each parcel of real estate that any of the Division and the Division Subsidiaries leases or subleases and which is listed on §3(l)(ii) of the Disclosure Schedule as a property for which a title insurance policy is to be procured, an ALTA Leasehold Owner's Policy of Title Insurance Form B-1987 (or equivalent policy [reasonably] acceptable to the Buyer if the real property is located in a state in which an ALTA Leasehold Owner's Policy of Title Insurance Form B-1987 is not available) issued by a title insurer [reasonably] satisfactory to the Buyer (and, if requested by the Buyer, reinsured in whole or in part by one or more insurance companies and pursuant to a direct access agreement [reasonably] acceptable to the Buyer) in such amount as the Buyer [reasonably] may determine (taking into account the time cost of money using the Applicable Rate as the discount rate and such other factors as whether the fair market rental value of the premises exceeds the stipulated consideration in the lease or sublease, whether the tenant or subtenant has any option to renew or extend, whether the tenant or subtenant owns any improvements located on the premises, whether the tenant or subtenant is permitted to sublease, and whether the tenant or subtenant would owe any amount under the

---

[50] Sample acquisition agreement 2004.2 (the *pro-seller* divisional asset purchase agreement) gives the Target Stockholders, the Target, its Subsidiaries, and their directors and officers greater latitude to respond to unsolicited proposals.

[51] These provisions concerning title insurance are relatively long and detailed. A condensed version may be more appropriate when, for example, the real property of the Division and the Division Subsidiaries is relatively insignificant.

Sample acquisition agreement 2004.2 (the *pro-seller* divisional asset purchase agreement) does not have any title insurance closing condition for the benefit of the Buyer and contemplates that the Buyer will obtain any title insurance it requires independently and at its own expense.

lease or sublease if evicted), insuring title to the leasehold or subleasehold estate to be in the Buyer or the Subsidiary as of the Closing (subject only to the title exceptions described above in §3(l)(ii) and in §3(l)(ii) of the Disclosure Schedule).

Each title insurance policy delivered under §5(h)(i) and §5(h)(ii) above shall (A) insure title to the real property and all recorded easements benefitting such real property, (B) contain an "extended coverage endorsement" insuring over the general exceptions contained customarily in such policies, (C) contain an ALTA Zoning Endorsement 3.1 (or equivalent), (D) contain an endorsement insuring that the real property described in the title insurance policy is the same real estate as shown on the Survey delivered with respect to such property, (E) contain an endorsement insuring that each street adjacent to the real property is a public street and that there is direct and unencumbered pedestrian and vehicular access to such street from the real property, (F) contain an inflation endorsement providing for annual adjustments in the amount of coverage corresponding to the annual percentage increase, if any, in the United States Department of Commerce Composite Construction Cost Index (Base Year = _____), (G) if the real property consists of more than one record parcel, contain a "contiguity" endorsement insuring that all of the record parcels are contiguous to one another, and (H) contain a "non-imputation" endorsement to the effect that title defects known to the officers, directors, and stockholders of the owner prior to the Closing shall not be deemed "facts known to the insured" for purposes of the policy.

(i) *Surveys.*[52] With respect to each parcel of real property that any of the Division and the Division Subsidiaries owns, leases, or subleases, and as to which a title insurance policy is to be procured pursuant to §5(h) above, the Target will cause the Division and the Division Subsidiaries to procure in preparation for the Closing a current survey of the real property certified to the Buyer, prepared by a licensed surveyor and conforming to current ALTA Minimum Detail Requirements for Land Title Surveys, disclosing the location of all improvements, easements, party walls, sidewalks, roadways, utility lines, and other matters shown customarily on such surveys, and showing access affirmatively to public streets and roads (the *"Survey"*). The Survey shall not disclose any survey defect or encroachment from or onto the real property which has not been cured or insured over prior to the Closing.

6. *Post-Closing Covenants.*[53] The Parties agree as follows with respect to the period following the Closing.

---

[52] Sample acquisition agreement 2004.2 (the *pro-seller* divisional asset purchase agreement) does not have any survey closing condition for the benefit of the Buyer and contemplates that the Buyer will obtain any surveys it requires independently and at its own expense.

[53] The Target may seek to obtain additional covenants from the Buyer and its Subsidiaries (e.g., the typical covenants contained in a loan agreement or an indenture) because the Buyer is issuing the Buyer Note to the Target as part of the Purchase Price. Any such covenants would remain applicable so long as the Buyer Note remained outstanding.

(a) *General.* In case at any time after the Closing any further action is necessary [or desirable] to carry out the purposes of this Agreement, each of the Parties will take such further action (including the execution and delivery of such further instruments and documents) as the other Party [reasonably] may request, all the sole cost and expense of the requesting Party (unless the requesting Party is entitled to indemnification therefor under §8 below).[54] The Target acknowledges and agrees that from and after the Closing the Buyer will be entitled to possession of all documents, books, records (including Tax records), agreements, and financial data of any sort relating to the Division and the Division Subsidiaries.

(b) *Litigation Support.* In the event and for so long as any Party actively is contesting or defending against any action, suit, proceeding, hearing, investigation, charge, complaint, claim, or demand in connection with (i) any transaction contemplated under this Agreement or (ii) any fact, situation, circumstance, status, condition, activity, practice, plan, occurrence, event, incident, action, failure to act, or transaction on or prior to the Closing Date involving any of the Division and the Division Subsidiaries, the other Party will cooperate with the contesting or defending Party and its counsel in the contest or defense, make available its personnel, and provide such testimony and access to its books and records as shall be necessary in connection with the contest or defense, all at the sole cost and expense of the contesting or defending Party (unless the contesting or defending Party is entitled to indemnification therefor under §8 below).[55]

(c) *Transition.* The Target will not take any action that is designed or intended to have the effect of discouraging any lessor, licensor, customer, supplier, or other business associate of any of the Division and the Division Subsidiaries from maintaining the same business relationships with the Buyer and the Division Subsidiaries after the Closing as it maintained with the Division and the Division Subsidiaries prior to the Closing. The Target will refer all customer inquiries relating to the businesses of the Division and the Division Subsidiaries to the Buyer from and after the Closing.

(d) *Confidentiality.*[56] The Target will treat and hold as such all of the Confidential Information, refrain from using any of the Confidential Information except in connection with this Agreement, and deliver promptly to the Buyer or destroy, at the request and option of the Buyer, all tangible embodiments (and all copies)

---

[54] The Parties may prefer to allocate responsibility for these particular costs and expenses in some other manner (e.g., the Party incurring the costs and expenses might be responsible for their payment; the Parties might share the costs and expenses in a predetermined ratio; or one Party might be responsible for the costs and expenses up to a specified aggregate ceiling and the other Party responsible for any excess).

Compare §10(k) (which allocates responsibility between the Buyer and the Target for their costs and expenses through the Closing).

[55] The Parties may prefer to allocate responsibility for these particular costs and expenses in some other manner as discussed in the preceding footnote.

[56] Sample acquisition agreement 2004.2 (the *pro-seller* divisional asset purchase agreement) lacks a comparable confidentiality provision affecting the Target after the Closing.

of the Confidential Information which are in its possession. In the event that the Target is requested or required (by oral question or request for information or documents in any legal proceeding, interrogatory, subpoena, civil investigative demand, or similar process) to disclose any Confidential Information, the Target will notify the Buyer promptly of the request or requirement so that the Buyer may seek an appropriate protective order or waive compliance with the provisions of this §6(d). If, in the absence of a protective order or the receipt of a waiver hereunder, the Target is, on the advice of counsel, compelled to disclose any Confidential Information to any tribunal or else stand liable for contempt, the Target may disclose the Confidential Information to the tribunal; *provided, however,* that the Target shall use its [reasonable] best efforts to obtain, at the [reasonable] request of the Buyer, an order or other assurance that confidential treatment will be accorded to such portion of the Confidential Information required to be disclosed as the Buyer shall designate.

(e) *Covenant Not to Compete.*[57] For a period of [five years] from and after the Closing Date, the Target will not engage directly or indirectly in any business that any of the Division and the Division Subsidiaries conducts as of the Closing Date [in any geographic area in which any of the Division and the Division Subsidiaries conducts that business as of the Closing Date]; *provided, however,* that no owner of less than 1% of the outstanding stock of any publicly traded corporation shall be deemed to engage solely by reason thereof in any of its businesses. If the final judgment of a court of competent jurisdiction declares that any term or provision of this §6(e) is invalid or unenforceable, the Parties agree that the court making the determination of invalidity or unenforceability shall have the power to reduce the scope, duration, or area of the term or provision, to delete specific words or phrases, or to replace any invalid or unenforceable term or provision with a term or provision that is valid and enforceable and that comes closest to expressing the intention of the invalid or unenforceable term or provision, and this Agreement shall be enforceable as so modified after the expiration of the time within which the judgment may be appealed.

(f) *Buyer Note.* The Buyer Note will be imprinted with a legend substantially in the following form:

The payment of principal and interest on this Note is subject to certain recoupment provisions set forth in an Asset Purchase Agreement dated as of _____, 19____ (the "Agreement") between the issuer of this Note and the person to which this Note originally was issued. This Note was originally issued on _____, 19____, and has not been registered under the Securities Act of 1933, as amended. The transfer of this Note is subject to certain restrictions set forth in the Agreement. The issuer of this Note will furnish a copy of these provisions to the holder hereof without charge upon written request.

---

[57] Note that unless this Agreement allocates a specified amount of consideration to the covenant not to compete, applicable tax cases will preclude the Buyer from seeking to allocate a portion of the Purchase Price to the covenant and amortizing such amount over the covenant's life.

Each holder desiring to transfer a Buyer Note first must furnish the Buyer with (i) a written opinion [reasonably] satisfactory to the Buyer in form and substance from counsel [reasonably] satisfactory to the Buyer by reason of experience to the effect that the holder may transfer the Buyer Note as desired without registration under the Securities Act and (ii) a written undertaking executed by the desired transferee [reasonably] satisfactory to the Buyer in form and substance agreeing to be bound by the recoupment provisions and the restrictions on transfer contained herein.[58]

7. *Conditions to Obligation to Close.*

(a) *Conditions to Obligation of the Buyer.* The obligation of the Buyer to consummate the transactions to be performed by it in connection with the Closing is subject to satisfaction of the following conditions:[59]

(i) the representations and warranties set forth in §3 above shall be true and correct in all material respects at and as of the Closing Date;[60]

(ii) the Target shall have performed and complied with all of its covenants hereunder in all material respects through the Closing;

(iii) the Target and the Division Subsidiaries shall have procured all of the third party consents specified in §5(b) above, all of the title insurance commitments, policies, and riders specified in §5(h) above, and all of the surveys specified in §5(i) above;[61]

(iv) no action, suit, or proceeding shall be pending [or threatened] before any court or quasi-judicial or administrative agency of any federal, state, local, or foreign jurisdiction [or before any arbitrator] wherein an unfavorable injunction, judgment, order, decree, ruling, or charge would (A) prevent consummation of any of the transactions contemplated by this Agreement, (B) cause any of the transactions contemplated by this Agreement to be rescinded following consummation, (C) affect adversely the right of the Buyer to own the Acquired

---

[58] Certain provisions in §6(f) contemplate that the Buyer will issue the Buyer Note pursuant to an exemption from securities registration under the Securities Act. These provisions must be eliminated if the Buyer will issue the Buyer Note in an offering registered under the Securities Act.

[59] Note the provision in §9(a)(ii) giving the Buyer the right to terminate this Agreement within a specified period after signing if the Buyer is not [reasonably] satisfied with the results of its continuing business, legal, and accounting due diligence concerning the Division and the Division Subsidiaries. If this termination right were to continue through the Closing, it could be recast as an additional closing condition in §7(a).

[60] Note that this provision will not give the Buyer any closing condition with respect to any adverse matter that the Target may disclose in the Disclosure Schedule. This is because the disclosure will cure any misrepresentation or breach of warranty that might otherwise have existed. Thus, if the Target discloses an adverse matter in the Disclosure Schedule, the Buyer may seek to add a specific closing condition requiring an acceptable resolution of the matter.

[61] Sample acquisition agreement 2004.2 (the *pro-seller* divisional asset purchase agreement) lacks a comparable closing condition with respect to third party consents, title insurance, and surveys.

Assets, to operate the former businesses of the Division, and to control the Division Subsidiaries, or (D) affect adversely the right of any of the Division Subsidiaries to own its assets and to operate its businesses (and no such injunction, judgment, order, decree, ruling, or charge shall be in effect);[62]

(v) the Target shall have delivered to the Buyer a certificate to the effect that each of the conditions specified above in §7(a)(i)-(iv) is satisfied in all respects;

(vi) [all applicable waiting periods (and any extensions thereof) under the Hart-Scott-Rodino Act shall have expired or otherwise been terminated and the Target, the Division Subsidiaries, and the Buyer shall have received all other authorizations, consents, and approvals of governments and governmental agencies referred to in §3(c) and §4(c) above];

(vii) the relevant parties shall have entered into side agreements in form and substance as set forth in Exhibits F-1 through F-_____ attached hereto and the same shall be in full force and effect;[63]

(viii) the Buyer shall have received from counsel to the Target an opinion in form and substance as set forth in Exhibit G attached hereto, addressed to the Buyer, and dated as of the Closing Date;

(ix) the Buyer shall have received the resignations, effective as of the Closing, of each director and officer of the Division Subsidiaries other than those whom the Buyer shall have specified in writing at least [five] business days prior to the Closing;[64]

(x) the Buyer shall have obtained on terms and conditions [reasonably] satisfactory to it all of the financing it needs in order to consummate the transactions contemplated hereby [and fund the working capital requirements of the acquired businesses after the Closing];[65]

(xi) all actions to be taken by the Target in connection with consummation of the transactions contemplated hereby and all certificates, opinions, instruments,

---

[62] Sample acquisition agreement 2004.2 (the *pro-seller* divisional asset purchase agreement) contains a narrower closing condition requiring only that there not be in effect any injunction, judgment, order, decree, ruling, or charge preventing consummation of the transactions contemplated by this Agreement.

[63] If the Buyer is acquiring a division of Bigco, the Buyer may require significant transition assistance. This might be the case when Bigco performs substantial services for its divisions and/or when Bigco owns various tangible and intangible assets used by its divisions. For example, the Buyer may require real estate leases, intellectual property licenses, and accounting, purchasing, payroll, risk management, and data processing services from Bigco.

[64] Sample acquisition agreement 2004.2 (the *pro-seller* divisional asset purchase agreement) lacks a comparable closing condition concerning the receipt of director and officer resignations.

[65] Sample acquisition agreement 2004.2 (the *pro-seller* divisional asset purchase agreement) lacks a comparable closing condition concerning the availability of financing for the transaction.

and other documents required to effect the transactions contemplated hereby will be [reasonably] satisfactory in form and substance to the Buyer.

The Buyer may waive any condition specified in this §7(a) if it executes a writing so stating at or prior to the Closing.

(b) *Conditions to Obligation of the Target.* The obligation of the Target to consummate the transactions to be performed by it in connection with the Closing is subject to satisfaction of the following conditions:

(i) the representations and warranties set forth in §4 above shall be true and correct in all material respects at and as of the Closing Date;

(ii) the Buyer shall have performed and complied with all of its covenants hereunder in all material respects through the Closing;

(iii) no action, suit, or proceeding shall be pending [or threatened] before any court or quasi-judicial or administrative agency of any federal, state, local, or foreign jurisdiction [or before any arbitrator] wherein an unfavorable injunction, judgment, order, decree, ruling, or charge would (A) prevent consummation of any of the transactions contemplated by this Agreement or (B) cause any of the transactions contemplated by this Agreement to be rescinded following consummation (and no such injunction, judgment, order, decree, ruling, or charge shall be in effect);[66]

(iv) the Buyer shall have delivered to the Target a certificate to the effect that each of the conditions specified above in §7(b)(i)-(iii) is satisfied in all respects;

(v) [all applicable waiting periods (and any extensions thereof) under the Hart-Scott-Rodino Act shall have expired or otherwise been terminated and the Target, the Division Subsidiaries, and the Buyer shall have received all other authorizations, consents, and approvals of governments and governmental agencies referred to in §3(c) and §4(c) above];

(vi) the relevant parties shall have entered into side agreements in form and substance as set forth in Exhibits F-_____, F-_____, . . . and F-_____ and the same shall be in full force and effect;

(vii) the Target shall have received from counsel to the Buyer an opinion in form and substance as set forth in Exhibit H attached hereto, addressed to the Target, and dated as of the Closing Date; and

---

[66] Because this Target's closing condition conforms in part to the comparable Buyer's closing condition in §7(a)(iv), it leaves the Target with a relatively broad "out." Thus, the Buyer may prefer to narrow the respective closing conditions. Compare the narrower closing conditions in sample acquisition agreement 2004.2 (the *pro-seller* divisional asset purchase agreement).

(viii) all actions to be taken by the Buyer in connection with consummation of the transactions contemplated hereby and all certificates, opinions, instruments, and other documents required to effect the transactions contemplated hereby will be [reasonably] satisfactory in form and substance to the Target.

The Target may waive any condition specified in this §7(b) if it executes a writing so stating at or prior to the Closing.

8. *Remedies for Breaches of This Agreement.*[67]

(a) *Survival of Representations and Warranties.*[68]

[ALTERNATIVE A (FULL INDEMNIFICATION): All of the representations and warranties of the Buyer and the Target contained in this Agreement shall survive the Closing (even if the damaged Party knew or had reason to know of any misrepresentation or breach of warranty at the time of Closing) and continue in full force and effect forever thereafter (subject to any applicable statutes of limitations).]

[ALTERNATIVE B (LIMITED INDEMNIFICATION): All of the representations and warranties of the Target contained in §3(g)-(j) and §3(l)-(cc) of this Agreement

---

[67] The Buyer may seek some form of additional security covering the obligation of the Target to indemnify the Buyer after the Closing. The recoupment provisions contained in §8(f) below provide security up to the principal amount outstanding from time to time under the Buyer Note. The Buyer may seek additional provisions calling for (a) the Target to deposit a portion of the Purchase Price with a third party escrow agent, (b) the Buyer to hold back a portion of the Purchase Price (to be paid later with interest), or (c) the Buyer to obtain a security interest in certain assets of the Target.

[68] This *pro-buyer* Agreement contains alternative provisions for (a) *full indemnification* to the Buyer for breaches of the Target's representations and warranties (i.e., all representations and warranties survive indefinitely, and there is no deductible, threshold, or ceiling with respect to indemnification against breaches thereof) and (b) *limited indemnification* to the Buyer for breaches of the Target's representations and warranties (i.e., the representations and warranties with respect to the transaction itself and with respect to taxes survive indefinitely; the other representations and warranties survive only for [three years]; and there is a threshold, but not a deductible or ceiling, with respect to indemnification against breaches of the latter).

Sample acquisition agreement 2004.2 (the *pro-seller* divisional asset purchase agreement), on the other hand, contains alternative provisions for (a) *minimal indemnification* to the Buyer for breaches of the Target's representations and warranties (i.e., only the representations and warranties concerning the transaction itself survive the Closing) and (b) *limited indemnification* to the Buyer for breaches of the Target's representations and warranties (i.e., the representations and warranties with respect to the transaction itself survive indefinitely; the other representations and warranties survive only for [one year]; and there is a deductible and a ceiling with respect to indemnification against breaches of the latter).

This *pro-buyer* Agreement provides that the representations and warranties will survive the Closing (*even if* the damaged Party knew or had reason to know of the misrepresentation or breach of warranty at the time of Closing).

Sample acquisition agreement 2004.2 (the *pro-seller* divisional asset purchase agreement), on the other hand, provides that the representations and warranties of the Parties will survive the Closing (*unless* the damaged Party knew or had reason to know of the misrepresentation or breach of warranty at the time of Closing).

shall survive the Closing (even if the Buyer knew or had reason to know of any misrepresentation or breach of warranty at the time of Closing) and continue in full force and effect for a period of [three years] thereafter. All of the other representations and warranties of the Buyer and the Target contained in this Agreement (including the representations and warranties of the Target contained in §3(a)-(f) and §3(k) hereof) shall survive the Closing (even if the damaged Party knew or had reason to know of any misrepresentation or breach of warranty at the time of Closing) and continue in full force and effect forever thereafter (subject to any applicable statutes of limitations).]

(b) *Indemnification Provisions for Benefit of the Buyer.*[69]

(i) In the event the Target breaches (or in the event any third party alleges facts that, if true, would mean the Target has breached) any of its representations, warranties, and covenants contained in this Agreement, and, if there is an applicable survival period pursuant to §8(a) above, provided that the Buyer makes a written claim for indemnification against the Target pursuant to §10(g) below within such survival period, then the Target agrees to indemnify the Buyer from and against the entirety of any Adverse Consequences the Buyer may suffer through and after the date of the claim for indemnification (including any Adverse Consequences the Buyer may suffer after the end of any applicable survival period) resulting from, arising out of, relating to, in the nature of, or caused by the breach (or the alleged breach)[70] [[*ALTERNATIVE B (LIMITED*

---

[69] The Buyer will become indirectly responsible for all of the liabilities of the *Division Subsidiaries* if the Buyer acquires their capital stock as part of the Acquired Assets. For this reason, the Buyer may seek (a) to purchase assets from the Target *and from each of the Division Subsidiaries* (i.e., a multiple entity asset sale) or (b) to have the Target liquidate and dissolve the Division Subsidiaries tax free under Code §332 (to the extent they are United States corporations) and sell their assets to the Buyer.

In addition, this Agreement provides that the Buyer will assume certain specified liabilities of the *Division. See* the definition of Assumed Liabilities in §1 (and in particular the provision making the Buyer responsible for certain liabilities the Target reveals in the Disclosure Schedule).

Finally, the Buyer may be exposed for certain liabilities of the *Division* by operation of law if the Target does not pay them (e.g., under applicable bulk sales statutes and common law doctrines of de facto merger and successor liability). *See* ¶2001.2.2.2.

These post-Closing indemnification provisions are designed to work in conjunction with the narrow definition of Assumed Liabilities in §1 and the extensive representations and warranties in §3 to protect the Buyer against liabilities it does not intend to assume.

[70] This *pro-buyer* Agreement requires an indemnifying party (presumably, but not necessarily, the Target) to indemnify an indemnified party (presumably, but not necessarily, the Buyer) from and against any Adverse Consequences the indemnified party *may* suffer through and after the date of the claim for indemnification (*including* any Adverse Consequences the indemnified party may suffer after the end of any applicable survival period) *resulting from, arising out of, relating to, in the nature of, or caused by* certain breaches by the indemnifying party of its representations, warranties, and covenants.

The *pro-seller* Agreement (sample acquisition agreement 2004.2), on the other hand, requires an indemnifying party to indemnify an indemnified party from and against any Adverse Consequences the indemnified party *shall* suffer through and after the date of the claim for indemnification (but *excluding* any Adverse Consequences the indemnified party shall suffer after the end of any applicable survival period) *caused [proximately] by* certain breaches by the indemnifying party of its representations, warranties, and covenants.

INDEMNIFICATION): ; *provided, however,* that the Target shall not have any obligation to indemnify the Buyer from and against any Adverse Consequences resulting from, arising out of, relating to, in the nature of, or caused by the breach (or alleged breach) of any representation or warranty of the Target contained in §3(g)-(j) and §3(l)-(cc) above until the Buyer has suffered Adverse Consequences by reason of all such breaches (or alleged breaches) in excess of a $_____ aggregate threshold (at which point the Target will be obligated to indemnify the Buyer from and against all such Adverse Consequences relating back to the first dollar).][71]

(ii) The Target agrees to indemnify the Buyer from and against the entirety of any Adverse Consequences the Buyer may suffer resulting from, arising out of, relating to, in the nature of, or caused by:

(A) any Liability of the Target which is not an Assumed Liability (including any Liability of the Target that becomes a Liability of the Buyer under any bulk transfer law of any jurisdiction, under any common law doctrine of de facto merger or successor liability, under Environmental, Health, and Safety Requirements, or otherwise by operation of law);[72]

(B) any Liability of any of the Division Subsidiaries for unpaid Taxes with respect to any Tax year or portion thereof ending on or before the Closing Date (or for any Tax year beginning before and ending after the Closing Date to the extent allocable to the portion of such period beginning before and ending on the Closing Date);[73] or

(C) any Liability of any of the Division Subsidiaries for the unpaid Taxes of any Person (including the Target and its Subsidiaries) under Reg. §1.1502-6 (or any similar provision of state, local, or foreign law), as a transferee or successor, by contract, or otherwise.[74]

---

[71] The Target may seek to substitute a deductible (with no relation back to the first dollar) for the threshold in this proviso and to impose an aggregate ceiling on indemnification. *Compare* the *pro-seller* Agreement (sample acquisition agreement 2004.2). The Target may also seek to impose an additional *per claim* deductible.

[72] The Buyer may be exposed for certain liabilities of the Target by operation of law if the Target does not pay them (e.g., under applicable bulk sales statutes, common law doctrines of de facto merger and successor liability, and environmental laws). *See* ¶2001.2.2.2. This post-Closing indemnification provision is designed to protect the Buyer against liabilities of the Target that the Buyer does not intend to assume.

[73] Clause (B) is consistent with the principle that Target is obligated to pay all pre-Closing Taxes of the Target and the Division Subsidiaries and is entitled to retain sufficient Cash to satisfy such obligation (see definition of "Acquired Assets" (item (k)) and §2(d)). This indemnity is limited to unpaid Taxes of the Subsidiaries. It does not cover unpaid Taxes of the Target itself, because Taxes of the Target are expressly excluded from the definition of "Assumed Liabilities" and therefore are indemnified under §8(b)(ii)(A).

[74] If any of the Division Subsidiaries has been a member of an Affiliated Group filing a consolidated federal income tax return (including, if applicable, the Target's Affiliated Group), such Division Subsidiary (or its successor) will be jointly and severally liable under Reg. §1.1502-6 for certain tax

(iii) The Target agrees to indemnify the Buyer from and against the entirety of any Adverse Consequences the Buyer may suffer resulting from, arising out of, relating to, in the nature of, or caused by _____.[75]

(c) *Indemnification Provisions for Benefit of the Target.*

(i) In the event the Buyer breaches (or in the event any third party alleges facts that, if true, would mean the Buyer has breached) any of its representations, warranties, and covenants contained in this Agreement, and, if there is an applicable survival period pursuant to §8(a) above, provided that the Target makes a written claim for indemnification against the Buyer pursuant to §10(g) below within such survival period, then the Buyer agrees to indemnify the Target from and against the entirety of any Adverse Consequences the Target may suffer through and after the date of the claim for indemnification (including any Adverse Consequences the Target may suffer after the end of any applicable survival period) resulting from, arising out of, relating to, in the nature of, or caused by the breach (or the alleged breach).

(ii) The Buyer agrees to indemnify the Target from and against the entirety of any Adverse Consequences the Target may suffer resulting from, arising out of, relating to, in the nature of, or caused by any Assumed Liability.

(d) *Matters Involving Third Parties.*[76]

---

liabilities incurred by such Affiliated Group for a tax year when such Division Subsidiary was a member of such Affiliated Group for all or part of such tax year. *See* ¶210.

A Division Subsidiary may also be liable for the unpaid taxes of third parties under similar provisions of state, local, or foreign law, as a transferee or successor, by contract (e.g., a tax sharing agreement), or otherwise.

After the Buyer acquires the stock of any such Division Subsidiary, the Division Subsidiary will remain liable for any such unpaid tax liabilities.

This post-Closing indemnification provision is designed to protect the Buyer against any liability for the unpaid taxes of any person (including the Target and its Subsidiaries).

In order to eliminate this risk altogether, the Buyer may seek (a) to purchase assets from the Target *and from each of the Division Subsidiaries* (i.e., a multiple entity asset sale) or (b) to have the Target liquidate and dissolve the Division Subsidiaries tax free under Code §332 (to the extent they are United States corporations) and sell their assets to the Buyer.

[75] Note that the indemnification provisions in clause (i) above will not give the Buyer any post-Closing indemnification rights with respect to any adverse matter that the Target may disclose in the Disclosure Schedule. This is because the disclosure will cure any misrepresentation or breach of warranty that might otherwise have existed.

Thus, when the Target discloses an adverse matter in the Disclosure Schedule, the Buyer may seek to add a provision conferring specific post-Closing indemnification rights with respect to the particular matter.

The Buyer normally would seek to draft such a provision so that the indemnification would not be subject to any survival period, threshold, deductible, and/or ceiling.

[76] An *indemnifying party* (presumably, but not necessarily, the Target) will normally seek to control the defense of any third party claim that may give rise to a claim for indemnification under §8. However, the *indemnified* party (presumably, but not necessarily, the Buyer) will not want the indemnifying party to control the defense of any third party claim in which the indemnified party will retain a meaningful interest. For example, the indemnifying party may seek to control the defense of a third party claim

(i) If any third party shall notify any Party (the *"Indemnified Party"*) with respect to any matter (a *"Third Party Claim"*) which may give rise to a claim for indemnification against the other Party (the *"Indemnifying Party"*) under this §8, then the Indemnified Party shall promptly notify the Indemnifying Party thereof in writing; *provided, however,* that no delay on the part of the Indemnified Party in notifying the Indemnifying Party shall relieve the Indemnifying Party from any obligation hereunder unless (and then solely to the extent) the Indemnifying Party thereby is prejudiced.

(ii) The Indemnifying Party will have the right to defend the Indemnified Party against the Third Party Claim with counsel of its choice [reasonably] satisfactory to the Indemnified Party so long as (A) the Indemnifying Party notifies the Indemnified Party in writing within [15 days] after the Indemnified Party has given notice of the Third Party Claim that the Indemnifying Party will indemnify the Indemnified Party from and against the entirety of any Adverse Consequences the Indemnified Party may suffer resulting from, arising out of, relating to, in the nature of, or caused by the Third Party Claim, (B) the Indemnifying Party provides the Indemnified Party with evidence [reasonably] acceptable to the Indemnified Party that the Indemnifying Party will have the financial resources to defend against the Third Party Claim and fulfill its indemnification obligations hereunder, (C) the Third Party Claim involves only money damages and does not seek an injunction or other equitable relief, (D) settlement of, or an adverse judgment with respect to, the Third Party Claim is not, in the good faith judgment of the Indemnified Party, likely to establish a precedential custom or practice [materially] adverse to the continuing business interests of the Indemnified Party, and (E) the Indemnifying Party conducts the defense of the Third Party Claim actively and diligently.

(iii) So long as the Indemnifying Party is conducting the defense of the Third Party Claim in accordance with §8(d)(ii) above, (A) the Indemnified Party may retain separate co-counsel at its sole cost and expense and participate in the defense of the Third Party Claim, (B) the Indemnified Party will not consent to the entry of any judgment or enter into any settlement with respect to the

---

if the third party seeks an injunction or other equitable relief or if it is not clear that the indemnifying party will bear the entirety of any money damages or amount paid in settlement.

This *pro-buyer* Agreement provides that the indemnified party will control the defense of any third party claim *unless* (a) the indemnifying party accepts full responsibility for the matter within [15 days], (b) the indemnifying party demonstrates it has the financial resources necessary to defend against the matter and fulfill its indemnification obligations, (c) the third party seeks only money damages (as opposed to an injunction or other equitable relief), (d) settlement of, or an adverse judgment with respect to, the third party claim is not likely to establish a precedent [materially] adverse to the indemnified party, and (e) the indemnifying party conducts the defense actively and diligently.

The *pro-seller* agreement (sample acquisition agreement 2004.2), on the other hand, provides that the indemnifying party may assume the defense of a third party claim *at any time* during the course of the defense and prevents the indemnified party from consenting to the entry of any judgment or entering into any settlement with respect to the matter without the consent of the indemnifying party [(not to be unreasonably withheld)].

Third Party Claim without the prior written consent of the Indemnifying Party [(not to be withheld unreasonably)], and (C) the Indemnifying Party will not consent to the entry of any judgment or enter into any settlement with respect to the Third Party Claim without the prior written consent of the Indemnified Party [(not to be withheld unreasonably)].

(iv) In the event any of the conditions in §8(d)(ii) above is or becomes unsatisfied, however, (A) the Indemnified Party may defend against, and consent to the entry of any judgment or enter into any settlement with respect to, the Third Party Claim in any manner it [reasonably] may deem appropriate (and the Indemnified Party need not consult with, or obtain any consent from, the Indemnifying Party in connection therewith), (B) the Indemnifying Party will reimburse the Indemnified Party promptly and periodically for the costs of defending against the Third Party Claim (including [reasonable] attorneys' fees and expenses), and (C) the Indemnifying Party will remain responsible for any Adverse Consequences the Indemnified Party may suffer resulting from, arising out of, relating to, in the nature of, or caused by the Third Party Claim to the fullest extent provided in this §8.

(e) *Determination of Adverse Consequences.* [The Parties shall take into account the time cost of money (using the Applicable Rate as the discount rate) in determining Adverse Consequences for purposes of this §8.] All indemnification payments under this §8 shall be deemed adjustments to the Purchase Price.

(f) *Recoupment Under Buyer Note.* The Buyer shall have the option of recouping all or any part of any Adverse Consequences it may suffer (in lieu of seeking any indemnification to which it is entitled under this §8) by notifying the Target that the Buyer is reducing the principal amount outstanding under the Buyer Note. This shall affect the timing and amount of payments required under the Buyer Note in the same manner as if the Buyer had made a permitted prepayment (without premium or penalty) thereunder.[77]

(g) *Other Indemnification Provisions.* The foregoing indemnification provisions are in addition to, and not in derogation of, any statutory, equitable, or common law remedy any Party may have for breach of representation, warranty, or covenant (including without limitation any such remedy arising under Environmental, Health, and Safety Requirements) any Party may have with respect to the Division, the Division Subsidiaries, or the transactions contemplated by this Agreement.[78]

---

[77] The *pro-seller* Agreement (sample acquisition agreement 2004.2) lacks a comparable provision giving the Buyer a right of recoupment against the Buyer Note.

[78] Sample acquisition agreement 2004.2 (the *pro-seller* divisional purchase agreement) states that (1) the remedies available to the Parties under the Agreement are exclusive (i.e., that the Buyer has no other statutory, equitable, or common law remedies) and (2) the Buyer specifically waives and releases the Target from, and indemnifies the Target with respect to, environmental, health, and safety matters.

Sample acquisition agreement 2004.3 (the *neutral* divisional purchase agreement) (1) states that the remedies available to the Parties under the Agreement are exclusive (i.e., that the Buyer has no other statutory, equitable, or common law remedies), (2) contains a waiver of extra-contractual

9. *Termination.*

(a) *Termination of Agreement.* Certain of the Parties may terminate this Agreement as provided below:

(i) the Buyer and the Target may terminate this Agreement by mutual written consent at any time prior to the Closing;

(ii) the Buyer may terminate this Agreement by giving written notice to the Target on or before the [30th] day following the date of this Agreement if the Buyer is not [reasonably] satisfied with the results of its continuing business, legal, environmental, and accounting due diligence regarding the Division and the Division Subsidiaries;[79]

(iii) the Buyer may terminate this Agreement by giving written notice to the Target at any time prior to the Closing (A) in the event the Target has breached any material representation, warranty, or covenant contained in this Agreement in any material respect, the Buyer has notified the Target of the breach, and the breach has continued without cure for a period of [30 days] after the notice of breach or (B) if the Closing shall not have occurred on or before _____, 19_____, by reason of the failure of any condition precedent under §7(a) hereof (unless the failure results primarily from the Buyer itself breaching any representation, warranty, or covenant contained in this Agreement); and

(iv) the Target may terminate this Agreement by giving written notice to the Buyer at any time prior to the Closing (A) in the event the Buyer has breached any material representation, warranty, or covenant contained in this Agreement in any material respect, the Target has notified the Buyer of the breach, and the breach has continued without cure for a period of [30 days] after the notice of breach or (B) if the Closing shall not have occurred on or before _____, 19_____, by reason of the failure of any condition precedent under §7(b) hereof (unless the failure results primarily from the Target itself breaching any representation, warranty, or covenant contained in this Agreement).

(b) *Effect of Termination.* If any Party terminates this Agreement pursuant to §9(a) above, all rights and obligations of the Parties hereunder shall terminate without any Liability of any Party to the other Party (except for any Liability of any Party then in breach).

---

environmental remedies, but (3) does not contain an environmental indemnification of the Target by the Buyer.

[79] Sample acquisition agreement 2004.2 (the *pro-seller* divisional asset purchase agreement) lacks a comparable provision giving the Buyer a right to terminate the agreement for a limited period after signing if the Buyer is not [reasonably] satisfied with the results of its continuing business, legal, environmental, and accounting due diligence concerning the Division and the Division Subsidiaries.

10. *Miscellaneous.*

(a) *Press Releases and Public Announcements.* No Party shall issue any press release or make any public announcement relating to the subject matter of this Agreement [prior to the Closing] without the prior written approval of the other Party; *provided, however,* that any Party may make any public disclosure it believes in good faith is required by applicable law or any listing or trading agreement concerning its publicly-traded securities (in which case the disclosing Party will use its [reasonable] best efforts to advise the other Party prior to making the disclosure).

(b) *No Third-Party Beneficiaries.* This Agreement shall not confer any rights or remedies upon any Person other than the Parties and their respective successors and permitted assigns.

(c) *Entire Agreement.* [This Agreement (including the documents referred to herein) constitutes the entire agreement between the Parties and supersedes any prior understandings, agreements, or representations by or between the Parties, written or oral, to the extent they have related in any way to the subject matter hereof].

(d) *Succession and Assignment.* This Agreement shall be binding upon and inure to the benefit of the Parties named herein and their respective successors and permitted assigns. No Party may assign either this Agreement or any of its rights, interests, or obligations hereunder without the prior written approval of the other Party; *provided however,* that the Buyer may (i) assign any or all of its rights and interests hereunder to one or more of its Affiliates and (ii) designate one or more of its Affiliates to perform its obligations hereunder (in any or all of which cases the Buyer nonetheless shall remain responsible for the performance of all of its obligations hereunder).

(e) *Counterparts.* This Agreement may be executed in one or more counterparts, each of which shall be deemed an original but all of which together will constitute one and the same instrument.

(f) *Headings.* The section headings contained in this Agreement are inserted for convenience only and shall not affect in any way the meaning or interpretation of this Agreement.

(g) *Notices.* All notices, requests, demands, claims, and other communications hereunder will be in writing. Any notice, request, demand, claim, or other communication hereunder shall be deemed duly given if (and then two business days after) it is sent by registered or certified mail, return receipt requested, postage prepaid, and addressed to the intended recipient as set forth below:

If to the Target:	*Copy to:*
If to the Buyer:	*Copy to:*
If to the Process Agent:	*Copy to:*

Any Party may send any notice, request, demand, claim, or other communication hereunder to the intended recipient at the address set forth above using any other means (including personal delivery, expedited courier, messenger service, telecopy, telex, ordinary mail, or electronic mail), but no such notice, request, demand, claim, or other communication shall be deemed to have been duly given unless and until it actually is received by the intended recipient. Any Party may change the address to which notices, requests, demands, claims, and other communications hereunder are to be delivered by giving the other Party notice in the manner herein set forth.

(h) *Governing Law. This Agreement shall be governed by and construed in accordance with the domestic laws of* _____ *the State of without giving effect to any choice or conflict of law provision or rule (whether of the State of* _____ *or any other jurisdiction) that would cause the application of the laws of any jurisdiction other than the State of* _____ .

(i) *Amendments and Waivers.* No amendment of any provision of this Agreement shall be valid unless the same shall be in writing and signed by the Buyer and the Target [The Target may consent to any such amendment at any time prior to the Closing with the prior authorization of its board of directors; *provided, however,* that any amendment effected after the Target Stockholders have approved this Agreement will be subject to the restrictions contained in the (APPLICABLE CORPORATION STATUTE)]. No waiver by any Party of any default, misrepresentation, or breach of warranty or covenant hereunder, whether intentional or not, shall be deemed to extend to any prior or subsequent default, misrepresentation, or breach of warranty or covenant hereunder or affect in any way any rights arising by virtue of any prior or subsequent such occurrence.

(j) *Severability.* Any term or provision of this Agreement that is invalid or unenforceable in any situation in any jurisdiction shall not affect the validity or enforceability of the remaining terms and provisions hereof or the validity or enforceability of the offending term or provision in any other situation or in any other jurisdiction.

(k) *Expenses.* Each of the Buyer, the Target, the Division Subsidiaries, and the Target Stockholders will bear his or its own costs and expenses (including legal fees and expenses) incurred in connection with this Agreement and the transactions contemplated hereby.[80] The Target agrees that the Division and the Division

---

[80] This Agreement makes the Division Subsidiaries responsible for their own transactional costs and expenses. This means the Buyer will bear these costs and expenses if it consummates the asset purchase.

Subsidiaries have not borne and will not bear any of the costs and expenses of the Target and the Target Stockholders (including any of their legal fees and expenses) in connection with this Agreement or any of the transactions contemplated hereby. The Target also agrees that the Division and the Division Subsidiaries have not paid any amount to any third party, and will not pay any amount to any third party, with respect to any of the costs and expenses of the Target and the Target Stockholders (including any of their legal fees and expenses) in connection with this Agreement or any of the transactions contemplated hereby.[81]

(l) *Construction.* [The Parties have participated jointly in the negotiation and drafting of this Agreement. In the event an ambiguity or question of intent or interpretation arises, this Agreement shall be construed as if drafted jointly by the Parties and no presumption or burden of proof shall arise favoring or disfavoring any Party by virtue of the authorship of any of the provisions of this Agreement.] Any reference to any federal, state, local, or foreign statute or law shall be deemed also to refer to all rules and regulations promulgated thereunder, unless the context requires otherwise. The word "including" shall mean including without limitation. Nothing in the Disclosure Schedule shall be deemed adequate to disclose an exception to a representation or warranty made herein unless the Disclosure Schedule identifies the exception with [reasonable] particularity and describes the relevant facts in [reasonable] detail. Without limiting the generality of the foregoing, the mere listing (or inclusion of a copy) of a document or other item shall not be deemed adequate to disclose an exception to a representation or warranty made herein (unless the representation or warranty has to do with the existence of the document or other item itself). The Parties intend that each representation, warranty, and covenant contained herein shall have independent significance. If any Party has breached any representation, warranty, or covenant contained herein in any respect, the fact that there exists another representation, warranty, or covenant relating to the same subject matter (regardless of the relative levels of specificity) which the Party has not breached shall not detract from or

---

The Division Subsidiaries may incur significant costs and expenses if they prepare portions of the Disclosure Schedule and the Financial Statements, give notices to third parties and obtain their consent, make filings under the Hart-Scott-Rodino Act and respond to requests for additional information, and/or obtain title insurance and surveys for the Closing.

For this reason, the Buyer may seek to have the Target reimburse the Division Subsidiaries for some or all of these costs and expenses (out of assets other than the assets of the Division).

The Target, on the other hand, may seek to make the Buyer responsible for some or all of the costs and expenses of the Target and the Target Stockholders. Sample acquisition agreement 2004.2 (the *pro-seller* divisional asset purchase agreement) contains provisions more favorable to the Target in this regard.

The Parties may settle on a compromise allocation of responsibility (such as sharing the costs and expenses in a predetermined ratio or making one Party responsible for the costs and expenses up to a specified aggregate ceiling and the other Party responsible for any excess).

[81] Notice that the Buyer will bear the costs and expenses of the Target and the Target Stockholders to the extent the Division pays any amount to a third party with respect thereto prior to the Closing. This is because the payment will reduce the amount of cash the Buyer otherwise would receive when it acquires the assets of the Division at the Closing. This provision is designed to protect the Buyer from having to bear any of the costs and expenses of the Target and the Target Stockholders.

mitigate the fact that the Party is in breach of the first representation, warranty, or covenant.[82]

(m) *Incorporation of Exhibits and Schedules.* The Exhibits and Schedules identified in this Agreement are incorporated herein by reference and made a part hereof.

(n) *Specific Performance.* Each of the Parties acknowledges and agrees that the other Party would be damaged irreparably in the event any of the provisions of this Agreement are not performed in accordance with their specific terms or otherwise are breached. Accordingly, each of the Parties agrees that the other Party shall be entitled to an injunction or injunctions to prevent breaches of the provisions of this Agreement and to enforce specifically this Agreement and the terms and provisions hereof in any action instituted in any court of the United States or any state thereof having jurisdiction over the Parties and the matter [(subject to the provisions set forth in §10(o) below)], in addition to any other remedy to which it may be entitled, at law or in equity.[83]

(o) *Submission to Jurisdiction.*[84] Each of the Parties submits to the jurisdiction of any state or federal court sitting in _____, _____ in any action or proceeding arising out of or relating to this Agreement and agrees that all claims in respect of the action or proceeding may be heard and determined in any such court. [Each Party also agrees not to bring any action or proceeding arising out of or relating to this Agreement in any other court.] Each of the Parties waives any defense of inconvenient forum to the maintenance of any action or proceeding so brought and waives any bond, surety, or other security that might be required of any other Party with respect thereto. Each Party appoints _____ (the *"Process Agent"*) as its agent to receive on its behalf service of copies of the summons and complaint and any other process that might be served in the action or proceeding. Any Party may make service on the other Party by sending or delivering a copy of the process (i) to the Party to be served at the address and in the manner provided for the giving of notices in §10(g) above or (ii) to the Party to be served in care of the Process Agent at the address and in the manner provided for the giving of notices in §10(g) above. Nothing in this §10(o), however, shall affect the right of any Party [to bring any action or proceeding arising out of or relating to this Agreement in any other court or] to serve legal process in any other manner permitted by law or in equity. Each Party agrees that a final judgment in any action or proceeding so brought shall be conclusive and may be enforced by suit on the judgment or in any other manner provided by law or in equity.[85]

---

[82] Sample acquisition agreement 2004.2 (the *pro-seller* divisional asset purchase agreement) omits the last four sentences of this paragraph.

[83] Sample acquisition agreement 2004.2 (the *pro-seller* divisional asset purchase agreement) omits this specific performance provision.

[84] The Parties may want to add a provision calling for optional or mandatory arbitration with respect to all or certain issues.

[85] Sample acquisition agreement 2004.2 (the *pro-seller* divisional asset purchase agreement) omits this submission to jurisdiction provision.

(p) *Tax Matters.*[86]

[(i) Any agreement between the Target and any of the Division Subsidiaries regarding allocation or payment of Taxes or amounts in lieu of Taxes shall be deemed terminated at and as of the Closing.

(ii) The Target will be responsible for the preparation and filing of all Tax Returns for the Target for all periods as to which Tax Returns are due after the Closing Date (including the consolidated, unitary, and combined Tax Returns for the Target which include the operations of the Division and the Division Subsidiaries for any period ending on or before the Closing Date). The Target will make all payments required with respect to any such Tax Return.

(iii) The Buyer will be responsible for the preparation and filing of all Tax Returns for the Division and the Division Subsidiaries for all periods as to which Tax Returns are due after the Closing Date (other than for Taxes with respect to periods for which the consolidated, unitary, and combined Tax Returns of the Target will include the operations of the Division and the Division Subsidiaries). The Buyer will make all payments required with respect to any such Tax Return; *provided, however,* that the Target will reimburse the Buyer concurrently therewith to the extent any payment the Buyer is making relates to the operations of any of the Division and the Division Subsidiaries for any period ending on or before the Closing Date.

(iv) The Buyer and the Target will (A) cooperate in the preparation and filing of an election under Code §338(h)(10) with respect to the sale of the stock of the Division Subsidiaries hereunder[87] and (B) take all such action as is required in order to give effect to the election for state, local, and foreign Tax purposes to the greatest extent permitted by law.]

(q) *Employee Benefits Matters.* [The Buyer will adopt and assume at and as of the Closing each of the Employee Benefit Plans that the Division maintains and

---

[86] This Agreement contains a considerably abbreviated version of the tax provisions found in sample acquisition agreement 2002.4 (sale of subsidiary out of consolidated group). The Parties may wish to incorporate some or all of the unabridged provisions from sample acquisition agreement 2002.4 into this Agreement.

[87] The Buyer may seek to have the Parties make an election under Code §338(h)(10) (i.e., to have the sale of the stock of the Division Subsidiaries taxed as though the Division Subsidiaries instead had sold their *assets* to the Buyer). *See* ¶205.

This differs from any other election the Buyer might make under Code §338 in that the *Target* will be responsible for any federal income tax on the deemed sale of assets. Note, however, that the Target will incur no federal income tax on the sale of the *stock* of the Division Subsidiaries (i.e., only on the deemed sale of their *assets*) if the Parties make a Code §338(h)(10) election.

This Agreement provides that the Target will remain responsible for any incremental tax arising out of the Code §338(h)(10) election. See the definition of Assumed Liabilities in §1. The Target, of course, will seek to make the Buyer responsible for the incremental tax. Sample acquisition agreement 2004.2 (the *pro-seller* divisional asset purchase agreement) contains provisions more favorable to the Target in this regard.

each trust, insurance contract, annuity contract, or other funding arrangement that the Division has established with respect thereto. The Target will transfer (or cause the plan administrators to transfer) at and as of the Closing all of the corresponding assets associated with the Employee Benefit Plans that the Buyer is adopting and assuming. With respect to each Multiemployer Plan, the Parties shall take all actions necessary to comply with the requirements of ERISA §4204.][88]

(r) *Bulk Transfer Laws.* The Buyer acknowledges that the Target will not comply with the provisions of any bulk transfer laws of any jurisdiction in connection with the transactions contemplated by this Agreement.[89]

*   *   *   *   *

IN WITNESS WHEREOF, the Parties hereto have executed this Agreement on [as of] the date first above written.

[BUYER]

By: _____

Title: _____

[TARGET]

By: _____

Title: _____

---

[88] This Agreement provides for a transfer of all Employee Benefit Plan assets (including overfundings) and liabilities (including underfundings) to the Buyer. There are many other approaches to splitting and matching plan assets and liabilities which would cause the Buyer to share to various degrees in plan overfundings and underfundings.

If the Buyer did not want to share in any plan overfundings and underfundings, the Buyer could establish substantially identical plans for future benefit accruals and count past service with any of the Division and the Division Subsidiaries for purposes of eligibility and vesting thereunder. The Target would then continue its previously established plans on a "frozen" basis and retain the benefit of any overfunding (or the detriment of any underfunding) thereunder.

If the Buyer wanted to share in only certain plan overfundings and underfundings, the Buyer and the Target could proceed as set forth in the preceding paragraph except that the Buyer would assume the liability for certain past service benefits under the Division plans as of the Closing Date and the Target would transfer certain corresponding plan assets to the Buyer.

In any event, the Purchase Price should reflect the intended disposition of employee benefit plan assets and liabilities.

[89] The Buyer may seek to have the Target comply with the applicable bulk transfer laws in certain circumstances. *See* ¶2001.2.2.2.

¶2004.2   Pro-Seller Divisional Purchase

Sample acquisition agreement 2004.2 (*pro-seller* divisional asset purchase) contains provisions favoring T in such areas as (i) the extent to which T will retain the divisional cash (net of unpaid taxes) at the time of the closing, (ii) the extent to which P will bear the burden of the divisional liabilities and obligations at the time of the closing, (iii) the extent to which P will lack conditions to its obligation to close, (iv) the extent to which T will be required to give representations and warranties, and (v) the extent to which T will be required to indemnify P against breaches of those representations and warranties.

Sample acquisition agreement 2004.2 provides that T will (i) retain all of the divisional cash at the closing and (ii) remain liable for the unpaid divisional taxes for periods up to the closing. This means that T will retain the divisional cash (net of unpaid taxes) at the time of the closing.

Sample acquisition agreement 2004.2 provides that P will assume substantially all of the divisional obligations and liabilities (whether known or unknown, and whether absolute or contingent). Thus, P would generally assume such undisclosed divisional liabilities as environmental cleanup, employment discrimination, antitrust violations, product liability, product warranty, and other claims and lawsuits.

Sample acquisition agreement 2004.2 contains limited representations and warranties from T concerning (i) the historical divisional financial statements, (ii) intervening events, (iii) litigation, (iv) tax matters, (v) pension and welfare benefit plans, (vi) environmental, health, and safety matters, and (vii) compliance with federal, state, local, and foreign laws.

Sample acquisition agreement 2004.2 *does not* contain a specific representation and warranty concerning undisclosed divisional liabilities.

Sample acquisition agreement 2004.2 also contains limited representations and warranties from T concerning (i) authorization with respect to the transaction, (ii) title to the assets being sold, (iii) required governmental and third party consents (and noncontravention generally), (iv) organization, (v) real estate matters, (vi) intellectual property matters, (vii) leases and contracts, and (viii) brokerage fees.

T's representations and warranties are qualified frequently with references to materiality and to the actual knowledge of T's shareholders, but not, for example, T's directors, officers, and employees, *without any duty of independent investigation.*

Sample acquisition agreement 2004.2 contains alternative provisions for (i) minimal indemnification to P for breaches of T's representations and warranties (i.e., none of the representations and warranties concerning the division survive the closing and there is no indemnification for breaches thereof)[1] *or* (ii) limited indemnification to P for breaches of T's representations and warranties (i.e., the representations and warranties concerning the division survive only for one year

---

¶2004.2   [1] This is referred to as *minimal* indemnification (rather than *no* indemnification) because T's representations and warranties about the transaction itself (e.g., organization of T, authorization of the transaction, noncontravention, absence of brokers' fees, ownership of the divisional assets, etc.) do survive the closing and may give rise to indemnification.

and there is a deductible and a ceiling with respect to indemnification for breaches thereof).

P *does not* have any right to recoup its losses against the P notes in lieu of seeking indemnification from T.

P's obligation to close is subject to minimal conditions such as (i) compliance with T's representations, warranties, and covenants, (ii) absence of a material adverse change, (iii) absence of an injunction affecting the transaction, (iv) delivery of any side agreements, and (v) delivery of an opinion of T's legal counsel.

P *does not* have any closing condition concerning its ability to secure financing for the transaction *or* any right to terminate the purchase agreement after signing if it is not satisfied with the results of its continuing business, legal, and accounting due diligence review.

There are a number of other important differences between sample acquisition agreement 2004.1 (*pro-buyer* divisional asset purchase) and sample acquisition agreement 2004.2 (*pro-seller* divisional asset purchase). Each of these sample acquisition agreements contains extensive footnotes with cross-references pointing out the differences.

ASSET PURCHASE AGREEMENT[2]

BETWEEN

_____

AND

_____

_____, 19____

TABLE OF CONTENTS

---

[2] The Buyer generally will obtain a cost basis (i.e., the Purchase Price *plus* the Assumed Liabilities *plus* the expenses of the transaction) in the Acquired Assets.

A purchase of assets in which the consideration is primarily cash and notes is generally treated for accounting purposes as a purchase rather than as a pooling of interests. *See* ¶1503.

Some LBO structures prejudice the Target's creditors and hence might permit payments, transfers, liens, and obligations arising out of the LBO to be attacked under fraudulent conveyance law. *See* ¶1506.

Exhibit A—Form of Buyer Note
Exhibit B—Forms of Assignments
Exhibit C—Form of Assumption
Exhibit D—Allocation Schedule
Exhibit E—Historical Financial Statements
Exhibit F—Forms of Side Agreements
Exhibit G—Form of Opinion of Counsel to the Target
Exhibit H—Form of Opinion of Counsel to the Buyer
Disclosure Schedule—Exceptions to Representations and Warranties

[EXHIBITS AND SCHEDULES HAVE BEEN OMITTED FROM THIS SAMPLE ACQUISITION AGREEMENT 2004.2]

Agreement entered into on [as of] _____, 19____, by and between _____, a _____ corporation (the *"Buyer"*), and _____, a _____ corporation (the *"Target"*). The Buyer and the Target are referred to collectively herein as the *"Parties."*

This Agreement contemplates a transaction in which the Buyer will purchase substantially all of the assets (and assume substantially all of the liabilities) of the _____ Division of the Target in return for cash and the Buyer Note.[3]

---

[3] When the Buyer purchases a division of the Target, the Target will generally retain those assets and rights which it does not transfer and assign to the Buyer, and the Target will generally remain responsible for those liabilities and obligations not assumed by the Buyer.

It is generally necessary to prepare asset transfer documents and liability assumption documents in an asset purchase (whether a purchase of all the Target's assets or a purchase of the Target's division), which would not be required if the Buyer purchased the Target's *stock.*

The Buyer's contractual assumption of certain divisional liabilities and obligations generally will not preclude a third party to whom the Target owed the liabilities and obligations from suing the Target (if the Buyer has failed to pay or perform) unless the third party consents to the Buyer's assumption and agrees to look only to the Buyer for satisfaction (i.e., enters into a novation agreement). This means that, if the Buyer fails to satisfy the assumed liabilities and obligations, nonconsenting third parties to whom the Target owed the liabilities and obligations may have a cause of action against the Target or, if the Target has liquidated and dissolved, against the Target's stockholders and/or directors.

Now, therefore, in consideration of the premises and the mutual promises herein made, and in consideration of the representations, warranties, and covenants herein contained, the Parties agree as follows.

1. *Definitions.*

"Accredited Investor" has the meaning set forth in Regulation D promulgated under the Securities Act.

"Acquired Assets" means all of the right, title, and interest that the Target possesses and has the right to transfer in and to all of the assets constituting the Division,[4] *including* all of its (a) real property, leaseholds and subleaseholds therein, improvements, fixtures, and fittings thereon, and easements, rights-of-way, and other appurtenants thereto (such as appurtenant rights in and to public streets), (b) tangible personal property (such as machinery, equipment, inventories of raw materials and supplies, manufactured and purchased parts, goods in process and finished goods, furniture, automobiles, trucks, tractors, trailers, tools, jigs, and dies), (c) intellectual property, goodwill associated therewith, licenses and sublicenses granted and obtained with respect thereto, and rights thereunder, remedies against infringements thereof, and rights to protection of interests therein under the laws of all jurisdictions, (d) leases, subleases, and rights thereunder, (e) agreements, contracts, indentures, mortgages, instruments, Security Interests, guaranties, other similar arrangements, and rights thereunder, (f) accounts, notes, and other receivables, (g) securities (such as the capital stock in the Division Subsidiaries), (h) claims, deposits, prepayments, refunds, causes of action, choses in action, rights of recovery, rights of set off, and rights of recoupment (including any such item relating to the payment of taxes), (i) franchises, approvals, permits, licenses, orders, registrations, certificates, variances, and similar rights obtained from governments and governmental agencies, (j) books, records, ledgers, files, documents, correspondence, lists, plats, architectural plans, drawings, and specifications, creative materials, advertising and promotional materials, studies, reports, and other printed or written materials, and (k) [rights in and with respect to the assets associated with its Employee Benefit Plans];[5] *provided, however,* that the Acquired Assets shall not include (i) the corporate charter, qualifications to conduct business as a foreign corporation, arrangements with registered agents relating to foreign qualifications, taxpayer and other identification numbers, seals, minute books, stock transfer books, blank stock certificates, and other documents relating to the organization, maintenance, and existence of the Target as a corporation, (ii) any Cash,[6] or (iii) any of the rights of the Target under this Agreement

---

[4] The Buyer may seek to have the definition of Acquired Assets broadened to include *all* right, title, and interest in and to the divisional assets (rather than only so much as the Target possesses and has the right to transfer). Sample acquisition agreement 2004.1 (the *pro-buyer* divisional asset purchase agreement) contains provisions which are more favorable to the Buyer in this regard.

[5] See the provisions in §10(o) below with respect to employee benefits matters.

[6] This Agreement provides that the Target will retain the consolidated cash of the Division and the Division Subsidiaries. §2(d) below permits the Target to cause the Division Subsidiaries to distribute all of their cash to the Target at the Closing in order to facilitate the intended cash retention.

(or under any side agreement between the Target on the one hand and the Buyer on the other hand entered into on or after the date of this Agreement).[7]

"Adverse Consequences" means all actions, suits, proceedings, hearings, investigations, charges, complaints, claims, demands, injunctions, judgments, orders, decrees, rulings, damages, dues, penalties, fines, costs, [reasonable amounts paid in settlement,] liabilities, obligations, taxes, liens, losses, expenses, and fees, including court costs and [reasonable] attorneys' fees and expenses.

"Affiliate" has the meaning set forth in Rule 12b-2 of the regulations promulgated under the Securities Exchange Act.

"Affiliated Group" means any affiliated group within the meaning of Code §1504 [or any similar group defined under a similar provision of state, local, or foreign law].

"Applicable Rate" means the corporate base rate of interest publicly announced from time to time by [FINANCIAL INSTITUTION] [plus/minus ____% per annum].

"Assumed Liabilities"[8] means all liabilities and obligations of the Division (whether known or unknown, whether asserted or unasserted, whether absolute or contingent, whether accrued or unaccrued, whether liquidated or unliquidated, and whether due or to become due), including (a) all liabilities of the Target for transfer, sales, use, and other non-income taxes arising in connection with the consummation of the transactions contemplated hereby, (b) all liabilities of the Target for any incremental Income Taxes arising because any of the Division Subsidiaries is deemed to be transferring its assets pursuant to an election under Code §338(h)(10), (c) all liabilities of the Target for costs and expenses (including legal fees and expenses) the Target and the Target Stockholders have incurred in connection with this Agreement and the transactions contemplated hereby, (d) all liabilities and obligations of the Division under the agreements, contracts, leases, licenses, and other arrangements referred to in the definition of Acquired Assets, (e) [all liabilities and obligations of the Division under its Employee Benefit Plans],[9] (f) all liabilities and obligations of or relating to the Division with respect

---

The Buyer normally will seek to obtain this consolidated cash (net of unpaid taxes at the Closing for which the Target will remain liable). Sample acquisition agreement 2004.1 (the *pro-buyer* divisional asset purchase agreement) contains provisions which are more favorable to the Buyer in this regard.

[7] It may be difficult to identify and describe those rights, assets, obligations, and liabilities of the Target which constitute the Division. This is especially likely where the Target does not segregate cash in a separate account for the Division or where the Division shares rights, assets, obligations, and liabilities with the Target and its Affiliates. The Parties may wish to expand upon the definitions of Acquired Assets and Assumed Liabilities to include schedules showing the disposition of specific items.

[8] See the footnote to §2(b) below for an important discussion of certain tax issues which may affect the drafting of this definition as it concerns liabilities of the Division which have not yet matured into a deduction for tax purposes.

[9] See the provisions in §10(o) below with respect to employee benefits matters.

to environmental matters, including without limitation those arising under Environmental, Health, and Safety Requirements,[10] (g) [all obligations of the Division to indemnify any Person by reason of the fact that he or it was a director, officer, employee, or agent of the Division or was serving at the request of the Division as a partner, trustee, director, officer, employee, or agent of another entity (whether such indemnification is for judgments, damages, penalties, fines, costs, amounts paid in settlement, losses, expenses, or otherwise and whether such indemnification is pursuant to any statute, charter document, bylaw, agreement, or otherwise)],[11] and (h) all other liabilities and obligations of the Division set forth in the Disclosure Schedule; *provided, however*, that the Assumed Liabilities shall not include (i) any liability of the Target for unpaid taxes (with respect to the Division or otherwise) for periods prior to the Closing, (ii) any liability of the Target for any Income Taxes arising because the Target is transferring the Acquired Assets, because the Target has an Excess Loss Account in the stock of any of the Division Subsidiaries, or because the Target has deferred gain on any Deferred Intercompany Transaction, or (iii) any liability or obligation of the Target under this Agreement (or under any side agreement between the Target on the one hand and the Buyer on the other hand entered into on or after the date of this Agreement).[12]

"Buyer" has the meaning set forth in the preface above.

"Buyer Note" has the meaning set forth in §2(c) below.

"Cash" means cash and cash equivalents (including marketable securities and short term investments) calculated in accordance with GAAP applied on a basis consistent with the preparation of the Financial Statements.

---

[10] This provision requires the Buyer to assume all environmental liabilities relating to the Division.

Sample acquisition agreement 2004.1 (the *pro-buyer* divisional purchase agreement) leaves with the Target all environmental liabilities (other than those shown on the face of the Most Recent Balance Sheet) of the Division.

Sample acquisition agreement 2004.3 (the *neutral* divisional purchase agreement) states that the Buyer assumes those environmental liabilities specifically set forth on the Disclosure Schedule to that agreement.

[11] This *pro-seller* divisional asset purchase agreement contains bracketed language providing that the Buyer will assume all obligations of the Division to indemnify any Person, by reason of the fact that such Person was, before the asset purchase, a director or other officeholder of the Division entitled to indemnification from the Division, with respect to any matter whatsoever. *This provision is unusually favorable to the Target, and would be inappropriate in most transactions involving the purchase of a division.*

Compare sample acquisition agreement 2004.1 (the *pro-buyer* divisional asset purchase agreement), which provides that the Buyer will not assume such obligations. The buyer will likely seek such a provision even in this pro-seller agreement, and such a provision may well be appropriate.

These provisions relate marginally to the surprising decision in Heffernan v. Pacific Dunlop GNB Corporation, 965 F.2d 369 (7th Cir. 1992). *See* §8(g) of sample acquisition agreement 2002.1 (the pro-buyer *stock* purchase agreement) and the footnote thereto. Although *Heffernan* involved a purchase of stock, rather than a purchase of divisional assets, the instant structure presents some of the same concerns.

[12] This definition of Assumed Liabilities is relatively broad. The Buyer is assuming substantially all of the liabilities and obligations of the Division (whether known or unknown, whether asserted

"Closing" has the meaning set forth in §2(e) below.

"Closing Date" has the meaning set forth in §2(e) below.

"COBRA" means the requirements of Part 6 of Subtitle B of Title I of ERISA and Code §4980B and of any similar state law.

"Code" means the Internal Revenue Code of 1986, as amended.

*"Confidential Information"*means any information concerning the businesses and affairs of the Division and the Division Subsidiaries that is not already generally available to the public.

"Deferred Intercompany Transaction" has the meaning set forth in Reg. §1.1502-13.

"Disclosure Schedule" has the meaning set forth in §3 below.

"Division" means the Target with respect to its _____ Division.

"Division Subsidiary" means any Subsidiary of the Target included within the Division.

"Employee Benefit Plan" means any "employee benefit plan" (as such term is defined in ERISA §3(3)) and any other [material] employee benefit plan, program or arrangement of any kind.

"Employee Pension Benefit Plan" has the meaning set forth in ERISA §3(2).

"Employee Welfare Benefit Plan" has the meaning set forth in ERISA §3(1).

---

or unasserted, whether absolute or contingent, whether accrued or unaccrued, whether liquidated or unliquidated, and whether due or to become due), including (i) transfer, sales, use, and other non-income taxes arising in connection with the transaction, (ii) incremental income taxes arising in connection with any Code §338(h)(10) election, (iii) costs and expenses arising in connection with the transaction, (iv) contracts with third parties, (v) employee benefit plans, and (vi) matters set forth in the Disclosure Schedule.

The Buyer is not, however, assuming (a) any liability for unpaid taxes with respect to periods prior to the Closing or (b) any liability for income taxes (except as noted in the previous paragraph) arising in connection with the transaction.

The Buyer may seek to assume only certain specified liabilities and obligations. Sample acquisition agreement 2004.1 (the *pro-buyer* divisional asset purchase agreement) contains a narrower definition of Assumed Liabilities.

"Environmental, Health, and Safety Requirements" shall mean all federal, state, local and foreign statutes, regulations, and ordinances concerning public health and safety, worker health and safety, and pollution or protection of the environment, including without limitation all those relating to the presence, use, production, generation, handling, transportation, treatment, storage, disposal, distribution, labeling, testing, processing, discharge, release, threatened release, control, or cleanup of any hazardous materials, substances or wastes, as such requirements are enacted and in effect on or prior to the Closing Date.[13]

"ERISA" means the Employee Retirement Income Security Act of 1974, as amended.

"ERISA Affiliate" means each entity which is treated as a single employer with the Target for purposes of Code §414.

"Excess Loss Account" has the meaning set forth in Reg. §1.1502-19.

"Financial Statement" has the meaning set forth in §3(g) below.

"GAAP" means United States generally accepted accounting principles as in effect from time to time.

"Hart-Scott-Rodino Act" means the Hart-Scott-Rodino Antitrust Improvements Act of 1976, as amended.

"Income Tax" means any federal, state, local, or foreign income tax, including any interest, penalty, or addition thereto, whether disputed or not.

"Income Tax Return" means any return, declaration, report, claim for refund, or information return or statement relating to Income Taxes, including any schedule or attachment thereto.

"Indemnified Party" has the meaning set forth in §8(d) below.

"Indemnifying Party" has the meaning set forth in §8(d) below.

"Knowledge" means actual knowledge without independent investigation.[14]

---

[13] Sample acquisition agreement 2004.1 (the *pro-buyer* divisional purchase agreement) explicitly extends this definition to include legal requirements enacted and in effect prior to, on, or after the Closing Date and also includes within this definition contractual obligations and common law.

Sample acquisition agreement 2004.3 (the *neutral* divisional purchase agreement) is silent as to the time frame for enactment of covered Environmental, Health, and Safety Requirements and also includes within this definition common law.

[14] Sample acquisition agreement 2004.1 (the *pro-buyer* divisional asset purchase agreement) defines "Knowledge" as actual knowledge after reasonable investigation.

"Most Recent Financial Statements" has the meaning set forth in §3(g) below.

"Most Recent Fiscal Month End" has the meaning set forth in §3(g) below.

"Multiemployer Plan" has the meaning set forth in ERISA §3(37).

"Ordinary Course of Business" means the ordinary course of business consistent with past custom and practice (including with respect to quantity and frequency).

"Party" has the meaning set forth in the preface above.

"PBGC" means the Pension Benefit Guaranty Corporation.

"Person" means an individual, a partnership, a corporation, an association, a joint stock company, a trust, a joint venture, an unincorporated organization, or a governmental entity (or any department, agency, or political subdivision thereof).

"Purchase Price" has the meaning set forth in §2(c) below.

"Reportable Event" has the meaning set forth in ERISA §4043.

"Securities Act" means the Securities Act of 1933, as amended.

"Securities Exchange Act" means the Securities Exchange Act of 1934, as amended.

"Security Interest" means any mortgage, pledge, lien, encumbrance, charge, or other security interest, *other than* (a) mechanic's, materialmen's, and similar liens, (b) liens for taxes not yet due and payable [or for taxes that the taxpayer is contesting in good faith through appropriate proceedings], (c) purchase money liens and liens securing rental payments under capital lease arrangements, and (d) other liens arising in the Ordinary Course of Business and not incurred in connection with the borrowing of money.

"Subsidiary" means any corporation with respect to which a specified Person (or a Subsidiary thereof) owns a majority of the common stock or has the power to vote or direct the voting of sufficient securities to elect a majority of the directors.[15]

"Target" has the meaning set forth in the preface above.

"Target Share" means any share of the Common Stock, par value $_____ per share, of the Target.[16]

---

[15] It may be necessary to revise this definition if, for example, the Division has subsidiary *partnerships*.

[16] It may be necessary to revise this definition if the Target has additional classes of capital stock.

"Target Stockholder" means any person who or which holds any Target Shares.

"Third Party Claim" has the meaning set forth in §8(d) below.

2. *Basic Transaction.*

(a) *Purchase and Sale of Assets.* On and subject to the terms and conditions of this Agreement, the Buyer agrees to purchase from the Target, and the Target agrees to sell, transfer, convey, and deliver to the Buyer, all of the Acquired Assets at the Closing for the consideration specified below in this §2.

(b) *Assumption of Liabilities.* On and subject to the terms and conditions of this Agreement, the Buyer agrees to assume and become responsible for all of the Assumed Liabilities at the Closing. The Buyer will not assume or have any responsibility, however, with respect to any other obligation or liability of the Target not included within the definition of Assumed Liabilities.[17]

---

[17] In a taxable purchase of the Target's divisional assets, the Division may have liabilities which have not yet matured into a deduction for tax purposes. For example, (1) a cash method Target may have accrued (but unpaid) operating liabilities, (2) a cash method or an accrual method Target may have contingent liabilities, (3) a cash method or an accrual method Target may have unfunded pension liabilities, and (4) an accrual method Target may have liabilities as to which the "all events" test has been satisfied but as to which "economic performance" (e.g., payment) has not yet occurred. The tax treatment of these and other liabilities which have not yet matured into deductions is somewhat surprising. *See* ¶304.

Under Code §461(h), an accrual method Target can deduct liabilities which otherwise satisfy the all events test (i.e., "Code §461(h) Liabilities") only as economic performance occurs. With respect to many such liabilities, economic performance occurs under the Code §461(h) regulations only when the Target has made payment with respect to the liability. *See* ¶304.4.

Reg. §§1.461-4(d)(5) and -4(g)(1)(ii)(C) seem to provide that when the Target sells the Buyer a trade or business and, as part of the sale, the Buyer *"expressly assumes"* a Code §461(h) Liability, the Target can deduct that liability (assuming that the Code §461(h) regulations make payment the proper test for economic performance) in the taxable year in which the sale occurred. This favorable tax result follows from the fact that the Target will be deemed to have made payment with respect to the liability when the amount of the liability (assumed by the Buyer) is included in the Target's amount realized on the sale of divisional assets. The regulation is, however, unclear on the meaning of the phrase "expressly assumes." *See* ¶304.4.

Cautious taxpayers should accordingly consider taking some or all of the following steps: (i) the Parties should specifically enumerate in this Agreement as many as practicable of the Code §461(h) Liabilities which the Buyer is assuming; (ii) the Parties should specifically state in this Agreement that the Buyer is "expressly assuming" not only these enumerated liabilities but also any categories of *unenumerated* Code §461(h) Liabilities which the Buyer is assuming; and (iii) the boards of directors of the respective Parties should adopt resolutions specifically stating that the Buyer is "expressly assuming" these Code §461(h) Liabilities.

Reg. §§1.461-4(d)(5) and -4(g)(1)(ii)(C) are applicable by their terms only with respect to Code §461(h) Liabilities. However, their premise that the Target will be deemed to have made payment with respect to a liability when the amount of the liability (assumed by the Buyer) is included in the Target's amount realized on the sale of divisional assets may have a broader application. For this reason, cautious taxpayers may want to apply the advice in the preceding paragraph of this footnote to cover *all* liabilities which the Buyer is assuming as to which the Target has not yet become entitled to a deduction under the Code.

(c) *Purchase Price.*[18] The Buyer agrees to pay to the Target at the Closing $_____ (the *"Purchase Price"*) by delivery of (i) its promissory note (the *"Buyer Note"*) in the form of Exhibit A attached hereto in the principal amount of $_____ and (ii) cash for the balance of the Purchase Price payable by wire transfer or delivery of other immediately available funds.[19]

(d) *Cash Payment to Target.*[20] Immediately prior to the Closing, the Target will cause the Division Subsidiaries to pay the Target an aggregate amount equal to the consolidated Cash of the Division Subsidiaries as of the Closing. The Target may cause any of the Division Subsidiaries to make any such payment to the Target in the form of a dividend or a redemption.[21]

(e) *The Closing.* The closing of the transactions contemplated by this Agreement (the *"Closing"*) shall take place at the offices of _____ in _____, _____ , commencing at 9:00 a.m. local time on the [second] business day following the satisfaction or waiver of all conditions to the obligations of the Parties to consummate the transactions contemplated hereby (other than conditions with respect to actions the respective Parties will take at the Closing itself) or such other date as the Parties may mutually determine (the *"Closing Date"*); *provided, however,* that the Closing Date shall be no earlier than _____, 19_____.

(f) *Deliveries at the Closing.* At the Closing, (i) the Target will deliver to the Buyer the various certificates, instruments, and documents referred to in §7(a) below; (ii)

---

[18] The Target may seek to have the Buyer make an earnest money deposit upon execution of this Agreement. If the transaction were thereafter completed, the deposit would be applied to the Purchase Price. If the transaction were thereafter aborted, the deposit would be refunded to the Buyer or paid to the Target as liquidated damages depending on the terms of this Agreement and the reasons for the termination.

[19] Sample acquisition agreement 2002.5 contains additional provisions for use where there is to be a post-Closing Purchase Price adjustment based on the consolidated net book value for the Division and the Division Subsidiaries as of the Closing. That sample acquisition agreement can be adapted for other post-Closing Purchase Price adjustments (such as a comparison of consolidated working capital with consolidated liabilities as of the Closing *or* a contingent earnout based on consolidated earnings for a specified period after the Closing).

Sample acquisition agreement 2002.5 is, however, intended for use with sample acquisition agreements 2002.1, 2002.2, and 2002.3 (the *stock* purchase agreements) and must be modified prior to use with this *asset* purchase agreement.

[20] This *pro-seller* agreement provides that the Target will retain *all* of the consolidated cash of the Division and the Division Subsidiaries. *See* the definition of Acquired Assets in §1 above. This §2(d) permits the Target to cause the Division Subsidiaries to distribute all of their cash to the Target at the Closing in order to facilitate the intended cash retention.

Sample acquisition agreement 2004.1 (the *pro-buyer* divisional asset purchase agreement), on the other hand, provides that the Target will retain only so much of the consolidated cash of the Division and the Division Subsidiaries as will cover their aggregate unpaid taxes up to the Closing for which the Target will remain liable. *See* the definition of Acquired Assets in §1 thereof and the provision for a partial cash distribution from the Division Subsidiaries to the Target in §2(d) thereof.

[21] The Parties should determine whether there is any external restriction or prohibition on the type of cash payment by the Division Subsidiaries contemplated by this §2(d) (such as a loan covenant or a statutory provision concerning dividends and stock redemptions). The Parties should also consider any possible difference in tax treatment between a cash dividend and a partial stock redemption.

the Buyer will deliver to the Target the various certificates, instruments, and documents referred to in §7(b) below; (iii) the Target will execute, acknowledge (if appropriate), and deliver to the Buyer (A) assignments (including real property and intellectual property transfer documents) in the forms attached hereto as Exhibits B-1 through B-____ and (B) such other instruments of sale, transfer, conveyance, and assignment as the Buyer and its counsel [reasonably] may request; (iv) the Buyer will execute, acknowledge (if appropriate), and deliver to the Target (A) an assumption in the form attached hereto as Exhibit C and (B) such other instruments of assumption as the Target and its counsel [reasonably] may request; and (v) the Buyer will deliver to the Target the consideration specified in §2(c) above.

(g) *Allocation.* [The Parties agree to allocate the Purchase Price (and all other capitalizable costs) among the Acquired Assets for all purposes (including financial accounting and tax purposes) in accordance with the allocation schedule attached hereto as Exhibit D.][22]

3. *Representations and Warranties of the Target.*[23] The Target represents and warrants to the Buyer that the statements contained in this §3 are correct and complete as of the date of this Agreement and will be correct and complete as of the Closing Date (as though made then and as though the Closing Date were substituted for the date of this Agreement throughout this §3), except as set forth in the disclosure schedule accompanying this Agreement and initialed by the Parties (the "Disclosure Schedule").[24] The Disclosure Schedule will be arranged in paragraphs corresponding to the lettered and numbered paragraphs contained in this §3.

---

[22] The 1986 Act generally requires the Buyer and the Target to allocate the Buyer's aggregate basis (i.e., the Purchase Price *plus* the Assumed Liabilities *plus* the expenses of the transaction) among the Acquired Assets using the residual method. *See* ¶403. The Parties should omit this provision if they do not reach agreement on a particular allocation schedule.

[23] This *pro-seller* §3 contains relatively few representations and warranties concerning the Division and the Division Subsidiaries, and is qualified frequently with references to "knowledge" (defined as the actual knowledge of any Target Stockholder without independent investigation) and "materiality" (defined generally as having a material adverse effect on the financial condition of the Division and the Division Subsidiaries taken as a whole or on the ability of the Parties to consummate the transactions contemplated by this Agreement).

The Buyer will seek to have the Target make extensive representations and warranties concerning the Division and the Division Subsidiaries, without any qualification as to materiality and with only occasional references to knowledge (defined in a manner more favorable to the Buyer as the actual knowledge of any Target Stockholder or any director, officer, or employee of any of the Target and its Subsidiaries after reasonable investigation). Sample acquisition agreement 2004.1 (the *pro-buyer* divisional asset purchase agreement) contains comparable representations and warranties which are more favorable to the Buyer.

[24] The Buyer will have a closing condition (*see* §7(a)(i) below) and post-Closing indemnification rights (*see* §8(b) below) with respect to certain misrepresentations and breaches of warranty. The Buyer will not, however, have a closing condition or post-Closing indemnification rights with respect to any adverse matter which the Target discloses in the Disclosure Schedule. This is because the disclosure will cure any misrepresentation or breach of warranty that might otherwise have existed. Thus, where the Target discloses an adverse matter in the Disclosure Schedule, the Buyer may seek (a) to avoid assuming responsibility for the matter (see the definition of Assumed Liabilities in §1 above), (b) to add a specific closing condition requiring an acceptable resolution of the matter, and/or (c) to obtain specific post-Closing indemnification against the matter.

(a) *Organization of the Target.* The Target is a corporation duly organized, validly existing, and in good standing under the laws of the jurisdiction of its incorporation.

(b) *Authorization of Transaction.* The Target has full power and authority (including full corporate power and authority) to execute and deliver this Agreement and to perform its obligations hereunder. [Without limiting the generality of the foregoing, the board of directors of the Target and the Target Stockholders have duly authorized the execution, delivery, and performance of this Agreement by the Target.][25] This Agreement constitutes the valid and legally binding obligation of the Target, enforceable in accordance with its terms and conditions.

(c) *Noncontravention.* [To the Knowledge of any of the Target Stockholders,] neither the execution and the delivery of this Agreement, nor the consummation of the transactions contemplated hereby (including the assignments and assumptions referred to in §2 above), will [(i)] violate any constitution, statute, regulation, rule, injunction, judgment, order, decree, ruling, charge, or other restriction of any government, governmental agency, or court to which any of the Target and the Division Subsidiaries is subject or any provision of the charter or bylaws of any of the Target and the Division Subsidiaries [or (ii) conflict with, result in a breach of, constitute a default under, result in the acceleration of, create in any party the right to accelerate, terminate, modify, or cancel, or require any notice under any agreement, contract, lease, license, instrument, or other arrangement to which any of the Target and the Division Subsidiaries is a party or by which it is bound or to which any of its assets is subject (or result in the imposition of any Security Interest upon any of its assets), except where the violation, conflict, breach, default, acceleration, termination, modification, cancellation, failure to give notice, or Security Interest would not have a material adverse effect on the financial condition of the Division and the Division Subsidiaries taken as a whole or on the ability of the Parties to consummate the transactions contemplated by this Agreement]. [To the Knowledge of any of the Target Stockholders,] none of the Target and the Division Subsidiaries needs to give any notice to, make any filing with, or obtain any authorization, consent, or approval

---

Sample acquisition agreement 2004.1 (the *pro-buyer* divisional asset purchase agreement) contains additional provisions to the effect that the Target's disclosures will be ineffective unless they meet specified standards for particularity and detail. *See* §10(l) of sample acquisition agreement 2004.1.

[25] The Target must obtain the approval of its board of directors *and* the approval of its stockholders in order to sell all or substantially all of its assets. *See* ¶2001.2.2.2. A sale of the divisional assets may trigger this requirement, depending on the size of the *divisional* assets relative to the Target's other assets.

This Agreement assumes the Target has already obtained any requisite corporate approvals.

If such approval of the Target's stockholders is necessary, but the Parties wish to enter into this Agreement before the Target has obtained such approval, the Parties should revise this Agreement to include (a) a covenant calling for the Target to obtain such approval prior to the Closing and (b) a closing condition for each of the Parties to the effect that the Target *has* obtained such approval. *Compare* sample acquisition agreement 2005 (the reverse subsidiary merger agreement), which contemplates the Target corporation will obtain the approval of its stockholders between the signing of the merger agreement and the Closing.

The Parties generally will not enter into an asset purchase agreement (or for that matter a merger agreement) until the Target has obtained any requisite approval of its *board of directors*.

of any government or governmental agency in order for the Parties to consummate the transactions contemplated by this Agreement (including the assignments and assumptions referred to in §2 above) [, except where the failure to give notice, to file, or to obtain any authorization, consent, or approval would not have a material adverse effect on the financial condition of the Division and the Division Subsidiaries taken as a whole or on the ability of the Parties to consummate the transactions contemplated by this Agreement].[26]

(d) *Brokers' Fees.* The Target has no liability or obligation to pay any fees or commissions to any broker, finder, or agent with respect to the transactions contemplated by this Agreement for which the Buyer could become liable or obligated. None of the Division Subsidiaries has any liability or obligation to pay any fees or commissions to any broker, finder, or agent with respect to the transactions contemplated by this Agreement.

(e) *Title to Tangible Assets.* The Division and the Division Subsidiaries have good title to, or a valid leasehold interest in, the material tangible assets they use regularly in the conduct of their businesses.

(f) *Subsidiaries.* §3(f) of the Disclosure Schedule sets forth for each Division Subsidiary (i) its name and jurisdiction of incorporation, (ii) the number of shares of authorized capital stock of each class of its capital stock, (iii) the number of issued and outstanding shares of each class of its capital stock, the names of the holders thereof, and the number of shares held by each such holder, (iv) the number of shares of its capital stock held in treasury, and (v) its directors and officers. Each Division Subsidiary is a corporation duly organized, validly existing, and in good standing under the laws of the jurisdiction of its incorporation. Each Division Subsidiary is duly authorized to conduct business and is in good standing under the laws of each jurisdiction where such qualification is required, except where the lack of such qualification would not have a material adverse effect on the financial condition of the Division and the Division Subsidiaries taken as a whole. Each Division Subsidiary has full corporate power and authority to carry on the businesses in which it is engaged and to own and use the properties owned and used by it. All of the issued and outstanding shares of capital stock of each Division Subsidiary have been duly authorized and are validly issued, fully paid, and nonassessable. One of the Division and the Division Subsidiaries holds of record and owns beneficially all of the outstanding shares of each Division Subsidiary.

---

[26] The Buyer may seek to have the Target include the bracketed language concerning required notices and consents under arrangements with third parties. The Target, on the other hand, may seek to include the bracketed language concerning knowledge and materiality (particularly if the language concerning required notices and consents is included). *Compare* the representation and warranty from the *Buyer* in §4(c) below.

(g) *Financial Statements.*[27] Attached hereto as Exhibit E are the following financial statements (collectively the *"Financial Statements"*): (i) audited consolidated balance sheets and statements of income, changes in control account, and cash flow as of and for the fiscal years ended _____, 19____, _____, 19____, _____, 19____, _____, 19____, and _____, 19____ for the Division and the Division Subsidiaries; and (ii) unaudited consolidated balance sheets and statements of income, changes in control account, and cash flow (the *"Most Recent Financial Statements"*) as of and for the ____ months ended _____, 19____ (the *"Most Recent Fiscal Month End"*) for the Division and the Division Subsidiaries.[28] The Financial Statements (including the notes thereto) have been prepared in accordance with GAAP applied on a consistent basis throughout the periods covered thereby and present fairly the financial condition of the Division and the Division Subsidiaries as of such dates and the results of operations of the Division and the Division Subsidiaries for such periods;[29] *provided, however,* that the Most Recent Financial Statements are subject to normal year-end adjustments and lack footnotes and other presentation items. The Target maintains a separate Cash account for the Division (into which the Target deposits all of the receipts of the Division and out of which the Target makes all of the disbursements of the Division).

(h) *Events Subsequent to Most Recent Fiscal Month End.* Since the Most Recent Fiscal Month End, there has not been any material adverse change in the financial condition of the Division and the Division Subsidiaries taken as a whole. Without limiting the generality of the foregoing, since that date none of the Target and its Subsidiaries has engaged in any practice, taken any action, or entered into any transaction outside the Ordinary Course of Business the primary purpose or effect of which has been to generate or preserve Cash.[30]

(i) *Legal Compliance.* To the Knowledge of any of the Target Stockholders, each of the Division and the Division Subsidiaries has complied with all applicable laws

---

[27] This *pro-seller* divisional asset purchase agreement does not contain a representation and warranty concerning undisclosed liabilities. *See* sample acquisition agreement 2004.1 (the *pro-buyer* divisional asset purchase agreement) for an example of such a provision.

[28] In the event the Target is unable to satisfy its retained liabilities and obligations after the Closing (i.e., the liabilities and obligations the Buyer did not assume), the Buyer may be exposed for certain of those liabilities and obligations by operation of law (e.g., under statutes and common law doctrines imposing successor liability). *See* ¶2001.2.2.2.

For this reason, the Buyer may seek additional representations and warranties about the *Target's* financial statements and undisclosed liabilities. *Compare* sample acquisition agreement 2003.2 (the *pro-seller* asset purchase agreement), which contains representations and warranties for use when the Buyer is acquiring *all* of the assets of a target corporation.

[29] Sample acquisition agreement 2004.1 (the *pro-buyer* divisional asset purchase agreement) contains additional representations and warranties to the effect that the financial statements are correct and complete and consistent with the books and records of the Division and the Division Subsidiaries.

[30] The requirement to disclose certain matters which have had an effect on the amount of cash relates to the fact that the Target will retain the consolidated cash of the Division and the Division Subsidiaries. See §2(d) above and the definition of Acquired Assets in §1 above.

This disclosure requirement is designed to uncover pre-Closing activities of the Division and the Division Subsidiaries which were outside the Ordinary Course of Business and either (a) intended to generate cash (such as borrowings, sales of assets, and collections of accounts receivable) or (b)

(including rules, regulations, codes, plans, injunctions, judgments, orders, decrees, rulings, and charges thereunder) of federal, state, local, and foreign governments (and all agencies thereof), except where the failure to comply would not have a material adverse effect upon the financial condition of the Division and the Division Subsidiaries taken as a whole.

(j) *Tax Matters.*[31]

(i) Each of the Division and the Division Subsidiaries[32] has filed all Income Tax Returns that it was required to file, and has paid all Income Taxes shown thereon as owing, except where the failure to file Income Tax Returns or to pay Income Taxes would not have a material adverse effect on the financial condition of the Division and the Division Subsidiaries taken as a whole.[33]

(ii) §3(j) of the Disclosure Schedule lists all Income Tax Returns filed with respect to any of the Division and the Division Subsidiaries for taxable periods ended on or after _____, 19_____, indicates those Income Tax Returns that have been audited, and indicates those Income Tax Returns that currently are the subject of audit. The Target has delivered to the Buyer correct and complete copies of all federal Income Tax Returns, examination reports, and statements of deficiencies assessed against or agreed to by any of the Division and the Division Subsidiaries since _____, 19_____.

---

intended to eliminate expenditures (such as failures to make loan repayments, purchase assets, pay accounts payable, perform maintenance and repairs, conduct research and development, and engage in advertising and promotion).

[31] This Agreement provides that the Buyer will not assume any liability of the *Target* (*including the Division*) for unpaid taxes through the Closing. See the definition of Assumed Liabilities in §1 above. This Agreement also provides that the Target will be responsible for the unpaid taxes of the *Division Subsidiaries* through the Closing. See the tax allocation provisions in §10(n) below.

The Buyer may, however, have (i) exposure for the tax liabilities of the Target (including the Division) by operation of law if the Target does not pay them (e.g., under applicable bulk sales statutes and common law doctrines of de facto merger and successor liability) and (ii) indirect exposure for the tax liabilities of the Division Subsidiaries not paid by the Target when the Buyer acquires their capital stock as part of the Acquired Assets. In order to eliminate the latter risk, the Buyer may seek (a) to purchase assets from the Target *and from each of the Division Subsidiaries* (i.e., a multiple entity asset sale) or (b) to have the Target liquidate and dissolve the Division Subsidiaries tax free under Code §332 (to the extent they are United States corporations) and sell their assets to the Buyer.

[32] This Agreement contains a considerably abbreviated version of the tax provisions found in sample acquisition agreement 2002.4 (sale of subsidiary out of consolidated group). The Parties may wish to incorporate some or all of the unabridged provisions from sample acquisition agreement 2002.4 into this Agreement.

[33] Sample acquisition agreement 2004.1 (the *pro-buyer* divisional asset purchase agreement) contains a broader representation to the effect that each of the Division and the Division Subsidiaries has filed all Tax Returns that it was required to file, that all such Tax Returns were correct and complete in all respects, and that all taxes owed by any of the Division and the Division Subsidiaries (whether or not shown on any Tax Return) have been paid.

(iii) None of the Division and the Division Subsidiaries has waived any statute of limitations in respect of Income Taxes or agreed to any extension of time with respect to an Income Tax assessment or deficiency.

(iv) None of the Division and the Division Subsidiaries is a party to any Income Tax allocation or sharing agreement.

(v) [To the Knowledge of any of the Target Stockholders, none of the Division Subsidiaries has been a member of an Affiliated Group filing a consolidated federal Income Tax Return (other than a group the common parent of which was the Target).][34]

(k) *Real Property.*

(i) §3(k)(i) of the Disclosure Schedule lists all real property that any of the Division and the Division Subsidiaries owns. With respect to each such parcel of owned real property, and except for matters which would not have a material adverse effect on the financial condition of the Division and the Division Subsidiaries taken as a whole:

(A) the identified owner has good and marketable title to the parcel of real property, free and clear of any Security Interest, easement, covenant, or other restriction, except for installments of special assessments not yet delinquent, recorded easements, covenants, and other restrictions, and utility easements, building restrictions, zoning restrictions, and other easements and restrictions existing generally with respect to properties of a similar character;

(B) there are no leases, subleases, licenses, concessions, or other agreements granting to any party or parties the right of use or occupancy of any portion of the parcel of real property; and

(C) there are no outstanding options or rights of first refusal to purchase the parcel of real property, or any portion thereof or interest therein.

---

[34] If a Division Subsidiary has been a member of an Affiliated Group filing a consolidated federal income tax return, such corporation (or its successor) will be jointly and severally liable under Reg. §1.1502-6 for certain tax liabilities incurred by such Affiliated Group for a tax year when such corporation was member of such Affiliated Group for all or part of such tax year. *See* ¶210.

A Division Subsidiary may also be liable for the unpaid taxes of third parties under similar provisions of state, local, or foreign law, as a transferee or successor, by contract (e.g., a tax sharing agreement), or otherwise.

The Buyer will become indirectly responsible for any such liability of the Division Subsidiaries when the Buyer acquires their capital stock as part of the Acquired Assets.

The Buyer may seek additional protection from the Target against any liability for the unpaid taxes of third parties. Sample acquisition agreement 2004.1 (the *pro-buyer* divisional asset purchase agreement), for example, contains a broader representation and warranty and specific post-Closing indemnification provisions in this regard. *See* §3(k)(v) and §8(b)(ii) of sample acquisition agreement 2004.1.

(ii) §3(k)(ii) of the Disclosure Schedule lists all real property leased or subleased to any of the Division and the Division Subsidiaries. The Target has delivered to the Buyer correct and complete copies of the leases and subleases listed in §3(k)(ii) of the Disclosure Schedule (as amended to date). To the Knowledge of any of the Target Stockholders, each lease and sublease listed in §3(k)(ii) of the Disclosure Schedule is legal, valid, binding, enforceable, and in full force and effect, except where the illegality, invalidity, nonbinding nature, unenforceability, or ineffectiveness would not have a material adverse effect on the financial condition of the Division and the Division Subsidiaries taken as a whole.

(l) *Intellectual Property.* §3(l) of the Disclosure Schedule identifies each patent or registration which has been issued to any of the Division and the Division Subsidiaries with respect to any of its intellectual property, identifies each pending patent application or application for registration which any of the Division and the Division Subsidiaries has made with respect to any of its intellectual property, [and identifies each license, agreement, or other permission which any of the Division and the Division Subsidiaries has granted to any third party with respect to any of its intellectual property].

(m) *Contracts.* §3(m) of the Disclosure Schedule lists all written contracts and other written agreements to which any of the Division and the Division Subsidiaries is a party the performance of which will involve consideration in excess of $_____. The Target has delivered to the Buyer a correct and complete copy of each contract or other agreement listed in §3(m) of the Disclosure Schedule (as amended to date).

(n) *Powers of Attorney.* To the Knowledge of any of the Target Stockholders, there are no outstanding powers of attorney executed on behalf of any of the Division and the Division Subsidiaries.

(o) *Litigation.* §3(o) of the Disclosure Schedule sets forth each instance in which any of the Division and the Division Subsidiaries (i) is subject to any outstanding injunction, judgment, order, decree, ruling, or charge or (ii) is a party to any action, suit, proceeding, hearing, or investigation of, in, or before any court or quasi-judicial or administrative agency of any federal, state, local, or foreign jurisdiction, except where the injunction, judgment, order, decree, ruling, action, suit, proceeding, hearing, or investigation would not have a material adverse effect on the financial condition of the Division and the Division Subsidiaries taken as a whole.

(p) *Employee Benefits.*

(i) §3(p) of the Disclosure Schedule lists each Employee Benefit Plan that any of the Division and the Division Subsidiaries maintains or to which any of the Division and the Division Subsidiaries contributes.

(A) To the Knowledge of any of the Target Stockholders, each such Employee Benefit Plan (and each related trust, insurance contract, or fund) has been maintained, funded and administered in accordance with the terms of such Employee Benefit Plan and complies in form and in operation in all respects with the applicable requirements of ERISA and the Code, except where the failure to comply would not have a material adverse effect on the financial condition of the Division and the Division Subsidiaries taken as a whole.

(B) All contributions (including all employer contributions and employee salary reduction contributions) which are due have been made to each such Employee Benefit Plan which is an Employee Pension Benefit Plan. All premiums or other payments which are due have been paid with respect to each such Employee Benefit Plan which is an Employee Welfare Benefit Plan.

(C) Each such Employee Benefit Plan which is intended to meet the requirements of a "qualified plan" under Code §401(a) has received a determination letter from the Internal Revenue Service to the effect that it meets the requirements of Code §401(a).

(D) As of the last day of the most recent prior plan year, the market value of assets under each such Employee Benefit Plan which is an Employee Pension Benefit Plan (other than any Multiemployer Plan) equaled or exceeded the present value of liabilities thereunder (determined in accordance with then current funding assumptions).

(E) The Target has delivered to the Buyer correct and complete copies of the plan documents and summary plan descriptions, the most recent determination letter received from the Internal Revenue Service, the most recent annual report (IRS Form 5500), and all related trust agreements, insurance contracts, and other funding arrangements which implement each such Employee Benefit Plan.

(ii) [With respect to each Employee Benefit Plan that any of the Division and the Division Subsidiaries or any ERISA Affiliate maintains or has maintained during the prior six years or to which any of them contributes, or has been required to contribute during the prior six years:

(A) No action, suit, proceeding, hearing, or investigation with respect to the administration or the investment of the assets of any such Employee Benefit Plan (other than routine claims for benefits) is pending, except where the action, suit, proceeding, hearing, or investigation would not have a material adverse effect on the financial condition of the Division and the Division Subsidiaries taken as a whole.

(B) None of the Division and the Division Subsidiaries has incurred any liability to the PBGC (other than PBGC premium payments) or otherwise under Title IV of ERISA (including any withdrawal liability) with respect to any such Employee Benefit Plan which is an Employee Pension Benefit Plan.][35]

(q) *Environmental, Health, and Safety Matters.*[36]

(i) To the Knowledge of any of the Target Stockholders, the Division and the Division Subsidiaries are in compliance with Environmental, Health, and Safety Requirements, except for such noncompliance as would not have a material adverse effect on the financial condition of the Division and the Division Subsidiaries taken as a whole.

(ii) To the Knowledge of any of the Target Stockholders, the Division and the Division Subsidiaries have not received any written notice, report or other information regarding any actual or alleged material violation of Environmental, Health, and Safety Requirements, or any material liabilities or potential material liabilities (whether accrued, absolute, contingent, unliquidated or otherwise), including any investigatory, remedial or corrective obligations, relating to the Division or the Division Subsidiaries or their facilities arising under Environmental, Health, and Safety Requirements, the subject of which would have a material adverse effect on the financial condition of the Division and the Division Subsidiaries taken as a whole.

(iii) This Section 3(q) contains the sole and exclusive representations and warranties of the Target with respect to any environmental, health, or safety matters, including without limitation any arising under any Environmental, Health, and Safety Requirements.

(r) *Certain Business Relationships with the Division and the Division Subsidiaries.* None of the Target Stockholders and their Affiliates has been involved in any mate-

---

[35] The Target may seek to delete or qualify some or all of this §3(p)(ii).

[36] These representations and warranties concerning environmental, health, and safety matters are relatively long and detailed. A condensed version may be more appropriate when, for example, the operations of the Division and the Division Subsidiaries appear to have had a relatively insignificant effect upon the environment or upon public or employee health and safety.

The environmental representations in this *pro-seller* divisional purchase agreement (1) are limited to matters within the Target Stockholder's knowledge, (2) are consistently limited to matters that would have a material adverse effect, (3) do not extend to strict liability for site cleanup under CERCLA or common law liability, (4) otherwise limit the disclosure and indemnification obligations of the Target, and (5) state that these environmental representations constitute the sole representation of the Target with respect to environmental, health, and safety matters.

Sample acquisition agreement 2004.1 (the *pro-buyer* divisional purchase agreement) contain broader environmental, health, and safety representations, which (1) contain neither knowledge nor materiality limitations, (2) impose a broader disclosure obligation upon the Target, and (3) extend to strict liability for site cleanup under CERCLA and common law liability under current and future Environmental, Health, and Safety Requirements.

Sample acquisition agreement 2004.3 (the *neutral* divisional purchase agreement) contains environmental representations which are (1) subject to certain materiality limitations and (2) are slightly more limited and focused than the corresponding *pro-buyer* representations.

rial business arrangement or relationship with any of the Division and the Division Subsidiaries within the past 12 months, and none of the Target Stockholders and their Affiliates owns any material asset, tangible or intangible, which is used in the business of any of the Division and the Division Subsidiaries.

(s) *Investment.* The Target (i) understands that the Buyer Note has not been, and will not be, registered under the Securities Act, or under any state securities laws, and is being offered and sold in reliance upon federal and state exemptions for transactions not involving any public offering, (ii) is acquiring the Buyer Note solely for its own account for investment purposes, and not with a view to the distribution thereof, (iii) is a sophisticated investor with knowledge and experience in business and financial matters, (iv) has received certain information concerning the Buyer and has had the opportunity to obtain additional information as desired in order to evaluate the merits and the risks inherent in holding the Buyer Note, (v) is able to bear the economic risk and lack of liquidity inherent in holding the Buyer Note, and (vi) is an Accredited Investor for the reasons set forth in §3(r) of the Disclosure Schedule.[37]

(t) *Disclaimer of Other Representations and Warranties.* Except as expressly set forth in this Section 3, the Target makes no representation or warranty, express or implied, at law or in equity, in respect of any of its assets (including, without limitation, the Acquired Assets), liabilities or operations, including, without limitation, with respect to merchantability or fitness for any particular purpose, and any such other representations or warranties are hereby expressly disclaimed. Buyer hereby acknowledges and agrees that, except to the extent specifically set forth in this Section 3, the Buyer is purchasing the Acquired Assets on an "as-is, where-is" basis. Without limiting the generality of the foregoing, the Target makes no representation or warranty regarding any assets other than the Acquired Assets or any liabilities other than the Assumed Liabilities, and none shall be implied at law or in equity.[38]

4. *Representations and Warranties of the Buyer.*[39] The Buyer represents and warrants to the Target that the statements contained in this §4 are correct and complete as of the date of this Agreement and will be correct and complete as of the Closing Date (as though made then and as though the Closing Date were substituted for the date

---

[37] This provision contemplates that the Buyer will issue the Buyer Note pursuant to the exemption from registration under the Securities Act contained in Regulation D. The Parties should determine whether this exemption is available in a particular transaction. If it is not, the Agreement must be modified as necessary to reflect the issuance of the Buyer Note under a different exemption from securities registration or in an offering registered under the Securities Act.

[38] Consideration should be given to highlighting this subsection by printing it in all capital letters, particularly in jurisdictions where statutory or common law rights (e.g., implied representations and warranties) are being waived.

[39] The Target may seek to obtain additional representations and warranties concerning the Buyer and its Subsidiaries (e.g., the typical representations and warranties contained in a loan agreement or an underwriting agreement) because the Buyer is issuing the Buyer Note to the Target as part of the Purchase Price. Any such representations and warranties would normally survive the Closing and remain applicable for so long as the Buyer Note remained outstanding.

of this Agreement throughout this §4), except as set forth in the Disclosure Schedule. The Disclosure Schedule will be arranged in paragraphs corresponding to the lettered and numbered paragraphs contained in this §4.

(a) *Organization of the Buyer.* The Buyer is a corporation duly organized, validly existing, and in good standing under the laws of the jurisdiction of its incorporation.

(b) *Authorization of Transaction.* The Buyer has full power and authority (including full corporate power and authority) to execute and deliver this Agreement and to perform its obligations hereunder. This Agreement constitutes the valid and legally binding obligation of the Buyer, enforceable in accordance with its terms and conditions.

(c) *Noncontravention.* Neither the execution and the delivery of this Agreement, nor the consummation of the transactions contemplated hereby (including the assignments and assumptions referred to in §2 above), will [(i)] violate any constitution, statute, regulation, rule, injunction, judgment, order, decree, ruling, charge, or other restriction of any government, governmental agency, or court to which the Buyer is subject or any provision of its charter or bylaws [or (ii) conflict with, result in a breach of, constitute a default under, result in the acceleration of, create in any party the right to accelerate, terminate, modify, or cancel, or require any notice under any agreement, contract, lease, license, instrument, or other arrangement to which the Buyer is a party or by which it is bound or to which any of its assets is subject]. The Buyer does not need to give any notice to, make any filing with, or obtain any authorization, consent, or approval of any government or governmental agency in order for the Parties to consummate the transactions contemplated by this Agreement (including the assignments and assumptions referred to in §2 above).

(d) *Brokers' Fees.* The Buyer has no liability or obligation to pay any fees or commissions to any broker, finder, or agent with respect to the transactions contemplated by this Agreement for which the Target could become liable or obligated.

5. *Pre-Closing Covenants.*[40] The Parties agree as follows with respect to the period between the execution of this Agreement and the Closing.

(a) *General.* Each of the Parties will use its reasonable best efforts to take all action and to do all things necessary[, proper, or advisable] in order to consummate and make effective the transactions contemplated by this Agreement (including satisfaction, but not waiver, of the closing conditions set forth in §7 below).

(b) *Notices and Consents.* [The Target will give (and will cause each of the Division Subsidiaries to give) any notices to third parties, and the Target will use its reasonable best efforts (and will cause each of the Division Subsidiaries to use its reasonable

---

[40] Sample acquisition agreement 2004.1 (the *pro-buyer* divisional asset purchase agreement) contains additional pre-Closing covenants concerning preservation of the business and obtaining title insurance and surveys in preparation for the Closing.

best efforts) to obtain any third party consents, that the Buyer reasonably may request in connection with the matters referred to in §3(c) above.] Each of the Parties will (and the Target will cause each of the Division Subsidiaries to) give any notices to, make any filings with, and use its reasonable best efforts to obtain any authorizations, consents, and approvals of governments and governmental agencies in connection with the matters referred to in §3(c) and §4(c) above. Without limiting the generality of the foregoing, each of the Parties will file (and the Target will cause each of the Division Subsidiaries to file) any Notification and Report Forms and related material that it may be required to file with the Federal Trade Commission and the Antitrust Division of the United States Department of Justice under the Hart-Scott-Rodino Act, will use its reasonable best efforts to obtain (and the Target will cause each of the Division Subsidiaries to use its reasonable best efforts to obtain) a waiver from the applicable waiting period, and will make (and the Target will cause each of the Division Subsidiaries to make) any further filings pursuant thereto that may be necessary[, proper, or advisable] in connection therewith.

(c) *Operation of Business.* [The Target will not cause or permit any of the Division and the Division Subsidiaries to engage in any practice, take any action, or enter into any transaction outside the Ordinary Course of Business.[41] Without limiting the generality of the foregoing,] the Target will not cause or permit any of the Division and the Division Subsidiaries to engage in any practice, take any action, or enter into any transaction outside the Ordinary Course of Business the primary purpose or effect of which will be to generate or preserve Cash.[42]

(d) *Full Access.* [The Target will permit (and will cause each of the Division and the Division Subsidiaries to permit) representatives of the Buyer to have full access at all reasonable times, and in a manner so as not to interfere with the normal business operations of the Division and the Division Subsidiaries, to all premises, properties, personnel, books, records (including tax records), contracts, and documents of or pertaining to each of the Division and the Division Subsidiaries. The Buyer will treat and hold as such any Confidential Information it receives from any of the Target Stockholders, the Target, and its Subsidiaries in the course of the reviews contemplated by this §5(d), will not use any of the Confidential Information except in connection with this Agreement, and, if this Agreement is terminated for any reason whatsoever, will return to the Target all tangible embodiments (and all copies) of the Confidential Information which are in its possession.]

---

[41] The Buyer may seek to have this covenant restrict a number of specific practices, actions, and transactions. Sample acquisition agreement 2004.1 (the *pro-buyer* divisional asset purchase agreement) contains provisions which are more favorable to the Buyer in this regard.

[42] This covenant relates to the fact that the Target will retain the consolidated cash of the Division and the Division Subsidiaries. *See* §2(d) above and the definition of Acquired Assets in §1 above. The covenant is designed to prevent pre-Closing activities of the Division and the Division Subsidiaries which would be outside the Ordinary Course of Business and either (a) intended to generate cash (such as borrowing, sale of assets, and collections of accounts receivable) or (b) intended to eliminate expenditures (such as failures to make loan repayments, purchase assets, pay accounts payable, perform maintenance and repairs, conduct research and development, and engage in advertising and promotion).

(e) *Notice of Developments.*

(i) The Target may elect at any time to notify the Buyer of any development causing a breach of any of its representations and warranties in §3(g)-(p) above. Unless the Buyer has the right to terminate this Agreement pursuant to §9(a)(ii) below by reason of the development and exercises that right within the period of [10 business days] referred to in §9(a)(ii) below, the written notice pursuant to this §5(e)(i) will be deemed to have amended the Disclosure Schedule, to have qualified the representations and warranties contained in §3 above, and to have cured any misrepresentation or breach of warranty that otherwise might have existed hereunder by reason of the development.[43]

(ii) Each Party will give prompt written notice to the other Party of any material adverse development causing a breach of any of its own representations and warranties in §3(a)-(f) and §4 above. No disclosure by any Party pursuant to this §5(e)(ii), however, shall be deemed to amend or supplement the Disclosure Schedule or to prevent or cure any misrepresentation or breach of warranty.[44]

(f) *Exclusivity.* The Target will not (and will not cause or permit any of the Division and the Division Subsidiaries to) solicit, initiate, or encourage the submission of any proposal or offer from any Person relating to the acquisition of all or substantially all of the capital stock or assets of any of the Division and the Division Subsidiaries (including any acquisition structured as a merger, consolidation, or share exchange); *provided, however,* that the Target, its Subsidiaries, and their directors and officers will remain free to participate in any discussions or negotiations regarding, furnish any information with respect to, assist or participate in, or facilitate in any other manner any effort or attempt by any Person to do or seek any of the foregoing to the extent their fiduciary duties may require.[45]

6. *Post-Closing Covenants.*[46] The Parties agree as follows with respect to the period following the Closing.

---

[43] This §5(e)(i) permits the Target to notify the Buyer of any development prior to the Closing that causes a breach of the representations and warranties in §3(g)-(p) above concerning the Division and the Division Subsidiaries. If the development gives the Buyer any right to terminate this Agreement pursuant to §9(a)(ii) below, the Buyer must exercise its termination right within [10 business days] after the notice. Unless the Buyer has such a termination right and exercises it within that period, the notice will be deemed to have cured any such breach of the representations and warranties that otherwise would have existed.

[44] Sample acquisition agreement 2004.1 (the *pro-buyer* divisional asset purchase agreement) provides that *no* disclosure (presumably, but not necessarily, by the Target) between signing and Closing will supplement the previous disclosures or cure any misrepresentation or breach of warranty.

[45] Sample acquisition agreement 2004.1 (the *pro-buyer* divisional asset purchase agreement) lacks a comparable proviso permitting these persons to respond to unsolicited proposals to the extent their fiduciary duties may require.

[46] Sample acquisition agreement 2004.1 (the *pro-buyer* divisional asset purchase agreement) contains an additional covenant requiring the Target to keep certain information regarding the Division and the Division Subsidiaries confidential after the Closing.

The Target may seek to obtain additional covenants from the Buyer and its Subsidiaries (e.g., the typical covenants contained in a loan agreement or an indenture) because the Buyer is issuing the

(a) *General.* In case at any time after the Closing any further action is necessary [or desirable] to carry out the purposes of this Agreement, each of the Parties will take such further action (including the execution and delivery of such further instruments and documents) as the other Party [reasonably] may request, all the sole cost and expense of the requesting Party (unless the requesting Party is entitled to indemnification therefor under §8 below).[47]

(b) *Litigation Support.* In the event and for so long as any Party actively is contesting or defending against any action, suit, proceeding, hearing, investigation, charge, complaint, claim, or demand in connection with (i) any transaction contemplated under this Agreement or (ii) any fact, situation, circumstance, status, condition, activity, practice, plan, occurrence, event, incident, action, failure to act, or transaction on or prior to the Closing Date involving any of the Division and the Division Subsidiaries, the other Party will cooperate with the contesting or defending Party and its counsel in the contest or defense, make available its personnel, and provide such testimony and access to its books and records as shall be necessary in connection with the contest or defense, all at the sole cost and expense of the contesting or defending Party (unless the contesting or defending Party is entitled to indemnification therefor under §8 below).[48]

(c) *Transition.* [The Target will not take any action that is designed or intended to have the effect of discouraging any lessor, licensor, customer, supplier, or other business associate of any of the Division and the Division Subsidiaries from maintaining the same business relationships with the Buyer and the Division Subsidiaries after the Closing as it maintained with the Division and the Division Subsidiaries prior to the Closing.]

(d) *Covenant Not to Compete.*[49] [For a period of one year from and after the Closing Date, the Target will not engage directly or indirectly in any business that any of the Division and the Division Subsidiaries conducts as of the Closing Date in any geographic area in which any of the Division and the Division Subsidiaries conducts that business as of the Closing Date; *provided, however,* that no owner of less than 5% of the outstanding stock of any publicly traded corporation shall be deemed to

---

Buyer Note to the Target as part of the Purchase Price. Any such covenants would remain applicable so long as the Buyer Note remained outstanding.

[47] The Parties may prefer to allocate responsibility for these particular costs and expenses in some other manner (e.g., the Party incurring the costs and expenses might be responsible for their payment, the Parties might share the costs and expenses in a predetermined ratio, or one Party might be responsible for the costs and expenses up to a specified aggregate ceiling and the other Party responsible for any excess).

Compare §10(k) below (which allocates responsibility between the Buyer and the Target for their costs and expenses through the Closing).

[48] The Parties may prefer to allocate responsibility for these particular costs and expenses in some other manner as discussed in the preceding footnote.

[49] Note that unless this Agreement allocates a specified amount of consideration to the covenant not to compete, applicable tax cases will preclude the Buyer from seeking to allocate a portion of the Purchase Price to the covenant and amortizing such amount over the covenant's life.

engage solely by reason thereof in any of its businesses. If the final judgment of a court of competent jurisdiction declares that any term or provision of this §6(d) is invalid or unenforceable, the Parties agree that the court making the determination of invalidity or unenforceability shall have the power to reduce the scope, duration, or area of the term or provision, to delete specific words or phrases, or to replace any invalid or unenforceable term or provision with a term or provision that is valid and enforceable and that comes closest to expressing the intention of the invalid or unenforceable term or provision, and this Agreement shall be enforceable as so modified after the expiration of the time within which the judgment may be appealed.]

(e) *Buyer Note.* The Buyer Note will be imprinted with a legend substantially in the following form:

This Note was originally issued on _____, 19_____, and has not been registered under the Securities Act of 1933, as amended.

7. *Conditions to Obligation to Close.*

(a) *Conditions to Obligation of the Buyer.*[50] The obligation of the Buyer to consummate the transactions to be performed by it in connection with the Closing is subject to satisfaction of the following conditions:

(i) the representations and warranties set forth in §3 above shall be true and correct in all material respects at and as of the Closing Date;[51]

(ii) the Target shall have performed and complied with all of its covenants hereunder in all material respects through the Closing;

[50] Sample acquisition agreement 2004.1 (the *pro-buyer* divisional asset purchase agreement) contains additional closing conditions for the benefit of the Buyer concerning third party consents, title insurance, surveys, director and officer resignations, and the receipt of financing for the transaction.

[51] Note that this provision will not give the Buyer any closing condition with respect to any adverse matter which the Target may disclose in the Disclosure Schedule. This is because the disclosure will cure any misrepresentation or breach of warranty that might otherwise have existed. Thus, where the Target discloses an adverse matter in the Disclosure Schedule, the Buyer may seek to add a specific closing condition requiring an acceptable resolution of the matter.

Section 5(e)(i) above permits the Target to notify the Buyer of any development prior to the Closing that causes a breach of its representations and warranties in §3(g)-(p) above concerning the Division and the Division Subsidiaries. If the development gives the Buyer any right to terminate this Agreement pursuant to §9(a)(ii) below, the Buyer must exercise its termination right within [10 business days] after the notice. Unless the Buyer has such a termination right and exercises it within that period, the notice will be deemed to have cured any such breach of the representations and warranties that otherwise would have existed.

(iii) there shall not be any injunction, judgment, order, decree, ruling, or charge in effect preventing consummation of any of the transactions contemplated by this Agreement;[52]

(iv) the Target shall have delivered to the Buyer a certificate to the effect that each of the conditions specified above in §7(a)(i)-(iii) is satisfied in all respects;

(v) [all applicable waiting periods (and any extensions thereof) under the Hart-Scott-Rodino Act shall have expired or otherwise been terminated and the Target, the Division Subsidiaries, and the Buyer shall have received all other authorizations, consents, and approvals of governments and governmental agencies referred to in §3(c) and §4(c) above];

(vi) the relevant parties shall have entered into side agreements in form and substance as set forth in Exhibits through F-_____ attached hereto and the same shall be in full force and effect;[53]

(vii) the Buyer shall have received from counsel to the Target an opinion in form and substance as set forth in Exhibit G attached hereto, addressed to the Buyer, and dated as of the Closing Date; and

(viii) all actions to be taken by the Target in connection with consummation of the transactions contemplated hereby and all certificates, opinions, instruments, and other documents required to effect the transactions contemplated hereby will be [reasonably] satisfactory in form and substance to the Buyer.

The Buyer may waive any condition specified in this §7(a) if it executes a writing so stating at or prior to the Closing.

(b) *Conditions to Obligation of the Target.* The obligation of the Target to consummate the transactions to be performed by it in connection with the Closing is subject to satisfaction of the following conditions:

(i) the representations and warranties set forth in §4 above shall be true and correct in all material respects at and as of the Closing Date;

(ii) the Buyer shall have performed and complied with all of its covenants hereunder in all material respects through the Closing;

---

[52] Sample acquisition agreement 2004.1 (the *pro-buyer* divisional asset purchase agreement) contains a broader closing condition requiring also that there not be any pending [or threatened] litigation.

[53] Where the Target is acquiring a division of Bigco, the Buyer may require significant transition assistance. This might be the case where Bigco performs substantial services for its divisions and/or where Bigco owns various tangible and intangible assets used by its divisions. For example, the Buyer may require real estate leases, intellectual property licenses, and accounting, purchasing, payroll, risk management, and data processing services from Bigco.

(iii) there shall not be any injunction, judgment, order, decree, ruling, or charge in effect preventing consummation of any of the transactions contemplated by this Agreement;[54]

(iv) the Buyer shall have delivered to the Target a certificate to the effect that each of the conditions specified above in §7(b)(i)-(iii) is satisfied in all respects;

(v) [all applicable waiting periods (and any extensions thereof) under the Hart-Scott-Rodino Act shall have expired or otherwise been terminated and the Target, the Division Subsidiaries, and the Buyer shall have received all other authorizations, consents, and approvals of governments and governmental agencies referred to in §3(c) and §4(c) above];

(vi) the relevant parties shall have entered into side agreements in form and substance as set forth in Exhibits F-_____, F-_____, . . . and F-_____ and the same shall be in full force and effect;

(vii) the Target shall have received from counsel to the Buyer an opinion in form and substance as set forth in Exhibit H attached hereto, addressed to the Target, and dated as of the Closing Date; and

(viii) all actions to be taken by the Buyer in connection with consummation of the transactions contemplated hereby and all certificates, opinions, instruments, and other documents required to effect the transactions contemplated hereby will be [reasonably] satisfactory in form and substance to the Target.

The Target may waive any condition specified in this §7(b) if it executes a writing so stating at or prior to the Closing.

8. *Remedies for Breaches of This Agreement.*[55]

(a) *Survival of Representations and Warranties.*[56]

---

[54] Because this Target's closing condition conforms to the comparable Buyer's closing condition in §7(a)(iii) above, it leaves the Target with a relatively narrow "out." Thus, the Target may prefer to broaden the respective closing conditions. Compare the broader closing conditions in sample acquisition agreement 2004.1 (the *pro-buyer* divisional asset purchase agreement).

[55] The Buyer may seek some form of additional security covering the obligation of the Target to indemnify the Buyer after the Closing. This may include provisions calling for (a) the Buyer to have a recoupment remedy with respect to the Buyer Note, (b) the Target to deposit a portion of the Purchase Price with a third party escrow agent, (c) the Buyer to hold back a portion of the Purchase Price (to be paid later with interest), or (d) the Buyer to obtain a security interest in certain assets of the Target Stockholders. Sample acquisition agreement 2004.1 (the *pro-buyer* divisional asset purchase agreement), for example, contains recoupment provisions applicable to the Buyer Note.

[56] This *pro-seller* Agreement contains alternative provisions for (a) *minimal indemnification* to the Buyer for breaches of the Target's representations and warranties (i.e., only the representations and warranties concerning the transaction itself survive the Closing) and (b) *limited indemnification* to the Buyer for breaches of the Target's representations and warranties (i.e., the representations and warranties with respect to the transaction itself survive indefinitely, the other representations and warranties

ALTERNATIVE A (MINIMAL INDEMNIFICATION): None of the representations and warranties of the Target contained in §3(g)-(r) of this Agreement shall survive the Closing. All of the other representations and warranties of the Buyer and the Target contained in this Agreement (including the representations and warranties of the Target contained in §3(a)-(f) hereof) shall survive the Closing (unless the damaged Party knew or had reason to know of any misrepresentation or breach of warranty or covenant at the time of Closing) and continue in full force and effect forever thereafter (subject to any applicable statutes of limitations).

ALTERNATIVE B (LIMITED INDEMNIFICATION): All of the representations and warranties of the Target contained in §3(g)-(r) of this Agreement shall survive the Closing (unless the Buyer knew or had reason to know of any misrepresentation or breach of warranty at the time of Closing) and continue in full force and effect for a period of [one year] thereafter. All of the other representations and warranties of the Buyer and the Target contained in this Agreement (including the representations and warranties of the Target contained in §3(a)-(f) hereof) shall survive the Closing (unless the damaged Party knew or had reason to know of any misrepresentation or breach of warranty at the time of Closing) and continue in full force and effect forever thereafter (subject to any applicable statutes of limitations).

(b) *Indemnification Provisions for Benefit of the Buyer.*[57]

---

survive only for [one year], and there is a deductible and a ceiling with respect to indemnification against breaches of the latter).

Sample acquisition agreement 2004.1 (the *pro-buyer* divisional asset purchase agreement) on the other hand, contains alternative provisions for (a) *full indemnification* to the Buyer for breaches of the Target's representations and warranties (i.e., all representations and warranties survive indefinitely and there is no deductible, threshold, or ceiling with respect to indemnification against breaches thereof) and (b) *limited indemnification* to the Buyer for breaches of the Target's representations and warranties (i.e., the representations and warranties with respect to the transaction itself and with respect to taxes survive indefinitely, the other representations and warranties survive only for [three years], and there is a threshold, but not a deductible or ceiling, with respect to indemnification against breaches of the latter).

This *pro-seller* Agreement provides that the representations and warranties of the Parties will survive the Closing (*unless* the damaged Party knew or had reason to know of the misrepresentation or breach of warranty at the time of Closing).

Sample acquisition agreement 2004.1 (the *pro-buyer* divisional asset purchase agreement), on the other hand, provides that the representations and warranties will survive the Closing (*even if* the damaged Party knew or had reason to know of the misrepresentation or breach of warranty at the time of Closing).

[57] The Buyer will become indirectly responsible for all of the liabilities of the *Division Subsidiaries* if the Buyer acquires their capital stock as part of the Acquired Assets. For this reason, the Buyer may seek (a) to purchase assets from the Target *and from each of the Division Subsidiaries* (i.e., a multiple entity asset sale) or (b) to have the Target liquidate and dissolve the Division Subsidiaries tax free under Code §332 (to the extent they are United States corporations) and sell their assets to the Buyer.

In addition, this Agreement provides that the Buyer will assume substantially all of the liabilities of the *Division* (whether known or unknown, whether asserted or unasserted, whether absolute or contingent, whether accrued or unaccrued, whether liquidated or unliquidated, and whether due or to become due). See the definition of Assumed Liabilities in §1 above.

Finally, the Buyer may be exposed for certain liabilities of the *Division* by operation of law if the Target does not pay them (e.g., under applicable bulk sales statutes and common law doctrines of de facto merger and successor liability). *See* ¶2001.2.2.2.

(i) In the event the Target breaches any of its representations, warranties, and covenants contained in this Agreement,[58] and, if there is an applicable survival period pursuant to §8(a) above, provided that the Buyer makes a written claim for indemnification against the Target pursuant to §10(g) below within such survival period, then the Target agrees to indemnify the Buyer from and against the entirety of any Adverse Consequences the Buyer shall suffer through and after the date of the claim for indemnification (but *excluding* any Adverse Consequences the Buyer shall suffer after the end of any applicable survival period) caused [proximately] by the breach;[59] *provided, however*, that the Target shall not have any obligation to indemnify the Buyer from and against any Adverse Consequences caused by the breach of any representation or warranty of the Target contained in §3(g)-(p) above [ALTERNATIVE B (LIMITED INDEMNIFICATION]: (A) until the Buyer has suffered Adverse Consequences by reason of all such breaches in excess of a $_____ aggregate deductible (after which point the Target will be obligated only to indemnify the Buyer from and against further such Adverse Consequences)[60] or thereafter (B) to the extent the Adverse Consequences the Buyer has suffered by reason of all such breaches exceeds a $_____ aggregate ceiling (after which point the Target will have no obligation to indemnify the Buyer from and against further such Adverse Consequences)].[61]

(ii) The Target agrees to indemnify the Buyer from and against the entirety of any Adverse Consequences the Buyer shall suffer caused [proximately] by any liability of the Target which is not an Assumed Liability (including any liability

---

These post-Closing indemnification provisions are designed to work in conjunction with the definition of Assumed Liabilities in §1 above and the representations and warranties in §3 above to protect the Buyer against liabilities it does not intend to assume.

[58] Section 5(e)(i) above permits the Target to notify the Buyer of any development prior to the Closing that causes a breach of the representations and warranties in §3(g)-(p) above concerning the Division and the Division Subsidiaries. If the development gives the Buyer any right to terminate this Agreement pursuant to §9(a)(ii) below, the Buyer must exercise its termination right within [10 business days] after the notice. Unless the Buyer has such a termination right and exercises it within that period, the notice will be deemed to have cured any such breach of the representations and warranties that otherwise would have existed.

[59] This *pro-seller* Agreement requires an indemnifying party (presumably, but not necessarily, the Target) to indemnify an Indemnified party (presumably, but not necessarily, the Buyer) from and against any Adverse Consequences the indemnified party *shall* suffer through and after the date of the claim for indemnification (but *excluding* any Adverse Consequences the indemnified party shall suffer after the end of any applicable survival period) *caused [proximately] by* certain breaches by the indemnifying party of its representations, warranties, and covenants.

The *pro-buyer* Agreement (sample acquisition agreement 2004.1), on the other hand, requires an indemnifying party to indemnify an Indemnified party from and against any Adverse Consequences the indemnified party *may* suffer through and after the date of the claim for indemnification (*including* any Adverse Consequences the indemnified party may suffer after the end of any applicable survival period) *resulting from, arising out of, relating to, in the nature of, or caused by* certain breaches by the indemnifying party of its representations, warranties, and covenants.

[60] The Target may also seek to impose a *per claim* deductible.

[61] The Buyer may seek to substitute a threshold (with relation back to the first dollar once the threshold is exceeded) for the deductible in this proviso and also seek to eliminate the ceiling on indemnification. *Compare* the *pro-buyer* Agreement (sample acquisition agreement 2004.1).

of the Target that becomes a liability of the Buyer under any bulk transfer law of any jurisdiction, under any common law doctrine of de facto merger or successor liability, or otherwise by operation of law).[62]

(c) *Indemnification Provisions for Benefit of the Target.*

(i) In the event the Buyer breaches any of its representations, warranties, and covenants contained in this Agreement, and, if there is an applicable survival period pursuant to §8(a) above, provided that the Target makes a written claim for indemnification against the Buyer pursuant to §10(g) below within such survival period, then the Buyer agrees to indemnify the Target from and against the entirety of any Adverse Consequences the Target shall suffer through and after the date of the claim for indemnification (but *excluding* any Adverse Consequences the Target shall suffer after the end of any applicable survival period) caused [proximately] by the breach.

(ii) The Buyer agrees to indemnify the Target from and against the entirety of any Adverse Consequences the Target shall suffer caused [proximately] by any liability of the Target which is an Assumed Liability.

(d) *Matters Involving Third Parties.*[63]

(i) If any third party shall notify any Party (the *"Indemnified Party"*) with respect to any matter (a *"Third Party Claim"*) which may give rise to a claim for indemnification against the other Party (the *"Indemnifying Party"*) under this §8, then the Indemnified Party shall promptly (and in any event within [five business days]

---

[62] The Buyer may be exposed for certain liabilities of the Division by operation of law if the Target does not pay them (e.g., under applicable bulk sales statutes and common law doctrines of de facto merger and successor liability). *See* ¶2001.2.2.2. This post-Closing indemnification provision is designed to protect the Buyer against liabilities of the Target which the Buyer does not intend to assume.

[63] An *indemnifying* party (presumably, but not necessarily, the Target) will normally seek to control the defense of any third party claim that may give rise to a claim for indemnification under this §8. However, the *indemnified* party (presumably, but not necessarily, the Buyer) will not want the indemnifying party to control the defense of any third party claim in which the indemnified party will retain a meaningful interest. For example, the indemnified party may seek to control the defense of a third party claim if the third party seeks an injunction or other equitable relief or if it is not clear that the indemnifying party will bear the entirety of any money damages or amount paid in settlement.

This *pro-seller* Agreement provides that the indemnifying party may assume the defense of a third party claim at *any time* during the course of the defense, and prevents the indemnified party from consenting to the entry of any judgment or entering into any settlement with respect to the matter without the consent of the indemnifying party [(not to be unreasonably withheld)].

The *pro-buyer* Agreement (sample acquisition agreement 2004.1), on the other hand, provides that the indemnified party will control the defense of any third party claim *unless* (a) the indemnifying party accepts full responsibility for the matter within [15 days], (b) the indemnifying party demonstrates it has the financial resources necessary to defend against the matter and fulfill its indemnification obligations, (c) the third party seeks only money damages (as opposed to an injunction or other equitable relief), (d) settlement of, or an adverse judgment with respect to, the third party claim is not likely to establish a precedent [materially] adverse to the indemnified party, and (e) the indemnifying party conducts the defense actively and diligently.

after receiving notice of the Third Party Claim) notify the Indemnifying Party thereof in writing.

(ii) The Indemnifying Party will have the right at any time to assume and thereafter conduct the defense of the Third Party Claim with counsel of its choice [reasonably satisfactory to the Indemnified Party; *provided, however*, that the Indemnifying Party will not consent to the entry of any judgment or enter into any settlement with respect to the Third Party Claim without the prior written consent of the Indemnified Party (not to be withheld unreasonably) unless the judgment or proposed settlement involves only the payment of money damages and does not impose an injunction or other equitable relief upon the Indemnified Party].

(iii) Unless and until the Indemnifying Party assumes the defense of the Third Party Claim as provided in §8(d)(ii) above, however, the Indemnified Party may defend against the Third Party Claim in any manner it reasonably may deem appropriate.

(iv) In no event will the Indemnified Party consent to the entry of any judgment or enter into any settlement with respect to the Third Party Claim without the prior written consent of the Indemnifying Party [(not to be withheld unreasonably)].

(e) *Determination of Adverse Consequences.* The Parties shall make appropriate adjustments for tax benefits and insurance coverage [and take into account the time cost of money (using the Applicable Rate as the discount rate)] in determining Adverse Consequences for purposes of this §8. All indemnification payments under this §8 shall be deemed adjustments to the Purchase Price.

(f) *Exclusive Remedy.* The Buyer and the Target acknowledge and agree that the foregoing indemnification provisions in this §4 shall be the exclusive remedy of the Buyer and the Target with respect to the Division, the Division Subsidiaries, and the transactions contemplated by this Agreement. [ALTERNATIVE A (MINIMAL INDEMNIFICATION): Without limiting the generality of the foregoing, the Buyer acknowledges and agrees that it shall not have any remedy after the Closing for any breach of the representations and warranties in §3(g)-(q) above.] [*ALTERNATIVE B (LIMITED INDEMNIFICATION): OMIT ALTERNATIVE A LANGUAGE ABOVE.*][64]

---

[64] Sample acquisition agreement 2004.1 (the *pro-buyer* divisional purchase agreement) states that the indemnification provisions in the Agreement are in addition to and not in derogation of any other statutory, equitable, or common law remedies (including any such remedies relating to environmental matters).

Sample acquisition agreement 2004.3 (the *neutral* divisional purchase agreement) states, as does (f) above, that the remedies available to the parties under the Agreement are exclusive (i.e., that the Buyer has no other statutory, equitable, or common law remedies) and also sets forth a waiver of extra-contractual environmental remedies, but does not contain an environmental indemnification of the Target by the Buyer of the sort set forth in §8(g) of this *pro-seller* divisional purchase agreement.

Although not so stated in this *pro-seller* divisional purchase agreement, the Target could seek to have its own statutory, equitable, and common law remedies survive while the Buyer's analogous rights are explicitly negated, although this would be unusual.

(g) *Environmental Remedies.*[65]

[ALTERNATIVE A (MINIMAL INDEMNIFICATION): Without limiting the generality of (f), above, the Buyer hereby waives any right, whether arising at law or in equity, to seek contribution, cost recovery, damages, or any other recourse or remedy from the Target, and hereby releases the Target, from any claim, demand or liability, with respect to any environmental, health, or safety matter relating to the past, current or future facilities, properties or operations of the Division, the Division Subsidiaries, and all of their respective predecessors or Affiliates, including without limitation any such matter arising under any Environmental, Health, and Safety Requirements and including, without limitation, any arising under the Comprehensive Environmental Response, Compensation, and Liability Act ("CERCLA"), any analogous state law, or the common law. The Buyer hereby unconditionally agrees to indemnify, defend, and hold harmless the Target from any and all liability, loss, cost or expense with respect to any such environmental, health, or safety matter (including any arising under any Environmental, Health, and Safety Requirements and including, without limitation, CERCLA, any analogous state law, or the common law).]

[ALTERNATIVE B (LIMITED INDEMNIFICATION): Without limiting the generality of (f), above, the Buyer understands and agrees that its right to indemnification under §8(b) for breach of the representations and warranties contained in §3(q) shall constitute its sole and exclusive remedy against the Target with respect to any environmental, health, or safety matter relating to the past, current or future facilities, properties or operations of the Division, the Division Subsidiaries, and all of their respective predecessors or Affiliates, including without limitation any such matter arising under any Environmental, Health, and Safety Requirements. Aside from such right to indemnification, the Buyer hereby waives any right, whether arising at law or in equity, to seek contribution, cost recovery, damages, or any other recourse or remedy from the Target, and hereby releases the Target from any claim, demand or liability, with respect to any such environmental, health, or safety matter (including without limitation any arising under any Environmental, Health, and Safety Requirements and including without limitation any arising under the Comprehensive Environmental Response, Compensation, and Liability Act ("CERCLA"), any analogous state law, or the common law. Except as set forth above, the Buyer hereby unconditionally agrees to indemnify, defend, and hold harmless the Target from any and all liability, loss, cost or expense with respect to any such environmental, health, or safety matter (including without limitation any arising under any Environmental, Health, and Safety Requirements and including without limitation CERCLA, any analogous state law, and the common law).]

---

[65] This provision (1) limits the Buyer's recourse against the Target for environmental, health, or safety matters to the Buyer's right, if any, to indemnification for breach of the environmental, health, and safety representation, and (2) grants the Target indemnification by the Buyer for environmental, health, and safety matters.

9. *Termination.*

(a) *Termination of Agreement.*[66] Certain of the Parties may terminate this Agreement as provided below:

(i) the Buyer and the Target may terminate this Agreement by mutual written consent at any time prior to the Closing;

(ii) the Buyer may terminate this Agreement by giving written notice to the Target at any time prior to the Closing in the event (A) the Target has within the then previous [10 business days] given the Buyer any notice pursuant to §5(e)(i) above and (B) the development that is the subject of the notice has had a material adverse effect upon the financial condition of the Division and the Division Subsidiaries taken as a whole;[67]

(iii) the Buyer may terminate this Agreement by giving written notice to the Target at any time prior to the Closing (A) in the event the Target has breached any material representation, warranty, or covenant contained in this Agreement (other than the representations and warranties in §3(g)-(p) above) in any material respect, the Buyer has notified the Target of the breach, and the breach has continued without cure for a period of [30 days] after the notice of breach or (B) if the Closing shall not have occurred on or before _____, 19_____, by reason of the failure of any condition precedent under §7(a) hereof (unless the failure results primarily from the Buyer itself breaching any representation, warranty, or covenant contained in this Agreement); and

(iv) the Target may terminate this Agreement by giving written notice to the Buyer at any time prior to the Closing (A) in the event the Buyer has breached any material representation, warranty, or covenant contained in this Agreement in any material respect, the Target has notified the Buyer of the breach, and the breach has continued without cure for a period of [30 days] after the notice of breach or (B) if the Closing shall not have occurred on or before _____, 19_____, by reason of the failure of any condition precedent under §7(b) hereof (unless the failure results primarily from the Target itself breaching any representation, warranty, or covenant contained in this Agreement).

(b) *Effect of Termination.* If any Party terminates this Agreement pursuant to §9(a) above, all rights and obligations of the Parties hereunder shall terminate without

---

[66] Sample acquisition agreement 2004.1 (the *pro-buyer* divisional asset purchase agreement) contains a provision giving the Buyer a right to terminate the agreement for a limited period after signing if the Buyer is not [reasonably] satisfied with the results of its continuing business, legal, environmental, and accounting due diligence concerning the Division and the Division Subsidiaries.

[67] Section 5(e)(i) above permits the Target to notify the Buyer of any development prior to the Closing that causes a breach of the representations and warranties in §3(g)-(p) above concerning the Division and the Division Subsidiaries. If the development gives the Buyer any right to terminate this Agreement pursuant to this §9(a)(ii), the Buyer must exercise its termination right within [10 business days] after the notice. Unless the Buyer has such a termination right and exercises it within

any liability of any Party to the other Party (except for any liability of any Party then in breach); *provided, however,* that the confidentiality provisions contained in §5(d) above shall survive termination.

10. *Miscellaneous.*[68]

(a) *Press Releases and Public Announcements.* No Party shall issue any press release or make any public announcement relating to the subject matter of this Agreement [prior to the Closing] without the prior written approval of the other Party; *provided, however,* that any Party may make any public disclosure it believes in good faith is required by applicable law or any listing or trading agreement concerning its publicly-traded securities (in which case the disclosing Party will use its [reasonable] best efforts to advise the other Party prior to making the disclosure).

(b) *No Third-Party Beneficiaries.* This Agreement shall not confer any rights or remedies upon any Person other than the Parties and their respective successors and permitted assigns.

(c) *Entire Agreement.* [This Agreement (including the documents referred to herein) constitutes the entire agreement between the Parties and supersedes any prior understandings, agreements, or representations by or between the Parties, written or oral, to the extent they related in any way to the subject matter hereof.]

(d) *Succession and Assignment.* This Agreement shall be binding upon and inure to the benefit of the Parties named herein and their respective successors and permitted assigns. No Party may assign either this Agreement or any of its rights, interests, or obligations hereunder without the prior written approval of the other Party [; *provided, however,* that the Buyer may (i) assign any or all of its rights and interests hereunder to one or more of its Affiliates and (ii) designate one or more of its Affiliates to perform its obligations hereunder (in any or all of which cases the Buyer nonetheless shall remain responsible for the performance of all of its obligations hereunder)].

(e) *Counterparts.* This Agreement may be executed in one or more counterparts, each of which shall be deemed an original but all of which together will constitute one and the same instrument.

(f) *Headings.* The section headings contained in this Agreement are inserted for convenience only and shall not affect in any way the meaning or interpretation of this Agreement.

---

that period, the notice will be deemed to have cured any such breach of the representations and warranties that otherwise would have existed.

[68] The Buyer may seek to add provisions whereby the Parties agree to specific performance, agree to service of process on an agent, and submit to the [exclusive] jurisdiction of the state and federal courts in a particular city. Sample acquisition agreement 2004.1 (the pro-buyer divisional asset purchase agreement) contains examples of these provisions.

(g) *Notices.* All notices, requests, demands, claims, and other communications hereunder will be in writing. Any notice, request, demand, claim, or other communication hereunder shall be deemed duly given if (and then two business days after) it is sent by registered or certified mail, return receipt requested, postage prepaid, and addressed to the intended recipient as set forth below:

If to the Target: *Copy to:*

If to the Buyer: *Copy to:*

Any Party may send any notice, request, demand, claim, or other communication hereunder to the intended recipient at the address set forth above using any other means (including personal delivery, expedited courier, messenger service, telecopy, telex, ordinary mail, or electronic mail), but no such notice, request, demand, claim, or other communication shall be deemed to have been duly given unless and until it actually is received by the intended recipient. Any Party may change the address to which notices, requests, demands, claims, and other communications hereunder are to be delivered by giving the other Party notice in the manner herein set forth.

(h) *Governing Law. This Agreement shall be governed by and construed in accordance with the domestic laws of the State of _____ without giving effect to any choice or conflict of law provision or rule (whether of the State of _____ or any other jurisdiction) that would cause the application of the laws of any jurisdiction other than the State of _____.*

(i) *Amendments and Waivers.* No amendment of any provision of this Agreement shall be valid unless the same shall be in writing and signed by the Buyer and the Target. [The Target may consent to any such amendment at any time prior to the Closing with the prior authorization of its board of directors; *provided, however*, that any amendment effected after the Target Stockholders have approved this Agreement will be subject to the restrictions contained in the (APPLICABLE CORPORATION STATUTE).] No waiver by any Party of any default, misrepresentation, or breach of warranty or covenant hereunder, whether intentional or not, shall be deemed to extend to any prior or subsequent default, misrepresentation, or breach of warranty or covenant hereunder or affect in any way any rights arising by virtue of any prior or subsequent such occurrence.

(j) *Severability.* Any term or provision of this Agreement that is invalid or unenforceable in any situation in any jurisdiction shall not affect the validity or enforceability of the remaining terms and provisions hereof or the validity or enforceability of the offending term or provision in any other situation or in any other jurisdiction.

(k) *Expenses.* Each of the Target, the Division Subsidiaries, and the Buyer will bear its own costs and expenses (including legal fees and expenses) incurred in

---

The Parties may want to add a provision calling for optional or mandatory arbitration with respect to all or certain issues.

connection with this Agreement and the transactions contemplated hereby. The Target will also bear all of the costs and expenses of the Target Stockholders (including all of their legal fees and expenses) incurred in connection with this Agreement and the transactions contemplated hereby.[69]

(l) *Construction.* [The Parties have participated jointly in the negotiation and drafting of this Agreement. In the event an ambiguity or question of intent or interpretation arises, this Agreement shall be construed as if drafted jointly by the Parties and no presumption or burden of proof shall arise favoring or disfavoring any Party by virtue of the authorship of any of the provisions of this Agreement.] Any reference to any federal, state, local, or foreign statute or law shall be deemed also to refer to all rules and regulations promulgated thereunder, unless the context requires otherwise. The word "including" shall mean including without limitation.[70]

(m) *Incorporation of Exhibits and Schedules.* The Exhibits and Schedules identified in this Agreement are incorporated herein by reference and made a part hereof.

(n) *Tax Matters.*[71]

---

[69] This Agreement makes the Target responsible for the transactional costs and expenses of the Target and the Target Stockholders, but treats these costs and expenses as Assumed Liabilities. This means that the Buyer will bear these costs and expenses if it consummates the asset purchase. *See* §2(b) above and the related definition of "Assumed Liabilities" in §1 above.

Furthermore, this Agreement leaves the Division Subsidiaries responsible for their own transactional costs and expenses. This means that the Buyer will bear these costs and expenses if it acquires their capital stock as part of the Acquired Assets.

Note, however, that allocating transactional costs and expenses to the Division and the Division Subsidiaries may reduce the amount of cash the Target will be entitled to retain at the Closing. See §§2(a) and 2(d) above and the related definition of "Acquired Assets" in §1 above. Furthermore, any assumption of the Target Stockholders' costs and expenses by the Target may be deemed a dividend for federal income tax purposes.

The Target may seek to make the Buyer *directly* responsible for these costs and expenses. In the unlikely event the Buyer agreed to this arrangement, it would be responsible for the costs and expenses of the Target Stockholders, the Target, and the Division Subsidiaries whether or not it consummated the asset purchase.

The Buyer may seek to make the Target and the Target Stockholders responsible for their own costs and expenses. Sample acquisition agreement 2004.1 (the *pro-buyer* divisional asset purchase agreement) contains provisions more favorable to the Buyer in this regard.

The Parties may settle on a compromise allocation of responsibility (such as sharing the costs and expenses in a predetermined ratio or making one Party responsible for the costs and expenses up to a specified aggregate ceiling and the other Party responsible for any excess).

[70] Sample acquisition agreement 2004.1 (the *pro-buyer* divisional asset purchase agreement) contains additional language construing the representations, warranties, and covenants herein in a manner more favorable to the Buyer.

[71] This Agreement contains a considerably abbreviated version of the tax provisions found in sample acquisition agreement 2002.4 (sale of subsidiary out of consolidated group). The Parties may wish to incorporate some or all of the unabridged provisions from sample acquisition agreement 2002.4 into this Agreement.

(i) Any agreement between the Target and any of the Division Subsidiaries regarding allocation or payment of taxes or amounts in lieu of taxes shall be deemed terminated at and as of the Closing.

(ii) The Target will be responsible for the preparation and filing of all tax returns for the Target for all periods as to which tax returns are due after the Closing Date (including the consolidated, unitary, and combined tax returns for the Target which include the operations of the Division and the Division Subsidiaries for any period ending on or before the Closing Date). The Target will make all payments required with respect to any such tax return.

(iii) The Buyer will be responsible for the preparation and filing of all tax returns for the Division and the Division Subsidiaries for all periods as to which tax returns are due after the Closing Date (other than for taxes with respect to periods for which the consolidated, unitary, and combined tax returns of the Target will include the operations of the Division and the Division Subsidiaries). The Buyer will make all payments required with respect to any such tax return; *provided, however*, that the Target will reimburse the Buyer concurrently therewith to the extent any payment the Buyer is making relates to the operations of any of the Division and the Division Subsidiaries for any period ending on or before the Closing Date.

(iv) The Buyer and the Target will (A) cooperate in the preparation and filing of an election under Code §338(h)(10) with respect to the sale of the stock of the Division Subsidiaries hereunder[72] and (B) take all such action as is required in order to give effect to the election for state, local, and foreign tax purposes to the greatest extent permitted by law.]

(o) *Employee Benefits Matters.* [The Buyer will adopt and assume at and as of the Closing each of the Employee Benefit Plans that the Division maintains and each trust, insurance contract, annuity contract, or other funding arrangement that the Division has established with respect thereto. The Target will transfer (or cause the plan administrators to transfer) at and as of the Closing all of the corresponding assets associated with the Employee Benefit Plans that the Buyer is adopting and

---

[72] The Buyer may seek to have the Parties make an election under Code §338(h)(10) (i.e., to have the sale of the stock of the Division Subsidiaries taxed as though the Division Subsidiaries instead had sold their *assets* to the Buyer). *See* ¶205.

This differs from any other election the Buyer might make under Code §338 in that the *Target* will be responsible for any federal income tax on the deemed sale of assets. Note, however, that the Target will incur no federal income tax on the sale of the *stock* of the Division Subsidiaries (i.e., only on the deemed sale of their *assets*) if the Parties make a Code §338(h)(10) election.

This Agreement makes the Buyer responsible for any incremental tax arising out of the Code §338(h)(10) election. See the definition of Assumed Liabilities in §1 above. The Buyer, of course, will seek to make the Target responsible for the incremental tax. Sample acquisition agreement 2004.1 (the *pro-buyer* divisional asset purchase agreement) contains provisions which are more favorable to the Buyer in this regard.

assuming. With respect to each Multiemployer Plan, the Parties shall take all actions necessary to comply with the requirements of ERISA §4204.][73]

(p) *Bulk Transfer Laws.* The Buyer acknowledges that the Target will not comply with the provisions of any bulk transfer laws of any jurisdiction in connection with the transactions contemplated by this Agreement.[74]

* * * * *

IN WITNESS WHEREOF, the Parties hereto have executed this Agreement on [as of] the date first above written.

[BUYER]

By: _____

Title: _____

[TARGET]

By: _____

Title: _____

---

[73] This Agreement provides for a transfer of all Employee Benefit Plan Assets (including overfundings) and liabilities (including underfundings) to the Buyer. There are many other approaches to splitting and matching plan assets and liabilities which would cause the Buyer to share to various degrees in plan overfundings and underfundings.

If the Buyer did not want to share in any plan overfundings and underfundings, the Buyer could establish substantially identical plans for future benefit accruals and count past service with any of the Division and the Division Subsidiaries for purposes of eligibility and vesting thereunder. The Target would then continue its previously established plans on a "frozen" basis and retain the benefit of any overfunding (or the detriment of any underfunding) thereunder.

If the Buyer wanted to share in only certain plan overfundings and underfundings, the Buyer and the Target could proceed as set forth in the preceding paragraph, except that the Buyer would assume the liability for certain past service benefits under the Division plans as of the Closing Date and the Target would transfer certain corresponding plan assets to the Buyer.

In any event, the Purchase Price should reflect the intended disposition of employee benefit plan assets and liabilities.

[74] The Buyer may seek to have the Target comply with the applicable bulk transfer laws in certain circumstances. *See* ¶2001.2.2.2.

¶2004.3   Neutral Divisional Purchase

Sample acquisition agreement 2004.3 (*neutral* divisional asset purchase) is intended to strike a reasonable balance between the conflicting interests of P and T in such areas as (i) the extent to which P will receive divisional cash (net of unpaid taxes) at the time of the closing, (ii) the extent to which T will bear the burden of the divisional liabilities and obligations after the closing, (iii) the extent to which P will have conditions to its obligation to close, (iv) the extent to which T will be required to give representations and warranties, and (v) the extent to which T will be required to indemnify P against breaches of those representations and warranties.

Sample acquisition agreement 2004.3 provides that T will retain only so much of the divisional cash at the closing as will cover the unpaid divisional taxes with respect to periods up to the closing for which T will remain liable. This means that P will receive the divisional cash (net of unpaid taxes) at the time of the closing.

Sample acquisition agreement 2004.3 provides that the only T liabilities P will assume are those divisional liabilities (i) shown on the last divisional balance sheet reviewed by P before signing the contract, (ii) incurred in the ordinary course of business thereafter (but not including claims and lawsuits), (iii) involving employee benefit plans and executory contracts, or (iv) listed on a disclosure schedule. Thus, P would generally *not* assume such undisclosed divisional liabilities as environmental cleanup, employment discrimination, antitrust violations, product liability, product warranty, tax deficiencies, and other claims and lawsuits.

Sample acquisition agreement 2004.3 contains fairly extensive representations and warranties from T concerning (i) the historical divisional financial statements, (ii) intervening material adverse changes in the divisional business, (iii) litigation and material undisclosed liabilities, (iv) tax matters, (v) pension and welfare benefit plans, (vi) compliance with federal, state, local, and foreign laws, (vii) environmental matters, and (viii) product liability and warranties.

Sample acquisition agreement 2004.3 also contains fairly extensive representations and warranties from T concerning (i) authorization with respect to the transaction, (ii) title to the assets being sold, (iii) required governmental and third party consents (and noncontravention generally), (iv) organization, (v) adequacy and condition of the divisional tangible assets, (vi) real estate matters, (vii) intellectual property matters, (viii) leases, licenses, and contracts, (ix) inventory and accounts receivable, (x) insurance, (xi) brokerage fees, and (xii) material misstatements and omissions.

T's representations and warranties are, however, qualified with relatively frequent references to knowledge (defined as the actual knowledge of its shareholders, directors, and officers after reasonable investigation) and materiality.

Sample acquisition agreement 2004.3 provides that the representations and warranties with respect to the transaction itself and with respect to taxes will survive indefinitely, that the environmental representations and warranties will survive for five years, that the other representations and warranties will survive for two years, and that there will be a deductible and a ceiling with respect to indemnification against breaches of any representations and warranties that do not concern the transaction itself.

P *does not* have any right to recoup its losses against the P notes in lieu of seeking indemnification from T.

P's obligation to close is subject to several conditions such as (i) compliance with T's representations, warranties, and covenants, (ii) absence of a material adverse change, (iii) absence of litigation affecting the transaction, (iv) receipt of governmental approvals, (v) delivery of title insurance, surveys, and material third party consents, (vi) delivery of any side agreements, and (vii) delivery of an opinion of T's legal counsel.

P *does not* have any closing condition concerning its ability to secure financing for the transaction *or* any right to terminate the purchase agreement after signing if it is not satisfied with the results of its continuing business, legal, and accounting due diligence review.

It is important to note that some of the provisions in sample acquisition agreement 2004.3 are neutral only in the context of the overall agreement. In part, this is due to the interplay between T's representations and warranties (which are fairly extensive, but qualified with references to knowledge and materiality) on the one hand and the indemnification obligations of T's stockholders (which are subject to various deductibles, ceilings, and survival periods) on the other. Accordingly, it is not always possible to remove a provision from sample acquisition agreement 2004.3 for use in another agreement and have the provision remain neutral.

Finally, the choice of neutral provisions for sample acquisition agreement 2004.3 was necessarily subjective. Thus, in any particular transaction, it may be necessary to modify the agreement so that it strikes a different balance between the interests of P and T.

There are a number of other important differences among sample acquisition agreement 2004.1 (*pro-buyer* divisional asset purchase), sample acquisition agreement 2004.2 (*pro-seller* divisional asset purchase), and sample acquisition agreement 2004.3 (*neutral* divisional asset purchase). Each of these sample acquisition agreements contains extensive footnotes with cross-references pointing out the differences.

ASSET PURCHASE AGREEMENT[1]

BETWEEN

_____

AND

_____

_____, 19_____

TABLE OF CONTENTS

¶2004.3   [1] The Buyer generally will obtain a cost basis (i.e., the Purchase Price _plus_ the Assumed Liabilities _plus_ the expenses of the transaction) in the Acquired Assets.

A purchase of assets in which the consideration is primarily cash and notes is generally treated for accounting purposes as a purchase rather than as a pooling of interests. _See_ ¶1503.

Some LBO structures prejudice the Target's creditors and hence might permit payments, transfers, liens, and obligations arising out of the LBO to be attacked under fraudulent conveyance law. _See_ ¶1506.

Exhibit A—Form of Buyer Note
Exhibit B—Forms of Assignments
Exhibit C—Form of Assumption
Exhibit D—Allocation Schedule
Exhibit E—Historical Financial Statements
Exhibit F—Forms of Side Agreements
Exhibit G—Form of Opinion of Counsel to the Target
Exhibit H—Form of Opinion of Counsel to the Buyer
Disclosure Schedule—Exceptions to Representations and Warranties

[EXHIBITS AND SCHEDULES HAVE BEEN OMITTED FROM THIS SAMPLE ACQUISITION AGREEMENT 2004.3]

Agreement entered into on [as of] _____, 19____, by and between _____, a _____ corporation (the *"Buyer"*), and _____, a corporation (the *"Target"*). The Buyer and the Target are referred to collectively herein as the *"Parties."*

This Agreement contemplates a transaction in which the Buyer will purchase all of the assets (and assume certain of the liabilities) of the _____ Division of the Target in return for cash and the Buyer Notes.[2]

Now, therefore, in consideration of the premises and the mutual promises herein made, and in consideration of the representations, warranties, and covenants herein contained, the Parties agree as follows.

1. *Definitions.*

"Accredited Investor" has the meaning set forth in Regulation D promulgated under the Securities Act.

"Acquired Assets" means all right, title, and interest in and to all of the assets constituting the Division,[3] *including* all of its (a) real property, leaseholds and subleaseholds therein, improvements, fixtures, and fittings thereon, and easements, rights-of-way, and other appurtenants thereto (such as appurtenant rights in and to public streets), (b) tangible personal property (such as machinery, equipment, inventories of raw materials and supplies, manufactured and purchased parts, goods in process and finished goods, furniture, automobiles, trucks, tractors, trailers, tools, jigs, and dies), (c) Intellectual Property, goodwill associated therewith, licenses and sublicenses granted and obtained with respect thereto, and rights thereunder, remedies against infringements thereof, and rights to protection of interests therein under the laws of all jurisdictions, (d) leases, subleases, and rights thereunder, (e) agreements, contracts, indentures, mortgages, instruments, Security Interests, guaranties, other similar arrangements, and rights thereunder, (f) accounts, notes, and other receivables, (g) securities (such as the capital stock in the Division Subsidiaries), (h) claims, deposits, prepayments, refunds, causes of action, choses in action, rights of recovery, rights of set off, and rights of recoupment (including

---

[2] When the Buyer purchases a division of the Target, the Target will generally retain those assets and rights which it does not transfer and assign to the Buyer, and the Target will generally remain responsible for those liabilities and obligations not assumed by the Buyer.

It is generally necessary to prepare asset transfer documents and liability assumption documents in an asset purchase (whether a purchase of all the Target's assets or a purchase of the Target's division), which would not be required if the Buyer purchased the Target's *stock.*

The Buyer's contractual assumption of certain divisional liabilities and obligations generally will not preclude a third party to whom the Target owed the liabilities and obligations from suing the Target (if the Buyer has failed to pay or perform) unless the third party consents to the Buyer's assumption and agrees to look only to the Buyer for satisfaction (i.e., enters into a novation agreement). This means that, if the Buyer fails to satisfy the assumed liabilities and obligations, nonconsenting third parties to whom the Target owed the liabilities and obligations may have a cause of action against the Target or, if the Target has liquidated and dissolved, against the Target's stockholders and/or directors.

[3] This Agreement, like sample acquisition agreement 2004.1 (the *pro-buyer* divisional asset purchase agreement), defines "Acquired Assets" broadly to include all right, title, and interest in and to the divisional assets.

Sample acquisition agreement 2004.2 (the *pro-seller* divisional asset purchase agreement), on the other hand, defines "Acquired Assets" more narrowly to include only so much of the Target's right, title, and interest in and to the divisional assets *as it possesses and has the right to transfer.*

any such item relating to the payment of taxes), (i) franchises, approvals, permits, licenses, orders, registrations, certificates, variances, and similar rights obtained from governments and governmental agencies, (j) books, records, ledgers, files, documents, correspondence, lists, plats, architectural plans, drawings, and specifications, creative materials, advertising and promotional materials, studies, reports, and other printed or written materials, (k) any Cash in excess of an amount equal to the Target's good faith estimate of the unpaid taxes of the Division and the Division Subsidiaries (net of any amount the Division and the Division Subsidiaries shall have paid to the Target with respect thereto under any tax sharing arrangement) with respect to periods prior to the Closing for which the return is due after the Closing[4] (computed on a pro forma stand-alone basis in accordance with the past custom and practice of the Division and the Division Subsidiaries in filing their tax returns),[5] and (l) [rights in and with respect to the assets associated with its Employee Benefit Plans];[6] *provided, however*, that the Acquired Assets shall not include (i) the corporate charter, qualifications to conduct business as a foreign corporation, arrangements with registered agents relating to foreign qualifications, taxpayer and other identification numbers, seals, minute books, stock transfer books, blank stock certificates, and other documents relating to the organization, maintenance, and existence of the Target as a corporation or (ii) any of the rights of the Target under this Agreement (or under any side agreement between the Target on the one hand and the Buyer on the other hand entered into on or after the date of this Agreement).[7]

"*Adverse Consequences*" means all actions, suits, proceedings, hearings, investigations, charges, complaints, claims, demands, injunctions, judgments, orders, de-

---

[4] This Agreement, like sample acquisition agreement 2004.1 (the *pro-buyer* divisional asset purchase agreement), provides that the Buyer will acquire the consolidated cash of the Division and the Division Subsidiaries (net of unpaid taxes up to the Closing for which the Target will remain liable). §2(d) below permits the Target to cause the Division Subsidiaries to distribute some or all of their cash to the Target as of the Closing in order to facilitate the intended cash retention for unpaid taxes. This would be necessary if, for example, the Division itself lacked sufficient cash to cover the aggregate unpaid taxes for the Division and the Division Subsidiaries.

Sample acquisition agreement 2004.2 (the *pro-seller* divisional asset purchase agreement), on the other hand, provides that the Target will retain all of the consolidated cash of the Division and the Division Subsidiaries.

The Parties may want to introduce a post-Closing adjustment to the Purchase Price based on the difference between the Target's good faith estimate of the consolidated cash (net of unpaid taxes through the Closing) and the actual amount as determined later. *See* sample acquisition agreement 2002.5 for analogous provisions concerning a different type of post-Closing Purchase Price adjustment.

[5] This definition provides that the unpaid taxes of the Division and the Division Subsidiaries will be computed on a pro forma *stand-alone* basis in accordance with their past custom and practice in filing their tax returns. This means that the unpaid taxes of the Division and the Division Subsidiaries will not be reduced by any net operating loss attributable to other divisions and subsidiaries of the Target.

[6] *See* the provisions in §10(o) below with respect to employee benefits matters.

[7] It may be difficult to identify and describe those rights, assets, obligations, and liabilities of the Target which constitute the Division. This is especially likely where the Target does not segregate cash in a separate account for the Division or where the Division shares rights, assets, obligations, and liabilities with the Target and its Affiliates. The Parties may wish to expand upon the definitions of Acquired Assets and Assumed Liabilities to include schedules showing the disposition of specific items.

crees, rulings, damages, dues, penalties, fines, costs, [reasonable amounts paid in settlement], liabilities, obligations, taxes, liens, losses, expenses, and fees, including court costs and [reasonable] attorneys' fees and expenses.

"*Affiliate*" has the meaning set forth in Rule 12b-2 of the regulations promulgated under the Securities Exchange Act.

"*Affiliated Group*" means any affiliated group within the meaning of Code §1504(a) [or any similar group defined under a similar provision of state, local, or foreign law].

"*Applicable Rate*" means the corporate base rate of interest announced from time to time by [FINANCIAL INSTITUTION] [plus/minus _____% per annum].

"*Assumed Liabilities*"[8] means (a) all liabilities of the Division set forth on the face of the Most Recent Balance Sheet (rather than in any notes thereto), (b) all liabilities of the Division which have arisen after the Most Recent Fiscal Month End in the Ordinary Course of Business (other than any liability resulting from, arising out of, relating to, in the nature of, or caused by any breach of contract, breach of warranty, tort, infringement, violation of law, or environmental matter, including without limitation those arising under Environmental, Health, and Safety Requirements), (c) all obligations of the Division under the agreements, contracts, leases, licenses, and other arrangements referred to in the definition of Acquired Assets either (i) to furnish goods, services, and other non-Cash benefits to another party after the Closing or (ii) to pay for goods, services, and other non-Cash benefits that another party will furnish to it after the Closing, (d) [all liabilities and obligations of the Division under its Employee Benefit Plans],[9] and (e) [all other liabilities and obligations of or relating to the Division (including such liabilities and obligations relating to environmental matters[10]) specifically set forth in an appendix to the Disclosure Schedule under an express statement (that the Buyer has initialled) to the effect that the definition of Assumed Liabilities will include the liabilities and obligations so disclosed]; *provided, however*, that the Assumed Liabilities shall not include (i) any liability of the Target for unpaid taxes (with respect to the Division or otherwise) for periods prior to the Closing, (ii) any liability of the Target for income, transfer, sales, use, and other taxes arising in connection with the consummation of the transactions contemplated hereby (including any Income Taxes arising because the Target is

---

[8] *See* the footnote to §2(b) below for an important discussion of certain tax issues which may affect the drafting of this definition as it concerns liabilities of the Division which have not yet matured into a deduction for tax purposes.

[9] *See* the provisions in §10(o) below with respect to employee benefits matters.

[10] This provision states that Buyer assumes liabilities and obligations (including those relating to environmental matters) specifically set forth in the Disclosure Schedule.

Sample acquisition agreement 2004.1 (the *pro-buyer* divisional purchase agreement) leaves with the Target all environmental liabilities (other than those shown on the face of the Most Recent Balance Sheet) of the Division.

Sample acquisition agreement 2004.2 (the *pro-seller* divisional purchase agreement) requires the Buyer to assume all environmental liabilities relating to the Division.

transferring the Acquired Assets, because any of its Subsidiaries is deemed to be transferring its assets pursuant to an election under Code §338(h)(10), because the Target has an Excess Loss Account in the stock of any of its Subsidiaries, or because the Target has deferred gain on any Deferred Intercompany Transaction), (iii) any liability of the Target for the unpaid taxes of any Person other than the Target under Reg. §1.1502-6 (or any similar provision of state, local, or foreign law), as a transferee or successor, by contract, or otherwise,[11] (iv) any obligation of the Target to indemnify any Person by reason of the fact that such Person was a director, officer, employee, or agent of the Target or was serving at the request of the Target as a partner, trustee, director, officer, employee, or agent of another entity (whether such indemnification is for judgments, damages, penalties, fines, costs, amounts paid in settlement, losses, expenses, or otherwise and whether such indemnification is pursuant to any statute, charter document, bylaw, agreement, or otherwise),[12] (v) any liability of the Target for costs and expenses incurred in connection with this Agreement and the transactions contemplated hereby, or (vi) any liability or obligation of the Target under this Agreement (or under any side agreement between the Target on the one hand and the Buyer on the other hand entered into on or after the date of this Agreement).[13]

---

[11] If the Target has been a member of an Affiliated Group filing a consolidated federal income tax return, the Target (or its successor) will be jointly and severally liable under Reg. §1.1502-6 for certain tax liabilities incurred by such Affiliated Group for a tax year when the Target was a member of such Affiliated Group for all or part of such tax year. *See* ¶210.

The Target may also be liable for the unpaid taxes of third parties under similar provisions of state, local, or foreign law, as a transferee or successor, by contract (e.g., a tax sharing agreement), or otherwise.

This provision is designed to protect the Buyer against assuming any liability for the unpaid taxes of any person other than the Target.

[12] This Agreement, like sample acquisition agreement 2004.1 (the *pro-buyer* divisional asset purchase agreement), provides that the Buyer will not assume any obligation of the Target to indemnify its directors and other officeholders.

Sample acquisition agreement 2004.2 (the *pro-seller* divisional asset purchase agreement), on the other hand, contains bracketed language providing that the Buyer will assume all obligations of the Division to indemnify any Person, by reason of the fact that such Person was, before the asset purchase, a director or other officeholder of the Division entitled to indemnification from the Division, with respect to any matter whatsoever. The provision in the *pro-seller* agreement is unusually favorable to the Target, and would be inappropriate in most transactions involving the purchase of a division.

These provisions relate marginally to the surprising decision in Heffernan v. Pacific Dunlop GNB Corporation, 965 F.2d 369 (7th Cir. 1992). *See* §8(g) of sample acquisition agreement 2002.1 (the pro-buyer *stock* purchase agreement) and the footnote thereto. Although *Heffernan* involved a purchase of stock, rather than a purchase of divisional assets, the instant structure presents some of the same concerns.

[13] This Agreement, like sample acquisition agreement 2004.1 (the *pro-buyer* divisional asset purchase agreement), contains a relatively narrow definition of Assumed Liabilities. The Buyer is assuming only those liabilities set forth on the face of the Most Recent Balance Sheet or incurred thereafter in the Ordinary Course of Business *plus* certain specified liabilities and obligations involving employee benefit plans and executory contracts *plus* certain liabilities and obligations identified in the Disclosure Schedule. The Buyer is *not* assuming any undisclosed liabilities (with certain exceptions as noted in the preceding sentence), any liabilities set forth in the Disclosure Schedule (unless the Disclosure Schedule contains an express assumption initialled by the Buyer), or any liability for unpaid taxes with respect to periods prior to the Closing.

Sample acquisition agreement 2004.2 (the *pro-seller* divisional asset purchase agreement), on the other hand, contains a broad definition of Assumed Liabilities. In that sample acquisition agreement,

"Basis" means any past or present fact, situation, circumstance, status, condition, activity, practice, plan, occurrence, event, incident, action, failure to act, or transaction that forms or could form the basis for any specified consequence.

"Buyer" has the meaning set forth in the preface above.

"Buyer Note" has the meaning set forth in §2(c) below.

"Cash" means cash and cash equivalents (including marketable securities and short term investments) calculated in accordance with GAAP applied on a basis consistent with the preparation of the Financial Statements.

"Closing" has the meaning set forth in §2(e) below.

"Closing Date" has the meaning set forth in §2(e) below.

"COBRA" means the requirements of Part 6 of Subtitle B of Title I of ERISA and Code §4980B and of any similar state law.

"Code" means the Internal Revenue Code of 1986, as amended.

"Confidential Information" means any information concerning the businesses and affairs of the Division and the Division Subsidiaries that is not already generally available to the public.

"Controlled Group" has the meaning set forth in Code §1563.

"Deferred Intercompany Transaction" has the meaning set forth in Reg. §1.1502-13.

"Disclosure Schedule" has the meaning set forth in §3 below.

"Division" means the Target with respect to its _____ Division.

"Division Subsidiary" means any Subsidiary of the Target included within the Division.

---

the Buyer assumes substantially all liabilities and obligations of the Division (whether known or unknown, whether asserted or unasserted, whether absolute or contingent, whether accrued or unaccrued, whether liquidated or unliquidated, and whether due or to become due), including (i) transfer, sales, use, and other non-income taxes arising in connection with the transaction, (ii) incremental income taxes arising in connection with any Code §338(h)(10) election, (iii) costs and expenses arising in connection with the transaction, (iv) contracts with third parties, (v) employee benefit plans, and (vi) matters set forth in the Disclosure Schedule. The Buyer in that *pro-seller* form does not, however, assume (a) any liability for unpaid taxes with respect to periods prior to the Closing or (b) any liability for income taxes (other than as noted above with respect to any Code §338(h)(10) election) arising in connection with the transaction.

"Employee Benefit Plan" means any "employee benefit plan" (as such term is defined in ERISA §3(3)) and any other [material] employee benefit plan, program or arrangement of any kind.

"Employee Pension Benefit Plan" has the meaning set forth in ERISA §3(2).

"Employee Welfare Benefit Plan" has the meaning set forth in ERISA §3(1).

"Environmental, Health, and Safety Requirements"[14] shall mean all federal, state, local and foreign statutes, regulations, ordinances and similar provisions having the force or effect of law, all judicial and administrative orders and determinations, and all common law concerning public health and safety, worker health and safety, and pollution or protection of the environment, including without limitation all those relating to the presence, use, production, generation, handling, transportation, treatment, storage, disposal, distribution, labeling, testing, processing, discharge, release, threatened release, control, or cleanup of any hazardous materials, substances or wastes, chemical substances or mixtures, pesticides, pollutants, contaminants, toxic chemicals, petroleum products or byproducts, asbestos, polychlorinated biphenyls, noise or radiation.

"ERISA" means the Employee Retirement Income Security Act of 1974, as amended.

"ERISA Affiliate" means each entity which is treated as a single employer with the Target for purposes of Code §414.

"Excess Loss Account" has the meaning set forth in Reg. §1.1502-19.

"Fiduciary" has the meaning set forth in ERISA §3(21).

"Financial Statement" has the meaning set forth in §3(g) below.

"GAAP" means United States generally accepted accounting principles as in effect from time to time.

"Hart-Scott-Rodino Act" means the Hart-Scott-Rodino Antitrust Improvements Act of 1976, as amended.

---

[14] Sample acquisition agreement 2004.1 (the *pro-buyer* divisional purchase agreement) explicitly extends this definition to include legal requirements enacted and in effect prior to, on, or after the Closing Date and also includes within this definition contractual obligations.

Sample acquisition agreement 2004.2 (the *pro-seller* divisional purchase agreement) does not include either contractual obligations or common law in this definition and explicitly limits this definition to laws as enacted and in effect on or prior to the Closing Date.

"Income Tax" means any federal, state, local, or foreign income tax, including any interest, penalty, or addition thereto, whether disputed or not.[15]

"Income Tax Return" means any return, declaration, report, claim for refund, or information return or statement relating to Income Taxes, including any schedule or attachment thereto, and including any amendment thereof.

"Indemnified Party" has the meaning set forth in §8(d) below.

"Indemnifying Party" has the meaning set forth in §8(d) below.

"Intellectual Property" means (a) all inventions (whether patentable or unpatentable and whether or not reduced to practice), all improvements thereto, and all patents, patent applications, and patent disclosures, together with all reissuances, continuations, continuations-in-part, revisions, extensions, and reexaminations thereof, (b) all trademarks, service marks, trade dress, logos, trade names, and corporate names, together with all translations, adaptations, derivations, and combinations thereof and including all goodwill associated therewith, and all applications, registrations, and renewals in connection therewith, (c) all copyrightable works, all copyrights, and all applications, registrations, and renewals in connection therewith, (d) all mask works and all applications, registrations, and renewals in connection therewith, (e) all trade secrets and confidential business information (including ideas, research and development, know-how, formulas, compositions, manufacturing and production processes and techniques, technical data, designs, drawings, specifications, customer and supplier lists, pricing and cost information, and business and marketing plans and proposals), (f) all computer software (including data and related documentation), (g) all other proprietary rights, and (h) all copies and tangible embodiments thereof (in whatever form or medium).

"Knowledge" means actual knowledge after reasonable investigation.[16]

"Most Recent Balance Sheet" means the balance sheet contained within the Most Recent Financial Statements.

"Most Recent Financial Statements" has the meaning set forth in §3(g) below.

"Most Recent Fiscal Month End" has the meaning set forth in §3(g) below.

"Most Recent Fiscal Year End" has the meaning set forth in §3(g) below.

---

[15] This Agreement, like sample acquisition agreement 2004.2 (the *pro-seller* divisional asset purchase agreement), uses the term "Income Tax," which is defined narrowly to include only federal, state, local, and foreign income taxes. Sample acquisition agreement 2004.1 (the *pro-buyer* divisional asset purchase agreement), on the other hand, uses the term "Tax," which is defined broadly to include taxes of all descriptions.

[16] This Agreement, like sample acquisition agreement 2004.1 (the *pro-buyer* divisional asset purchase agreement), defines "Knowledge" as actual knowledge after reasonable investigation. Sample acquisi-

"Multiemployer Plan" has the meaning set forth in ERISA §3(37).

"Ordinary Course of Business" means the ordinary course of business consistent with past custom and practice (including with respect to quantity and frequency).

"Party" has the meaning set forth in the preface above.

"PBGC" means the Pension Benefit Guaranty Corporation.

"Person" means an individual, a partnership, a corporation, an association, a joint stock company, a trust, a joint venture, an unincorporated organization, or a governmental entity (or any department, agency, or political subdivision thereof).

"Prohibited Transaction" has the meaning set forth in ERISA §406 and Code §4975.

"Purchase Price" has the meaning set forth in §2(c) below.

"Reportable Event" has the meaning set forth in ERISA §4043.

"Securities Act" means the Securities Act of 1933, as amended.

"Securities Exchange Act" means the Securities Exchange Act of 1934, as amended.

"Security Interest" means any mortgage, pledge, lien, encumbrance, charge, or other security interest, *other than* (a) mechanic's, materialmen's, and similar liens, (b) liens for taxes not yet due and payable [or for taxes that the taxpayer is contesting in good faith through appropriate proceedings], (c) purchase money liens and liens securing rental payments under capital lease arrangements, and (d) other liens arising in the Ordinary Course of Business and not incurred in connection with the borrowing of money.

"Subsidiary" means any corporation with respect to which a specified Person (or a Subsidiary thereof) owns a majority of the common stock or has the power to vote or direct the voting of sufficient securities to elect a majority of the directors.[17]

"Survey" has the meaning set forth in §5(i) below.

"Target" has the meaning set forth in the preface above.

"Target Share" means any share of the Common Stock, par value $_____ per share, of the Target.[18]

---

tion agreement 2004.2 (the *pro-seller* divisional asset purchase agreement), on the other hand, defines "Knowledge" as actual knowledge without independent investigation.

[17] It may be necessary to revise this definition if, for example, the Target has subsidiary *partnerships*.

[18] It may be necessary to revise this definition if the Target has additional classes of capital stock.

"Target Stockholder" means any person who or which holds any Target Shares.

"Third Party Claim" has the meaning set forth in §8(d) below.

2. *Basic Transaction.*

(a) *Purchase and Sale of Assets.* On and subject to the terms and conditions of this Agreement, the Buyer agrees to purchase from the Target, and the Target agrees to sell, transfer, convey, and deliver to the Buyer, all of the Acquired Assets at the Closing for the consideration specified below in this §2.

(b) *Assumption of Liabilities.* On and subject to the terms and conditions of this Agreement, the Buyer agrees to assume and become responsible for all of the Assumed Liabilities at the Closing. The Buyer will not assume or have any responsibility, however, with respect to any other obligation or liability of the Target not included within the definition of Assumed Liabilities.[19]

---

[19] In a taxable purchase of the Target's divisional assets, the Division may have liabilities which have not yet matured into a deduction for tax purposes. For example, (1) a cash method Target may have accrued (but unpaid) operating liabilities, (2) a cash method or an accrual method Target may have contingent liabilities, (3) a cash method or an accrual method Target may have unfunded pension liabilities, and (4) an accrual method Target may have liabilities as to which the "all events" test has been satisfied but as to which "economic performance" (e.g., payment) has not yet occurred. The tax treatment of these and other liabilities which have not yet matured into deductions is somewhat surprising. *See* ¶304.

Under Code §461(h), an accrual method Target can deduct liabilities which otherwise satisfy the all events test (i.e., "Code §461(h) Liabilities") only as economic performance occurs. With respect to many such liabilities, economic performance occurs under the proposed Code §461(h) regulations only when the Target has made payment with respect to the liability. *See* ¶304.4.

Reg. §§1.461-4(d)(5) and -4(g)(1)(ii)(C) seem to provide that when the Target sells the Buyer a trade or business and, as part of the sale, the Buyer *"expressly assumes"* a Code §461(h) Liability, the Target can deduct that liability (assuming that the Code §461(h) regulations make payment the proper test for economic performance) in the taxable year in which the sale occurred. This favorable tax result follows from the fact that the Target will be deemed to have made payment with respect to the liability when the amount of the liability (assumed by the Buyer) is included in the Target's amount realized on the sale of divisional assets. The proposed regulation is, however, unclear on the meaning of the phrase "expressly assumes." *See* ¶304.4.

Cautious taxpayers should accordingly consider taking some or all of the following steps: (i) the Parties should specifically enumerate in this Agreement as many as practicable of the Code §461(h) Liabilities which the Buyer is assuming; (ii) the Parties should specifically state in this Agreement that the Buyer is "expressly assuming" not only these enumerated liabilities but also any categories of *unenumerated* Code §461(h) Liabilities which the Buyer is assuming; and (iii) the boards of directors of the respective Parties should adopt resolutions specifically stating that the Buyer is "expressly assuming" these Code §461(h) Liabilities.

Reg. §§1.461-4(d)(5) and 1.461-4(g)(1)(ii)(C) are applicable by their terms only with respect to Code §461(h) Liabilities. However, their premise that the Target will be deemed to have made payment with respect to a liability when the amount of the liability (assumed by the Buyer) is included in the Target's amount realized on the sale of divisional assets may have a broader application. For this reason, cautious taxpayers may want to apply the advice in the preceding paragraph of this footnote to cover *all* liabilities which the Buyer is assuming as to which the Target has not yet become entitled to a deduction under the Code.

(c) *Purchase Price.*[20]   The Buyer agrees to pay to the Target at the Closing $_____ (the *"Purchase Price"*) by delivery of (i) its promissory note (the *"Buyer Note"*) in the form of Exhibit A attached hereto in the principal amount of $_____ and (ii) cash for the balance of the Purchase Price payable by wire transfer or delivery of other immediately available funds.[21]

(d) *Cash Distribution to Target.*[22]   Immediately prior to the Closing, the Target may cause one or more of the Division Subsidiaries to pay the Target an aggregate amount equal to the Target's good faith estimate of the amount by which the unpaid taxes of the Division and the Division Subsidiaries (net of any amount the Division and the Division Subsidiaries shall have paid to the Target with respect thereto under any tax sharing arrangement) with respect to periods prior to the Closing for which the return is due after the Closing (computed on a pro forma stand-alone basis in accordance with the past custom and practice of the Division and the Division Subsidiaries in filing their Income Tax Returns)[23] exceeds the Cash of the Division.[24]

---

[20] The Target may seek to have the Buyer make an earnest money deposit upon execution of this Agreement. If the transaction were thereafter completed, the deposit would be applied to the Purchase Price. If the transaction were thereafter aborted, the deposit would be refunded to the Buyer or paid to the Target as liquidated damages depending on the terms of this Agreement and the reasons for the termination.

[21] Sample acquisition agreement 2002.5 contains additional provisions for use where there is to be a post-Closing Purchase Price adjustment based on the consolidated net book value for the Target and its Subsidiaries as of the Closing. That sample acquisition agreement can be adapted for other post-Closing Purchase Price adjustments (such as a comparison of consolidated working capital with consolidated liabilities as of the Closing *or* a contingent earnout based on consolidated earnings for a specified period after the Closing).

Sample acquisition agreement 2002.5 is, however, intended for use with sample acquisition agreements 2002.1, 2002.2, and 2002.3 (the *stock* purchase agreements) and must be modified prior to use with this *divisional asset* purchase agreement.

[22] This Agreement, like sample acquisition agreement 2004.1 (the *pro-buyer* divisional asset purchase agreement), provides that the Target will retain only so much of the consolidated cash of the Division and the Division Subsidiaries as will cover their aggregate unpaid taxes up to the Closing for which the Target will remain liable. *See* the definition of Acquired Assets in §1 above. This §2(d) permits the Target to cause the Division Subsidiaries to distribute some or all of their cash to the Target at the Closing if the cash of the Division alone will not be enough to cover the aggregate unpaid taxes of the Division and the Division Subsidiaries.

Sample acquisition agreement 2004.2 (the *pro-seller* divisional asset purchase agreement), on the other hand, provides that the Target will retain *all* of the consolidated cash of the Division and the Division Subsidiaries. *See* the definition of Acquired Assets in §1 thereof and the provision for a cash distribution from the Division Subsidiaries to the Target in §2(d) thereof.

[23] This definition provides that the unpaid taxes of the Division and the Division Subsidiaries will be computed on a pro forma *stand-alone* basis in accordance with their past custom and practice in filing their tax returns. This means that the unpaid taxes of the Division and the Division Subsidiaries will not be reduced by any net operating loss attributable to other divisions and subsidiaries of the Target.

[24] The Parties may want to introduce a post-Closing adjustment to the Purchase Price based on the difference between the amount of cash the Target will retain at the Closing (i.e., the Target's good faith estimate of the consolidated cash net of unpaid taxes through the Closing) and the actual amount as determined later. *See* sample acquisition agreement 2002.5 for analogous provisions concerning a different type of post-Closing Purchase Price adjustment.

The Target may cause any of the Division Subsidiaries to make any such payment to the Target in the form of a dividend or a redemption.[25]

(e) *The Closing.* The closing of the transactions contemplated by this Agreement (the *"Closing"*) shall take place at the offices of _____ in _____, commencing at 9:00 a.m. local time on the [second] business day following the satisfaction or waiver of all conditions to the obligations of the Parties to consummate the transactions contemplated hereby (other than conditions with respect to actions the respective Parties will take at the Closing itself) or such other date as the Parties may mutually determine (the *"Closing Date"*); *provided, however,* that the Closing Date shall be no earlier than _____, 19____.

(f) *Deliveries at the Closing.* At the Closing, (i) the Target will deliver to the Buyer the various certificates, instruments, and documents referred to in §7(a) below; (ii) the Buyer will deliver to the Target the various certificates, instruments, and documents referred to in §7(b) below; (iii) the Target will execute, acknowledge (if appropriate), and deliver to the Buyer (A) assignments (including real property and Intellectual Property transfer documents) in the forms attached hereto as Exhibits B-1 through B-____ and (B) such other instruments of sale, transfer, conveyance, and assignment as the Buyer and its counsel [reasonably] may request; (iv) the Buyer will execute, acknowledge (if appropriate), and deliver to the Target (A) an assumption in the form attached hereto as Exhibit C and (B) such other instruments of assumption as the Target and its counsel [reasonably] may request; and (v) the Buyer will deliver to the Target the consideration specified in §2(c) above.

(g) *Allocation.* [The Parties agree to allocate the Purchase Price (and all other capitalizable costs) among the Acquired Assets for all purposes (including financial accounting and tax purposes) in accordance with the allocation schedule attached hereto as Exhibit D.][26]

3. *Representations and Warranties of the Target.*[27] The Target represents and warrants to the Buyer that the statements contained in this §3 are correct and

---

[25] The Parties should determine whether there is any external restriction or prohibition on the type of cash payment by the Division Subsidiaries contemplated by this §2(d) (such as a loan covenant or a statutory provision concerning dividends and stock redemptions). The Parties should also consider any possible difference in tax treatment between a cash dividend and a partial stock redemption.

[26] The 1986 Act generally requires the Buyer and the Target to allocate the Buyer's aggregate basis (i.e., the Purchase Price *plus* the Assumed Liabilities *plus* the expenses of the transaction) among the Acquired Assets using the residual method. *See* ¶403. The Parties should omit this provision if they do not reach agreement on a particular allocation schedule.

[27] The Buyer will seek to have the Target make extensive representations and warranties concerning the Division and the Division Subsidiaries, with only occasional qualifications as to knowledge and without any qualification as to materiality. *See* §3 of sample acquisition agreement 2004.1 (the *pro-buyer* divisional asset purchase agreement).

The Target, on the other hand, will seek to give fewer representations and warranties concerning the Division and the Division Subsidiaries, with frequent qualifications as to knowledge and materiality. *See* §3 of sample acquisition agreement 2004.2 (the *pro-seller* divisional asset purchase agreement).

complete as of the date of this Agreement and will be correct and complete as of the Closing Date (as though made then and as though the Closing Date were substituted for the date of this Agreement throughout this §3), except as set forth in the disclosure schedule accompanying this Agreement and initialed by the Parties (the *"Disclosure Schedule"*).[28] The Disclosure Schedule will be arranged in paragraphs corresponding to the lettered and numbered paragraphs contained in this §3.[29]

(a) *Organization of the Target.* The Target is a corporation duly organized, validly existing, and in good standing under the laws of the jurisdiction of its incorporation.

(b) *Authorization of Transaction.* The Target has full power and authority (including full corporate power and authority) to execute and deliver this Agreement and to perform its obligations hereunder. [Without limiting the generality of the foregoing, the board of directors of the Target and the Target Stockholders have duly authorized the execution, delivery, and performance of this Agreement by the Target.][30] This Agreement constitutes the valid and legally binding obligation of the Target, enforceable in accordance with its terms and conditions.

(c) *Noncontravention.* Neither the execution and the delivery of this Agreement, nor the consummation of the transactions contemplated hereby (including the

---

This Agreement, which is intended to favor neither the Buyer nor the Target, contains fairly extensive representations and warranties *and* relatively frequent qualifications as to knowledge and materiality.

[28] The Buyer will have a closing condition (*see* §7(a)(i) below) and post-Closing indemnification rights (*see* §8(b) below) with respect to certain misrepresentations and breaches of warranty. The Buyer will not, however, have a closing condition or post-Closing indemnification rights with respect to any adverse matter which the Target discloses in the Disclosure Schedule. This is because the disclosure will cure any misrepresentation or breach of warranty that might otherwise have existed. Thus, where the Target discloses an adverse matter in the Disclosure Schedule, the Buyer may seek (a) to avoid assuming responsibility for the matter (*see* the definition of Assumed Liabilities in §1 above), (b) to add a specific closing condition requiring an acceptable resolution of the matter, and/or (c) to obtain specific post-Closing indemnification against the matter.

[29] Sample acquisition agreement 2004.1 (the *pro-buyer* divisional asset purchase agreement) contains additional provisions to the effect that the Target's disclosures will be ineffective unless they meet specified standards for particularity and detail. This Agreement, like sample acquisition agreement 2004.2 (the *pro-seller* divisional asset purchase agreement), lacks such provisions.

[30] The Target must obtain the approval of its board of directors *and* the approval of its stockholders in order to sell all or substantially all of its assets. *See* ¶2001.2.2.2. A sale of the *divisional* assets may trigger this requirement, depending on the size of the divisional assets relative to the Target's other assets.

This Agreement assumes the Target has already obtained any requisite corporate approvals.

If approval of the Target's stockholders is necessary, but the Parties wish to enter into this Agreement before the Target has obtained such approval, the Parties should revise this Agreement to include (a) a covenant calling for the Target to obtain such approval prior to the Closing and (b) a closing condition for each of the Parties to the effect that the Target *has* obtained such approval. *Compare* sample acquisition agreement 2005 (the reverse subsidiary merger agreement) which contemplates the target corporation will obtain the approval of its stockholders between the signing of the merger agreement and the Closing.

assignments and assumptions referred to in §2 above), will (i) violate any constitution, statute, regulation, rule, injunction, judgment, order, decree, ruling, charge, or other restriction of any government, governmental agency, or court to which any of the Target and the Division Subsidiaries is subject or any provision of the charter or bylaws of any of the Target and the Division Subsidiaries or (ii) conflict with, result in a breach of, constitute a default under, result in the acceleration of, create in any party the right to accelerate, terminate, modify, or cancel, or require any notice under any agreement, contract, lease, license, instrument, or other arrangement to which any of the Target and the Division Subsidiaries is a party or by which it is bound or to which any of its assets is subject (or result in the imposition of any Security Interest upon any of its assets), except where the violation, conflict, breach, default, acceleration, termination, modification, cancellation, failure to give notice, or Security Interest would not have a material adverse effect on the business, financial condition, operations, results of operations, or future prospects of the Division and the Division Subsidiaries or on the ability of the Parties to consummate the transactions contemplated by this Agreement. None of the Target and the Division Subsidiaries needs to give any notice to, make any filing with, or obtain any authorization, consent, or approval of any government or governmental agency in order for the Parties to consummate the transactions contemplated by this Agreement (including the assignments and assumptions referred to in §2 above), except where the failure to give notice, to file, or to obtain any authorization, consent, or approval would not have a material adverse effect on the business, financial condition, operations, results of operations, or future prospects of the Division and the Division Subsidiaries or on the ability of the Parties to consummate the transactions contemplated by this Agreement.

(d) *Brokers' Fees.* The Target has no liability or obligation to pay any fees or commissions to any broker, finder, or agent with respect to the transactions contemplated by this Agreement for which the Buyer could become liable or obligated. None of the Division Subsidiaries has any liability or obligation to pay any fees or commissions to any broker, finder, or agent with respect to the transactions contemplated by this Agreement.

(e) *Title to Assets.* The Division and the Division Subsidiaries have good and marketable title to, or a valid leasehold interest in, the properties and assets used by them, located on their premises, or shown on the Most Recent Balance Sheet or acquired after the date thereof, free and clear of all Security Interests, except for properties and assets disposed of in the Ordinary Course of Business since the date of the Most Recent Balance Sheet. Without limiting the generality of the foregoing, the Division has good and marketable title to all of the Acquired Assets, free and clear of any Security Interest or restriction on transfer.

The Parties generally will not enter into an asset purchase agreement (or for that matter a merger agreement) until the Target has obtained any requisite approval of its *board of directors.*

(f) *Subsidiaries.* §3(f) of the Disclosure Schedule sets forth for each Division Subsidiary (i) its name and jurisdiction of incorporation, (ii) the number of shares of authorized capital stock of each class of its capital stock, (iii) the number of issued and outstanding shares of each class of its capital stock, the names of the holders thereof, and the number of shares held by each such holder, (iv) the number of shares of its capital stock held in treasury, and (v) its directors and officers. Each Division Subsidiary is a corporation duly organized, validly existing, and in good standing under the laws of the jurisdiction of its incorporation. Each Division Subsidiary is duly authorized to conduct business and is in good standing under the laws of each jurisdiction where such qualification is required, except where the lack of such qualification would not have a material adverse effect on the business, financial condition, operations, results of operations, or future prospects of the Division and the Division Subsidiaries. Each Division Subsidiary has full corporate power and authority to carry on the businesses in which it is engaged and to own and use the properties owned and used by it. All of the issued and outstanding shares of capital stock of each Division Subsidiary have been duly authorized and are validly issued, fully paid, and nonassessable. One of the Target and the Division Subsidiaries holds of record and owns beneficially all of the outstanding shares of each Division Subsidiary, free and clear of any restrictions on transfer (other than restrictions under the Securities Act and state securities laws), taxes, Security Interests, options, warrants, purchase rights, contracts, commitments, equities, claims, and demands. There are no outstanding or authorized options, warrants, purchase rights, subscription rights, conversion rights, exchange rights, or other contracts or commitments that could require any of the Target and its Subsidiaries to sell, transfer, or otherwise dispose of any capital stock of any of the Division Subsidiaries or that could require any Division Subsidiary to issue, sell, or otherwise cause to become outstanding any of its own capital stock (other than this Agreement). There are no outstanding stock appreciation, phantom stock, profit participation, or similar rights with respect to any Division Subsidiary. There are no voting trusts, proxies, or other agreements or understandings with respect to the voting of any capital stock of any Division Subsidiary. None of the Target and the Division Subsidiaries controls directly or indirectly or has any direct or indirect equity participation in any corporation, partnership, trust, or other business association with respect to the Division which is not a Division Subsidiary.

(g) *Financial Statements.* Attached hereto as Exhibit E are the following financial statements (collectively the *"Financial Statements"*): (i) audited consolidated balance sheets and statements of income, changes in control account, and cash flow as of and for the fiscal years ended _____, 19_____, _____, 19_____, _____, 19_____, _____, 19_____, and _____, 19_____ (the *"Most Recent Fiscal Year End"*) for the Division and the Division Subsidiaries; and (ii) unaudited consolidated balance sheets and statements of income, changes in control account, and cash flow (the *"Most Recent Financial Statements "*) as of and for the _____ months ended _____, 19_____ (the *"Most Recent Fiscal Month*

End ") for the Division and the Division Subsidiaries.[31] The Financial Statements (including the notes thereto) have been prepared in accordance with GAAP applied on a consistent basis throughout the periods covered thereby and present fairly the financial condition of the Division and the Division Subsidiaries as of such dates and the results of operations of the Division and the Division Subsidiaries for such periods;[32] *provided, however,* that the Most Recent Financial Statements are subject to normal year-end adjustments (which will not be material individually or in the aggregate) and lack footnotes and other presentation items. The Target maintains a separate Cash account for the Division (into which the Target deposits all of the receipts of the Division and out of which the Target makes all of the disbursements of the Division).

(h) *Events Subsequent to Most Recent Fiscal Year End.* Since the Most Recent Fiscal Year End, there has not been any material adverse change in the business, financial condition, operations, results of operations, or future prospects of the Division and the Division Subsidiaries taken as a whole. Without limiting the generality of the foregoing, since that date:

(i) none of the Division and the Division Subsidiaries has sold, leased, transferred, or assigned any material assets, tangible or intangible, outside the Ordinary Course of Business;

(ii) none of the Division and the Division Subsidiaries has entered into any material agreement, contract, lease, or license outside the Ordinary Course of Business;

(iii) no party (including any of the Division and the Division Subsidiaries) has accelerated, terminated, made material modifications to, or cancelled any material agreement, contract, lease, or license to which any of the Division and the Division Subsidiaries is a party or by which any of them is bound;

(iv) none of the Division and the Division Subsidiaries has imposed any Security Interest upon any of its assets, tangible or intangible;

---

[31] In the event the Target is unable to satisfy its retained liabilities and obligations after the Closing (i.e., the liabilities and obligations the Buyer did not assume), the Buyer may be exposed for certain of those liabilities and obligations by operation of law (e.g., under statutes and common law doctrines imposing successor liability). See ¶2001.2.2.2.

For this reason, the Buyer may seek additional representations and warranties about the *Target's* financial statements and undisclosed liabilities. *Compare* sample acquisition agreement 2003.1 (the *pro-buyer* asset purchase agreement) which contains representations and warranties for use when the Buyer is acquiring *all* of the assets of a target corporation.

[32] This Agreement, like sample acquisition agreement 2004.2 (the *pro-seller* divisional asset purchase agreement), contains a representation and warranty to the effect that the Financial Statements have been prepared in accordance with GAAP consistently applied and fairly present the financial condition and the results of operations of the Division and the Division Subsidiaries. Sample acquisition agreement 2004.1 (the *pro-buyer* divisional asset purchase agreement), on the other hand, contains additional representations and warranties to the effect that the Financial Statements are correct and complete and consistent with the books and records of the Division and the Division Subsidiaries.

(v) none of the Division and the Division Subsidiaries has made any material capital expenditures outside the Ordinary Course of Business;

(vi) none of the Division and the Division Subsidiaries has made any material capital investment in, or any material loan to, any other Person outside the Ordinary Course of Business;

(vii) the Division and the Division Subsidiaries have not created, incurred, assumed, or guaranteed more than $_____ in aggregate indebtedness for borrowed money and capitalized lease obligations;

(viii) none of the Division and the Division Subsidiaries has granted any license or sublicense of any material rights under or with respect to any Intellectual Property;

(ix) there has been no change made or authorized in the charter or bylaws of any of the Division Subsidiaries;

(x) none of the Division Subsidiaries has issued, sold, or otherwise disposed of any of its capital stock, or granted any options, warrants, or other rights to purchase or obtain (including upon conversion, exchange, or exercise) any of its capital stock;

(xi) none of the Division Subsidiaries has declared, set aside, or paid any dividend or made any distribution with respect to its capital stock (whether in cash or in kind) or redeemed, purchased, or otherwise acquired any of its capital stock;

(xii) none of the Division and the Division Subsidiaries has experienced any material damage, destruction, or loss (whether or not covered by insurance) to its property;

(xiii) none of the Division and the Division Subsidiaries has made any loan to, or entered into any other transaction with, any of the directors, officers, and employees of the Target and its Subsidiaries (including the Division Subsidiaries) outside the Ordinary Course of Business;

(xiv) none of the Division and the Division Subsidiaries has entered into any employment contract or collective bargaining agreement, written or oral, or modified the terms of any existing such contract or agreement;

(xv) none of the Division and the Division Subsidiaries has granted any increase in the base compensation of any of the directors, officers, and employees of the Target and its Subsidiaries (including the Division Subsidiaries) outside the Ordinary Course of Business;

(xvi) none of the Division and the Division Subsidiaries has adopted, amended, modified, or terminated any bonus, profit-sharing, incentive, severance, or other plan, contract, or commitment for the benefit of any of the directors, officers, and employees of the Target and its Subsidiaries (including the Division Subsidiaries), or taken any such action with respect to any other Employee Benefit Plan;

(xvii) none of the Division and the Division Subsidiaries has made any other material change in employment terms for any of the directors, officers, and employees of the Target and its Subsidiaries (including the Division Subsidiaries) outside the Ordinary Course of Business;

(xviii) the Division has not paid any amount to any third party with respect to any liability or obligation (including any costs and expenses the Target has incurred or may incur in connection with this Agreement and the transactions contemplated hereby) which would not constitute an Assumed Liability if in existence as of the Closing;[33] and

(xix) none of the Division and the Division Subsidiaries has committed to any of the foregoing.

(i) *Undisclosed Liabilities.* None of the Division and the Division Subsidiaries has any material liability (whether known or unknown, whether asserted or unasserted, whether absolute or contingent, whether accrued or unaccrued, whether liquidated or unliquidated, and whether due or to become due, including any liability for taxes), except for (i) liabilities set forth on the face of the Most Recent Balance Sheet (rather than in any notes thereto) and (ii) liabilities which have arisen after the Most Recent Fiscal Month End in the Ordinary Course of Business.[34]

---

[33] Notice that the Buyer will bear the cost of (i.e., will in effect assume) any liability or obligation to the extent the Division pays any amount to a third party with respect thereto prior to the Closing. This is because the payment will reduce the amount of cash the Buyer otherwise would receive when it acquires the assets of the Division at the Closing. The Buyer therefore will seek to prevent the Division from making any payment with respect to a liability or obligation the Buyer is not assuming.

This representation and warranty is designed to uncover whether the Division has made any such payment between the Most Recent Fiscal Year End and the date of this Agreement. §5(c) below contains a comparable covenant prohibiting the Division from making any such payment between the date of this Agreement and the Closing.

[34] This Agreement, like sample acquisition agreement 2004.1 (the *pro-buyer* divisional asset purchase agreement), contains representations regarding undisclosed liabilities. Sample acquisition agreement 2004.2 (the *pro-seller* divisional asset purchase agreement), on the other hand, lacks such a representation.

By way of background, this Agreement provides that the Buyer will assume certain specified liabilities of the *Division*. *See* the definition of Assumed Liabilities in §1 above (and in particular the provision making the Buyer responsible for certain liabilities the Target reveals in the Disclosure Schedule).

In addition, the Buyer may be exposed for certain liabilities of the *Division* by operation of law if the Target does not pay them (e.g., under applicable bulk sales statutes and common law doctrines of de facto merger and successor liability). *See* ¶2001.2.2.2.

(j) *Legal Compliance.* Each of the Division and the Division Subsidiaries has complied with all applicable laws (including rules, regulations, codes, plans, injunctions, judgments, orders, decrees, rulings, and charges thereunder) of federal, state, local, and foreign governments (and all agencies thereof), and no action, suit, proceeding, hearing, investigation, charge, complaint, claim, demand, or notice has been filed or commenced against any of them alleging any failure so to comply, except where the failure to comply would not have a material adverse effect on the business, financial condition, operations, results of operations, or future prospects of the Division and the Division Subsidiaries.

(k) *Tax Matters.*[35]

(i) Each of the Division and the Division Subsidiaries[36] has filed all Income Tax Returns that it was required to file. All such Income Tax Returns were correct and complete in all material respects. All Income Taxes owed by any of the Division and the Division Subsidiaries (whether or not shown on any

---

Finally, the Buyer will become indirectly responsible for all of the liabilities of the *Division Subsidiaries* not paid by the Target when the Buyer acquires their capital stock as part of the Acquired Assets. For this reason, the Buyer may seek (a) to purchase assets from the Target *and from each of the Division Subsidiaries* (i.e., a multiple entity asset sale) or (b) to have the Target liquidate and dissolve the Division Subsidiaries tax free under Code §332 (to the extent they are United States corporations) and sell their assets to the Buyer.

These representations regarding undisclosed liabilities (and the post-Closing indemnification provisions in §8(b) below) are designed to work in conjunction with the narrow definition of Assumed Liabilities in §1 above to protect the Buyer against liabilities it does not intend to assume.

[35] This Agreement provides that the Buyer will not assume any liability of the *Target (including the Division)* for unpaid taxes through the Closing. *See* the definition of Assumed Liabilities in §1 above. This Agreement also provides that the Target will be responsible for the unpaid taxes of the *Division Subsidiaries* through the Closing. *See* the tax allocation provisions in §10(n) below. Sample acquisition agreement 2004.1 (the *pro-buyer* divisional asset purchase agreement) and sample acquisition agreement 2004.2 (the *pro-seller* divisional asset purchase agreement) are alike in this respect, and contain similar provisions.

The Buyer may, however, have (i) exposure for the tax liabilities of the Target (including the Division) by operation of law if the Target does not pay them (e.g., under applicable bulk sales statutes and common law doctrines of de facto merger and successor liability) and (ii) indirect exposure for the tax liabilities of the Division Subsidiaries not paid by the Target when the Buyer acquires their capital stock as part of the Acquired Assets. In order to eliminate the latter risk, the Buyer may seek (a) to purchase assets from the Target *and from each of the Division Subsidiaries* (i.e., a multiple entity asset sale) or (b) to have the Target liquidate and dissolve the Division Subsidiaries tax free under Code §332 (to the extent they are United States corporations) and sell their assets to the Buyer.

[36] This Agreement contains a considerably abbreviated version of the tax provisions found in sample acquisition agreement 2002.4 (sale of subsidiary out of consolidated group). The Parties may wish to incorporate some or all of the unabridged provisions from sample acquisition agreement 2002.4 into this Agreement.

Income Tax Return) have been paid.[37] None of the Division and the Division Subsidiaries currently is the beneficiary of any extension of time within which to file any Income Tax Return.

(ii) There is no material dispute or claim concerning any Income Tax liability of any of the Division and the Division Subsidiaries either (A) claimed or raised by any authority in writing or (B) as to which any of the Target Stockholders and the directors and officers of the Target and its Subsidiaries has Knowledge based upon personal contact with any agent of such authority.

(iii) §3(k) of the Disclosure Schedule lists all federal, state, local, and foreign Income Tax Returns filed with respect to any of the Division and the Division Subsidiaries for taxable periods ended on or after _____, 19_____, indicates those Income Tax Returns that have been audited, and indicates those Income Tax Returns that currently are the subject of audit. The Target has delivered to the Buyer correct and complete copies of all federal Income Tax Returns, examination reports, and statements of deficiencies assessed against or agreed to by any of the Division and the Division Subsidiaries since _____, 19_____. None of the Division and the Division Subsidiaries has waived any statute of limitations in respect of Income Taxes or agreed to any extension of time with respect to an Income Tax assessment or deficiency.

(iv) None of the Division and the Division Subsidiaries has filed a consent under Code §341(f) concerning collapsible corporations. None of the Division and the Division Subsidiaries has made any material payments, is obligated to make any material payments, or is a party to any agreement that under certain circumstances could obligate it to make any material payments that will not be deductible under Code §280G. None of the Division and the Division Subsidiaries has been a United States real property holding corporation within the meaning of Code §897(c)(2) during the applicable period specified in Code §897(c)(1)(A)(ii). None of the Division and the Division Subsidiaries is a party to any tax allocation or sharing agreement. None of the Target and its Subsidiaries (A) has been a member of an Affiliated Group filing a consolidated federal

---

[37] Sample acquisition agreement 2004.1 (the *pro-buyer* divisional asset purchase agreement) contains a broad representation and warranty to the effect that each of the Division and the Division Subsidiaries has filed all tax returns that it was required to file, that all such tax returns were correct and complete in all respects, and that all taxes owed by any of the Division and the Division Subsidiaries (whether or not shown on any return) have been paid.

Sample acquisition agreement 2004.2 (the *pro-seller* divisional asset purchase agreement), on the other hand, contains a narrow representation to the effect that each of the Division and the Division Subsidiaries has filed all *income* tax returns that it was required to file and has paid all *income* taxes *shown thereon as owing*.

This Agreement, which is intended to favor neither the Buyer nor the Target, contains a fairly broad representation and warranty to the effect that each of the Division and the Division Subsidiaries has filed all *income* tax returns that it was required to file, that all such *income* tax returns were correct and complete in all *material* respects, and that all *income* taxes owed by any of the Division and the Division Subsidiaries (whether or not shown on any return) have been paid.

Income Tax Return (other than a group the common parent of which was the Target) or (B) has any liability for the taxes of any Person (other than any of the Target and its Subsidiaries) under Reg. §1.1502-6 (or any similar provision of state, local, or foreign law), as a transferee or successor, by contract, or otherwise.[38]

(v) The unpaid Income Taxes of the Division and the Division Subsidiaries (A) did not, as of the Most Recent Fiscal Month End, exceed by any material amount the reserve for Income Tax liability (rather than any reserve for deferred taxes established to reflect timing differences between book and tax income) set forth on the face of the Most Recent Balance Sheet (rather than in any notes thereto) and (B) will not exceed by any material amount that reserve as adjusted for operations and transactions through the Closing Date in accordance with the past custom and practice of the Division and the Division Subsidiaries in filing their Income Tax Returns.

(l) *Real Property.*[39]

(i) §3(l)(i) of the Disclosure Schedule lists and describes briefly all real property that any of the Division and the Division Subsidiaries owns. With respect to each such parcel of owned real property:

---

[38] If the Target or a Subsidiary has been a member of an Affiliated Group filing a consolidated federal income tax return, such corporation (or its successor) will be jointly and severally liable under Reg. §1.1502-6 for certain tax liabilities incurred by such Affiliated Group for a tax year when such corporation was a member of such Affiliated Group for all or part of such tax year. *See* ¶210.

The Target or a Subsidiary may also be liable for the unpaid taxes of third parties under similar provisions of state, local, or foreign law, as a transferee or successor, by contract (e.g., a tax sharing agreement), or otherwise.

This Agreement provides that the Buyer will not assume any liability of the *Target* for the unpaid taxes of the Target or any other person. See the definition of "Assumed Liabilities" in §1 above. Sample acquisition agreement 2004.1 (the *pro-buyer* divisional asset purchase agreement) and sample acquisition agreement 2004.2 (the *pro-seller* divisional asset purchase agreement) are alike in this respect, and contain similar provisions.

However, the Buyer will become indirectly responsible for any such liability of the *Division Subsidiaries* when the Buyer acquires their capital stock as part of the Acquired Assets. In order to eliminate this risk altogether, the Buyer may seek (a) to purchase assets from the Target *and from each of the Division Subsidiaries* (i.e., a multiple entity asset sale) or (b) to have the Target liquidate and dissolve the Division Subsidiaries tax free under Code §332 (to the extent they are United States corporations) and sell their assets to the Buyer.

This Agreement, like sample acquisition agreement 2004.1 (the *pro-buyer* divisional asset purchase agreement), contains a relative broad representation (as set forth above) and a specific indemnification provision (*see* §8(b)(ii) below) designed to protect the Buyer against any such liability for the unpaid taxes of the Target or any other person.

Sample acquisition agreement 2004.2 (the *pro-seller* divisional asset purchase agreement), on the other hand, contains only a representation that, to the knowledge of the Target Stockholders, none of the Division Subsidiaries has been a member of any Affiliated Group filing a consolidated federal income tax return (other than a group the common parent of which was the Target).

[39] These representations and warranties concerning real property are relatively long and detailed. A condensed version of these provisions may be more appropriate where, for example, the real property of the Division and the Division Subsidiaries is relatively insignificant.

(A) the identified owner has good and marketable title to the parcel of real property, free and clear of any Security Interest, easement, covenant, or other restriction, except for installments of special assessments not yet delinquent, recorded easements, covenants, and other restrictions, and utility easements, building restrictions, zoning restrictions, and other easements and restrictions existing generally with respect to properties of a similar character which do not affect materially and adversely the current use, occupancy, or value, or the marketability of title, of the property subject thereto;

(B) there are no pending or, to the Knowledge of any of the Target Stockholders and the directors and officers of the Target and its Subsidiaries, threatened condemnation proceedings, law suits, or administrative actions relating to the property, or other matters affecting materially and adversely the current use, occupancy, or value thereof;

(C) the legal description for the parcel contained in the deed thereof describes such parcel fully and adequately, the buildings and improvements are located within the boundary lines of the described parcels of land, are not in material violation of applicable setback requirements, zoning laws, and ordinances (and none of the properties or buildings or improvements thereon are subject to "permitted non-conforming use" or "permitted non-conforming structure" classifications), and do not encroach on any easement which may burden the land;

(D) all facilities have received all approvals of governmental authorities (including material licenses and permits) required in connection with the ownership or operation thereof, and have been operated and maintained in accordance with applicable laws, rules, and regulations in all material respects;

(E) there are no leases, subleases, licenses, concessions, or other agreements, written or oral, granting to any party or parties the right of use or occupancy of any portion of the parcel of real property;

(F) there are no outstanding options or rights of first refusal to purchase the parcel of real property, or any portion thereof or interest therein; and

(G) there are no parties (other than the Division and the Division Subsidiaries) in possession of the parcel of real property, other than tenants under any leases disclosed in §3(l)(i) of the Disclosure Schedule who are in possession of space to which they are entitled.

(ii) §3(l)(ii) of the Disclosure Schedule lists and describes briefly all real property leased or subleased to any of the Division and the Division Subsidiaries. §3(l)(ii) of the Disclosure Schedule also identifies the leased or subleased properties for which title insurance policies are to be procured in accordance with §5(h)(ii) below. The Target has delivered to the Buyer correct and complete copies of the leases and subleases listed in §3(l)(ii) of the Disclosure Schedule (as amended to date). With respect to each material lease and sublease listed in §3(l)(ii) of the Disclosure Schedule:

(A) the lease or sublease is legal, valid, binding, enforceable, and in full force and effect in all material respects;

(B) no party to the lease or sublease is in material breach or default, and no event has occurred which, with notice or lapse of time, would constitute a material breach or default or permit termination, modification, or acceleration thereunder;

(C) no party to the lease or sublease has repudiated any material provision thereof;

(D) there are no material disputes, oral agreements, or forbearance programs in effect as to the lease or sublease;

(E) none of the Division and the Division Subsidiaries has assigned, transferred, conveyed, mortgaged, deeded in trust, or encumbered any interest in the leasehold or subleasehold; and

(F) all facilities leased or subleased thereunder have received all approvals of governmental authorities (including material licenses and permits) required in connection with the operation thereof, and have been operated and maintained in accordance with applicable laws, rules, and regulations in all material respects.

(m) *Intellectual Property.*[40]

(i) None of the Division and the Division Subsidiaries has interfered with, infringed upon, misappropriated, or violated any material Intellectual Property rights of third parties in any material respect, and none of the Target Stockholders and the directors and officers of the Target and its Subsidiaries has ever received any charge, complaint, claim, demand, or notice alleging any such interference, infringement, misappropriation, or violation (including any claim that any of the Division and the Division Subsidiaries must license or refrain from using any Intellectual Property rights of any third party). To the Knowledge of any of the Target Stockholders and the directors and officers of the Target and its Subsidiaries, no third party has interfered with, infringed upon,

---

[40] These representations and warranties concerning intellectual property are relatively long and detailed. A condensed version of these provisions may be more appropriate where, for example, the intellectual property of the Division and the Division Subsidiaries is relatively insignificant.

misappropriated, or violated any material Intellectual Property rights of any of the Division and the Division Subsidiaries in any material respect.

(ii) §3(m)(ii) of the Disclosure Schedule identifies each patent or registration which has been issued to any of the Division and the Division Subsidiaries with respect to any of its Intellectual Property, identifies each pending patent application or application for registration which any of the Division and the Division Subsidiaries has made with respect to any of its Intellectual Property, and identifies each material license, agreement, or other permission which any of the Division and the Division Subsidiaries has granted to any third party with respect to any of its Intellectual Property (together with any exceptions). The Target has delivered to the Buyer correct and complete copies of all such patents, registrations, applications, licenses, agreements, and permissions (as amended to date). §3(m)(ii) of the Disclosure Schedule also identifies each material trade name or unregistered trademark used by any of the Division and the Division Subsidiaries in connection with any of its businesses. With respect to each item of Intellectual Property required to be identified in §3(m)(ii) of the Disclosure Schedule:

(A) the Division and the Division Subsidiaries possess all right, title, and interest in and to the item, free and clear of any Security Interest, license, or other restriction;

(B) the item is not subject to any outstanding injunction, judgment, order, decree, ruling, or charge;

(C) no action, suit, proceeding, hearing, investigation, charge, complaint, claim, or demand is pending or, to the Knowledge of any of the Target Stockholders and the directors and officers of the Target and its Subsidiaries, is threatened which challenges the legality, validity, enforceability, use, or ownership of the item; and

(D) none of the Division and the Division Subsidiaries has ever agreed to indemnify any Person for or against any interference, infringement, misappropriation, or other conflict with respect to the item.

(iii) §3(m)(iii) of the Disclosure Schedule identifies each material item of Intellectual Property that any third party owns and that any of the Division and the Division Subsidiaries uses pursuant to license, sublicense, agreement, or permission. The Target has delivered to the Buyer correct and complete copies of all such licenses, sublicenses, agreements, and permissions (as amended to date). With respect to each item of Intellectual Property required to be identified in §3(m)(iii) of the Disclosure Schedule:

(A) the license, sublicense, agreement, or permission covering the item is legal, valid, binding, enforceable, and in full force and effect in all material respects;

(B) no party to the license, sublicense, agreement, or permission is in material breach or default, and no event has occurred which with notice or lapse of time would constitute a material breach or default or permit termination, modification, or acceleration thereunder;

(C) no party to the license, sublicense, agreement, or permission has repudiated any material provision thereof; and

(D) none of the Division and the Division Subsidiaries has granted any sublicense or similar right with respect to the license, sublicense, agreement, or permission.

(n) *Tangible Assets.* The buildings, machinery, equipment, and other tangible assets that the Division and the Division Subsidiaries own and lease are free from material defects (patent and latent), have been maintained in accordance with normal industry practice, and are in good operating condition and repair (subject to normal wear and tear).

(o) *Inventory.* The inventory of the Division and the Division Subsidiaries consists of raw materials and supplies, manufactured and processed parts, work in process, and finished goods, all of which is merchantable and fit for the purpose for which it was procured or manufactured, and none of which is slow-moving, obsolete, damaged, or defective, subject only to the reserve for inventory writedown set forth on the face of the Most Recent Balance Sheet (rather than in any notes thereto) as adjusted for operations and transactions through the Closing Date in accordance with the past custom and practice of the Division and the Division Subsidiaries.

(p) *Contracts.* §3(p) of the Disclosure Schedule lists the following contracts and other agreements to which any of the Division and the Division Subsidiaries is a party:

(i) any agreement (or group of related agreements) for the lease of personal property to or from any Person providing for lease payments in excess of $_____ per annum;

(ii) any agreement (or group of related agreements) for the purchase or sale of raw materials, commodities, supplies, products, or other personal property, or for the furnishing or receipt of services, the performance of which will extend over a period of more than one year, or involve consideration in excess of $_____;

(iii) any agreement concerning a partnership or joint venture;

(iv) any agreement (or group of related agreements) under which it has created, incurred, assumed, or guaranteed any indebtedness for borrowed money, or any capitalized lease obligation, in excess of $_____ or under which it has imposed a Security Interest on any of its assets, tangible or intangible;

(v) any material agreement concerning confidentiality or noncompetition;

(vi) any material agreement involving any of the Target Stockholders and their Affiliates (including the Target and its Subsidiaries other than the Division Subsidiaries);

(vii) any profit sharing, stock option, stock purchase, stock appreciation, deferred compensation, severance, or other material plan or arrangement for the benefit of the current or former directors, officers, and employees of the Target and its Subsidiaries (including the Division Subsidiaries);

(viii) any collective bargaining agreement;

(ix) any agreement for the employment of any individual on a full-time, part-time, consulting, or other basis providing annual compensation in excess of $_____ or providing material severance benefits;

(x) any agreement under which it has advanced or loaned any amount to any of the directors, officers, and employees of the Target and its Subsidiaries (including the Division Subsidiaries) outside the Ordinary Course of Business;

(xi) any agreement under which the consequences of a default or termination could have a material adverse effect on the business, financial condition, operations, results of operations, or future prospects of the Division and the Division Subsidiaries; or

(xii) any other agreement (or group of related agreements) the performance of which involves consideration in excess of $_____.

The Target has delivered to the Buyer a correct and complete copy of each written agreement listed in §3(p) of the Disclosure Schedule (as amended to date) and a written summary setting forth the material terms and conditions of each oral agreement referred to in §3(p) of the Disclosure Schedule. With respect to each such agreement: (A) the agreement is legal, valid, binding, enforceable, and in full force and effect in all material respects; (B) no party is in material breach or default, and no event has occurred which with notice or lapse of time would constitute a material breach or default, or permit termination, modification, or acceleration, under the agreement; and (C) no party has repudiated any material provision of the agreement.

(q) *Notes and Accounts Receivable.* All notes and accounts receivable of the Division and the Division Subsidiaries are reflected properly on their books and records, are valid receivables subject to no setoffs or counterclaims, are current and collectible, and will be collected in accordance with their terms at their recorded amounts, subject only to the reserve for bad debts set forth on the face of the Most Recent Balance Sheet (rather than in any notes thereto) as adjusted for operations and transactions through the Closing Date in accordance with the past custom and practice of the Division and the Division Subsidiaries.

(r) *Powers of Attorney.* To the Knowledge of any of the Target Stockholders and the directors and officers of the Target and its Subsidiaries, there are no material outstanding powers of attorney executed on behalf of any of the Division and the Division Subsidiaries.

(s) *Insurance.* §3(s) of the Disclosure Schedule sets forth the following information with respect to each material insurance policy (including policies providing property, casualty, liability, and workers' compensation coverage and bond and surety arrangements) with respect to which any of the Division and the Division Subsidiaries is a party, a named insured, or otherwise the beneficiary of coverage:

   (i) the name, address, and telephone number of the agent;

   (ii) the name of the insurer, the name of the policyholder, and the name of each covered insured;

   (iii) the policy number and the period of coverage;

   (iv) the scope (including an indication of whether the coverage is on a claims made, occurrence, or other basis) and amount (including a description of how deductibles and ceilings are calculated and operate) of coverage; and

   (v) a description of any retroactive premium adjustments or other material loss-sharing arrangements.

With respect to each such insurance policy: (A) the policy is legal, valid, binding, enforceable, and in full force and effect in all material respects; (B) neither any of the Division and the Division Subsidiaries nor any other party to the policy is in material breach or default (including with respect to the payment of premiums or the giving of notices), and no event has occurred which, with notice or the lapse of time, would constitute such a material breach or default, or permit termination, modification, or acceleration, under the policy; and (C) no party to the policy has repudiated any material provision thereof. §3(s) of the Disclosure

Schedule describes any material self-insurance arrangements affecting any of the Division and the Division Subsidiaries.

(t) *Litigation.* §3(t) of the Disclosure Schedule sets forth each instance in which any of the Division and the Division Subsidiaries (i) is subject to any outstanding injunction, judgment, order, decree, ruling, or charge or (ii) is a party or, to the Knowledge of any of the Target Stockholders and the directors and officers of the Target and its Subsidiaries, is threatened to be made a party to any action, suit, proceeding, hearing, or investigation of, in, or before any court or quasi-judicial or administrative agency of any federal, state, local, or foreign jurisdiction or before any arbitrator.

(u) *Product Warranty.* Substantially all of the products manufactured, sold, leased, and delivered by the Division and the Division Subsidiaries have conformed in all material respects with all applicable contractual commitments and all express and implied warranties, and none of the Division and the Division Subsidiaries has any material liability (whether known or unknown, whether asserted or unasserted, whether absolute or contingent, whether accrued or unaccrued, whether liquidated or unliquidated, and whether due or to become due) for replacement or repair thereof or other damages in connection therewith, subject only to the reserve for product warranty claims set forth on the face of the Most Recent Balance Sheet (rather than in any notes thereto) as adjusted for operations and transactions through the Closing Date in accordance with the past custom and practice of the Division and the Division Subsidiaries. Substantially all of the products manufactured, sold, leased, or delivered by the Division and the Division Subsidiaries are subject to standard terms and conditions of sale or lease. §3(u) of the Disclosure Schedule includes copies of the standard terms and conditions of sale or lease for each of the Division and the Division Subsidiaries (containing applicable guaranty, warranty, and indemnity provisions).

(v) *Product Liability.* None of the Division and the Division Subsidiaries has any material liability (whether known or unknown, whether asserted or unasserted, whether absolute or contingent, whether accrued or unaccrued, whether liquidated or unliquidated, and whether due or to become due) arising out of any injury to individuals or property as a result of the ownership, possession, or use of any product manufactured, sold, leased, or delivered by any of the Division and the Division Subsidiaries.

(w) *Employees.* To the Knowledge of any of the Target Stockholders and the directors and officers of the Division and the Division Subsidiaries, no executive, key employee, or significant group of employees plans to terminate employment with any of the Division and the Division Subsidiaries during the next 12 months. None of the Division and the Division Subsidiaries is a party to or bound by any collective bargaining agreement, nor has any of them experienced any strike or material grievance, claim of unfair labor practices, or other collective bargaining dispute within the past [three] years. None of the Division and the Division

Subsidiaries has committed any material unfair labor practice. None of the Target Stockholders and the directors and officers of the Target and its Subsidiaries has any Knowledge of any organizational effort presently being made or threatened by or on behalf of any labor union with respect to employees of any of the Division and the Division Subsidiaries.

(x) *Employee Benefits.*[41]

(i) §3(x) of the Disclosure Schedule lists each Employee Benefit Plan that any of the Division and the Division Subsidiaries maintains or to which any of the Division and the Division Subsidiaries contributes or has any obligation to contribute.

(A) Each such Employee Benefit Plan (and each related trust, insurance contract, or fund) has been maintained, funded and administered in accordance with the terms of such Employee Benefit Plan and complies in form and in operation in all material respects with the applicable requirements of ERISA, the Code, and other applicable laws.

(B) All required reports and descriptions (including annual reports (IRS Form 5500), summary annual reports, and summary plan descriptions) have been timely filed and/or distributed in accordance with the applicable requirements of ERISA and the Code with respect to each such Employee Benefit Plan. The requirements of COBRA have been met in all material respects with respect to each such Employee Benefit Plan which is an Employee Welfare Benefit Plan subject to COBRA.

(C) All contributions (including all employer contributions and employee salary reduction contributions) which are due have been made within the time period prescribed by ERISA to each such Employee Benefit Plan which is an Employee Pension Benefit Plan and all contributions for any period ending on or before the Closing Date which are not yet due have been made to each such Employee Pension Benefit Plan or accrued in accordance with the past custom and practice of the Division and the Division Subsidiaries. All premiums or other payments for all periods ending on or before the Closing Date have been paid with respect to each such Employee Benefit Plan which is an Employee Welfare Benefit Plan.

(D) Each such Employee Benefit Plan intended to meet the requirements of a "qualified plan" under Code §401(a) has received a favorable determination letter from the Internal Revenue Service that it is a "qualified plan," and the Target Stockholders are not aware of any facts or circumstances that could adversely affect the qualified status of any such Employee Benefit Plan.

---

[41] These representations and warranties concerning employee benefits are relatively long and detailed. A condensed version of these provisions may be more appropriate where, for example, the Division and the Division Subsidiaries have relatively insignificant employee benefit plans.

(E) The market value of assets under each such Employee Benefit Plan which is an Employee Pension Benefit Plan (other than any Multiemployer Plan) equals or exceeds the present value of all vested and nonvested liabilities thereunder (determined in accordance with then current funding assumptions).

(F) The Target has delivered to the Buyer correct and complete copies of the plan documents and summary plan descriptions, the most recent determination letter received from the Internal Revenue Service, the most recent annual report (IRS Form 5500, with all applicable attachments), and all related trust agreements, insurance contracts, and other funding arrangements which implement each such Employee Benefit Plan.

(ii) With respect to each Employee Benefit Plan that any of the Division, the Division Subsidiaries, and any ERISA affiliate maintains, to which any of them contributes, or has any obligation to contribute, or with respect to which any of them has any [material] liability or potential liability:

(A) No such Employee Benefit Plan which is an Employee Pension Benefit Plan (other than any Multiemployer Plan) has been completely or partially terminated or been the subject of a Reportable Event as to which notices would be required to be filed with the PBGC. No proceeding by the PBGC to terminate any such Employee Pension Benefit Plan (other than any Multiemployer Plan) has been instituted or, to the Knowledge of any of the Target Stockholders and the directors and officers of the Target and its Subsidiaries, threatened.

(B) There have been no Prohibited Transactions with respect to any such Employee Benefit Plan. No Fiduciary has any liability for material breach of fiduciary duty or any other material failure to act or comply in connection with the administration or investment of the assets of any such Employee Benefit Plan. No action, suit, proceeding, hearing, or investigation with respect to the administration or the investment of the assets of any such Employee Benefit Plan (other than routine claims for benefits) is pending or, to the Knowledge of any of the Target Stockholders and the directors and officers of the Target and its Subsidiaries, threatened.

(C) None of the Division and the Division Subsidiaries has incurred any material liability (whether known or unknown, whether asserted or unasserted, whether absolute or contingent, whether accrued or unaccrued, whether liquidated or unliquidated, and whether due or to become due) to the PBGC (other than with respect to PBGC premium payments not yet due) or otherwise under Title IV of ERISA (including any withdrawal liability as defined in ERISA §4201) or under the Code with respect to any such Employee Benefit Plan which is an Employee Pension Benefit Plan, or under

COBRA with respect to any such Employee Benefit Plan which is an Employee Welfare Benefit Plan.

(iii) None of the Division, the Division Subsidiaries, and any ERISA Affiliate contributes to, has any obligation to contribute to, or has any material liability (whether known or unknown, whether asserted or unasserted, whether absolute or contingent, whether accrued or unaccrued, whether liquidated or unliquidated, and whether due or to become due), including withdrawal liability (as defined in ERISA §4201), under or with respect to any Multiemployer Plan.

(iv) None of the Division and the Division Subsidiaries maintains, contributes to or has an obligation to contribute to, or has any [material] liability or potential liability with respect to, any Employee Welfare Benefit Plan providing medical, health, or life insurance or other welfare-type benefits for current or future retired or terminated employees, their spouses, or their dependents (other than in accordance with COBRA).

(y) *Guaranties.* None of the Division and the Division Subsidiaries is a guarantor or otherwise is responsible for any liability or obligation (including indebtedness) of any other Person.

(z) *Environment, Health, and Safety Matters.*[42]

(i) Each of the Division, the Division Subsidiaries, and their respective predecessors and Affiliates has complied and is in compliance, in each case in all material respects, with all Environmental, Health, and Safety Requirements.

(ii) Without limiting the generality of the foregoing, each of the Division, the Division Subsidiaries, and their respective Affiliates, has obtained, has complied, and is in compliance with, in each case in all material respects, all material permits, licenses and other authorizations that are required pursuant to Environmental, Health, and Safety Requirements for the occupation of its facilities and the operation of its business; a list of all such material permits, licenses and other authorizations is set forth on the attached *"Environmental and Safety Permits Schedule."*

---

[42] These representations and warranties concerning environmental, health, and safety matters are relatively long and detailed. A condensed version may be more appropriate when, for example, the operations of the Division and the Division Subsidiaries appear to have had a relatively insignificant effect upon the environment or upon public or employee health and safety.

While quite comprehensive (including coverage for strict liability for site cleanup under CERCLA and common law liability), these environmental representations and warranties contain a consistent materiality limitation and are otherwise generally more limited and narrowly focused than those in sample acquisition agreement 2004.1 (the *pro-buyer* divisional purchase agreement).

The environmental representations and warranties in sample acquisition agreement 2004.2 (the *pro-seller* divisional purchase agreement) are further limited to matters within the Target Stockholder's knowledge, do not extend to strict liability for site cleanup under CERCLA or common law liability, and otherwise limit the disclosure and indemnification obligations of the Target.

(iii) None of the Division, the Division Subsidiaries, or their respective Affiliates has received any written or oral notice, report or other information regarding any actual or alleged material violation of Environmental, Health, and Safety Requirements, or any material liabilities or potential material liabilities (whether accrued, absolute, contingent, unliquidated or otherwise), including any material investigatory, remedial or corrective obligations, relating to any of them or its facilities arising under Environmental, Health, and Safety Requirements.

(iv) Except as set forth on the attached *"Environmental and Safety Matters Schedule,"* none of the following exists at any property or facility owned or operated by the Division or the Division Subsidiaries: (1) underground storage tanks, (2) asbestos-containing material in any friable and damaged form or condition, (3) materials or equipment containing polychlorinated biphenyls, or (4) landfills, surface impoundments, or disposal areas.

(v) None of the Division, the Division Subsidiaries, or any of their respective predecessors or Affiliates has treated, stored, disposed of, arranged for or permitted the disposal of, transported, handled, or released any substance, including without limitation any hazardous substance, or owned or operated any property or facility (and no such property or facility is contaminated by any such substance) in a manner that has given or would give rise to material liabilities, including any material liability for response costs, corrective action costs, personal injury, property damage, natural resources damages or attorney fees, pursuant to the Comprehensive Environmental Response, Compensation and Liability Act of 1980, as amended ("CERCLA") or the Solid Waste Disposal Act, as amended ("SWDA") or any other Environmental, Health, and Safety Requirements.

(vi) Neither this Agreement nor the consummation of the transaction that is the subject of this Agreement will result in any material obligations for site investigation or cleanup, or notification to or consent of government agencies or third parties, pursuant to any of the so-called "transaction-triggered" or "responsible property transfer" Environmental, Health, and Safety Requirements.

(aa) *Year 2000.* None of the computer software, computer firmware, computer hardware (whether general or special purpose) or other similar or related items of automated, computerized or software systems that are material to the businesses of the Division or a Division Subsidiary, will malfunction, cease to function, generate incorrect data or produce incorrect results when processing, providing or receiving (i) date-related data from, into and between the twentieth and twenty-first centuries or (ii) date-related data in connection with any valid date in the twentieth and twenty-first centuries.[43]

(bb) *Certain Business Relationships with the Division and the Division Subsidiaries.* None of the Target Stockholders and their Affiliates has been involved in any material business arrangement or relationship with any of the Division and the Division Subsidiaries within the past 12 months, and none of the Target Stockholders and their Affiliates owns any material asset, tangible or intangible, which is used in the business of any of the Division and the Division Subsidiaries.

(cc) *Disclosure.* The representations and warranties contained in this §3 do not contain any untrue statement of a material fact or omit to state any material fact necessary in order to make the statements and information contained in this §3 not misleading.

(dd) *Investment.* The Target (i) understands that the Buyer Note has not been, and will not be, registered under the Securities Act, or under any state securities laws, and is being offered and sold in reliance upon federal and state exemptions for transactions not involving any public offering, (ii) is acquiring the Buyer Note solely for its own account for investment purposes, and not with a view to the distribution thereof, (iii) is a sophisticated investor with knowledge and experience in business and financial matters, (iv) has received certain information concerning the Buyer and has had the opportunity to obtain additional information as desired in order to evaluate the merits and the risks inherent in holding the Buyer Note, (v) is able to bear the economic risk and lack of liquidity inherent in holding the Buyer Note, and (vi) is an Accredited Investor for the reasons set forth in §3(cc) of the Disclosure Schedule.[44]

4. *Representations and Warranties of the Buyer.*[45] The Buyer represents and warrants to the Target that the statements contained in this §4 are correct and complete as of the date of this Agreement and will be correct and complete as of the Closing

---

[43] This representation can be omitted for agreements entered into a sufficient period after approximately 3/1/00 so that Buyer has been able to verify that the Division and the Division Subsidiaries have no Y2K problem.

Sample acquisition agreement 2004.1 (the *pro-buyer* divisional purchase agreement) contains a more extensive representation on this topic and 2004.2 (the *pro-seller* divisional purchase agreement) contains no representation on this topic.

[44] This provision contemplates that the Buyer will issue the Buyer Note pursuant to the exemption from registration under the Securities Act contained in Regulation D. The Parties should determine whether this exemption is available in a particular transaction. If it is not, the Agreement must be modified as necessary to reflect the issuance of the Buyer Note under a different exemption from securities registration or in an offering registered under the Securities Act.

[45] The Target may seek to obtain additional representations and warranties concerning the Buyer and its Subsidiaries (e.g., the typical representations and warranties contained in a loan agreement or an underwriting agreement) because the Buyer is issuing the Buyer Note to the Target as part of the Purchase Price. Any such representations and warranties would normally survive the Closing and remain applicable for so long as the Buyer Note remained outstanding.

Date (as though made then and as though the Closing Date were substituted for the date of this Agreement throughout this §4), except as set forth in the Disclosure Schedule. The Disclosure Schedule will be arranged in paragraphs corresponding to the lettered and numbered paragraphs contained in this §4.

(a) *Organization of the Buyer.* The Buyer is a corporation duly organized, validly existing, and in good standing under the laws of the jurisdiction of its incorporation.

(b) *Authorization of Transaction.* The Buyer has full power and authority (including full corporate power and authority) to execute and deliver this Agreement and to perform its obligations hereunder. This Agreement constitutes the valid and legally binding obligation of the Buyer, enforceable in accordance with its terms and conditions.

(c) *Noncontravention.* Neither the execution and the delivery of this Agreement, nor the consummation of the transactions contemplated hereby (including the assignments and assumptions referred to in §2 above), will (i) violate any constitution, statute, regulation, rule, injunction, judgment, order, decree, ruling, charge, or other restriction of any government, governmental agency, or court to which the Buyer is subject or any provision of its charter or bylaws or (ii) conflict with, result in a breach of, constitute a default under, result in the acceleration of, create in any party the right to accelerate, terminate, modify, or cancel, or require any notice under any agreement, contract, lease, license, instrument, or other arrangement to which the Buyer is a party or by which it is bound or to which any of its assets is subject, except where the violation, conflict, breach, default, acceleration, termination, modification, cancellation, failure to give notice, or Security Interest would not have a material adverse effect on the ability of the Parties to consummate the transactions contemplated by this Agreement. The Buyer does not need to give any notice to, make any filing with, or obtain any authorization, consent, or approval of any government or governmental agency in order for the Parties to consummate the transactions contemplated by this Agreement (including the assignments and assumptions referred to in §2 above), except where the failure to give notice, to file, or to obtain any authorization, consent, or approval would not have a material adverse effect on the ability of the Parties to consummate the transactions contemplated by this Agreement.

(d) *Brokers' Fees.* The Buyer has no liability or obligation to pay any fees or commissions to any broker, finder, or agent with respect to the transactions contemplated by this Agreement for which the Target could become liable or obligated.

5. *Pre-Closing Covenants.* The Parties agree as follows with respect to the period between the execution of this Agreement and the Closing.

(a) *General.* Each of the Parties will use its reasonable best efforts to take all action and to do all things necessary [, proper, or advisable] in order to consummate and make effective the transactions contemplated by this Agreement (including satisfaction, but not waiver, of the closing conditions set forth in §7 below).

(b) *Notices and Consents.* The Target will give (and will cause each of the Division Subsidiaries to give) any notices to third parties, and the Target will use its reasonable best efforts (and will cause each of the Division Subsidiaries to use its reasonable best efforts) to obtain any third party consents, that the Buyer reasonably may request in connection with the matters referred to in §3(c) above. Each of the Parties will (and the Target will cause each of the Division Subsidiaries to) give any notices to, make any filings with, and use its reasonable best efforts to obtain any authorizations, consents, and approvals of governments and governmental agencies in connection with the matters referred to in §3(c) and §4(c) above. Without limiting the generality of the foregoing, each of the Parties will file (and the Target will cause each of the Division Subsidiaries to file) any Notification and Report Forms and related material that it may be required to file with the Federal Trade Commission and the Antitrust Division of the United States Department of Justice under the Hart-Scott-Rodino Act, will use its reasonable best efforts to obtain (and the Target will cause each of the Division Subsidiaries to use its reasonable best efforts to obtain) a waiver from the applicable waiting period, and will make (and the Target will cause each of the Division Subsidiaries to make) any further filings pursuant thereto that may be necessary [, proper, or advisable] in connection therewith.

(c) *Operation of Business.* The Target will not cause or permit any of the Division and the Division Subsidiaries to engage in any practice, take any action, or enter into any transaction outside the Ordinary Course of Business. Without limiting the generality of the foregoing, the Target will not cause or permit any of the Division and the Division Subsidiaries to (i) pay any amount to any third party with respect to any liability or obligation (including any costs and expenses the Target and its Subsidiaries have incurred or may incur in connection with this Agreement and the transactions contemplated hereby) which would not constitute an Assumed Liability if in existence as of the Closing, (ii) _____, or (iii) otherwise engage in any practice, take any action, or enter into any transaction of the sort described in §3(h) above.[46]

(d) *Preservation of Business.* The Target will cause each of the Division and the Division Subsidiaries to keep its business and properties substantially intact,

---

[46] The Parties may prefer to revise this covenant so that it recites specific prohibitions (rather than incorporating the matters in §3(h) above by reference).

including its present operations, physical facilities, working conditions, and relationships with lessors, licensors, suppliers, customers, and employees.[47]

(e) *Full Access.* The Target will permit (and will cause each of the Division and the Division Subsidiaries to permit) representatives of the Buyer to have full access at all reasonable times, and in a manner so as not to interfere with the normal business operations of the Division and the Division Subsidiaries, to all premises, properties, personnel, books, records (including tax records), contracts, and documents of or pertaining to each of the Division and the Division Subsidiaries. The Buyer will treat and hold as such any Confidential Information it receives from any of the Target Stockholders, the Target, and its Subsidiaries in the course of the reviews contemplated by this §5(e), will not use any of the Confidential Information except in connection with this Agreement, and, if this Agreement is terminated for any reason whatsoever, will return to the Target Stockholders, the Target, and its Subsidiaries all tangible embodiments (and all copies) of the Confidential Information which are in its possession.[48]

(f) *Notice of Developments.* Each Party will give prompt written notice to the other Party of any material adverse development causing a breach of any of its own representations and warranties in §3 and §4 above.[49] No disclosure by any Party pursuant to this §5(f), however, shall be deemed to amend or supplement the Disclosure Schedule or to prevent or cure any misrepresentation, breach of warranty, or breach of covenant.[50]

(g) *Exclusivity.* The Target will not (and the Target will not cause or permit any of the Division and the Division Subsidiaries to)(i) solicit, initiate, or encourage

[47] This Agreement, like sample acquisition agreement 2004.1 (the *pro-buyer* divisional asset purchase agreement), contains a provision regarding preservation of the business of the Division and the Division Subsidiaries. Sample acquisition agreement 2004.2 (the *pro-seller* divisional asset purchase agreement), on the other hand, lacks such a provision.

[48] This Agreement, like sample acquisition agreement 2004.2 (the *pro-seller* divisional asset purchase agreement), contains a confidentiality and nonuse provision protecting the Confidential Information until the Buyer actually purchases the divisional assets. Sample acquisition agreement 2004.1 (the *pro-buyer* divisional asset purchase agreement), on the other hand, lacks such a provision.

[49] This Agreement, like sample acquisition agreement 2004.1 (the *pro-buyer* divisional asset purchase agreement), requires the Target to notify the Buyer of any material adverse development prior to the Closing that causes a breach of any of the representations and warranties in §3 above.

Sample acquisition agreement 2004.2 (the *pro-seller* divisional asset purchase agreement), on the other hand, permits (but does not require) the Target to notify the Buyer of any such development. Moreover, if the development gives the Buyer any right to terminate the *pro-seller* agreement, the Buyer must exercise its termination right within [10 business days] after the notice. Unless the Buyer has such a termination right under the *pro-seller* agreement and exercises it within such period, the notice will be deemed to have cured any breach of the representations and warranties that otherwise would have existed by reason of the adverse development.

[50] This Agreement, like sample acquisition agreement 2004.1 (the *pro-buyer* divisional asset purchase agreement), provides that no disclosure (presumably, but not necessarily, by the Target) between signing and Closing shall be deemed to supplement the previous disclosures or to cure any breach of the Agreement. Sample acquisition agreement 2004.2 (the *pro-seller* divisional asset purchase agreement), on the other hand, provides that certain such disclosures *will* supplement the previous

the submission of any proposal or offer from any Person relating to the acquisition of any capital stock or other voting securities, or any substantial portion of the assets, of any of the Division and the Division Subsidiaries (including any acquisition structured as a merger, consolidation, or share exchange) or (ii) participate in any discussions or negotiations regarding, furnish any information with respect to, assist or participate in, or facilitate in any other manner any effort or attempt by any Person to do or seek any of the foregoing.[51]

(h) *Title Insurance.* [52] The Target will cause each of the Division and the Division Subsidiaries to obtain the following title insurance commitments, policies, and riders in preparation for the Closing:

(i) with respect to each parcel of real estate that any of the Division and the Division Subsidiaries owns, an ALTA Owner's Policy of Title Insurance Form B-1987 (or equivalent policy reasonably acceptable to the Buyer if the real property is located in a state in which an ALTA Owner's Policy of Title Insurance Form B-1987 is not available) issued by a title insurer reasonably satisfactory to the Buyer (and, if requested by the Buyer, reinsured in whole or in part by one or more insurance companies and pursuant to a direct access agreement reasonably acceptable to the Buyer), in such amount as the Buyer reasonably may determine to be the fair market value of such real property (including all improvements located thereon), insuring title to such real property to be in the Buyer or the Subsidiary as of the Closing (subject only to the title exceptions described above in §3(l)(i) and in §3(l)(i) of the Disclosure Schedule); and

(ii) with respect to each parcel of real estate that any of the Division and the Division Subsidiaries leases or subleases and which is listed on §3(l)(ii) of the Disclosure Schedule as a property for which a title insurance policy is to be procured, an ALTA Leasehold Owner's Policy of Title Insurance-1987 (or equivalent policy reasonably acceptable to the Buyer if the real property is located in a state in which an ALTA Leasehold Owner's Policy of Title Insurance-1987 is not available) issued by a title insurer reasonably satisfactory to the Buyer (and, if requested by the Buyer, reinsured in whole or in part by one or more insurance companies and pursuant to a direct access agreement

---

disclosures and cure breaches of the Agreement. *See* the discussion in the immediately preceding footnote.

[51] Sample acquisition agreement 2004.2 (the *pro-seller* divisional asset purchase agreement) permits the Target, its Subsidiaries, and their directors and officers to respond to unsolicited proposals to the extent their fiduciary duties may require. This Agreement, like sample acquisition agreement 2004.1 (the *pro-buyer* divisional purchase agreement), lacks such a provision.

[52] This Agreement, like sample acquisition agreement 2004.1 (the *pro-buyer* divisional asset purchase agreement), contains relatively long and detailed provisions concerning title insurance. A condensed version may be more appropriate where, for example, the real property of the Division and the Division Subsidiaries is relatively insignificant.

Sample acquisition agreement 2004.2 (the *pro-seller* divisional asset purchase agreement), on the other hand, does not have *any* such provisions and contemplates that the Buyer will obtain any title insurance it requires independently and at its own expense.

reasonably acceptable to the Buyer) in such amount as the Buyer reasonably may determine (taking into account the time cost of money using the Applicable Rate as the discount rate and such other factors as whether the fair market rental value of the premises exceeds the stipulated consideration in the lease or sublease, whether the tenant or subtenant has any option to renew or extend, whether the tenant or subtenant owns any improvements located on the premises, whether the tenant or subtenant is permitted to sublease, and whether the tenant or subtenant would owe any amount under the lease or sublease if evicted), insuring title to the leasehold or subleasehold estate to be in the Buyer or the Subsidiary as of the Closing (subject only to the title exceptions described above in §3(l)(ii) and in §3(l)(ii) of the Disclosure Schedule).

Each title insurance policy delivered under §5(h)(i) and §5(h)(ii) above shall (A) insure title to the real property and all recorded easements benefitting such real property, (B) contain an "extended coverage endorsement" insuring over the general exceptions contained customarily in such policies, (C) contain an ALTA Zoning Endorsement 3.1 (or equivalent), (D) contain an endorsement insuring that the real property described in the title insurance policy is the same real estate as shown on the Survey delivered with respect to such property, (E) contain an endorsement insuring that each street adjacent to the real property is a public street and that there is direct and unencumbered pedestrian and vehicular access to such street from the real property, (F) contain an inflation endorsement providing for annual adjustments in the amount of coverage corresponding to the annual percentage increase, if any, in the United States Department of Commerce Composite Construction Cost Index (Base Year = _____, (G) if the real property consists of more than one record parcel, contain a "contiguity" endorsement insuring that all of the record parcels are contiguous to one another, and (H) contain a "non-imputation" endorsement to the effect that title defects known to the officers, directors, and stockholders of the owner prior to the Closing shall not be deemed "facts known to the insured" for purposes of the policy.

(i) *Surveys.*[53] With respect to each parcel of real property that any of the Division and the Division Subsidiaries owns, leases, or subleases, and as to which a title insurance policy is to be procured pursuant to §5(h) above, the Target will cause the Division and the Division Subsidiaries to procure in preparation for the Closing a current survey of the real property certified to the Buyer, prepared by a licensed surveyor and conforming to current ALTA Minimum Detail Requirements for Land Title Surveys, disclosing the location of all improvements, easements, party walls, sidewalks, roadways, utility lines, and other matters shown

---

[53] This Agreement, like sample acquisition agreement 2004.1 (the *pro-buyer* divisional asset purchase agreement), contains relatively long and detailed provisions concerning real property surveys. A condensed version may be more appropriate where, for example, the real property of the Division and the Division subsidiaries is relatively insignificant.

Sample acquisition agreement 2004.2 (the *pro-seller* divisional asset purchase agreement), on the other hand, does not have *any* such provisions and contemplates that the Buyer will obtain any surveys it requires independently and at its own expense.

customarily on such surveys, and showing access affirmatively to public streets and roads (the *"Survey"*). The Survey shall not disclose any survey defect or encroachment from or onto the real property which has not been cured or insured over prior to the Closing.

6. *Post-Closing Covenants.*[54] The Parties agree as follows with respect to the period following the Closing.

(a) *General.* In case at any time after the Closing any further action is necessary to carry out the purposes of this Agreement, each of the Parties will take such further action (including the execution and delivery of such further instruments and documents) as the other Party [reasonably] may request, all at the sole cost and expense of the requesting Party (unless the requesting Party is entitled to indemnification therefor under §8 below).[55] The Target acknowledges and agrees that from and after the Closing the Buyer will be entitled to possession of all documents, books, records (including tax records), agreements, and financial data of any sort relating to the Division and the Division Subsidiaries.

(b) *Litigation Support.* In the event and for so long as any Party actively is contesting or defending against any action, suit, proceeding, hearing, investigation, charge, complaint, claim, or demand in connection with (i) any transaction contemplated under this Agreement or (ii) any fact, situation, circumstance, status, condition, activity, practice, plan, occurrence, event, incident, action, failure to act, or transaction on or prior to the Closing Date involving any of the Division and the Division Subsidiaries, the other Party will cooperate with the contesting or defending Party and its counsel in the contest or defense, make available its personnel, and provide such testimony and access to its books and records as shall be necessary in connection with the contest or defense, all at the sole cost and expense of the contesting or defending Party (unless the contesting or defending Party is entitled to indemnification therefor under §8 below).[56]

(c) *Transition.* The Target will not take any action that is designed or intended to have the effect of discouraging any lessor, licensor, customer, supplier, or other business associate of any of the Division and the Division Subsidiaries from

---

[54] The Target may seek to obtain additional covenants from the Buyer and its Subsidiaries (e.g., the typical covenants contained in a loan agreement or an indenture) because the Buyer is issuing the Buyer Note to the Target as part of the Purchase Price. Any such covenants would remain applicable so long as the Buyer Note remained outstanding.

[55] The Parties may prefer to allocate responsibility for these particular costs and expenses in some other manner (e.g., the Party incurring the costs and expenses might be responsible for their payment, the Parties might share the costs and expenses in a predetermined ratio, or one Party might be responsible for the costs and expenses up to a specified aggregate ceiling and the other Party responsible for any excess).

Compare §10(k) below (which allocates responsibility between the Buyer and the Target for their costs and expenses through the Closing).

[56] The Parties may prefer to allocate responsibility for these particular costs and expenses in some other manner as discussed in the preceding footnote.

maintaining the same business relationships with the Buyer and the Division Subsidiaries after the Closing as it maintained with the Division and the Division Subsidiaries prior to the Closing.

(d) *Confidentiality.*[57] The Target will treat and hold as such all of the Confidential Information, refrain from using any of the Confidential Information except in connection with this Agreement, and deliver promptly to the Buyer or destroy, at the request and option of the Buyer, all tangible embodiments (and all copies) of the Confidential Information which are in its possession. In the event that the Target is requested or required (by oral question or request for information or documents in any legal proceeding, interrogatory, subpoena, civil investigative demand, or similar process) to disclose any Confidential Information, the Target will notify the Buyer promptly of the request or requirement so that the Buyer may seek an appropriate protective order or waive compliance with the provisions of this §6(d). If, in the absence of a protective order or the receipt of a waiver hereunder, the Target is, on the advice of counsel, compelled to disclose any Confidential Information to any tribunal or else stand liable for contempt, the Target may disclose the Confidential Information to the tribunal; *provided, however,* that the Target shall use its [reasonable] best efforts to obtain, at the [reasonable] request of the Buyer, an order or other assurance that confidential treatment will be accorded to such portion of the Confidential Information required to be disclosed as the Buyer shall designate.

(e) *Covenant Not to Compete.*[58] For a period of [three years] from and after the Closing Date, the Target will not engage directly or indirectly in any business that any of the Division and the Division Subsidiaries conducts as of the Closing Date in any geographic area in which any of the Division and the Division Subsidiaries conducts that business as of the Closing Date; *provided, however,* that no owner of less than 1% of the outstanding stock of any publicly traded corporation shall be deemed to engage solely by reason thereof in any of its businesses. If the final judgment of a court of competent jurisdiction declares that any term or provision of this §6(e) is invalid or unenforceable, the Parties agree that the court making the determination of invalidity or unenforceability shall have the power to reduce the scope, duration, or area of the term or provision, to delete specific words or phrases, or to replace any invalid or unenforceable term or provision with a term or provision that is valid and enforceable and that comes closest to expressing the intention of the invalid or unenforceable term or provision, and this Agreement shall be enforceable as so modified after the expiration of the time within which the judgment may be appealed.

---

[57] This Agreement, like sample acquisition agreement 2004.1 (the *pro-buyer* divisional asset purchase agreement), requires the Target to keep certain information regarding the Division and the Division Subsidiaries confidential after the Closing. Sample acquisition agreement 2004.2 (the *pro-seller* divisional asset purchase agreement), on the other hand, lacks such a provision.

[58] Note that unless this Agreement allocates a specified amount of consideration to the covenant not to compete, applicable tax cases will preclude the Buyer from seeking to allocate a portion of the Purchase Price to the covenant and amortizing such amount over the covenant's life.

(f) *Buyer Note.* The Buyer Note will be imprinted with a legend substantially in the following form:

This Note was originally issued on _____, 19_____, and has not been registered under the Securities Act of 1933, as amended. The transfer of this Note is subject to certain restrictions set forth in the Agreement. The issuer of this Note will furnish a copy of these provisions to the holder hereof without charge upon written request.

Each holder desiring to transfer a Buyer Note first must furnish the Buyer with (i) a written opinion reasonably satisfactory to the Buyer in form and substance from counsel reasonably satisfactory to the Buyer by reason of experience to the effect that the holder may transfer the Buyer Note as desired without registration under the Securities Act and (ii) a written undertaking executed by the desired transferee reasonably satisfactory to the Buyer in form and substance agreeing to be bound by the restrictions on transfer contained herein.[59]

7. *Conditions to Obligation to Close.*

(a) *Conditions to Obligation of the Buyer.* The obligation of the Buyer to consummate the transactions to be performed by it in connection with the Closing is subject to satisfaction of the following conditions:[60]

(i) the representations and warranties set forth in §3 above shall be true and correct in all material respects at and as of the Closing Date;[61]

(ii) the Target shall have performed and complied with all of its covenants hereunder in all material respects through the Closing;

(iii) the Target and the Division Subsidiaries shall have procured all of the material third party consents specified in §5(b) above, all of the title insurance

---

[59] This Agreement, like sample acquisition agreement 2004.1 (the *pro-buyer* divisional asset purchase agreement), calls for a legend on the Buyer Note and provides that any holder who wishes to transfer the Buyer Note must first obtain an opinion of counsel and an undertaking of the transferee (in each case as to securities law matters). Sample acquisition agreement 2004.2 (the *pro-seller* divisional asset purchase agreement), on the other hand, only calls for a legend on the Buyer Note. Note that any such provision would be inappropriate if the Buyer will issue the Buyer Note in an offering registered under the Securities Act.

[60] Sample acquisition agreement 2004.1 (the *pro-buyer* divisional asset purchase agreement) contains an additional closing condition for the benefit of the Buyer concerning the receipt of financing for the transaction. This Agreement, like sample acquisition agreement 2004.2 (the *pro-seller* divisional asset purchase agreement), lacks a comparable provision.

[61] Note that this provision will not give the Buyer any closing condition with respect to any adverse matter which the Target may disclose in the Disclosure Schedule. This is because the disclosure will cure any misrepresentation or breach of warranty that might otherwise have existed. Thus, where the Target discloses an adverse matter in the Disclosure Schedule, the Buyer may seek to add a specific closing condition requiring an acceptable resolution of the matter.

commitments, policies, and riders specified in §5(h) above, and all of the surveys specified in §5(i) above;[62]

(iv) no action, suit, or proceeding shall be pending before any court or quasi-judicial or administrative agency of any federal, state, local, or foreign jurisdiction or before any arbitrator wherein an unfavorable injunction, judgment, order, decree, ruling, or charge would (A) prevent consummation of any of the transactions contemplated by this Agreement, (B) cause any of the transactions contemplated by this Agreement to be rescinded following consummation, (C) affect adversely the right of the Buyer to own the Acquired Assets, to operate the former businesses of the Division, and to control the Division Subsidiaries, or (D) affect materially and adversely the right of any of the Division Subsidiaries to own its assets and to operate its businesses (and no such injunction, judgment, order, decree, ruling, or charge shall be in effect);[63]

(v) the Target shall have delivered to the Buyer a certificate to the effect that each of the conditions specified above in §7(a)(i)-(iv) is satisfied in all respects;

(vi) all applicable waiting periods (and any extensions thereof) under the Hart-Scott-Rodino Act shall have expired or otherwise been terminated and the Target, the Division Subsidiaries, and the Buyer shall have received all other material authorizations, consents, and approvals of governments and governmental agencies referred to in §3(c) and §4(c) above;

(vii) the relevant parties shall have entered into side agreements in form and substance as set forth in Exhibits through F-_____ attached hereto and the same shall be in full force and effect;[64]

(viii) the Buyer shall have received from counsel to the Target an opinion in form and substance as set forth in Exhibit G attached hereto, addressed to the Buyer, and dated as of the Closing Date;

[62] This Agreement, like sample acquisition agreement 2004.1 (the *pro-buyer* divisional asset purchase agreement), includes a closing condition for the benefit of the Buyer regarding third party consents, title insurance, and surveys. Unlike sample acquisition agreement 2004.1, however, the closing condition in this Agreement refers only to *material* third party consents. Sample acquisition agreement 2004.2 (the *pro-seller* divisional asset purchase agreement), on the other hand, lacks a comparable closing condition altogether.

[63] This Agreement, like sample acquisition agreement 2004.1 (the *pro-buyer* divisional asset purchase agreement), contains a broad closing condition regarding injunctions, judgments, orders, and pending actions, suits, and proceedings that prevent or could have an adverse effect upon the transactions contemplated by the Agreement. Unlike sample acquisition agreement 2004.1, however, the closing condition in this Agreement does not cover actions, suits, and proceedings that are only threatened. Sample acquisition agreement 2004.2 (the *pro-seller* divisional asset purchase agreement), on the other hand, contains a narrower closing condition covering only injunctions, judgments, and orders that prevent consummation of the transactions.

[64] Where the Buyer is acquiring a division of Bigco, the Buyer may require significant transition assistance. This might be the case where Bigco performs substantial services for its divisions and/or

(ix) the Buyer shall have received the resignations, effective as of the Closing, of each director and officer of the Division Subsidiaries;[65] and

(x) all actions to be taken by the Target in connection with consummation of the transactions contemplated hereby and all certificates, opinions, instruments, and other documents required to effect the transactions contemplated hereby will be reasonably satisfactory in form and substance to the Buyer.

The Buyer may waive any condition specified in this §7(a) if it executes a writing so stating at or prior to the Closing.

(b) *Conditions to Obligation of the Target.* The obligation of the Target to consummate the transactions to be performed by it in connection with the Closing is subject to satisfaction of the following conditions:

(i) the representations and warranties set forth in §4 above shall be true and correct in all material respects at and as of the Closing Date;

(ii) the Buyer shall have performed and complied with all of its covenants hereunder in all material respects through the Closing;

(iii) no action, suit, or proceeding shall be pending before any court or quasi-judicial or administrative agency of any federal, state, local, or foreign jurisdiction or before any arbitrator wherein an unfavorable injunction, judgment, order, decree, ruling, or charge would (A) prevent consummation of any of the transactions contemplated by this Agreement or (B) cause any of the transactions contemplated by this Agreement to be rescinded following consummation (and no such injunction, judgment, order, decree, ruling, or charge shall be in effect);[66]

(iv) the Buyer shall have delivered to the Target a certificate to the effect that each of the conditions specified above in §7(b)(i)-(iii) is satisfied in all respects;

---

where Bigco owns various tangible and intangible assets used by its divisions. For example, the Buyer may require real estate leases, intellectual property licenses, and accounting, purchasing, payroll, risk management, and data processing services from Bigco.

[65] This Agreement, like sample acquisition agreement 2004.1 (the *pro-buyer* divisional asset purchase agreement), contains a closing condition regarding the receipt of director and officer resignations. Sample acquisition agreement 2004.2 (the *pro-seller* divisional asset purchase agreement), on the other hand, lacks a comparable closing condition.

[66] Because this Target's closing condition conforms in part to the comparable Buyer's closing condition in §7(a)(iv) above, it leaves the Target with a relatively broad "out." Thus, the Buyer may prefer to narrow the respective closing conditions. *Compare* the narrower closing conditions in sample acquisition agreement 2004.2 (the *pro-seller* divisional asset purchase agreement) and the even broader closing conditions in sample acquisition agreement 2004.1 (the *pro-buyer* divisional asset purchase agreement).

(v) all applicable waiting periods (and any extensions thereof) under the Hart-Scott-Rodino Act shall have expired or otherwise been terminated and the Target, the Division Subsidiaries, and the Buyer shall have received all other material authorizations, consents, and approvals of governments and governmental agencies referred to in §3(c) and §4(c) above;

(vi) the relevant parties shall have entered into side agreements in form and substance as set forth in Exhibits F-_____, F-_____, . . . and F-_____ and the same shall be in full force and effect;

(vii) the Target shall have received from counsel to the Buyer an opinion in form and substance as set forth in Exhibit H attached hereto, addressed to the Target, and dated as of the Closing Date; and

(viii) all actions to be taken by the Buyer in connection with consummation of the transactions contemplated hereby and all certificates, opinions, instruments, and other documents required to effect the transactions contemplated hereby will be reasonably satisfactory in form and substance to the Target.

The Target may waive any condition specified in this §7(b) if it executes a writing so stating at or prior to the Closing.

8. *Remedies for Breaches of This Agreement.*[67]

(a) *Survival of Representations and Warranties.*[68] All of the representations and warranties of the Target contained in §3(g)-(j) and §3(l)-(cc) above shall survive the Closing (even if the Buyer knew or had reason to know of any misrepresentation or

---

[67] The Buyer may seek some form of additional security covering the obligation of the Target to indemnify the Buyer after the Closing. This may include provisions calling for (a) the Buyer to have a recoupment remedy with respect to the Buyer Note, (b) the Target to deposit a portion of the Purchase Price with a third party escrow agent, (c) the Buyer to hold back a portion of the Purchase Price (to be paid later with interest), or (d) the Buyer to obtain a security interest in certain assets of the Target. Sample acquisition agreement 2004.1 (the *pro-buyer* divisional asset purchase agreement), for example, contains recoupment provisions applicable to the Buyer Note.

[68] Sample acquisition agreement 2004.1 (the *pro-buyer* divisional asset purchase agreement) contains alternative provisions for (A) *full indemnification* (the representations and warranties survive indefinitely and there is no deductible, threshold, or ceiling with respect to indemnification against breaches thereof) and (B) *limited indemnification* (the representations and warranties with respect to the transaction itself and with respect to taxes survive indefinitely, the other representations and warranties survive only for [three years], and there is a threshold, but not a deductible or ceiling, with respect to indemnification against breaches of the latter). The *pro-buyer* Agreement also provides that a particular representation and warranty will survive the Closing *even if* the damaged Party knew or had reason to know of a breach thereof at the time of Closing.

Sample acquisition agreement 2004.2 (the *pro-seller* divisional asset purchase agreement), on the other hand, contains alternative provisions for (A) *minimal indemnification* (only the representations and warranties concerning the transaction itself survive the Closing) and (B) *limited indemnification* (the representations and warranties with respect to the transaction itself survive indefinitely, the other representations and warranties survive only for [one year], and there is a deductible and a ceiling with respect to indemnification against breaches of the latter). The *pro-seller* Agreement provides,

breach of warranty at the time of Closing) and continue in full force and effect for a period of [two years] thereafter; *provided, however*, that the representations and warranties contained in §3(z) above shall survive the Closing (even if the Buyer knew or had reason to know of any misrepresentation or breach of warranty at the time of Closing) and continue in full force and effect for a period of [five years] thereafter. All of the other representations and warranties of the Parties contained in this Agreement (including the representations and warranties of the Target contained in §3(a)-(f) and §3(k) above) shall survive the Closing (even if the damaged Party knew or had reason to know of any misrepresentation or breach of warranty at the time of Closing) and continue in full force and effect forever thereafter (subject to any applicable statutes of limitations).

(b) *Indemnification Provisions for Benefit of the Buyer.*[69]

(i) In the event the Target breaches any of its representations, warranties, and covenants contained in this Agreement, and, if there is an applicable survival period pursuant to §8(a) above, provided that the Buyer makes a written claim for indemnification against the Target pursuant to §10(g) below within such survival period, then the Target agrees to indemnify the Buyer from and against the entirety of any Adverse Consequences the Buyer may suffer through and after the date of the claim for indemnification (including any Adverse Consequences the Buyer may suffer after the end of any applicable survival period) resulting from, arising out of, relating to, in the nature of, or

---

however, that a particular representation and warranty will *not* survive the Closing if the damaged Party knew or had reason to know of a breach thereof at the time of Closing.

This Agreement, which is intended to favor neither the Buyer nor the Target, provides that the representations and warranties with respect to the transaction itself and with respect to taxes will survive indefinitely, the environmental representations and warranties will survive for [five years], the other representations and warranties will survive for [two years], and there will be a deductible and a ceiling with respect to indemnification against breaches of any representations and warranties that do not concern the transaction itself. This Agreement, like the *pro-buyer* Agreement, also provides that a particular representation and warranty will survive the Closing *even if* the damaged Party knew or had reason to know of a breach thereof at the time of Closing.

[69] The Buyer will become indirectly responsible for all of the liabilities of the *Division Subsidiaries* if the Buyer acquires their capital stock as part of the Acquired Assets. For this reason, the Buyer may seek (a) to purchase assets from the Target *and from each of the Division Subsidiaries* (i.e., a multiple entity asset sale) or (b) to have the Target liquidate and dissolve the Division Subsidiaries tax free under Code §332 (to the extent they are United States corporations) and sell their assets to the Buyer.

In addition, this Agreement provides that the Buyer will assume certain specified liabilities of the Division. *See* the definition of Assumed Liabilities in §1 above (and in particular the provision making the Buyer responsible for certain liabilities the Target reveals in the Disclosure Schedule).

Finally, the Buyer may be exposed for certain liabilities of the *Division* by operation of law if the Target does not pay them (e.g., under applicable bulk sales statutes and common law doctrines of de facto merger and successor liability). *See* ¶2001.2.2.2.

These post-Closing indemnification provisions are designed to work in conjunction with the definition of Assumed Liabilities in §1 above and the representations and warranties in §3 above to protect the Buyer against liabilities it does not intend to assume.

caused by the breach;[70] *provided, however,* that (A) the Target shall not have any obligation to indemnify the Buyer from and against any Adverse Consequences resulting from, arising out of, relating to, in the nature of, or caused by the breach of any representation or warranty of the Target contained in §3(g)-(cc) above until the Buyer has suffered Adverse Consequences by reason of all such breaches in excess of a \$_____ aggregate deductible (after which point the Target will be obligated only to indemnify the Buyer from and against further such Adverse Consequences)[71] and (B) there will be a \$_____ aggregate ceiling on the obligation of the Target to indemnify the Buyer from and against Adverse Consequences resulting from, arising out of, relating to, in the nature of, or caused by breaches of the representations and warranties of the Target contained in §3(g)-(cc) above.[72]

(ii) The Target agrees to indemnify the Buyer from and against the entirety of any Adverse Consequences the Buyer may suffer resulting from, arising out of, relating to, in the nature of, or caused by:

(A) any liability of the Target which is not an Assumed Liability (including any liability of the Target that becomes a liability of the Buyer under any bulk transfer law of any jurisdiction, under any common law doctrine of de facto merger or successor liability, or otherwise by operation of law);[73]

(B) any liability of any of the Division Subsidiaries for unpaid Income Taxes or other unpaid taxes with respect to any Tax year or portion thereof ending on or before the Closing Date (or for any Tax year beginning before

---

[70] This Agreement, like sample acquisition agreement 2004.1 (the *pro-buyer* divisional asset purchase agreement), requires an indemnifying party (presumably, but not necessarily, the Target) to indemnify an indemnified party (presumably, but not necessarily, the Buyer) from and against any Adverse Consequences the indemnified party *may* suffer through and after the date of the claim for indemnification (*including* any Adverse Consequences the indemnified party may suffer after the end of any applicable survival period) *resulting from, arising out of, relating to, in the nature of, or caused by* certain breaches by the indemnifying party of his or its representations, warranties, and covenants.

Sample acquisition agreement 2004.2 (the *pro-seller* divisional asset purchase agreement), on the other hand, provides that the indemnifying party (presumably, but not necessarily, the Target) must indemnify the indemnified party (presumably, but not necessarily, the Buyer) from and against Adverse Consequences the indemnified party *shall* suffer *caused [proximately] by* certain breaches by the indemnifying party of his or its representations, warranties, and covenants.

[71] The Target may also seek to impose a *per claim* deductible.

[72] This Agreement, like sample acquisition agreement 2004.2 (the *pro-seller* divisional asset purchase agreement), imposes a deductible and a ceiling on indemnification for breaches of the representations and warranties in §3 above. Sample acquisition agreement 2004.1 (the *pro-buyer* divisional asset purchase agreement), on the other hand, substitutes a threshold (with relation back to the first dollar once the threshold is exceeded) for the deductible and also eliminates the ceiling on indemnification.

[73] The Buyer may be exposed for certain liabilities of the Target by operation of law if the Target does not pay them (e.g., under applicable bulk sales statutes and common law doctrines of de facto merger and successor liability). *See* ¶2001.2.2.2. This indemnification provision is designed to protect the Buyer against liabilities arising by operation of law which it does not intend to assume.

and ending after the Closing Date to the extent allocable to the portion of such period beginning before and ending on the Closing Date);[74] or

(C) any liability of any of the Division Subsidiaries for the unpaid taxes of any Person (including the Target and its Subsidiaries) under Reg. §1.1502-6 (or any similar provision of state, local, or foreign law), as a transferee or successor, by contract, or otherwise.[75]

(iii) The Target agrees to indemnify the Buyer from and against the entirety of any Adverse Consequences the Buyer may suffer resulting from, arising out of, relating to, in the nature of, or caused by _____.[76]

(c) *Indemnification Provisions for Benefit of the Target.*

(i) In the event the Buyer breaches any of its representations, warranties, and covenants contained in this Agreement, and, if there is an applicable survival period pursuant to §8(a) above, provided that the Target makes a written claim for indemnification against the Buyer pursuant to §10(g) below

---

[74] Clause (B) is consistent with the principle that Target is obligated to pay all pre-Closing taxes of the Target and any Division Subsidiaries and is entitled to retain sufficient Cash to satisfy such obligation (see definition of "Acquired Assets" (item (k) and §2(d)). This indemnity is limited to unpaid taxes of the Subsidiaries. It does not cover unpaid taxes of the Target itself, because taxes of the Target are expressly excluded from the definition of "Assumed Liabilities" and therefore are indemnified under §8(b)(ii)(A).

[75] If a Division Subsidiary has been a member of an Affiliated Group filing a consolidated federal income tax return, such corporation (or its successor) will be jointly and severally liable under Reg. §1.1502-6 for certain tax liabilities incurred by such Affiliated Group for a tax year when such corporation was a member of such Affiliated Group for all or part of such tax year. *See* ¶210.

A Division Subsidiary may also be liable for the unpaid taxes of third parties under similar provisions of state, local, or foreign law, as a transferee or successor, by contract (e.g., a tax sharing agreement), or otherwise.

After the Buyer acquires the stock of any such Division Subsidiary, the Division Subsidiary will remain liable for any such unpaid tax liabilities.

This Agreement, like sample acquisition agreement 2004.1 (the *pro-buyer* divisional asset purchase agreement), contains an indemnification provision designed to protect the Buyer against any liability for the unpaid taxes of any person (including the Target and its Subsidiaries). Sample acquisition agreement 2004.2 (the *pro-seller* divisional asset purchase agreement), on the other hand, contains no such provision.

[76] Note that the indemnification provisions in clause (i) above will not give the Buyer any post-Closing indemnification rights with respect to any adverse matter which the Target may disclose in the Disclosure Schedule. This is because the disclosure will cure any misrepresentation or breach of warranty that might otherwise have existed.

Thus, where the Target discloses an adverse matter in the Disclosure Schedule, the Buyer may seek to add a provision conferring specific post-Closing indemnification rights with respect to the particular matter.

The Buyer normally would seek to draft such a provision so that the indemnification would not be subject to any survival period, threshold, deductible, and/or ceiling.

This Agreement, like sample acquisition agreement 2004.1 (the *pro-buyer* divisional asset purchase agreement), provides for such indemnification with respect to particular matters. Sample acquisition agreement 2004.2 (the *pro-seller* divisional asset purchase agreement), on the other hand, lacks a comparable provision.

within such survival period, then the Buyer agrees to indemnify the Target from and against the entirety of any Adverse Consequences the Target may suffer through and after the date of the claim for indemnification (including any Adverse Consequences the Target may suffer after the end of any applicable survival period) resulting from, arising out of, relating to, in the nature of, or caused by the breach.

(ii) The Buyer agrees to indemnify the Target from and against the entirety of any Adverse Consequences the Target may suffer resulting from, arising out of, relating to, in the nature of, or caused by any Assumed Liability.

(d) *Matters Involving Third Parties.*

(i) If any third party shall notify any Party (the *"Indemnified Party"*) with respect to any matter (a *"Third Party Claim"*) which may give rise to a claim for indemnification against the other Party (the *"Indemnifying Party"*) under this §8, then the Indemnified Party shall promptly notify the Indemnifying Party thereof in writing; *provided, however,* that no delay on the part of the Indemnified Party in notifying the Indemnifying Party shall relieve the Indemnifying Party from any obligation hereunder unless (and then solely to the extent) the Indemnifying Party thereby is prejudiced.

(ii) The Indemnifying Party will have the right to assume the defense of the Third Party Claim with counsel of its choice reasonably satisfactory to the Indemnified Party at any time within 15 days after the Indemnified Party has given notice of the Third Party Claim; *provided, however,* that the Indemnifying Party must conduct the defense of the Third Party Claim actively and diligently thereafter in order to preserve its rights in this regard; and *provided further* that the Indemnified Party may retain separate co-counsel at its sole cost and expense and participate in the defense of the Third Party Claim.[77]

(iii) So long as the Indemnifying Party has assumed and is conducting the defense of the Third Party Claim in accordance with §8(d)(ii) above, (A) the

[77] An *indemnifying* party (presumably, but not necessarily, the Target) will normally seek to control the defense of any third party claim that may give rise to a claim for indemnification under this §8. However, the *indemnified* party (presumably, but not necessarily, the Buyer) will not want the indemnifying party to control the defense of any third party claim in which the indemnified party will retain a meaningful interest. For example, the indemnified party may seek to control the defense of a third party claim if the third party seeks an injunction or other equitable relief or if it is not clear that the indemnifying party will bear the entirety of any money damages or amount paid in settlement.

Sample acquisition agreement 2004.1 (the *pro-buyer* divisional asset purchase agreement) provides that the indemnified party will control the defense of any third party claim *unless* (a) an indemnifying party accepts full responsibility for the matter within [15 days], (b) the indemnifying party demonstrates it has the financial resources necessary to defend against the matter and fulfill its indemnification obligations, (c) the third party seeks only money damages (as opposed to an injunction or other equitable relief), (d) settlement of, or an adverse judgment with respect to, the third party claim is not likely to establish a precedent [materially] adverse to the indemnified party, and (e) the indemnifying party conducts the defense actively and diligently.

Indemnifying Party will not consent to the entry of any judgment or enter into any settlement with respect to the Third Party Claim without the prior written consent of the Indemnified Party (not to be withheld unreasonably) unless the judgment or proposed settlement involves only the payment of money damages by the Indemnifying Party and does not impose an injunction or other equitable relief upon the Indemnified Party and (B) the Indemnified Party will not consent to the entry of any judgment or enter into any settlement with respect to the Third Party Claim without the prior written consent of the Indemnifying Party (not to be withheld unreasonably).

(iv) In the event the Indemnifying Party does not assume and conduct the defense of the Third Party Claim in accordance with §8(d)(ii) above, however, (A) the Indemnified Party may defend against, and consent to the entry of any judgment or enter into any settlement with respect to, the Third Party Claim in any manner it reasonably may deem appropriate (and the Indemnified Party need not consult with, or obtain any consent from, the Indemnifying Party in connection therewith) and (B) the Indemnifying Party will remain responsible for any Adverse Consequences the Indemnified Party may suffer resulting from, arising out of, relating to, in the nature of, or caused by the Third Party Claim to the fullest extent provided in this §8.[78]

(e) *Determination of Adverse Consequences.* The Parties shall make appropriate adjustments for tax consequences and insurance coverage and take into account

---

Sample acquisition agreement 2004.2 (the *pro-seller* divisional asset purchase agreement), on the other hand, provides that an indemnifying party may assume the defense of a third party claim *at any time* during the course of the defense.

This Agreement, which is intended to favor neither the Buyer nor the Target, provides that an indemnifying party may assume the defense of a third party claim at any time within 15 days after the indemnified party has given notice of the third party claim, but requires the indemnifying party to conduct the defense of the third party claim actively and diligently thereafter.

[78] This Agreement, like sample acquisition agreement 2004.1 (the *pro-buyer* divisional asset purchase agreement), provides that the *indemnified party* will not consent to the entry of any judgment or enter into any settlement with respect to the third party claim without the prior written consent of the indemnifying party (not to be withheld unreasonably) unless the indemnifying party fails to assume and conduct the defense of the third party claim. Sample acquisition agreement 2004.2 (the *pro-seller* divisional asset purchase agreement), on the other hand, provides that the indemnified party will not consent to the entry of any judgment or enter into any settlement with respect to the third party claim without the prior written consent of the indemnifying party (not to be withheld unreasonably) under any circumstances.

This Agreement, like sample acquisition agreement 2004.2 (the *pro-seller* divisional asset purchase agreement), also provides that the *indemnifying party* will not consent to the entry of any judgment or enter into any settlement with respect to the third party claim without the prior written consent of the indemnified party (not to be withheld unreasonably) unless the judgment or proposed settlement involves only the payment of money damages by one or more of the indemnifying parties and does not impose an injunction or other equitable relief upon the indemnified party. Sample acquisition agreement 2004.1 (the *pro-buyer* divisional asset purchase agreement), on the other hand, provides that the indemnifying party will not consent to the entry of any judgment or enter into any settlement with respect to the third party claim without the prior written consent of the indemnified party (not to be withheld unreasonably) under any circumstances.

the time cost of money (using the Applicable Rate as the discount rate) in determining Adverse Consequences for purposes of this §8. All indemnification payments under this §8 shall be deemed adjustments to the Purchase Price.

(f) *Exclusive Remedy.*[79] The Buyer and the Target acknowledge and agree that the foregoing indemnification provisions in this §8 shall be the exclusive remedy of the Buyer and the Target with respect to the Division, the Division Subsidiaries, and the transactions contemplated by this Agreement. Without limiting the generality of the foregoing, the Buyer and the Target hereby waive any statutory, equitable, or common law rights or remedies relating to any environmental matters, including without limitation any such matters arising under any Environmental, Health, and Safety Requirements and including without limitation any arising under the Comprehensive Environmental Response, Compensation, and Liability Act ("CERCLA").

9. *Termination.*[80]

(a) *Termination of Agreement.* Certain of the Parties may terminate this Agreement as provided below:

(i) the Buyer and the Target may terminate this Agreement by mutual written consent at any time prior to the Closing;

(ii) the Buyer may terminate this Agreement by giving written notice to the Target at any time prior to the Closing (A) in the event the Target has breached any material representation, warranty, or covenant contained in this Agreement in any material respect, the Buyer has notified the Target of the breach, and the breach has continued without cure for a period of [30 days] after the notice of breach or (B) if the Closing shall not have occurred on or before _____, 19____, by reason of the failure of any condition precedent under §7(a) hereof (unless the failure results primarily from the Buyer itself breaching any representation, warranty, or covenant contained in this Agreement); and

---

[79] Sample acquisition agreement 2004.1 (the *pro-buyer* divisional purchase agreement) states that the indemnification provisions in the Agreement are in addition to and not in derogation of any other statutory, equitable, or common law remedies (including any such remedies relating to environmental matters).

As does this *neutral* divisional purchase agreement, sample acquisition agreement 2003.2 (the *pro-seller* divisional purchase agreement) states that the remedies available to the Parties under the Agreement are exclusive (i.e., that the Buyer has no other statutory, equitable, or common law remedies) and also contains an additional provision by which the Buyer specifically waives and releases the Target from, and agrees to indemnify the Target with respect to, any environmental liabilities.

[80] Sample acquisition agreement 2004.1 (the *pro-buyer* divisional asset purchase agreement) contains a provision giving the Buyer a right to terminate the agreement for a limited period after signing if the Buyer is not [reasonably] satisfied with the results of its continuing business, legal, environmental, and accounting due diligence concerning the Division and the Division Subsidiaries. This Agreement,

(iii) the Target may terminate this Agreement by giving written notice to the Buyer at any time prior to the Closing (A) in the event the Buyer has breached any material representation, warranty, or covenant contained in this Agreement in any material respect, the Target has notified the Buyer of the breach, and the breach has continued without cure for a period of [30 days] after the notice of breach or (B) if the Closing shall not have occurred on or before _____, 19____, by reason of the failure of any condition precedent under §7(b) hereof (unless the failure results primarily from the Target itself breaching any representation, warranty, or covenant contained in this Agreement).

(b) *Effect of Termination.* If any Party terminates this Agreement pursuant to §9(a) above, all rights and obligations of the Parties hereunder shall terminate without any liability of any Party to the other Party (except for any liability of any Party then in breach); *provided, however*, that the confidentiality provisions contained in §5(e) above shall survive termination.

10. *Miscellaneous.*[81]

(a) *Press Releases and Public Announcements.* No Party shall issue any press release or public announcement relating to the subject matter of this Agreement [prior to the Closing] without the prior written approval of the other Party; *provided, however*, that any Party may make any public disclosure it believes in good faith is required by applicable law or any listing or trading agreement concerning its publicly-traded securities (in which case the disclosing Party will use its [reasonable] best efforts to advise the other Party prior to making the disclosure).

(b) *No Third-Party Beneficiaries.* This Agreement shall not confer any rights or remedies upon any Person other than the Parties and their respective successors and permitted assigns.

(c) *Entire Agreement.* [This Agreement (including the documents referred to herein) constitutes the entire agreement between the Parties and supersedes any prior understandings, agreements, or representations by or between the Parties, written or oral, to the extent they related in any way to the subject matter hereof].

(d) *Succession and Assignment.* This Agreement shall be binding upon and inure to the benefit of the Parties named herein and their respective successors

---

like sample acquisition agreement 2004.2 (the *pro-seller* divisional asset purchase agreement), lacks a comparable provision.

[81] Sample acquisition agreement 2004.1 (the *pro-buyer* divisional asset purchase agreement) contains provisions whereby the Parties agree to specific performance, agree to service of process on an agent, and submit to the [exclusive] jurisdiction of the state and federal courts in a particular city. This Agreement, like sample acquisition agreement 2004.2 (the *pro-seller* divisional asset purchase agreement), lacks comparable provisions.

and permitted assigns. No Party may assign either this Agreement or any of its rights, interests, or obligations hereunder without the prior written approval of the other Party; *provided, however,* that the Buyer may (i) assign any or all of its rights and interests hereunder to one or more of its Affiliates and (ii) designate one or more of its Affiliates to perform its obligations hereunder (in any or all of which cases the Buyer nonetheless shall remain responsible for the performance of all of its obligations hereunder).

(e) *Counterparts.* This Agreement may be executed in one or more counterparts, each of which shall be deemed an original but all of which together will constitute one and the same instrument.

(f) *Headings.* The section headings contained in this Agreement are inserted for convenience only and shall not affect in any way the meaning or interpretation of this Agreement.

(g) *Notices.* All notices, requests, demands, claims, and other communications hereunder will be in writing. Any notice, request, demand, claim, or other communication hereunder shall be deemed duly given if (and then two business days after) it is sent by registered or certified mail, return receipt requested, postage prepaid, and addressed to the intended recipient as set forth below:

If to the Target:　　　　　　*Copy to:*

If to the Buyer:　　　　　　*Copy to:*

Any Party may send any notice, request, demand, claim, or other communication hereunder to the intended recipient at the address set forth above using any other means (including personal delivery, expedited courier, messenger service, telecopy, telex, ordinary mail, or electronic mail), but no such notice, request, demand, claim, or other communication shall be deemed to have been duly given unless and until it actually is received by the intended recipient. Any Party may change the address to which notices, requests, demands, claims, and other communications hereunder are to be delivered by giving the other Party notice in the manner herein set forth.

(h) *Governing Law. This Agreement shall be governed by and construed in accordance with the domestic laws of the State of_____without giving effect to any choice or conflict of law provision or rule (whether of the State of _____ or any other jurisdiction) that would cause the application of the laws of any jurisdiction other than the State of _____.*

The Parties may want to add a provision calling for optional or mandatory arbitration with respect to all or certain issues.

(i) *Amendments and Waivers.* No amendment of any provision of this Agreement shall be valid unless the same shall be in writing and signed by the Buyer and the Target. [The Target may consent to any such amendment at any time prior to the Closing with the prior authorization of its board of directors; *provided, however,* that any amendment effected after the Target Stockholders have approved this Agreement will be subject to the restrictions contained in the (APPLICABLE CORPORATION STATUTE)]. No waiver by any Party of any default, misrepresentation, or breach of warranty or covenant hereunder, whether intentional or not, shall be deemed to extend to any prior or subsequent default, misrepresentation, or breach of warranty or covenant hereunder or affect in any way any rights arising by virtue of any prior or subsequent such occurrence.

(j) *Severability.* Any term or provision of this Agreement that is invalid or unenforceable in any situation in any jurisdiction shall not affect the validity or enforceability of the remaining terms and provisions hereof or the validity or enforceability of the offending term or provision in any other situation or in any other jurisdiction.

(k) *Expenses.* Each of the Buyer, the Target, the Division Subsidiaries, and the Target Stockholders will bear his or its own costs and expenses (including legal fees and expenses) incurred in connection with this Agreement and the transactions contemplated hereby.[82] The Target agrees that the Division and the Division Subsidiaries have not borne and will not bear any of the costs and expenses of the Target and the Target Stockholders (including any of their legal fees and expenses) in connection with this Agreement or any of the transactions contemplated hereby. The Target also agrees that the Division and the Division Subsidiaries have not paid any amount to any third party, and will not pay any amount

---

[82] This Agreement, like sample acquisition agreement 2004.1 (the *pro-buyer* divisional asset purchase agreement), makes the Division Subsidiaries responsible for their own transactional costs and expenses. This means the Buyer will bear these costs and expenses if it consummates the asset purchase. The Division Subsidiaries may incur significant costs and expenses if they prepare portions of the Disclosure Schedule and the Financial Statements, give notices to third parties and obtain their consent, make filings under the Hart-Scott-Rodino Act and respond to requests for additional information, and/or obtain title insurance and surveys for the Closing. For this reason, the Buyer may seek to have the Target reimburse the Division Subsidiaries for some or all of these costs and expenses (out of assets other than the assets of the Division).

Sample acquisition agreement 2004.2 (the *pro-seller* divisional asset purchase agreement), on the other hand, makes the Target responsible for the transactional costs and expenses of the Target and the Target Stockholders, but treats these costs and expenses as Assumed Liabilities. This means that the Buyer will bear these costs and expenses if it consummates the asset purchase. Furthermore, the *pro-seller* agreement leaves the Division Subsidiaries responsible for their own transactional costs and expenses (so that the Buyer will bear these costs and expenses if it acquires their capital stock as part of the Acquired Assets). Finally, the Target may seek to make the Buyer *directly* responsible for these costs and expenses. In the unlikely event the Buyer agreed to this arrangement, it would be responsible for the costs and expenses of the Target Stockholders, the Target, and the Division Subsidiaries whether or not it consummated the asset purchase.

The Parties may settle on a compromise allocation of responsibility (such as sharing the costs and expenses in a predetermined ratio or making one Party responsible for the costs and expenses up to a specified aggregate ceiling and the other Party responsible for any excess).

to any third party, with respect to any of the costs and expenses of the Target and the Target Stockholders (including any of their legal fees and expenses) in connection with this Agreement or any of the transactions contemplated hereby.[83]

(l) *Construction.* The Parties have participated jointly in the negotiation and drafting of this Agreement. In the event an ambiguity or question of intent or interpretation arises, this Agreement shall be construed as if drafted jointly by the Parties and no presumption or burden of proof shall arise favoring or disfavoring any Party by virtue of the authorship of any of the provisions of this Agreement. Any reference to any federal, state, local, or foreign statute or law shall be deemed also to refer to all rules and regulations promulgated thereunder, unless the context requires otherwise. The word "including" shall mean including without limitation.[84]

(m) *Incorporation of Exhibits and Schedules.* The Exhibits and Schedules identified in this Agreement are incorporated herein by reference and made a part hereof.

(n) *Tax Matters.*[85]

[(i) Any agreement between the Target and any of the Division Subsidiaries regarding allocation or payment of taxes or amounts in lieu of taxes shall be deemed terminated at and as of the Closing.

(ii) The Target will be responsible for the preparation and filing of all Income Tax Returns for the Target for all periods as to which Income Tax Returns are due after the Closing Date (including the consolidated, unitary, and combined Income Tax Returns for the Target which include the operations of the Division and the Division Subsidiaries for any period ending on or before the Closing Date). The Target will make all payments required with respect to any such Income Tax Return.

(iii) The Buyer will be responsible for the preparation and filing of all Income Tax Returns for the Division and the Division Subsidiaries for all periods as to which Income Tax Returns are due after the Closing Date (other than for

---

[83] Notice that the Buyer will bear the costs and expenses of the Target and the Target Stockholders to the extent the Division pays any amount to a third party with respect thereto prior to the Closing. This is because the payment will reduce the amount of cash the Buyer otherwise would receive when it acquires the assets of the Division at the Closing. This provision is designed to protect the Buyer from having to bear any of the costs and expenses of the Target and the Target Stockholders.

[84] Sample acquisition agreement 2004.1 (the *pro-buyer* divisional asset purchase agreement) contains additional provisions construing the representations, warranties, and covenants in a manner more favorable to the Buyer. This Agreement, like sample acquisition agreement 2004.2 (the *pro-seller* divisional asset purchase agreement), lacks comparable provisions.

[85] This Agreement contains a considerably abbreviated version of the tax provisions found in sample acquisition agreement 2002.4 (sale of subsidiary out of consolidated group). The Parties may wish to incorporate some or all of the unabridged provisions from sample acquisition agreement 2002.4 into this Agreement.

Income Taxes with respect to periods for which the consolidated, unitary, and combined Income Tax Returns of the Target will include the operations of the Division and the Division Subsidiaries). The Buyer will make all payments required with respect to any such Income Tax Return; *provided, however,* that the Target will reimburse the Buyer concurrently therewith to the extent any payment the Buyer is making relates to the operations of any of the Division and the Division Subsidiaries for any period ending on or before the Closing Date.

(iv) The Buyer and the Target will (A) cooperate in the preparation and filing of an election under Code §338(h)(10) with respect to the sale of the stock of the Division Subsidiaries hereunder[86] and (B) take all such action as is required in order to give effect to the election for state, local, and foreign Income Tax purposes to the greatest extent permitted by law.]

(o) *Employee Benefits Matters.* [The Buyer will adopt and assume at and as of the Closing each of the Employee Benefit Plans that the Division maintains and each trust, insurance contract, annuity contract, or other funding arrangement that the Division has established with respect thereto. The Buyer will ensure that the Employee Benefit Plans treat employment with any of the Division and the Division Subsidiaries prior to the Closing Date the same as employment with any of the Buyer and the Division Subsidiaries from and after the Closing Date for purposes of eligibility, vesting, and benefit accrual. The Target will transfer (or cause the plan administrators to transfer) at and as of the Closing all of the corresponding assets associated with the Employee Benefit Plans that the Buyer is adopting and assuming. With respect to each Multiemployer Plan, the Parties shall take all actions necessary to comply with the requirements of ERISA §4204.][87]

---

[86] The Buyer may seek to have the Parties make an election under Code §338(h)(10) (i.e., to have the sale of the stock of the Division Subsidiaries taxed as though the Division Subsidiaries instead had sold their *assets* to the Buyer). *See* ¶205.

This differs from any other election the Buyer might make under Code §338 in that the *Target* will be responsible for any federal income tax on the deemed sale of assets. Note, however, that the Target will incur no federal income tax on the sale of the *stock* of the Division Subsidiaries (i.e., only on the deemed sale of their *assets*) if the Parties make a Code §338(h)(10) election.

This Agreement, like sample acquisition agreement 2004.1 (the *pro-buyer* divisional asset purchase agreement), provides that the Target will remain responsible for any incremental tax arising out of the Code §338(h)(10) election. *See* the definition of "Assumed Liabilities" in §1 above.

Sample acquisition agreement 2004.2 (the *pro-seller* divisional asset purchase agreement), on the other hand, provides that the Buyer will be responsible for any such incremental tax. *See* the definition of "Assumed Liabilities" in §1 of the *pro-seller* agreement.

[87] This Agreement provides for a transfer of all Employee Benefit Plan assets (including overfundings) and liabilities (including underfundings) to the Buyer. There are many other approaches to splitting and matching plan assets and liabilities which would cause the Buyer to share to various degrees in plan overfundings and underfundings.

If the Buyer did not want to share in any plan overfundings and underfundings, the Buyer could establish substantially identical plans for future benefit accruals and count past service with any of the Division and the Division Subsidiaries for purposes of eligibility and vesting thereunder. The Target would then continue its previously established plans on a "frozen" basis and retain the benefit of any overfunding (or the detriment of any underfunding) thereunder.

If the Buyer wanted to share in only certain plan overfundings and underfundings, the Buyer and the Target could proceed as set forth in the preceding paragraph, except that the Buyer would assume

(p) *Bulk Transfer Laws.* The Buyer acknowledges that the Target will not comply with the provisions of any bulk transfer laws of any jurisdiction in connection with the transactions contemplated by this Agreement.[88]

* * * * *

IN WITNESS WHEREOF, the Parties hereto have executed this Agreement on [as of] the date first above written.

[BUYER]

By: _____

Title: _____

[TARGET]

By: _____

Title: _____

---

the liability for certain past service benefits under the Division plans as of the Closing Date and the Target would transfer certain corresponding plan assets to the Buyer.

In any event, the Purchase Price should reflect the intended disposition of Employee Benefit Plan assets and liabilities.

[88] The Buyer may seek to have the Target comply with the applicable bulk transfer laws in certain circumstances. *See* ¶2001.2.2.2.

Taxable Reverse Subsidiary Merger

¶2005 REVERSE SUBSIDIARY MERGER OF P's TRANSITORY SUBSIDIARY INTO T FOR CASH AND NOTES

Sample acquisition agreement 2005 is a taxable reverse subsidiary merger agreement (in which T's shareholders receive cash and notes) for use where T is a public reporting company and is not a subsidiary member of a consolidated group. Because this sample acquisition agreement assumes that T is a publicly held company, it contains very limited representations and warranties about T (based primarily on T's SEC filings) and no post-closing indemnification from T's shareholders.

This arrangement is typical in public company acquisitions for two reasons. *First*, P will have the comfort of the substantial public information about T available in T's SEC filings and hence P needs less in the way of representations and warranties. *Second*, the merger consideration will generally be disbursed to T's shareholders as soon as the merger is effective. Although an escrow for a portion of the merger consideration is feasible, it is not frequently used.

If T is *not* a publicly held company, P may seek extensive representations and warranties about T and post-closing indemnification from T's shareholders against any breaches thereof. Sample acquisition agreements 2002.1, 2002.2, and 2002.3 (the stock purchase agreements) contain provisions which are more favorable to P in this respect than the provisions in sample acquisition agreement 2005.

Additionally, if T is either an S corporation or a member of an affiliated or consolidated group of corporations, P may seek to have T's shareholders join in making a Code §338(h)(10) election. For such a provision, see §9 of the pro-buyer stock purchase form in ¶2002.01.

If T is a subsidiary member of a consolidated group, the parties should consider the issues raised in ¶2002.4.

Naturally the acquisition documents covering an actual transaction must be carefully tailored to the economic terms and the risk-sharing arrangements agreed upon by the parties. It is therefore unlikely that any sample acquisition agreement will ever be appropriate in its entirety for a particular negotiated transaction. Indeed, in preparing the acquisition documents for a particular negotiated transaction, it will frequently be necessary to mix and match between sample acquisition agreements, i.e., to use parts of several. When one portion of a sample acquisition agreement is changed, however, care is necessary to make sure that all appropriate changes are made in other parts of the sample acquisition agreement, because many clauses of a sample acquisition agreement are often interrelated.

Sample acquisition agreement 2005 contemplates that P will acquire all of T's outstanding shares for cash and notes through the mechanism of a reverse subsidiary merger (i.e., a merger of P's transitory subsidiary S with and into T). For tax purposes, this merger is treated as if P purchased T stock from T's shareholders directly for cash and notes (the existence of the transitory subsidiary S and the merger are disregarded).[1] The reverse subsidiary merger technique is used when T has so many shareholders that it would be unwieldy for all of them to become parties to a stock purchase agreement (or when T has only a few shareholders, but some minority shareholders decline to participate).[2] If P is to pay the entire purchase price in cash (i.e., no P notes are being issued to T's shareholders in the merger), all of the provisions relating to the P notes can be deleted.

After S merges into T, T will become a subsidiary of P. T will generally retain all of its assets and rights and remain responsible for all of its liabilities and obligations. It is generally not necessary to prepare asset transfer documents or liability assumption documents in a merger, as it is in a purchase of assets.

See ¶2001.2.3 for a further description of the principal tax and other issues associated with a merger.

Sample acquisition agreement 2002.5 (purchase price adjustment) contains additional provisions for use where there is to be a post-closing purchase price adjustment based on T's net book value as of the closing. This sample acquisition agreement can be adapted for other post-closing purchase price adjustments (such as a comparison of working capital with liabilities as of the closing *or* a contingent earnout based on earnings for a specified period after the closing). Sample acquisition agreement 2002.5 is, however, intended for use with sample acquisition agreements 2002.1, 2002.2, and 2002.3 (the *stock purchase* agreements) and must be modified prior to use with sample acquisition agreement 2005 (the reverse subsidiary *merger* agreement).

The parties must address a number of general issues in preparing any acquisition document. See ¶2001.1 for a discussion of these key issues.

¶2005   [1] Rev. Rul. 73-427, 1973-2 C.B. 301. *See* ¶202.

[2] Sample acquisition agreement 2005 contemplates a single-step reverse subsidiary merger. The parties would have to modify the agreement accordingly if the transaction involved a first-step tender offer followed by a second-step merger. *See* ¶1502.7.

MERGER PURCHASE AGREEMENT[3]

AMONG

_____

AND

_____, _____,

AND_____

_____, 19____

TABLE OF CONTENTS

[3] A reverse subsidiary merger will generally be treated as a sale of stock for federal income tax purposes. *See* ¶202. The Buyer may choose to make a Code §338 election on a timely basis after an acquisition structured as a taxable reverse subsidiary merger. *See* ¶¶107.1, 204, 205, 403, and 405.

If the Buyer makes a timely Code §338 election, the Target in effect becomes "New Target" immediately following the acquisition date: the Target's basis in its assets is stepped up (or down) so that the Target's aggregate asset basis equals the purchase price (plus the Target's liabilities, including tax liabilities generated in the transaction, and the Buyer's expenses of the acquisition), and "Old Target's" corporate attributes—e.g., earnings and profits and tax accounting methods—are expunged. Concomitantly, effective upon the close of the acquisition date, "Old Target" is taxed as if it had sold its assets, i.e., the Target is taxed on its full gain or loss inherent in its tangible and intangible assets (including goodwill), with the Target's gain or loss on each asset being ordinary or capital in character, depending on the nature of each asset treated as sold.

If the Buyer intends to make a Code §338 election, it may well be desirable to add language to this Agreement (and to have the board of directors of the Target adopt resolutions) stating that the New Target "expressly assumes" certain enumerated liabilities (and all other unenumerated liabilities) of the Target which have not yet matured into tax deductions. *See* ¶304 and the related footnote to ¶2001.2.1.1(1).

A reverse subsidiary merger in which the consideration is primarily cash and notes is generally treated for accounting purposes as a purchase rather than as a pooling of interests. *See* ¶1503.

Some LBO structures prejudice the Target's creditors and hence might permit payments, transfers, liens, and obligations arising out of the LBO to be attacked under fraudulent conveyance law. *See* ¶1506.

Exhibit A—Certificate of Merger
Exhibit B—Form of Indenture
Exhibit C—Form of Letter of Transmittal
Exhibit D—Permitted Investments
Exhibit E—Form of Opinion of Counsel to the Target
Exhibit F—Form of Opinion of Counsel to the Buyer and the Transitory Subsidiary
Disclosure Schedule—Exceptions to Representations and Warranties

[EXHIBITS AND SCHEDULES HAVE BEEN OMITTED FROM THIS SAMPLE ACQUISITION AGREEMENT 2005]

Agreement entered into on [as of] _____, 19____, by and among _____, a _____ corporation (the "*Buyer*"), _____, a [Delaware] corporation and a wholly-owned Subsidiary of the Buyer (the "*Transitory Subsidiary*"), and _____, a [Delaware] corporation (the "*Target*"). The Buyer, the Transitory Subsidiary, and the Target are referred to collectively herein as the "*Parties.*"[4]

This Agreement contemplates a transaction in which the Buyer will acquire all of the outstanding capital stock of the Target for cash and debentures through a reverse subsidiary merger of the Transitory Subsidiary with and into the Target.[5]

Now, therefore, in consideration of the premises and the mutual promises herein made, and in consideration of the representations, warranties, and covenants herein contained, the Parties agree as follows.

---

[4]This Agreement contemplates that the Buyer will acquire all of the outstanding Target Shares for cash and debentures through the mechanism of a reverse subsidiary merger (i.e., a merger of the Transitory Subsidiary with and into the Target).

The reverse subsidiary merger technique is used when the Target has so many shareholders that it would be unwieldy for all of them to become parties to a stock purchase agreement (or when the Target has only a few shareholders, but some minority shareholders decline to participate).

This Agreement contemplates a single-step reverse subsidiary merger. The Parties would have to modify the Agreement accordingly if the transaction involved a first-step tender offer followed by a second-step merger. See ¶1502.7.

[5]After the Transitory Subsidiary merges into the Target, the Target will become a subsidiary of the Buyer (assuming the Buyer is a corporation). The Target will generally retain all of its assets and rights and remain responsible for all of its liabilities and obligations. Thus it is generally not necessary to prepare asset transfer documents or liability assumption documents in a reverse subsidiary merger, as it is in a purchase of assets.

1. *Definitions.*

"Affiliate" has the meaning set forth in Rule 12b-2 of the regulations promulgated under the Securities Exchange Act.

"Buyer" has the meaning set forth in the preface above.

"Buyer-owned Share" means any Target Share that the Buyer or the Transitory Subsidiary owns beneficially.

"Buyer Comfort Letter" has the meaning set forth in §5(d) below.

"Buyer Debenture" has the meaning set forth in §2(d)(v) below.

"Certificate of Merger" has the meaning set forth in §2(c) below.

"Closing" has the meaning set forth in §2(b) below.

"Closing Date" has the meaning set forth in §2(b) below.

"Confidential Information" means any information concerning the businesses and affairs of the Target and its Subsidiaries that is not already generally available to the public.

"Definitive Financing Agreements" has the meaning set forth in §5(e) below.

"Definitive Proxy Materials" means the definitive proxy materials relating to the Special Meeting.

"Delaware General Corporation Law" means the General Corporation Law of the State of Delaware, as amended.[6]

"Disclosure Schedule" has the meaning set forth in §3 below.

"Dissenting Share" means any Target Share which any stockholder who or which has exercised his or its appraisal rights under the Delaware General Corporation Law holds of record.

"Effective Time" has the meaning set forth in §2(d)(i) below.

"Fairness Opinion" has the meaning set forth in §5(d) below.

"Financing Commitment" has the meaning set forth in §4(b) below.

---

[6] This Agreement assumes that the Target and the Transitory Subsidiary are Delaware corporations. The Parties will have to modify the Agreement accordingly if the Target or the Transitory Subsidiary is incorporated under the laws of another jurisdiction.

"Form T-1" has the meaning set forth in §5(c)(i) below.

"GAAP" means United States generally accepted accounting principles as in effect from time to time.

"Hart-Scott-Rodino Act" means the Hart-Scott-Rodino Antitrust Improvements Act of 1976, as amended.

"Indenture" has the meaning set forth in §2(d)(v) below.

"Joint Disclosure Document" means the disclosure document combining the Prospectus and the Definitive Proxy Materials.

"Knowledge" means actual knowledge [PRO-BUYER: after reasonable investigation] [PRO-SELLER: without independent investigation].

"Merger" has the meaning set forth in §2(a) below.

"Merger Consideration" has the meaning set forth in §2(d)(v) below.

"Most Recent Fiscal Quarter End" has the meaning set forth in §3(f) below.

"Ordinary Course of Business" means the ordinary course of business consistent with past custom and practice (including with respect to quantity and frequency).

"Party" has the meaning set forth in the preface above.

"Paying Agent" has the meaning set forth in §2(e) below.

"Payment Fund" has the meaning set forth in §2(e) below.

"Person" means an individual, a partnership, a corporation, an association, a joint stock company, a trust, a joint venture, an unincorporated organization, or a governmental entity (or any department, agency, or political subdivision thereof).

"Prospectus" means the final prospectus relating to the registration of the Buyer Debentures under the Securities Act.

"Public Report" has the meaning set forth in §3(e) below.

"Registration Statement" has the meaning set forth in §5(c)(i) below.

"Requisite Stockholder Approval" means the affirmative vote of the holders of [a majority] of the Target Shares in favor of this Agreement and the Merger.[7]

"SEC" means the Securities and Exchange Commission.

"Securities Act" means the Securities Act of 1933, as amended.

"Securities Exchange Act" means the Securities Exchange Act of 1934, as amended.

"Security Interest" means any mortgage, pledge, lien, encumbrance, charge, or other security interest, *other than* (a) mechanic's, materialman's, and similar liens, (b) liens for taxes not yet due and payable or for taxes that the taxpayer is contesting in good faith through appropriate proceedings, (c) purchase money liens and liens securing rental payments under capital lease arrangements, and (d) other liens arising in the Ordinary Course of Business and not incurred in connection with the borrowing of money.

"Special Meeting" has the meaning set forth in §5(c)(ii) below.

"Subsidiary" means any corporation with respect to which a specified Person (or a Subsidiary thereof) owns a majority of the common stock or has the power to vote or direct the voting of sufficient securities to elect a majority of the directors.[8]

"Surviving Corporation" has the meaning set forth in §2(a) below.

"Target" has the meaning set forth in the preface above.

"Target Comfort Letter" has the meaning set forth in §5(d) below.

"Target Share" means any share of the Common Stock, $_____ par value per share, of the Target.[9]

"Target Stockholder" means any Person who or which holds any Target Shares.

"Transitory Subsidiary" has the meaning set forth in the preface above.

"Trust Indenture Act" means the Trust Indenture Act of 1939, as amended.

---

[7] The Parties should determine whether any statute (e.g., the Delaware General Corporation Law) or corporate document (e.g., the charter or bylaws of the Target) imposes any supermajority or class vote requirement with respect to the Merger.

It may be necessary to revise this definition if the Target has additional classes of capital stock.

[8] It may be necessary to revise this definition if, for example, the Target has subsidiary *partnerships*.

[9] It may be necessary to revise this definition if the Target has additional classes of capital stock.

2. *Basic Transaction.*[10]

(a) *The Merger.* On and subject to the terms and conditions of this Agreement, the Transitory Subsidiary will merge with and into the Target (the *"Merger"*) at the Effective Time. The Target shall be the corporation surviving the Merger (the *"Surviving Corporation"*).

(b) *The Closing.* The closing of the transactions contemplated by this Agreement (the *"Closing"*) shall take place at the offices of _____, in _____, _____, commencing at 9:00 a.m. local time on the [second] business day following the satisfaction or waiver of all conditions to the obligations of the Parties to consummate the transactions contemplated hereby (other than conditions with respect to actions the respective Parties will take at the Closing itself) or such other date as the Parties may mutually determine (the *"Closing Date"*); *provided, however,* that the Closing Date shall be no earlier than _____, 19____.

(c) *Actions at the Closing.* At the Closing, (i) the Target will deliver to the Buyer and the Transitory Subsidiary the various certificates, instruments, and documents referred to in §6(a) below, (ii) the Buyer and the Transitory Subsidiary will deliver to the Target the various certificates, instruments, and documents referred to in §6(b) below, (iii) the Target and the Transitory Subsidiary will file with the Secretary of State of the State of [Delaware] a Certificate of Merger in the form attached hereto as Exhibit A (the *"Certificate of Merger"*), and (iv) the Buyer will cause the Surviving Corporation to deliver the Payment Fund to the Paying Agent in the manner provided below in this §2.

(d) *Effect of Merger.*

(i) *General.* The Merger shall become effective at the time (the *"Effective Time"*) the Target and the Transitory Subsidiary file the Certificate of Merger with the Secretary of State of the State of [Delaware]. The Merger shall have the effect set forth in the Delaware General Corporation Law. The Surviving Corporation may, at any time after the Effective Time, take any action (including executing and delivering any document) in the name and on behalf of either the Target or the Transitory Subsidiary in order to carry out and effectuate the transactions contemplated by this Agreement.

(ii) *Certificate of Incorporation.* The Certificate of Incorporation of the Surviving Corporation shall be amended and restated at and as of the Effective Time to read as did the Certificate of Incorporation of the Transitory Subsidiary

---

[10] The Target may seek to have the Buyer make an earnest money deposit upon execution of this Agreement. If the Merger were thereafter completed, the deposit would be applied against the Merger Consideration. If the Merger were thereafter aborted, the deposit would be refunded to the Buyer or paid to the Target as liquidated damages depending upon the terms of this Agreement and the reasons for the termination.

immediately prior to the Effective Time (except that the name of the Surviving Corporation will remain unchanged).

(iii) *Bylaws.* The Bylaws of the Surviving Corporation shall be amended and restated at and as of the Effective Time to read as did the Bylaws of the Transitory Subsidiary immediately prior to the Effective Time (except that the name of the Surviving Corporation will remain unchanged).

(iv) *Directors and Officers.* The directors and officers of the Transitory Subsidiary shall become the directors and officers of the Surviving Corporation at and as of the Effective Time (retaining their respective positions and terms of office).

(v) *Conversion of Target Shares.*[11] At and as of the Effective Time, (A) each Target Share (other than any Dissenting Share or Buyer-owned Share) shall be converted into the right to receive an amount (the *"Merger Consideration"*) equal to $_____ in cash (without interest) plus $_____ in principal amount of debentures (the *"Buyer Debentures"*) issued by the Buyer and having the terms and provisions set forth in an indenture in the form attached hereto as Exhibit B (the *"Indenture"*), (B) each Dissenting Share shall be converted into the right to receive payment from the Surviving Corporation with respect thereto in accordance with the provisions of the Delaware General Corporation Law, and (C) each Buyer-owned Share shall be cancelled; *provided, however,* that the Merger Consideration shall be subject to equitable adjustment in the event of any stock split, stock dividend, reverse stock split, or other change in the number of Target Shares outstanding. No Target Share shall be deemed to be outstanding or to have any rights other than those set forth above in this §2(d)(v) after the Effective Time.[12]

(vi) *Conversion of Capital Stock of the Transitory Subsidiary.* At and as of the Effective Time, each share of Common Stock, $_____ par value per share, of the Transitory Subsidiary shall be converted into one share of Common Stock, $_____ par value per share, of the Surviving Corporation.

(e) *Procedure for Payment.*

(i) Immediately after the Effective Time, (A) the Buyer will cause the Surviving Corporation to furnish to _____ (the *"Paying Agent"*) a corpus (the *"Payment Fund"*) consisting of cash and Buyer Debentures (registered in

---

[11] It may be necessary to revise this §2(d)(v) if the Target has additional classes of capital stock. *See* the definition of Target Shares in §1 above.

[12] It may be necessary or desirable to issue the Buyer Debentures only in integral multiples of $1,000. In that event, the Parties will have to address the disposition of fractional interests (e.g., the Buyer could cause the Paying Agent to sell the aggregate fractional interest in the public market and distribute the cash proceeds pro rata among the former Target Stockholders who or which otherwise would have been entitled to receive the fractional interests).

the name of the Paying Agent or its nominee) sufficient in the aggregate for the Paying Agent to make full payment of the Merger Consideration to the holders of all of the outstanding Target Shares (other than any Dissenting Shares and Buyer-owned Shares) and (B) the Buyer will cause the Paying Agent to mail a letter of transmittal (with instructions for its use) in the form attached hereto as Exhibit C to each record holder of outstanding Target Shares for the holder to use in surrendering the certificates which represented his or its Target Shares against payment of the Merger Consideration. No interest will accrue or be paid to the holder of any outstanding Target Shares (other than any interest on the Buyer Debentures in accordance with their terms).

(ii) The Buyer may cause the Paying Agent to invest the cash included in the Payment Fund in one or more of the permitted investments set forth on Exhibit D attached hereto; *provided, however*, that the terms and conditions of the investments shall be such as to permit the Paying Agent to make prompt payment of the Merger Consideration as necessary. The Buyer may cause the Paying Agent to pay over to the Surviving Corporation any net earnings with respect to the investments, and the Buyer will cause the Surviving Corporation to replace promptly any portion of the Payment Fund which the Paying Agent loses through investments.

(iii) The Buyer may cause the Paying Agent to pay over to the Surviving Corporation any portion of the Payment Fund (including any earnings thereon) remaining [180 days] after the Effective Time, and thereafter all former stockholders shall be entitled to look to the Surviving Corporation (subject to abandoned property, escheat, and other similar laws) as general creditors thereof with respect to the cash and Buyer Debentures payable upon surrender of their certificates.

(iv) The Buyer shall cause the Surviving Corporation to pay all charges and expenses of the Paying Agent.

(f) *Closing of Transfer Records.* After the close of business on the Closing Date, transfers of Target Shares outstanding prior to the Effective Time shall not be made on the stock transfer books of the Surviving Corporation.

3. *Representations and Warranties of the Target.*[13] The Target represents and warrants to the Buyer and the Transitory Subsidiary that the statements contained

---

[13] This Agreement assumes that the Target is a publicly held company, and as a result contains very limited representations and warranties about the Target and its Subsidiaries (based primarily on the Public Reports) and no post-Closing indemnification from the Target Stockholders.

This arrangement is typical in public company acquisitions for two reasons. *First,* the Buyer will have the comfort of the substantial public information about the Target and its Subsidiaries available in the Public Reports and hence the Buyer needs less in the way of representations and warranties. *Second,* the Merger Consideration will generally be disbursed to the Target Stockholders as soon as the Merger is effective. Although an escrow for a portion of the Merger Consideration is feasible, it is not frequently used.

in this §3 are correct and complete as of the date of this Agreement and will be correct and complete as of the Closing Date (as though made then and as though the Closing Date were substituted for the date of this Agreement throughout this §3), except as set forth in the disclosure schedule accompanying this Agreement and initialed by the Parties (the *"Disclosure Schedule"*).[14] The Disclosure Schedule will be arranged in paragraphs corresponding to the lettered and numbered paragraphs contained in this §3.

(a) *Organization, Qualification, and Corporate Power.* Each of the Target and its Subsidiaries is a corporation duly organized, validly existing, and in good standing under the laws of the jurisdiction of its incorporation. Each of the Target and its Subsidiaries is duly authorized to conduct business and is in good standing under the laws of each jurisdiction where such qualification is required [PRO-SELLER:, except where the lack of such qualification would not have a material adverse effect on the financial condition of the Target and its Subsidiaries taken as a whole or on the ability of the Parties to consummate the transactions contemplated by this Agreement].[15] Each of the Target and its Subsidiaries has full corporate power and authority to carry on the businesses in which it is engaged and to own and use the properties owned and used by it.

If the Target is *not* a publicly held company, the Buyer may seek extensive representations and warranties about the Target and its Subsidiaries and post-Closing indemnification from the Target stockholders against any breaches thereof. Sample acquisition agreement 2002.1 (the *pro-buyer* stock purchase agreement) contains provisions which are more favorable to the Buyer in this respect than the provisions in this sample acquisition agreement 2005. Indeed, even sample acquisition agreement 2002.2 (the *pro-seller* stock purchase agreement) contains provisions which are more favorable to the Buyer in this respect than the provisions in this sample acquisition agreement 2005 (but of course not as favorable to the Buyer as the provisions in sample acquisition agreement 2002.1).

Naturally the acquisition documents covering an actual transaction must be carefully tailored to the economic terms and the risk-sharing arrangements agreed upon by the parties. It is therefore unlikely that any sample acquisition agreement will ever be appropriate in its entirety for a particular negotiated transaction. Indeed, in preparing the acquisition documents for a particular negotiated transaction, it will frequently be necessary to mix and match between sample acquisition agreements, i.e., to use parts of several. When one portion of a sample acquisition agreement is changed, however, care is necessary to make sure that all appropriate changes are made in other parts of the sample acquisition agreement, because many clauses of a sample acquisition agreement are often interrelated.

[14] Because the Target Stockholders will have no obligation to indemnify the Buyer after the Closing for any breach of this Agreement, these representations and warranties will in effect serve only as closing conditions for the Buyer. See the closing condition in §6(a)(iii) below.

The Buyer will not, however, have any closing condition with respect to any adverse matter which the Target discloses in the Disclosure Schedule. This is because the disclosure will cure any misrepresentation or breach of warranty that might otherwise have existed. Thus, if the Target reveals an adverse matter in the Disclosure Schedule, the Buyer may seek to add a specific closing condition requiring an acceptable resolution of the matter.

[15] There are several references to materiality throughout these representations and warranties. Since the relevant closing condition in §6(a)(iii) below is already qualified as to materiality, and since the representations and warranties will not survive the Closing so as to serve any other purpose, these references to materiality are redundant. The Buyer may seek to eliminate this redundancy out of concern that the double materiality will somehow narrow its closing condition.

(b) *Capitalization.* The entire authorized capital stock of the Target consists of _____ Target Shares, of which _____ Target Shares are issued and outstanding and _____ Target Shares are held in treasury.[16] All of the issued and outstanding Target Shares have been duly authorized and are validly issued, fully paid, and nonassessable. There are no outstanding or authorized options, warrants, purchase rights, subscription rights, conversion rights, exchange rights, or other contracts or commitments that could require the Target to issue, sell, or otherwise cause to become outstanding any of its capital stock. There are no outstanding or authorized stock appreciation, phantom stock, profit participation, or similar rights with respect to the Target.

(c) *Authorization of Transaction.* The Target has full power and authority (including full corporate power and authority) to execute and deliver this Agreement and to perform its obligations hereunder; *provided, however,* that the Target cannot consummate the Merger unless and until it receives the Requisite Stockholder Approval. This Agreement constitutes the valid and legally binding obligation of the Target, enforceable in accordance with its terms and conditions.

(d) *Noncontravention.* [PRO-SELLER: To the Knowledge of any director or officer of the Target,] neither the execution and the delivery of this Agreement, nor the consummation of the transactions contemplated hereby, will (i) violate any constitution, statute, regulation, rule, injunction, judgment, order, decree, ruling, charge, or other restriction of any government, governmental agency, or court to which any of the Target and its Subsidiaries is subject or any provision of the charter or bylaws of any of the Target and its Subsidiaries or (ii) conflict with, result in a breach of, constitute a default under, result in the acceleration of, create in any party the right to accelerate, terminate, modify, or cancel, or require any notice under any agreement, contract, lease, license, instrument, or other arrangement to which any of the Target and its Subsidiaries is a party or by which it is bound or to which any of its assets is subject (or result in the imposition of any Security Interest upon any of its assets) [PRO-SELLER:, except where the violation, conflict, breach, default, acceleration, termination, modification, cancellation, failure to give notice, or Security Interest would not have a material adverse effect on the financial condition of the Target and its Subsidiaries taken as a whole or on the ability of the Parties to consummate the transactions contemplated by this Agreement]. [PRO-SELLER: To the Knowledge of any director or officer of the Target, and] other than in connection with the provisions of the Hart-Scott-Rodino Act, the Delaware General Corporation Law, the Securities Exchange Act, the Securities Act, the Trust Indenture Act, and the state securities laws, none of the Target and its Subsidiaries needs to give any notice to, make any filing with, or obtain any authorization, consent, or approval of any government or governmental agency in order for the Parties to consummate the transactions contemplated by this Agreement [PRO-SELLER:, except where the failure to give

---

[16] It may be necessary to revise this sentence if the Target has more than one class of capital stock. See the definition of Target Shares in §1 above.

notice, to file, or to obtain any authorization, consent, or approval would not have a material adverse effect on the financial condition of the Target and its Subsidiaries taken as a whole or on the ability of the Parties to consummate the transactions contemplated by this Agreement.]

(e) *Filings with the SEC.* The Target has made all filings with the SEC that it has been required to make [PRO-SELLER: within the past [three] years] under the Securities Act and the Securities Exchange Act (collectively the *"Public Reports"*). Each of the Public Reports has complied with the Securities Act and the Securities Exchange Act in all material respects. None of the Public Reports, as of their respective dates, contained any untrue statement of a material fact or omitted to state a material fact necessary in order to make the statements made therein, in light of the circumstances under which they were made, not misleading. The Target has delivered to the Buyer a correct and complete copy of each Public Report (together with all exhibits and schedules thereto and as amended to date).

(f) *Financial Statements.* The Target has filed Quarterly Reports on Form 10-Q for the fiscal quarters ended _____, 19_____ (the *"Most Recent Fiscal Quarter End"*), _____, 19_____, and _____, 19_____ and an Annual Report on Form 10-K for the fiscal year ended _____, 19_____. The financial statements included in or incorporated by reference into these Public Reports (including the related notes and schedules) have been prepared in accordance with GAAP applied on a consistent basis throughout the periods covered thereby [,] [and] present fairly the financial condition of the Target and its Subsidiaries as of the indicated dates and the results of operations of the Target and its Subsidiaries for the indicated periods [PRO-BUYER:, are correct and complete in all respects, and are consistent with the books and records of the Target and its Subsidiaries]; *provided, however*, that the interim statements are subject to normal year-end adjustments.

(g) *Events Subsequent to Most Recent Fiscal Quarter End.* Since the Most Recent Fiscal Quarter End, there has not been any [PRO-BUYER: material adverse change in the business, financial condition, operations, results of operations, or future prospects] [PRO-SELLER: material adverse change in the financial condition] of the Target and its Subsidiaries taken as a whole.[17]

(h) *Undisclosed Liabilities.* [PRO-BUYER: None of the Target and its Subsidiaries has any liability (whether known or unknown, whether asserted or unasserted, whether absolute or contingent, whether accrued or unaccrued, whether liquidated or unliquidated, and whether due or to become due), including any liability for taxes, except for (i) liabilities set forth on the face of the balance sheet dated as of the Most Recent Fiscal Quarter End (rather than in any notes thereto) and (ii) liabilities which have arisen after the Most Recent Fiscal Quarter End in the

---

[17] The Buyer may seek to expand upon this representation and warranty, since it covers a period with respect to which there may be material undisclosed developments. Sample acquisition agreement 2002.1 (the pro-buyer stock purchase agreement) contains a version of this representation and warranty which is more favorable to the Buyer.

Ordinary Course of Business (none of which results from, arises out of, relates to, is in the nature of, or was caused by any breach of contract, breach of warranty, tort, infringement, or violation of law).]

(i) *Brokers' Fees.* None of the Target and its Subsidiaries has any liability or obligation to pay any fees or commissions to any broker, finder, or agent with respect to the transactions contemplated by this Agreement.

(j) *Disclosure.* The Definitive Proxy Materials will comply with the Securities Exchange Act in all material respects. The Definitive Proxy Materials will not contain any untrue statement of a material fact or omit to state a material fact necessary in order to make the statements made therein, in the light of the circumstances under which they will be made, not misleading; *provided, however,* that the Target makes no representation or warranty with respect to any information that the Buyer and the Transitory Subsidiary will supply specifically for use in the Definitive Proxy Materials. None of the information that the Target will supply specifically for use in the Registration Statement or the Prospectus will contain any untrue statement of a material fact or omit to state a material fact necessary in order to make the statements made therein, in the light of the circumstances under which they will be made, not misleading.

4. *Representations and Warranties of the Buyer and the Transitory Subsidiary.*[18] Each of the Buyer and the Transitory Subsidiary represents and warrants to the Target that the statements contained in this §4 are correct and complete as of the date of this Agreement and will be correct and complete as of the Closing Date (as though made then and as though the Closing Date were substituted for the date of this Agreement throughout this §4), except as set forth in the Disclosure Schedule.[19] The Disclosure Schedule will be arranged in paragraphs corresponding to the numbered and lettered paragraphs contained in this §4.

(a) *Organization.* Each of the Buyer and the Transitory Subsidiary is a corporation duly organized, validly existing, and in good standing under the laws of the jurisdiction of its incorporation.

(b) *Financing.* [The Buyer has furnished to the Target correct and complete copies of written commitments from third parties (the *"Financing Commitments"*)

---

[18] The Target may seek to obtain additional representations and warranties concerning the Buyer and its Subsidiaries (e.g., the typical representations and warranties contained in a loan agreement or an underwriting agreement) because to the Target Stockholders are receiving the Buyer Debentures in the Merger as part of the Merger Consideration. Any such representations and warranties would normally survive the Closing and remain applicable for so long as the Buyer Debentures remained outstanding.

[19] Because the Buyer will have no obligation to indemnify the Target Stockholders after the Closing for any breach of this Agreement, these representations and warranties will in effect serve only as closing conditions for the Target. See the closing condition in §6(b)(iii) below.

The Target will not, however, have any closing condition with respect to any adverse matter which the Buyer reveals in the Disclosure Schedule. This is because the disclosure will cure any

committing to provide the Buyer and the Transitory Subsidiary with all of the financing they will require in order to consummate the Merger and fund the working capital needs of the Surviving Corporation and its Subsidiaries after the Closing.][20]

(c) *Authorization of Transaction.* Each of the Buyer and the Transitory Subsidiary has full power and authority (including full corporate power and authority) to execute and deliver this Agreement and to perform its obligations hereunder. This Agreement constitutes the valid and legally binding obligation of each of the Buyer and the Transitory Subsidiary, enforceable in accordance with its terms and conditions.

(d) *Noncontravention.* [PRO-BUYER: To the Knowledge of any director or officer of the Buyer,] neither the execution and the delivery of this Agreement, nor the consummation of the transactions contemplated hereby, will (i) violate any constitution, statute, regulation, rule, injunction, judgment, order, decree, ruling, charge, or other restriction of any government, governmental agency, or court to which either the Buyer or the Transitory Subsidiary is subject or any provision of the charter or bylaws of either the Buyer or the Transitory Subsidiary or (ii) conflict with, result in a breach of, constitute a default under, result in the acceleration of, create in any party the right to accelerate, terminate, modify, or cancel, or require any notice under any agreement, contract, lease, license, instrument, or other arrangement to which either the Buyer or the Transitory Subsidiary is a party or by which it is bound or to which any of its assets is subject [PRO-BUYER:, except where the violation, conflict, breach, default, acceleration, termination, modification, cancellation, or failure to give notice would not have a material adverse effect on the ability of the Parties to consummate the transactions contemplated by this Agreement]. [PRO-BUYER: To the Knowledge of any director or officer of the Buyer, and] other than in connection with the provisions of the Hart-Scott-Rodino Act, the Delaware General Corporation Law, the Securities Exchange Act, the Securities Act, the Trust Indenture Act, and the state securities laws, neither the Buyer nor the Transitory Subsidiary needs to give any notice to, make any filing with, or obtain any authorization, consent, or approval of any government or governmental agency in order for the Parties to consummate the transactions contemplated by this Agreement [PRO-BUYER:, except where the failure to give notice, to file, or to obtain any authorization, consent, or approval would not have a material adverse effect on the ability of the Parties to consummate the transactions contemplated by this Agreement.]

(e) *Brokers' Fees.* Neither the Buyer nor the Transitory Subsidiary has any liability or obligation to pay any fees or commissions to any broker, finder, or

---

misrepresentation or breach of warranty that might otherwise have existed. Thus, if the Buyer reveals an adverse matter in the Disclosure Schedule, the Target may seek to add a specific closing condition requiring an acceptable resolution of the matter.

[20] If the Target agrees to give the Buyer a closing condition concerning financing, the Target in return may seek a representation and warranty to the effect that the Buyer has already obtained

agent with respect to the transactions contemplated by this Agreement for which any of the Target and its Subsidiaries could become liable or obligated.

(f) *Disclosure.* The Registration Statement and the Prospectus will comply with the Securities Act in all material respects. The Registration Statement and the Prospectus will not contain any untrue statement of a material fact or omit to state a material fact necessary in order to make the statements made therein, in the light of the circumstances under which they will be made, not misleading; *provided, however,* that the Buyer and the Transitory Subsidiary make no representation or warranty with respect to any information that the Target will supply specifically for use in the Registration Statement and the Prospectus. None of the information that the Buyer and the Transitory Subsidiary will supply specifically for use in the Definitive Proxy Materials will contain any untrue statement of a material fact or omit to state a material fact necessary in order to make the statements made therein, in the light of the circumstances under which they will be made, not misleading.

5. *Covenants.*[21] The Parties agree as follows with respect to the period from and after the execution of this Agreement.[22]

(a) *General.* Each of the Parties will use its [reasonable] best efforts to take all action and to do all things necessary [, proper, or advisable] in order to consummate and make effective the transactions contemplated by this Agreement (including satisfaction, but not waiver, of the closing conditions set forth in §6 below).

(b) *Notices and Consents.* The Target will give any notices (and will cause each of its Subsidiaries to give any notices) to third parties, and will use its [reasonable] best efforts to obtain (and will cause each of its Subsidiaries to use its [reasonable] best efforts to obtain) any third party consents, that the Buyer [reasonably] may request in connection with the matters referred to in §3(d) above.

(c) *Regulatory Matters and Approvals.* Each of the Parties will (and the Target will cause each of its Subsidiaries to) give any notices to, make any filings with,

---

financing commitments and a covenant to the effect that the Buyer will use its [reasonable] best efforts to enter into definitive financing agreements as soon as practicable. *See* §5(e) and §6(a)(xi) below.

[21] The Target Stockholders may seek to obtain additional covenants from the Buyer and its Subsidiaries (e.g., the typical covenants contained in a loan agreement or indenture) because the Buyer is issuing the Buyer Debentures to the Target Stockholders in the Merger as part of the Merger Consideration. Any such covenants would remain applicable so long as the Buyer Debentures remained outstanding.

[22] The Parties are likely to incur significant costs and expenses in connection with the transaction. For example, the Parties and their agents will have to (a) prepare and/or review this Agreement, the Disclosure Schedule, and the Joint Disclosure Document, (b) make filings under the Securities Act and the Securities Exchange Act and respond to comments thereon, (c) make filings under the Hart-Scott-Rodino Act and respond to requests for additional information, (d) obtain the Fairness Opinion, the Target Comfort Letter, and the Buyer Comfort Letter, and (e) give notices to third parties and obtain their consents.

§8(l) below allocates responsibility among the respective parties for these costs and expenses through the Closing.

and use its [reasonable] best efforts to obtain any authorizations, consents, and approvals of governments and governmental agencies in connection with the matters referred to in §3(d) and §4(d) above. Without limiting the generality of the foregoing:

(i) *Securities Act, Securities Exchange Act, Trust Indenture Act, and State Securities Laws.* The Target will prepare and file with the SEC preliminary proxy materials under the Securities Exchange Act relating to the Special Meeting. The Buyer will prepare and file with the SEC a registration statement under the Securities Act relating to the offering and issuance of the Buyer Debentures (the *"Registration Statement"*) and a statement of eligibility and qualification under the Trust Indenture Act (the *"Form T-I"*) relating to the trustee under the Indenture. The filing Party in each instance will use its [reasonable] best efforts to respond to the comments of the SEC thereon and will make any further filings (including amendments and supplements) in connection therewith that may be necessary [, proper, or advisable]. The Buyer will provide the Target, and the Target will provide the Buyer, with whatever information and assistance in connection with the foregoing filings that the filing Party [reasonably] may request. The Buyer will take all actions that may be necessary [, proper, or advisable] under state securities laws in connection with the offering and issuance of the Buyer Debentures.[23]

(ii) *Delaware General Corporation Law.* The Target will call a special meeting of its stockholders (the *"Special Meeting"*), as soon as [reasonably] practicable in order that the stockholders may consider and vote upon the adoption of this Agreement and the approval of the Merger in accordance with the Delaware General Corporation Law. The Target will mail the Joint Disclosure Document to its stockholders as soon as [reasonably] practicable. The Joint Disclosure Document will contain the affirmative recommendation of the board of directors of the Target in favor of the adoption of this Agreement and the approval of the Merger; *provided, however,* that no director or officer of the Target shall be required to violate any fiduciary duty or other requirement imposed by law in connection therewith.

(iii) *Hart-Scott-Rodino Act.* Each of the Parties will file (and the Target will cause each of its Subsidiaries to file) any Notification and Report Forms and related material that it may be required to file with the Federal Trade Commission and the Antitrust Division of the United States Department of Justice under the Hart-Scott-Rodino Act, will use its [reasonable] best efforts to obtain (and the Target will cause each of its Subsidiaries to use its [reasonable] best efforts to obtain) an early termination of the applicable waiting period, and

---

[23] The Parties should determine whether any additional filings will be required under the Securities Act, the Securities Exchange Act, the Trust Indenture Act, and state securities laws (such as reports of ownership on Schedule 13D and transaction statements on Schedule 13E-3). This especially might be the case in transactions with management participation.

will make (and the Target will cause each of its Subsidiaries to make) any further filings pursuant thereto that may be necessary [, proper, or advisable].

(d) *Fairness Opinion and Comfort Letters.* The Target will deliver to the Buyer and the Transitory Subsidiary on or before the date the Joint Disclosure Document is mailed to the stockholders of the Target (i) an opinion of [TARGET'S INVEST-MENT BANK] as to the fairness of the Merger to the Target Stockholders from a financial point of view (the *"Fairness Opinion"*) and (ii) a letter of [TARGET'S ACCOUNTING FIRM] stating their conclusions as to the accuracy of certain information derived from the financial records of the Target and its Subsidiaries and contained in the Joint Disclosure Document (the *"Target Comfort Letter"*). Each of the Fairness Opinion and the Target Comfort Letter shall be [reasonably] satisfactory to the Buyer and the Transitory Subsidiary in form and substance. The Buyer and the Transitory Subsidiary will deliver to the Target on or before the date the Joint Disclosure Document is mailed to the stockholders of the Target a letter of [BUYER'S ACCOUNTING FIRM] stating their conclusions as to the accuracy of certain information derived from the financial records of the Buyer and its Subsidiaries and contained in the Joint Disclosure Document (the *"Buyer Comfort Letter"*). The Buyer Comfort Letter shall be [reasonably] satisfactory to the Target in form and substance.

(e) *Financing.* [The Buyer and the Transitory Subsidiary will use their [reasonable] best efforts to enter into definitive agreements (the *"Definitive Financing Agreements"*) as soon as [reasonably] practicable on terms and conditions substantially in accordance with the Financing Commitments. The Buyer will furnish correct and complete copies of the Definitive Financing Agreements to the Target. In the event any or all of the financing becomes unavailable for any reason, the Buyer will use its [reasonable] best efforts to obtain replacement financing on substantially equivalent terms and conditions from alternative sources. Any provision of this Agreement to the contrary notwithstanding, the Target will not have any obligation to mail the Joint Disclosure Document to its stockholders until the Buyer has delivered copies of the Definitive Financing Agreements to the Target.][24]

(f) *Operation of Business.*[25] The Target will not (and will not cause or permit any of its Subsidiaries to) engage in any practice, take any action, or enter into any transaction outside the Ordinary Course of Business. Without limiting the generality of the foregoing:

---

[24] If the Target agrees to give the Buyer a closing condition concerning financing, the Target in return may seek a representation and warranty to the effect that the Buyer has already obtained financing commitments and a covenant to the effect that the Buyer will use its [reasonable] best efforts to enter into definitive financing agreements as soon as practicable. *See* §4(b) above and §6(a)(xi) below.

[25] The Buyer may seek to expand upon the specific prohibitions in this covenant. Sample acquisition agreement 2002.1 (the pro-buyer stock purchase agreement) contains provisions more favorable to the Buyer in this regard.

The Target may seek to narrow (or even eliminate) the specific prohibitions in this covenant. Sample acquisition agreement 2002.2 (the pro-seller stock purchase agreement) contains provisions more favorable to the Target in this regard.

(i) none of the Target and its Subsidiaries will authorize or effect any change in its charter or bylaws;

(ii) none of the Target and its Subsidiaries will grant any options, warrants, or other rights to purchase or obtain any of its capital stock or issue, sell, or otherwise dispose of any of its capital stock (except upon the conversion or exercise of options, warrants, and other rights currently outstanding);

(iii) none of the Target and its Subsidiaries will declare, set aside, or pay any dividend or distribution with respect to its capital stock (whether in cash or in kind), or redeem, repurchase, or otherwise acquire any of its capital stock [, in either case outside the Ordinary Course of Business];

(iv) none of the Target and its Subsidiaries will issue any note, bond, or other debt security or create, incur, assume, or guarantee any indebtedness for borrowed money or capitalized lease obligation outside the Ordinary Course of Business;

(v) none of the Target and its Subsidiaries will impose any Security Interest upon any of its assets outside the Ordinary Course of Business;

(vi) none of the Target and its Subsidiaries will make any capital investment in, make any loan to, or acquire the securities or assets of any other Person outside the Ordinary Course of Business;

(vii) none of the Target and its Subsidiaries will make any change in employment terms for any of its directors, officers, and employees outside the Ordinary Course of Business; and

(viii) none of the Target and its Subsidiaries will commit to any of the foregoing.

(g) *Full Access.* The Target will (and will cause each of its Subsidiaries to) permit representatives of the Buyer to have full access [PRO-SELLER: at all reasonable times, and in a manner so as not to interfere with the normal business operations of the Target and its Subsidiaries,] to all premises, properties, personnel, books, records (including tax records), contracts, and documents of or pertaining to each of the Target and its Subsidiaries. Each of the Buyer and the Transitory Subsidiary will treat and hold as such any Confidential Information it receives from any of the Target and its Subsidiaries in the course of the reviews contemplated by this §5(g), will not use any of the Confidential Information except in connection with this Agreement, and, if this Agreement is terminated for any reason whatsoever, agrees to return to the Target all tangible embodiments (and all copies) thereof which are in its possession.

(h) *Notice of Developments.* Each Party will give prompt written notice to the others of any material adverse development causing a breach of any of its own representations and warranties in §3 and §4 above. No disclosure by any Party pursuant to this §5(h), however, shall be deemed to amend or supplement the Disclosure Schedule or to prevent or cure any misrepresentation, breach of warranty, or breach of covenant.

(i) *Exclusivity.* The Target will not (and will not cause or permit any of its Subsidiaries to) solicit, initiate, or encourage the submission of any proposal or offer from any Person relating to the acquisition of all or substantially all of the capital stock or assets of any of the Target and its Subsidiaries (including any acquisition structured as a merger, consolidation, or share exchange); *provided, however*, that the Target, its Subsidiaries, and their directors and officers will remain free to participate in any discussions or negotiations regarding, furnish any information with respect to, assist or participate in, or facilitate in any other manner any effort or attempt by any Person to do or seek any of the foregoing to the extent their fiduciary duties may require. [PRO-BUYER: The Target shall notify the Buyer immediately if any Person makes any proposal, offer, inquiry, or contact with respect to any of the foregoing.]

(j) *Insurance and Indemnification.*

(i) [PRO-SELLER: The Buyer will provide each individual who served as a director or officer of the Target at any time prior to the Effective Time with liability insurance for a period of [48 months] after the Effective Time no less favorable in coverage and amount than any applicable insurance in effect immediately prior to the Effective Time] [PRO-BUYER: ; *provided, however*, that the Buyer may reduce the coverage and amount of liability insurance to the extent the cost of liability insurance having the full coverage and amount would exceed $_____ per annum].

(ii) The Buyer will not take any action to alter or impair any exculpatory or indemnification provisions now existing in the certificate of incorporation or bylaws of the Target for the benefit of any individual who served as a director or officer of the Target at any time prior to the Effective Time.

(iii) [PRO-SELLER: The Buyer will indemnify each individual who served as a director or officer of the Target at any time prior to the Effective Time from and against any and all actions, suits, proceedings, hearings, investigations, charges, complaints, claims, demands, injunctions, judgments, orders, decrees, rulings, damages, dues, penalties, fines, costs, amounts paid in settlement, liabilities, obligations, taxes, liens, losses, expenses, and fees, including all court costs and [reasonable] attorneys' fees and expenses, resulting from, arising out of, relating to, in the nature of, or caused by this Agreement or any of the transactions contemplated herein.]

6. *Conditions to Obligation to Close.*

(a) *Conditions to Obligation of the Buyer and the Transitory Subsidiary.* The obligation of each of the Buyer and the Transitory Subsidiary to consummate the transactions to be performed by it in connection with the Closing is subject to satisfaction of the following conditions:

(i) this Agreement and the Merger shall have received the Requisite Stockholder Approval [PRO-BUYER: and the number of Dissenting Shares shall not exceed _____% of the number of outstanding Target Shares];

(ii) [PRO-BUYER: the Target and its Subsidiaries shall have procured all of the third party consents specified in §5(b) above;][26]

(iii) the representations and warranties set forth in §3 above shall be true and correct in all material respects at and as of the Closing Date;[27]

(iv) the Target shall have performed and complied with all of its covenants hereunder in all material respects through the Closing;

(v) [PRO-BUYER: no action, suit, or proceeding shall be pending or threatened before any court or quasi-judicial or administrative agency of any federal, state, local, or foreign jurisdiction or before any arbitrator wherein an unfavorable injunction, judgment, order, decree, ruling, or charge would (A) prevent consummation of any of the transactions contemplated by this Agreement, (B) cause any of the transactions contemplated by this Agreement to be rescinded following consummation, (C) affect adversely the right of the Buyer to own the capital stock of the Surviving Corporation and to control the Surviving Corporation and its Subsidiaries, or (D) affect adversely the right of any of the Surviving Corporation and its Subsidiaries to own its assets and to operate its businesses (and no such injunction, judgment, order, decree, ruling, or charge shall be in effect);] [PRO-SELLER: there shall not be any judgment, order, decree, stipulation, injunction, or charge in effect preventing consummation of any of the transactions contemplated by this Agreement;]

(vi) the Target shall have delivered to the Buyer and the Transitory Subsidiary a certificate to the effect that each of the conditions specified above in §6(a)(i)-(v) is satisfied in all respects;

---

[26] The Buyer may also seek covenants and closing conditions concerning title insurance and surveys to be delivered at the Closing. Sample acquisition agreement 2002.1 (the pro-buyer stock purchase agreement) contains provisions which are more favorable to the Buyer in this regard.

[27] Note that this provision will not give the Buyer any closing condition with respect to any adverse matter which the Target may disclose in the Disclosure Schedule. This is because the disclosure will cure any misrepresentation or breach of warranty that might otherwise have existed. Thus, if the Target discloses an adverse matter in the Disclosure Schedule, the Buyer may seek to add a specific closing condition requiring an acceptable resolution of the matter.

(vii) the Registration Statement shall have become effective under the Securities Act;

(viii) [all applicable waiting periods (and any extensions thereof) under the Hart-Scott-Rodino Act shall have expired or otherwise been terminated and the Parties shall have received all other authorizations, consents, and approvals of governments and governmental agencies referred to in §3(d) and §4(d) above];

(ix) the Buyer and the Transitory Subsidiary shall have received from counsel to the Target an opinion in form and substance as set forth in Exhibit E attached hereto, addressed to the Buyer and the Transitory Subsidiary, and dated as of the Closing Date;

(x) [PRO-BUYER: the Buyer and the Transitory Subsidiary shall have received the resignations, effective as of the Closing, of each director and officer of the Target and its Subsidiaries other than those whom the Buyer shall have specified in writing at least [five] business days prior to the Closing;]

(xi) [PRO-BUYER: the Buyer and the Transitory Subsidiary shall have obtained all of the financing they will require in order to consummate the Merger and fund the working capital needs of the Surviving Corporation and its Subsidiaries after the Closing on terms and conditions substantially in accordance with the Financing Commitments;][28] and

(xii) all actions to be taken by the Target in connection with consummation of the transactions contemplated hereby and all certificates, opinions, instruments, and other documents required to effect the transactions contemplated hereby will be [reasonably] satisfactory in form and substance to the Buyer and the Transitory Subsidiary.

The Buyer and the Transitory Subsidiary may waive any condition specified in this §6(a) if they execute a writing so stating at or prior to the Closing.

(b) *Conditions to Obligation of the Target.* The obligation of the Target to consummate the transactions to be performed by it in connection with the Closing is subject to satisfaction of the following conditions:

(i) the Registration Statement shall have become effective under the Securities Act;

---

[28] If the Target agrees to give the Buyer a closing condition concerning financing, the Target in return may seek a representation and warranty to the effect that the Buyer has already obtained financing commitments and a covenant to the effect that the Buyer will use its [reasonable] best efforts to enter into definitive financing agreements as soon as practicable. *See* §4(b) and §5(e) above.

(ii) [CONFORM TO THE BUYER'S CLOSING CONDITION IN §6(a)(xi) ABOVE];

(iii) the representations and warranties set forth in §4 above shall be true and correct in all material respects at and as of the Closing Date;

(iv) each of the Buyer and the Transitory Subsidiary shall have performed and complied with all of its covenants hereunder in all material respects through the Closing;

(v) [CONFORM TO THE BUYER'S CLOSING CONDITION IN §6(a)(v) ABOVE];

(vi) each of the Buyer and the Transitory Subsidiary shall have delivered to the Target a certificate to the effect that each of the conditions specified above in §6(b)(i)-(v) is satisfied in all respects;

(vii) this Agreement and the Merger shall have received the Requisite Stockholder Approval;

(viii) [all applicable waiting periods (and any extensions thereof) under the Hart-Scott-Rodino Act shall have expired or otherwise been terminated and the Parties shall have received all other authorizations, consents, and approvals of governments and governmental agencies referred to in §3(d) and §4(d) above];

(ix) the Target shall have received from counsel to the Buyer and the Transitory Subsidiary an opinion in form and substance as set forth in Exhibit F attached hereto, addressed to the Target, and dated as of the Closing Date; and

(x) all actions to be taken by the Buyer and the Transitory Subsidiary in connection with consummation of the transactions contemplated hereby and all certificates, opinions, instruments, and other documents required to effect the transactions contemplated hereby will be [reasonably] satisfactory in form and substance to the Target.

The Target may waive any condition specified in this §6(b) if it executes a writing so stating at or prior to the Closing.

7. *Termination.*

(a) *Termination of Agreement.* Any of the Parties may terminate this Agreement with the prior authorization of its board of directors (whether before or after stockholder approval) as provided below:

(i) the Parties may terminate this Agreement by mutual written consent at any time prior to the Effective Time;

(ii) the Buyer and the Transitory Subsidiary may terminate this Agreement by giving written notice to the Target at any time prior to the Effective Time (A) in the event the Target has breached any material representation, warranty, or covenant contained in this Agreement in any material respect, the Buyer or the Transitory Subsidiary has notified the Target of the breach, and the breach has continued without cure for a period of [30 days] after the notice of breach or (B) if the Closing shall not have occurred on or before _____, 19_____, by reason of the failure of any condition precedent under §6(a) hereof (unless the failure results primarily from the Buyer or the Transitory Subsidiary breaching any representation, warranty, or covenant contained in this Agreement);

(iii) the Target may terminate this Agreement by giving written notice to the Buyer and the Transitory Subsidiary at any time prior to the Effective Time (A) in the event the Buyer or the Transitory Subsidiary has breached any material representation, warranty, or covenant contained in this Agreement in any material respect, the Target has notified the Buyer and the Transitory Subsidiary of the breach, and the breach has continued without cure for a period of [30 days] after the notice of breach or (B) if the Closing shall not have occurred on or before _____, 19_____, by reason of the failure of any condition precedent under §6(b) hereof (unless the failure results primarily from the Target breaching any representation, warranty, or covenant contained in this Agreement);

(iv) [PRO-SELLER: the Target may terminate this Agreement by giving written notice to the Buyer and the Transitory Subsidiary at any time prior to the Effective Time in the event the Target's board of directors concludes that termination would be in the best interests of the Target and its stockholders;][29]

(v) any Party may terminate this Agreement by giving written notice to the other Parties at any time prior to the Effective Time in the event the Fairness Opinion is withdrawn; or

---

[29] This Agreement does not contain any breakup fee, lockup option, or similar provision for the benefit of the Buyer (other than the limited exclusivity provisions in §5(i) above) designed to address the threat of competing transactions when the Target is a publicly held company.

The Buyer might, for example, seek to have the Target pay the Buyer a breakup fee (e.g., the Buyer's costs and expenses, a fixed dollar amount, or a formula amount based on the spread between the Merger Consideration and a subsequent superior offer) in the event the Parties terminate this Agreement under certain specified circumstances.

The Buyer might also seek to have the Target give the Buyer an option to acquire Target Shares (with an exercise price at or below the Merger Consideration) or an option (sometimes referred to as a "Crown Jewel" option) to acquire certain desirable assets of the Target (with an exercise price at or below fair market value) in the event the Parties terminate this Agreement under certain specified circumstances.

(vi) any Party may terminate this Agreement by giving written notice to the other Parties at any time after the Special Meeting in the event this Agreement and the Merger fail to receive the Requisite Stockholder Approval.

(b) *Effect of Termination.* If any Party terminates this Agreement pursuant to §7(a) above, all rights and obligations of the Parties hereunder shall terminate without any liability of any Party to any other Party (except for any liability of any Party then in breach); *provided, however,* that the confidentiality provisions contained in §5(g) above shall survive any such termination.

8. *Miscellaneous.*

(a) *Survival.* None of the representations, warranties, and covenants of the Parties (other than the provisions in §2 above concerning payment of the Merger Consideration and the provisions in §5(j) above concerning insurance and indemnification) will survive the Effective Time.

(b) *Press Releases and Public Announcements.* No Party shall issue any press release or make any public announcement relating to the subject matter of this Agreement without the prior written approval of the other Parties; *provided, however,* that any Party may make any public disclosure it believes in good faith is required by applicable law or any listing or trading agreement concerning its publicly-traded securities (in which case the disclosing Party will use its [reasonable] best efforts to advise the other Party prior to making the disclosure).

(c) *No Third-Party Beneficiaries.* This Agreement shall not confer any rights or remedies upon any Person other than the Parties and their respective successors and permitted assigns; *provided, however,* that (i) the provisions in §2 above concerning payment of the Merger Consideration are intended for the benefit of the Target Stockholders and (ii) the provisions in §5(j) above concerning insurance and indemnification are intended for the benefit of the individuals specified therein and their respective legal representatives.

(d) *Entire Agreement.* [This Agreement (including the documents referred to herein) constitutes the entire agreement among the Parties and supersedes any prior understandings, agreements, or representations by or among the Parties, written or oral, to the extent they related in any way to the subject matter hereof.]

(e) *Succession and Assignment.* This Agreement shall be binding upon and inure to the benefit of the Parties named herein and their respective successors and permitted assigns. No Party may assign either this Agreement or any of its rights, interests, or obligations hereunder without the prior written approval of the other Parties.

These provisions come in many forms, raise complex issues concerning the fiduciary duties of directors and officers, and generally are negotiated extensively.

(f) *Counterparts.* This Agreement may be executed in one or more counterparts, each of which shall be deemed an original but all of which together will constitute one and the same instrument.

(g) *Headings.* The section headings contained in this Agreement are inserted for convenience only and shall not affect in any way the meaning or interpretation of this Agreement.

(h) *Notices.* All notices, requests, demands, claims, and other communications hereunder will be in writing. Any notice, request, demand, claim, or other communication hereunder shall be deemed duly given if (and then two business days after) it is sent by registered or certified mail, return receipt requested, postage prepaid, and addressed to the intended recipient as set forth below:

If to the Target: *Copy to:*

If to the Buyer: *Copy to:*

If to the Transitory Subsidiary: *Copy to:*

Any Party may send any notice, request, demand, claim, or other communication hereunder to the intended recipient at the address set forth above using any other means (including personal delivery, expedited courier, messenger service, telecopy, telex, ordinary mail, or electronic mail), but no such notice, request, demand, claim, or other communication shall be deemed to have been duly given unless and until it actually is received by the intended recipient. Any Party may change the address to which notices, requests, demands, claims, and other communications hereunder are to be delivered by giving the other Parties notice in the manner herein set forth.

(i) *Governing Law. This Agreement shall be governed by and construed in accordance with the domestic laws of the State of [Delaware] without giving effect to any choice or conflict of law provision or rule (whether of the State of [Delaware] or any other jurisdiction) that would cause the application of the laws of any jurisdiction other than the State of [Delaware].*

(j) *Amendments and Waivers.* The Parties may mutually amend any provision of this Agreement at any time prior to the Effective Time with the prior authorization of their respective boards of directors; *provided, however,* that any amendment effected subsequent to stockholder approval will be subject to the restrictions contained in the Delaware General Corporation Law. No amendment of any provision of this Agreement shall be valid unless the same shall be in writing and signed by all of the Parties. No waiver by any Party of any default, misrepresentation, or breach of warranty or covenant hereunder, whether intentional or not, shall be deemed to extend to any prior or subsequent default, misrepresentation, or breach of warranty or covenant hereunder or affect in any way any rights arising by virtue of any prior or subsequent such occurrence.

(k) *Severability.* Any term or provision of this Agreement that is invalid or unenforceable in any situation in any jurisdiction shall not affect the validity or enforceability of the remaining terms and provisions hereof or the validity or enforceability of the offending term or provision in any other situation or in any other jurisdiction.

(l) *Expenses.* Each of the Parties will bear its own costs and expenses (including legal fees and expenses) incurred in connection with this Agreement and the transactions contemplated hereby.[30]

(m) *Construction.* [The Parties have participated jointly in the negotiation and drafting of this Agreement. In the event an ambiguity or question of intent or interpretation arises, this Agreement shall be construed as if drafted jointly by the Parties and no presumption or burden of proof shall arise favoring or disfavoring any Party by virtue of the authorship of any of the provisions of this Agreement.] Any reference to any federal, state, local, or foreign statute or law shall be deemed also to refer to all rules and regulations promulgated thereunder, unless the context otherwise requires. The word *"including"* shall mean including without limitation.

(n) *Incorporation of Exhibits and Schedules.* The Exhibits and Schedules identified in this Agreement are incorporated herein by reference and made a part hereof.

*   *   *   *   *

---

[30] This Agreement makes each of the Parties responsible for its own costs and expenses whether or not the Merger is consummated. This means the Buyer will inherit the costs and expenses of the Target and its Subsidiaries if the Merger is consummated, but will be responsible for only its own costs and expenses if the Merger is aborted.

The Buyer may seek reimbursement from the Target for the Buyer's costs and expenses if the Merger is aborted under certain specified circumstances. Similarly, the Target may seek reimbursement from the Buyer for the Target's costs and expenses if the Merger is aborted under certain other specified circumstances. The Parties may settle on a compromise allocation of responsibility for costs and expenses if the Merger is aborted (such as sharing the costs and expenses in a predetermined ratio or making one Party responsible for the costs and expenses up to a specified aggregate ceiling and the other Party responsible for any excess).

IN WITNESS WHEREOF, the Parties hereto have executed this Agreement on [as of] the date first above written.

[BUYER]

By: _____

Title: _____

[TARGET]

By: _____

Title: _____

[TRANSITORY SUBSIDIARY]

By: _____

Title: _____

Tax-Free Merger

¶2006 TAX-FREE MERGER OF T INTO P FOR P STOCK

Sample acquisition agreement 2006 is a tax-free merger agreement for use where T is a public reporting company. Because this sample acquisition agreement assumes that T is a publicly held company, it contains very limited representations and warranties about T (based primarily on T's SEC filings) and no post-closing indemnification from T's shareholders.

This arrangement is typical in public company acquisitions for two reasons. *First*, P will have the comfort of the substantial public information about T available in T's SEC filings, and hence P needs less in the way of representations and warranties. *Second*, the merger consideration will generally be disbursed to T's shareholders as soon as the merger is effective. Although an escrow for a portion of the merger consideration is feasible, it is not frequently used.

If T is *not* a publicly held company, P may seek extensive representations and warranties about T and post-closing indemnification from T's shareholders against any breaches thereof. Sample acquisition agreements 2003.1, 2003.2, and 2003.3 (the asset purchase agreements) contain provisions that are more favorable to P in this respect than the provisions in this sample acquisition agreement 2006.

Naturally the acquisition documents covering an actual transaction must be carefully tailored to the economic terms and the risk-sharing arrangements agreed upon by the parties. It is therefore unlikely that any sample acquisition agreement will ever be appropriate in its entirety for a particular negotiated transaction. Indeed, in preparing the acquisition documents for a particular negotiated transaction, it will frequently be necessary to mix and match between sample acquisition agreements, i.e., to use parts of several. When one portion of a sample acquisition agreement is changed, however, care is necessary to make sure that all appropriate changes are made in other parts of the sample acquisition agreement, because many clauses of a form are often interrelated.

Sample acquisition agreement 2006 contemplates a tax-free merger of T into P (e.g., a two-party "A" reorganization pursuant to Code §368(a)(1)(A)), with T's shareholders receiving capital stock of P in exchange for their capital stock in T. See ¶801 for a discussion of the requirements for and consequences of an "A" reorganization (including the circumstances under which P may distribute cash or other "boot" to T's shareholders in addition to P stock).[1]

There are alternative tax-free acquisition structures that P and T may wish to consider. See Chapters 6, 7, and 8 for a discussion of stock-for-stock exchanges, stock-for-assets exchanges, forward subsidiary mergers, and reverse subsidiary mergers. See also Chapter 9 for a discussion of evolving acquisition techniques using Code §351.

All tax-free reorganizations (including the two-party "A" reorganization) must satisfy three requirements: (i) business purpose, (ii) continuity of shareholder interest, and (iii) continuity of business enterprise. See ¶¶609, 610, and 611. Unless the merger of T into P satisfies all three of these requirements, the transaction will not qualify as a tax-free reorganization and instead will constitute a taxable sale of assets from T to P followed by a complete liquidation of T. See Rev. Rul. 69-6, 1969-1 C.B. 104, discussed at ¶301. For example, if too much of the consideration paid to T's shareholders is cash or other boot (i.e., too little of the consideration is P stock), so that the continuity of shareholder interest requirement is not satisfied, the transaction will be treated as such a taxable sale of assets.

After T merges into P, P will generally acquire all of T's assets and rights, and assume all of T's liabilities and obligations, by operation of law.

It is generally not necessary to prepare asset transfer documents or liability assumption documents in a merger, as it is in a purchase of assets.

See ¶2001.2.3 for a further description of the principal tax and other issues associated with a merger.

Sample acquisition agreement 2002.5 (purchase price adjustment) contains additional provisions for use where there is to be a post-closing purchase price adjustment based on T's net book value as of the closing. This form can be adapted for other post-closing purchase price adjustments (such as a comparison of working capital with liabilities as of the closing *or* a contingent earnout based on earnings for a specified period after the closing). Sample acquisition agreement 2002.5 is, however, intended for use with sample acquisition agreements 2002.1, 2002.2, and 2002.3 (the taxable *stock purchase* agreements) and must be modified prior to use with sample acquisition agreement 2006 (the tax-free *merger* agreement).

The parties must address a number of general issues in preparing any acquisition document. See ¶2001.1 for a discussion of these key issues.

¶2006   [1] A transaction which is a tax-free reorganization for tax purposes (so that the basis of T in its assets carries over to P) also may constitute a *pooling of interests* for GAAP purposes (so that the book value of T for its assets carries over to P) if it meets the very rigorous pooling requirements described at ¶1503. If the parties wish to structure the transaction as a pooling of interests for GAAP purposes, it will be necessary to add representations, warranties, covenants, and other provisions addressing the pooling requirements.

AGREEMENT AND PLAN OF MERGER[2]

AMONG

_____

AND

_____, _____,

AND_____

_____, 19____

TABLE OF CONTENTS

[2] This Agreement contemplates a tax-free merger of the Target into the Buyer (e.g., a two-party "A" reorganization pursuant to Code §368(a)(1)(A)), with the Target Stockholders receiving capital stock of the Buyer in exchange for their capital stock in the Target. *See* ¶801 for a discussion of the requirements for and consequences of an "A" reorganization (including the circumstances under which the Buyer may distribute cash or other "boot" to the Target Stockholders in addition to the Buyer stock).

There are alternative tax-free acquisition structures that the Parties may wish to consider. *See* Chapters 6, 7, and 8 for a discussion of stock-for-stock exchanges, stock-for-assets exchanges, forward subsidiary mergers, and reverse subsidiary mergers. *See* also Chapter 9 for a discussion of evolving acquisition techniques using Code §351.

A transaction which is a tax-free reorganization for tax purposes (so that the basis of the Target in its assets carries over to the Buyer) also may constitute a *pooling of interests* for GAAP purposes (so that the book value of the Target for its assets carries over to the Buyer) if it meets the very rigorous pooling requirements described at ¶1503. If the Parties wish to structure the transaction as a pooling of interests for GAAP purposes, it will be necessary to add representations, warranties, covenants, and other provisions to the Agreement addressing the pooling requirements.

Although a leveraged buyout is usually a taxable transaction, occasionally an LBO may be structured as a tax-free reorganization. Some LBO structures prejudice the Target's creditors and hence might permit payments, transfers, liens, and obligations arising out of the LBO to be attacked under fraudulent conveyance law. *See* ¶1506.

[EXHIBITS AND SCHEDULES HAVE BEEN OMITTED FROM THIS SAMPLE ACQUISITION AGREEMENT 2006]

Agreement entered into on [as of] _____, 19____ by and between _____, a [Delaware] corporation (the *"Buyer"*), and _____, a [Delaware] corporation (the *"Target"*). The Buyer and the Target are referred to collectively herein as the *"Parties."*

This Agreement contemplates a tax-free merger of the Target with and into the Buyer in a reorganization pursuant to Code §368(a)(1)(A).[3] The Target Stockholders will receive capital stock in the Buyer in exchange for their capital stock

---

[3] All tax-free reorganizations (including the two-party "A" reorganization) must satisfy three requirements: (i) business purpose, (ii) continuity of shareholder interest, and (iii) continuity of business enterprise. *See* ¶¶609, 610, and 611. Unless the merger of the Target into the Buyer satisfies all three of these requirements, the transaction will not qualify as a tax-free reorganization and instead will constitute a taxable sale of assets from the Target to the Buyer followed by a complete liquidation of the Target. *See* Rev. Rul. 69-6, 1969-1 C.B. 104, discussed at ¶301. For example, if too much of the consideration paid to the Target Stockholders is cash or other boot (i.e., too little of the consideration is Buyer stock), so that the continuity of shareholder interest requirement is not satisfied, the transaction will be treated as such a taxable sale of assets.

This Agreement accordingly contains (a) a statement regarding the business purpose for the Merger (*see* the preamble below), (b) a brief description of certain representations, warranties, and covenants the Parties might wish to obtain from the Target Stockholders regarding continuity of shareholder interest (*see* Exhibit A hereto), and (c) certain representations, warranties, and covenants from the Buyer and the Target regarding continuity of the business enterprise (*see* §§3(j), 4(f), and 5(k) below).

The Parties might also wish to condition their respective obligations to close on the receipt of a private letter ruling from the IRS to the effect that the Merger will qualify as a tax-free reorganization. *See* §§6(a)(xii) and 6(b)(xi) below.

in the Target.[4] [The Parties expect that the Merger will further certain of their business objectives (including, without limitation, _____).][5]

Now, therefore, in consideration of the premises and the mutual promises herein made, and in consideration of the representations, warranties, and covenants herein contained, the Parties agree as follows.

1. *Definitions.*

"Affiliate" has the meaning set forth in Rule 12b-2 of the regulations promulgated under the Securities Exchange Act.

"Buyer" has the meaning set forth in the preface above.

"Buyer-owned Share" means any Target Share that the Buyer owns beneficially.

"Buyer Comfort Letter" has the meaning set forth in §5(d) below.

"Buyer Share" means any share of the Common Stock, $_____ par value per share, of the Buyer.[6]

"Certificate of Merger" has the meaning set forth in §2(c) below.

"Closing" has the meaning set forth in §2(b) below.

"Closing Date" has the meaning set forth in §2(b) below.

"Confidential Information" means any information concerning the businesses and affairs of the Target and its Subsidiaries that is not already generally available to the public.

"Conversion Ratio" has the meaning set forth in §2(d)(v) below.

"Definitive Buyer Proxy Materials" means the definitive proxy materials relating to the Special Buyer Meeting.

"Definitive Target Proxy Materials" means the definitive proxy materials relating to the Special Target Meeting.

---

[4] After the Target merges into the Buyer, the Buyer will generally acquire all of the Target's assets and rights, and assume all of the Target's liabilities and obligations, by operation of law. Thus, it is generally not necessary to prepare asset transfer documents or liability assumption documents in a merger, as it is in a purchase of assets.

[5] The Merger will not qualify as a tax-free reorganization unless the Parties have a valid business purpose for the transaction. *See* ¶609. The Parties therefore may wish to record certain of their business objectives in this preamble to the Agreement.

[6] It may be necessary to revise this definition if the Buyer has additional classes of capital stock.

"Delaware General Corporation Law" means the General Corporation Law of the State of Delaware, as amended.[7]

"Disclosure Schedule" has the meaning set forth in §3 below.

"Dissenting Share" means any Target Share which any stockholder who or which has exercised his or its appraisal rights under the Delaware General Corporation Law holds of record.

"Effective Time" has the meaning set forth in §2(d)(i) below.

"Exchange Agent" has the meaning set forth in §2(e) below.

"Fairness Opinion" has the meaning set forth in §5(d) below.

"GAAP" means United States generally accepted accounting principles as in effect from time to time.

"Hart-Scott-Rodino Act" means the Hart-Scott-Rodino Antitrust Improvements Act of 1976, as amended.

"IRS" means the Internal Revenue Service.

"Joint Disclosure Document" means the disclosure document combining the Prospectus, the Definitive Buyer Proxy Materials, and the Definitive Target Proxy Materials.

"Knowledge" means actual knowledge [PRO-BUYER: after reasonable investigation] [PRO-SELLER: without independent investigation].

"Merger" has the meaning set forth in §2(a) below.

"Most Recent Fiscal Quarter End" has the meaning set forth in §3(f) below.

"Ordinary Course of Business" means the ordinary course of business consistent with past custom and practice (including with respect to quantity and frequency).

"Party" has the meaning set forth in the preface above.

"Person" means an individual, a partnership, a corporation, an association, a joint stock company, a trust, a joint venture, an unincorporated organization, or a governmental entity (or any department, agency, or political subdivision thereof).

---

[7] This Agreement assumes that the Buyer and the Target are Delaware corporations. The Parties will have to modify the Agreement accordingly if the Buyer or the Target is incorporated under the laws of another jurisdiction.

"Prospectus" means the final prospectus relating to the registration of the Buyer Shares under the Securities Act.

"Public Report" has the meaning set forth in §3(e) below.

"Registration Statement" has the meaning set forth in §5(c)(i) below.

"Requisite Buyer Stockholder Approval" means the affirmative vote of the holders of [a majority] of the Buyer Shares in favor of this Agreement and the Merger.[8]

"Requisite Target Stockholder Approval" means the affirmative vote of the holders of [a majority] of the Target Shares in favor of this Agreement and the Merger.[9]

"SEC" means the Securities and Exchange Commission.

"Securities Act" means the Securities Act of 1933, as amended.

"Securities Exchange Act" means the Securities Exchange Act of 1934, as amended.

"Security Interest" means any mortgage, pledge, lien, encumbrance, charge, or other security interest, *other than* (a) mechanic's, materialmen's, and similar liens, (b) liens for taxes not yet due and payable or for taxes that the taxpayer is contesting in good faith through appropriate proceedings, (c) purchase money liens and liens securing rental payments under capital lease arrangements, and (d) other liens arising in the Ordinary Course of Business and not incurred in connection with the borrowing of money.

"Special Buyer Meeting" has the meaning set forth in §5(c)(ii) below.

"Special Target Meeting" has the meaning set forth in §5(c)(ii) below.

"Subsidiary" means any corporation with respect to which a specified Person (or a Subsidiary thereof) owns a majority of the common stock or has the power to vote or direct the voting of sufficient securities to elect a majority of the directors.[10]

"Surviving Corporation" has the meaning set forth in §2(a) below.

---

[8] The Parties should determine whether the Buyer stockholders must approve the Merger (as this Agreement assumes) and, if so, whether any statute (e.g., the Delaware General Corporation Law) or corporate document (e.g., the charter or bylaws of the Buyer) imposes any supermajority or class vote requirement. *See* ¶2001.2.3.2(7).

It may be necessary to revise this definition if the Buyer has additional classes of capital stock.

[9] The Parties should determine whether any statute (e.g., the Delaware General Corporation Law) or corporate document (e.g., the charter or bylaws of the Target) imposes any supermajority or class vote requirement with respect to the Merger.

It may be necessary to revise this definition if the Target has additional classes of capital stock.

[10] It may be necessary to revise this definition if, for example, the Target has subsidiary *partnerships*.

"Target" has the meaning set forth in the preface above.

"Target Comfort Letter" has the meaning set forth in §5(d) below.

"Target Share" means any share of the Common Stock, $_____ par value per share, of the Target.[11]

"Target Stockholder" means any Person who or which holds any Target Shares.

2. *Basic Transaction.*[12]

(a) *The Merger.* On and subject to the terms and conditions of this Agreement, the Target will merge with and into the Buyer (the *"Merger"*) at the Effective Time. The Buyer shall be the corporation surviving the Merger (the *"Surviving Corporation"*).

(b) *The Closing.* The closing of the transactions contemplated by this Agreement (the *"Closing"*) shall take place at the offices of _____ in _____, _____, commencing at 9:00 a.m. local time on the [second] business day following the satisfaction or waiver of all conditions to the obligations of the Parties to consummate the transactions contemplated hereby (other than conditions with respect to actions the respective Parties will take at the Closing itself) or such other date as the Parties may mutually determine (the *"Closing Date"*); *provided, however,* that the Closing Date shall be no earlier than _____, 19____.

(c) *Actions at the Closing.* At the Closing, (i) the Target will deliver to the Buyer the various certificates, instruments, and documents referred to in §6(a) below, (ii) the Buyer will deliver to the Target the various certificates, instruments, and documents referred to in §6(b) below, (iii) the Buyer and the Target will file with the Secretary of State of the State of [Delaware] a Certificate of Merger in the form attached hereto as Exhibit B (the *"Certificate of Merger"*), and (iv) the Buyer will deliver to the Exchange Agent in the manner provided below in this §2 the certificate evidencing the Buyer Shares issued in the Merger.

(d) *Effect of Merger.*

(i) *General.* The Merger shall become effective at the time (the *"Effective Time"*) the Buyer and the Target file the Certificate of Merger with the Secretary of State of the State of [Delaware]. The Merger shall have the effect set forth in the Delaware General Corporation Law. The Surviving Corporation may, at

---

[11] It may be necessary to revise this definition if the Target has additional classes of capital stock.

[12] The Target may seek to have the Buyer make an earnest money deposit upon execution of this Agreement. If the Merger were thereafter completed, the Buyer would recover the deposit. If the Merger were thereafter aborted, the deposit would be refunded to the Buyer or paid to the Target as liquidated damages depending upon the terms of this Agreement and the reasons for the termination.

any time after the Effective Time, take any action (including executing and delivering any document) in the name and on behalf of either the Buyer or the Target in order to carry out and effectuate the transactions contemplated by this Agreement.

(ii) *Certificate of Incorporation.* The Certificate of Incorporation of the Buyer in effect at and as of the Effective Time will remain the Certificate of Incorporation of the Surviving Corporation without any modification or amendment in the Merger.[13]

(iii) *Bylaws.* The Bylaws of the Buyer in effect at and as of the Effective Time will remain the Bylaws of the Surviving Corporation without any modification or amendment in the Merger.

(iv) *Directors and Officers.* The directors and officers of the Buyer in office at and as of the Effective Time will remain the directors and officers of the Surviving Corporation (retaining their respective positions and terms of office).

(v) *Conversion of Target Shares.*[14] At and as of the Effective Time, (A) each Target Share (other than any Dissenting Share or Buyer-owned Share) shall be converted into the right to receive _____ Buyer Shares (the ratio of _____ Buyer Shares to one Target Share is referred to herein as the *"Conversion Ratio"*), (B) each Dissenting Share shall be converted into the right to receive payment from the Surviving Corporation with respect thereto in accordance with the provisions of the Delaware General Corporation Law, and (C) each Buyer-owned Share shall be canceled; *provided, however*, that the Conversion Ratio shall be subject to equitable adjustment in the event of any stock split, stock dividend, reverse stock split, or other change in the number of Target Shares outstanding. No Target Share shall be deemed to be outstanding or to have any rights other than those set forth above in this §2(d)(v) after the Effective Time.[15]

(vi) *Buyer Shares.* Each Buyer Share issued and outstanding at and as of the Effective Time will remain issued and outstanding.

---

[13] The Parties should determine whether the Buyer will have the authorized but unissued Buyer Shares required in order to consummate the Merger. If not, the board of directors and stockholders of the Buyer will have to amend its Certificate of Incorporation in order to authorize the requisite additional Buyer Shares.

[14] It may be necessary to revise this §2(d)(v) if the Target has additional classes of capital stock. *See* the definition of Target Shares in §1 above.

[15] It may be necessary or desirable to issue only whole Buyer Shares. In that event, the Parties will have to address the disposition of fractional interests (e.g., the Buyer could cause the Exchange Agent to sell the aggregate fractional interest in the public market and distribute the cash proceeds pro rata among the former Target Stockholders who or which otherwise would have been entitled to receive the fractional interests).

(e) *Procedure for Payment.*

(i) Immediately after the Effective Time, (A) the Buyer will furnish to _____ (the *"Exchange Agent"*) a stock certificate (issued in the name of the Exchange Agent or its nominee) representing that number of Buyer Shares equal to the product of (I) the Conversion Ratio *times* (II) the number of outstanding Target Shares (other than any Dissenting Shares and Buyer-owned Shares) and (B) the Buyer will cause the Exchange Agent to mail a letter of transmittal (with instructions for its use) in the form attached hereto as Exhibit C to each record holder of outstanding Target Shares for the holder to use in surrendering the certificates which represented his or its Target Shares in exchange for a certificate representing the number of Buyer Shares to which he or it is entitled.

(ii) The Buyer will not pay any dividend or make any distribution on Buyer Shares (with a record date at or after the Effective Time) to any record holder of outstanding Target Shares until the holder surrenders for exchange his or its certificates which represented Target Shares. The Buyer instead will pay the dividend or make the distribution to the Exchange Agent in trust for the benefit of the holder pending surrender and exchange. The Buyer may cause the Exchange Agent to invest any cash the Exchange Agent receives from the Buyer as a dividend or distribution in one or more of the permitted investments set forth on Exhibit D attached hereto; *provided, however,* that the terms and conditions of the investments shall be such as to permit the Exchange Agent to make prompt payments of cash to the holders of outstanding Target Shares as necessary. The Buyer may cause the Exchange Agent to pay over to the Buyer any net earnings with respect to the investments, and the Buyer will replace promptly any cash which the Exchange Agent loses through investments. In no event, however, will any holder of outstanding Target Shares be entitled to any interest or earnings on the dividend or distribution pending receipt.

(iii) The Buyer may cause the Exchange Agent to return any Buyer Shares and dividends and distributions thereon remaining unclaimed [180 days] after the Effective Time, and thereafter each remaining record holder of outstanding Target Shares shall be entitled to look to the Buyer (subject to abandoned property, escheat, and other similar laws) as a general creditor thereof with respect to the Buyer Shares and dividends and distributions thereon to which he or it is entitled upon surrender of his or its certificates.

(iv) The Buyer shall pay all charges and expenses of the Exchange Agent.

(f) *Closing of Transfer Records.* After the close of business on the Closing Date, transfers of Target Shares outstanding prior to the Effective Time shall not be made on the stock transfer books of the Surviving Corporation.

3. *Representations and Warranties of the Target.*[16] The Target represents and warrants to the Buyer that the statements contained in this §3 are correct and complete as of the date of this Agreement and will be correct and complete as of the Closing Date (as though made then and as though the Closing Date were substituted for the date of this Agreement throughout this §3), except as set forth in the disclosure schedule accompanying this Agreement and initialed by the Parties (the *"Disclosure Schedule"*).[17] The Disclosure Schedule will be arranged in paragraphs corresponding to the lettered and numbered paragraphs contained in this §3.

(a) *Organization, Qualification, and Corporate Power.* Each of the Target and its Subsidiaries is a corporation duly organized, validly existing, and in good standing under the laws of the jurisdiction of its incorporation. Each of the Target and its Subsidiaries is duly authorized to conduct business and is in good standing under the laws of each jurisdiction where such qualification is required [PRO-SELLER: except where the lack of such qualification would not have a material adverse effect on the financial condition of the Target and its Subsidiaries taken as a whole or on the ability of the Parties to consummate the transactions contemplated by

---

[16] This Agreement assumes that the Target is a publicly held company, and as a result contains very limited representations and warranties about the Target and its Subsidiaries (based primarily on the Public Reports) and no post-Closing indemnification from the Target Stockholders.

This arrangement is typical in public company acquisitions for two reasons. *First*, the Buyer will have the comfort of the substantial public information about the Target and its Subsidiaries available in the Public Reports, and hence the Buyer needs less in the way of representations and warranties. *Second*, the Buyer Shares will generally be disbursed to the Target Stockholders as soon as the Merger is effective. Although an escrow for a portion of the Buyer Shares is feasible, it is not frequently used.

If the Target is *not* a publicly held company, the Buyer may seek extensive representations and warranties about the Target and its Subsidiaries and post-Closing indemnification from the Target Stockholders against any breaches thereof. Sample acquisition agreement 2003.1 (the *pro-buyer* asset purchase agreement) contains provisions which are more favorable to the Buyer in this respect than the provisions in this sample acquisition agreement 2006. Indeed, even sample acquisition agreement 2003.2 (the *pro-seller* asset purchase agreement) contains provisions which are more favorable to the Buyer in this respect than the provisions in this sample acquisition agreement 2006 (but of course not as favorable to the Buyer as the provisions in sample acquisition agreement 2003.1).

Naturally the acquisition documents covering an actual transaction must be carefully tailored to the economic terms and the risk-sharing arrangements agreed upon by the parties. It is therefore unlikely that any sample acquisition agreement will ever be appropriate in its entirety for a particular negotiated transaction. Indeed, in preparing the acquisition documents for a particular negotiated transaction, it will frequently be necessary to mix and match between sample acquisition agreements, i.e., to use parts of several. When one portion of a sample acquisition agreement is changed, however, care is necessary to make sure that all appropriate changes are made in other parts of the sample acquisition agreement, because many clauses of a sample acquisition agreement are often interrelated.

[17] Because the Target Stockholders will have no obligation to indemnify the Buyer after the Closing for any breach of this Agreement, these representations and warranties will in effect serve only as closing conditions for the Buyer. See the closing condition in §6(a)(iii) below.

The Buyer will not, however, have any closing condition with respect to any adverse matter which the Target discloses in the Disclosure Schedule. This is because the disclosure will cure any misrepresentation or breach of warranty that might otherwise have existed. Thus, where the Target reveals an adverse matter in the Disclosure Schedule, the Buyer may seek to add a specific closing condition requiring an acceptable resolution of the matter.

this Agreement].[18] Each of the Target and its Subsidiaries has full corporate power and authority to carry on the businesses in which it is engaged and to own and use the properties owned and used by it.

(b) *Capitalization.* The entire authorized capital stock of the Target consists of _____ Target Shares, of which _____ Target Shares are issued and outstanding and _____ Target Shares are held in treasury.[19] All of the issued and outstanding Target Shares have been duly authorized and are validly issued, fully paid, and nonassessable. There are no outstanding or authorized options, warrants, purchase rights, subscription rights, conversion rights, exchange rights, or other contracts or commitments that could require the Target to issue, sell, or otherwise cause to become outstanding any of its capital stock. There are no outstanding or authorized stock appreciation, phantom stock, profit participation, or similar rights with respect to the Target.

(c) *Authorization of Transaction.* The Target has full power and authority (including full corporate power and authority) to execute and deliver this Agreement and to perform its obligations hereunder; *provided, however,* that the Target cannot consummate the Merger unless and until it receives the Requisite Target Stockholder Approval. This Agreement constitutes the valid and legally binding obligation of the Target, enforceable in accordance with its terms and conditions.

(d) *Noncontravention.* [PRO-SELLER: To the Knowledge of any director or officer of the Target,] neither the execution and the delivery of this Agreement, nor the consummation of the transactions contemplated hereby, will (i) violate any constitution, statute, regulation, rule, injunction, judgment, order, decree, ruling, charge, or other restriction of any government, governmental agency, or court to which any of the Target and its Subsidiaries is subject or any provision of the charter or bylaws of any of the Target and its Subsidiaries or (ii) conflict with, result in a breach of, constitute a default under, result in the acceleration of, create in any party the right to accelerate, terminate, modify, or cancel, or require any notice under any agreement, contract, lease, license, instrument or other arrangement to which any of the Target and its Subsidiaries is a party or by which it is bound or to which any of its assets is subject (or result in the imposition of any Security Interest upon any of its assets) [PRO-SELLER: except where the violation, conflict, breach, default, acceleration, termination, modification, cancellation, failure to give notice, or Security Interest would not have a material adverse effect on the financial condition of the Target and its Subsidiaries taken as a whole or on the ability of the Parties to consummate the transactions

---

[18] There are several references to materiality throughout these representations and warranties. Since the relevant closing condition in §6(a)(iii) below is already qualified as to materiality, and since the representations and warranties will not survive the Closing so as to serve any other purpose, these references to materiality are redundant. The Buyer may seek to eliminate this redundancy out of concern that the double materiality will somehow narrow its closing condition.

[19] It may be necessary to revise this sentence if the Target has more than one class of capital stock. See the definition of Target Shares in §1 above.

contemplated by this Agreement]. [PRO-SELLER: To the Knowledge of any director or officer of the Target, and] other than in connection with the provisions of the Hart-Scott-Rodino Act, the Delaware General Corporation Law, the Securities Exchange Act, the Securities Act, and the state securities laws, none of the Target and its Subsidiaries needs to give any notice to, make any filing with, or obtain any authorization, consent, or approval of any government or governmental agency in order for the Parties to consummate the transactions contemplated by this Agreement [PRO-SELLER:, except where the failure to give notice, to file, or to obtain any authorization, consent, or approval would not have a material adverse effect on the Target and its Subsidiaries taken as a whole or on the ability of the Parties to consummate the transactions contemplated by this Agreement.]

(e) *Filings with the SEC.* The Target has made all filings with the SEC that it has been required to make [PRO-SELLER: within the past [three] years] under the Securities Act and the Securities Exchange Act (collectively the *"Public Reports"*). Each of the Public Reports has complied with the Securities Act and the Securities Exchange Act in all material respects. None of the Public Reports, as of their respective dates, contained any untrue statement of a material fact or omitted to state a material fact necessary in order to make the statements made therein, in light of the circumstances under which they were made, not misleading. The Target has delivered to the Buyer a correct and complete copy of each Public Report (together with all exhibits and schedules thereto and as amended to date).

(f) *Financial Statements.* The Target has filed Quarterly Reports on Form 10-Q for the fiscal quarters ended _____, 19____ (the *"Most Recent Fiscal Quarter End"*), _____, 19____, and _____, 19____ and an Annual Report on Form 10-K for the fiscal year ended _____, 19____. The financial statements included in or incorporated by reference into these Public Reports (including the related notes and schedules) have been prepared in accordance with GAAP applied on a consistent basis throughout the periods covered thereby [,] [and] present fairly the financial condition of the Target and its Subsidiaries as of the indicated dates and the results of operations of the Target and its Subsidiaries for the indicated periods [PRO-BUYER: are correct and complete in all respects, and are consistent with the books and records of the Target and its Subsidiaries]; *provided, however,* that the interim statements are subject to normal year-end adjustments.

(g) *Events Subsequent to Most Recent Fiscal Quarter End.* Since the Most Recent Fiscal Quarter End, there has not been any [PRO-BUYER: material adverse change in the business, financial condition, operations, results of operations, or future prospects] [PRO-SELLER: material adverse change in the financial condition] of the Target and its Subsidiaries taken as a whole.[20]

---

[20] The Buyer may seek to expand upon this representation and warranty, since it covers a period with respect to which there may be material undisclosed developments. Sample acquisition agreement 2003.1 (the pro-buyer asset purchase agreement) contains a version of this representation and warranty which is more favorable to the Buyer.

(h) *Undisclosed Liabilities.* [PRO-BUYER: None of the Target and its Subsidiaries has any liability (whether known or unknown, whether asserted or unasserted, whether absolute or contingent, whether accrued or unaccrued, whether liquidated or unliquidated, and whether due or to become due), including any liability for taxes, except for (i) liabilities set forth on the face of the balance sheet dated as of the Most Recent Fiscal Quarter End (rather than in any notes thereto) and (ii) liabilities which have arisen after the Most Recent Fiscal Quarter End in the Ordinary Course of Business (none of which results from, arises out of, relates to, is in the nature of, or was caused by any breach of contract, breach of warranty, tort, infringement, or violation of law).]

(i) *Brokers' Fees.* None of the Target and its Subsidiaries has any liability or obligation to pay any fees or commissions to any broker, finder, or agent with respect to the transactions contemplated by this Agreement.

(j) *Continuity of Business Enterprise.* [The Target operates at least one significant historic business line, or owns at least a significant portion of its historic business assets, in each case within the meaning of Reg. §1.368-1(d).][21]

(k) *Disclosure.* The Definitive Target Proxy Materials will comply with the Securities Exchange Act in all material respects. The Definitive Target Proxy Materials will not contain any untrue statement of a material fact or omit to state a material fact necessary in order to make the statements made therein, in the light of the circumstances under which they will be made, not misleading; *provided, however*, that the Target makes no representation or warranty with respect to any

---

[21] The Merger will not qualify as a tax-free reorganization unless the Buyer either (a) continues a significant historic business line of the Target or (b) uses a significant portion of the Target's historic business assets in a business. Under 1/98 regulations, such continuity may be maintained (i) directly by the Buyer, (ii) through one or more Code §368(c) 80% controlled subsidiaries that are members of the Buyer's "qualified group," or (iii) through a partnership in which (A) one or more members of the Buyer's "qualified group" have active and substantial management functions as a partner with respect to the business or (B) members of the Buyer's "qualified group" in the aggregate own an interest in the partnership representing a significant interest in the business. *See* Reg. §1.368-1(d) and ¶611. The starting point in this analysis is whether the Target itself operates at least one significant historic business line or owns at least a significant portion of its historic business assets. If this is true, it generally will suffice that the Buyer *presently intends* to continue a significant historic business line or use a significant portion of the historic business assets in a business after the reorganization, either directly or indirectly, as described above. *See* §4(f) below. The Target (and indirectly the Target Stockholders) nonetheless may wish to obtain a covenant from the Buyer that it *actually will* continue a significant historic business line or use a significant portion of the historic business assets in a business after the reorganization (in order to avoid future disputes with IRS that might arise should the Buyer ever depart from its stated present intention). *See* §5(k) below.

This representation and warranty contains certain terms such as *"significant historic business line"* and *"significant portion* of its *historic business assets"* that are undefined except for the general cross-reference to Reg. §1.368-1(d). The Parties may prefer to define some or all of these terms by reference to specific quantitative tests. Reg. §1.368-1(d)(5) contains five examples which the Parties may find helpful in this regard. Notice, however, that despite these examples the test for continuity of the business enterprise requires the Parties to consider all of the relevant facts and circumstances. *See* Reg. §1.368-1(d)(1)-(4).

information that the Buyer will supply specifically for use in the Definitive Target Proxy Materials. None of the information that the Target will supply specifically for use in the Registration Statement, the Prospectus, or the Definitive Buyer Proxy Materials will contain any untrue statement of a material fact or omit to state a material fact necessary in order to make the statements made therein, in the light of the circumstances under which they will be made, not misleading.

4. *Representations and Warranties of the Buyer.*[22] The Buyer represents and warrants to the Target that the statements contained in this §4 are correct and complete as of the date of this Agreement and will be correct and complete as of the Closing Date (as though made then and as though the Closing Date were substituted for the date of this Agreement throughout this §4), except as set forth in the Disclosure Schedule.[23] The Disclosure Schedule will be arranged in paragraphs corresponding to the numbered and lettered paragraphs contained in this §4.

(a) *Organization.* The Buyer is a corporation duly organized, validly existing, and in good standing under the laws of the jurisdiction of its incorporation.

(b) *Capitalization.* The entire authorized capital stock of the Buyer consists of _____ Buyer Shares, of which _____ Buyer Shares are issued and outstanding and _____ Buyer Shares are held in treasury.[24] All of the Buyer Shares to be issued in the Merger have been duly authorized and, upon consummation of the Merger, will be validly issued, fully paid, and nonassessable.

(c) *Authorization of Transaction.* The Buyer has full power and authority (including full corporate power and authority) to execute and deliver this Agreement and to perform its obligations hereunder; *provided, however,* that the Buyer cannot consummate the Merger unless and until it receives the Requisite Buyer Stockholder Approval. This Agreement constitutes the valid and legally binding obligation of the Buyer, enforceable in accordance with its terms and conditions.

---

[22] The Target may seek to obtain additional representations and warranties concerning the Buyer and its Subsidiaries (e.g., the typical representations and warranties contained in a stock purchase agreement) because the Target Stockholders are receiving the Buyer Shares in the Merger in exchange for their Target Shares. *See, e.g.,* sample acquisition agreements 2002.1 (the pro-buyer stock purchase agreement) and 2002.2 (the pro-seller stock purchase agreement). *See also* sample acquisition agreement 2005 (reverse subsidiary merger).

[23] Because the Buyer will have no obligation to indemnify the Target Stockholders after the Closing for any breach of this Agreement, these representations and warranties will in effect serve only as closing conditions for the Target. See the closing condition in §6(b)(iv) below.

The Target will not, however, have any closing condition with respect to any adverse matter which the Buyer reveals in the Disclosure Schedule. This is because the disclosure will cure any misrepresentation or breach of warranty that might otherwise have existed. Thus, where the Buyer reveals an adverse matter in the Disclosure Schedule, the Target may seek to add a specific closing condition requiring an acceptable resolution of the matter.

[24] It may be necessary to revise this sentence if the Buyer has more than one class of capital stock. See the definition of Buyer Shares in §1 above.

(d) *Noncontravention.* [PRO-BUYER: To the Knowledge of any director or officer of the Buyer,] neither the execution and the delivery of this Agreement, nor the consummation of the transactions contemplated hereby, will (i) violate any constitution, statute, regulation, rule, injunction, judgment, order, decree, ruling, charge, or other restriction of any government, governmental agency, or court to which the Buyer is subject or any provision of the charter or bylaws of the Buyer or (ii) conflict with, result in a breach of, constitute a default under, result in the acceleration of, create in any party the right to accelerate, terminate, modify, or cancel, or require any notice under any agreement, contract, lease, license, instrument or other arrangement to which the Buyer is a party or by which it is bound or to which any of its assets is subject [PRO-BUYER: , except where the violation, conflict, breach, default, acceleration, termination, modification, cancellation, or failure to give notice would not have a material adverse effect on the ability of the Parties to consummate the transactions contemplated by this Agreement]. [PRO-BUYER: To the Knowledge of any director or officer of the Buyer, and] other than in connection with the provisions of the Hart-Scott-Rodino Act, the Delaware General Corporation Law, the Securities Exchange Act, the Securities Act, and the state securities laws, the Buyer does not need to give any notice to, make any filing with, or obtain any authorization, consent, or approval of any government or governmental agency in order for the Parties to consummate the transactions contemplated by this Agreement [PRO-BUYER: , except where the failure to give notice, to file, or to obtain any authorization, consent, or approval would not have a material adverse effect on the ability of the Parties to consummate the transactions contemplated by this Agreement.]

(e) *Brokers' Fees.* The Buyer does not have any liability or obligation to pay any fees or commissions to any broker, finder, or agent with respect to the transactions contemplated by this Agreement for which any of the Target and its Subsidiaries could become liable or obligated.

(f) *Continuity of Business Enterprise.* [It is the present intention of the Buyer to continue at least one significant historic business line of the Target, or to use at least a significant portion of the Target's historic business assets in a business, in each case within the meaning of Reg. §1.368-1(d).][25]

---

[25] The Merger will not qualify as a tax-free reorganization unless the Buyer either (a) continues a significant historic business line of the Target or (b) uses a significant portion of the Target's historic business assets in a business. Under 1/98 regulations, such continuity may be maintained (i) directly by the Buyer, (ii) through one or more Code §368(c) 80% controlled subsidiaries that are members of the Buyer's "qualified group," or (iii) through a partnership in which (A) one or more members of the Buyer's "qualified group" have active and substantial management functions as a partner with respect to the business or (B) members of the Buyer's "qualified group" in the aggregate own an interest in the partnership representing a significant interest in the business. *See* Reg. §1.368-1(d) and ¶611. The starting point in this analysis is whether the Target itself operates at least one significant historic business line or owns at least a significant portion of its historic business assets. *See* §3(j) above. If this is true, it generally will suffice that the Buyer *presently intends* to continue a significant historic business line or use a significant portion of the historic business assets in a business after the reorganization, either directly or indirectly, as described above. The Target (and indirectly the Target Stockholders) nonetheless may wish to obtain a covenant from the Buyer that it *actually will* continue

(g) *Disclosure.* The Registration Statement, the Prospectus, and the Definitive Buyer Proxy Materials will comply with the Securities Act and the Securities Exchange Act in all material respects. The Registration Statement, the Prospectus, and the Definitive Buyer Proxy Materials will not contain any untrue statement of a material fact or omit to state a material fact necessary in order to make the statements made therein, in the light of the circumstances under which they will be made, not misleading; *provided, however,* that the Buyer makes no representation or warranty with respect to any information that the Target will supply specifically for use in the Registration Statement, the Prospectus, and the Definitive Buyer Proxy Materials. None of the information that the Buyer will supply specifically for use in the Definitive Target Proxy Materials will contain any untrue statement of a material fact or omit to state a material fact necessary in order to make the statements made therein, in the light of the circumstances under which they will be made, not misleading.

5. *Covenants.* The Parties agree as follows with respect to the period from and after the execution of this Agreement.[26]

(a) *General.* Each of the Parties will use its [reasonable] best efforts to take all action and to do all things necessary [, proper, or advisable] in order to consummate and make effective the transactions contemplated by this Agreement (including satisfaction, but not waiver, of the closing conditions set forth in §6 below).

(b) *Notices and Consents.* The Target will give any notices (and will cause each of its Subsidiaries to give any notices) to third parties, and will use its [reasonable] best efforts to obtain (and will cause each of its Subsidiaries to use its [reasonable] best efforts to obtain) any third party consents, that the Buyer [reasonably] may request in connection with the matters referred to in §3(d) above.

(c) *Regulatory Matters and Approvals.* Each of the Parties will (and the Target will cause each of its Subsidiaries to) give any notices to, make any filings with,

---

a significant historic business line or use a significant portion of the historic business assets in a business after the reorganization (in order to avoid future disputes with the IRS that might arise should the Buyer ever depart from its stated present intention). *See* §5(k) below.

   This representation and warranty contains certain terms such as "*continue* at least one *significant historic business line* of the Target" and "*use* at least a *significant portion* of the Target's *historic business assets in a business*" that are undefined except for the general cross-reference to Reg. §1.368-1(d). The Parties may prefer to define some or all of these terms by reference to specific quantitative tests. Reg. §1.368-1(d)(5) contains five examples which the Parties may find helpful in this regard. Notice, however, that despite these examples the test for continuity of the business enterprise requires the Parties to consider all of the relevant facts and circumstances. *See* Reg. §1.368-1(d)(1)-(4).

   [26] The Parties are likely to incur significant costs and expenses in connection with the transaction. For example, the Parties and their agents will have to (a) prepare and/or review this Agreement, the Disclosure Schedule, and the Joint Disclosure Document, (b) make filings under the Securities Act and the Securities Exchange Act and respond to comments thereon, (c) make filings under the Hart-Scott-Rodino Act and respond to requests for additional information, (d) obtain the Fairness Opinion, the Target Comfort Letter, and the Buyer Comfort Letter, and (e) give notices to third parties and obtain their consents.

and use its [reasonable] best efforts to obtain any authorizations, consents, and approvals of governments and governmental agencies in connection with the matters referred to in §3(d) and §4(d) above. Without limiting the generality of the foregoing:

(i) *Securities Act, Securities Exchange Act, and State Securities Laws.* The Target will prepare and file with the SEC preliminary proxy materials under the Securities Exchange Act relating to the Special Target Meeting. The Buyer will prepare and file with the SEC a registration statement under the Securities Act relating to the offering and issuance of the Buyer Shares (the *"Registration Statement"*) and preliminary proxy materials under the Securities Exchange Act relating to the Special Buyer Meeting. The filing Party in each instance will use its [reasonable] best efforts to respond to the comments of the SEC thereon and will make any further filings (including amendments and supplements) in connection therewith that may be necessary [, proper, or advisable]. The Buyer will provide the Target, and the Target will provide the Buyer, with whatever information and assistance in connection with the foregoing filings that the filing Party [reasonably] may request. The Buyer will take all actions that may be necessary [, proper, or advisable] under state securities laws in connection with the offering and issuance of the Buyer Shares.[27]

(ii) *Delaware General Corporation Law.* The Target will call a special meeting of its stockholders (the *"Special Target Meeting"*) as soon as [reasonably] practicable in order that the stockholders may consider and vote upon the adoption of this Agreement and the approval of the Merger in accordance with the Delaware General Corporation Law. The Buyer will call a special meeting of its stockholders (the *"Special Buyer Meeting"*) as soon as [reasonably] practicable in order that the stockholders may consider and vote upon the adoption of this Agreement and the approval of the Merger in accordance with the Delaware General Corporation Law. The Parties will mail the Joint Disclosure Document to their respective stockholders simultaneously and as soon as [reasonably] practicable. The Joint Disclosure Document will contain the affirmative recommendations of the respective boards of directors of the Parties in favor of the adoption of this Agreement and the approval of the Merger; *provided, however,* that no director or officer of either Party shall be required to violate any fiduciary duty or other requirement imposed by law in connection therewith.

(iii) *Hart-Scott-Rodino Act.* Each of the Parties will file (and the Target will cause each of its Subsidiaries to file) any Notification and Report Forms and related material that it may be required to file with the Federal Trade Commis-

---

Section 8(l) below allocates responsibility between the respective parties for these costs and expenses through the Closing.

[27] The Parties should determine whether any additional filings will be required under the Securities Act, the Securities Exchange Act, and state securities laws (such as reports of ownership on Schedule 13D and transaction statements on Schedule 13E-3). This especially might be the case in transactions with management participation.

sion and the Antitrust Division of the United States Department of Justice under the Hart-Scott-Rodino Act, will use its [reasonable] best efforts to obtain (and the Target will cause each of its Subsidiaries to use its [reasonable] best efforts to obtain) an early termination of the applicable waiting period, and will make (and the Target will cause each of its Subsidiaries to make) any further filings pursuant thereto that may be necessary [, proper, or advisable].

(d) *Fairness Opinion and Comfort Letters.* The Target will deliver to the Buyer on or before the date the Joint Disclosure Document is mailed to their respective stockholders (i) an opinion of [TARGET'S INVESTMENT BANK] as to the fairness of the Merger to the Target Stockholders from a financial point of view (the *"Fairness Opinion"*) and (ii) a letter of [TARGET'S ACCOUNTING FIRM] stating their conclusions as to the accuracy of certain information derived from the financial records of the Target and its Subsidiaries and contained in the Joint Disclosure Document (the *"Target Comfort Letter"*). Each of the Fairness Opinion and the Target Comfort Letter shall be [reasonably] satisfactory to the Buyer in form and substance. The Buyer will deliver to the Target on or before the date the Joint Disclosure Document is mailed to their respective stockholders a letter of [BUYER'S ACCOUNTING FIRM] stating their conclusions as to the accuracy of certain information derived from the financial records of the Buyer and its Subsidiaries and contained in the Joint Disclosure Document (the *"Buyer Comfort Letter"*). The Buyer Comfort Letter shall be [reasonably] satisfactory to the Target in form and substance.

(e) *Listing of Buyer Shares.* The Buyer will use its [reasonable] best efforts to cause the Buyer Shares that will be issued in the Merger to be approved for listing on the [New York Stock Exchange], subject to official notice of issuance, prior to the Effective Time.

(f) *Operation of Business.*[28] The Target will not (and will not cause or permit any of its Subsidiaries to) engage in any practice, take any action, or enter into any transaction outside the Ordinary Course of Business. Without limiting the generality of the foregoing:

(i) none of the Target and its Subsidiaries will authorize or effect any change in its charter or bylaws;

(ii) none of the Target and its Subsidiaries will grant any options, warrants, or other rights to purchase or obtain any of its capital stock or issue, sell, or

---

[28] The Buyer may seek to expand upon the specific prohibitions in this covenant. Sample acquisition agreement 2003.1 (the pro-buyer asset purchase agreement) contains provisions more favorable to the Buyer in this regard.

The Target may seek to narrow (or even eliminate) the specific prohibitions in this covenant. Sample acquisition agreement 2003.2 (the pro-seller asset purchase agreement) contains provisions more favorable to the Target in this regard.

otherwise dispose of any of its capital stock (except upon the conversion or exercise of options, warrants, and other rights currently outstanding);

(iii) none of the Target and its Subsidiaries will declare, set aside, or pay any dividend or distribution with respect to its capital stock (whether in cash or in kind), or redeem, repurchase, or otherwise acquire any of its capital stock [, in either case outside the Ordinary Course of Business];

(iv) none of the Target and its Subsidiaries will issue any note, bond, or other debt security or create, incur, assume, or guarantee any indebtedness for borrowed money or capitalized lease obligation outside the Ordinary Course of Business;

(v) none of the Target and its Subsidiaries will impose any Security Interest upon any of its assets outside the Ordinary Course of Business;

(vi) none of the Target and its Subsidiaries will make any capital investment in, make any loan to, or acquire the securities or assets of any other Person outside the Ordinary Course of Business;

(vii) none of the Target and its Subsidiaries will make any change in employment terms for any of its directors, officers, and employees outside the Ordinary Course of Business; and

(viii) none of the Target and its Subsidiaries will commit to any of the foregoing.

(g) *Full Access.* The Target will (and will cause each of its Subsidiaries to) permit representatives of the Buyer to have full access [PRO-SELLER: at all reasonable times, and in a manner so as not to interfere with the normal business operations of the Target and its Subsidiaries,] to all premises, properties, personnel, books, records (including tax records), contracts, and documents of or pertaining to each of the Target and its Subsidiaries. The Buyer will treat and hold as such any Confidential Information it receives from any of the Target and its Subsidiaries in the course of the reviews contemplated by this §5(g), will not use any of the Confidential Information except in connection with this Agreement, and, if this Agreement is terminated for any reason whatsoever, agrees to return to the Target all tangible embodiments (and all copies) thereof which are in its possession.

(h) *Notice of Developments.* Each Party will give prompt written notice to the other of any material adverse development causing a breach of any of its own representations and warranties in §3 and §4 above. No disclosure by any Party pursuant to this §5(h), however, shall be deemed to amend or supplement the Disclosure Schedule or to prevent or cure any misrepresentation, breach of warranty, or breach of covenant.

(i) *Exclusivity.* The Target will not (and will not cause or permit any of its Subsidiaries to) solicit, initiate, or encourage the submission of any proposal or offer from any Person relating to the acquisition of all or substantially all of the capital stock or assets of any of the Target and its Subsidiaries (including any acquisition structured as a merger, consolidation, or share exchange); *provided, however,* that the Target, its Subsidiaries, and their directors and officers will remain free to participate in any discussions or negotiations regarding, furnish any information with respect to, assist or participate in, or facilitate in any other manner any effort or attempt by any Person to do or seek any of the foregoing to the extent their fiduciary duties may require. [PRO-BUYER: The Target shall notify the Buyer immediately if any Person makes any proposal, offer, inquiry, or contact with respect to any of the foregoing.]

(j) *Insurance and Indemnification.*

(i) [PRO-SELLER: The Buyer will provide each individual who served as a director or officer of the Target at any time prior to the Effective Time with liability insurance for a period of [48 months] after the Effective Time no less favorable in coverage and amount than any applicable insurance in effect immediately prior to the Effective Time] [PRO-BUYER: ; *provided, however,* that the Buyer may reduce the coverage and amount of liability insurance to the extent the cost of liability insurance having the full coverage and amount would exceed $_____ per annum].

(ii) The Buyer, as the Surviving Corporation in the Merger, will observe any indemnification provisions now existing in the certificate of incorporation or bylaws of the Target for the benefit of any individual who served as a director or officer of the Target at any time prior to the Effective Time.

(iii) [PRO-SELLER: The Buyer will indemnify each individual who served as a director or officer of the Target at any time prior to the Effective Time from and against any and all actions, suits, proceedings, hearings, investigations, charges, complaints, claims, demands, injunctions, judgments, orders, decrees, rulings, damages, dues, penalties, fines, costs, amounts paid in settlement, liabilities, obligations, taxes, liens, losses, expenses, and fees, including all court costs and [reasonable] attorneys' fees and expenses, resulting from, arising out of, relating to, in the nature of, or caused by this Agreement or any of the transactions contemplated herein.]

(k) *Continuity of Business Enterprise.* [PRO-SELLER: The Buyer will continue at least one significant historic business line of the Target, or use at least a significant portion of the Target's historic business assets in a business, in each case within the meaning of Reg. §1.368-1(d), except that the Buyer may transfer the Target's historic business assets (i) to a corporation that is a member of the Buyer's "qualified group," within the meaning of Reg. §1.368-1(d)(4)(ii), or (ii) to a partnership if (A) one or more members of the Buyer's "qualified group" have active and substantial management functions as a partner with respect to the Target's historic business or (B) members of the Buyer's "qualified group" in the aggregate own an interest in the partnership representing a significant interest in the Target's historic business, in each case within the meaning of Reg. §1.368-1(d)(4)(iii).[29]][30]

6. *Conditions to Obligation to Close.*

(a) *Conditions to Obligation of the Buyer.* The obligation of the Buyer to consummate the transactions to be performed by it in connection with the Closing is subject to satisfaction of the following conditions:

(i) this Agreement and the Merger shall have received the Requisite Target Stockholder Approval [PRO-BUYER: and the number of Dissenting Shares shall not exceed _____% of the number of outstanding Target Shares];

---

[29] If the Buyer (or its subsidiary) acquires the Target's stock in a Code §368(a)(2)(E) Reverse Subsidiary Merger or a "B" reorganization, the Buyer (or its subsidiary) should not transfer the Target's stock to (i) a corporation that is not a member of the Buyer's qualified group or (ii) a partnership (even if members of the Buyer's qualified group hold 100% of the interests in the partnership) because a transfer of the type described in (i) or (ii) immediately above would create a step-transaction risk of causing the acquisition of the Target's stock to fail as a tax-free reorganization. *See* Reg. §1.368-2(k) example (3) and ¶611.2.2. For a similar reason, where the Buyer's subsidiary acquires the Target's stock, the Buyer should not transfer the subsidiary's stock to a corporation that is not a member of the Buyer's qualified group or to a partnership. The Target Stockholders may wish to obtain a covenant from the Buyer that it will not make such transfers after the reorganization.

[30] The Merger will not qualify as a tax-free reorganization unless the Buyer either (a) continues a significant historic business line of the Target or (b) uses a significant portion of the Target's historic business assets in a business. Under 1/98 regulations, such continuity may be maintained (i) directly by the Buyer, (ii) through one or more Code §368(c) 80% controlled subsidiaries that are members of the Buyer's "qualified group," or (iii) through a partnership in which (A) one or more members of the Buyer's "qualified group" have active and substantial management functions as a partner with respect to the business or (B) members of the Buyer's "qualified group" in the aggregate own an interest in the partnership representing a significant interest in the business. *See* Reg. §1.368-1(d) and ¶611. The starting point in this analysis is whether the Target itself operates at least one significant historic business line or owns at least a significant portion of its historic business assets. *See* §3(j) above. If this is true, it generally will suffice that the Buyer *presently intends* to continue a significant historic business line or use a significant portion of the historic business assets in a business after the reorganization, either directly or indirectly, as described above. *See* §4(f) above. The Target (and indirectly the Target Stockholders) nonetheless may wish to obtain a covenant from the Buyer that it *actually will* continue a significant historic business line or use a significant portion of the historic business assets in a business after the reorganization (in order to avoid future disputes with the IRS that might arise should the Buyer ever depart from its stated present intention).

This *pro-seller* covenant contains certain terms such as "*continue* at least one *significant historic business line* of the Target" and "*use* at least a *significant portion* of the Target's *historic business assets in a business*" that are undefined except for the general cross-reference to Reg. §1.368-1(d). The Parties may prefer to define some or all of these terms by reference to specific quantitative tests. Reg. §1.368-1(d)(5) contains five examples which the Parties may find helpful in this regard. Notice, however, that despite these examples the test for continuity of the business enterprise requires the Parties to consider all of the relevant facts and circumstances. *See* Reg. §1.368-1(d)(1)-(4).

(ii) [PRO-BUYER: the Target and its Subsidiaries shall have procured all of the third party consents specified in §5(b) above;][31]

(iii) the representations and warranties set forth in §3 above shall be true and correct in all material respects at and as of the Closing Date;[32]

(iv) the Target shall have performed and complied with all of its covenants hereunder in all material respects through the Closing;

(v) [PRO-BUYER: no action, suit, or proceeding shall be pending or threatened before any court or quasi-judicial or administrative agency of any federal, state, local, or foreign jurisdiction or before any arbitrator wherein an unfavorable injunction, judgment, order, decree, ruling, or charge would (A) prevent consummation of any of the transactions contemplated by this Agreement, (B) cause any of the transactions contemplated by this Agreement to be rescinded following consummation, (C) affect adversely the right of the Surviving Corporation to own the former assets, to operate the former businesses, and to control the former Subsidiaries of the Target, or (D) affect adversely the right of any of the former Subsidiaries of the Target to own its assets and to operate its businesses (and no such injunction, judgment, order, decree, ruling, or charge shall be in effect);] [PRO-SELLER: there shall not be any judgment, order, decree, stipulation, injunction, or charge in effect preventing consummation of any of the transactions contemplated by this Agreement;]

(vi) the Target shall have delivered to the Buyer a certificate to the effect that each of the conditions specified above in §6(a)(i)-(v) is satisfied in all respects;

(vii) this Agreement and the Merger shall have received the Requisite Buyer Stockholder Approval;

(viii) the Registration Statement shall have become effective under the Securities Act;

(ix) the Buyer Shares that will be issued in the Merger shall have been approved for listing on the [New York Stock Exchange], subject to official notice of issuance;

---

[31] The Buyer may also seek covenants and closing conditions concerning title insurance and surveys to be delivered at the Closing. Sample acquisition agreement 2003.1 (the pro-buyer asset purchase agreement) contains provisions which are more favorable to the Buyer in this regard.

[32] Note that this provision will not give the Buyer any closing condition with respect to any adverse matter which the Target may disclose in the Disclosure Schedule. This is because the disclosure will cure any misrepresentation or breach of warranty that might otherwise have existed. Thus, where the Target discloses an adverse matter in the Disclosure Schedule, the Buyer may seek to add a specific closing condition requiring an acceptable resolution of the matter.

(x) [all applicable waiting periods (and any extensions thereof) under the Hart-Scott-Rodino Act shall have expired or otherwise been terminated and the Parties shall have received all other authorizations, consents, and approvals of governments and governmental agencies referred to in §3(d) and §4(d) above];

(xi) the Buyer shall have received from counsel to the Target an opinion in form and substance as set forth in Exhibit E attached hereto, addressed to the Buyer, and Dated as of the Closing Date;

(xii) [the Buyer shall have received from the IRS a private letter ruling to the effect that the Merger will constitute a tax-free reorganization pursuant to Code §368(a)(1)(A);][33]

(xiii) [PRO-BUYER: the Buyer shall have received the resignations, effective as of the Closing, of each director and officer of the Target and its Subsidiaries other than those whom the Buyer shall have specified in writing at least [five] business days prior to the Closing;] and

(xiv) all actions to be taken by the Target in connection with consummation of the transactions contemplated hereby and all certificates, opinions, instruments, and other documents required to effect the transactions contemplated hereby will be [reasonably] satisfactory in form and substance to the Buyer.

The Buyer may waive any condition specified in this §6(a) if it executes a writing so stating at or prior to the Closing.

(b) *Conditions to Obligation of the Target.* The obligation of the Target to consummate the transactions to be performed by it in connection with the Closing is subject to satisfaction of the following conditions:

(i) this Agreement and the Merger shall have received the Requisite Buyer Stockholder Approval;

(ii) the Registration Statement shall have become effective under the Securities Act;

(iii) the Buyer Shares that will be issued in the Merger shall have been approved for listing on the [New York Stock Exchange], subject to official notice of issuance;

(iv) the representations and warranties set forth in §4 above shall be true and correct in all material respects at and as of the Closing Date;

[33] The Buyer alternatively may wish to obtain an opinion of tax counsel addressing this issue.

(v) the Buyer shall have performed and complied with all of its covenants hereunder in all material respects through the Closing;

(vi) [CONFORM TO THE BUYER'S CLOSING CONDITION IN §6(a)(v) ABOVE];

(vii) the Buyer shall have delivered to the Target a certificate to the effect that each of the conditions specified above in §6(b)(i)-(vi) is satisfied in all respects;

(viii) this Agreement and the Merger shall have received the Requisite Target Stockholder Approval;

(ix) [all applicable waiting periods (and any extensions thereof) under the Hart-Scott-Rodino Act shall have expired or otherwise been terminated and the Parties shall have received all other authorizations, consents, and approvals of governments and governmental agencies referred to in §3(d) and §4(d) above];

(x) the Target shall have received from counsel to the Buyer an opinion in form and substance as set forth in Exhibit F attached hereto, addressed to the Target, and dated as of the Closing Date;

(xi) [the Target shall have received from the IRS a private letter ruling to the effect that the Merger will constitute a tax-free reorganization pursuant to Code §368(a)(1)(A);][34] and

(xii) all actions to be taken by the Buyer in connection with consummation of the transactions contemplated hereby and all certificates, opinions, instruments, and other documents required to effect the transactions contemplated hereby will be [reasonably] satisfactory in form and substance to the Target.

The Target may waive any condition specified in this §6(b) if it executes a writing so stating at or prior to the Closing.

7. *Termination.*

(a) *Termination of Agreement.* Either of the Parties may terminate this Agreement with the prior authorization of its board of directors (whether before or after stockholder approval) as provided below:

(i) the Parties may terminate this Agreement by mutual written consent at any time prior to the Effective Time;

[34] The Target alternatively may wish to obtain an opinion of tax counsel addressing this issue.

(ii) the Buyer may terminate this Agreement by giving written notice to the Target at any time prior to the Effective Time (A) in the event the Target has breached any material representation, warranty, or covenant contained in this Agreement in any material respect, the Buyer has notified the Target of the breach, and the breach has continued without cure for a period of [30 days] after the notice of breach or (B) if the Closing shall not have occurred on or before _____, 19____, by reason of the failure of any condition precedent under §6(a) hereof (unless the failure results primarily from the Buyer breaching any representation, warranty, or covenant contained in this Agreement);

(iii) the Target may terminate this Agreement by giving written notice to the Buyer at any time prior to the Effective Time (A) in the event the Buyer has breached any material representation, warranty, or covenant contained in this Agreement in any material respect, the Target has notified the Buyer of the breach, and the breach has continued without cure for a period of [30 days] after the notice of breach or (B) if the Closing shall not have occurred on or before _____, 19____, by reason of the failure of any condition precedent under §6(b) hereof (unless the failure results primarily from the Target breaching any representation, warranty, or covenant contained in this Agreement);

(iv) [PRO-SELLER: the Target may terminate this Agreement by giving written notice to the Buyer at any time prior to the Effective Time in the event the Target's board of directors concludes that termination would be in the best interests of the Target and its stockholders;][35]

(v) any Party may terminate this Agreement by giving written notice to the other Party at any time prior to the Effective Time in the event the Fairness Opinion is withdrawn; or

(vi) any Party may terminate this Agreement by giving written notice to the other Party at any time after the Special Buyer Meeting or the Special Target Meeting in the event this Agreement and the Merger fail to receive the Requisite Buyer Stockholder Approval or the Requisite Target Stockholder Approval respectively.

---

[35] This Agreement does not contain any breakup fee, lockup option, or similar provision for the benefit of the Buyer (other than the limited exclusivity provisions in §5(i) above) designed to address the threat of competing transactions when the Target is a publicly held company.

The Buyer might, for example, seek to have the Target pay the Buyer a breakup fee (e.g., the Buyer's costs and expenses, a fixed dollar amount, or a formula amount based on the consideration in a subsequent superior offer) in the event the Parties terminate this Agreement under certain specified circumstances.

The Buyer might also seek to have the Target give the Buyer an option to acquire Target Shares (with an exercise price at or below the Merger Consideration) or an option (sometimes referred to as a "Crown Jewel" option) to acquire certain desirable assets of the Target (with an exercise price at or below fair market value) in the event the Parties terminate this Agreement under certain specified circumstances.

(b) *Effect of Termination.* If any Party terminates this Agreement pursuant to §7(a) above, all rights and obligations of the Parties hereunder shall terminate without any liability of any Party to any other Party (except for any liability of any Party then in breach); *provided, however,* that the confidentiality provisions contained in §5(g) above shall survive any such termination.

8. *Miscellaneous.*

(a) *Survival.* None of the representations, warranties, and covenants of the Parties (other than the provisions in §2 above concerning issuance of the Buyer Shares, the provisions in §5(j) above concerning insurance and indemnification, and [PRO-SELLER: the provisions in §5(k) above concerning certain requirements for a tax-free reorganization]) will survive the Effective Time.

(b) *Press Releases and Public Announcements.* No Party shall issue any press release or make any public announcement relating to the subject matter of this Agreement without the prior written approval of the other Party; *provided, however,* that any Party may make any public disclosure it believes in good faith is required by applicable law or any listing or trading agreement concerning its publicly-traded securities (in which case the disclosing Party will use its [reasonable] best efforts to advise the other Party prior to making the disclosure).

(c) *No Third-Party Beneficiaries.* This Agreement shall not confer any rights or remedies upon any Person other than the Parties and their respective successors and permitted assigns; *provided, however,* that (i) the provisions in §2 above concerning issuance of the Buyer Shares and [PRO-SELLER: the provisions in §5(k) above concerning certain requirements for a tax-free reorganization] are intended for the benefit of the Target Stockholders and (ii) the provisions in §5(j) above concerning insurance and indemnification are intended for the benefit of the individuals specified therein and their respective legal representatives.

(d) *Entire Agreement.* [This Agreement (including the documents referred to herein) constitutes the entire agreement between the Parties and supersedes any prior understandings, agreements, or representations by or between the Parties, written or oral, to the extent they related in any way to the subject matter hereof.]

(e) *Succession and Assignment.* This Agreement shall be binding upon and inure to the benefit of the Parties named herein and their respective successors and permitted assigns. No Party may assign either this Agreement or any of its rights, interests, or obligations hereunder without the prior written approval of the other Party.

These provisions come in many forms, raise complex issues concerning the fiduciary duties of directors and officers, and generally are negotiated extensively.

(f) *Counterparts.* This Agreement may be executed in one or more counterparts, each of which shall be deemed an original but all of which together will constitute one and the same instrument.

(g) *Headings.* The section headings contained in this Agreement are inserted for convenience only and shall not affect in any way the meaning or interpretation of this Agreement.

(h) *Notices.* All notices, requests, demands, claims, and other communications hereunder will be in writing. Any notice, request, demand, claim, or other communication hereunder shall be deemed duly given if (and then two business days after) it is sent by registered or certified mail, return receipt requested, postage prepaid, and addressed to the intended recipient as set forth below:

If to the Target: *Copy to:*

If to the Buyer: *Copy to:*

Any Party may send any notice, request, demand, claim, or other communication hereunder to the intended recipient at the address set forth above using any other means (including personal delivery, expedited courier, messenger service, telecopy, telex, ordinary mail, or electronic mail), but no such notice, request, demand, claim, or other communication shall be deemed to have been duly given unless and until it actually is received by the intended recipient. Any Party may change the address to which notices, requests, demands, claims, and other communications hereunder are to be delivered by giving the other Party notice in the manner herein set forth.

(i) *Governing Law. This Agreement shall be governed by and construed in accordance with the domestic laws of the State of [Delaware] without giving effect to any choice or conflict of law provision or rule (whether of the State of [Delaware] or any other jurisdiction) that would cause the application of the laws of any jurisdiction other than the State of [Delaware].*

(j) *Amendments and Waivers.* The Parties may mutually amend any provision of this Agreement at any time prior to the Effective Time with the prior authorization of their respective boards of directors; *provided, however,* that any amendment effected subsequent to stockholder approval will be subject to the restrictions contained in the Delaware General Corporation Law. No amendment of any provision of this Agreement shall be valid unless the same shall be in writing and signed by both of the Parties. No waiver by any Party of any default, misrepresentation, or breach of warranty or covenant hereunder, whether intentional or not, shall be deemed to extend to any prior or subsequent default, misrepresentation, or breach of warranty or covenant hereunder or affect in any way any rights arising by virtue of any prior or subsequent such occurrence.

(k) *Severability.* Any term or provision of this Agreement that is invalid or unenforceable in any situation in any jurisdiction shall not affect the validity or enforceability of the remaining terms and provisions hereof or the validity or enforceability of the offending term or provision in any other situation or in any other jurisdiction.

(l) *Expenses.* Each of the Parties will bear its own costs and expenses (including legal fees and expenses) incurred in connection with this Agreement and the transactions contemplated hereby.[36]

(m) *Construction.* [The Parties have participated jointly in the negotiation and drafting of this Agreement. In the event an ambiguity or question of intent or interpretation arises, this Agreement shall be construed as if drafted jointly by the Parties and no presumption or burden of proof shall arise favoring or disfavoring any Party by virtue of the authorship of any of the provisions of this Agreement.] Any reference to any federal, state, local, or foreign statute or law shall be deemed also to refer to all rules and regulations promulgated thereunder, unless the context otherwise requires. The word "including" shall mean including without limitation.

(n) *Incorporation of Exhibits and Schedules.* The Exhibits and Schedules identified in this Agreement are incorporated herein by reference and made a part hereof.

*   *   *   *   *

IN WITNESS WHEREOF, the Parties hereto have executed this Agreement on [as of] the date first above written.

[BUYER]

By: _____

Title: _____

[TARGET]

By: _____

Title: _____

---

[36] This Agreement makes each of the Parties responsible for its own costs and expenses whether or not the Merger is consummated. This means the Buyer will inherit the costs and expenses of the Target and its Subsidiaries if the Merger is consummated, but will be responsible for only its own costs and expenses if the Merger is aborted.

The Buyer may seek reimbursement from the Target for the Buyer's costs and expenses if the Merger is aborted under certain specified circumstances. Similarly, the Target may seek reimbursement from the Buyer for the Target's costs and expenses if the Merger is aborted under certain other specified circumstances. The Parties may settle on a compromise allocation of responsibility for costs and expenses if the Merger is aborted (such as sharing the costs and expenses in a predetermined ratio or making one Party responsible for the costs and expenses up to a specified aggregate ceiling and the other Party responsible for any excess).

EXHIBIT A[37]—AGREEMENT REGARDING CONTINUITY OF SHAREHOLDER INTEREST

As discussed in ¶610, Treasury on 1/23/98 issued final, temporary, and proposed regulations under Code §368 which changed dramatically the application of the continuity of interest requirement for corporate reorganizations.[38] These regulations (final, temporary, and proposed) apply to transactions after 1/28/98, excluding transactions carried out pursuant to a written agreement which (subject to customary conditions) was binding on and at all times after 1/28/98.

This Exhibit A contains suggestions for drafting an agreement between P on the one hand and some or all of T's shareholders on the other hand regarding continuity of shareholder interest under both the pre- and post-1/28/98 doctrines. It does *not* contain an actual model agreement for use in this context.

Sample acquisition agreement 2006 contemplates a tax-free merger of T into P (e.g., a two-party "A" reorganization pursuant to Code §368(a)(1)(A)), with T's shareholders receiving stock of P in exchange for their stock in T. See ¶801 for a discussion of the requirements for and consequences of an "A" reorganization (including the circumstances under which P may distribute cash or other "boot" to T's shareholders in addition to P stock).

All tax-free reorganizations (including the two-party "A" reorganization) must satisfy three requirements: (i) business purpose, (ii) continuity of shareholder interest, and (iii) continuity of business enterprise. See ¶¶609, 610, and 611. A merger of T into P which does not satisfy all three of these requirements does not qualify as a tax-free reorganization and instead constitutes a taxable sale of assets from T to P followed by a complete liquidation of T. See Rev. Rul. 69-6, 1969-1 C.B. 104, discussed at ¶301.

For example, if too much of the consideration paid to T's shareholders in the merger is cash or other boot (i.e., too little of the consideration is P stock), or if (under pre-1/28/98 doctrine) T's shareholders fail to retain a sufficient quantity of the P stock received in the merger for a sufficient period of time after the merger, the continuity of shareholder interest requirement is not satisfied and the transaction fails to qualify as a tax-free reorganization.

Under new Reg. §1.368-1(e), the continuity of interest requirement is applied solely by reference to the consideration P gives to T's shareholders, so that the issue of post-reorganization continuity largely disappears. Thus a post-reorganization disposition of P stock, even if pursuant to a plan does not adversely affect continuity.[39]

Although the 1/98 regulations largely abolish the post-reorganization continuity of interest requirement, three caveats remain, as described in more detail in ¶610:

---

[37] This is Exhibit A to sample acquisition agreement 2006 (the tax-free merger agreement).

[38] T.D. 8760, 8761.

[39] The 1/98 final continuity of interest regulations do not apply to "D" reorganizations and Code §355 transactions; hence, post-reorganization continuity of interest may (for "D" reorganizations) or will (for Code §355 transactions) persist as a relevant doctrine for such transactions.

First, any new P stock sold by an old T shareholder to a person related to P sufficiently soon after the P-T acquisition so as to be stepped together with the P-T transaction will not constitute good continuity. A purchaser of P stock is related to P for this purpose only if such purchaser is (1) a corporation which is a member of P's affiliated group under Code §1504 (applied without regard to the exceptions in Code §1504(b)) or (2) a corporation whose purchase of P's stock would be treated as a redemption under Code §304(a)(2) (in general, where T owns or is treated as owning 50% or more of the corporation's stock measured by vote or value).[40]

Second, a proprietary interest in T is not preserved to the extent that, prior to and in connection with P's acquisition of T, the interest is redeemed or an extraordinary distribution is made with respect to the interest (i.e., T redeems some of its stock or makes an extraordinary distribution on its stock in anticipation of the P-T acquisition).[41]

Third, continuity of interest is not maintained with respect to any T stock that is acquired prior to and in connection with the P-T acquisition by a corporation related to T.[42] For this purpose, a corporation is related to T if a purchase of T stock by the corporation would be treated as a redemption under Code §304(a)(2) (in general, where T owns or is treated as owning 50% or more of the corporation's stock measured by vote or value).

In a failed two-party "A" reorganization, T is taxed as if it had sold all of its assets in a taxable transaction, triggering a GU Repeal tax on its assets, and P inherits T's tax liability under state merger law. In addition, as in any failed tax-free acquisition, T's shareholders are taxed on the exchange of their T stock for P stock. Thus, both P and T's shareholders have an interest in satisfying the continuity of shareholder interest test.

The continuity of shareholder interest doctrine is explained in detail at ¶610.

In light of the 1/98 regulations, P as acquiring party in the merger may seek certain representations and warranties regarding the T's shareholders' pre-transaction stock ownership in order to have some comfort that the post-1/28/98 continuity of shareholder interest test will be met.[43] Three possible representations and warranties are set forth below, with the first representation and warranty being the least specific (and hence the "loosest") and with each succeeding one being somewhat more specific (and hence "tighter"):

1. *Least Specific.* Prior to the merger, T's shareholders did not dispose of any T stock, or receive any distribution from T, in a manner that would cause the merger to violate the continuity of shareholder interest requirement set forth in Reg. §1.368-1(e).

2. *More Specific.* Prior to the merger, T's shareholders neither had portions of their T interests redeemed by T, nor received extraordinary distributions with

---

[40] Reg. §1.368-1(e)(3).

[41] Temp. Reg. §1.368-1T(e)(1)(ii)(A).

[42] Temp. Reg. §1.368-1T(e)(2)(ii).

[43] If T's stock is publicly traded, the parties will generally request only T's insiders (i.e., members of T's management, its control group, and their relatives) and T's 5% shareholders to make a representation and warranty regarding continuity of shareholder interest. *See* ¶610.10.

respect to their T interests, and no corporation related to T within the meaning of Reg. §1.368-1(e)(3)(i)(B) acquired any T stock, where such dispositions or acquisitions would reduce the aggregate FV of the P stock to be received by T's shareholders as a group (with such FV measured as of the merger date) to an amount less than [ ][44] % of the aggregate FV of T's stock determined immediately before any of such distributions, dispositions or acquisitions.

3. *Most Specific.* Prior to the merger, no T shareholder had a portion of such shareholder's T interest redeemed by T, or received an extraordinary distribution with respect to its T interest, and no corporation related to T within the meaning of Reg. §1.368-1(e)(3)(i)(B) acquired any stock of T held by such T shareholder, where such disposition or acquisition would reduce the aggregate FV of the P stock to be received by such T shareholder (with such FV measured as of the merger date) to an amount less than [ ][45] % of the FV of the T stock held by such T shareholder immediately before any of such distribution, disposition or acquisition.

Reorganization covered by pre-1/28/98 regulations. The remainder of this Exhibit A contains suggestions for drafting an agreement between P on the one hand and some or all of T's shareholders on the other hand regarding continuity of shareholder interest under the pre-1/28/98 continuity of interest doctrine. Under the 1/98 regulations (Reg. §1.368-1(e)), such an agreement is advisable only for a transaction occurring pursuant to a written agreement binding on or before and at all times after 1/28/98 (and for a "D" reorganization or a Code §355 transaction).

In such a transaction, the parties to the merger will generally want T's shareholders to make certain representations and warranties regarding their *present intent* in order to have some comfort that the continuity of shareholder interest test will be met.[46] Three possible representations and warranties are set forth below, with the first representation and warranty being the least specific (and hence the "loosest") and with each succeeding one being somewhat more specific (and hence "tighter"):

1. *Least Specific.* T's shareholders have no present plan, intention, or arrangement to dispose of any of the P stock received in the merger in a manner that would cause the merger to violate the continuity of shareholder interest requirement set forth in the pre-1/28/98 version of Reg. §1.368-1.

2. *More Specific.* T's shareholders as a group have no present plan, intention, or arrangement to dispose of any of the P stock received in the merger if such disposition would reduce the aggregate FV of the P stock retained by T's share-

---

[44] As discussed in ¶610.2, this percentage will normally fall between 40% and 50%, depending on the parties' aggressiveness.

[45] As discussed in ¶610.2, this percentage will normally fall between 40% and 50%, depending on the parties' aggressiveness.

[46] If T's stock is publicly traded, then the parties generally will ask only T's insiders (i.e., members of T's management, its control group, and their relatives) to make a representation and warranty regarding continuity of shareholder interest. *See* ¶610.10.

holders as a group (with such FV measured as of the merger date) to an amount less than [ ]⁴⁷ % of the aggregate FV of T's stock immediately before the merger.

3. *Most Specific.* No T shareholder has any present plan, intention, or arrangement to dispose of any of the P stock received by such shareholder in the merger if such disposition would reduce the FV of the P stock retained by such T shareholder (with such FV measured as of the merger date) to an amount less than [ ]⁴⁸ percent of the FV of the T stock held by such T shareholder immediately before the merger.

In addition, the parties to the merger may want T's shareholders to make certain covenants regarding their *future conduct* in order to ensure that the continuity of shareholder interest test (under pre-1/28/98 doctrine) will be met.⁴⁹ Three possible covenants are set forth below (corresponding to the three possible representations and warranties as to their present intent set forth above), with the first covenant being the least specific (and hence the "loosest") and with each succeeding one being somewhat more specific (and hence "tighter"):

1. *Least Specific.* T's shareholders will not dispose of any of the P stock received in the merger in a manner that would cause the merger to violate the continuity of shareholder interest requirement set forth in the pre-1/28/98 version of Reg. §1.368-1. Any T shareholder wishing to dispose of any shares of P stock received in the merger shall provide written notice to P, not less than [ ] days prior to the intended date of disposition, specifying the number of shares of which the T shareholder proposes to dispose.

2. *More Specific.* T's shareholders as a group will not dispose of any of the P stock received in the merger⁵⁰ within [ ]⁵¹ years after the merger if such disposition would reduce the aggregate FV of the P stock retained by T's shareholders as a group (with such FV measured as of the merger date) to an amount less than [ ]⁵² % of the aggregate FV of T's stock immediately before the merger, unless the T shareholder obtains an opinion of counsel reasonably satisfactory to P that such transfer will not violate the continuity of shareholder interest requirement set forth in the pre-1/28/98 version of Reg. §1.368-1. Any T shareholder wishing to dispose of any shares of P stock received in the merger shall provide written notice to P, not less than [ ] days prior to the intended date of disposition, specifying the number of P shares intended to be disposed of.

---

⁴⁷ As discussed in ¶610.2, this percentage will normally fall between 40% and 50%, depending on the parties' aggressiveness.

⁴⁸ As discussed in ¶610.2, this percentage will normally fall between 40% and 50%, depending on the parties' aggressiveness.

⁴⁹ If T's stock is publicly traded, then the parties generally will ask only T's insiders (i.e., members of T's management, its control group, and their relatives) to make a covenant regarding continuity of shareholder interest. *See* ¶610.10.

⁵⁰ While the law is not wholly clear, it appears that transfers by gift, bequest, and similar means do not destroy continuity of shareholder interest under the pre-1/28/98 *See* ¶610.11.3. Thus, the parties may wish to provide an explicit exception to the covenant for such transfers.

⁵¹ As discussed in ¶610.5, this time period will normally fall between one and five years, depending on the parties' aggressiveness.

⁵² As discussed in ¶610.2, this percentage will normally fall between 40% and 50%, depending on the parties' aggressiveness.

3. *Most Specific.* No T shareholder will dispose of any of the P stock received in the merger[53] within [ ][54] years after the merger if such disposition would reduce the FV of the P stock retained by such T shareholder (with such FV measured as of the merger date) to an amount less than [ ][55] percent of the FV of the T stock held by such T shareholder immediately before the merger, unless the T shareholder obtains an opinion of counsel reasonably satisfactory to P that such transfer will not violate the continuity of shareholder interest requirement set forth in the pre-1/28/98 version Reg. §1.368-1. Any T shareholder wishing to dispose of any shares of P stock received in the merger shall provide written notice to P, not less than [ ] days prior to the intended date of disposition, specifying the number of P shares intended to be disposed of.

---

[53] While the law is not wholly clear, it appears that transfers by gift, bequest, and similar means do not destroy continuity of shareholder interest under the pre-1/28/98 doctrine. *See* ¶610.11.3. Thus, the parties may wish to provide an exception to the covenant for such transfers.

[54] As discussed in ¶610.5, this time period will normally fall between one and five years, depending on the parties' aggressiveness.

[55] As discussed in ¶610.2, this percentage will normally fall between 40% and 50%, depending on the parties' aggressiveness.